Global Financial Institutions and Markets

In Loving Memory of Ida W. Kelly and Lucille V. Johnson

Global Financial Institutions and Markets

HAZEL J. JOHNSON

UNIVERSITY OF LOUISVILLE

BLACKWELL
Business

Copyright © Hazel J. Johnson 2000

The right of Hazel J. Johnson to be identified as the author of this work has been asserted in accordance with the Copyright, Designs and Patents Act 1988.

First published 2000

2 4 6 8 10 9 7 5 3 1

Blackwell Publishers Inc.
350 Main Street
Malden, Massachusetts 02148
USA

Blackwell Publishers Ltd
108 Cowley Road
Oxford OX4 1JF
UK

Library of Congress Cataloging-in-Publication Data

Johnson, Hazel J.
    Global financial institutions and markets / Hazel J. Johnson.
        p.   cm.
    Includes bibliographical references and index.
    ISBN 1–55786–992–8 (alk. paper). — ISBN 1–55786–993–6 (pbk. :
alk. paper)
        1. International finance.   2. Financial institutions,
International.   3. Capital market.   4. Banks and banking,
International.   I. Title.
    HG3881.J5833   1999
    332.1′5—dc21   99–30909
                                                              CIP

British Library Cataloguing in Publication Data

A CIP catalogue record for this book is available from the British Library.

Typeset in 10 on 11^1/$_2$pt Ehrhardt
by Graphicraft Limited, Hong Kong
Printed in Great Britain by TJ International, Padstow, Cornwall.

This book is printed on acid-free paper.

Contents in Brief

Contents in Detail

contents

♦ ♦ ♦

preface

◆ ◆ ◆

Preface

Financial markets make it possible for resources to be devoted to productive uses for the benefit of society. The most familiar financial institutions that help accomplish resource allocation are commercial banks, mutual funds, pension funds, and insurance companies.

However, the global financial system is undergoing significant change:

- Banks are offering an increasing array of securities-related products, such as mutual funds.
- The securitization of traditional loans has created an active market involving both banks and securities firms.
- Consolidation in the banking industry has reduced the number of US banks from approximately 15,000 in the mid-1980s to less than 9,000 in 1998 – and this consolidation is far from complete.
- Technological innovation is changing basic methods of financial product delivery – now more geared to telephone and other electronic means, including the Internet.
- The mutual fund sector of the financial services industry has experienced tremendous growth and is part of the redefinition of pension plans and other retirement savings.
- Increasing emphasis on market valuation of financial institutions requires an enhanced appreciation for the way financial instruments, indeed, entire financial services companies, are valued.
- In the United States, the historical separation of commercial banking, investment banking, and insurance is ending.
- Countries such as Canada, Japan, Germany, the United Kingdom have long permitted nation-wide branching of commercial banks. In the late 1990s, US banks were given the authority (through federal legislation) to branch nationwide.
- Regional trade agreements (such as the EU, NAFTA, ASEAN, and Mercosur) not only have profound implications for the flow of goods and services, but also for the provision of financial services. These affect the powers of existing financial services firms, and opportunities for expansion.
- Increasing cross-border transactions require an appreciation for cultural differences in the methods of doing business.

- Technology, such as the Internet, is making instantaneous global communication increasingly possible. In the financial services industry, this necessitates an appreciation for the similarities and differences in institutions and markets.

In order to be competitive in the financial services labor market, practitioners must understand these dynamics.

In several respects, these issues have been addressed in *Global Financial Institutions and Markets*.

- The financial structure and management of commercial banks, thrifts, investment companies (mutual funds and closed-end funds), pension funds, insurance companies, and finance companies are analyzed.
- A full description of asset-backed securities has been incorporated, including pass-through and pay-through securities.
- Three chapters of the book address management issues in the context of commercial banking, which can be applied to other financial institutions. Management issues include profitability, liquidity, liability management, the securities portfolio, the loan portfolio, capital, and asset/liability management.
- The formation of the European Union and the process of monetary union are explained.
- Comparative interest and inflation rates are examined over time in the United States, the United Kingdom, Germany, France, Italy, and Japan.
- The financial practices and regulatory systems of a wide range of countries are discussed.
- The book includes the topics of Islamic banking and socialist banking.
- Separate chapters have been devoted to the topics of investment banking, financial derivatives, bank valuation, regional trade agreements, technological change in banking, and securities activities of commercial banks.

Thus, the material in *Global Financial Institutions and Markets* is both quantitative and descriptive. This mix supports the learning experience to help the reader become more technically competent and culturally prepared.

Hazel J. Johnson

How To Use This Book

Global Financial Institutions and Markets is organized to help you gain an overview of each chapter quickly and then to develop an understanding of the content in detail.

- The Chapter Overview describes the concepts that you will learn in the chapter.
- Key Terms gives you a checklist of new words and phrases that are used and defined in the chapter. This list is helpful when studying the material, perhaps for an examination. The list is also useful when using the book as a reference, that is, to find material on a particular topic.
- Throughout the chapter, the definitions of the Key Terms are shown in boxes for ease of identification in the sections associated with the terms.
- The Chapter Outline is a section-by-section sequence of the chapter.
- The International Comparisons portion of the Chapter Outline highlights the country coverage of each chapter. Specific country coverage helps you to understand not only the technical practices in the countries highlighted, but also enables you to gain insight into the culture of business in these countries.
- In those chapters with quantitative material, numerical examples illustrate the use of formulas and are helpful study aids.
- Throughout the book, the composition of assets and liabilities of financial industries is highlighted from the 1960s to the present. You can use these tables to help understand the trend of each of these industries.

While each reader of the book may use it in the manner most comfortable for the individual, the following approach will generally help the reader to master the material:

1. Read the chapter overview.
2. Read the text of the chapter.
3. Study the terms in the definition boxes.
4. Study the trend data in tables and/or graphs.
5. Rework any numerical examples provided in the chapter.
6. Answer end-of-chapter questions and problems, as applicable.

7   Draw parallels between and among different industries that may compete for the same clientele. These comparisons will often involve analysis of two or more chapters.

For exercises that are assigned for oral presentation or for research projects:

1   Identify the relevant concepts in the text.
2   Define the relevant terms.
3   Make liberal use of the data in tables and graphs to illustrate the assignment or research project.
4   Search the Internet for the organizations cited in tables and graphs to find additional research support.

Global Financial Institutions and Markets is a comprehensive, flexible text that can be used for background material, quantitative analysis, and trends.

Overview of the Financial Services Industry

chapter 1

CHAPTER OVERVIEW

This chapter:
- Analyzes the role of financial institutions in society.
- Describes the process of financial intermediation.
- Differentiates direct and indirect financing.
- Outlines recent changes in the financial services industry in terms of domestic and international competition.

KEY TERMS

barter system
capital market
deficit savings unit
denomination intermediation
direct financing
financial institutions
financial intermediation
indirect financing

information intermediation
maturity intermediation
net interest margin
primary security
risk intermediation
secondary security
surplus savings unit

CHAPTER OUTLINE

Introduction

Financial institutions facilitate economic growth in modern society by performing essential intermediation and distribution functions. When they act as intermediaries, financial institutions channel funds to productive uses while providing investors with a variety of outlets for their savings. Securities brokers and dealers efficiently distribute securities that companies issue to finance productive undertakings. Smooth-running and well developed financial markets facilitate this process. As efficient as US financial markets have become, they face significant change in a time of new alignments in domestic markets and increased international competition. US banks are undergoing significant restructuring, as the industry consolidates while broadening its offering of services. Mutual funds are redefining the investment activity of individuals and households.

 The Role of Financial Institutions

The term *financial institutions* describes a wide array of firms. The most familiar financial institution is probably a commercial bank. In fact, commercial banks are the oldest financial institutions in most countries and they handle a significant portion of every country's financial assets. Financial institutions include:

Commercial banks
Savings and loan associations
Mutual savings banks
Credit unions
Insurance companies
Pension funds
Investment companies
Investment bankers
Securities brokers and dealers
Finance companies

Why do financial institutions exist and why are they so diverse? In fact, they share common attributes. All have at least some contact with the general public; all accept money and provide services in return. The discussion of their development starts with a simple world that assumes the existence of money and works toward the complex system of financial markets today.

② Example of a Financial Transaction

2.1 SAVINGS UNITS

First, assume a tiny economy, a world populated by only two people – Person A and Person B. Person A works throughout the year to obtain all necessities of life – food, shelter, and clothing. Person A now has $100 of excess resources, that is, assets of $100. Assuming no liabilities, Person A has wealth (net worth) of $100, or $W_0 = \$100$. Since income exceeded expenditures for the year, Person A is a *surplus savings unit*.

> **Surplus savings unit (SSU):**
>   An economic entity whose income for a particular period exceeds
>   expenditures.

The amount of Person A's wealth will stay the same without any productive application for the funds, that is, without investment opportunities.

Now consider Person B, who also has worked successfully during the year to satisfy basic needs, but without accumulating excess resources like Person A. Person B's current wealth is zero. Hence, the sum of wealth of the two citizens of this small economy is $100.

However, B, has a concept for a one-year project that promises to return 20 percent on investment. Yet, with no funds available for investment, B will be unable to take advantage of the lucrative opportunity. All other things being equal, the wealth of this society one year from now, W_1, will be identical to its current wealth, as noted in Exhibit 1.1.

Without Direct Financing		
Person	W_0	W_1
A	$100	$100
B	0	0
Economy	$100	$100
With Direct Financing		
Person	W_0	W_1
A	$100	$110
B	0	10
Economy	$100	$120

◆ **Exhibit 1.1: A two-person world**

2.2 DIRECT FINANCING

The clear solution to this dilemma is for Person A to lend Person B the funds necessary for the project. If this happens, Person B becomes a *deficit savings unit*.

> **Deficit savings unit (DSU):**
> An economic unit whose current income is less than current expenditures.

When the ultimate user of funds – a DSU or an entrepreneur – obtains necessary resources from an investor or SSU, the process is called *direct financing*.

> **Direct financing:**
> The provision of funds for investment to the ultimate user of the funds (DSU) by an ultimate investor (SSU).

This arrangement makes it possible for a person with an idea or an opportunity to undertake a worthwhile project that would, otherwise, have been forgone. The benefits of direct financing reach beyond one individual, however. They are an important source of growth in an economy.

If we assume that Person A is willing to provide financing in the amount of $100 at an agreed-upon rate of 10 percent (probably documented in a promissory note signed by Person B), A earns $10; total wealth of Person A one year from now will be $110 [$100(1.10) = $110], or W_1 = $110, as also shown in Exhibit 1.1. B's wealth also increases. After repayment of principal and interest, Person B's wealth will have increased to $10 [$100(1.20) − $110 = $10]. On an aggregate basis then, the wealth of the economy grows to $120, increasing by the 20 percent return on B's project. In the absence of financing, this growth would not have occurred. Notice that the economy grows by the rate of return available from investment (20 percent), and that this rate of return is shared, in negotiated proportions, between SSUs and DSUs.

Direct financing works only when *mutual* agreement on all terms of the arrangement is possible. In this example, Person A had confidence in the proposed project and did not object to the required holding period. Person B agreed to the 10 percent interest rate.

Financial Intermediation

3.1 AN EXPANDED EXAMPLE

Direct financing in a world of more than a handful of people can be an inefficient way to allocate capital. Suppose there are 100 SSUs and 100 DSUs, all of them as interested in financing their projects at favorable terms as the original Person B. If each DSU investigates a direct financing arrangement with each ultimate investor, search and information costs become unreasonable (up to 10,000 searches, with 100 DSUs each investigating 100 SSUs). If each of the ultimate investors also looks for the "right" investment, information costs will mount even faster.

Now suppose that a financial intermediary, a commercial bank, is introduced as shown in Exhibit 1.2. The bank, not the individuals, can analyze each of the projects proposed by the entrepreneurs (B_1 through B_{100}). Because no more than 100 "feasibility studies" are required for the potential projects proposed by the entrepreneurs, information costs are reduced. In fact, the bank may be able to offer the ultimate investors (A_1 through A_{100}) a wider range of financial opportunities than would have been available through direct financing. This process is *indirect financing*.

```
Entrepreneurs              Financial intermediary              Investors

                              Commercial bank
                           _____

B₁                  $                          $              A₁
B₂            ←───────────                ←───────────        A₂
B₃                                                            A₃
.                 note                        deposit         .
.            ───────────→                ───────────→         .
.                                                             .
B₁₀₀                       _____          A₁₀₀
```

◆ **Exhibit 1.2:** Expanded world with financial intermediation and indirect financing

> **Indirect financing:**
> The process by which entrepreneurs (deficit savings units) obtain money for investment from a financial intermediary who, in turn, has accumulated the funds from ultimate investors (surplus savings units).

Exhibit 1.2 illustrates how investment dollars flow from SSUs through the intermediary to the entrepreneurs, producing essentially the same net result as direct financing. The distinction is that the commercial bank holds promissory notes, that is, the obligations of the entrepreneurs. The ultimate investor now holds a bank deposit, a different financial instrument. The promissory note is a *primary security*; the deposit is a *secondary security*.

> **Primary security:**
> A financial claim issued by the ultimate user of the funds, the DSU.

> **Secondary security:**
> A financial claim issued by a financial intermediary.

The changes in the financial instruments held by ultimate investors are the essence of *financial intermediation*.

> **Financial intermediation:**
> The process of facilitating the flow of funds from surplus savings units (SSUs) to deficit savings units (DSUs), with primary securities (issued by DSUs) held by financial institutions and secondary securities (issued by financial institutions) held by SSUs.

3.2 FORMS OF FINANCIAL INTERMEDIATION

Indirect financing through financial intermediaries, like direct financing, facilitates economic growth by allowing capital to be channeled to investment projects. The effect of indirect financing is a significant change in the type of securities held by the investing public. The type of intermediation, or change, that occurs may be described in four broad categories:

1. *Denomination intermediation*: The amount of the necessary investment changes. A number of relatively small investments may be pooled together to finance projects that require large amounts of capital. Alternatively, a large investment can be distributed to a number of smaller projects.

2. *Maturity intermediation*: The length of time that an ultimate investor is required to stay invested changes. Deposits and other secondary securities may have short terms to maturity, and may, in fact, be payable upon demand, while financing made available to DSUs has a maturity more appropriate for the project involved (frequently longer term).

3. *Risk intermediation*: The risk absorbed by the ultimate investor changes. SSUs do not bear direct risk of default (nonpayment of principal or interest) by DSUs. The secondary securities issued to the SSU are backed by the financial strength of the intermediary (and, in the case of bank deposits, by a federal insurance facility).

4. *Information intermediation*: The amount of information gathering required by the ultimate investors changes. SSUs need not research all projects in which they ultimately invest. Investors instead may rely on the management skill and financial position of the intermediary.

3.3 OTHER FINANCIAL INTERMEDIARIES – BRIEFLY

Banks are not the only financial institutions that perform intermediation functions and serve an industrial economy. Other financial intermediaries are savings and loan associations, mutual savings banks, credit unions, investment companies, pension funds, insurance companies, and finance companies.

3.3.1 DEPOSITORY INSTITUTIONS

Commercial banks, savings and loan associations, mutual savings banks, and credit unions are *depository institutions*. That is, they all issue secondary securities in the form of the customer's deposit, money that can be withdrawn upon demand or according to terms of the deposit agreement. Mutual savings and loan associations, mutual savings banks, and credit unions technically issue ownership shares, not deposits.

Savings and loan associations (S&Ls) were established to provide real estate finance by accepting small savers' deposits and investing in residential mortgages. To this traditional function has been added consumer and commercial loans. S&Ls now also accept checking and large-denomination deposits. Some S&Ls have converted to bank charters and those that have not offer many of the same services as commercial banks.

Mutual savings banks were also originally geared to the small investor. These institutions made mortgage loans and accepted primarily savings deposits. Their activities have grown in ways similar to S&Ls.

Like S&Ls and mutual savings banks, *credit unions* provide a savings vehicle for the small investor. Historically, they invested these funds in small consumer loans for purposes other than residential housing. Members of credit unions share some form of common bond, frequently employment or occupation. As credit unions have evolved, they too have begun to offer a full range of consumer services, including home mortgage loans.

3.3.2 NON-DEPOSITORY FINANCIAL INSTITUTIONS

Investment companies, pension funds, insurance companies, and *finance companies* are financial intermediaries that are not depository institutions. Thus, the secondary securities that they issue to ultimate investors are different. *Investment companies* (for example, Fidelity mutual funds) pool money in small denominations to make large purchases of corporate and government securities. To this extent, they are similar to commercial banks, but investment companies issue ownership shares, not deposits, to their investors. The rate of return from an investment company share depends on the rate of return of the securities in which the company invests, with no guarantee or insurance for the investor.

Pension funds offer the secondary security of deferred income. Contributors to pension funds receive the promise of lump-sum or periodic payments at or during retirement from employment. Contributions into pension funds are made by both employers and employees. Pension funds are major providers of money for industrial expansion.

Insurance companies promise protection from a variety of specified risks in exchange for investor funds. This promised protection is documented in an insurance policy. The two major types of insurance companies are life insurers and property and casualty insurers. Life insurers protect investors from death and disability during the term of the policy. (Some life insurance policies also include a savings component.) Property and casualty insurers protect against all other risks – automobile insurance is an example. Like pension funds, insurance companies invest policyholder funds in loans to and securities of commercial enterprises.

Finance companies cater to both consumers and businesses. In this sense, they offer services that are similar to those of commercial banks, although finance companies generally make riskier loans than banks – that is, there is often a higher probability of non-repayment of loans that finance companies make. As a result, finance company loan rates are higher than bank loan rates. Another difference is that finance companies do not accept deposits, but issue securities similar to those of nonfinancial firms.

These financial intermediaries, together with commercial banks, control a large share of the financial assets of the economy. While the secondary security varies, depending on the institution, the process of intermediation is much the same.

An Analysis of Financial Intermediation

This section provides an introductory analysis of intermediation by examining one transaction in which a commercial bank acts as intermediary, with a variety of changes in the financial position of all parties.

4.1 THE BALANCE SHEET

This example illustrates the flow of funds in financial intermediation by tracing a $10,000 deposit made by an investor (A) through the balance sheet of a commercial bank to the balance sheet of an entrepreneur (B). Exhibit 1.3 shows that investor A has Cash on Hand (a liquid asset) in the amount of $10,000. When A deposits the money in the bank, A's liquid asset is reclassified as Cash in Bank, and the bank's Vault Cash (asset) and Deposits (liability) accounts both increase by $10,000.

The bank then makes a loan of $10,000 to a third party, entrepreneur B. After the loan is made, the bank's $10,000 addition to Vault Cash changes to an addition to Loans. On B's balance sheet,

	A	Commercial Bank	B
Before transaction			
Assets			
Cash on hand	10,000		
Liabilities			
After deposit			
Assets			
Cash in bank	10,000		
Vault cash		+10,000	
Liabilities			
Deposits		+10,000	
After loan			
Assets			
Cash in bank	10,000		+10,000
Loans		+10,000	
Liabilities			
Deposits		+10,000	
Notes payable			+10,000

◆ **Exhibit 1.3: Balance sheet impact of financial intermediation**

Cash in Bank (asset) and Notes Payable (liability) accounts both increase by $10,000. Without the intermediary – that is, if A had provided direct loan financing to B – A's and B's balance sheets would have changed in exactly the same *amount*, but the asset held by A would have been a promissory note executed by B, not a bank deposit.

4.2 INCOME AND EXPENSE

To analyze the compensation to each of the parties in the intermediation process, assume first that these balances are unchanged for one year. Also assume that the bank pays interest on deposits at 8 percent and charges 11 percent interest on loans, and that B's investment project has a rate of return of 20 percent.

According to Exhibit 1.4, A earns $800 (8 percent of the $10,000), which the bank is obligated to pay because of its contractual commitment. Once the bank enters into this contract with A, the

	A	Bank	B
Bank deposit interest	800	<800>	
Bank loan interest		1,100	<1,100>
Project return			2,000
Net returns	800	300	900

◆ **Exhibit 1.4: Compensation to participants in financial intermediation**

liability of the bank to A is not affected by the bank's investment decision. Yet because interest expense for the bank (interest *income* for A) begins accruing immediately on deposit, it is in the bank's best interest to put the $10,000 to productive use as soon as possible. Assuming that the bank makes the loan to B on the day of A's deposit, the bank's interest income from the loan to B (interest *expense* for B) begins accruing right away. Likewise, B promptly invests the loan proceeds in the proposed project.

At the end of the year, the bank's (pretax) net interest earnings are $300 – the $1,100 loan income less $800 deposit interest expense payable to A. B's earnings before taxes are $900 – $2,000 in project revenues less $1,100 in interest expense. The total amount earned depends on the return on B's investment, assumed here to be 20 percent, or $2,000. That $2,000 is distributed among the three participants in the intermediation process: $800 + $300 + $900.

In large part, the bank's earnings depend on the *spread*, or the difference between the bank's cost of money (the deposit rate in this example) and its investment rate of return (the loan rate). In the case of commercial banks, the spread is referred to as *net interest margin*.

Net interest margin:
The difference between the average rate earned on earning assets and the average rate paid on interest-bearing liabilities.

The spread or net interest margin is a basic measure of profitability for a financial intermediary and is the institution's compensation for lending risks – for example, the risk of nonrepayment. The intermediary incurs additional expense in the form of information gathering and customer service that also must be covered by the spread. Moreover, it cannot lend all its assets on a long-term basis. To ensure that customers can withdraw cash on demand, the bank must invest some deposits (its liabilities) in assets that can be converted quickly to cash. These more liquid assets do not earn as high a rate of return as loans to entrepreneurs and other clients, reducing the intermediary's profitability. (See also Exhibit 1.5.)

The example above (Exhibit 1.2) shows how a financial intermediary facilitates the productive investment function of the economy and illustrates the reason why financial intermediaries exist. They perform services that transform the financial instruments available to the public so that they have more appealing denomination, maturity, and risk characteristics. They are sources of information that the public needs to evaluate investment instruments. For these services, financial intermediaries earn the spread (and fee income for other services) reduced by the cost of doing business (information processing and customer service).

⑤ Direct Financing

Not all financial institutions are intermediaries, that is, not all change the security held by the ultimate investor. Other financial institutions that are not intermediaries perform vital roles in the distribution of primary securities, that is, securities issued by the ultimate user of the funds or DSUs. *Investment bankers* and *securities brokers and dealers* sell to the public the same debt and equity securities issued by nonfinancial firms.

Investment bankers advise corporations on the terms and conditions of issuing securities, including the proper timing, pricing, and maturity. Securities issued in this way include stocks, bonds (long-term debt), and commercial paper (short-term debt). As compensation for their security-issuing

Ernst Baltensperger's bank theory overview[1] classifies models in three basic categories: (1) those that assume that the bank is a price setter in deposit and credit markets, (2) those that apply portfolio theory and rely heavily on the assumption of risk aversion, and (3) those that emphasize the real resource cost of providing banking services. Many of these models do not address the issue of scale, that is, the bank's optimal size.

Baltensperger's synthesis of the earlier work develops a model addressing both the bank's asset mix and scale. The bank's expected profit is specified as:

$$E(\pi) = rE - iD - C - L$$

where $E(\pi)$ = the bank's expected profit
r = rate of return on earning assets
E = dollar amount of earning assets (such as securities and loans)
i = rate of interest paid on deposits
D = dollar amount of deposits
C = dollar production cost (especially labor cost) of providing real resource banking services (such as check clearing, credit evaluation, safekeeping, and bookkeeping)
L = opportunity cost of holding liquid assets

The bank's deposits (D) are assumed to equal earning assets (E) plus reserves (R). Baltensperger shows that the bank will maximize expected profit with respect to R and D (and thus E) by investing in earning assets until marginal revenue exactly equals the sum of marginal production and liquidity costs. To finance these investments, deposits should expand until marginal revenue and costs become equal.

As fee income from deposit accounts, brokerage activities, mutual fund sales, and other activities becomes a larger part of bank revenues, the model can be adapted to incorporate this aspect of bank services. Also, given the extent to which banking services are delivered via electronic means (for example, automated teller machines and telephone banking), the model also can accommodate the cost of providing services without the intervention of a human teller.

$$E(\pi) = rE + F - iD - C - L$$

where F = fee income not related to earning assets
C = dollar production cost including labor and service-providing technology

This model also can be applied beyond commercial banking. Because a number of financial institutions offer deposit and loan services, Baltensperger's framework can be useful in analyzing the general case of financial intermediaries.

◆ **Exhibit 1.5: The theory of financial intermediation**

◆ *Notes*:   1   Baltensperger, Ernst. "Alternative Approaches to the Theory of the Banking Firm," *Journal of Monetary Economics*, vol. 6 (1980), pp. 1–37.

services, investment bankers receive fees. They also underwrite securities or assume the risk of selling all, or part, of the issue. Compensation for this service is the underwriters spread, that is, the difference between the price the investment bank pays the issuing firm for the security and the price at which it sells the security to the investing public.

While not engaging in intermediation, *securities brokers and dealers* perform a vital function by placing securities issues in the hands of new investors. After stocks and bonds have been issued, investors may resell securities (to other investors) through brokers. Brokers do not technically take title to securities. Instead, they bring the buyer and seller together, earning a commission in the process. Dealers actually take title to the securities and earn the difference between (1) the price that they pay for securities and (2) the price for which they resell them. Smoothly functioning markets, which allow investors to convert stock or bond holdings into cash or more liquid assets, facilitate the sale of additional securities whenever they are offered by the issuing firms.

⑥ The Changing Face of Financial Intermediation

All financial intermediaries originally operated in market niches in which they generally specialized. Historically, for example, commercial banks have been an important part of the economy's payments system and a major source of short-term finance for industry. Banks now offer consumer, real estate, and longer-term commercial services. Many of the products offered by banks are related to securities rather than deposits. Likewise, many securities firms now offer products that have traditionally been associated with banks – such as the Merrill Lynch Cash Management Account, essentially an interest-bearing checking account. Investment companies (mutual funds) offer rates of return to small investors that are often more attractive than rates available at depository institutions. Thus, over time, financial institutions have diversified to such an extent that many functions now overlap. This competition in financial services also has blurred the difference between many formerly distinct institutions.

6.1 CHANGING MARKET NICHES

While the US financial system continues to be one of the world's most advanced, the effect of the blurring of niches has been a shift in the relative importance of financial institutions. Exhibit 1.6 shows the change. In 1964, depository institutions had 58 percent of the total financial assets held by financial institutions. By 1989, their share had dropped to 49 percent and by 1998 to 33 percent. The primary beneficiaries of this shift have been investment companies (from 3 to 20 percent) and pension funds (from 11 to 26 percent). The competitive rates of return available through investment companies have clearly attracted ultimate investors, particularly small investors, away from depository institutions. At the same time, the significant growth in assets under management at both investment companies and pension funds has created even larger pools of funds that provide alternatives to bank loans. Thus, banks today face threats to both their deposit base and loan portfolio.

The savings and loan industry has been perhaps the hardest hit by these changes. The number of S&Ls declined from 4,098 in 1960 to 2,819 in 1990 to 1,728 in 1998 (as of Dec. 31, except for 1998 (June 30)). The income on long-term, fixed-rate mortgage loans was insufficient to cover the cost of maintaining their deposit base as money market interest rates rose dramatically during the 1970s. During the 1980s, S&Ls were permitted to engage in other forms of financial services that yielded higher rates of return so that they might improve the spread. However, in most cases, these investments also were much riskier. As a result, many loans were not collected and savings

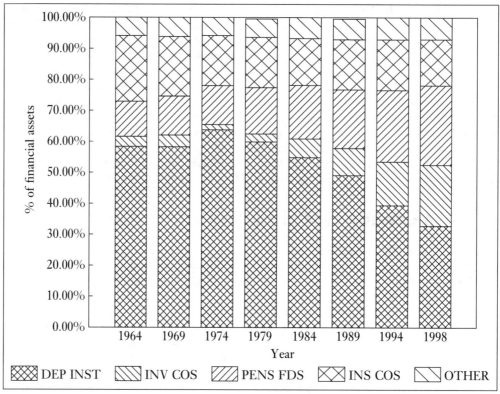

◆ **Exhibit 1.6:** Share of financial assets held by financial institutions, 1964–98

◆ *Notes*:   DEP INST   Depository institutions (commercial banks, savings and loan associations, mutual savings banks, and credit unions)
          INV COS   Investment companies
          PENS FDS Pension funds
          INS COS   Insurance companies
          OTHER   Finance companies and securities brokers and dealers

◆ *Source*:   Derrick Johnson of H. J. Johnson & Associates based on data from: Board of Governors of the Federal Reserve System. *Flow of Funds Accounts; Flows and Outstandings.*

institutions failed. Failures reached record levels and the industry regulatory structure was completely revamped.

Banks are affected as well. They lost much of their low-cost deposits and top-tier corporate loan business. At the heart of this effect is a change in the interest rate environment that has produced a trend toward direct financing of corporate America. Major corporate clients have found it more economical to borrow short-term funds in the commercial paper market directly from the investing public rather than to borrow from a bank. Commercial paper allows large, creditworthy firms borrow for periods of up to 270 days. Exhibit 1.7 shows that the commercial paper rate has been only slightly higher than the Treasury bill rate (the lowest short-term rate available) since 1975, while the prime rate (bank loan rate charged to the best corporate customers) has been significantly higher.

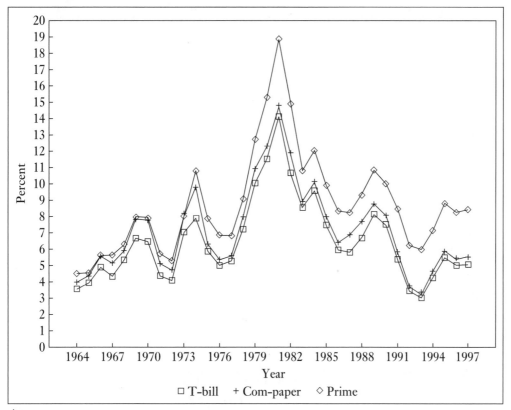

◆ **Exhibit 1.7:** Interest rates: T-bill, commercial paper, and prime, 1964–97

◆ *Source*: Derrick Johnson of H. J. Johnson & Associates based on data from: United States Department of Commerce, Bureau of Economic Analysis, *Business Statistics 1961–88* and *Survey of Current Business, April 1991*; Board of Governors of the Federal Reserve System, *Federal Reserve Bulletin*, various issues.

As Exhibit 1.8 shows, the amount of commercial paper outstanding represented less than 5 percent of the amount of domestic bank loans in 1964. This percentage increased steadily, until 1989 commercial paper totaled almost 29 percent of the dollar value of outstanding bank loans. In the early 1990s, the average was 28 to 29 percent, rising to 39 percent of domestic bank loans by 1998. This trend has contributed to a decline in commercial bank market share.

Commercial banks partially have counteracted this shrinkage in market share by offering other financial products, notably, mutual funds – products developed by the banks themselves (proprietary mutual funds) or products of investment companies (nonproprietary mutual funds). In the early 1990s, banks sold shares of funds backed by pools of long-term debt or bonds (40–50 percent), stock (20–30 percent), and short-term debt or money market instruments (the remainder). Unlike the market share of assets of financial institutions, the share of bank sales of mutual funds is increasing.

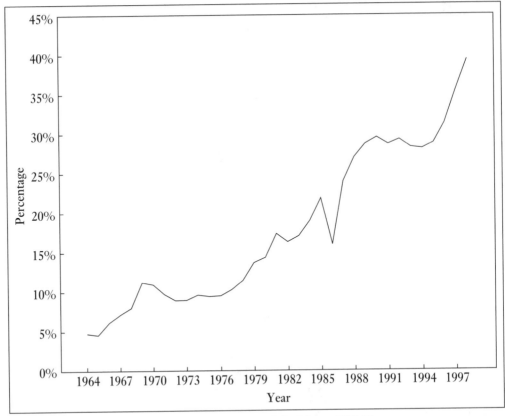

◆ **Exhibit 1.8:** **Commercial paper as a percentage of domestic bank loans, 1964–98**

◆ *Source*:   Derrick Johnson of H. J. Johnson & Associates based on data from: Board of Governors of the Federal Reserve System, *Flow of Funds Accounts; Financial Assets and Liabilities*, various issues.

6.2 CHANGING BANKING INDUSTRY STRUCTURE

Volatile interests, the loss of a low-cost deposit base, the flight of major corporate clients, the expansion of other financial institutions into once-traditional banking services, and the inability of commercial banks to expand into other profitable activities created tremendous pressure on banks in the 1980s. In fact, these pressures are undoubtedly at the root of the highest rate of bank failures since the Great Depression of the 1930s. Exhibit 1.9 shows that after the Second World War (1939–45), annual commercial bank failures numbered fewer than 20 per year. During the 1980s, this number rose to over 200. During the 1990s, the failure rate subsided as interest rates moderated and banking industry returned to more consistent profitability. In 1997, only one US commercial bank failed.

At the same time, the number of commercial banks also has declined significantly. This phenomenon is primarily attributable to mergers and acquisitions. While mergers (not associated with financial distress) averaged 132 during the 1970s, the average rose to 504 for the period from 1990

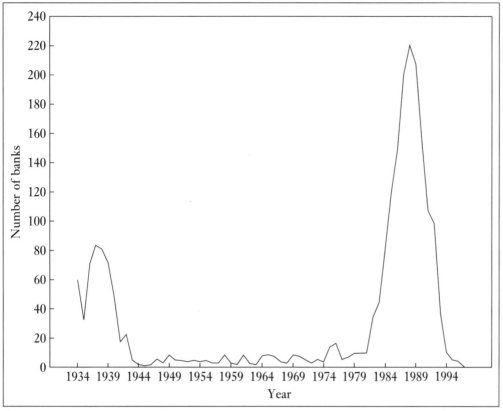

◆ **Exhibit 1.9:   Commercial bank failures, 1934–97**

◆ *Source*:   Derrick Johnson of H. J. Johnson & Associates based on data from: Federal Deposit
Insurance Corporation, *1988 Annual Report*, *FDIC Quarterly Banking Profile* (4Q 1988 and
4Q 1989), and *Statistics on Banking* (various issues).

through 1997. As a result of this massive consolidation, the number of commercial banks in the
United States declined from 14,000 in 1975 to 9,149 at the end of 1997.

6.3 A MORE GLOBAL INDUSTRY

The ability of financial institutions to compete is critical as global markets continue to develop.
Domestic commercial banks compete at home not only with other domestic financial institutions,
but also increasingly with foreign banks. Exhibit 1.10 indicates that foreign bank loans during the
1960s represented less than 2 percent of the amount of domestic bank loans. Twenty-eight years
later, in 1992, the percentage was 15 percent. From 1992 through 1998, the foreign bank loans
consistently represented more than 13 percent of domestic bank loans.

The financial services industry is undergoing significant change in terms of product mix and
competition. Investors are more knowledgeable about investment alternatives. Different types of

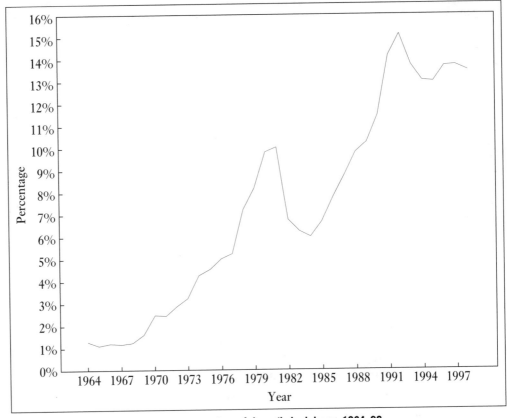

◆ **Exhibit 1.10:** **Commercial paper as a percentage of domestic bank loans, 1964–98**

◆ *Source*:   Derrick Johnson of H. J. Johnson & Associates based on data from: Board of Governors of the Federal Reserve System, *Flow of Funds Accounts; Financial Assets and Liabilities*, various issues.

financial institutions offer similar types of products. Technology is changing the manner in which financial products are offered by all firms, while the impact of international competition is an increasingly significant factor.

 ## Summary

Financial institutions continue to evolve. Although the provider may change, the needed services remain fairly constant. Liquidity and capital investment funds must be channeled from surplus savings units to deficit savings units. Depository institutions (commercial banks, savings and loan associations, mutual savings banks, and credit unions) are now competing with other institutions for market share. Traditional banking services now may be obtained from any number of financial institutions – including investment companies, insurance companies, pension funds, and finance companies. One consequence is that savings and loan associations and commercial banks failed at alarming rates before the interest rate volatility of the 1980s moderated in the 1990s.

Competition between domestic and foreign institutions is becoming much keener. From negligible levels in the 1960s, foreign banks are now a significant presence in the US market. The economies of the world clearly are becoming more integrated. If anything is a constant in the changing financial services industry, it may be the continuing trend toward integration of institutions, markets, and economies.

End-of-chapter Questions

1. What is the difference between a surplus saving economic unit and a deficit savings unit?
2. How do financial intermediaries affect transactions between surplus savings units and deficit savings units?
3. The government and business sectors of the US economy are both deficit savings sectors. Do you think there is a difference in the nature of the two sectors' expenditures?
4. Describe the four types of financial intermediation.
5. a. Why have nonfinancial corporations begun to depend more on direct (vs. indirect) financing?
   b. What financial instrument has made short-term direct financing more feasible?
   c. What financial institutions help nonfinancial corporations to engage in direct financing?
6. In what way are commercial banks, savings and loan associations, mutual savings banks, and credit unions different from other financial institutions?
7. All financial intermediaries issue secondary securities. What is the nature of the secondary securities of:
   a. Investment companies
   b. Pension funds
   c. Insurance companies
   d. Finance companies
8. What is a financial intermediary's spread?
9. All other things being equal, what impact does an increase in deposit interest rates have on a bank's net interest margin (spread)?
10. What happens to a bank's spread if an increase in bank deposit rates is "passed on" to the bank's loan customers?
11. What financial institutions have offered alternatives for small depositors that have seriously eroded commercial bank market share?
12. Describe the recent trend in commercial bank failures.
13. Since 1964, how has the mix of domestic vs. foreign bank loans changed in the United States?

14. **Obtain the literature that describes mutual fund offerings of:**
    a. **A local commercial bank**
    b. **Fidelity Investments (Boston, Massachusetts)**
    Compare the variety of funds offered by the two institutions.
15. **Refer to the "Money Rates" and the "Treasury Bonds, Notes & Bills" quotations of a recent edition of *The Wall Street Journal* (Section C). Determine:**
    a. **The prime rate**
    b. **The commercial paper rates**
    c. **The Treasury bill rates**
    Compare these rates to those in Exhibit 1.7.

Selected References

Baltensperger, Ernst. "Alternative Approaches to the Theory of the Banking Firm," *Journal of Monetary Economics*, vol. 6 (1980), pp. 1–17.

Barth, James R., R. Dan Brumbaugh, Jr., and Robert E. Litan. *Banking Industry in Turmoil: A Report on the Condition of the US Banking Industry and the Bank Insurance Fund*, US Government Printing Office, Washington, DC, December 1990.

Board of Governors of the Federal Reserve System. *Flow of Funds Accounts; Financial Assets and Liabilities*, Washington, DC.

Federal Deposit Insurance Corporation. *1988 Annual Report, 1989 Annual Report*, Washington, DC.

Federal Deposit Insurance Corporation. *FDIC Quarterly Banking Profile*, Washington, DC.

Investment Company Institute Research Department, "Fundamentals – Mutual Fund Research in Brief," Investment Company Institute, Washington, DC, September/October 1995.

Selgin, George A. "Commercial Banks as Pure Intermediaries: Between 'Old' and 'New' Views," *Southern Economic Journal*, vol. 56, no. 1 (1989), pp. 80–6.

Task Force on the International Competitiveness of US Financial Institutions. *Report of the Subcommittee on Financial Institutions Supervision, Regulation, and Insurance*, US Government Printing Office, Washington, DC, October 1990.

US Department of Commerce, Bureau of Economic Analysis. *Business Statistics 1961–1988*, Washington, DC.

US Department of Commerce, Bureau of Economic Analysis. *Survey of Current Business, April 1991*, Washington, DC.

Walsh, Carl E. and Peter R. Hartley. "Financial Intermediation, Monetary Policy, and Equilibrium Business Cycles," *Federal Reserve Bank of San Francisco Economic Review*, issue 4 (Fall 1988), pp. 19–28.

PART I
Domestic Money
Markets

Money

chapter 2

CHAPTER OVERVIEW

This chapter:
- Discusses the characteristics of money.
- Traces the development of money to the present day.
- Establishes the link between the banking system and the money supply.
- Defines the current specifications of money supply and recent changes in its composition.

KEY TERMS

barter system
checks
demand deposit
double coincidence of want
excess reserves
fractional reserves
full-bodied money
medium of exchange
monetary standard

money
money supply
paper money system
parity value of a currency
reserve assets
standard for deferred payments
store of value
unit of account

CHAPTER OUTLINE

1   The Functions of Money
2   Monetary Systems
   2.1   Barter System
   2.2   Full-bodied Money
   2.3   Paper Money
   2.4   Deposit Money
   2.5   Electronic Money

Introduction

At the heart of any financial system is money. Money is the common bond that ties financial institutions in the United States to each other and to institutions in other countries. Money functions as a medium of exchange, a unit of account, a store of value, and a standard for deferred payments. Monetary systems have evolved over time from barter economies to gold and silver coin to paper money to deposits, which dominate now both because of the scarcity of precious metal and the need for a flexible money supply.

Today, methods of payment go beyond currency and coin. For example, bank checking accounts, credit union share draft accounts, and money market fund shares are all forms of money. As a result, the money supply is now affected by a wide circle of financial institutions. Increasingly, electronic means of payment are replacing traditional forms of money. This chapter describes domestic and international money issues – the functions of money, development of international monetary standards, and money creation by financial institutions.

 The Functions of Money

Money allows people to satisfy individual needs through access to goods and services produced by other members of society, according to their particular aptitude or occupation. Most people, for example, buy food by exchanging money for specific items sold in stores. The store, in turn, buys these items through a similar exchange with a distributor. The distributor, too, relies on other sources, eventually traceable to a company or individual actually producing food. This chain of events is repeated in the delivery of any number of products. In this way, an individual can work in a specialized field or profession, but still satisfy his or her need for the necessities of life. This specialization enhances individual productivity and the productiveness of society as a whole.

> **Money:**
>   Anything accepted as a legal means of payment in financial transactions.

Money serves three functions that make this arrangement possible:

- Medium of exchange
- Unit of account
- Store of value

In the case of acceptance of money in exchange for goods and services, money functions as a *medium of exchange*. As a medium of exchange, money must be recognized as an acceptable payment (1) by all who trade goods and services and (2) for debts owned to creditors.

> **Medium of exchange:**
> The function of money that permits its universal exchange for other commodities.

Second, money is a *unit of account* – an abstract, intangible concept, in the same sense that "length" is an intangible concept. Effectively, a unit of account describes the price or relative value of items that are bought and sold. The price of an object specifies the appropriate *amount* of money to purchase it, not the value of the money itself. For this reason, we can say that money is a standard of value for all other goods and services in the economy.

> **Unit of account:**
> The function of money that results in the pricing of other commodities in terms of units of an economy's money.

Throughout history, a country's medium of exchange and unit of account generally have been incorporated into the same monetary instrument. A graphic example of the problems associated with the separation of medium of exchange and unit of account diverge may be found in Germany in the early 1920s, as shown in Exhibit 2.1.

> After the First World War, the German economy underwent a period of hyperinflation that simultaneously affected the money supply, the general level of prices, and the foreign exchange rate of the German mark. From December 1918 to June 1923, currency in circulation increased from 33.1 billion marks to 17.4 trillion marks, representing an average annual increase of 284 percent. The average annual increase in wholesale prices for the two-year period ended June 1923 was 3,725 percent. The average annual devaluation of the mark (relative to the US dollar) during the same two-year period was 3,884 percent.
>
> Wages and prices were stated in terms of a commodity, for example, the number of marks that were necessary to purchase a specified quantity of wheat, milk, or butter, at the time of payment. For example, in 1922, a state floated a bond issue that was denominated in rye. In 1923, a German firm issued a loan in the amount of 200,000 kilograms of flax. When one of these instruments matured, the lender received interest and principal in the number of marks necessary to purchase the stated amounts of rye or flax.
>
> Such examples of separation of the functions of medium of exchange and unit of account are rare. This unfortunate period in German history underscores the need for money to also act as a store of value.

◆ **Exhibit 2.1:** **The post-Second World War monetary distress of Germany**

◆ *Sources*:   Kindleberger, Charles P., *A Financial History of Western Europe*, 1984, pp. 312–13. Struthers, J. and H. Speight, *Money: Institutions, Theory and Policy*, 1986, p. 7.

> **Store of value:**
> The function of money that prevents its purchasing power from declining over time, that is, a way to transfer wealth into the future.

The third function of money is as a *store of value*. To serve an economy's needs effectively, money must retain its purchasing power so that it can be used after it is earned. If money were not a store of value, people would be forced to invest all cash proceeds immediately in assets that *did* retain value. Inflation threatens the store of value function because each unit of money buys fewer goods and services as time passes. That is, $1.00 received today will not be enough to buy $1.00's worth of goods one year from now. (Inflation and price changes are described in chapter 10.)

② Monetary Systems

Monetary systems are the general mechanisms for exchange of goods and services. There are five types of monetary systems incorporating, at various levels of efficiency, all the functions of money described above. In ascending order of efficiency, these are:

- Barter
- Full-bodied money
- Paper money
- Deposit money
- Electronic money

2.1 BARTER SYSTEM

A *barter system* restricts ultimate users to the exchange of commodities, an arrangement that requires a *double coincidence of want*. Suppose that a farmer has produced 10 bales of hay and that the farmer needs 5 yards of material for clothing. Under the barter system, the farmer must find an individual who both needs hay *and* possesses the cloth. Assuming success in finding this match, the next obstacle to overcome is mutual agreement on price. In terms of hay, what is the price of cloth? In terms of cloth, what is the price of hay? This dilemma is not uncommon in Russia and other Eastern European countries that frequently engage in barter in order to obtain Western goods. In barter transactions, large quantities of commodities or raw materials (such as crude oil, cotton, or grain) often are exchanged for manufactured products.

> **Double coincidence of want (in barter):**
> The situation in which each of two parties seeks to obtain the product or commodity that the other possesses.

The search for double coincidence of want and negotiation of relative prices is repeated whenever a producer needs anything other than the commodity produced. Thus, search and information costs in a purely barter economy quickly become prohibitive. The high costs restrict the free flow of goods and services by which we characterize more developed economic systems.[1] The denomination of commodities in terms of money results in more efficiency. Money reduces the transactions cost of exchange. The double coincidence of want is no longer necessary and the farmer can sell hay to anyone who needs it. Later, the farmer may exchange the money for other commodities.

2.2 FULL-BODIED MONEY

The first systems of modern *full-bodied* money used coins made of precious metals, usually gold or silver. Full-bodied money systems date back to 560 BC during the era of Croesus, King of Lydia, an ancient kingdom in what is now Turkey. The first coins were made of electrum, an alloy of gold and silver.

> **Full-bodied money:**
> Money (medium of exchange) with an intrinsic value that is equal to its value as a unit of account. Many commodities have been used as full-bodied money, but the most common have been precious metals.

Over time, a number of items have been used as full-bodied money – for example, stones, shells, ivory, wampum beads, tobacco, furs, and dried fish. However, metal coins have been favored as full-bodied money because of their portability (ease of carrying), durability (good condition after much handling), divisibility (ease of use in transactions of different amounts), and high intrinsic value (high value in a relatively small amount of coins). (See also Exhibit 2.2.)

Historically, gold was used in England beginning in the late seventeenth century. On the other hand, the French generally preferred silver or a combination of gold and silver, called bimetallism. Although there was some debate in Europe as to the more appropriate metal – gold, silver, or some combination – trading nations found it necessary to use a form of money whose value corresponded to its metallic content. In this way, trading was easier because all parties agreed on the value of the money used in trade.

In the United States, full-bodied metallic coins were used from 1792 until 1965, when the government discontinued the use of silver in newly minted dimes and quarters. By 1970, no

---

The following is an excerpt from *Money and Banking in Africa* by J. K. Onoh:

In primitive chiefdoms and kingdoms the only mode of transaction was the barter system. This was because there were no organized political and economic institutions to impart legal tender status to standard commodities that could then serve as money. Consequently, a number of commodities were adopted as exchange media in Africa, America, Asia, Australia and Europe. Cattle represented one of the oldest commodities used as money. Cattle were used widely by the Romans as a means for striking a bargain. The Latin word *pecunia* (money) is derived from *pecus* (cattle). Salt also served as money in ancient Rome. Salary is derived from the Latin word *salarium* (salt). The American Red Indians used the feathers of rare birds as money and the Arabs used dates and tea. Other commodities which were also widely used as money in primitive Europe included oil, wheat, furs and wine.

◆ **Exhibit 2.2: Full-bodied systems of the world**

◆ *Source*: Onoh, J. K. *Money and Banking in Africa*, 1982, p. 1.

precious metal was used in US coins that circulated as money. (Precious metal coins may still be used as investments and as collector's items.)

While metallic coins performed all the functions of money, the system presented some problems. In some cases, people melted down the coins to hoard the precious metals. Also, the weight of the coins made large transactions cumbersome. Coin counterfeiting and shortages of gold in the nineteenth century also threatened the full-bodied money system.

2.3 Paper Money

Early goldsmiths have been credited with the creation of *paper money*. When they served as custodians of gold for their customers, they issued receipts for the gold held in safekeeping. Later, to redeem their property, patrons presented these receipts to the goldsmith and received their gold. As the receipts were fully collateralized by gold, their implicit value was understood by all and the receipts were easier to exchange than the underlying gold. Gold receipts began to circulate as money. Goldsmiths, thus, became the world's first bankers – issuers of early paper money.

Until the early 1930s, most paper money (by then issued primarily by sovereign governments) remained convertible into gold. For many years thereafter, only the US dollar was convertible into gold. Finally, in 1971, the United States suspended gold convertibility of the dollar as described in the sections below under the heading "Monetary Standards."

2.4 Deposit Money

Beginning in the 1860s, banks encouraged the use of checks and *demand deposit (checking) accounts*. (See also chapter 12, section entitled "National Bank Act of 1863" for a description of the regulatory environment that encouraged the development of checking accounts.) A check is payable in either currency (paper money) or coin, but may also be added to the bank account of the payee by depositing the check. Checks are negotiable, that is, can be transferred to another person if the payee endorses (signs the back of) the check.

Check:
> Demand for payment drawn on a bank payable to either the maker/drawer (writer of the check) or to a third party. A check instructs a bank to "pay to the order of" a person, company, or other entity.

Deposit money adds efficiency to the payments system by permitting large transactions to the effected with the transfer of a single piece of the paper – the check. The use of deposit money is possible because banks have devised a system of recognizing and collecting checks drawn on other banks. (See chapter 23, section entitled "Check Clearing.") Today, savings and loan associations, credit unions, brokerage firms, and mutual funds offer accounts that are subject to withdrawal by checks.

2.5 Electronic Money

With the advent of computers and advanced telecommunications networks, *electronic money* has become commonplace. Electronic money can be transmitted through a variety of means, including credit cards, debit cards, and smart cards.

First, merchants accepted *credit cards* that contain a magnetic strip. Through the information contained in the magnetic strip, the amount of a transaction is added to the deposit account of the merchant. The customer (holder of the card) is then billed by the card company.

Now *debit cards* are increasing in use and popularity. A debit card operates like a check in that the cardholder may present the card for payment against funds held in a deposit account. The card is similar to a credit card in that it contains a magnetic strip with all pertinent information. However, a debit card transaction causes an immediate withdrawal from (decrease in) the cardholder's account and an immediate deposit (increase) in the merchant's account.

The *smart card* has a computer chip instead of a magnetic strip. As a result, the smart card can store value – like an electronic wallet or purse. The value stored on the card can be increased in a number of ways – such as paying in advance (as in the case of telephone or public transportation smart cards) or loading the card from a personal computer with an Internet link to a bank. The value stored on the card is reduced whenever a purchase is made.

The evolution of monetary systems has facilitated the exchange of goods and services across national boundaries. Cross-border purchases can be made easily with credit or debit cards because card-issuing banks settle the currency exchange for the customer and the merchant. Clearly, the ease of such transactions would not be possible if exchange markets and monetary standards had not been coordinated on an international basis.

Monetary Standards

The *monetary standard* of a country is the specific physical form of money the country adopts. In general, the form is either:

- commodity standard, that is, value linked to a commodity, or
- noncommodity standard, that is, paper money.

Historically, the most important commodity standards have been:

- gold coin
- gold bullion
- gold exchange
- silver

In the case of adoption of a *gold coin* standard, mints freely accept gold from the public and manufacture coins as prescribed by law. Gold coin is legal tender – that is, must be accepted as payment.

The *gold bullion* standard requires that paper money (bank or government liabilities) be convertible into gold bullion. A number of countries switched to this standard after the First World War (1914–18) in an effort to conserve their gold reserves. A gold bullion (bar) contains considerably more gold than a coin, making conversion an expensive exercise in paper money terms, thereby discouraging gold conversions. At the same time, the conversion feature permitted standardized payment settlements and facilitated trade between those countries that used the gold bullion standard.

A *gold exchange* standard does not obligate the adopting country to convert its currency into gold in any form. Instead, the paper money is legal tender and convertible into drafts (similar to checks) that are payable in the currency of a country that *has* adopted either the gold coin or gold bullion standard. Countries on a gold exchange standard maintain reserves of (1) gold bullion and (2) the gold-bullion-standard currency. The monetary authorities purchase gold-bullion-standard currency with gold from the foreign country that is on the gold bullion standard. The use of "gold drafts" in this case eliminates the expense of shipping and handling gold bullion.

The principles of operating on a *silver standard* would be similar to operating on a gold standard. While some countries have successively adopted a silver standard, a gold standard, or both standards (bimetallism), the silver standard became progressively less attractive as the market value of silver declined relative to the market value of gold.

Most of the countries of the world have adopted a *paper (noncommodity)* standard. A noncommodity standard is either an *inconvertible* paper standard or a *controlled* paper standard. As one might guess, a country adopting an *inconvertible* paper standard permits no conversion of the currency into either gold or silver. Unlimited conversion into foreign currencies is possible, however, as long as the foreign countries do not restrict such conversion. A *controlled* paper standard allows limited conversion into gold or silver. Historically, the controlled paper standard has discouraged international trade (foreign parties have difficulty converting the currency) and encouraged illegal foreign currency exchange (black market) activities.

The Adoption of Monetary Standards

Today's monetary standards are the result of both national and international economic developments. Progression to the current, international monetary system, at times, has not been smooth and the pattern of adopted standards has changed dramatically over the past century. By 1933, after the Great Depression and accompanying banking crises here and abroad, many countries no longer used a gold coin or gold bullion standard. The countries which remained on a gold standard were the United States and the so-called gold block of France, Belgium, the Netherlands, Switzerland, and Italy.

4.1 Bretton Woods, 1944

Before the end of the Second World War (1939–45), the 1944 Bretton Woods Articles of Agreement established the International Monetary Fund (IMF), whose current membership is 181 countries. (See also chapter 20 for a description of the IMF.) The original IMF charter required members to (1) agree with the IMF upon a currency exchange rate (the official par value of a country's currency) and (2) take appropriate action to maintain the value of their currencies within a narrow band around that par value (1 percent above or below), called a "tunnel." (Foreign currency markets and currency exchange rate patterns are discussed in chapters 8 and 11.)

Parity value of a currency:
> The official exchange rate of a currency, or the equality of purchasing power established between (1) one currency and another currency or between (2) one currency and another commodity of value. This concept is also known as par value of a currency.

Member countries were to maintain these *parities* in terms of gold or in terms of the US dollar. Even though parity or par values were expressed in terms of gold, all currencies were effectively pegged to the US dollar, with one ounce of gold equivalent to US$35.[2] Members were required to maintain their currency values within ±1 percent of the agreed upon parity. That is, if a member currency were to become more than 1 percent weaker than the parity exchange rate against the dollar, the member country was obligated to correct the situation, perhaps by entering the currency markets and buying their currency while selling dollars. Conversely, a stronger currency would also require action by the member country, perhaps selling the member currency and buying dollars. In any event, this agreement ended reliance on a gold bullion standard for all countries, except the United States, and established a *gold exchange standard*.[3]

Gold convertibility of the US dollar proved to be unsustainable. Between 1947 and 1956, short-term holdings of US dollars by foreign entities rose from $4.8 billion to $13 billion. Given US gold reserves then valued at $22 billion, these relatively large foreign holdings of dollars were not seen as a serious threat – until European banks (especially in England and Switzerland) began to trade US dollars in what came to be known as Eurodollar markets. (See chapter 9 for a discussion of the Euromarkets.) In 1958, an alarming $2.3 billion in gold was drained from US reserves. Despite measures taken by the US government to halt the outflow, this trend continued throughout the 1960s.

In the late 1960s, speculators, anticipating a decline in the value of the dollar because of this gold drain, borrowed dollars in the Eurodollar market and quickly sold them for other relatively more valuable currencies.[4] This dollar selling put downward pressure on the value of the dollar and upward pressure on the value of other currencies. Monetary officials in other countries were forced to sell their own currencies and buy dollars in order to try to maintain the parities (exchange rates) mandated by the Bretton Woods charter. Foreign official coffers were soon flooded with US dollars. At the same time, US corporate treasurers, also fearful of devaluation, converted massive amounts of US-dollar-denominated liquid assets into other currencies. US gold reserves were severely strained.

4.2 THE SMITHSONIAN AGREEMENT, 1971

By 1971, foreign financial institutions held dollar claims in the amount of $36 billion – twice the amount of gold reserves held by the US government for international convertibility ($18 billion). In August 1971, the United States suspended gold convertibility of the dollar. In December of the same year, the G-10 countries met and negotiated the Smithsonian Agreement, which placed the G-10 countries on an *inconvertible paper standard*, the "dollar standard."[5] Nine currencies were revalued relative to the US dollar, making them convertible into the dollar, with the dollar not convertible into gold. With the exception of Canada, the countries agreed to revaluations from 7.5 to 16.9 percent above the par values that had been stipulated prior to the Smithsonian meeting and the 1 percent band around par value (the tunnel) became 2.25 percent. The Canadian dollar was allowed to float; that is, the Canadian dollar was no longer pegged to the US dollar. Although this agreement effectively reduced the value of the dollar relative to other currencies, the change was expressed in terms of an increase in the price of gold from $35 an ounce to $38. The official explanation was that the dollar had depreciated in terms of gold, not in terms of the other currencies.

4.3 THE SNAKE IN THE TUNNEL

At the same time, the European Community (EC), which had been created by the 1957 Treaty of Rome, sought a closer coordination of their currency values (monetary integration) than the

Smithsonian Agreement provided.[6] In accordance with recommendations of the 1970 Werner Report, an official EC report, the EC in 1971 established a maximum band around par values that was half the size of the Smithsonian band – the colorfully named "snake in the tunnel."

4.4 FLOATING EXCHANGE RATES, 1973

Meanwhile, confidence in the Smithsonian Agreement faltered. The United States, following three years of large trade surpluses, posted substantial trade deficits in 1971 and 1972.[7] US dollars were exchanged in large amounts for the foreign currencies needed to pay for the excess of imports over exports. That is, the supply of dollars increased on the world markets. Domestically, expansion of the money supply in 1972 (creation of more dollars within the United States) was roughly 25 percent faster than in 1971.

As the market value of the dollar fell in light of these trade deficits and money supply statistics, central banks in other countries were forced to intervene in currency markets to maintain the agreed-upon parities. This meant buying the US dollar and selling their own and other foreign currencies. The demand for the dollar generated by these central bank purchases was intended to stimulate increases in the value of the US dollar. The governments of Germany and Japan, in particular, accumulated large reserves of US dollars. General market consensus was that the 1971 US dollar devaluation had not been sufficient to avoid the need for this kind of market intervention. In the United States, sentiments grew that the special role of the dollar was no longer appropriate and that the currency should be allowed to float.

In March 1973, after a number of monetary crises, the G-10 countries and Switzerland, Denmark, Luxembourg, and Ireland met and abandoned the dollar standard. The United States made the suspension of gold convertibility (begun in 1971) a permanent arrangement. France, Germany, Belgium, the Netherlands, Luxembourg, Sweden, and Norway agreed to a joint float. Currencies of the United States, Canada, the United Kingdom, Japan, Switzerland, and Ireland were allowed to float. Essentially, the monetary relationships established in March 1973 remain unchanged today. (See Exhibit 2.3.)

Currency pegged to:		
US dollar	French franc	Other currency
Antigua & Barbuda	Benin	Bhutan (Indian rupee)
Argentina	Burkina Faso	Bosnia and Herzegovina
The Bahamas	Cameroon	(deutsche mark)
Barbados	Central African Republic	Brunei Därussalam
Belize	Chad	(Singapore dollar)
Djibouti	Comoros	Estonia (deutsche mark)
Dominica	Congo	Kiribati (Australian dollar)
Grenada	Côte d'Ivoire	Lesotho (South African rand)
Iraq	Equatorial Guinea	Namibia (South African rand)
Liberia	Gabon	San Marino (Italian lira)
Lithuania	Mali	Swaziland (South African rand)

US dollar	French franc	Other currency
Marshall Islands	Niger	
Micronesia, Fed. states of	Senegal	
Nigeria	Togo	
Oman Panama		
St. Kitts & Nevis		
St. Lucia		
St. Vincent and the Grenadines		
Syrian Arab Rep.		

SDR	Other composite[2]	
Libya	Bangladesh	Malta
Myanmar	Botswana	Morocco
	Burundi	Nepal
	Cape Verde	Seychelles
	Cyprus	Slovak Republic
	Czech Republic	Solomon Islands
	Fiji	Thailand
	Iceland	Tonga
	Jordan	Vanuatu
	Kuwait	Western Samoa

Flexibility limited in terms of a single currency or group of currencies

Single currency[3]	Cooperative Arrangement[4]
Bahrain	Austria
Qatar	Belgium
Saudi Arabia	Denmark
United Arab Emirates	France
	Germany
	Ireland
	Luxembourg
	Netherlands
	Portugal
	Spain

More Flexible		
Adjusted according to a set of indicators[5]		
Chile Nicaragua		

Other managed floating	Independently floating	
Algeria	Afghanistan, Islamic State of	Moldova
Angola	Albania	Mongolia
Belarus	Armenia	Mozambique
Brazil	Australia	New Zealand
Cambodia	Azerbaijan[6]	Papua New Guinea
China, People's Republic of	Bolivia	Paraguay
Colombia	Bulgaria	Peru
Costa Rica	Canada	Philippines
Croatia	Ethiopia	Romania
Dominican Republic	Finland	Rwanda
Ecuador	The Gambia	Sáo Tomé and Principe
Egypt	Ghana	Sierra Leone
El Salvador	Guatemala	Somalia
Eritea	Guines	South Africa
Georgia	Guyana	Sudan
Greece	Haiti	Sweden
Guinea-Bissau	India	Switzerland
Honduras	Italy	Tajikistan, Rep.
Hungary	Jamaica	Tanzania
Indonesia	Japan	Trinidad and Tobago
Iran, Islamic Republic of	Kazakstan	Uganda
Israel	Kenya	United Kingdom
Korea	Lao P.D. Rep.	United States
Kyrgyz Rep.	Lebanon	Yemen, Republic of
Latvia	Madisgascar	Zaire
Macedonia, FYR of	Malawi	Zambia
Malaysia	Mauritania	Zimbabwe
Maldives	Mexico	
Mauritius		
Norway		
Pakistan		
Poland		
Russia		
Singapore		
Slovenia		
Sri Lanka		
Suriname		
Tunisia		
Turkmenistan		

Other managed floating	*Independently floating*
Turkey Ukraine Uruguay Uzbekistan Venezuela Vietnam	

♦ **Exhibit 2.3:** Exchange rate arrangements, as of June 30, 1996[1]

♦ *Notes*:
1 For members with dual or multiple exchange markets, the arrangement shown is that in the major market.
2 Comprises currencies that are pegged to various "baskets" of currencies of the members' own choice, as distinct from the SDR basket.
3 Exchange rates of all currencies have shown limited flexibility in terms of the US dollar.
4 Refers to the cooperative arrangement maintained under the European Monetary System.
5 Includes exchange arrangements under which the exchange rate is adjusted at relatively frequent intervals, on the basis of indicators determined by the respective member countries.
6 Starting May 24, 1994, the Azerbaijan authorities ceased to peg the manat to the Russian ruble and the exchange arrangement was reclassified to "Independently floating."

♦ *Source*:   *International Financial Statistics*, International Monetary Fund, Sept. 1996.

The evolution of monetary standards illustrates several points:

- Ultimately, the international value of money will depend on underlying economic and financial factors within a country. For example, the United States was unable to maintain an external monetary value that was inconsistent with the state of US fiscal and monetary affairs and the US trade balance.
- Management of a country's money supply will be affected by political considerations, some of which may be international political considerations, as with the European coordination of exchange rates.
- A money supply that is tied to the supply of a commodity such as gold (commodity standard) is not flexible and, history shows, unsustainable.

⑤ Expansion of the Money Supply by Banks

Within the global monetary system, financial institutions help to meet capital investment needs by providing liquidity and expanding the money supply. (This section discusses the role of private financial institutions in money supply changes. Chapters 13 and 14 describe government monetary policy.) This may best be seen in the case of banks by returning to history's first bankers, the goldsmiths (discussed earlier in the chapter). As long as the goldsmiths' total receipts issued (their liabilities) equaled the value of the gold they held in safekeeping (their assets), the gold receipts – even though they circulated as money – did not increase the money supply. In banking terms, receipts were deposits, and the gold was held against future redemption requests or withdrawals. Over time, this basic safekeeping system developed to allow issuance of receipts that were not completely backed by gold, which had the effect of increasing the money supply, that is, the number of gold receipts in circulation.

5.1 Bank Reserves

Gold initially was a reserve asset, representing 100 percent of the goldsmith's liabilities (deposits).

> **Reserve assets (historical sense):**
> Assets (cash and other liquid instruments) held for the satisfaction of future requests for cash (withdrawals) that are related to specific liabilities (deposits).

When the receipts themselves began to be used as money, redemption requests for the gold became less frequent and more predictable. In fact, the amount of gold actually needed to satisfy withdrawals was considerably less than total outstanding gold receipts. In other words, *required* reserves were less than 100 percent of deposits. The goldsmiths, could conceivably lend any *excess reserves*, or, alternatively, issue gold receipts that were not backed by gold (earning interest on the loans, in either case). When excess reserves are loaned, the money supply increases. In fact, this process is at the heart of our modern banking system.

> **Excess reserves:**
> The amount by which actual reserve assets exceed required reserves.

Today, required reserves are established by the Federal Reserve for US banks. In other countries, the central bank or other bank regulators specify the amount of liquid assets that must be held at all times.

5.2 Money Supply Expansion

Banking practice and regulation expressly permit maintenance of *fractional reserves*; banks are not required to keep reserve assets to match 100 percent of deposits. The fractional reserve requirement means that a deposit of liquid assets into the banking system expands the money supply by an amount that is more than the amount of the deposit. This deposit has a magnifying effect.

To see this, assume that required reserves for each institution in the system are 10 percent of deposits. Let the variable r represent this required reserve percentage. Assume further that the Federal Reserve injects $100 in liquidity into the system through a $100 deposit in a demand deposit account at Bank A on January 2.

> **Demand deposit:**
> Depository institution account that may be withdrawn upon demand via check or other means.

Date
Jan. 2

Bank A			
Reserves	100	Deposits	100

Jan. 3

Bank A			
Reserves	10	Deposits	100
Loans	90		

Bank B			
Reserves	90	Deposits	90

Jan. 4

Bank A			
Reserves	10	Deposits	100
Loans	90		

Bank B			
Reserves	9	Deposits	90
Loans	81		

Bank C			
Reserves	81	Deposits	81

Jan. 5

Bank A			
Reserves	10	Deposits	100
Loans	90		

Bank B			
Reserves	9	Deposits	90
Loans	81		

Bank C			
Reserves	8.10	Deposits	81
Loans	72.90		

Bank D			
Reserves	72.90	Deposits	72.90

◆ **Exhibit 2.4: Money supply expansion by banking system**

Refer to Exhibit 2.4. Notice that, immediately after the deposit of $100 in cash, both assets and liabilities of Bank A increase by the amount of the deposit. With a 10 percent reserve requirement, at the close of business January 2, Bank A has $90 in excess reserves, [total reserves minus required reserves equals $100 − r($100)], or [$100(1 − r)].

The following day, January 3, Bank A lends that $90 in excess reserves to a customer by crediting the customer's demand deposit account by $90, and recording a loan in the same amount. The same day, the customer writes a $90 check to a vendor who presents the check to Bank A for payment and deposits the cash into an account at Bank B. The accounting entries on the books of both banks are as follows:

	Debit	Credit
Bank A		
1. Loans	90	
Deposits		90
(Loan to second customer)		
2. Deposits	90	
Reserves		90
(Payment of check to vendor)		
Bank B		
Reserves	90	
Deposits		90
(Deposit by vendor)		

At the close of business on January 3, Bank A has no excess reserves, because reserves are now exactly 10 percent of deposits. Bank B, however, has $81 in excess reserves, [$90(1 − r)]. On January 4, Bank B lends its excess reserves and the process begins again. By the end of the day, Bank C has $72.90 in excess reserves, [$81(1 − r)]. At the close of business on January 5, Bank C's excess reserves, similarly, are invested in loans. This continues until no bank in the system has excess reserves. Note that each deposit, D, creates excess reserves of D(1 − r).

The total effect on the money supply of the initial $100 deposit is the change in deposits in the entire banking system or the total of the changes in each institution's deposits.

$$D_t = D_A + D_B + D_C + D_D + \ldots$$
$$= 100 + 100(1 − r) + 100(1 − r)^2 + 100(1 − r)^3 \ldots$$
$$= 100[1 + (1 − r) + (1 − r)^2 + (1 − r)^3 \ldots] \tag{2.1}$$

where D_t = total change in deposits or the effect on money supply
$\quad D_i$ = increase in deposits at Bank i
$\quad 100$ = the amount of the original infusion of liquidity
$\quad r$ = required reserve percentage

The total effect on money supply reduces to the following relationship.[8]

$$D_t = L/r \tag{2.2}$$

where L = the amount of the liquidity infusion ($100 in the example above).

With a 10 percent reserve requirement, a $100 cash deposit into the banking system eventually increases the money supply by $1,000.[9] This happens whenever cash is converted into banking system deposits.[10]

When the transaction occurs in the opposite direction, the money supply *contracts*. The amount of the contraction is a multiple of the amount of the transaction, as in the case of the bank deposit. Again, the multiple equals the inverse of the reserve requirement.[11]

5.3 DEFINING THE MONEY SUPPLY

Deposits of commercial banks are an integral part of the money supply because they serve all the necessary functions of money – medium of exchange, unit of account, and store of value. Other financial institutions offer accounts (liabilities on their books) with features that are virtually identical to commercial bank demand deposits, including NOW (negotiable order of withdrawal) accounts, share draft accounts in credit unions, and brokerage firm transactions accounts. The money supply includes these and other liquid financial instruments.

The three main components of the money supply are M_1, M_2, and M_3, with the most liquid being M_1.

M_1:

Currency and coin in circulation, demand deposits in commercial banks, transactions accounts at other depository institutions (NOW accounts, Super NOW accounts, Automatic Transfer Service (ATS) accounts), and traveler's checks.

M_2:

M_1 plus savings accounts, money market deposit accounts at depository institutions, certificates of deposit and repurchase agreements in amounts under $100,000, overnight repurchase agreements of commercial banks, overnight Eurodollars issued to US residents (excluding financial institutions), and retail money market fund balances (owned by individual investors).

Please note that Eurodollar deposits are issued in US dollars by a bank or bank branch outside the United States. A small amount of Eurodollar deposits are recorded in International Banking Facilities (IBFs) which are special, international divisions of banks within the United States. (See also chapter 9 (for Eurodollars) and chapter 18 (IBFs).)

M_3:

M_2 plus certificates of deposit and repurchase agreements in denominations greater than $100,000, institutional money market fund balances (owned by institutions), and term Eurodollars issued to US residents (excluding financial institutions).

L is an additional money supply component.

L:

Monetary liquid assets which include M_3, commercial paper (short-term obligations of corporations), bankers' acceptances (short-term obligations guaranteed by banks), US savings bonds (not traded in financial markets), and marketable US Treasury securities (traded in financial markets).

Exhibit 2.5 illustrates the growth in each of the money supply aggregates from 1964 through 1998. M_3 grew from $425 billion in 1964 to $5.8 trillion in 1998. In 1964, cash and transactions

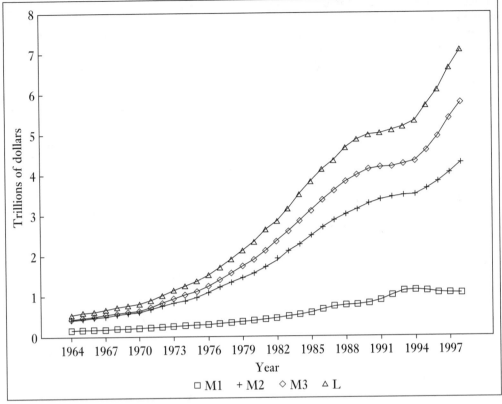

◆ **Exhibit 2.5:** Money supply, 1964–98

◆ *Source*:   United States Department of Commerce, Bureau of Economic Analysis, *Business Statistic 1961–88*, *Survey of Current Business, April 1991*, and *Federal Reserve Bulletin*, various issues.

accounts, M_1, represented 37 percent of total money supply (M_3). Thirty-four years later, this percentage was only 19 percent (of M_3).

The largest segment of the money supply in 1998 consisted of the less liquid assets in M_2, primarily composed of small time deposits, money market deposit accounts, savings accounts, and retail money market fund balances – accounts controlled by individuals. These consumer-related financial instruments grew from $253 billion in 1964 to $3.2 trillion in 1998. Over the same period, there was little change in the percentage that the consumer-related instruments represented of M_3 (59 percent in 1964 and 56 percent in 1998). However, large-denomination deposits and institutional money market fund balances ($[M_3 - M_2]$) increased from $15 billion in 1964 (4 percent of M_3) to $1.5 trillion in 1998 (26 percent of MM_3).

The increase in M_3 has come at the expense of the more liquid M_1 segment (37 percent of M_3 in 1964, but only 19 percent by 1998).[12] Basically, this shift is an indication of substantial growth in interest-rate-sensitive instruments, which represents a corresponding loss in funding for commercial banks and thrifts from traditional interest-free demand deposit accounts.[13] Also, the inclusion of interest-bearing transactions accounts (NOW accounts) in M_1 compounds this effect. To some extent, the factors that led to these changes in the money supply have affected all the financial institutions and markets that are discussed in this text.

 **Summary**

Money links financial institutions to each other and to the customers that they serve. Money is a medium of exchange, a unit of account, and a store of value. In a less developed economy, the method of exchanging goods and services – the monetary system – may be based on barter. In more advanced economies, the monetary system is full-bodied money, paper money, deposit money, or electronic money (with the last three having the advantages of ease of transport and convenience in large transactions).

Monetary standards describe the physical attributes of money with the two primary classifications being commodity and noncommodity (paper) standards. Commodity standards usually involve gold. Gold coin, as full-bodied money, has value in its own right. The gold bullion standard uses paper money that is convertible into gold. The gold exchange standard uses paper money that may be exchanged for another currency that, in turn, may be converted into gold. Silver standards have similar definitions but have been less frequently adopted.

Today, monetary standards that have been adopted are primarily noncommodity (paper) standards. An inconvertible paper standard allows conversion into other currencies, but not into gold or silver. A controlled paper standard does not even allow conversion into other currencies. Most countries have adopted the inconvertible paper standard.

At one time, commercial banks were the only private financial institutions that issued money. In addition to currency and coin (issued by government monetary authorities), demand deposits and bank savings accounts were primary components of the money supply. Today, the money supply includes demand deposit accounts; transactions accounts of savings institutions, credit unions, and securities firms; large and small time deposits; and money market fund shares. As a result, a wide range of institutions now influence the money supply.

 End-of-chapter Questions

1. What are the primary functions of money?
2. Explain the advantages of a modern monetary system over a barter system.
3. What is full-bodied money?
4. Differentiate among gold coin, gold bullion, and gold exchange monetary standards.
5. Why do you suppose that the Bretton Woods arrangement was agreed to in the year 1944?
6. Describe the actions of the European Community (EC) with respect to the 1971 Smithsonian Agreement.
7. What problems for a country can be caused by wild fluctuations in the foreign exchange rate of its currency?
8. What events led to the suspension of gold convertibility of the US dollar?

9. Explain expansion of the money supply in connection with the maintenance of fractional bank reserves.

10. The money supply is an important element in a country's economic development. What impact would an inadequate money supply have on the economy?

11. Refer to *International Financial Statistics* (International Monetary Fund) in your school's library. Prepare two charts (line graphs) for the United States, Germany, Japan, and the United Kingdom from 1965 through 1985 for the following economic factors:
    a. Annual change in the consumer price index (inflation rate).
    b. Average currency exchange rate for the non-US countries (number of units of currency that are the equivalent of one US dollar).
    On your charts, identify the years associated with significant developments in the international monetary system. What changes do you think may be associated with the events discussed in this chapter?

End-of-chapter Problems

1. Suppose that a country operates under a barter system. If five yards of textile material have the same value as 10 bales of hay, what is the price of:
   a. one yard of textile material?
   b. one bale of hay?

2. Suppose that a foreign currency speculator borrows $100,000 and converts them into British pounds (£s) when the exchange rate is $1.85 = £1 ($1 = £0.5405) and repays the dollar loan when the exchange rate is $1.90 = £1 ($1 = £0.5263). Ignoring interest on the loan, did the speculator profit from this transaction? If so, by how much?

3. If the money supply increases by $600 million after a liquidity infusion of $72 million, what is the implied reserve requirement?

4. Refer to the *Federal Reserve Bulletin*. Determine:
   a. The dollar amount of change in M_1, M_2, M_3, and L during the most recent 12-month period.
   b. The percentage change in each.

NOTES

1   Even if these conditions *are* met, the total number of prices in a system with *n* commodities is n(n − 1)/2, the total of all possible combinations of *n* items. When one of the commodities is modern money, the number of prices is reduced to n − 1. Every other commodity is denominated in terms of money.

2   US dollar conversion into gold was possible only for governments at the time of the Bretton Woods Conference. The Gold Act of 1934 prohibited gold conversion by individuals.

3   In the case of the exchange of non-US currencies for *other* non-US currencies, a more appropriate designation is inconvertible paper standard. (See discussion of Monetary Standards in earlier section.)

4   If a speculator anticipates a decline in the value of the US dollar, the speculator would borrow US dollars and convert the dollars into another currency. If the US dollar declines in value, the speculator needs less foreign currency to purchase the US dollars necessary to repay the dollar loan. The speculator realizes profit equal to the difference between (1) the amount of currency into which the borrowed dollars originally were converted and (2) the amount of currency necessary to repay the dollar loan.

5   The "Group of Ten" are Belgium, Canada, France, Germany, Italy, Japan, the Netherlands, Sweden, the United Kingdom, and the United States. Switzerland is an associate member.

6   Under terms of the Maastricht Treaty of 1992, the association of these countries is now referred to as the European Union.

7   From 1968 to 1970, the US trade surplus (excess of exports over imports) grew from $1.4 to $3.8 billion. This situation reversed in 1971 and 1972 with trade deficits (excess of imports over exports) of $0.9 and $5.2 billion, respectively.

8   The bracketed term in Equation (1) is a geometric series in which each successive term increases by the multiplicative factor, q, that, in this case, has the value $(1 − r)$. The value of this term converges to:

$$(1 − (q^\infty))/(1 − q) = (1 − (1 − r))/(1 − (1 − r))$$
$$= (1 − 0)/(1 − 1 + r) = 1/r$$

9   The $1,000 expansion will occur as long as there are no "leaks" in the process such as time deposits (instead of demand account deposits) or excess reserves held by banks.

10   This also happens when government expenditures exceed government receipts – that is, (1) when the government spends more for goods and services than it collects in taxes and other revenues or (2) when a government agency purchases more government securities on the open market than it sells. This effect is not limited to American depositors with US dollars. The money supply also expands when a check drawn on a non-dollar-denominated account is deposited in a US bank. Such a transaction is roughly equivalent to the sale of foreign currency for US dollars and the deposit of those dollars into the banking system. For example, suppose that a Japanese customer opens an account in a US bank with a check drawn on a Japanese bank and denominated in Japanese yen. The US bank presents the check to the Japanese bank and receives credit; the yen must be converted into dollars and credited to the customer's US account. These dollars are a liquidity infusion into the banking system as much as a domestic cash deposit.

11   Reduction of the money supply results when deposits are converted to cash (and *not* redeposited), when government receipts exceed expenditures, when a government agency sells more government securities than it purchases, and when US dollar-denominated deposits are transferred to bank accounts denominated in other currencies.

12   In 1964, the difference between L and M_3 – representing savings bonds, marketable Treasury securities, commercial paper, and bankers' acceptances – was 27 percent of M_3 and 21 percent of L. In 1998, the corresponding percentages were 22 and 18 percent, respectively.

13   Thrift institutions are savings and loan associations, mutual savings banks, and credit unions.

SELECTED REFERENCES

Fitch, Thomas. *Dictionary of Banking Terms*, Barron's Educational Series, Hauppauge, NY, 1990.

Greider, William. *Secrets of the Temple: How the Federal Reserve Runs the Country*, Touchstone/Simon & Schuster, New York, 1987.

Kaufman, Hugo M. *Germany's International Monetary Policy and the European Monetary System*, Columbia University Press, New York, 1985.

Kindleberger, Charles P. *A Financial History of Western Europe*, George Allen & Unwin (Publishers) Ltd., London, 1984.

International Financial Statistics. International Monetary Fund, September 1996.

Mullineux, Andrew. *International Banking and Financial Systems: A Comparison*, Graham & Trotman Ltd., London, 1987.

Onoh, J. K. *Money and Banking in Africa*, Longman Group Limited, London, 1982.

Rosenberg, Jerry M. *Dictionary of International Trade*, John Wiley & Sons, New York, 1994.

Struthers, J. and H. Speight. *Money; Institutions, Theory and Policy*, Longman Group Ltd., London, 1986.

Money Markets

chapter 3

CHAPTER OVERVIEW

This chapter:
- Defines money markets.
- Explains the roles of money market participants.
- Describes financial instruments traded in money markets and analyzes their pricing.
- Addresses issues of adequate control in the government securities market.
- Examines recent trends in US money markets.

KEY TERMS

banker's acceptance
basis point
bid–asked spread
bill discounting
bill of exchange
book-entry system
call money
commercial paper
competitive bid
discount house
discount pricing
federal funds
gilt-edged market
government agency securities
government securities dealer

immediately available funds
interbank market
letter of credit
liquid assets
money market
negotiable certificate of deposit
noncompetitive bid
opportunity cost of holding cash
repurchase agreement
sterling money markets
Tanshi company
tender system
tiered custodial system
Treasury bills (T-bills)

CHAPTER OUTLINE

Introduction

Smoothly functioning financial markets allow financial institutions to perform distribution and intermediation functions efficiently and effectively. Financial markets are either *money* or *capital* markets, depending on the maturity of the specific financial instruments that are traded. This chapter discusses money markets which are markets for short-term transactions and chapters 4 and 5 describe capital markets.

US money markets are based on a foundation of *Treasury bills*, which are US government liabilities of less than one year in original maturity. T-bills are auctioned in the primary market and traded in an active secondary market created by government securities dealers. A number of other financial instruments have evolved to complement the T-bill market. Commercial banks and other depository institutions (and more recently, securities dealers and real estate funds) participate in markets for *federal funds* and *repurchase agreements*, both of which constitute short-term agreements to borrow and lend. *Negotiable certificates of deposit*, issued by banks and savings and loans, are widely held as liquid assets by nonfinancial corporations, personal trusts, pension funds, state and local governments, and others. *Commercial paper* (short-term liabilities of corporations) is another vehicle for short-term financing that has grown rapidly in recent years, with finance companies, nonfinancial corporations, and bank holding companies being primary issuers of commercial paper. *Banker's acceptances* (bank liabilities) accommodate financing needs associated primarily with international trade.

These markets, or markets like them, are found in virtually every industrialized country. In some countries, interbank transactions formed the core of the money markets – Japan and Hong Kong are examples. In other countries, institutions with no equivalent in the United States play vital roles in the smooth operation of money markets. Japanese *Tanshi* companies and British *discount houses* perform what would be considered governmental functions in the United States.

While the configuration of money markets may vary from one country to another, whatever their format, money markets are the mechanism allowing a variety of participants to meet a wide range of liquidity objectives in any economy.

 ## What is a Money Market?

The maturity of financial instruments that are traded is one way to differentiate markets. If the securities traded are short-term instruments, the market is called a *money market*. When maturities exceed one year, the market is considered a *capital market* (the subject of chapters 4 and 5).

Another differentiation is whether the securities are new (offered in the *primary* market) or already existing (traded in the *secondary* market). For example, when US Treasury bills (T-bills) are sold to the public for the first time, the sale takes place in a primary money market. When investors buy or sell already existing T-bills through dealers, these transactions occur in a secondary money market. Money markets enable market participants to borrow or lend liquid assets, and thereby meet needs for cash or investment of cash.

Money market:
    A market in which financial instruments with remaining maturities up to one year are bought and sold.

Liquid assets:
    Assets that may be converted into cash quickly, without significant loss of value.

Investing excess liquid assets – that is, lending – reduces the opportunity cost of holding cash or cash equivalents. Borrowing short-term funds eliminates disruption that would be caused by temporary cash flow deficits, that is, outflows that temporarily exceed inflows.

Opportunity cost of holding cash:
>That rate of return that could be earned if the next best alternative to cash were held by an investor, that is, that rate of return that is forgone when an investor holds cash.

Money Market Participants

2.1 THE UNITED STATES

The major money market participants are:

- The US Treasury
- The Federal Reserve System
- Government securities dealers
- Commercial banks
- Nonfinancial corporations

The *US Treasury* issues the Treasury bills and other securities that are the foundation of the money market. Short-term issues enable the government (1) to raise money to make necessary expenditures between the receipts of tax revenue and (2) to refinance maturing issues. These short-term issues are liabilities of the US Treasury.

The *Federal Reserve System* historically holds over 75 percent of its financial assets in the form of US government securities (10 percent of the total outstanding in 1996) and its role in the operation of money markets is crucial. As the fiscal agent for the Treasury, the Federal Reserve distributes all government securities in the primary market. In addition, the Federal Reserve uses these securities to carry out its monetary policy. Its ultimate responsibility for the money supply makes the Federal Reserve the single most influential participant in US money markets.

Government securities dealers make markets in Treasury securities by buying large blocks of securities from the Federal Reserve in the primary market and distributing them to customers. The dealers hold inventories of securities (assets) that facilitate secondary trading by their customers. Dealers also buy and sell for their own accounts, further helping to support an active and liquid market.

In the United States, *commercial banks* are major money market participants. In 1996, they accounted for 83 percent of negotiable certificates of deposit (CDs) outstanding and 66 percent of federal funds and repurchase agreements (liabilities).[1] Bank holding companies accounted for approximately 5 percent of commercial paper outstanding (liabilities) in 1996. Also, banks extend lines of credit supporting the commercial paper of nonfinancial firms, making the paper safer and more appealing to investors. (In this case, a bank issues a *standby* line of credit that is used only if the issuer of the commercial paper fails to repay.) As a group, banks hold a larger percentage of US government securities (assets) than any other group of financial institutions (approximately 8 percent in 1996).

Nonfinancial corporations are also major participants in US money markets. In 1996, these companies accounted for 25 percent of all commercial paper outstanding (liabilities).

2.2 THE UNITED KINGDOM AND JAPAN

In many other countries the money market functions of commercial banks, government entities, and securities dealers parallel those of their US counterparts. Such markets may vary in degree of development, but the basic functions take place in a comparable fashion. Two financial systems, however, have institutions for which there are no US parallels. In the United Kingdom, *discount houses* act as intermediaries between the government and the commercial (clearing) banks. These private firms absorb the entire weekly UK Treasury bill offering, can borrow from the Bank of England (UK's central bank), are active dealers in short-term government securities, and make a secondary market with merchant banks in negotiable CDs and acceptances.

In the United States, commercial banks may borrow directly from the Federal Reserve. British clearing banks must make their liquidity adjustments through the discount houses; they may not borrow directly from the Bank of England. It is this function of UK discount houses that distinguishes them from any US financial institution. The Bank of England carries out its monetary policy largely by purchase and sale of Treasury and commercial bills through the intermediary discount houses. Only in connection with the "big bang" of 1986 did banks gain the right to operate in the government securities market as US banks do. The UK discount house model is also used in countries that have British-style banking systems – for example, Singapore and Nigeria.

Another unique set of financial firms is the *Tanshi houses* of Japan. The Japanese government has licensed these six private companies in perpetuity to act as intermediaries in all money markets except the *gensaki* (repurchase agreement) market. Like discount houses, these nonbank firms may borrow from the central bank (the Bank of Japan), which frequently carries out its monetary policy through the *Tanshi*. They are the primary means through which large banks maintain reserve requirements. Because of their close relationship with the Bank of Japan, these nongovernmental companies essentially supervise bill-discount (high-quality corporate promissory note) and call money (interbank funds) markets – important components of Japan's money markets.

 Money Market Instruments

In the United States, the most widely traded money market instruments are:

- US Treasury bills
- Federal funds
- Repurchase agreements
- Negotiable certificates of deposit
- Commercial paper
- Banker's acceptances

Money market instruments share certain qualities that make them useful for wholesale (large) transactions:

- *Liquidity* – which describes the ability to convert an asset into cash with relative ease while not significantly depressing its price in the process – is perhaps the most important quality.
- *Default risk* – which is the risk of nonpayment of principal or interest – must be minimal in order for the security to be considered a safe haven for excess liquidity.

	Amount[1]		%[2]
Treasury Securities			
Treasury Bills	$641.1		
Others[3]	553.8	$1,194.9	32.0%
Federal Funds and Repurchase Agreements[4]		865.4	23.1
Negotiable Certificates of Deposit		564.8	15.1
Commercial Paper		1,098.4	29.4
Bankers' Acceptances		14.3	0.4
		$3,737.8	100.0%

◆ **Exhibit 3.1:** **Money market instruments outstanding, United States, as of June 30, 1998**

◆ *Notes*:   1   Billions of dollars
2   Percentage of total money market instruments outstanding
3   Treasury notes and bonds with less than one year to maturity remaining
4   Federal Reserve statistics do not separate federal funds and repurchase agreements

◆ *Sources*:   Board of Governors of the Federal Reserve System, *Flow of Funds Accounts; Flows and Outstandings.* Department of the Treasury, *Monthly Statement of the Public Debt of the United States, August 31, 1996.*

- *Short time to maturity* – given that adverse price movements attributable to interest rate changes are smaller for shorter-term assets – helps to ensure that interest rate changes will not affect the security's market value materially.

Exhibit 3.1 summarizes the amount of each US money market instrument outstanding as of mid-1998.

3.1 TREASURY SECURITIES

Treasury securities are obligations of the US government. They are issued to cover government budget deficits (excess of expenditures over revenues) and to refinance maturing government debt. The United States government sells Treasury securities through a *bid* or *tender* system.

> **Bid or tender system:**
> A predetermined quantity of securities is offered for sale and sold or "tendered" to the highest bidders.

The most common marketable government securities are *bills*, *notes*, and *bonds*. (The US Treasury also issues nonmarketable securities such as retirement bonds and savings bonds.) T-bills have original maturities of one year or less, while notes are for one to 10 years, and bonds have maturities greater than 10 years.

Treasury bills and other Treasury securities (with less than one year remaining life) are the most important instruments in US money markets. Exhibit 3.1 shows that, in 1998, these short-term instruments represented over 32 percent of all money market instruments outstanding, a larger share than any other single instrument.

> **Treasury bills (T-bills):**
> Short-term obligations of the US Treasury Department with original maturities of one year or less.

3.1.1 THE PRIMARY MARKET

The Bidding Process

The Treasury Department auctions an announced quantity of new bills through Federal Reserve district banks and their branches.

- 13-week and 26-week T-bills are auctioned each week.
- The 52-week bills are auctioned every fourth week.
- Essentially cash management bills follow the same auction schedule as 13-week and 26-week bills.

Bids for Treasury securities may be submitted by government securities dealers (for clients or for their own accounts), individuals, or financial and nonfinancial corporations. On the date of an auction, bids are submitted to the Federal Reserve Bank in New York, other Federal Reserve district banks, or the Bureau of the Public Debt (Treasury Department). Most of these bids are submitted by primary government securities dealers, but others may participate as well. Two types of bids are submitted:

- *Competitive bids* include the amount of securities and yield. The deadline for these bids is 1:00 p.m. ET. The yield is the minimum rate of return that the bidder wants to accept and must be stated in two decimal places, for example, 5.12 percent. Large investors usually submit competitive bids, which make up the bulk of the aggregate dollar value of total bids. However, Treasury rules prohibit any single bidder from obtaining more than 35 percent of any new issue.
- *Noncompetitive bids* include an amount only. The deadline for these bids is 12:00 noon ET. Noncompetitive bidders understand that they will receive a yield that is based on the outcome of the competitive bidding process. Most individual investors submit noncompetitive bids. Noncompetitive bids are limited to $1 million or less. Historically, noncompetitive bids have constituted 10 percent to 25 percent of the total.

The day of the auction, Federal Reserve banks and branches accept bids until 1:00 p.m. Eastern time, when all bids are forwarded to the Treasury. Noncompetitive bids are "accepted" before competitive bids in the sense that the amount of available securities is effectively reduced by the amount of noncompetitive bids before competitive bids are considered. For example, a $11 billion auction with $4 billion in noncompetitive bids will result in the allocation of only $7 billion to competitive bidders.

Competitive bids are accepted in ascending order of yield, that is, descending order of price. The highest bid (lowest price) that is accepted is referred to as the *stop out bid*. When this yield is translated into a price, that price is referred to as the *stop out price*. The discount rate is then set based on the accepted competitive bids. The discount rate is set so that the average price paid for the T-bills is as close to par as possible. The actual price paid by the competitive bidders will be based on the yield of their bid and the issue's discount rate. Under this system, some of the competitive bidders pay a premium for the securities, others pay a discount and still others pay close to par. All noncompetitive bidders receive their securities at the average yield of competitive bids.

By 3:00 p.m. ET of the auction day, the results of the auction are announced. The information that is released includes the stop out bid, parties that received allocations, the average yield accepted, and the lowest yield accepted. If the auction is for a Treasury note or bond, the coupon rate is also announced. In addition, a measure which describes the success of the auction is included. The *tail* is the difference between the stop out bid and the average bid. The tail is a measure of the difference between the highest bid (lowest price) and the average yield. The size of the tail reflects the range of yields offered for the securities. If the tail is large, the auction is considered weak because it was necessary to accept relatively high yields in order to sell all the securities. On the other hand, if the tail is zero, the auction is considered very strong because there was significant demand within a tight range of interest rates.

International Participation

Foreign and international monetary authorities also participate in Treasury auctions. These parties are permitted to submit noncompetitive bids. However, instead of reducing the amount of securities offered during the auction, foreign noncompetitive bids add to the allocation. For example, if $11 billion in securities are to be auctioned, foreign noncompetitive bids will result in more than $11 billion being issued. Assuming that there are $4 billion in domestic noncompetitive bids, and $2 billion in foreign noncompetitive bids, securities totalling $13 billion will be issued:

- $7 billion to competitive bidders.
- $4 billion to domestic noncompetitive bidders.
- $2 billion to foreign noncompetitive bidders.

The additional securities offered through the auction are referred to as *add-ons*.

T-bill Pricing and Delivery

Treasury bills are sold at a *discount* price. Interest earned is the difference between the price paid to purchase the instrument and the amount received upon maturity. A T-bill price is face value (e.g., $10,000) less applicable discount according to the given rate of interest. The discount is based on a 360–day year and the number of days between date of purchase and maturity date and is quoted per $100 of face value. Once the interest rate is set through the auction, the price is determined by this formula:

$$P = 100 - discount$$

$$= 100 - 100\,(k)\left(\frac{N}{360}\right)$$

$$= 100\left[1 - (k)\left(\frac{N}{360}\right)\right] \tag{3.1}$$

where P = price per $100 of face value
k = appropriate interest rate
N = number of days to maturity

> **Discount pricing:**
> Setting the price of a financial instrument at the face value less the amount of interest that will be earned through the maturity date.

At an interest rate of 8 percent for three-month bills (91 days to maturity), the Treasury bill price would be $97.9778 per $100 face value. Rounded to three decimals, the cost to purchase $1 million in bills is $979,780 [$97.978 × 10,000 = $979,780] and, upon maturity, the interest earned totals $20,220 [$1 million − 979,780].

Treasury bill purchases are recorded in a *book-entry system*. Physical securities are never delivered. Instead, a record of transactions is maintained electronically by the Treasury and the Federal Reserve system. This arrangement significantly reduces transactions costs by eliminating the need to handle, ship, or store physical documents.

Once the Treasury auction is complete, settlement (that is, payment and delivery) is accomplished through a *tiered custodial system*.[2]

> **Tiered custodial system:**
> System that segments ownership records of T-bills. The Treasury Department records ownership by the relevant Federal Reserve bank. The particular Federal Reserve bank records ownership for a depository institution. Only the depository institution maintains records of ultimate ownership.

3.1.2 THE SECONDARY MARKET

The United States

The secondary market in Treasury bills is a vast and exceedingly efficient telecommunications network, whose major participants are *primary government securities dealers*, 37 financial institutions so designated by the Federal Reserve. These banks, brokerage firms, and bond houses buy and sell Treasury bills for their own and their customers' accounts. Customers include depository institutions, insurance companies, pension funds, nonfinancial firms, and state and local governments.

Government dealers help to maintain an orderly market mechanism through trades of Treasury bills for their own accounts. They earn profits based on the difference between the price at which they are willing to purchase Treasury bills, the *bid price*, and the price at which they will sell them, the *asked price*. The efficiency of the market is evidenced by narrow *bid–asked spreads*, typically ranging from two to four *basis points*. Thus, the customary spread is approximately $50 to $100 per $1 million of three-month bills.[3]

> **Bid–asked spread:**
> Dealer profit in a T-bill transaction; the difference between the purchase and sales prices that a dealer will accept.

> **Basis point:**
> One hundredth of one percent.

During the 1960s and 1970s, there were only five primary government securities dealers and the industry was essentially self-regulating, as these dealers were exempt from federal oversight until the U.S. Treasury Department was given rule-making authority in 1986. Currently, the number of primary dealers is 37, but the industry remains highly concentrated with Salomon Brothers historically commanding the most significant role.

Because of the importance of a handful of primary dealers, there have long been suspicions that the bidding process was not as competitive as it should be. In some cases, such suspicions seemed credible; for example, in a 1979 auction of $3.3 billion in Treasury securities, all primary dealers bid exactly the same price.

In 1991, Salomon Brothers' activity in the market violated the Treasury Department rule with respect to purchases by a single dealer for its own account. On several occasions, the firm gained control of more than 35 percent of new issues by using customers' accounts – sometimes with their knowledge and consent and sometimes without. The motive for this behavior is excess profits that may be generated by "cornering the market":

- The firm places a bid for 35 percent of the issue at a price sufficiently high to ensure acceptance by the Treasury Department (primary market).
- Simultaneously, the firm places orders on behalf of its largest clients at a similarly high price (primary market).
- The Treasury accepts the bids.
- The firm then purchases the customers' securities at cost, thus controlling a significant share of the total new issue (secondary market).
- When other bond dealers wish to purchase the securities, the firm can charge a monopoly-like premium over cost and earn excess profits.

An investigation led to disclosure of Salomon's role in such market manipulation. One particularly graphic example of misconduct was a May 1991 auction in which Salomon gained control of 94 percent of an $11 billion issue. Criminal charges and civil lawsuits were brought against the firm and there were calls for regulatory reform of the industry.

Nevertheless, the market is so large that even this scandal had relatively little impact on market stability. (In 1991, Salomon Brothers owned less than 2 percent of all Treasury securities outstanding.) The most significant outcome of the Salomon Brothers scandal was conversion to an electronic bidding process that is monitored on a weekly basis. The review of market activity is performed jointly by the Federal Reserve Bank of New York, the US Treasury Department, and the Securities and Exchange Commission.

◆ **Exhibit 3.2: The case of Salomon Brothers: scandal in the government securities market**

While the US government securities market is the largest and most liquid market in the world, there have been problems. Exhibit 3.2 describes challenges associated with maintaining integrity in the market and the reforms that resulted.

As the core of the US money market, the US Treasury bill market attracts both domestic and international investors. The Treasury has sold three-month maturities since 1929 and six-month and one-year maturities since the late 1950s.

Exhibit 3.3 provides a list of the current primary government securities dealers. The group of 37 firms is roughly equally divided among commercial bank affiliates and securities firms. There is also representation by foreign institutions, primarily commercial bank affiliates.

BA Securities, Inc.
Barclays de Zoete Wedd Securities Inc.
Bear, Stearns & Co., Inc.
BT Securities Corporation
Chase Securities Inc.
Chemical Securities Inc.
Citicorp Securities, Inc.
CS First Boston Corporation
Daiwa Securities America, Inc.
Dean Witter Reynolds Inc.
Deutsche Bank Securities Corporation
Dillon, Read & Co. Inc.
Donaldson, Lufkin & Jenrette Securities Corporation
Eastbridge Capital Inc.
First Chicago Capital Markets, Inc.
Fuji Securities Inc.
Goldman, Sachs & Co.
Greenwich Capital Markets, Inc.
HSBC Securities, Inc.
Aubrey G. Lanston & Co., Inc.
Lehman Brothers Inc.
Merrill Lynch Government Securities Inc.
J. P. Morgan Securities, Inc.
Morgan Stanley & Co. Incorporated
NationsBanc Capital Markets, Inc.
Nesbitt Burns Securities Inc.
The Nikko Securities Co. International, Inc.
Nomura Securities International, Inc.
Paine Webber Incorporated
Prudential Securities Incorporated
Saloman Brothers Inc.
Sanwa Securities (USA) Co., L.P.
Smith Barney Inc.
SBC Capital Markets Inc.
UBS Securities Inc.
Yamaichi International (America), Inc.
Zions First National Bank

◆ **Exhibit 3.3:** Primary US government securities dealers

◆ *Source*:   Market Reports Division, Federal Reserve Bank of New York, July 11, 1996.

The United Kingdom

In Europe, T–bills have an even longer history than in the United States, with the United Kingdom (location of the world's largest money market) first issuing Treasury bills in 1877. All UK bills have original maturities of 91 days and are bought and sold through discount houses, the financial institutions that act as intermediaries between British clearing (commercial) banks and the Bank of England, the central bank.

Since the "big bang" of 1986, which involved major deregulation of the financial markets, domestic and foreign banks have been permitted to operate as primary dealers in the medium- and long-term government securities market, the *gilt-edged* market. With this new status, banks may now also bid on, but not act as primary dealers for, Treasury bills in the primary market.

Gilt-edged market:
> The market for medium- and long-term government securities in the United Kingdom.

Asia

While the US government securities market operates a bid or tender system, an alternative method of selling government securities is through the *tap* system.

Tap system:
> The government sells only those securities that the public requests.

Singapore made government securities available on a tap basis beginning in 1923, but the Singapore money market did not expand dramatically until three discount houses began operation in 1972 and Treasury bill sales were converted to the tender system in 1973. These factors and government initiatives to develop secondary markets in other money market instruments helped double the size of the money market in the five years that followed.

While many countries' money markets have developed around Treasury bills, others have evolved using other dominant liquid assets. Hong Kong, as a British colony (until 1997, when the People's Republic of China resumed power), had neither a central bank nor an indigenous government securities market. Thus, *call money*, the equivalent of US federal funds, long formed the core of the money markets of Hong Kong. Japan also has had a long tradition of a market in call money.

3.2 FEDERAL FUNDS

Federal funds are not formal securities. They are immediately available funds that are loaned or borrowed among financial institutions.

Immediately available funds:
> Funds on deposit in a commercial bank or other depository institution that may be withdrawn with no delay.

Federal funds:
> Immediately available short-term funds transferred (loaned or borrowed) between financial institutions, usually for a period of one day.

Recall from chapter 2 that US banks and (since 1980) other depository institutions that are federally insured are required to maintain *reserves*, that is, liquid assets to back deposit liabilities at levels specified by the Federal Reserve. These reserves may consist of vault cash or deposits at a Federal Reserve bank. As deposits at Federal Reserve banks earn no interest, banks have an incentive to redeploy any excess reserves. The federal funds market developed as a way to do this.

3.2.1 THE MARKET

The federal funds market began in the 1920s when banks with excess reserves loaned the excess to banks that needed reserves at a "Fed funds" rate close to the rate that financial institutions pay to borrow directly from the Federal Reserve. The institution that borrows federal funds records a liability, *federal funds purchased*. The lending institution records an asset, *federal funds sold*.

Federal funds transactions take two forms. If both institutions have Federal Reserve bank accounts, they may instruct the Federal Reserve to transfer funds from the account of the lender to the account of the borrower over Fedwire, the wire-transfer system of the Federal Reserve. Either party may initiate a transaction. Alternatively, an institution (respondent) may maintain an account with an institution acting as a federal funds broker (correspondent). In this case, the respondent bank informs the correspondent of its desire to sell federal funds, at which point the correspondent reclassifies the respondent's balance (liability on the books of the correspondent) from Demand Deposits to Federal Funds Purchased. The correspondent frequently resells the funds to a third party in the market.

3.2.2 DURATION

The maturity of a federal funds transaction is usually one day – *overnight*.

- When both banks have Federal Reserve accounts (liabilities for the Federal Reserve Bank), the transaction is reversed on the following day. The Federal Reserve bank debits the account of the borrower (reduces the balance of the borrower's reserve bank account) and credits the account of the lender (increases the balance of the lender's account) for the principal amount of the transaction plus interest earned.
- If the transaction was brokered, the transaction is reversed when the correspondent debits Federal Funds Purchased (liability) in the amount of the transaction and Interest Expense for the interest to be paid, crediting the respondent's Demand Deposit account.

Banks may also negotiate *term federal funds* loans, usually for a period of 90 days or less. An institution may choose this arrangement if it expects liquidity needs to persist longer than overnight, or if it anticipates a rise in interest rates in the near future. *Continuing contract federal funds* are, in effect, a continuous rollover of overnight federal funds at the rate that applies each day. This can evolve into a longer-term arrangement with a variable interest rate. (Because either party may withdraw from the contract, this arrangement may also be short-term.)

3.2.3 TERMS

Most federal funds borrowings are unsecured. In fact, most are supported only by oral agreements made by telephone. This procedure is possible because the parties have long-standing business relationships or because the broker has no doubt about the institution's creditworthiness.

When federal funds are explicitly secured, the borrower places securities in the possession (custody account) of the lender. At the time the loan is repaid, custody of the securities is returned to the borrower. Title to the securities never changes, however.

Japan

The US federal funds market has a counterpart in several other countries. The *call money market* in Japan has operated since the turn of the century.

Call money:
> Loaned funds that are repayable upon the request of either party.

All transactions go through one of nine *Tanshi* companies licensed by the Japanese Ministry of Finance. The term of a call money loan can range from a half-day to seven days. *Half-day* money is borrowed at 9:00 a.m. and repaid at 1:00 p.m. or borrowed at 1:00 p.m. and repaid at 3:00 p.m. *Unconditional* money is repaid the following day. *Fixed maturity* money is repaid in two to seven days.

Hong Kong

In Hong Kong, the *interbank market* participants are licensed Hong Kong banks and authorized brokers. Overnight call and other short-term deposits are the common vehicles, and collateral is rarely required. The larger Hong Kong banks had long conducted short-term transactions of this nature, but it was not until the late 1950s that the market became active. A comparable interbank market was the only way to adjust liquidity in Singapore until discount houses were established.

Interbank market:
> Money market transactions (short-term exchange of liquid assets) between banks with no intermediary.

The United Kingdom

Discount houses in the United Kingdom have traditionally served to provide short-term credit in the UK banking system by entering into call money arrangements with individual banks. Banks with surplus funds lent them to discount houses and banks in need of liquidity called in their discount house loans. More recently, however, a parallel set of money markets has developed, one of which is the interbank market. Late in the 1960s clearing banks began to establish subsidiaries (nonclearing banks) to operate in the interbank market. Transactions generated by these and other institutions have since become dominant in the *sterling money markets*.

Sterling money market:
> Short-term market for funds denominated in British pounds.

Thus, while the call money markets of Hong Kong, Singapore, Japan, and the United Kingdom have common features, the markets have developed in somewhat different ways. The call money market of Hong Kong has functioned in much the same way as the US federal funds market, without any institutional intermediary. Singapore money markets did not become active until discount houses began operations and government securities were offered on a tender basis. Japan has maintained vigorous call money markets with the *Tanshi* houses as intermediaries since the turn of the century. Beginning in 1986, British call money markets with discount house intermediaries have had less impact because of deregulation and the growth of parallel, interbank markets. The British experience suggests that, in some cases, the more robust markets will be those that are developed outside the guidance of government agencies or affiliates. Thus, deregulation is a central theme in the financial markets of many countries.

3.3 Repurchase Agreements

The United States

Repurchase agreements, also referred to as repos, are agreements to sell securities and, later, to reverse the sale. These transactions commonly involve Treasury securities, but they may also involve government agency securities.

> **Repurchase agreement (repo):**
> An agreement between buyer and seller in the sale of securities to reverse the transaction in the future at a specified date and price.

> **Government agency securities:**
> Securities issued by an agency of the US federal government, with implicit backing of the federal government.

Repurchase agreements are essentially collateralized loans. A financial institution with large holdings of Treasury securities sells some portion of them for a predetermined period of time to obtain liquidity, and promise to repurchase the securities at the end of that period. Of course, on the other side of the transaction is an institution with excess liquidity. The amount of the transaction is relatively large, and the interest rate is below the federal funds rate. The lower rate is justified, because the transaction is collateralized by government securities.

Repurchase agreements are typically as short-term in nature as federal funds (or call money). Overnight, term, or continuing basis repurchase agreements are all negotiated. Unlike collateralized federal funds transactions, in which title to the securities does not change, in a repurchase agreement title *does transfer* to the purchaser.

In the United States, government securities dealers frequently engage in repurchase agreements for their own account to manage liquidity and to capitalize on anticipated changes in interest rates. If a dealer sells securities to a bank in one of these arrangements, the bank is said to have entered into a *reverse repo*. In fact, whichever party initially sells the securities enters a repo agreement, and the initial purchaser enters a reverse repo – one is simply the mirror image of the other. These transactions are commonly designated from the perspective of the securities dealer: if the dealer is the initial seller, the transaction is a repo; if the dealer is the initial purchaser, it is a reverse repo.

Japan

A Japanese counterpart to the repurchase agreement is the Japanese *gensaki*. While term repurchase agreements rarely exceed 30 days in the United States, the most common maturities in Japan are 30 to 60 days. Further, in the United States, nonfinancial corporations hold less than 25 percent of repurchase agreements. Nonfinancial corporations in Japan contribute over 60 percent to *gensaki* lending, exemplifying the close relationship between Japanese financial institutions and their corporate clients.

3.4 NEGOTIABLE CERTIFICATES OF DEPOSIT

Banks have issued certificates of deposits for many years, but it was not until the 1960s, when they were first issued in negotiable form, that certificates of deposit with original maturities of six months or less assumed a significant role in money markets.

Negotiable certificate of deposit (CD):
> A financial instrument issued by a bank documenting a deposit, with principal and interest repayable to the bearer at a specified future date.

Note that a negotiable certificate of deposit is a bearer instrument and a term (not demand) deposit. In the 1950s, nonnegotiable, large-denomination CDs were unattractive because significant interest penalties were levied upon early withdrawal. (This is still true for many small-denomination nonnegotiable certificates, such as those held by individual bank customers.) Also at that time, bank demand deposits (checking accounts) paid no interest. As corporate treasurers became more sophisticated cash managers and sought alternatives to demand deposits (assets) as outlets for liquidity, the result was a severe reduction in demand deposit balances held by corporations.

3.4.1 THE BIRTH OF NEGOTIABLE CDs IN THE US AND ABROAD

The negotiable CD was the banks' response to this deposit drain. In 1961, what is now Citibank issued the first negotiable CDs in amounts greater than $100,000. Although subject to interest rate ceilings as specified by a Federal Reserve limitation called Regulation Q, the negotiable CD offered an alternative to noninterest-bearing demand deposits. Its enthusiastic reception helped banks regain a good measure of the funding that had been lost. (See also Exhibit 3.4.)

Banks were able to increase the rate paid on negotiable CDs to attract more deposits as the need arose. This innovation brought widespread adoption of *bank liability management*, which enables banks to attract funds by offering higher interest rates thereby changing their deposit base. (See chapter 15 for discussion of liability management.) The interest rate ceiling was not a binding constraint until 1966 when Treasury bill interest rates rose to the point that they exceeded the maximum rate that could be paid on negotiable CDs. This meant that investors would not purchase more of the CDs as they matured, placing the banks in a "credit crunch." The banks reacted by offering competitively priced CDs *offshore* (that is, overseas) where Regulation Q was not applicable. So began the Eurodollar market. (See chapter 9 for a discussion of Euromarkets.)

In 1970, Regulation Q interest rate ceilings were lifted for CDs over $100,000. By 1972, certificates of deposit represented approximately 40 percent of all bank deposits. Negotiable CDs

In 1960, the first "Bankers Certificate" was offered by the Overseas Division of First National City Bank. The $1 million certificate was issued to Union Bank of Switzerland and was described as "marketable." In fact, Union Bank found that there was no market for the new instrument.

Walter Wriston, head of the Overseas Division, suggested to Discount Corporation, a government securities dealer, that it start a market in the new certificates. Discount Corporation was willing to do so *if* First National City provided the dealer with a $10 million unsecured loan (no collateral) to finance the operation. First National City overlooked its long-standing rule of not lending to securities dealers on an unsecured basis, and the market for bankers certificates was born.

On February 20, 1961, First National City announced the new bankers certificate to be sold in units of not less than $1 million with Discount Corporation agreeing to make a market. Walter Wriston would go on to become President and later Chairman of the nation's largest bank, now called Citibank. The new certificate would become one of the most important money market instruments in the United States and a model for similar instruments issued throughout the world.

◆ **Exhibit 3.4: Walter Wriston and the negotiable CD**

◆ *Source*:   Cleveland, Harold and Thomas Huertas. *Citibank 1812–1970*, Harvard University Press, Cambridge, Mass., 1985.

are now one of the most important instruments in US money markets. The negotiable CD is a major contribution by depository institutions to money markets in the United States and abroad.

When US banks went offshore in 1966, they selected London as the location for offering dollar-denominated negotiable CDs. The instrument was readily accepted there – so much so, that in 1968 the first sterling-denominated negotiable CDs were introduced. Negotiable CDs in domestic currency were first sold in Singapore in 1975 and in Hong Kong in 1977. The first yen-denominated negotiable CDs were sold in 1979.

3.4.2 CD PRICING

The clear appeal of these instruments *vis-à-vis* other time deposits is their negotiability. Once issued, negotiable CDs may be sold through brokers, generally in round lots of $1 million. While the CD is originally issued at face value, its price in the secondary market depends on prevailing rates and the remaining time to maturity. Pricing is most easily analyzed in the context of the time value of money. Consider first three basic relationships:

$$FV_n = PV(1 + k)^n \tag{3.2a}$$

$$PV = \frac{FV_n}{(1 + k)^n} \tag{3.2b}$$

$$k = \left(\frac{FV_n}{PV}\right)^{\left(\frac{1}{n}\right)} - 1 \tag{3.2c}$$

where FV_n = future value of an investment
    PV = present value of an investment
     k = rate of return
     n = number of periods the investment is held

Equation (3.2a) means that the value of an investment at some future time is a function of the initial investment, the rate of return being earned, and the length of time the investment is held. Equation (3.2b) is a variation of Equation (3.2a) and represents the current value of an investment with one specified future payoff. Equation (3.2c) computes the rate of return for an investment when the price is given and the future payoff is specified.

To illustrate the pricing of a negotiable CD, assume that on Day 0 a CD is issued at 8 percent with a maturity of 182 days (six months). The original investor, I^1, presumably will hold this CD for 182/365 of a year, so that the payoff of principal and interest on day 182 will be \$103,912.09, according to Equation (3.2a):

$$FV_{182} = 100,000(1 + .08)^{\frac{182}{365}}$$

$$= 103,912.09$$

But suppose I^1 decides to sell the CD to another investor, I^2, on day 92, when 90 days remain to maturity and CDs of this risk classification are yielding 7.5 percent. Applying Equation (3.2b), the price of the CD on day 92, P_{92}, is \$102,075.50:

$$P_{92} = \frac{103,912.09}{(1 + .075)^{90/365}}$$

$$= 102,075.50$$

This is exactly the price that will yield investor I^2 a rate of return of 7.5 percent.

$$k = \left(\frac{103,912.09}{102,075.50}\right)^{365/90} - 1$$

$$= 0.075$$

Equation (3.2b), can be adapted to generalize the price of a negotiable CD:

$$P_t = \frac{\left[P_0(1 + k_0)^{\left(\frac{N}{365}\right)}\right]}{(1 + k_t)^{\left(\frac{N-t}{365}\right)}} \tag{3.3}$$

where P_t = price at time t
$\quad P_0$ = face value of CD
$\quad k_0$ = interest rate at time of CD issue
$\quad N$ = original days to maturity
$\quad k_t$ = interest rate at time of CD sale

3.5 COMMERCIAL PAPER

3.5.1 HISTORY OF ISSUANCE

Another financial instrument that has significantly enhanced the alternatives for short-term liquidity adjustments is commercial paper. Commercial paper dates back to the beginning of trade in colonial America, even before banks were organized. The first form of commercial paper was bills of exchange.

> **Bill of exchange:**
> An order written by the seller of goods instructing the purchaser to pay the seller (or the bearer of the bill) a specified amount on a specified future date.

Bills of exchange essentially provide short-term loans to purchasers for a period of time between the sale of goods and the date of payment. They were used to smooth seasonal cash flow fluctuations. Bills of exchange could be *discounted* prior to the specified future date when the seller accepted the face amount of the bill less interest.

> **Bill discounting:**
> Receiving payment on a bill of exchange prior to the bill's maturity by surrendering the bill for face value less applicable interest for the time remaining to maturity.

The modern version of this instrument is called *commercial paper*, which is issued in large denominations, primarily by the most creditworthy firms. Commercial paper is a convenient way to raise short-term funds, because registration with the US Securities and Exchange Commission (SEC) is not necessary, as it is in the case of issuing other securities for sale to the public. In order to be exempt from SEC registration, the issue must have an original maturity of 270 days or less and be intended for current transactions. The most common maturities of commercial paper are between 20 and 45 days. Like bills of exchange and Treasury bills, most commercial paper is issued on a discounted basis.

> **Commercial paper:**
> Unsecured promissory notes, issued by corporations, with an original maturity of 270 days or less.

3.5.2 GROWTH AND MARKETABILITY

The amount of commercial paper outstanding increased dramatically in the early 1980s, when short-term bank loans became prohibitively expensive, and commercial paper represented a much less costly source of funds. In 1980, for example, the difference between the prime bank loan rate and the commercial paper rate exceeded 6.5 percent. Although the spread has since narrowed, commercial paper remains an important segment of US money markets.

Because commercial paper is unsecured, the credit rating of the issuing company is a critical factor in the marketability of the issues. Three credit-rating firms rate the issues – Standard & Poor's Corporation (S&P), Moody's Investors Service, and fitch Investor Service. S&P designates investment grade (high-quality) commercial paper as A-1 (highest investment grade), A-2 (high investment grade), and A-3 (good investment grade). Moody's comparable ratings are P-1, P-2, and P-3, while fitch rates better-quality paper F-1, F-2, or F-3. Over 70 percent of the commercial paper rated by these firms receives the highest rating and 98 percent receives the highest two ratings, which gives some measure of the importance of creditworthiness for successful marketing.

Banks play a vital role in these high average ratings. In most instances, issuing firms have backup lines of credit that cover 100 percent of the issue. When the credit of the issuing firm does not justify one of the top ratings, the firm may obtain a *letter of credit* from a bank with a top credit rating.

Letter of credit:
> A letter issued by a bank or other firm indicating that a firm has arranged
> to obtain financing up to a specified amount.

A letter of credit backing the commercial paper in effect substitutes the credit rating of the bank for the credit rating of the issuer. This is called a *support arrangement* and the commercial paper is called "commercial paper supported by letter of credit" or a "documented discount note." In addition to banks, supporting are insurance companies and parent companies (in the case of subsidiaries).

3.5.3 SECONDARY MARKETS

The United States

Compared to the market for Treasury bills and negotiable CDs, the secondary market for commercial paper is not as extensive. Dealers and direct issuers will redeem an issue prior to maturity if the investor is in dire need of funds, but early redemption is not encouraged. Of course, given that original maturities are so short, early redemption is generally not necessary.

Other Countries

Commercial paper markets outside the United States are in various stages of development. In the United Kingdom, bill-brokers originally facilitated discounting of bills of exchange by working through banks and wealthy individuals. Discount houses perform this function now by accepting call money from clearing banks, buying bills at discount, and rediscounting them at the Bank of England. Perhaps because of this long tradition of bill discounting, the sterling commercial paper market was not authorized until 1986. As the 1986 legislation effectively exempts firms that issue commercial paper from preparing a prospectus (as is true in the United States), it removes a significant impediment to development of the market.

In Hong Kong, where the call money market has traditionally played a critical domestic role, commercial paper has been introduced only recently. The first major issues did not appear until 1979.

Introduction of discount houses in Singapore in 1972 facilitated discounting of bills of exchange. Bills of exchange that have been approved by the Monetary Authority of Singapore (the equivalent of a central bank) may also be held as liquid assets by commercial banks. The commercial paper market started formally in 1984.

Japanese bills of exchange with maturities of from one to four months have long been discounted by banks, but until 1971, the activity was considered part of the call money market. Individual promissory notes have relatively small denominations, so they are packaged in larger aggregates and attached to a bank's accommodation bill with a face value equal to the sum of the accompanying promissory notes. The banks then trade these accommodation bills among themselves, with *Tanshi* companies acting as brokers.

A domestic commercial paper market has been slow to evolve in Japan, despite the fact that Japanese companies issue commercial paper in the United States and in Euromarkets. In 1982 Japanese banking laws were revised to permit the establishment of a domestic market, but the Ministry of finance formulated no regulations until 1987. These regulations classified commercial paper in the same category as commercial bills of exchange and designated banks and *Tanshi* companies as participants. Because commercial paper is unsecured debt, only corporations and banks with high credit ratings may issue this instrument in Japan.

3.6 BANKER'S ACCEPTANCES

Banker's acceptances are a subset of bills of exchange that are guaranteed by "accepting" banks. In these instruments, the credit of the bank substitutes for the credit of the purchaser and the seller is assured payment. Further, unlike an open trade credit arrangement (in which the seller provides credit for a period of time), the seller need not wait for payment. A banker's acceptance is immediately negotiable; the seller can either receive discounted payment at the accepting bank or hold the draft until the date of maturity. Banker's acceptances are particularly important in international trade. Maturities range from one to 6 months. Average maturity is three months.

Banker's acceptance:
> A time draft (post-dated instrument) payable to a seller of goods, with payment guaranteed by a bank.

3.6.1 CREATING A BANKER'S ACCEPTANCE

Creation of a banker's acceptance typically begins when an importer arranges a letter of credit through a bank, which then notifies an exporter (or the exporter's bank) that, once specific conditions have been satisfied, the exporter is entitled to draw (write) a draft on the importer's bank in the amount of the transaction. The conditions may include attaching documents to the draft verifying the shipment of goods.

Once the conditions have been satisfied, the exporter presents the documented draft to the importer's bank (perhaps through the exporter's bank). The importer's bank "accepts" the draft, and at that point the draft becomes a money market instrument. Payment to the exporter on the date of maturity is guaranteed, or, if the exporter decides to discount the draft immediately, payment is guaranteed to the holder of the acceptance.

Should the exporter decide to discount the acceptance, the importer's bank now has two alternatives. It simply can hold the acceptance in its portfolio (as an account receivable or loan) until maturity, at which time the importer repays the bank. In the interim, a loan is recorded on the books of importer's bank, as "customer's liability on acceptance outstanding." The accounting entry is:

	Debit	*Credit*
Customer's liability on acceptance O/S	X	
Cash		X

The second alternative is to sell the acceptance, in which case a liability, called "acceptance liability outstanding" is also created. In this case, a second entry is recorded:

	Debit	Credit
Cash	X	
Acceptance liability O/S		X

The second action is a way of funding the loan extended by the bank when the exporter decided to discount the acceptance prior to maturity.

There are other variations of acceptance creation. The draft may be drawn on the exporter's bank, especially if the importer's bank is relatively small. Alternatively, the importer's bank may arrange for a larger bank to accept the draft, and provide the third bank a guarantee against loss. Some acceptances do not involve the shipment of goods at all. Drafts drawn for working capital, for example, are referred to as *finance bills*.

In all cases, the accepting bank charges a commission that is a function of the time to maturity and the creditworthiness of the borrower. If the acceptance is held in the portfolio of the accepting bank, the bank also earns interest equivalent to the discount. Generally, the borrower absorbs these costs.

3.6.2 THE MARKET

The United States

In the secondary market, investors find banker's acceptances attractive because they are liquid and, although unsecured, have a historically low default rate. Investors include money market mutual funds, bank trust departments, state and local governments, insurance companies, pension funds, and commercial banks. Approximately 30 dealers and 12 brokers operate in the highly liquid US market for banker's acceptances.

From the perspective of accepting banks, acceptance financing is comparable to CD financing. The bank has an obligation to pay the holder of the acceptance, just as it has an obligation to pay the holder of a CD. Likewise, funds obtained in the sale of the acceptance finance the customer's loan, just as funds obtained in the CD market finance other loans. Because of these similarities, the discount rate on acceptances is consistently within 10 basis points of the interest rate on CDs. For example, if the CD rate is 8.00 percent, the banker's acceptance discount rate will fall between 7.90 percent and 8.10 percent.

Banker's acceptance liabilities are not subject to reserve requirements as long as they qualify as one of three kinds of *eligible acceptance*:

- Domestic trade
- US imports and exports
- Third-country

Acceptances that finance *domestic* trade have historically been a small portion of the total market. Before the 1960s, acceptances to finance *US imports and exports* were the most common, although currently they comprise less than half of all acceptance liabilities. The most common eligible category is now *third-country* acceptances, those that finance trade between countries outside the United States.

The growth of third-country acceptances was particularly strong during the 1970s, when non-US borrowers found the US acceptance market an attractive source of short-term financing. Most of these acceptances are *refinance bills* (working capital drafts). In these cases, the initial transactions between the two countries outside the United States are essentially the same as those described above. The refinance bill is created when the borrower's foreign bank holds the original draft drawn on it in its portfolio and draws another draft on a US bank to replenish its funds. When the US bank accepts this refinance bill, it then becomes a part of the US acceptance market.

In recent years, the US acceptance market has not expanded as markets for other money market instruments, primarily because US firms and their foreign counterparts have developed alternative sources of financing; commercial paper is an example. Elsewhere, the refinance bills of Japanese and other foreign banks have been replaced by borrowings in the Eurodollar markets.

The United Kingdom and Japan

Merchant banks are at the center of the UK banker's acceptance market (as distinguished from the discount house market). (Merchant banks are discussed in chapter 5.) While clearing banks maintain large branch networks of millions of individual depositors, merchant banks have made a niche for themselves by providing various financial services to businesses, including acceptance. But the acceptance business has experienced peaks and valleys as the government exerts and relaxes controls on other forms of lending.

The Japanese banker's acceptance market began in 1985, motivated by a desire to increase the demand for yen-denominated funds (very much in the interest of the United States because such an increase would help correct the then-overvalued dollar which made US exports to Japan expensive) and to give the Japanese government another instrument of monetary control. The growth of the market has been slower than anticipated, however, perhaps because of taxes imposed on banker's acceptances and the availability of other forms of short-term financing that are more competitively priced.

 Recent Trends

The 1970s were a period of financial innovation, driven partially by the high and volatile interest rates during the latter half of the decade. As a result, the expansion of private sector money market instruments outpaced the growth in government debt.

During the 1970s, as shown in Exhibit 3.5, the amount of money market instruments outstanding consistently grew at double-digit rates.

Exhibit 3.6 shows the aggregate dollar amounts of these private sector instruments in 1969, 1979, 1989, and 1998. Total instruments outstanding increased by a factor of 33 from 1969 ($74.6 billion) to 1998 ($2.5 trillion). Federal funds and repurchase agreements became a larger share of the total, while the remaining categories declined over the 29-year interval.

4.1 FEDERAL FUNDS AND REPOS

Exhibit 3.7 shows the share of total federal funds and repurchase agreement liabilities by issuer for 1969, 1979, 1989, and 1998. This market started as an exclusively interbank market. Later, savings institutions (savings and loan associations and mutual savings banks) and securities brokers and dealers have became more involved. As foreign banks entered the United States, they too have made their presence felt in the money markets. Most recently, real estate investment trusts (REITs) have become active participants in this market.

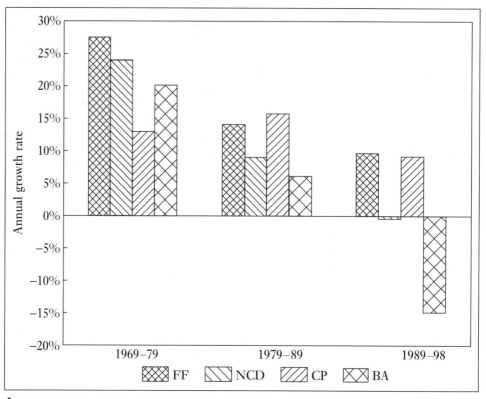

◆ **Exhibit 3.5:** Growth rates of four types of money market instruments 1969–79, 1979–89, and 1989–98

◆ *Notes:*   FF   Federal funds and repurchase agreements
             NCD   Negotiable certificates of deposit
             CP   Commercial paper
             BA   Banker's acceptances

◆ *Source:*   Author's calculations and graphic based on data from: Board of Governors of the Federal
             Reserve System, *Flow of Funds Accounts; Flows and Outstandings.*

	1969		1979		1989		1998	
	$	%	$	%	$	%	$	%
Fed. funds and repos	$8.7	11.7%	$98.6	20.5%	$367.6	24.7%	$865.4	34.0%
Neg. CDs	27.8	37.2	236.5	49.3	575.9	38.6	564.8	22.2
Comm. paper	32.6	43.7	110.9	23.1	486.8	32.6	1,098.4	43.2
BAs	5.5	7.4	34.1	7.1	61.6	4.1	14.3	0.6
	$74.6	100.0%	$480.1	100.0%	$1,491.9	100.0%	$2,542.9%	100.0%

◆ **Exhibit 3.6:** Mix of four money market instruments, 1969–98

◆ *Source:*   Author's calculations and graphic based on data from: Board of Governors of the Federal Reserve System,
             Flow of Funds Accounts; Flows and Outstandings.

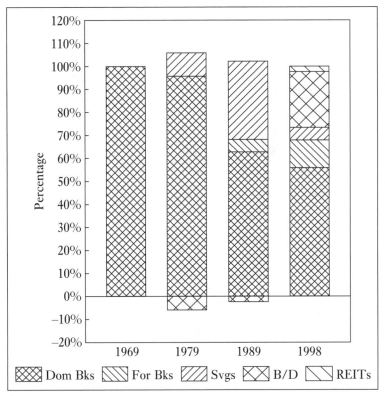

◆ **Exhibit 3.7:** Issuers of federal funds and repurchase agreements as a percentage of total outstanding 1969, 1979, 1989, and 1998

◆ *Notes*: Dom Bks   Domestic commercial banks
For Bks   Foreign commercial banks
Svgs   Savings institutions (savings and loan associations and mutual savings banks)
B/D   Securities brokers and dealers
REITs   Real estate investment trusts

In 1979 and 1989, brokers and dealers were net purchasers of federal funds and repurchase agreements, that is, the instruments were held as assets. For the other market participants, the instruments were liabilities.

◆ *Source*:   Author's calculations and graphic based on data from: Board of Governors of the Federal Reserve System, *Flow of Funds Accounts; Flows and Outstandings.*

4.2 NEGOTIABLE CERTIFICATES OF DEPOSIT

A similar trend has occurred in the negotiable CD market. As Exhibit 3.8 shows, domestic commercial banks issued 100 percent of the instruments outstanding in 1969. By 1998, this share was down to 55 percent.

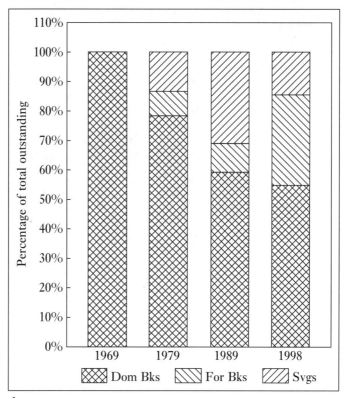

◆ **Exhibit 3.8:** **Issuers of negotiable certificates of deposit as a percentage of total outstanding, 1969, 1979, 1989, and 1998**

◆ *Notes*:   Dom Bks   Domestic commercial banks
              For Bks   Foreign commercial banks
              Svgs   Savings institutions (savings and
                         loan associations and mutual savings
                         banks)

◆ *Source*:   Author's calculations and graphic based on data
              from: Board of Governors of the Federal Reserve
              System, *Flow of Funds Accounts; Flows and
              Outstandings*.

4.3 COMMERCIAL PAPER

In the commercial paper market, finance companies have historically been the most significant issuers, accounting for over 70 percent of outstanding paper in 1969, as Exhibit 3.9 shows. The percentage dropped to 54.7 percent in 1979, was up again to almost 60 percent by 1989, but dropped to 26 percent in 1998.

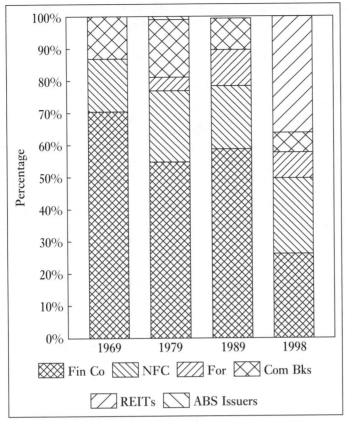

◆ **Exhibit 3.9:** **Issuers of commercial paper as a percentage of total outstanding, 1969, 1979, 1989, 1998**

◆ *Notes*:   Fin Co   Finance companies
              NFC   Nonfinancial corporations
              For   Foreign firms
              Com Bks   Commercial banks
              REITs   Real estate investment trusts
              ABS Issuers   Asset-backed securities issuers

◆ *Source*:   Author's calculations and graphic based on data from:
              Board of Governors of the Federal Reserve System, *Flow of Funds Accounts; Flows and Outstandings.*

 Summary

The short-term or *money markets* in the United States are centered first around Treasury bills, with negotiable CDs, federal funds and repurchase agreements, commercial paper, and banker's acceptances also important. Commercial banks, savings institutions, finance companies, government securities dealers, and foreign firms are the private sector entities that are the most significant participants. The US Treasury and the Federal Reserve are the biggest governmental participants.

In the United States, participants generally conduct transactions directly with each other, with the exception of primary transactions in the T-bill market. In Japan, private *Tanshi* houses oversee all transactions except *gensaki* (repurchase agreements). In the United Kingdom, discount houses have traditionally served a similar purpose. Only recently have parallel money markets begun to develop that do not require the intervention of discount houses.

The money markets of the United States, the United Kingdom, Japan, Hong Kong, and Singapore are among the world's largest. While T-bills have been the most important money market instrument in the United States, call money (the equivalent of federal funds) dominates in other countries, most notably Japan and Hong Kong. Negotiable CDs were introduced in the United States in 1961. In 1968, the United Kingdom had also introduced a sterling-denominated negotiable CD. During the mid-1970s Singapore and Hong Kong did so. A yen-denominated instrument was not created until 1979 and at first only in large denominations so as not to compete with the *gensaki* market.

The treatment of negotiable CDs in Japan is a good example of that country's approach to financial market regulation. Japanese corporations issued commercial paper in the United States during the early 1980s because the 1982 Japanese law permitting the issuance of commercial paper was not implemented until 1987. Similarly, there was no Japanese secondary market for banker's acceptances until 1985.

On the other hand, the governments of Singapore and Hong Kong have encouraged innovation in money markets in the interest of attracting financial services activities. The United Kingdom implemented similar deregulation in 1986.

In every country, money markets are dominated by large institutions engaging in large-denomination transactions. Generally, these markets are moving toward deregulation, with a wider variety of money market instruments becoming available to a greater assortment of institutions.

End-of-chapter Questions

1. What is the difference between money and capital markets?
2. Describe the US federal funds market and its equivalent in other countries.
3. Describe recent trends with respect to participants in the markets for:
   a. federal funds and repurchase agreements
   b. negotiable certificates of deposit
   c. commercial paper
4. a. What is a repurchase agreement?
   b. What precautionary measures should be taken when entering repurchase agreements?
5. a. What is a discount house?
   b. In which countries (described in this chapter) may they be found?
   c. What is their function?
6. What contributions to money market operations do government securities dealers make?

7. Commercial paper is an unsecured financial instrument. How is it possible that the commercial paper of a firm with less than a top credit rating can be given a top rating?

8. a. Differentiate a banker's acceptance for US imports and exports and a third-country acceptance.

    b. Under what circumstances would an acceptance be considered a refinance bill?

9. Discuss the role of the Federal Reserve as a money market participant.

10. In the primary market for Treasury securities, what is the difference between a tender system and a tap system?

11. Present evidence to support the statement that US money markets are becoming more internationalized.

12. a. How have negotiable CDs given commercial banks more flexibility?

    b. Why has the amount of negotiable CDs decreased in recent years despite the added flexibility that they give banks?

13. Obtain a recent edition of the *Wall Street Journal*.

    a. What is the prime interest rate?

    b. Compare the prime interest rate to the commercial paper rate. What is the implication of this difference?

14. Differentiate a competitive and a noncompetitive bid in the US primary T-bill market.

15. Why is a repurchase agreement like a collateralized loan?

 End-of-chapter Problems

1. Say that a noncompetitive bid for $1,000,000 in six-month (182-day) bills is submitted in a Treasury auction. If the weighted average interest rate of winning competitive bids is 7.75 percent, what is the total purchase price associated with this bid?

2. Suppose that you buy a $1,000,000 negotiable CD with an 8.5 percent interest rate that matures in three months (91 days). Assume further that you decide to sell this CD when there are 30 days left to maturity and the going interest rate is 9 percent.

    a. For what price will you be able to sell it?

    b. What rate of return will you earn?

    c. Show that the party to whom you sell the CD will earn 9 percent.

3. An individual places a noncompetitive bid for 30-day T-bills with a $1,000,000 face value through a commercial bank and the weighted average rate that applies is 7 percent.

   a. Show the T-accounts and their balances reflecting this transaction on the books of the commercial bank and the applicable Federal Reserve bank.

   b. Now assume the commercial bank enters a successful competitive bid of its own for $4,000,000 in T-bills and that the rate is 6.9 percent. How is this transaction reflected in the T-accounts of the commercial bank and the Federal Reserve bank?

4. An exporter presents a $500,000 draft to a commercial bank for payment due in 30 days. The draft is "accepted" and discounted, and the exporter is paid. If the discount rate is 6 percent, how much will the exporter be paid? Show the entry on the books of the bank that corresponds to this transaction.

5. If a government securities dealer asks a 6.96 percent discount on T-bills and bids a 7.00 percent discount, how much profit will be made on a purchase and sale of $2,000,000 in T-bills with 30 days left to maturity?

NOTES

1   Also in 1996, savings and loan associations and mutual savings banks were issuers of 16 percent of negotiable CDs outstanding and 5 percent of federal funds and repurchase agreements.

2   A Treasury Direct program also makes it possible for individuals to purchase government securities directly from the Treasury Department and receive disbursements through a book-entry account accessible through any Federal Reserve bank.

3   Calculation of the dollar amount of a two-basis-point spread on a $1 million, 91-day Treasury bill is comparable to calculation of the discount.

$$\text{Spread} = 1,000,000[k(N/360)]$$
$$= 1,000,000[.0002(91/360)]$$
$$= 50.56$$

SELECTED REFERENCES

Adams, T. F. M. and Iwao Hoshii. *A Financial History of the New Japan*, Kodansha International Tokyo, 1972.

Bronte, Stephen. *Japanese Finance: Markets and Institutions*, Euromoney Publications, London, 1982.

Clarke, William M. *How the City Works; An Introduction to its Financial Markets*, Waterlow Publishers, London, 1986.

Cook, Timothy Q. and Timothy D. Rowe, eds. *Instruments of the Money Market*, Federal Reserve Bank of Richmond, Richmond, Va., 1986.

Falkena, H. B., L. J. Fourie, and W. J. Kok, eds. *The Mechanics of the South African financial System*, Macmillan South Africa, Johannesburg, 1984.

Feldman, Robert Alan. *Japanese Financial Markets; Deficits, Dilemmas, and Deregulation*, MIT Press, London, 1986.

Fitch, Thomas. *Dictionary of Banking Terms*, Barron's Educational Series, Hauppauge, NY, 1990.

Fisher, Anne B. "Who's Hurt by Salomon's Greed?" *Fortune*, vol. 124, no. 7 (September 23, 1991), p. 71.

Fraser, Donald R. and Peter S. Rose, eds. *Financial Institutions and Markets in a Changing World*, 3rd edn, Business Publications, Plano, Tex., 1987.

Galen, Michele. "Salomon: Honesty is the Gutsiest Policy," *Business Week*, no. 3231 (September 16, 1991), pp. 100–1.

Grady, John and Martin Weale. *British Banking, 1960–85*, Macmillan Press London, 1986.

Havrilesky, Thomas M. and Robert Schweitzer, eds. *Contemporary Developments in Financial Institutions and Markets*, 2nd edn, Harlan Davidson, Arlington Heights, Ill., 1987.

Henderson, John and Jonathan P. Scott. *Securitization*, New York Institute of Finance, NY, 1988.

Hsu, Robert C. *The MIT Encyclopedia of the Japanese Economy*, MIT Press, Cambridge, Mass., 1994.

Huat, Tan Chwee. *Financial Institutions in Singapore*, 2nd edn, Singapore University Press, Singapore, 1981.

Johnson, Hazel J. *Bankers Guide to Investment Banking: Securities and Underwriting Activities in Commercial Banking*, Irwin Professional Publishing, Burr Ridge, Ill. (now McGraw-Hill, New York), 1996.

Jones, Frank J. and Frank J. Fabozzi. *The International Government Bond Markets*, Probus Publishing, Chicago (now McGraw-Hill, New York), 1992.

Lee, S. Y. and Y. C. Jao. *Financial Structures and Monetary Policies in Southeast Asia*, St. Martin's Press, New York, 1982.

Marshall, John F. and M. E. Ellis. *Investment Banking and Brokerage: The New Rules of the Game*, Probus Publishing, Chicago (now McGraw-Hill, New York), 1994.

McRae, Hamish and Frances Cairncross. *Capital City: London as a Financial Centre*, Methuen, London, 1984.

Mullineux, Andrew. *International Banking and Financial Systems: A Comparison*, Graham & Trotman, London, 1987.

Mullineux, A. W. *UK Banking After Deregulation*, Croom Helm, London, 1987.

Neufeld, E. P. *The Financial System of Canada*, St. Martin's Press, New York, 1972.

Skully, Michael T., ed. *Financial Institutions and Markets in the Far East: A Study of China, Hong Kong, Japan, South Korea, and Taiwan*, St. Martin's Press, New York, 1982.

—— . *Financial Institutions and Markets in Southeast Asia: A Study of Brunei, Indonesia, Malaysia, Philippines, Singapore and Thailand*, Macmillan Press, London, 1984.

—— . *Financial Institutions and Markets in the Southwest Pacific: A Study of Australia, Fiji, New Zealand, and Papua New Guinea*, Macmillan Press, London, 1985.

Srodes, James. "Rude Awakening: The Salomon Scandal Will Finally move Congress to Reform the Government Securities Market," *Financial World*, vol. 160, no. 19 (September 17, 1991), pp. 22–3.

Struthers, J. and H. Speight. *Money: Institutions, Theory and Policy*, Longman Group, London, 1986.

Viner, Aron. *Inside Japanese Financial Markets*, Dow Jones-Irwin, Homewood, Ill., 1988.

Weiss, Gary, Leah Nathans-Spiro, Jeffrey M. Laderman, Michael MacNamee, and Dean Foust. "The Salomon Shocker: How Bad will it Get?" *Business Week*, no. 3228 (August 26, 1991), pp. 54–7.

Wilson, J. S. G. *Banking Policy and Structure: A Comparative Analysis*, Croom Helm, London, 1986.

PART II
Domestic Capital Markets

Capital Market Instruments

CHAPTER OVERVIEW

This chapter:
- Defines capital markets.
- Analyzes capital market instruments in the United States.
- Outlines developments in secondary mortgage markets.
- Describes the process of securitization.

KEY TERMS

accrual bonds
amortization schedule
asset-backed bonds
asset-backed commercial paper
asset-backed preferred stock
bearer bonds
call protection
call provision
capital gains yield
collateralized mortgage obligations
common stock
consolidated bonds
debentures
Dutch auction system
equipment trust certificates
federal agency bonds
Federal Financing Bank
federally related institutions
federally sponsored agency

general obligation bonds
generic strips
government sponsored entities
indenture
index ratio
inflation–protection bonds
mortgage bonds
mortgage–backed bonds
mortgages
municipal bonds
participation certificate
pass–through certificates
pass–through securities
pay–through bonds
preferred stock
prepayment assumption
registered bonds
revenue bonds
securitization

stock warrants   variable rate bonds
subordinated debentures   yield to maturity
synthetic strips   Z-bonds
Treasury notes and bonds   zero-coupon bonds

 ## CHAPTER OUTLINE

1 Bonds
   1.1 Bond Valuation
   1.2 Bond Yields
   1.3 Special Features
   1.4 Types of Bonds
      1.4.1 Treasury Notes and Bonds
          Treasury Auctions
          A New Inflation-adjusted Bond
          Strips
      1.4.2 Federal Agency Bonds
      1.4.3 Municipal Bonds
          Municipal Bond Yields
          Municipal Bond Insurance
      1.4.4 Corporate Bonds
2 Corporate Stock
   2.1 Preferred Stock
   2.2 Common Stock
3 Mortgages
   3.1 Mortgage Payments
   3.2 Mortgage Pools
4 Securitization
   4.1 Asset-backed Securities
      4.1.1 Pass-through Securities
      4.1.2 Asset-backed Bonds
      4.1.3 Pay-through Bonds
      4.1.4 A Comparison
   4.2 Other Asset-backed Securities
   4.3 Advantages of Securitization

Introduction

The process of long-term, productive investment that was outlined in chapter 1 occurs in capital markets, where long-term financial instruments are traded. It is the long-term nature of the financial instruments that differentiates capital markets from money markets.

Capital markets:
     Markets in which financial instruments with maturities greater than one
     year are bought and sold.

Corporations secure financing through capital markets by selling long-term claims on their firms, whether in the form of bonds (liabilities) or stock (equity). Governments go to capital markets for operating funds and capital projects; households use them mainly for residential mortgage financing. This chapter describes the capital market instruments that are issued and traded within national boundaries.

Capital market instruments are classified in five categories:

- Government notes and bonds
- Municipal bonds
- Corporate bonds
- Corporate stock
- Mortgages

Exhibit 4.1 shows that there were $29 trillion in US capital market instruments in 1998. Corporate stock and mortgages are the largest categories, with $13.4 trillion and $5.5 trillion in securities outstanding, respectively. Corporate, government agency, and Treasury bonds are next in relative importance with 1998 outstanding amounts of $3.7 trillion, $3.0 trillion, and $2.2 trillion, respectively. Municipal bonds are the smallest category at $1.1 trillion. However, taken together, bonds ($10 trillion) represented roughly 74 percent of corporate stock in the US market in 1998.

	Amount[1]	%[2]
Government securities:		
Treasury notes and bonds:		
(with remaining maturities > one year)	$2,159.6	7.5%
Federally sponsored agencies	2,981.2	10.3
Municipal bonds	1,114.3	3.8
Corporate bonds	3,723.0	12.9
Corporate stock	13,443.5	46.5
Mortgages	5,505.8	19.0
	$28,927.4	100.0%

◆ **Exhibit 4.1: US capital market instruments outstanding, 1998**

◆ *Notes*:   1 Billions of dollars
             2 Percentage of total capital market instruments outstanding

◆ *Sources*: Board of Governors of the Federal Reserve System, *Flow of Funds
             Accounts: Flows and Outstandings*; Department of the Treasury, *Monthly
             Statement of the Public Debt of the United States.*

① Bonds

Corporations and government entities issue bonds to raise funds for operations or for capital projects. The buyer of the bond has a claim on the issuer, which owes the buyer a specified amount in the future as well as (usually) interest payments in the interim.

> **Bonds:**
> Contractual liabilities that obligate the issuer to pay a specified amount (the par, face, or maturity value) at a given date in the future (the maturity date), generally with periodic interest payments in the interim at a fixed rate (the coupon rate).

Bearer bonds are payable to whomever holds the securities; *registered bonds* are payable only to the owner specified in the issuer's records. Even though bonds have a definite term or life, investors often do not hold these instruments until they mature. Thus, the valuation of bonds prior to maturity is an important concept.

1.1 BOND VALUATION

The value of a bond is the present value of its future cash flows. Hence, the value or price is based on:

- Interest payments
- Maturity value
- Investor's minimum required rate of return

The cash flows of a bond are an *annuity of interest payments* during the life of the bond plus a single future payoff of the *maturity value*. These future cash flows are determined at the time that the bond is issued. The *required rate of return* is an investor's opportunity cost, that is, the rate of return on the next best investment opportunity. The rate is driven by financial market conditions and, thus, may change. A bond pricing formula values both the interest payments and the maturity value.

$$P_0 = I\left(\sum_{t=1}^{n}\left[\frac{1}{(1+k)^t}\right]\right) + M\left(\frac{1}{(1+k)^n}\right) \tag{4.1}$$

where P_0 = the current price of a bond
I = the amount of interest received each period

$\qquad = \dfrac{\text{maturity value} \times \text{coupon rate}}{\text{number of payments per year}}$

n = number of periods before bond matures
k = investor's minimum required rate of return p
M = bond maturity or par or face value

Consider a bond with a face value of $1,000, a coupon rate of 8 percent paid semiannually, and five years to maturity. Suppose that an investor wants to earn 10 percent at a minimum. This bond pays $80 per year in interest [$1,000 × 0.08], but the interest is paid semiannually, or two payments a year at $40 each. The required rate of return per six-month period is 5 percent [10%/2]. The number of six-month periods before the bond matures is 10 [5 years × 2 periods per year]. Applying Equation (4.1), the maximum price that the investor would pay for one of these bonds is $922.78.[1]

$$P_0 = 40\left(\sum_{t=1}^{10}\left[\frac{1}{(1.05)^t}\right]\right) + 1000\left(\frac{1}{(1.05)^{10}}\right)$$

$$= 40(PVIFA_{(.05,10)}) + 1000(PVIF_{(.05,10)})$$

$$= 40(7.7217) + 1000(0.61391)$$

$$= 308.87 + 613.91$$

$$= 922.78$$

1.2 Bond Yields

An investor who wants to earn 10 percent should pay less than the $1,000 par value. This is because the bond pays only 8 percent of the $1,000 face value each year. If the investor pays only $922.78, there will be a *capital gain* in addition to the interim interest payments. The *capital gains yield* in this case will be sufficient to bring the total return to 10 percent. The rate of return to a bond investor is determined both by interest payments and the change in value of the bond.

> **Capital gain:**
> The difference between the price that is originally paid for a bond and the cash proceeds realized at the time of maturity (the face value) or at the time of sale.

> **Capital gains yield:**
> Capital gain during a specific time period as a percentage of the value of a bond at the beginning of the period.

$$k_b = CY + CGY \tag{4.2}$$

where k_b = rate of return to a bond investor
   CY = current yield
   = annual interest payment as a percentage of bond value
   CGY = capital gains yield

On the 8 percent, five-year, $1,000 bond purchased for $922.78, the average annual capital gain is 1.6 percent.

$$CGY = (average\ return\ per\ period) \times (number\ of\ periods)$$

$$= \left[\left(\frac{FV}{PV}\right)^{\frac{1}{n}} - 1\right] \times 2$$

$$= \left[\left(\frac{1000}{922.78}\right)^{\frac{1}{10}} - 1\right] \times 2$$

$$= 0.016$$

For the first six months, the current yield is 4.3 percent [40/922.78], or approximately 8.6 percent for the year, for a total return of roughly 10.2 percent.[2]

If this bond had a coupon rate of 12 percent, instead of 8 percent, its price according to Equation (4.1) would be greater than its par value or $1,077.21.

$$P_0 = 60\left(\sum_{t=1}^{10}\left[\frac{1}{(1.05)^t}\right]\right) + 1000\left(\frac{1}{(1.05)^{10}}\right)$$

$$= 60(PVIFA_{(.05,10)}) + 1000(PVIF_{(.05,10)})$$

$$= 60(7.7217) + 1000(0.61391)$$

$$= 463.30 + 613.91$$

$$= 1077.21$$

The average annual change in price is a negative 1.5 percent[3] (capital loss), while the current yield in the first year is approximately 11.1 percent [(60/1,077.21) × 2]. This brings the total first year return to approximately 9.6 percent.

If a bond is sold at a stated market price, the unknown in Equation (4.1) is k, the rate of return, rather than P_0, the price. The rate, k, is then the yield to maturity, which is an expected rate of return, instead of the required rate of return.

Yield to maturity (YTM):
> The average annual rate of return to a bond investor who buys a bond today and holds it until it matures. The YTM is that rate of return that causes the market price to be exactly equal to the present value of the future cash flows (interest payments and maturity value).

The YTM measures *both* the current yield and the capital gains yield together. Because the bond pricing formula is complex, YTM must be found through a trial-and-error process, although a number of hand-held calculators are programmed to perform the necessary iterations. Manually, YTM is approximated using this formula:

$$YTM = \frac{\left[I + \frac{(M - P_0)}{n}\right]}{\left[\frac{(M + 2P_0)}{3}\right]} \tag{4.3}$$

where I = annual interest payment
n = number of years to maturity
M = bond maturity or par or face value
P_0 = current price of bond

Note that the two terms in the numerator of Equation (4.3) are the annual interest payment plus the average annual capital gain (or loss). The denominator is an approximate average investment in the bond – the maturity value plus two times the price, divided by 3. Applying Equation (4.3) to the 8 percent coupon bond in the example above, the YTM approximation is 10.06 percent, very close to the actual 10 percent YTM.

1.3 SPECIAL FEATURES

Some bonds have a *call provision* which may prevent investors from realizing the yield to maturity. Because a call is exercisable at the discretion of the issuer and deprives the investor of anticipated income, a *call premium* (the excess of the call price over par value) is often payable to the investor upon call. This is particularly true if the issuer calls the bond because current interest rates are significantly below the bond's coupon rate. If the issuer calls the bond in order to comply with sinking fund requirements (gradual bond retirement), the call premium is generally much lower. In any event, call premiums decline as the maturity date of the bond approaches. Often, bonds may not be called for several years after issuance; this period of time is referred to as *call protection*.

> **Call provision:**
> A feature of a bond that entitles the issuer to retire the bond before maturity.

While most bonds traded in the United States conform to the model described above, there are some variations. Some bonds do not pay periodic interest but are discounted in much the same way as commercial paper. These bonds are called *zero coupon bonds*. They have become more popular in recent years because of certain tax advantages that they offer particular borrowers, but they are still a relatively small part of the market. Other bonds carry a coupon rate that changes with market interest rates. These *variable rate bonds* serve to protect investors from adverse bond price changes, but they also prevent investors from locking in high rates of interest for extended periods of time. Variable rate bonds are less common in US markets than in Eurobond markets. (Eurobond and other international markets are discussed in chapters 7 and 8.)

1.4 TYPES OF BONDS

Government and private enterprises are active bond market participants. Exhibit 4.2 shows the rates of growth in the four categories of bonds for periods from 1969 to 1996.

1.4.1 TREASURY NOTES AND BONDS

T-notes are issued with original maturities of between 2 and 10 years. Specifically, notes with original maturities of 2, 5, and 10 years are issued. T-bonds have original maturities of between 10 years and 30 years, with 30-year bonds currently being issued. The government securities dealers that make markets for Treasury bills also make markets for Treasury notes and bonds. (See chapter 3 for coverage of government securities dealers.)

As is true with Treasury bills, note and bond prices are quoted as a percentage of $100 of face value, but the fractional values of bonds are expressed in 32nds of a percent. A price of 99 5/32 can also be written as 99.5 or 99:5. Since 1/32 is 0.03125 and 5/32 is 0.15625, the price for a $1,000 bond that is quoted at, for example, 99.5 is $991.56 [$P_0 = 10 \times 99.15625 = 991.56$].

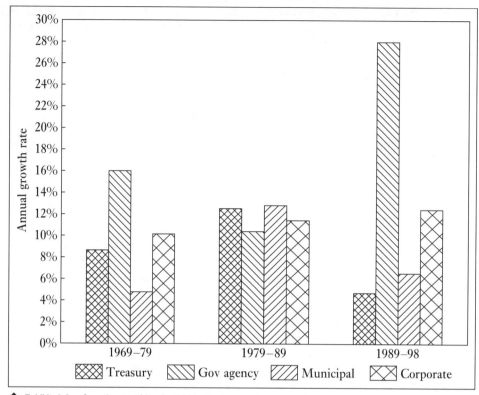

◆ **Exhibit 4.2:**   **Growth rate of bonds, 1969–79, 1979–89, 1989–98**

◆ *Source*:   Author's calculations and graphic based on data from: Board of Governors of the Federal Reserve System, *Flow of Funds Accounts; Flows and Outstandings.*

Chapter 3 described how the Federal Reserve auctions Treasury bills. The Fed also auctions Treasury notes and bonds in the primary market.

Treasury Auctions

The auction process is the same as that noted in chapter 3 (section 3.1.1, "The Bidding Process"). However, the frequency of issue differs.

- The 2-year notes are auctioned monthly.
- The 5-year and 10-year notes are auctioned in February, May, August, and November.
- The 30-year Treasury bond is issued in February, August, and November.

Individual noncompetitive bids for Treasury notes and bonds may not exceed $5 million. Competitive bids must include a yield to three decimal places, for example, 5.123 percent.

The multi-price auction process described in chapter 3 for T-bills is also used for 10-year notes and 30-year bonds. A different, single-price auction – a so-called *Dutch auction system* – is used for 2-year notes and 5-year notes. In this process, the yield to competitive bidders does not vary.

While bids are submitted and accepted in ascending order of yield, the yield to winning competitive bidders is set at the highest-accepted competitive bid rate or the lowest-accepted competitive bid price. At first glance, it appears that the Treasury may be paying a higher yield than would otherwise be the case. However, competitive bidders are motivated to enter a low enough yield bid to be included among the winners, while recognizing that they will be paid the highest yield (and pay the lowest price) among the winners. Essentially, the Dutch auction system means that all successful competitive bidders pay the stop out price. (See chapter 3 for a discussion of stop out price.) Since the coupon rate is determined in the same way as under the old system, the determination of coupon rate is not affected by this difference. Noncompetitive bidders receive their Treasuries at the same price as the competitive bidders.

A New Inflation-adjusted Bond

Beginning in January 1997, the Treasury began to offer *inflation-protection bonds*. The coupon rate on these bonds is fixed and paid semiannually. However, instead of a constant face value of $1,000, the face value of the inflation-protection is adjusted to compensate for inflation as measured by the consumer price index (CPI). (See chapter 10 for a discussion of inflation and price indexes.) Adjustment of the face value is accomplished by multiplying the original face value ($1,000) by an *index ratio*.

Index ratio:
Ratio of the CPI on the valuation date (after issuance) to the CPI on the date of issue.

The first inflation-protection securities were issued with an original maturity of 10 years and a face value of $1,000. Through the latter part of 1998, 5-year notes and 30-year bonds also were issued.

Strips

The Treasury does not issue zero-coupon bonds. However, in some cases, Treasury issues are converted to a series of zero-coupon instruments by separating the maturity value from the interest payments. For example, if 10-year, 8 percent notes in the amount of $200 million are treated in this way, that is, are *stripped*, 21 zero-coupon instruments will result – the 20 semiannual interest payments ($8 million each) and the maturity value ($200 million).

In 1982, Merrill Lynch and Salomon Brothers introduced these financial instruments by purchasing regular Treasury securities and issuing claims on the individual cash flows. Since the original obligations of the Treasury were not stripped, these first strips are *synthetic strips*. Merrill Lynch issues their strips under the acronym TIGR – Treasury Income Growth Receipts. In the case of Salomon Brothers, the instruments are called CATS – Certificates of Accrual on Treasury Securities.

Beginning in 1985, the Treasury Department issued Separate Trading of Registered Interest and Principal Securities (STRIPS). All Treasury securities with maturities of 10 years or more are eligible. These strips clear through the federal book-entry system. That is, sales are accounted for electronically. With the introduction of these *generic strips*, synthetic strips became a much less significant sector of the market.

1.4.2 FEDERAL AGENCY BONDS

Federal agencies fall into two general categories:

- *Federally sponsored agencies*, also known as *government sponsored entities*, are privately owned entities created by Congress to reduce the cost of borrowing in certain sectors considered important to the US economy. These institutions issue securities directly to the public.
- *Federally related institutions* are part of the federal government and do not issue securities directly to the public. Instead, since 1973, these institutions are funded indirectly through borrowings of the *Federal Financing Bank*, which was created in that year to centralize the borrowing of federally related institutions.[4]

The intermediation function of financial institutions that is described in chapter 1 is supported by the US government in certain sectors of the economy through federally sponsored agencies:

- Federal Home Loan Banks
- Federal National Mortgage Association
- Federal Home Loan Mortgage Corporation
- Farm Credit System
- Student Loan Marketing Association

The first three agencies channel funds into the mortgage market. The last two perform the same function in the agricultural sector and in higher education, respectively. All these agencies issue bonds.

In 1932 Congress created a *Federal Home Loan Bank* in each of 12 districts of the United States. These banks supervise federally chartered savings and loan associations and provide liquidity to member associations through their credit facility.

The *Federal National Mortgage Association* (Fannie Mae), established in 1938 as a federal government agency, started the secondary market in federally insured mortgages. In 1968 the agency became a separate entity, now owned completely by private investors.

The *Federal Home Loan Mortgage Corporation* (Freddie Mac) is a more recent addition to the list of federal agencies. In 1970 Freddie Mac was introduced into the Federal Home Loan Bank System to develop a secondary market in conventional mortgages, that is, those not federally guaranteed. The 12 Federal Home Loan District Banks and member S&L institutions are the agency's shareholders.

The *Farm Credit System* (including Farm Credit Banks and Banks for Cooperatives) dates back to 1917 when 12 Federal Land Banks were created. The Federal Intermediate Credit Banks and the Banks for Cooperatives originated in each district in 1923 and 1933, respectively. In addition, a Central Bank for Cooperatives helps to fund large loans or loans that involve more than one district.

Lenders under the Guaranteed Student Loan Program and individual investors own the stock of the *Student Loan Marketing Association* (Sallie Mae), created in 1970. The agency provides a secondary market for student loans that are guaranteed by the federal government and makes loans to institutions (called warehousing advances) so that they can offer more student loans.

The bonds issued by all these agencies are considered almost as safe as Treasury issues. Because of this, the yields on federal agency bonds are typically 10 to 150 basis points above Treasury securities of similar maturity, representing a more narrow spread than that which applies to many corporate bonds. There are a number of reasons for this rate behavior:

- Agency issues hold a number of advantages for investors:
  - Most interest income from government agency securities is exempt from state and local taxation, with the exception of Federal National Mortgage Association and of Federal Home Loan Mortgage Corporation issues.
  - Banks and savings and loan associations may use them as collateral when borrowing from the Federal Reserve.
  - While banks are restricted in terms of the extent to which they can trade certain securities, they may trade agency securities without limitation. S&Ls may use them to satisfy liquidity requirements.
- Federal agencies have lines of credit with the Treasury Department to use in the event that they have trouble meeting their obligations.
- Even without an explicit default guarantee, investors may feel that the federal government would not allow a federally sponsored agency to default on a debt obligation.

These factors combine to make federal agency bonds attractive investments.

1.4.3 MUNICIPAL BONDS

Municipal bonds include all debt instruments issued by local, county, and state governments. Issuers use proceeds from the sale of municipal bonds to finance public utilities, school construction, roads, transportation systems, and industrial development. An appealing feature is that most municipal bond interest payments to the holder are exempt from federal income taxation.

General obligation bonds (GOs) are backed by the full faith and credit of the issuer. Taxpayer approval is usually required for issuance because the taxing authority of the government body is pledged for the repayment. GOs are usually issued to finance non-revenue-producing projects such as schools, roads, and public buildings. *Revenue bonds* are backed only by cash flows from a specific project financed by the bond issue. If the income is not sufficient to service and retire the debt, tax revenues may not be allocated for this purpose. Projects financed with revenue bonds include toll bridges, toll highways, hospitals, and other public facilities that are revenue-generating. *Industrial revenue bonds* are issued by nonfinancial business concerns to help build the economic base of a political subdivision, that is, state or municipality. The political subdivision bears no liability for repayment. Credit risk is associated with the private corporation that is responsible for the project.

Municipal Bond Yields

To compare income from a tax-exempt municipal bond to that of a taxable bond, the *after-tax rate of interest* of a taxable bond must be identified.[5]

$$K_{AT} = K_{BT}(1 - t) \tag{4.4}$$

where k_{AT} = after-tax rate of interest of a taxable bond
k_{BT} = before-tax rate of interest of a taxable bond
t = marginal tax rate of the bond investor

This after-tax rate is the appropriate rate to compare with the municipal bond yield. All other things being equal, if the after-tax yield on a taxable bond is less than the yield of the municipal bond, the municipal bond is preferable.

Another way to analyze the interest from a tax-free bond is to determine the pretax rate for a taxable security that would cause an investor to be indifferent between the taxable bond and the municipal bond. This can be done by substituting the municipal bond yield for the after-tax rate in Equation (4.4) and solving for k_{BT}.

$$k_M = k_{BT}(1 - t)$$

$$\frac{k_M}{(1 - t)} = k_{BT} \tag{4.5}$$

where k_M = municipal bond yield

Municipal Bond Insurance

Only a few of the most actively traded municipal bonds are quoted in the financial press, that is, a fraction of the mutual bonds outstanding that have been floated by the approximately 50,000 issuers. Given the variability in available information, the vast number of issuers, and the lack of a centralized market for secondary trading, insurance coverage for the payment of municipal bond principal and interest is increasingly common.

From the issuer's perspective, insurance substitutes the credit worthiness of the insurer for the creditworthiness of the issuer. Thus, an issuer with something less than the top credit rating can obtain the top credit rating for its bond by purchasing insurance coverage from a company with the highest rating. The enhanced credit rating reduces borrowing cost for the issuer, often by more than the cost of insurance coverage. In the primary market, municipal bond insurers sell guarantees to bond issuers and, in the secondary market, sell guarantees to bond investors.

Six full-service municipal bond insurers currently provide coverage for the industry:

- AMBAC Indemnity Corporation
- Capital Guaranty Insurance Corporation (CGIC)
- Capital Markets Assurance Corporation (CapMAC)
- Financial Guaranty Insurance Corporation (FGIC)
- Financial Security Assurance, Inc. (FSA)
- Municipal Bond Investors Assurance Corporation (MBIA)

These companies carry the highest credit rating from the major credit rating agencies.

1.4.4 CORPORATE BONDS

Corporate bonds include all bonds that are not either government bonds (Treasury or federal agency) or municipal bonds. Corporations use the money raised by selling bonds for long-term purposes.

Bondholder rights and bond issuer responsibilities are included in the *indenture*.

Indenture:

    Written agreement specifying the terms and conditions for issuing bonds. The indenture states the form of the bond, interest to be paid, interest payment dates, maturity date, call provisions (as applicable), and any other condition that protects the rights of the bondholders (restrictive covenants).

The wide variety of corporate bonds includes:

- Mortgage bonds
- Equipment trust certificates
- Debentures
- Subordinated debentures

Some bonds allow conversion into common stock and some include warrants that can be exercised to buy common stock.

Firms issue *mortgage bonds* to finance specific projects. Once built or placed in operation, the project becomes collateral for the bond issue, making the issue *secured* debt. Power utility companies are frequent issuers of mortgage bonds. Should the issuer default on the obligation, bond holders may legally take title to the project (collateral) in order to satisfy the debt.

Tangible property also collateralizes *equipment trust certificates*. In this case, the property is specific pieces of large equipment, usually the rolling stock of railroads (railcars) and airplanes. The collateral of equipment trust certificates may be more readily marketable than that of mortgage bonds in the event of a bond default.

Debentures are long-term liabilities that are supported not by collateral but only by the general creditworthiness of the issuer. For this reason, they are riskier from an investor's perspective. In case of bankruptcy, while the collateral behind mortgage bonds and equipment trust certificates can be sold to satisfy the obligations of the secured debt, holders of debentures are general creditors of the firm; they receive distributions only after the secured creditors have been paid.

Subordinated debentures are also unsecured, but they are junior in rights to debentures. In the event of liquidation, subordinated debenture holders receive a cash distribution only after more senior debt (both secured and unsecured) has been repaid. If debentures are subordinated to bank loans, for example, bank loans would have to be completely satisfied in a liquidation before the subordinated debenture holders receive any of the proceeds from asset sales.

Corporate bonds may sometimes be exchanged for other securities. *Convertible bonds* may be exchanged for a specific number of shares of common stock of the issuing firm. An investor will not elect to surrender the bond and convert, however, unless the market value of the stock to which the investor is entitled exceeds the market value of the bond. In the case of widely traded issues, the price of the bond fluctuates to keep its market value roughly equivalent to the value of the stock into which it may be converted. However, regardless of the market value of the stock, the owner of a convertible bond will never be entitled to less than the principal and interest payments of the bond.

Bonds are sometimes issued with *stock warrants* attached. Warrants are options to purchase common stock at a specified price up to a specified date. Should the bondholder decide to exercise the option and purchase stock, it is not necessary to surrender the underlying bond. Again, bondholders will exercise their warrants only if the market value of the stock exceeds the specified (exercise) price of the warrant.

Bonds are an important source of capital for the federal government, states and municipalities, and private corporations. In the United States, however, private sector equity financing in the form of common stock has historically been a more important source of financing.

② Corporate Stock

The market value of common stock outstanding increased as fast as bonds during the 1980s and early 1990s. Exhibit 4.3 shows that the rate of increase of stock outstanding from 1969 to 1979 was just

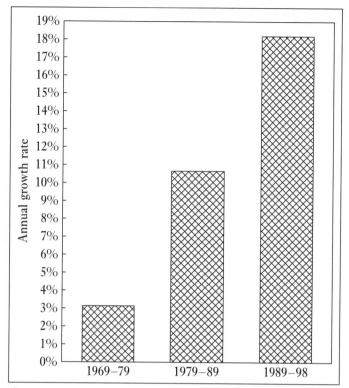

◆ **Exhibit 4.3:**   **Growth rate of corporate stock, 1969–79, 1979–89, 1989–98**

◆ *Source*:   Author's calculations and graphic based on data from: Board of Governors of the Federal Reserve System, *Flow of Funds Accounts; Flows and Outstandings.*

over 3 percent, much lower the 10 percent annual increase in corporate bonds (see Exhibit 4.2). From 1979 to 1989, however, the annual increase in stock outstanding was almost 11 percent. During the nine years ended 1998, outstanding corporate stock increased at the average annual rate of 18 percent. This relatively strong growth can be expected to continue to the extent that the secondary markets for stock remain strong, encouraging the issuance of new shares.

Holders of *corporate stock* have an ownership interest in the firm. Stock is recorded in the equity section of the firm's balance sheet. Corporate stock takes two forms:

- Preferred stock
- Common stock

Corporate stock:
    Financial claims on a corporation held by the owners of the firm.

2.1 Preferred Stock

Preferred stock is a hybrid instrument that represents an equity interest but pays a fixed dividend (just as a bond pays a fixed interest payment). Often preferred stock is *cumulative*, that is, all preferred dividends (unpaid in the past and currently due) must be paid before common shareholders may receive any dividend payments. Like the value of a bond, the value of preferred stock depends on the future cash flows to which the investor is entitled. Because the dividend is fixed, a preferred stockholder is entitled to a perpetual stream of level cash flows.

> **Dividends:**
> Periodic cash flows paid to owners of corporate stock (frequently paid on a quarterly basis).

$$P_0 = \sum_{t=1}^{\infty} \left[\frac{D}{(1+k)^t} \right] \tag{4.6}$$

where P_0 = price of a share of preferred stock today
D = fixed dividend per share
k = required rate of return

Equation (4.6) is a geometric series that converges to the valuation model for preferred stock:

$$P_0 = \frac{D}{k} \tag{4.7}$$

With the observed market price of preferred stock and the dividend per share, which is known, an investor's *expected rate of return* can be determined by solving for k in Equation (4.7).

> **Expected rate of return (k'):**
> The rate that causes an asset's present value of future cash flows to equal its market price. The expected rate of return is determined by substituting all known (or estimated) values into the asset's valuation formula and solving for k.

$$k' = \frac{D}{P_0} \tag{4.8}$$

Notice that the expected return for a investor in preferred stock is its dividend yield only (comparable to the current yield of a bond).

2.2 Common Stock

Common stock is an equity interest with dividend payments that are not fixed and that vary, usually increasing over time. In the event of liquidation, common shareholders have the lowest priority in terms of any cash distribution.[6] Because of this, owners of common stock have what is called a *residual* claim on the firm.

Assuming that dividends increase at a constant rate, the value of a share of common stock is the value of a constantly growing stream of cash flows:

$$P_0 = \frac{D_0(1+g)}{(1+k)} + \frac{D_0(1+g)^2}{(1+k)^2} + \ldots + \frac{D_0(1+g)^\infty}{(1+k)^\infty} \qquad (4.9)$$

where P_0 = price of a share of common stock today
D_0 = current dividend per share
g = constant growth rate of dividends
k = required rate of return, assuming $k < g$

Again, this relationship converges to:

$$P_0 = \frac{D_1}{(k-g)} \qquad (4.10)$$

where D_1 = dividend per share expected next period
$= D_0(1 + g)$

Solving Equation (4.10) for k, the result is the expected rate of return for a common shareholder when the price of the stock is known and a given growth rate has been estimated.

$$k' = \frac{D_1}{P_0} + g \qquad (4.11)$$

Common stock rate of return consists of the sum of dividend yield (D_1/P_0) and growth in the market price of the stock (capital gains yield). These components of return are comparable to the return components for bonds – current yield and capital gains.

Mortgages

US households generally obtain capital through mortgages. *Mortgages* are long-term loans that are secured by real property. Mortgages are issued to purchase real estate of four basic types:

- Homes
- Multifamily dwellings
- Commercial property
- Farms

> **Mortgages:**
> Long-term liabilities collateralized by real property. Commonly, monthly payments are made that fully repay both principal and interest over the term of the loan.

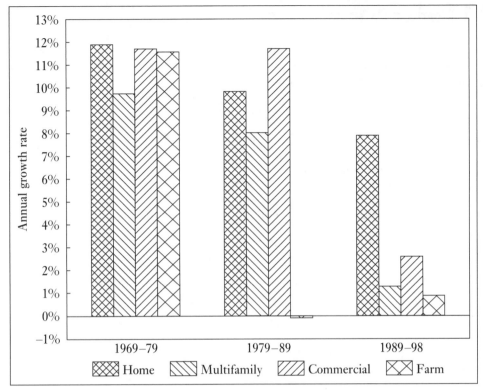

◆ **Exhibit 4.4: Growth rate of mortgages, 1969–79, 1979–89, 1989–98**

◆ *Source*:   Author's calculations and graphic based on data from: Board of Governors of the Federal Reserve System, *Flow of Funds Accounts; Flows and Outstandings.*

Exhibit 4.4 shows that home mortgages (used to purchase 1- to 4-family dwellings) have grown consistently at annual rates of between 8 percent and 12 percent since 1969.

Mortgages for multifamily dwellings are a smaller part of the market, having grown at an average annual rate of 10 percent from 1969 to 1979, 8.0 percent from 1979 to 1989, but only by 1 percent during the nine years ended 1998.

Commercial mortgages are used to finance real estate used for business purposes, such as office buildings and shopping malls. Commercial mortgages consistently grew faster than multifamily dwelling mortgages and even faster than home mortgages during the 1980s. However, the growth in excess of 11 percent per year (from 1969 to 1979 and again from 1979 to 1989) slowed to approximately 3 percent during the nine years ended 1998.

The growth rate in both multifamily and commercial mortgages has declined in recent years because of a soft real estate market in which many projects have high vacancy rates. This situation developed because of overbuilding during the 1980s.

Farm mortgages are the smallest part of the market. Having increased at a 12 percent rate from 1969 through 1979, farm mortgages declined slightly from 1979 to 1989. From 1989 to 1998, the average annual growth rate was a very low 0.9 percent. An overexpansion similar to that in the commercial sector occurred and the market is still correcting itself.

3.1 Mortgage Payments

Unlike corporate mortgage bond issuers who frequently pay only interest until the maturity date, households with mortgages most often pay equal monthly payments (an annuity) composed of both interest and partial principal repayment.

$$P = A(PVIFA_{(k,n)}) \tag{4.12}$$

where

P = principal amount of the loan
A = monthly payment
  = amount of annuity
k = periodic interest rate
n = number of periods in the term of the loan
$PVIFA_{(k,n)}$ = present value interest factor of an annuity

$$= \left(\frac{1}{k}\right) - \frac{1}{k(1+k)^n}$$

The monthly payment is determined by the amount, the term, and the interest rate of the loan.

$$A = \frac{P}{PVIFA_{(k,n)}} \tag{4.12a}$$

For example, a 30-year mortgage loan for $100,000 with a 10 percent interest rate requires monthly payments of $877.57.

$$A = \frac{100,000}{\left(\frac{1}{\left(\frac{.10}{12}\right)}\right) - \frac{1}{\left(\frac{.10}{12}\right)\left(1 + \left(\frac{.10}{12}\right)\right)^{360}}}$$

$$= \frac{100,000}{113.9507}$$

$$= 877.57$$

The first month's payment includes $833.33 of interest [100,000(.10/12)] on the unpaid principal of $100,000, and only $44.24 to reduce the balance of the loan. The principal reduction associated with the first payment leaves an unpaid principal to $99,955.76. The interest in the second payment is $832.96 [99,955.76(.10/12)], and the payment on principal is $44.61. Each month the portion of the payment allocated to interest is smaller because the unpaid principal is smaller. This process continues until the last payment brings the unpaid principal to zero.

A table that identifies the principal and interest components of each payment is called an *amortization schedule*. An amortization schedule can be constructed easily with the use of the formulas above and a computer spreadsheet program. (See end-of-chapter problems for an exercise constructing an amortization schedule.)

Recent innovations in the mortgage market include graduated payment mortgages (in which the early payments are calculated at rates of interest below market rates) and adjustable rate mortgages (that require payments to change when market interest rates change). A graduated mortgage makes it easier for a household to afford to make the payments in the early years of the mortgage. As the payments increase, household income also increases. An adjustable rate mortgage (ARM) is more affordable when interest rates are low, but payments increase when interest rates rise. An ARM helps ensure the lender of increasing interest income when interest rates rise, thereby shifting the exposure to interest rate risk from the lender to the borrower.[7]

3.2 MORTGAGE POOLS

Individual mortgages are not well suited for trading in capital markets, largely because the amounts of specific loans are not uniform; they are tied to the market value of underlying property. Also, information about the creditworthiness of individual borrowers is not as readily available as similar information for public companies. Federally sponsored agencies, however, have developed secondary markets for mortgages through creation of mortgage pools.

The Federal National Mortgage Association, the Federal Home Loan Mortgage Corporation, the Farmers Home Administration, and the Government National Mortgage Association (GNMA or Ginnie Mae – a division of Housing and Urban Development) issue debt securities to the public that represent claims on pools of mortgages. (Ginnie Mae securities are backed by the full faith and credit of the US government.) Investors in these mortgage pool securities receive pass-through certificates (agency liabilities), which entitle them to interest and principal payments according to their share of the pool.

Pass-through certificates have an element of uncertainty for investors, however. If the mortgages in the pool, the underlying mortgages, are refinanced, perhaps because mortgage interest rates decline significantly, the actual term of a pass-through certificate will be shorter than the investor anticipated at the time of purchase. This means that total investment return may be significantly less than first estimated.

In 1982, the Federal Home Loan Mortgage Corporation introduced *collateralized mortgage obligations (CMOs)* to address this concern. These early CMOs were divided into three groups, called *tranches*, A-1, A-2, and A-3. Holders of A-l CMOs received the customary pass-through of interest and principal payments, while A-2 and A-3 holders received interest only. When A-1 principal was completely repaid, A-2 began to receive distributions of principal. When A-2 was completely repaid, A-3 received principal payments. These arrangements reduce some of the uncertainty as to the actual maturity date and rate of return, especially for A-1 investors. This idea has been so well received that private firms now issue CMOs that are corporate bonds whose proceeds are invested in pass-through certificates. In each case, individual loans are converted into marketable securities through "securitization," a growing trend in the United States.

Securitization

Pass-through certificates and CMOs are examples of *securitized* assets. Questions that relate to the likely success of a securitization are:

- Are the credit issues relatively easy to understand and communicate?
- How easily can the cash flows of the underlying assets be estimated?
- Will the average life of the underlying assets be at least one year, ensuring an adequate return of interest payments?

- What are the historical default rates (nonpayment of scheduled interest and/or principal) of the underlying assets?
- Do the underlying assets totally amortize, that is, do the payments include principal and interest?
- Are the underlying assets based on a diverse pool?
- Can the collateral of the underlying assets (for example, the homes that are collateral for mortgages) be easily liquidated, as necessary?

> **Securitization:**
> The pooling of a group of loans with similar characteristics and the subsequent sale of interests in the pool to investors.

To the extent that the answers to these questions are favorable, the loans are good candidates for securitization.

4.1 ASSET-BACKED SECURITIES

An asset-backed security is the result of the securitization process. In essence, (1) loans are removed from the balance sheet of the issuer and (2) interests in the pool of loans are sold to investors. As a result, the issuer is able to become more liquid and originate even more loans. Typically, the issuer of asset-backed securities continues to accept payments, send statements, and perform other functions to service the loans. For these activities, the issuer of asset-backed securities is paid a fee, generally on the order of 50 basis points of the unpaid balance. (A basis point is one hundredth of one percent.)

The form of securitized assets varies. Generally, there are three basic categories:

- Pass-through securities
- Asset-backed bonds
- Pay-through bonds

4.1.1 PASS-THROUGH SECURITIES

Pass-through securities pay investors their proportional shares of cash flows generated by underlying assets. These cash flows include both principal and interest payments. A fee for servicing the underlying assets is deducted from each interest payment. A pass-through security, thus, represents ownership in a pool of assets. The assets are removed from the balance sheet of the originator of the loans and placed in a *trust*. In turn, the trust issues certificates of ownership to investors, the effective owners of the underlying assets.

Because the assets in the pool are typically mortgage loans and consumer receivables (automobile loans and credit card receivables), payments on the loans are generated monthly. All cash flows, with the exception of the servicing fee, flow to investors. These payments include interest, principal, and any prepayments of principal. Thus, cash flows from the underlying assets are said to be *dedicated* cash flows.

4.1.2 ASSET-BACKED BONDS

Asset-backed bonds remain on the balance sheet of the issuer. Underlying assets collateralize the bonds and also remain on the balance sheet of the issuer. The underlying assets may be loans or pass-through securities. As is true with other types of bonds, interest is paid semiannually and the face amount (par value or maturity value) is paid upon maturity. One frequent characteristic of asset-backed bonds is that they are typically overcollateralized, that is, the value of underlying assets is greater than the face value of asset-backed bonds (liabilities). Every three months, the value of the underlying assets (collateral) is assessed. If this amount is less than the amount specified in the bond indenture, additional loans or pass-through securities must be added to the collateral.

Unlike pass-through securities, asset-backed bonds do not have dedicated cash flows from the underlying assets. Also, because assets remain on the balance sheet of the issuer, no trust is formed.

4.1.3 PAY-THROUGH BONDS

Pay-through-bonds are a hybrid of pass-through securities and asset-backed bonds. Pay-through bonds are obligations of the issuer, as are asset-backed bonds. However, (1) all cash flows from the underlying assets are dedicated to servicing the obligation represented by pay-through bonds and (2) a separate entity is formed to hold the underlying assets, as is the case with pass-through securities. This separate entity also issues the bonds. Interest and principal payments are made monthly or quarterly.

Unlike either pass-through securities or asset-backed bonds, pay-through bonds are issued in different *tranches*. An *accrual* or *accretion bond* is similar to a zero-coupon bond, and is frequently referred to as a *Z-bond*. This tranche receives no interest or principal until it matures. Other tranches receive payments of interest at regular intervals. Commonly, only one tranche receives principal payments at a time. When principal has been repaid for the first tranche, then the second tranche begins to receive principal payments. When the second tranche has been completely repaid with respect to principal, the third tranche begins to receive principal payments.

This structure is intended to eliminate much of the uncertainty with respect to *prepayment risk*. Prepayment risk is the exposure that a long-term investor faces when purchasing an amortizing security that may be repaid much earlier than the original maturity date. While the investor may realize a gain on the early return of principal, the anticipated stream of interest payments can be drastically reduced. Pay-through bonds give investors relatively more control over this eventuality. Pay-through bonds may also contain a *residual tranche* which receives cash flows that are in excess of the obligations to the other tranches. This may occur, for example, when the rate of prepayment that is anticipated at the time of securitization exceeds the actual, realized rate of prepayment. In this case, total interest payments are greater than would otherwise have been the case. These "excess" interest payments accrue to the residual tranche investor.

4.1.4 A COMPARISON

Exhibit 4.5 provides a summary of the characteristics of the three types of asset-backed securities. (These are general characteristics which may differ considerably in actual application.) Pass-through securities represent the first "generation" of asset-backed securities. Pay-through bonds are the most recent innovation in the field and are decidedly more complex. All three types offer the advantage of an alternative funding source (instead of straight bonds or equity) that can be tapped relatively easily.

	Pass-through securities	Asset-backed bonds	Pay-through bonds
Payment frequency	Monthly	Semiannually	Monthly or quarterly
Recorded on the balance sheet of the issuer?	No	Yes	No
Cash flows from underlying assets dedicated to investors?	Yes	No	Yes
Trust or other separate entity created?	Yes	No	Yes
Classes of securities	Same for all investors	Same for all investors	Different tranches within one issue

◆ **Exhibit 4.5: Types of asset-backed securities**

4.2 OTHER ASSET-BACKED SECURITIES

Recall that government agencies played a major role in the development of the asset-backed securities market, having introduced pass-through securities in the 1970s. These initial issuances of mortgage-backed pass-throughs have been followed by private sector issues and innovation in terms of underlying assets which now include automobile loans, credit card receivables, commercial loans, computer and truck leases, loans for mobile homes, and other trade receivables.

In addition, commercial paper and preferred stock have been issued with asset backing. Usually, commercial paper is secured by credit card receivables, automobile and utility leases, and trade receivables. Preferred stock is frequently secured by mortgage-backed securities and trade receivables. Both asset-backed commercial paper and preferred stock have interest or dividend payments that are *not* tied to the cash flows of the *underlying* assets.

In the case of *asset-backed preferred stock*, the dividend rate is auction-rated. The dividends on this stock are paid and adjusted quarterly. These instruments have been issued by commercial bank holding companies since 1982 and pay interest that is based on a spread over Treasury rates. Because of this frequent change in the dividend rate, the market price of this preferred stock remains very close to par value. These adjustable-rate issues have no maturity date, but may often be called at the option of the issuer.

With respect to *asset-backed commercial paper*, these programs typically do not "unwind" when underlying assets amortize. Instead, new receivables are bought continually, with the net affect that the commercial paper is rolled over when it matures. There are a number of other differences between asset-backed commercial paper and other securitized assets:

- Commercial paper is issued in order to *purchase* underlying assets, not to facilitate their sale.
- Investment bankers (who help issuing firms bring stocks and bonds to market) typically provide credit enhancements or guarantees in the case of asset-backed commercial paper.
- In other cases, credit enhancement is typically provided by a third party, like an insurance company.
- While mortgage-backed securities are relatively liquid, asset-backed commercial paper is much less liquid because there is no active secondary market.

4.3 ADVANTAGES OF SECURITIZATION

Securitization provides a number of advantages for the issuing firms.

- Fully collateralized (secured) financing means that an issuer can obtain funds at a lower cost of capital.
- To the extent that the issuer services the underlying assets (that is, keeps records, sends statements, collects payments), an additional source of fee income is generated.
- Liquidity is much enhanced because loans and other receivables can be sold in a liquid secondary market despite the fact that the underlying assets, individually, may be highly illiquid.
- Securitization aids diversification in that an issuer can substitute a security backed by many loans for the same dollar cost that might be associated with only one or two individual loans.
- The credit rating of the certificates or bonds, to a great extent, will be determined by the creditworthiness of the underlying assets rather than the creditworthiness of the issuer. This feature enables companies with high-quality receivables or loans to issue highly rated bonds even if the company's credit rating is not the highest credit standard.

The growing variety of securitized assets indicates the advantages that the process of securitization offers. Selling mortgage loans to federal agencies lets savings and loan associations remove long-term assets from their books. As most of their deposits are short-term, sale of the mortgage loans helps S&Ls to match the average maturity of their assets to those of their liabilities more closely. Holding pass-throughs and CMOs lets S&Ls diversify their mortgage-related assets; in the case of CMOs, the S&Ls also shorten the average time to maturity of these holdings.

Life insurance companies have longer-term liabilities. From their perspective, investment in long-term residential mortgage assets would be advantageous. But *individual* mortgage loans would not be cost-effective because of the expense of administration. By investing in mortgage-backed pass-throughs, life insurance firms have the benefit of mortgage loan equivalents while avoiding administrative expense.

Securitization enables borrowers to access a source of low-cost funds. When a firm's overall credit rating is lower than the credit rating of its receivables, securitizing the receivables can reduce the borrower's rate of interest. Securitization also enables small and emerging companies to offer financing arrangements to their customers by selling on credit terms and then packaging the receivables for resale. For these and other reasons, securitization is likely to be an even more important component of capital market transactions in the future.

 Summary

Capital market instruments are long-term claims on governments, corporations, and households and they are classified as bonds, stock, or mortgages. The US Treasury issues bonds to finance the operations of the federal government. States and other political subdivisions issue municipal bonds to finance similar operations at the local level. Federal agencies issue bonds in order to purchase packages of mortgage loans and student loans from private lenders, thereby making more funds available for housing and education in the private sector. Corporations issue bonds and stock for long-term projects that will contribute to economic growth.

The value of capital market instruments is based on cash flows, required rate of interest, and timing of cash flows. Bonds and mortgages have a fixed term or time to maturity. Stock is a perpetual stream of payments. In each case, however, pricing formulas facilitate the valuation of these instruments. The formulas are also useful for computing an investor's expected return.

Capital market instruments totalled approximately $22 trillion in 1996. Corporate stock and mortgages represented the largest dollar value at $8.7 trillion and $4.9 trillion, respectively. Corporate bonds ($2.6 trillion), federal agency bonds ($2.5 trillion), Treasury notes and bonds ($2.3 trillion), and municipal bonds ($1.1 trillion) made up the remaining US capital market instruments.

Securitization has a significant trend in the recent development of the capital markets. Federal government agencies encouraged the process of securitization by purchasing pools of mortgage loans. Since then, the private sector has become actively involved as well. Now credit card, automobile, and business loans are packaged and sold, facilitating fresh infusions of funds into US capital markets.

End-of-chapter Questions

1. List and define the major financial instruments of the US capital markets.
2. What is the difference between a bond's yield to maturity and its current yield?
3. Differentiate between a debenture and a subordinated debenture.
4. How do federally sponsored agencies that operate in the secondary market for mortgages help to make more mortgage loans available in the primary market?
5. With respect to municipal bonds, why should a revenue bond yield a higher return than a general obligation bond?
6. What are the differences between common stock and preferred stock?
7. Which is more volatile in price: a fixed-rate, zero-coupon bond or a variable-rate bond that pays periodic interest?
8. How does a CMO differ from a pass-through certificate?
9. Securitization helps financial institutions be more liquid by selling portions of their loan portfolio. Do consumers benefit from securitization?
10. Identify the advantages and disadvantages of adjustable rate mortgages:
    a. From the perspective of borrowers.
    b. From the perspective of lenders.
11. What is a bond indenture?
12. How do pay-through bonds help to reduce risk for bondholders as compared to pass-through securities?
13. What are the cash flows for the "residual" class of investors in a CMO?
14. Explain the features of the inflation-protection bonds offered by the US Treasury.
15. Compare and contrast the Dutch-auction system and the multi-price auction system used by the US Treasury.

End-of-chapter Problems

1. What is the maximum price that you should be willing to pay for a bond with 7 years to maturity, a $1,000 par value, and an 8 percent coupon rate (paid semiannually) if your required rate of return is 12 percent?

2. If a 15-year zero coupon bond is selling for $239.39, what is its yield to maturity?

3. If your marginal tax rate is 28 percent, what corporate bond yield would make you indifferent to a 7 percent municipal bond?

4. If a share of stock is selling for $40, its last dividend was $2, and the firm's growth rate is expected to be 15 percent, what rate of return do you expect shareholders to earn next year?

5. Suppose that a corporate bond is convertible into 20 shares of common stock.
   a. If the bond is currently selling at par ($1,000), for what price should the stock be selling?
   b. If the stock were selling for $60 per share, for what price would you expect the bond to be selling?

6. An example in the chapter concerned an 8 percent coupon bond with a $1,000 face value that paid interest semiannually and matured in 5 years. With a required rate of return of 10 percent, the value of the bond was $922.78. Now suppose that the bond paid interest annually instead of semiannually.
   a. Compute the new value.
   b. Why is this value different?

7. A preferred stock pays an annual dividend of $4 and the required rate of return is 13 percent.
   a. What is the most you would be willing to pay for a share of this stock?
   b. Now suppose that another preferred stock is selling for $25 and that the required return is again 13 percent. What annual dividend should this stock be paying?

8. A common stock that paid a $3.24 dividend last year is selling for $50. If the required return is 15 percent, what should be this stock's growth rate?

9. Using either Excel, Lotus, or other spreadsheet software, set up a complete amortization schedule for the loan described in the chapter under "Mortgage Payments."

NOTES

1. PVIFA and PVIF are present value interest factors of an annuity and a single amount, respectively. See the time value of money tables in Appendix A at the back of the book.
2. This slight difference between the 10 percent required return and the 10.2 percent result is attributable to the use of 5 percent on a semiannual basis – an effective rate of 10.25 percent ($[1.05]^2 - 1$). To earn exactly 10 percent using semiannual compounding, only 4.88 percent is required semiannually.

$$1.10 = (1 + k)^2$$
$$k = (1.10)^{\frac{1}{2}} - 1$$
$$= 0.0488$$

   When this rate is used, the price of the bond is $931.65. The current yield is 8.6 percent which, when added to the average annual capital gain of 1.4 percent, yields a 10 percent rate of return.
3. $$CGY = [(1,000/1,077.21)^{1/10} - 1] \times 2$$
$$= -0.015$$

4. Included among federally related institutions are the Commodity Credit Corporation, the Export-Import Bank of the United States, the Farmers Home Administration, the General Services Administration, the Government National Mortgage Association, the Maritime Association, the Private Export Funding Corporation, the Rural Electrification Administration, the Rural Telephone Bank, the Small Business Administration, the Tennessee Valley Authority, and the Washington Metropolitan Area Transit Authority.
5. $$k_{AT} = k_{BT} - \text{tax}$$
$$k_{AT} = k_{BT} - k_{BT}(t)$$
$$= k_{BT}(1 - t)$$
6. After subordinated debentures, the next priority is preferred stock. After preferred stock claims are satisfied, common stock cash distributions are made.
7. Many ARMs contain protection for the borrower in the form of interest rate caps which limit both annual increases in interest rates and total increases over the life of the mortgage.

SELECTED REFERENCES

Carlson, John H. and Frank J. Fabozzi, eds. *The Trading and Securitization of Senior Bank Loans*, Probus Publishing, Chicago (now McGraw-Hill, New York), 1992.

Cohen, Jerome B., Edward D. Zinbarg, and Arthur Zeikel. *Investment Analysis and Portfolio Management*, 5th edn, Richard D. Irwin, Homewood, Ill., 1987.

Havrilesky, Thomas M. and Robert Schweitzer, eds. *Contemporary Developments in Financial Institutions and Markets*, Harlan Davidson, Arlington Heights, Ill., 1987.

Henderson, John and Jonathan P. Scott. *Securitization*, New York Institute of Finance, New York, 1988.

Johnson, Hazel J. *Bankers Guide to Investment Banking: Securities and Underwriting Activities in Commercial Banking*, Irwin Professional Publishing, Burr Ridge, Ill. (now McGraw-Hill, New York), 1996.

Mayo, Herbert B. *Investments: An Introduction*, Dryden Press, New York, 1984.

Pavel, Christine A. *Securitization: The Analysis and Development of the Loan-Based/Asset-Backed Securities Markets*, Chicago: Probus Publishing, 1989.

Peng, Scott Y. and Ravi E. Dattatreya. *The Structured Note Market: The Definitive Guide for Investors, Traders, and Issues*, Probus Publishing, Chicago (now McGraw-Hill, New York), 1995.

Stone, Charles, Anne Zissu, and Jess Lederman, eds. *The Global Asset Backed Securities Market: Structuring, Managing and Allocating Risk*, Probus Publishing, Chicago (now McGraw-Hill, New York), 1993.

Thau, Annette. *The Bond Book: Everything Investors Need to Know About Treasuries, Municipals, GNMAs, Corporates, Zeros, Bond Funds, Money Market Funds, and More*, Probus Publishing, Chicago (now McGraw-Hill, New York), 1992.

US Department of the Treasury. *Report of the Secretary of the Treasury on Government-Sponsored Enterprises*, Washington, DC, April 1991.

Capital Markets and International Diversification

chapter 5

CHAPTER OVERVIEW

This chapter:
- Differentiates the functions of primary and secondary capital markets.
- Introduces the investment banking process.
- Compares secondary markets in the United States.
- Highlights changes in the relative size of stock markets in developed countries and emerging markets.
- Describes the concepts of capital asset portfolio diversification.

KEY TERMS

American Stock Exchange
asset portfolio
capital markets
common stock
correlation coefficient
diversification
infrastructure fund
investment bank
market maker

merchant bank
National Association of Securities Dealers
New York Stock Exchange
organized stock exchange
OTC market
primary capital markets
secondary capital markets
Securities and Exchange Commission
specialist

CHAPTER OUTLINE

1 Primary Capital Markets
    1.1 Investment Banking
    1.2 New York Stock Exchange Listing
    1.3 American Stock Exchange Listing
    1.4 NASDAQ
    1.5 Privatization

INTERNATIONAL COMPARISONS:

Brazil	Malaysia
Canada	Mexico
France	Switzerland
Germany	Taiwan
India	Thailand
Japan	United Kingdom
Korea	

 Introduction

When the stocks and bonds described in chapter 4 are first issued, they are distributed to investors through primary markets. Investment bankers assist corporations in structuring the issues and take responsibility for selling the securities. These new issues of securities may be listed on organized exchanges or telecommunications networks. Once issued, the securities are bought and sold in secondary markets, again, on either organized exchanges or telecommunications networks.

Securities markets in Asia and other regions are developing more market-oriented practices. In addition, the need to raise large amounts of capital to "privatize" previously state-owned enterprises has great increased the incentives to encourage foreign investment. Greater access to such markets makes it possible for global investors to diversify their asset holdings beyond domestic investments and to improve risk/return tradeoffs. Continued expansion of international markets promises to make international diversification even easier.

① Primary Capital Markets

Financial securities are offered for the first time in *primary markets*. For US Treasury notes and bonds, initial issue is by periodic auctions through the New York Federal Reserve Bank and the US Treasury (described in chapters 3 and 4). For municipal bonds and corporate securities, primary markets operate in a different way, involving (1) investment banks in the United States, (2) merchant banks outside the United States, and (3) securities markets.

1.1 Investment Banking

Firms that facilitate the issue of stocks and bonds are called *investment banks*. The major investment banks in the United States are also called "bulge bracket" firms.[1] These firms are most active in helping to bring to market new debt, common stock, mortgage-backed securities, other asset-backed securities, preferred stock, and bonds issued by non-US issuers in the United States.[2]

Investment banks:
> Securities firms that (1) are retained to advise issuing entities on stock and bond offerings and (2) take an active role in distribution of the securities to ultimate investors.

In addition to bringing new securities to market, US investment banks participate in secondary market trading, corporate restructuring (changing the combination of debt and equity), advisory services, fund management, venture capital (for new high-growth-potential firms), and, since the 1980s, merchant banking. (See also chapter 6 for a discussion of investment banking.)

The *merchant bank* has long had a major role in primary securities markets outside the United States. Merchant banks operated in Italy as early as the fourteenth century. As the name implies, the first merchant bankers were European merchants who found that lending money and providing foreign exchange services made profitable and natural additions to their normal trading activities. Over time, England and northern Europe became centers for international trade, and London evolved as the hub of merchant banking, as it remains today. (See also Exhibit 5.1.)

Merchant bank:
> A bank that serves the needs of commercial enterprises by giving advice on financing alternatives and corporate mergers and underwriting new issues, as well as accepting bills of exchange, providing foreign currency exchange facilities, and operating in the money markets. A merchant bank invests its own capital in relatively short-term transactions associated with corporate restructurings and buyouts.

The London merchant banks are much smaller than clearing (commercial) banks, but both are licensed by the government. Merchant banks are primarily wholesale bankers; they lend funds in corporate and institutional markets. In recent years, they have focused more on primary market investment banking activities. Distinguishing characteristics of a merchant bank are that its staff is typically composed of a high proportion of professionals and that decisions are made quickly without recourse to bureaucratic chains of command, unlike the British clearing banks with large numbers of employees to staff numerous branches and a hierarchy to manage them.

Merchant banks operate in a number of countries and reflect the strong influence of the British model. In South Africa and Singapore, they are called merchant banks. In Australia they are referred to as *money market corporations* and in New Zealand as *unofficial money market corporations*. Merchant banks in Hong Kong are called *deposit-taking companies*. *Diversified financial institutions* are South Korea's equivalent, while the Japanese variation is *securities houses*. Like their names, the licensing of and legal specifications of merchant banks vary from one country to another.

Whether securities are brought to market through investment bankers or European-style merchant banks, the markets in which the securities are offered may be of two basic types – *organized exchanges* or *over-the-counter markets*. In the United States, the New York Stock Exchange (NYSE) and the American Stock Exchange (AMEX) are the national organized exchanges. In addition, there are a number of regional organized exchanges, including the Chicago Exchange, the Pacific Exchange, and those in Cincinnati, Philadelphia, and Boston. The national over-the-counter (OTC) is NASDAQ (National Association of Securities Dealers Automated Quotations).

Italian merchants began the long tradition of merchant banking. One of the most famous of these was Cosimo de Medici, who in the mid-fifteenth century established a network of operations beyond Italy with offices in London, Bruges (Belgium), and Avignon (France). As Italy lost its dominance in international commerce, merchant banking developed in northern Europe.

German merchant bankers became particularly well-known, with representation throughout Europe. By the 1700s, Mayer Amschel Rothschild, a clothing and coin merchant, had begun to diversify into financial services. Sending his sons to represent his interests, he established a Rothschild network including Frankfurt, London, Naples, Paris, and Vienna. These locations are the basis for the Rothschild corporate emblem, the Five Arrows, that is used today.

The oldest merchant bank in London is Barings Brothers; during the nineteenth century, it was the most prominent in Europe. This institution had considerable representation in North and South America (while Rothschild concentrated on Europe). In fact, when President Thomas Jefferson (1801–9) sought financing for the Louisiana Purchase in 1803, Barings Brothers arranged the $15 million needed. London continued to dominate international finance until the First World War, with merchant banks playing a vital role.[1] Much of the funding for the US railway system was provided by London merchant banks. While New York, Tokyo, and other centers have grown in significance with respect to various aspects of international finance, London remains the world center of merchant banking.

◆ **Exhibit 5.1:   Merchant Bankers of the Past**

◆ *Notes*:   1   In early 1995, Barings Brothers collapsed as the result of losses incurred from speculative transaction conducted by a trader in its Singapore office. Unauthorized transactions by this trader went unchecked until the equivalent of US$1.5 billion in losses had been realized. Barings was rescued by ING Bank of the Netherlands.

NASDAQ is a computerized network that links buyers and sellers through computer screens, rather than physical location. A larger number of stocks are listed on NASDAQ and an even greater number of stocks are reported without having met formal listing requirements. (See also the Secondary Capital Markets section below.)

1.2 New York Stock Exchange

Founded in 1792, the NYSE is the largest and oldest stock exchange in the United States, listing securities of major US corporations including the 30 firms included in the Dow Jones Industrial Average, a frequently quoted index. The exchange is located in New York City at 11 Wall Street, and is often referred to as the "Big Board." In 1995, the NYSE listed more than 2,675 stocks valued at $6 trillion (average value of $2.2 billion).

The requirements to list a stock on the NYSE are the most stringent and are contained in Exhibit 5.2. These requirements focus on the extent to which shares of a company are widely held, the size of the company, and profitability.

A firm that wishes to be considered for listing on the NYSE must meet the quantitative listing standards noted in Exhibit 5.2. For a firm that meets these standards, the first step in the process is a review by the NYSE, on a confidential basis. The NYSE reviews an applicant's case and advises as to whether the firm may list and identifies any reasons why a firm could not list. The NYSE review is at no cost to the firm.

	Minimum standards	Alternative minimum standards
Round-lot holders (number of holder of a unit of trading, usually 100 shares)	2,000[1]	Total shareholders of 2,200 *and* Average monthly trading volume of 100,000[2]
Public shares	1,100,000	n/a
Market value of public shares	$40,000,000	n/a
Net tangible assets	$40,000,000	n/a
Pretax income	Most recent year, $2,500,000 *and* Two preceding years, $2,000,000	Aggregate for last three years, $6,500,000 *and* Minimum in most recent year,[3] $4,500,000

◆ **Exhibit 5.2: New York Stock Exchange: listing requirements**

◆ *Notes*:   1   Number of shares held by nominees or depositories will be considered in addition to holders of record. In connection with initial public offerings, the NYSE will accept an undertaking that will be sold to a minimum of 2,000 round-lot holders.

2   For most recent 6 months.

3   All three years must be profitable.

n/a   Not applicable

◆ *Source*:   New York Stock Exchange, *Fact Book: 1995 Data.*

The NYSE also has other requirements for listing that are related to corporate governance. NYSE corporations must have a minimum of *two outside directors.* For those corporations that do not have the requisite outside directors, it is possible to appoint one at the time of listing and to have appointed the second within one year of listing. An outside director is one that is *not* an employee, an officer or former officer (of the corporation or a subsidiary), a relative of a principal executive officer, or an individual acting as an adviser, consultant, or legal counsel that receives compensation on a continuing basis in addition to director's fees.

In addition, each NYSE corporation must have an *audit committee.* The independence of this committee is critical. The audit committee must be composed of directors that are completely independent of the corporation's management.

Third, an NYSE corporation must maintain the integrity of shareholder *voting rights.* No action may be taken that would have the affect of nullifying, restricting, or disparately reducing the per share voting rights of an outstanding class of common stock.

The NYSE is also sensitive to the issue of *related party transactions.* A related party transaction may involve officers, directors, or shareholders of the company. Each corporation that applies for a listing on the NYSE will be required to confirm that it will appropriately review and oversee related party transactions on an ongoing basis. Such review may be conducted by the audit committee or by a comparable body.

In essence, the requirements for listing on the NYSE involve a wide shareholder base, a substantial balance sheet, reasonable profitability, and solid internal controls.

	Minimum standards	Alternative minimum standards
Public share holders	1) 800[1] or 2) 400 or 3) 400	1) 800[1] or 2) 400 or 3) 400
Public shares	1) 500,000 or 2) 1 million or 3) 500,000, with daily trading volume of at least 2,000 shares[2]	1) 500,000 or 2) 1 million or 3) 500,000, with daily trading volume of at least 2,000 shares[2]
Market value of public shares	$3,000,000	$15,000,000
Minimum price per share	$3	$3
Operating history	N/A	3 years
Shareholders equity	$4,000,000	$4,000,000
Pretax income	Most recent year or two of the last three years, $750,000	At least a three-year operating history (No income requirements)

◆ **Exhibit 5.3:** American Stock Exchange: listing requirements

◆ *Notes*:   1   Exclusive of the holdings of officers, directors, controlling shareholders, and other concentrated family holdings.
2   For prior six months.

◆ *Source*:   American Stock Exchange, *1996 AMEX Fact Book*.

1.3 AMERICAN STOCK EXCHANGE LISTING

AMEX is the second largest exchange in the United States. Since it first operated outdoors in New York City on various corners of the Wall Street district, this exchange was known first as the New York Curb Agency, then the New York Curb Market Association (from 1908 to 1921). This early organization concentrated on shares not listed on the NYSE. In 1921, the organization moved indoors at 86 Trinity Place and started a ticker (price quotation) service. In 1953, the exchange was renamed the American Stock Exchange.

AMEX continues to list securities of smaller firms as compared to the NYSE. In 1995, AMEX listed shares of 936 companies with a market capitalization of $137 billion (average value $146 million).

Exhibit 5.3 contains the listing requirements for AMEX. These are similar to the NYSE with the exception that the levels of publicly traded shares, assets, and income are lower. An applicant for listing on AMEX should be prepared to provide the same documents and to discuss the same governance issues as are relevant to an application for listing on the NYSE.

	Alternative 1	Alternative 2
Registration under Section 12(g) of the Securities Exchange Act of 1934 or equivalent	Yes	Yes
Net tangible assets[1]	$4 million	$12 million
Net income (In latest fiscal year or 2 of last 3 fiscal years)	$400,000	N/A
Pretax income (In latest fiscal year or 2 of last 3 fiscal years)	$750,000	N/A
Public float (shares)[2]	500,000	1 million
Market value of float	$3 million	$15 million
Operating history	N/A	3 years
Minimum bid price	$5	$3
Shareholders:		
If between 0.5 and 1 million shares publicly held	800	400
If more than 1 million shares publicly held	400	400
If more than 0.5 million shares held and average daily volume in excess of 2,000 shares	400	400
Number of market makers	2	2

◆ **Exhibit 5.4: NASDAQ: listing requirements**

◆ *Notes*:   1   Net tangible assets equal total assets minus intangible assets minus liabilities.

             2   Those shares *not* "held directly or indirectly by any officer or director of the issuer and by any person who is the beneficial owner of more than 10% of the total shares outstanding."

◆ *Source*:   The NASDAQ Stock Market, Inc., Oct. 1995.

1.4 NASDAQ

Until 1939, the over-the-counter market was essentially unorganized and unregulated. The Maloney Act amendments to the Securities Exchange Act permitted the creation of the National Association of Securities Dealers (NASD). The NASD is a self-regulating organization that has responsibilities in the OTC markets that are similar to those of organized stock markets. Stocks that are traded in the OTC market are separated into two classifications – those listed on NASDAQ (National Association of Securities Dealers Automated Quotations) and approximately 40,000 others. The more active stocks are listed on NASDAQ. In 1995, 5,122 companies were listed on NASDAQ with a market value of $1.2 trillion (average value $234 million).

Stocks that are listed on NASDAQ are either National Market System (NMS) or second-tier stocks. NMS stocks are the most widely held and actively traded among the NASDAQ listed stocks and number approximately 3,000. For NMS stocks, OTC dealers must provide information with respect to the last sale within 90 seconds of that trade. In the case of second-tier stocks, dealers must only report the aggregate trading volume at the end of each trading day. NASDAQ now has the second greatest trading volume in the United States, second only to the NYSE.

Exhibit 5.4 includes the minimum listing requirements for NASDAQ. There are two alternatives to obtain a NASDAQ listing. Alternative 1 places more emphasis on the operating results of the issuer in recent years and less emphasis on the size of the organization. On the other hand, Alternative 2 places more emphasis on market capitalization and the strength of the firm's balance sheet. (Market capitalization is the total market value of equity, as measured by the product of total shares outstanding and price per share.)

Under both alternatives, the listing firm must have a minimum of two *market makers* in place. However, since every dealer registered with NASDAQ can become a market maker and the average number of market makers is 11 per security, the two-market-maker requirement is not a binding constraint.

Market maker (NASDAQ):
> Independent securities dealer licensed by NASDAQ with the responsibility to execute buy and sell orders on behalf of customers or the dealer's own account.

If a firm does not qualify for listing as a NMS stock, it may qualify for listing in the NASDAQ SmallCap market. Exhibit 5.5 summarizes these requirements. While registration under the Securities Exchange Act of 1934 is required, there is temporary, automatic exemption for initial public offerings (IPOs).

	SmallCap
Registration under Section 12(g) of the Securities Exchange Act of 1934 or equivalent[1]	Yes
Total shareholders' equity	$2 million
Net income (In latest fiscal year or 2 of last 3 fiscal years)	N/A
Pretax income (In latest fiscal year or 2 of last 3 fiscal years)	N/A
Public float (shares)[2]	100,000
Market value of float	$1 million
Operating history	N/A
Minimum bid price	$3
Shareholders	300
Number of market makers	2
Total assets	$4 million

♦ **Exhibit 5.5: NASDAQ: SmallCap listing requirements**

♦ *Notes*:   1   A temporary, automatic exemption exists for initial public offerings.
              2   Those shares *not* "held directly or indirectly by any officer or director of the issuer and by any person who is the beneficial owner of more than 10% of the total shares outstanding."

♦ *Source*:   The NASDAQ Stock Market, Inc., *The Nasdaq Stock Market 1996 Fact Book*.

Nigeria has the largest population among the countries of Sub-Saharan Africa and is a major producer of crude oil. Although Nigeria remains a poor country by Western standards, the oil revenues have helped spur the development of a stock market. However, unlike prices in primary markets in the United States, Nigerian securities prices are set by the government. The Securities and Exchange Commission (SEC) determines market prices of securities. The Capital Issues Commission (CIC), established in 1973, like its ad-hoc predecessor, the Capital Issues Committee, attempts to set prices of publicly traded securities in order to protect the investors and to prevent price manipulation by market participants. The CIC's primary function is price-fixing in the primary market (an activity that some firms avoid by not offering their securities to the public) and it is not empowered to regulate the secondary market. The SEC, established in 1978, has the authority to require registration of *all* securities that ultimately may be held by investors other than those to whom they are originally sold and to supervise stock exchanges and securities firms.

Several factors are considered in setting the prices of equities. In general, the price is set so that the ratio of average annual earnings (over the preceding 5 years) to share price is 20 to 30 percent, depending on the industry. Another measure that is determined by the government is the net asset value per share (assets less liabilities divided by number of outstanding shares). The lower of (1) the price implied by the earnings/price ratio and (2) the net asset value per share, after adjustment for other relevant factors, becomes the price at which the stock may be sold.

In 1996, the Nigerian government moved toward greater free-market influence in the money and capital markets through a number of measures. Two of these – the Nigerian Investment Promotion Decree and the Foreign Exchange Monitoring Decree – removed previously imposed limits on foreign ownership of local companies and eased foreign exchange restrictions. Gradually, government control over Nigerian capital markets is being reduced.

◆ **Exhibit 5.6:** **The Nigerian primary capital market**

◆ *Sources*:   Nwankwo, G. O. *The Nigerian Financial System*, African Publishing Company, New York, 1980; Onoh, J. K., ed. *The Foundations of Nigeria's Financial Infrastructure*, Croom Helm, London, 1980; International Finance Corporation. *Emerging Stock Markets FactBook 1996*, Washington, DC, 1996.

Under a SmallCap listing, there is one requirement that is not included in the other alternatives. Total assets must amount to $4 million. This requirement, together with the requirement for minimum capital of $2 million suggests that the listing firm must have a debt ratio (debt-to-total-assets ratio) of no more than 50 percent. (See also Exhibit 5.6.)

An issuer of common stock has a wide range of alternatives to list on an organized exchange or in the OTC market. The appropriate choice clearly will be related to the size of the firm. Additional information that should be considered is the type of industry in which the issuing firm is engaged and the extent to which similar firms are traded either OTC or in organized exchanges. Another consideration for the decision to list is the investor market to which the issuer would like to appeal. If the company is of national interest, or potentially national interest, a national organized exchange or a NASDAQ National Market listing may be appropriate. On the other hand, if the stock is of primarily regional interest, listing on a regional exchange may be preferable and probably more efficient in terms of the expense of listing. (See also Exhibit 5.7.)

In 1998, the American Stock Exchange and NASDAQ merged. The new exchange is called NASDAQ-Amex.

1.5 PRIVATIZATION

A major trend in the global capital markets is the *privatization* of previously government-owned enterprises. Such conversions are undertaken for a number of reasons:

- Governments find that efficiency is hampered by government ownership and seek to infuse more private-sector practices.
- Major investment is needed in a government-controlled sector, such as crude oil exploration and drilling, but private capital cannot be obtained for a purely government-owned organization.
- Governments find that the liabilities associated with operating businesses that are sustaining losses cannot be met with existing government revenues.

The result of privatizations is the issuance of new stocks and bonds, which, in turn increases the outstanding supply of securities globally. However, the process sometimes can be complicated with issues of national sovereignty and national control of strategically important industries. Governments may resist the loss of control associated with privatization. Together, these entities often employ a large segment of the country's population and represent a significant share of GDP.

In Europe, large privatizations have taken place in several countries, including the United Kingdom (for example, British Telecom and British Coal) and France (Air France, Renault (automobiles), and Thomson Electronics). In 1996, a German privatization was introduced to the primary stock markets of the world after several years of planning. Deutsche Telekom (DT (telecommunications)) is the largest privatization offering to date.

Although the privatization trend may be observed in all regions of the world, privatizations in Asia (outside Japan) present an interesting case because of the high rate of economic growth in this region.[3] Asian countries need capital to build new telecommunications, energy, transportation, and water facilities. These and other major infrastructure projects are high on the list of privatizations.

To meet the infrastructure need, private-sector funds clearly will be necessary. At the same time, the private sector reasonably cannot be expected to absorb the total risk for such projects, given the public nature of the facilities and their high cost. Financing for these projects is typically structured with 25 percent equity and 75 percent debt. Generally, a high level of debt financing is acceptable for "public utilities" because cash flows from these large projects are often used to retire the debt. In Asia, the equity component for infrastructure projects has been greatly enhanced by the introduction of *infrastructure funds*. These funds were introduced after the Asian Development Bank completed an analysis in the early 1990s on the development and use of such vehicles.[4] Currently, Asian infrastructure funds include AIG Asian Infrastructure Fund, Global Power Investment Fund (affiliated with GE Capital, the International Finance Corporation, and the Quantum Fund), and the Peregrine Asian Infrastructure Fund.[5]

Infrastructure fund:
> A pool of funds invested in infrastructure projects (fixed assets such as roads, bridges, power plants, and telecommunications networks) with claims on the fund (liabilities) sold to the investing public.

However, problems raising the 75 percent debt portion of these projects center around several factors:

- Governments and supranational institutions (such as the World Bank) are not willing to assume such high levels of risk. (A supranational institution involves participation by a number of countries.) These are massive projects with high costs of completion.
- Commercial banks (that might, together, be able to raise the necessary debt funds) often are not prepared to take on the "completion risk" associated with infrastructure projects – that is, all of the risk associated with political and financial arrangements to bring a project to fruition.
- Funds cannot be completely dedicated to the project (which may take many years to complete) upon bond issuance. Instead, the funds are used over the period of time required to complete the infrastructure project. In some cases, this situation can result in negative arbitrage; that is, the borrowed funds that are not immediately needed can be invested only at rates (lending rates) which are below rates paid to obtain the funds (borrowing rates).
- Delays in project completion sometimes necessitate refinancing. If bonds were issued, assembling 300 or 400 bondholders to negotiate a refinancing clearly would not be feasible.
- Larger, institutional investors (mutual funds, pension funds, insurance companies), that might be expected to purchase bonds to finance the projects, may be less interested in the short maturities typically available in Asian bond markets. These institutions may prefer longer-term bonds (1) because of the investment philosophy of the mutual fund or (2) because the liabilities of the pension funds and insurance companies are long-term.

Thus, the key to successful privatizations in Asia outside Japan is for governments to create favorable macroeconomic conditions to attract needed investors. This includes developing an economic and regulatory environment that is internationally acceptable.

In general, privatizations in developing countries succeed when there is a favorable investment environment that will ensure investor confidence and adequate funds on an ongoing basis. Important steps toward achieving this goal include:

- Creating a competitive and transparent framework for the private sector, so that the terms of financial transactions are clearly understood.
- Defining a regulatory system that will apply to all parties.
- Establishing a reliable legal system that will fairly adjudicate rights and obligations.
- Establishing a transparent accounting system that is consistent with international standards.
- Developing local financial institutions that can tap local savings as a source of long-term finance.
- Developing domestic capital markets that become the primary source of finance for infrastructure and a viable mechanism for secondary trading of bonds and stocks.

The development of strong primary and secondary financial markets is often a critical step in a country's overall economic development.

Secondary Capital Markets

Once securities have been issued in the primary market, investors may sell or purchase them in *secondary markets*. In the United States, the secondary market for government securities, which are traded through government securities dealers, is quite active and liquid. Municipal bonds are traded primarily over-the-counter (OTC) and generally less frequently than federal government bonds. The secondary market for mortgages developed after initiatives taken by government agencies to sell interests in pools of mortgages. (See chapter 4, sections 3.2 and 4 (Mortgage pools and

Securitization).) Corporate bonds and stocks are traded either on an *organized stock exchange* or *over-the-counter (OTC)*.

2.1 ORGANIZED STOCK EXCHANGES

An organized exchange is a physical place where stocks and bonds are traded, with the help of specialists.

Organized stock exchange:
A specific location where stocks (and some bonds) are traded by exchange members who specialize in particular securities.

Specialists:
Exchange-assigned securities members that are obligated to maintain a fair and orderly market in the securities assigned to them. Specialists match buyers and sellers and maintain an orderly market by trading for their own account whenever there is an imbalance of buyers and sellers.

On both the NYSE and AMEX, specialists:

- Bring together buyers and sellers for their securities.
- Provide current price information concerning their securities.
- Maintain a "book" of buy and sell orders, given to them by other securities brokers, to be executed if and when the price of a security reaches a certain limit – so-called "limit orders."
- Buy or sell for their own account in the event of a shortage of sellers or buyers.

There are also regional exchanges, where securities of local firms trade. Over 90 percent of the securities listed on regional exchanges are also listed on either the NYSE or the AMEX. Regionals are the Chicago, Pacific, Boston, Philadelphia, and Cincinnati Stock Exchanges.

As shown in Exhibit 5.7, the breakdown of listed securities on the NYSE in 1994 was $4.2 trillion in common stock, $56 billion in preferred stock, and $2.3 trillion in bonds. On the AMEX in 1994, listed securities included common stock of $85 billion, preferred stock $1.6 billion, and bonds of $8 billion. In the same year, regional exchanges showed a similar pattern in that common stock was the most important listed security. Furthermore, the majority of listed stock was accounted for by the exchange in Boston ($2.9 billion), with Chicago ($535 million) and Pacific ($526 million) following. Also, the Pacific Exchange accounted for much of the preferred stock ($329 million) and almost all of the bonds ($1.1 billion) listed on the regional exchanges.

2.2 NASDAQ

On NASDAQ, market makers perform the same function as specialists on the NYSE and AMEX. These independent securities dealers compete with each other for investors' orders in a particular security. This arrangement is believed to ensure the best prices for investors in a security. The bids (prices at which market makers will buy) and offers (prices at which market makers will sell)

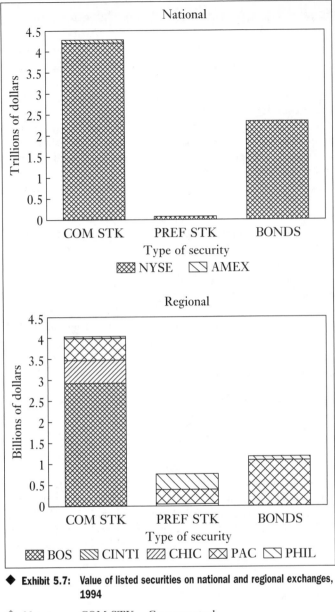

Exhibit 5.7: Value of listed securities on national and regional exchanges, 1994

Notes:

COM STK	Common stock
PREF STK	Preferred stock
BONDS	Corporate and municipal bonds
AMEX	American Stock Exchange
NYSE	New York Stock Exchange
BOS	Boston Stock Exchange
CINTI	Cincinnati Stock Exchange
CHIC	Chicago Stock Exchange
PAC	Pacific Stock Exchange
PHIL	Philadelphia Stock Exchange

Source: Derrick Johnson of H. J. Johnson & Associates, based on data from: *US Securities and Exchange Commission; 1995 Annual Report.*

for all registered market makers of NASDAQ are shown and continuously updated on this market's automated system. This makes it possible for a broker or a customer to identify the best price that is being quoted. Since any NASDAQ market dealer can be a market maker in any security simply by notifying NASDAQ of its intentions, an average of 11 market makers exist for each security traded on NASDAQ.

Previously, the 40,000 stocks that were not actually listed on NASDAQ (National Market or SmallCap) were quoted on a daily basis through printed media, the "Pink Sheets." Beginning in June 1990, this information was posted on an electronic Bulletin Board on which the dealers may post and update quotes.

The Bulletin Board should not be confused with the NASDAQ system. There are several differences.

- NASDAQ has specific minimum listing requirements, while the Bulletin Board does not. NASDAQ quotations are firm dealer commitments, which is not required for the Bulletin Board. Furthermore, dealers may even post indications of interest without including a price.
- NASDAQ transmits information to press wire services and to information service vendors; the Bulletin Board does not.
- NASDAQ is a telephone market supported by a computer system for quotation and execution of orders. Quotations are managed via leased telephone lines from the NASDAQ Central Processing Complex with collection and dissemination to dealers' desktop computer terminals.

Because of the speed and efficiency of the over-the-counter market, NASDAQ has grown rapidly.

2.3 Market Regulation

Both organized exchanges and OTC markets are regulated by the Securities and Exchange Commission (SEC) to prevent stock price manipulation, deception, and fraudulent practices. The National Association of Securities Dealers (NASD) is a self-regulatory body that licenses brokers and dealers and sets standards for ethical behavior. In 1996, the NASD responded to criticism of pricing practices in the OTC markets. At issue is alleged price manipulation that has the effect of increasing the prices paid by investors for virtually all stocks traded on NASDAQ. Thus, the issue of transparency and fairness of market conditions is as critical in US markets as it is in those countries that are currently undertaking large-scale privatizations.(See section 1.5, Privatization, above.)

2.4 International Comparisons

The US capital market has historically been the world's largest. As Exhibit 5.8 shows, as recently as 1980 the United States accounted for almost 55 percent of the value of securities listed on the stock markets (stock market capitalization) of all developed countries. Japan was then a distant second (14 percent) and the United Kingdom was third (8 percent). Canada, Germany, and France followed with less than a 5 percent share each.

During the following 15 years, the stock market capitalization of developed countries rose from $2.7 trillion in 1980 to $15.9 trillion by 1995. US capitalization increased more than 370 percent from $1.45 trillion to $6.86 trillion, while the Japanese market outstripped even this impressive growth. In 1980, Japanese capitalization was $380 billion. By 1995, it was up to $3.67 trillion, a more than 850 percent increase. In 1995, the United States share of market capitalization was

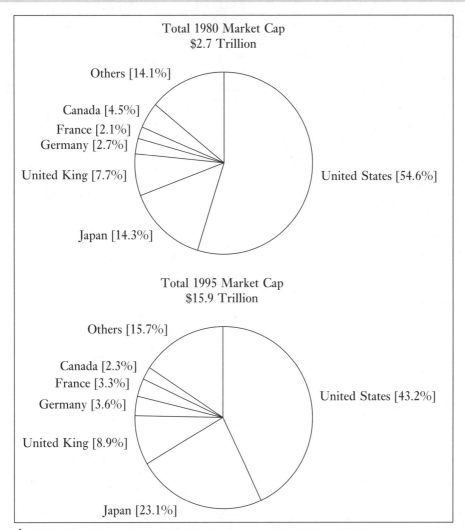

Total 1980 Market Cap
$2.7 Trillion

Others [14.1%]

Canada [4.5%]
France [2.1%]
Germany [2.7%]

United King [7.7%]

United States [54.6%]

Japan [14.3%]

Total 1995 Market Cap
$15.9 Trillion

Others [15.7%]

Canada [2.3%]
France [3.3%]

Germany [3.6%]

United States [43.2%]

United King [8.9%]

Japan [23.1%]

◆ **Exhibit 5.8: Stock market capitalization, developed countries, 1980 and 1995**

◆ *Source*:   Derrick Johnson of H. J. Johnson & Associates based on data from: International
Finance Corporation, *Emerging Stock Markets FactBook 1996*, Washington,
DC, 1996.

43.2 percent and that of Japan 23.1 percent. Large Japanese trade surpluses (excesses of exports
over imports) and a relatively strong Japanese currency contributed to this market expansion.

The economic expansion of the Newly Industrialized Countries (NICs) of Asia has had a similar
effect on their economies. Exhibit 5.9 shows the changes in stock market capitalization among
emerging economies, particularly the growing dominance of South Korea and Taiwan in this
group.[6] In 1980, when the total capitalization of emerging stock markets was $86 billion, Taiwan,
South Korea, Malaysia, Thailand, and India represented 36.1 percent. In the same year, Brazil
and Mexico accounted for 25.7 percent of emerging market capitalization. By 1995, emerging
market capitalization stood at $1.9 trillion.

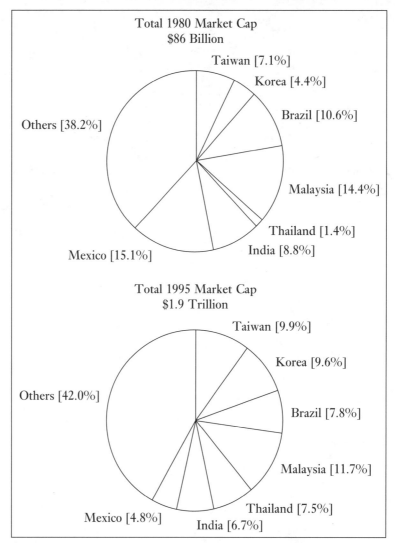

Total 1980 Market Cap
$86 Billion

Taiwan [7.1%]

Korea [4.4%]

Brazil [10.6%]

Others [38.2%]

Malaysia [14.4%]

Thailand [1.4%]

Mexico [15.1%]

India [8.8%]

Total 1995 Market Cap
$1.9 Trillion

Taiwan [9.9%]

Korea [9.6%]

Brazil [7.8%]

Others [42.0%]

Malaysia [11.7%]

Thailand [7.5%]

Mexico [4.8%]

India [6.7%]

◆ **Exhibit 5.9: Stock market capitalization, emerging markets, 1980 and 1995**

◆ *Source*:   Derrick Johnson of H. J. Johnson & Associates based on data
                   from: International Finance Corporation, *Emerging Stock Markets
                   FactBook 1996*, Washington, DC, 1996.

Large trade surpluses (as in the case of Japan) and high economic growth rates spurred growth in other Asian markets, with their share growing from 36.1 percent in 1980 to 45.4 percent in 1995, with Taiwan, Korea, and Thailand accounting for the increase in market share. At the same time, difficult economic conditions in Latin America are reflected in the decline of market capitalization of Brazil and Mexico from 25.7 percent in 1980 to 12.6 percent in 1995.[7]

Taken together, these trends indicate that the balance of economic power has begun to shift. Whether in developed or emerging markets, the stock markets of the western hemisphere are being outpaced by their Asian counterparts. These trends have significant implications for international investment diversification.

 International Diversification

Financial risk may be reduced through proper diversification of *asset portfolios* to help improve the risk/return tradeoff. These assets can include cash, short-term debt instruments, bonds, and stock. *Diversification* of assets limits risk by spreading investments over a number of companies, industries, and/or countries. Portfolio *variability* is the extent to which the actual returns may be different from *expected* returns. When the rates of return of assets in a portfolio do not move in the same way, negative returns of some assets can be offset by positive returns of other assets.

> **Asset portfolio:**
>> A combination of assets assembled to achieve certain investment objectives.

> **Diversification:**
>> Combining assets with the objective of reducing portfolio variability.

The *correlation coefficients* among the assets determine the degree to which diversification reduces overall portfolio risk.

> **Correlation coefficient:**
>> A measure of the degree to which the rates of return of two assets move together.[8]

The value of a correlation coefficient can range from +1 to –1. A correlation coefficient of +1 means that the returns of two assets move in identical ways. If $r_{i,j} = +1$, combining assets i and j does nothing to reduce total variability of the portfolio *vis-à-vis* the individual assets. These assets i and j are perfectly positively correlated.

Conversely, a correlation coefficient of –1 means that returns of the two assets move in opposite directions. When one asset performs poorly, the other compensates by performing well. Virtually all investment securities reflect, to some extent, the impact of economywide influences. There are not likely to be any perfectly negatively correlated assets. Instead, within a given country, most asset returns will be mildly positively correlated. Yet as long as assets are not perfectly positively correlated, *some measure* of diversification benefit is possible. Outside national borders, it may even be possible to identify assets or groups of assets with mildly negative correlations.

Exhibit 5.10 shows the correlation coefficients of seven national stock markets and two regions for the five years ended 1995, comparing the stock markets of the United States, the United Kingdom, developing regions of Asia and Latin America, and 7 individual emerging markets.

	US	UK	Asia	L.A.	TAI	KOR	BRAZ	MAL	THAI	IND	MEX
United States	1.0										
United Kingdom	.41	1.0									
Asia (region)	.21	.24	1.0								
Latin America (region)	.35	.20	.26	1.0							
Taiwan	.07	.29	.54	.17	1.0						
Korea	−.01	.16	.25	.23	.21	1.0					
Brazil	.42	.22	.08	.61	.14	−.05	1.0				
Malaysia	.18	.24	.95	.17	.41	.32	.02	1.0			
Thailand	.21	.06	.76	.22	.41	.17	.04	.60	1.0		
India	.01	−.02	.29	.40	.05	.26	.39	.15	.23	1.0	
Mexico	.21	.14	.30	.88	.14	−.04	.29	.24	.23	.27	1.0

◆ **Exhibit 5.10:** Stock market correlation coefficients, five years ended 1995

◆ *Source*:   International Finance Corporation. *Emerging Stock Markets FactBook 1996*, Washington, DC, 1996.

Note that the United States and the United Kingdom have a positive correlation of 0.41. In general, the correlations of these two markets with developing countries of Asia and Latin America are weaker than 0.41, suggesting potentially significant diversification benefits from combining investments in the United States or the United Kingdom with Asian or Latin American securities.

In some cases, the emerging markets showed high positive correlation with other markets. For example, the correlations of Malaysia (0.95) and Thailand (0.76) with Asia are high, as are the correlations of Malaysia with Thailand (0.60), Brazil with Latin America (0.61), and Mexico with Latin America (0.88).

In other cases, however, negative correlations can be observed:

- Korea with the United States (−0.01)
- India with the United Kingdom (−0.02)
- Korea with Brazil (−0.05)
- Korea with Mexico (−0.04)

In still other cases, correlations are only mildly positive, again, suggesting potentially significant diversification benefits associated with international capital market investments.

 Summary

Capital markets bring surplus savings units together with deficit savings units. Securities are sold for the first time in primary markets. In the United States, this process involves investment bankers that assume the risk of selling and distributing the stocks and bonds issued by corporations and government bodies.

Once issued, securities are traded among investors on secondary markets. In the United States, the New York Stock Exchange dominates all the others in terms of the value of traded securities.

The American Stock Exchange and NASDAQ represent the other national securities exchanges. Specialists and market makers work to ensure orderly and fair markets for investors.

Privatization will increase the activity in global stock and bond markets. This is particularly true in the case of Asia outside Japan where high rates of economic growth will be sustained only through the attraction and deployment of large amounts of capital.

A significant shift in market capitalization is occurring in developed and emerging markets. Asian markets (Japan and outside Japan) now represent the fast growing markets in terms of stock market capitalization.

International financial markets will likely continue to grow because they offer diversification possibilities that are not readily available in domestic markets. Some of the larger emerging stock markets have particular potential because they have weak positive or slightly negative correlations with the US and UK markets. As national markets continue to liberalize policies governing foreign involvement, these benefits should be easier to realize.

End-of-chapter Questions

1. What is an investment bank?

2. What is a primary market?

3. How does a commercial bank differ from a merchant bank?

4. Describe the general criteria that are considered by US organized exchanges in the area of quantitative listing requirements.

5. What do you believe has driven the large increases in stock market capitalization in Asian countries in recent years?

6. Do you think that the reduced importance of US markets in world finance can affect this country's standard of living? Why or why not?

7. As national financial markets become more open to cross-border investment, what impact might there be on the stock market correlations in Exhibit 5.10?

8. Describe the diversification benefits that may be derived when combining assets with a +1 correlation coefficient.

9. Referring to Exhibit 5.10, which emerging markets appear to have the most diversification benefits for an American investor?

10. Would you expect the correlations among various currencies to be stronger or weaker than the correlations among stock markets? Why or why not?

NOTES

1 The bulge bracket firms are Merrill Lynch, Goldman Sachs, Lehman Brothers, First Boston, Salomon Brothers, and Morgan Stanley.

2 Bonds issued by non-US residents in the United States, denominated in US dollars, with underwriting by a US investment bank are called foreign bonds, specifically, yankee bonds.

3 In late 1995, 1996 economic growth estimates (growth in gross domestic product or GDP) in the United States, the United Kingom, France, Germany, and Japan ranged from 1.4 to 3.0 percent. In Mexico, Argentina, Brazil, and Venezuela, GDP increases were estimated between 0.6 percent and 3.1 percent with the exception of Chile – estimated to grow at the rate of 6.6 percent. However, GDP growth estimates for Hong Kong (3.5 percent), Singapore (7.5 percent), China (8.6 percent), Malaysia (8.2 percent), Indonesia (8.5 percent), South Korea (7.7 percent), Taiwan (6.5 percent), Thailand (8.4 percent), and Vietnam (9.7 percent) were considerably higher than most countries outside Asia. In 1997, collapses in real estate prices and stock market values raised concerned about the continued rates of growth in Asia. However, the general consensus remained that long-term growth in the region would continue to outpace that in industrialized countries.

4 The Asian Development Bank was established in 1966 to facilitate development capital for Asia. It is headquartered in Manila, the Philippines.

5 The International Finance Corporation is affiliated with the World Bank Group as a facilitator in development of private-sector financial markets. The Quantum Fund is an offshore investment fund based in the Netherlands Antilles and established by international investor George Soros.

6 Asian NICs are Singapore, Hong Kong, South Korea, and Taiwan. Hong Kong and Singapore are small citystates that are considered developed regions and are not counted among developing countries or emerging markets. As of July 1997, the leadership of Hong Kong reverted to Beijing, People's Republic of China, after expiration of a long-term lease held by the British.

7 In 1997, a collapse in Asian real estate markets and stock markets combined with sizeable trade deficits to create instability in financial markets in the region.

8 $$r_{ij} = (\text{cov}(k_i,k_j))/(\sigma_i\sigma_j)$$

where cov (k_i,k_j) = covariance of returns of assets i and j

SELECTED REFERENCES

The American Stock Exchange. *1996 AMEX Fact Book*, 1996.

Clarke, William M. *How the City of London Works; An Introduction to its Financial Markets*, Waterlow Publishers, London, 1986.

Cohen, Jerome B., Edward D. Zinbarg, and Arthur Zeikel. *Investment Analysis and Portfolio Management*, 5th edn, Richard D. Irwin, Homewood, Ill., 1987.

Emerging Stock Markets Factbook 1996, International Finance Corporation, Washington, DC, 1996.

Falkena, H. B., L. J. Fourie, and W. J. Kok, eds. *The Mechanics of the South African Financial System: Financial Institutions, Instruments, and Markets*, Macmillan South Africa, Johannesburg, 1984.

Havrilesky, Thomas M. and Robert Schweitzer, eds. *Contemporary Developments in Financial Institutions and Markets*, Harlan Davidson, Arlington Heights, Ill., 1987.

Johnson, Hazel J. *Bankers Guide to Investment Banking: Securities and Underwriting Activities in Commercial Banking*, Irwin Professional Publishing, Burr Ridge, Ill. (now McGraw-Hill, New York), 1996.

Johnson, Hazel J. *Banking in Asia*, Lafferty, Dublin, 1997.

Mayo, Herbert B. *Investments: An Introduction*, Dryden Press, New York, 1984.

McRae, Hamish and Frances Cairncross. *Capital City: London as a Financial Centre*, Methuen, London, 1984.

The NASDAQ Stock Market, Inc. *The Nasdaq Stock Market 1996 Fact Book*, 1996.

The New York Stock Exchange. *Fact Book: 1995 Data*, 1996.

Nwankwo, G. O. *The Nigerian Financial System*, Africana Publishing Company, New York, 1980.

Onoh, J. K., ed. *The Foundations of Nigeria's Financial Infrastructure*, Croom Helm, London, 1980.

Rowley, Anthony. *Asian Stockmarkets: The Inside Story*, Far Eastern Economic Review, Hong Kong, 1987.

Skully, Michael T. *Merchant Banking in Australia*, Oxford University Press, Melbourne, 1987.

US Securities and Exchange Commission. *Internationalization of the Securities Markets; Report to the Senate Committee on Banking, Housing, and Urban Affairs and the House Committee on Energy and Commerce*, July 1987.

Viner, Aron. *Inside Japanese Financial Markets*, Dow Jones-Irwin, Homewood, Ill., 1988.

Investment Banking

chapter 6

CHAPTER OVERVIEW

This chapter:
- Describes the activities of investment bankers.
- Introduces the process of security registration.
- Describes formation and function of investment banking syndicates.
- Presents differences associated with underwriting municipal bonds.

KEY TERMS

best efforts agreement
blue sky laws
bookrunner
distribution syndicate
due diligence
firm commitment
initial public offering
investment bank
lead manager
management fee
offering date
originating house
primary market

private placement
prospectus
public offering
road show
selling concession
serial bonds
shelf registration
standby underwriting
syndicate
tombstone
underwriter's discount
underwriting fee
underwriting syndicate

CHAPTER OUTLINE

1   The Role of Investment Bankers
2   Public vs. Private Placement
3   The Public Offering

Introduction

A number of activities are appropriate for an investment banker, including securities underwriting, secondary market trading, secondary market making, corporate restructuring, financial engineering (zero-coupon securities, mortgage-backed securities, other asset-backed securities, and derivatives), merchant banking, and investment management. However, the most critical role of investment banking is bringing new securities to market to provide capital infusions for companies. This process includes advice as to structure and timing, as well as guaranteeing the sale of the securities, or underwriting the new financial instruments. Municipal securities are issued in a process that is similar to a corporate underwriting. However, the default risk of municipal bonds varies even more widely than that of corporate bonds.

The Role of Investment Bankers

An investment banker is a financial intermediary that is instrumental in the sale and distribution of newly issued securities. When a firm issues securities for the first time in the *primary market*, an investment banker gives advice as to the type of security that should be issued, the size and pricing of the offering, and even its timing. The client firm pays a fee for this service. The investment banker purchases securities from the issuer, as principal, and assumes the risk of distribution to ultimate investors. This process is referred to as *underwriting*.

> **Underwriting:**
> The initial distribution of securities by an entity other than the issuer, with the risk of price fluctuations borne to a greater or lesser extent by the distributor(s).

Often investment banks take full responsibility for selling the entire issue – the agreement between banker and issuer is a *firm commitment* in which the issuing firm is guaranteed a specific price and is relieved of the responsibility of marketing the securities. In a firm commitment arrangement, the underwriter assumes 100 percent of the risk and agrees to purchase 100 percent of the offering. The two parties work together to establish the right price for the securities and then negotiate the *underwriter's discount or spread*. The issuing firm receives the issue price less the discount. If it turns out that the securities cannot be sold to the public for at least the discounted price, the investment banker absorbs a loss.

> **Underwriter's discount or spread:**
> An investment banker's compensation for risk taking and distribution in connection with a new securities issue.

A *standby underwriting* is a commitment by the underwriter and the underwriting syndicate to purchase any securities that are not purchased by shareholders in connection with a rights offering or corporate reorganization.

> **Standby underwriting:**
> Arrangement in which the investment banker agrees to purchase any outstanding shares that have not been purchased after shareholders have exercised (1) their preemptive right to purchase new securities in a rights offering or (2) their right to receive new securities in exchange for old securities in a corporate restructuring.

In a rights offering, existing shareholders may exercise a "preemptive right" to maintain their proportional ownership of the firm when new shares are issued. The rights offering is frequently associated with a lower-than-market price for the shares and, typically, expires after a specified date. A standby underwriting assures the issuing firm that any shares not purchased by existing shareholders will be purchased by the investment banker and subsequently sold to investors or held in the accounts of the investment banker.

When the issuing firm is not well-known, the two parties may execute a *best efforts* agreement. As long as the sale of new securities meets the minimum price requirements of the issuer, the investment banker will be compensated on a pro-rata basis. For example, if only 20 percent of the securities are sold, the investment banker receives 20 percent of the total possible commission and is under no further obligation to the issuer. Best efforts underwritings are most often observed in the over-the-counter market for initial public offerings by new companies.

> **Best efforts agreement:**
> An agreement between the issuer of new securities and the investment banker that allows sharing of the risk; the investment banker sells the securities at the best market price it can obtain. This is essentially an agency arrangement.

To diversify the risk associated with underwriting new securities, investment bankers frequently form *syndicates* – groups of investment bankers that share the risks. Each member of the syndicate agrees to sell a certain portion of the new issue. The firm that negotiates with the issuing company is called either the *originating house*, or the *lead manager*, or the *bookrunner*.

Public vs. Private Placement

A *public offering* of securities is intended for sale to the general public. On the other hand, a *private placement* is sold to a small group of investors. Any public offering of securities in the United States that is offered to American investors is required to be registered with the Securities and Exchange Commission (SEC). In addition, public issues must comply with *blue sky laws* in the state of issue and sale. Although blue sky laws vary by state, most have similar provisions against fraud, require registration of all new securities issues (except municipal bonds), and are patterned after comparable federal provisions.

> **Blue sky laws:**
> State securities laws intended to safeguard investors from buying worthless securities.

The requirements of the federal SEC are the most comprehensive standards in a public offering. If a firm that has already issued public securities enters the primary market, a new issue of securities is referred to as a *public offering*. On the other hand, if the firm has never issued securities to the public at large, the offering is referred to as an *initial public offering (IPO)*. The SEC places stringent disclosure requirements on the issuer in both a public offering and an IPO. The objective is to insure that all potential investors have adequate information to make an informed decision. The only exceptions to this general rule are securities with an initial maturity of 270 days or less (commercial paper) or securities offered for private placement.

Because private placements bypass the process of SEC registration, they are faster and more flexible. The ability to offer a private placement is based on the Securities Act of 1933. In this legislation, the formal requirements for SEC registration were established. Within the same legislation, it was made clear that investors that could be considered knowledgeable and sophisticated need not be protected. The responsibility for obtaining adequate information prior to investment is shifted to investors in a private placement. In fact, the terms of a private placement are negotiated between the issuer and the investor. In this sense, a private placement is unlike a public offering in which the deal is structured and offered to the public after all features of the security have been decided.

While there is no limit to the number of potential investors that may be approached to purchase a private placement (since the 1982 issuance of SEC Regulation D), the SEC requires that these investors be able to demonstrate both the capacity and intent to hold the securities for an extended period of time. The investors that can make such commitments and demonstrate such capacity and intent are large financial institutions such as insurance companies, private pension funds, and public pension funds.

For the issuer, the advantage of a private placement is that the cost associated with a public offering may be reduced or avoided – flotation costs (underwriting spread and out-of-pocket expenses) and administrative costs of managing the issue. Also, issuers may place their securities more quickly than is possible with a public placement. In addition, deals can be customized to meet the needs of both the issuer and the investor without concerns for features that would make the securities more acceptable to a wider investor pool. Private placements may also be advisable if the firm has a limited credit history, that is, no credit rating or a credit rating that is less than investment grade.

The typical structure of a private placement will involve 35 or fewer investors, all of whom sign an *investment letter*. The investment letter states that securities will not be resold for a specific period of time, usually two years. However, the issue may be associated with a provision that permits registration with the SEC at a later time to improve its marketability. In addition, SEC Rule 144A makes it possible for privately held securities to be resold to institutional investors without registration with the SEC. It is the role of the investment banker to identify investors and to actively participate in the process of negotiating terms of the issue.

 # The Public Offering

The success of a public offering of securities depends on the ability of the investment banker to analyze the client, the potential investors, and market conditions. In addition, the investment banker has obligations to other investment banking firms that participate in the transaction as a part of the underwriting syndicate.

3.1 THE LEAD MANAGER AND THE PROSPECTUS

The investment bank that is chosen to manage an issue of new securities for a client is referred to as the *lead manager*, *bookrunner*, or *originating house*. It is the responsibility of the lead manager to ensure that the issuing firm complies with the disclosure requirements of the SEC. These disclosure requirements include an investigation into (1) the issuer of the securities and (2) the structure of the deal. In the terms used in the Securities Act of 1933, this investigation is referred to as *due diligence*. The law requires that the lead manager perform "a reasonable investigation" of the issuer. Failure to do so will result in the lead manager being held responsible for the consequences of such failure.

> **Due diligence:**
> The responsibility of investment bankers to investigate and disclose all relevant information concerning the issuer of public securities and the securities issue itself. Investment bankers are accountable to the SEC for such investigation and disclosure.

The results of the due diligence investigation are contained in the issuer's *prospectus*. The prospectus states the purpose of the security issue, including details with respect to the primary business of the issuer, the issuer's financial condition, and principal officers. The prospectus also describes the method of offering the securities for sale and any interest or dividends to be paid. Essentially, the prospectus is the method by which the lead manager and other participating investment bankers offer the securities to the public. However, it is the responsibility of the lead manager to ensure that all steps necessary to reach the public-offer stage are taken.

> **Prospectus:**
> An informational document describing a firm's intent to issue securities, as required by the SEC. The prospectus is an offer to sell securities to the public and is also referred to as an *offering circular*.

The issuer and the investment bank prepare a preliminary prospectus providing financial and other data about the firm, the securities being offered for sale, and the intended use of the funds to be raised. To alert prospective buyers that SEC approval is not final, the cover of the preliminary prospectus includes a statement to this effect in red lettering. This practice has led to the nickname for the preliminary prospectus – "red herring."

The second portion of the preliminary filing contains any supporting documentation that may be appropriate, including legal documents and a draft of the underwriting agreement. This portion of the preliminary filing is made available to the public at SEC offices.

The SEC allows the preliminary prospectus to clear within 20 days of its filing. If the SEC objects to the filing or requires more information, the 20-day waiting period begins again, unless the SEC grants an exception. After any required modifications and subsequent SEC approval, the final prospectus is prepared (now without the red lettering) and distributed to prospective buyers. State and municipal bonds need not be registered with the SEC and are exempt from the prospectus requirement, but no corporate stock or bonds may be sold in the US without an approved prospectus. The requirement for a prospectus is a common practice in most countries with developed securities markets.

The responsibilities of the lead manager in this process can generate tension between the lead manager and the issuer. Clearly, the investment banker that is selected as lead manager must have confidence in the viability of the new issue, but his or her enthusiasm should not be excessive, given the disclosure responsibilities. On the other hand, the issuing firm may adopt the most optimistic view of the prospects of the specific issue and of the firm in general. As a result, management of the firm may view the prospectus as a promotional vehicle.

The lead manager must resist the temptation to "promise too much" in the prospectus. In fact, the lead manager may prefer to de-emphasize optimistic future assessments of the firm to avoid later charges of misrepresentation. This is a delicate balance because the lead manager is simultaneously responsible for making sure that all of the new securities are sold (assuming a firm-commitment arrangement). The correct balance is to include all information that could have a possible impact on the decision-making process of investors. The objective facts of the firm, its market position, financial results, quality of management, and product innovations must be included to enable potential investors to assess the viability of the issue.

3.2 Shelf Registration

The public-offer process has been significantly streamlined since the introduction of shelf registration through SEC *Rule 415* in 1982. Rule 415 was an attempt, on an experimental basis, to streamline the registration process under the SEC. The objective was to reduce the cost of issuances in the United States and to speed the offering process. This shelf registration permits issuers to register securities that they expect to sell within two years of the initial effective date of approval, eliminating the need to file additional registration statements with each subsequent offering. For issuers, the advantage is that they may move quickly to issue securities when market

---

Shelf registration:
Registration of securities for public offer to be sold within two years of the effective date of the registration, without the necessity to file additional registration statements at the time of each offering.

conditions appear most favorable. (For example, issuers prefer to float bonds when interest rates are low, and to float stock when stock prices are strong.) Under this arrangement, issuers are required to report to the SEC any changes in financial condition during the two-year period. Under shelf registration, securities may be issued with as little as 24 hours' notice to the SEC.

Shelf registration was so well received that, in the year following its introduction, the experiment became a permanent rule. Since then, the SEC has approved the use of shelf registrations by limited partnership tax shelters, employee benefit plans, and issuers of mortgage pass-through certificates. SEC fees must be paid for all securities that are anticipated to be issued for the two-year period, however. To avoid paying excessive fees at the time of the Rule 415 filing, firms may file for only those securities that will be issued in the near term and then subsequently modify the filing when additional securities are to be issued.

3.3 Other Elements of the Public Offering

While the registration process is occurring, a number of other steps in the process are taking place:

- The red herring is being printed in sufficient quantities to distribute to the public.
- The appropriate filings under blue sky laws in those states in which the securities will be sold are initiated.
- Stock or bond certificates are printed.
- The lead manager forms the underwriting syndicate.
- The lead manager and members of the underwriting syndicate promote the issue in a *road show*.

During a road show, investment bankers and the issuing firms' management travel to various cities to speak to the investing public. Presentations are prepared that explain the company and its management. Both bankers and managers make themselves available to answer questions that arise.

While it is the primary responsibility of the lead manager to conduct the due diligence investigation and to coordinate the SEC filings, the syndicate shares the responsibility for purchasing from the issuer and distributing to the public the securities to be issued.

3.4 The Syndicate

The "syndicate" is a term that is applicable for the functions of *underwriting* and *distribution*.

> **Underwriting syndicate:**
> The group of investment bankers that take responsibility for selling the securities in a public offering, that is, assume underwriting risk.

> **Distribution syndicate:**
> Both the underwriting syndicate and a selling group for a public offering. The selling group bears no underwriting risk.

3.4.1 UNDERWRITING SYNDICATE

The underwriting syndicate reaches an agreement between the issuer and itself that the securities will be sold under a firm commitment, a best efforts, or a standby underwriting. The issuer and the syndicate must agree on the pricing of the securities, the quantity to be sold, and the proceeds to the issuer. Since the underwriters are compensated by the difference between the price charged to the investing public and the price promised to the issuer, there is a natural tendency for the underwriters to reduce the price paid to the issuer. On the other hand, there is a natural tendency for the issuer to maximize the price received. If this natural tension is not resolved, a firm commitment is unlikely. The issue may instead become a best efforts underwriting.

It should be noted that initial public offerings (IPOs) are difficult to price. There is no "seasoned" (already existing) security to which these new securities may be compared. Underwriters will resist pricing that is overly optimistic because the underwriting syndicate bears the ultimate risk and the degree of market uncertainty is large. As a result, IPOs are often associated with significant price increases after the initial underwriting.

To at least partially counterbalance this phenomenon, rules have been established by the National Association of Securities Dealers (NASD) that prohibit underwriters from selling the securities above the price indicated in the prospectus during the underwriting period. If the securities are priced substantially below the price at which the market is willing to purchase them, the syndicate is not permitted to increase the price and reap a windfall profit. Of course, if the market is softer than originally anticipated, that is, the market is willing to pay substantially less than the price indicated in the prospectus, the underwriting syndicate must absorb the loss.

While the issue is being approved by the SEC, negotiations as to price and terms continue between the issuer and the underwriting syndicate. Once final approval has been received from the SEC, the issuer and the syndicate engage in final negotiations of all underwriting terms. The date upon which this occurs is referred to as the *offering date*. The final terms include:

- Price of the offering
- Size of the offering
- Gross underwriting spread

> **Offering date:**
> Date on which the final terms of a public offering are negotiated between the issuer and the underwriting syndicate.

This information is provided to the SEC in an amendment to the prospectus. The following day a *tombstone* is published in the financial press. The tombstone is used to advise to the public that an offering of securities is being made. However, the securities are not formally offered through the tombstone advertisement. The prospectus is the only basis upon which sales of the securities may be made.

> **Tombstone:**
> Financial advertisement that lists the relevant information in connection with a public offering of securities. Included in the tombstone are (1) a description of the new securities and (2) the underwriters, in order of their participation.

3.4.2 DISTRIBUTION SYNDICATE

The distribution syndicate is composed of the underwriting syndicate and a selling group. The participants of the *underwriting syndicate* are:

- Managers
- Bulge bracket
- Major bracket
- Mezzanine bracket

The lead manager is a member of the group of managers. The lead manager is designated by the issuer and, with a consent of the issuer, forms the syndicate. Syndicate members are selected so that they represent a strong portfolio of all capabilities that will be required for successful underwriting. The managers' names appear first in a tombstone, with the lead manager generally listed first.

Next on the tombstone are the bulge bracket firms. The bulge bracket consists of the largest investment banking firms in the country. The term is derived from the appearance of their names when placed in tombstone advertisements – typically large and boldface.[1] The managers and the bulge bracket constitute the first tier of investment bankers.

The second tier of investment bankers is referred to as the major bracket. These are large firms that generally have the ability to distribute the securities widely. The mezzanine bracket consists of small firms that have special relationships with either the issuer or the lead manager.

All the firms are then divided into groups for the purpose of distribution of the securities. The breakdown of the *distribution syndicate* is:

- Managers
- Preferred group of dealers
- Nonpreferred dealers, or selling group

The managers are responsible for selling the bulk of the securities. The preferred group of dealers includes the managers and other members of the underwriting syndicate. The nonpreferred dealers, or selling group, accept no underwriting risk, even under a firm commitment arrangement.

The lead manager helps to stabilize the price of the security during the underwriting period by agreeing to purchase the securities at the offer price. This assures investors that there will be sufficient liquidity in the market. Often, the lead underwriter will continue to make a market in the securities after the underwriting period. The commitment of the lead manager to purchase securities at the offer price is referred to as a *stabilizing bid*.

3.4.3 COMPENSATION

The varying amount of risk accepted by the members of the distribution syndicate is reflected in the compensation arrangements of a securities issue.

- The *management fee* is compensation to the managers for their participation in preparing the securities offering. Accepting the responsibility for a thorough and diligent investigation is the primary basis for this compensation. Twenty percent of the gross underwriting spread (the difference between the offering price and the price paid to the issuer) typically is allocated for this purpose.

- The *underwriting fee* is also typically 20 percent of the gross underwriting spread. This portion of the compensation covers expenses such as advertising, legal expenses, postage, and other related out-of-pocket expenses. Expenses not covered by the underwriting fee are those which are the responsibility of the issuer, including fees for SEC filings, issuer-related legal fees, accounting fees, and printing fees. Any excess of the underwriting fees over the 20 percent allocation is covered by syndicate members based upon their participation in the issue. Should the 20 percent allocation exceed actual underwriting fees, the excess is allocated among participants in the same way.

- The *selling concession* is normally 60 percent of the underwriting spread. This compensation is allocated among the participants based on the securities for which they accept the responsibility to sell. Selling representatives within the firms of the syndicates will receive a portion of the selling concession. Should a syndicate member use a nonpreferred dealer, or selling group member, to sell part of the syndicate member's allocation of the securities, the selling group member may receive as much as half of the applicable concession.

④ The Municipal Offering

4.1 Municipal Underwriting

Municipal bonds are issued by states and other political subdivisions. (See also chapter 4 for a discussion of municipal bonds.) Municipal securities are rarely sold directly to the investing public. In most cases, an underwriting syndicate brings the bonds to market. In turn, the syndicate sells the municipal bonds to ultimate investors. Generally, the underwriting agreement is negotiated between the issuer and the underwriters, as discussed above. However, in some cases, state law requires that underwriting engagements be subject to a competitive bidding process. Most revenue bond issuances are negotiated, while general obligation bond issues are roughly divided equally between negotiated underwritings and competitive bid underwritings.

When the underwriting is competitive, potential underwriters do not meet with the issuers to suggest structure or terms of the issue as is true in corporate securities issues. Instead, the issuer first publishes an official notice of the sale that specifies size of the issue, maturity of the bonds, and conditions or restrictions that may apply.

Sometimes, municipal bonds are issued as *serial bonds*. Serial bonds are issues with maturity dates that are spread over a number of future periods. This creates several different tranches (segments, literally "slices") of the issue, one for each maturity date. At the same time, there may be a restriction that the tranches have coupon rates which are within a few basis points of each other. (A basis point is one hundredth of one percent.) This can present a problem for investment bankers in that such a restriction amounts to setting all interest rates at essentially the same level. That is, an intermediate-term bond (5 to 10 years) may have the same yield as a long-term bond (15 to 20 years). If long-term market interest rates are higher than intermediate-term rates (as they usually are), it may be necessary to sell some of the bonds at par while selling others above or below par. (See also chapter 4, sections 1.1 and 1.2 – "Bond Valuation" and "Bond Yields.") Such idiosyncracies cause municipal bond underwriting to be, in many ways, more challenging than corporate bond underwriting.

The underwriting process for municipal bonds follows much the same functional process as that for corporate bonds – origination, underwriting, and distribution. However, there are some differences. The US constitution forbids the federal government to interfere with the fundraising of states, and, by extension, local governments. This means that municipal bonds are not required to register with the SEC. Effectively, municipal issuers are exempt from the registration requirements

In April 1975, New York City was unable to pay the interest on a short-term note and deferred the payment. It should be noted that none of New York City's long-term bonds were ever involved in this problem. The interest was ultimately paid and no investor failed to receive the full amount of interest and payments as originally contracted. Of course, anyone who sold the bonds realized a capital loss because the market value declined significantly when New York City failed to pay the interest.

Resolution of the crisis involved the creation of the Municipal Assistance Corporation (MAC). This agency was empowered to issue bonds on behalf of New York City. MAC bonds were not obligations of the city, and were not backed by the taxing authority of the city. Instead, the state of New York backed the bonds in exchange for a lien on sales taxes within the city and on a stock transfer tax. When the bonds came to market, they yielded 200 basis points above the yields on comparable bonds at the time, that is, 10 percent when comparable bonds were yielding 8 percent.

The MAC bonds subsequently performed well with debt service coverage as high as 11 times. (This means that sales tax and stock transfer tax revenues were 11 times the amount necessary to pay the interest.) In fact, the performance was so good that the credit rating of the bonds was increased from A (third-best rating) to AA (second-best rating) by 1990. (See also chapter 11 for a description of bond ratings.) While the New York City case was satisfactorily resolved, the episode raised concerns about the safety of municipal bonds and the adequacy of investor protection.

◆ **Exhibit 6.1:** **Challenges in the New York municipal bond market**

of the Securities Act of 1933. (It should be noted, however, that municipal issuers are subject to the antifraud provisions of the Securities Exchange Act of 1934.)

The issuance of *official statements* by municipal securities underwriters has developed over time. Official statements take the place of a prospectus. The movement toward more "due diligence" on the part of municipal bond underwriters gained considerable momentum during the 1970s when New York City experienced a bond crisis. (See also Exhibit 6.1.)

In 1989, Rule 15c2-12 of the 1934 Securities Exchange Act was adopted, requiring that an underwriter of municipal securities deliver an official statement in connection with the primary issuance of municipal securities. The 1989 ruling was prompted largely by the failure of Washington Public Power System bonds and the belief that insufficient information had been provided to investors prior to bond purchases. (See also Exhibit 6.2.)

4.2 DISCLOSURE IN THE MUNICIPAL BOND MARKET

Because municipal securities are exempted from the Securities Act of 1933, disclosure requirements have been governed only by antifraud provisions of the law that prohibit fraudulent or deceptive practices in the issuance of municipal bonds. Specifically, disclosures by municipal bond issuers must not contain false or misleading statements of material (significant) facts. Also, material facts may not be omitted if the omission causes the statements to be misleading.

In the absence of federal regulation of disclosures, a number of voluntary guidelines have been established by associations involved in the municipal bond industry. Originally published in 1976 by the Government Finance Officers Association (GFOA, formerly the Municipal Finance Officers Association), the *Disclosure Guidelines for State and Local Government Securities* are composed of three sections – guidelines in connection with original offering of securities, ongoing

The Washington Public Power Supply System (WPPSS) was established by the state of Washington to produce and sell electric power to municipal and private power companies in the northwest region of the country. WPPSS issued revenue bonds in 1977 to finance two new nuclear power plants, Projects 4 and 5. The revenue bonds were supported by contracts to sell this power once the projects were completed. However, unforeseen cost overruns and lagging demand for power in the Northwest forced WPPSS to terminate construction of the plants in 1982. Bond holders were left holding worthless instruments.

In a case that was tried up through the Washington State Supreme Court, it was ruled that government authorities had no legal grounds upon which to pay principal and interest on the bonds from other revenue sources. This experience cost investors $2.25 billion and had a major impact on the revenue bond market. As a direct result, required yields on revenue bonds increased significantly, particularly those intended to finance wholesale power projects. The experience also had the effect of sharply escalating the concern for investor protection in the municipal bond industry.

◆ **Exhibit 6.2:   The failure of Washington Public Power System bonds**

disclosure, and procedures for distributing information to investors. The GFOA guidelines stress the voluntary nature of the suggestions and emphasize that adequate disclosure must always be from the viewpoint of the investor. These guidelines were revised in 1988 and 1991.

After the failure of the Washington Public Power System bonds, the Securities Exchange Commission (SEC) adopted Rule 15c2-12. As noted above, the rule requires that all municipal bond underwriters of primary market offerings of municipal bonds obtain and distribute to investors "official statements" from municipal issuers. Official statements are required for all bond issues of $1 million or more. Because the SEC, as an agency of the federal government, may not interfere with the financing arrangements of state and local governments, this rule was adopted as a way of "assisting" underwritings in meeting responsibilities under the more generalized antifraud provisions of the Securities Exchange of Act of 1934. Under Rule 15c2-12, an underwriter must:

- Obtain and review an issuers' official statement that is "deemed final" by an issuer prior to making any bid for purchase, offer, or sale of municipal bonds. That is, all terms and conditions must have been firmly agreed upon.
- Deliver upon request, copies of the final official statement for a specified period of time. This period of time begins at the time the official statement is available until the earlier of (1) 90 days from the beginning of the underwriting period or (2) the date when the official statement is made available to a Nationally Recognized Municipal Securities Information Repository. In no case shall this period be less than 25 days in length.
- Contract to receive, within a specified period of time, sufficient copies of the issuer's final official statement to comply with the delivery requirement.

There are three specific types of municipal bonds offerings which are exempted from these requirements. In each case, the offering of municipal bonds must be in denominations in $100,000 or more. Presumably, large denominations are purchased only by more sophisticated investors. In addition, any one of the three following conditions will exempt the issue from Rule 15c2-12:

- No more than 35 investors, each of whom the underwriter reasonably believes is capable of evaluating the investment and is not purchasing the investment with the intent to distribute.

- A maturity of nine months or less.
- The ability to tender to an issuer (redeem), at the option of the investor, at least as frequently as every nine months. This means that the investor can return the bonds to the issuer and receive payment for them at the discretion of the investor.

Three firms have been designated as Nationally Recognized Municipal Securities Information Repositories (NRMSIRs): American Banker Bond Buyer, J. J. Kenny Co., and Bloomberg LP. Supplying official statements to an NRMSIR reduces the length of time that a bond underwriter must supply the statements. As a result, many municipal bond underwriters have elected to make this information available to these repositories.

Because federal regulation may not interfere with the financing of states and local governments, there is no standard format for the official statements. As a result, there is wide variation in the content of the statements. Large municipal issuers typically provide thorough, highly detailed documents that meet or exceed the guidelines set by the Government Finance Officers Association. These statements typically include complete disclosure concerning the issuer, revenue sources, the use of funds to be raised, and the characteristics of the bonds to be issue. On the other hand, smaller issuers that are less frequent participants in a municipal bond market prepare less comprehensive statements. Some may include only a one- or two-page document that is geared primarily to assist in selling the issue.

 Summary

Securities underwriters need both (1) a strong perception of their clients' capabilities and financial position and (2) a keen awareness of market conditions. The ability to work within a syndicate environment requires good timing and good relationships. It is also necessary to have an appreciation for the likelihood of changes in the general economy, especially with respect to interest rates and economic expansion or recession. An underwriting team analyzes the overall market and the specific issue of new securities.

For a public offering of corporate securities, disclosure of all relevant information is accomplished through the prospectus which is approved by the SEC. While prospectus preparation and modification are the primary responsibilities of the lead manager, all the syndicate members share the responsibility of selling a public offering.

On the other hand, the municipal bond market is characterized by a myriad of issuers for which information is highly variable. Nevertheless, larger municipal bond issuers prepare documents, called official statements, that are often as detailed as corporate prospectuses.

 End-of-chapter Questions

1. How does a "firm commitment" differ from a "best efforts" underwriting arrangement?
2. The SEC does not attest to the value of a new security issue. Why, then, does the SEC require that the issuer prepare a prospectus?

3. Why would an investment banker organize an underwriting syndicate if the banker could make more profit by handling the new issue alone?

4. Explain how a "standby" underwriting is similar to a contingency when compared to a "firm commitment."

5. Is it always true that large investment banking firms have an advantage over smaller firms? Why or why not?

6. What is a lead manager in a public securities offering?

7. Describe the difference between a public placement and a private placement.

8. What is a "blue sky" law?

9. What is "due diligence"?

10. How is "due diligence" complicated in the case of new issues of municipal bonds?

11. Use the library resources at your institution and determine the most recent rankings ("league tables") of major investment bankers.

    a. What is the volume of underwritings in the reported period?

    b. Do these investment bankers exhibit differences in the mix of types of securities underwritten?

12. Obtain a recent copy of the *Wall Street Journal*. Identify a new securities issue tombstone, request prospectus information, and analyze the new issue from the perspective of an investor.

NOTE

1 The bulge bracket firms are responsible for the largest number of underwritings and dollar amount of securities issued. While rankings will vary by year and by classification of securities, common names in this category are Merrill Lynch, Goldman Sachs, Morgan Stanley, Salomon Brothers, and CS First Boston.

SELECTED REFERENCES

Fitch, Thomas. *Dictionary of Banking Terms*, Barron's Educational Series, Hauppauge, NY, 1990.

Heide, Susan C., Robert A. Klein, and Jess Lederman. *The Handbook of Municipal Bonds*, Probus Publishing, Chicago (now McGraw-Hill, New York), 1994.

Johnson, Hazel J. *Bankers Guide to Investment Banking: Securities and Underwriting Activities in Commercial Banking*, Irwin Professional Publishing, Burr Ridge, Ill. (now McGraw-Hill, New York), 1996.

Marshall, John F. and M. E. Ellis. *Investment Banking and Brokerage: The New Rules of the Game*, Probus Publishing, Chicago (now McGraw-Hill, New York), 1994.

Thau, Annette. *The Bond Book: Everything Investors Need to Know About Treasuries, Municipal, GMNAs, Corporates, Zeros, Bond Funds, Money Market Funds, and More*, Probus Publishing, Chicago (now McGraw-Hill, New York), 1994.

Derivative Securities

chapter 7

CHAPTER OVERVIEW

This chapter
- Describes the nature of derivative securities.
- Outlines the characteristics of specific derivative contracts – futures, options, and swaps.

KEY TERMS

American option
at-the-money option
call option
call swaption
cap
currency swap
derivative securities
European option
exercise or strike price
floor
futures contract
in-the-money option
index
initial margin
interest rate swap

margin call
marking to market
option contract
option expiration date
option premium
out-of-the-money option
payor swaption
put option
put swaption
receiver swaption
settlement frequency
swaption
underlying asset
variation margin

CHAPTER OUTLINE

Introduction

The United States has been most active in introducing innovations in derivative securities – financial futures, options, and swaps. It is now possible to purchase derivative securities based on stocks, bonds, and stock indices. Furthermore, swaps make it possible to restructure the cash flows of financial assets and liabilities.

 The Nature of Derivative Securities

Derivative securities are financial instruments that are based on other assets. In the sense that their value depends on other securities, derivatives are similar to securitized assets. However, derivative securities, unlike securitized assets, are not obligations backed by the original issuer of the underlying security. Instead, derivative securities are contracts between two parties other than the original issuer of the underlying security.

> **Derivative securities:**
> Securities whose value depends on other securities and, often, also depends on future events not yet known with certainty. Examples are futures contracts, option contracts, and swap contracts.

Derivative securities have evolved to help protect investors from certain risks:

- A manufacturer of cereal products is dependent on the grain market for inputs for its finished products. If the crops during a particular year are damaged by drought or other unfavorable conditions, the price of grain (and the manufacturer's cost of doing business) will increase.
- The owner of a large block of stock may fear that the stock's price will decline. If such a decline occurs, the investor will sustain large losses.
- A commercial bank may need to offer relatively long-term, fixed-rate loans in order to be competitive with other financial institutions. If interest rates increase significantly, the bank will incur a significant opportunity cost in the form of lost interest income.

All of these are *financial risks* that derivative securities can help to reduce. The food manufacturer can lock in the price of grain by buying a *futures* contract. The owner of the common stock can guard against losses by buying an *option* to sell the stock at a predetermined price. The commercial bank can enter into a *swap* contract to receive interest payments that vary with market conditions.

This chapter introduces the concept of derivative securities, a segment of the capital markets that is of increasing importance. The role of derivative securities in currency markets and foreign exchange risk management is described in chapter 8. The use of derivative securities to manage the interest rate risk associated with management of financial institutions is discussed and illustrated in chapter 17.

 Futures Contracts

Futures contracts are agreements to exchange a commodity or financial instrument at some date in the future. A futures contract buyer agrees to purchase the asset, the seller agrees to sell. Before the date of the future exchange, the market value of the underlying asset may change. If it increases, the value of the futures contract also increases. Thus, in the event that grain prices increase, the food manufacturer that holds a grain futures contract will realize a gain in the value of the futures contract to help offset the higher cost of doing business. Of course, if the value of the underlying asset falls, the futures contract value also declines.

> **Futures contract:**
> An agreement to exchange a standard quantity of an asset at a specified date in the future at a predetermined price.

Futures contracts are traded on organized exchanges. The seller of a futures contract can settle the obligation (open position) by delivering the underlying asset or by reentering the market and buying an offsetting contract through the exchange. Buyers may settle by taking delivery of the underlying asset or by selling offsetting contracts. In fact, most open positions (95 percent) are settled by offsetting contracts. That is, buyers of futures contracts subsequently sell futures contracts to close their positions, while sellers of futures contracts subsequently buy futures contracts to close their positions.

Parties in a futures contract are generally anonymous, that is, not known to one another. Risk of default is minimized in this case because the exchange guarantees the other side of the transaction. In the United States, futures contracts are actively traded on:

• The Chicago Board of Trade
• The International Monetary Market at the Chicago Mercantile Exchange
• The New York Futures Exchange

> **Initial margin (futures contract):**
> Minimum deposit for the buyer or seller of a futures contract paid to a broker as specified by the exchange upon which the futures contract is traded. Initial margin for futures contracts is similar to a good faith deposit.

To cover the guarantee provision, the exchange requires an *initial margin*, or deposit, of no more than 5 percent, by both the buyer and the seller of a futures contract. The initial margin is a kind of performance bond to assure settlement of the contract. The magnitude of the initial margin is slightly larger than the maximum daily price movement for the futures contract that is allowed by the exchange. The initial margin may be paid in cash or in US Treasury securities.

In addition, the exchange determines the adequacy of the margin each day by assessing the current value of the futures contract. Gains and losses in the value of the contract are then posted to each open position, that is, to each futures contract position that has not been settled. Such daily revaluation of an open contract is called *marking to market*. The change in value each day is called the *variation margin*. Before the beginning of trading the next day, the broker for each open futures contract position must settle (with the exchange) the variation margin determined at the end of the previous day's trading.

Marking to market (futures contract):
> Reflecting the actual market value of futures contracts in each futures account at the close of business each day.

Variation margin (futures contract):
> The daily change in market value of a futures contract position based on the settlement price of the contract at the end of the day.

If the value of the contract increased, the broker receives funds from the exchange for the futures account, that is, *receives* the variation margin. On the other hand, if the value of the contract declined on the previous trading day, the broker *pays* the variation margin. When the broker pays the variation margin, this is also referred to as a *margin call*. A margin call must be paid in cash.

Margin call (futures contract):
> The requirement to deposit more funds with the exchange to compensate for a decline in the value of a futures contract on the previous day's trading.

The first futures contracts were based on commodities such as agricultural crops. Government securities were the first futures contracts offered for financial instruments, then sold on the Chicago Board of Trade (CBOT). Today, futures contracts are traded on a number of underlying assets. For example, at the Chicago Mercantile Exchange, contracts are available with underlying assets that include interest rate instruments and currencies, as well as agricultural products. In addition, futures contracts now trade with indices as the underlying asset. For example, a stock index futures contract is based on a stock index (such as the S&P 500). Unlike Treasury or currency futures, there is no deliverable asset in the case of an index futures contract. Instead, the value of the contract is some multiple of the value of the index.

Index (securities):
> An indicator of financial market performance. For example, the S&P 500 is an index of the stocks of 500 major US industrial firms.

Exhibit 7.1 shows the four categories of futures contracts traded on the Chicago Mercantile Exchange – interest rate, currencies, indices, and agriculture. Also shown are the underlying assets or indices for specific contracts. (Currency futures are also discussed in Chapter 8, "Foreign Exchange Markets.")

 Options Contracts

Another area of American innovation in financial markets is the *option contract*. Like futures, options are traded on organized exchanges and guaranteed by the exchange on which they trade. To obtain the right associated with an option, an investor must pay an *option premium*. The right itself is exercisable at the discretion of the option owner. The asset that may be bought or sold is the *underlying asset*. Should the option owner elect to exercise the option, the price at which the transaction occurs is the *exercise or strike price*. The owner of the option has the right to exercise at the strike price until the option's *expiration date*.

> **Option contract:**
> An agreement that confers the right to buy or sell an asset at a set price through some future date. The right is exercisable at the discretion of the option buyer. The right to buy is a call option. The right to sell is a put option.

If the owner of the option has the right to purchase the underlying asset, the contract is a *call option*. On the other hand, if the owner of the option has the right to sell the underlying asset, the contract is a *put option*.

If the option can be exercised only at the expiration date, it is a *European option*. If it can be exercised at any time during the life of the option, it is an *American option*.

Interest Rate Contracts
Three-month Eurodollar time deposits
    (US dollar denominated deposits in banks outside the United States)
One-month LIBOR
    (London Interbank Offered Rate)
13-week US Treasury bills
One-year US Treasury bills
Three-month Euromark time deposits
    (German mark denominated deposits in banks outside Germany)

Currency Contracts
German deutsche mark
Japanese yen
Swiss franc
British pound
Canadian dollar
Australian dollar
French franc
German deutsche mark vs. Japanese yen

Index Contracts
Standard & Poor's 500 index
  (500 US stocks from a broad range of industries)
Standard & Poor's MidCap 400 index
  (400 US stocks with medium-range market value (average $700 million in 1991),
  representing industrials, utilities, financial, and transportation)
Major Market index[1]
  (20 well-known US stocks that represent a broad range of industries)
GSCI[2]
  (Goldman Sachs commodity index, representing 20 commodities)
Russell 2000 index
  (2,000 US stocks, representing the bottom 2,000 of the 3,000 largest US firms – that is,
  small firms)
Nikkei Stock index
  (225 leading Japanese companies listed on the Tokyo Stock Exchange)
FTSE 100 share index
  (100 largest stocks in the United Kingdom)

Agricultural Contracts
Live cattle
Live hog
Frozen pork bellies
Feeder cattle
Random length lumber
Broiler chicken

◆ **Exhibit 7.1:** **Futures contracts offered on the international monetary market of the Chicago Mercantile Exchange**

◆ *Notes*: 1 In the mid-1990s, the Major Market Index represented stock prices for: American
        Express, AT&T, Chevron, Coca-Cola, Walt Disney, Dow Chemical, DuPont, Eastman
        Kodak, Exxon, General Electric, General Motors, IBM, International Paper, Johnson &
        Johnson, McDonald's Corporation, Merck & Co., Minnesota Mining & Manufacturing,
        Philip Morris, Procter & Gamble, and Sears.
      2 The commodities included in the GSCI are copper, aluminum, nickel, zinc, gold, silver,
        platinum, live hogs, live cattle, wheat, corn, soybeans, sugar, coffee, cocoa, cotton,
        heating oil, unleaded gasoline, crude oil, and natural gas.

◆ *Sources*: Battley, Nick, ed. *The World's Futures & Options Markets*, 1993. Chicago Mercantile
        Exchange. *CME Futures and Options Contract Highlights*, 1994.

3.1 Intrinsic Value of Options

The *intrinsic value* of an option depends on the relationship between the market value of the underlying asset and the exercise or strike price of the option. (See also Exhibit 7.2.) Consider a call option.

• If the market value of an underlying asset exceeds the exercise price of a call option, the owner of such an option has the right to acquire the underlying asset at the strike price and then sell the asset in the market for a higher amount. For such a call option, the intrinsic value is positive and the option is said to be *in-the-money*.

	Call Option	Put Option
In-the-money	$MV > X$ Intrinsic value > 0	$X > MV$ Intrinsic value > 0
At-the-money	$MV = X$ Intrinsic value $= 0$	$X = MV$ Intrinsic value $= 0$
Out-of-the-money	$MV < X$ Intrinsic value $= 0$	$X < MV$ Intrinsic value $= 0$

◆ **Exhibit 7.2:** Intrinsic value of options for in-the-money, at-the-money, and out-of-the-money options

◆ *Notes*: MV Market value of underlying asset
                X Exercise price or strike price of the option

- If the market value of the underlying asset is less than the exercise price of the call option, the owner of such an option would be better off purchasing the asset in the market (for a lower price) and allowing the call option to expire unexercised. Exercising such an option would create economic loss for the option owner. That is, there is no intrinsic value and the option is said to be *out-of-the-money*.
- If the market value of the underlying asset and the exercise price of the call option are equal, all other things being equal, the owner of the call option is indifferent between exercising the option and purchasing the underlying asset in the market. Again, the call option has no intrinsic value. However, in this case, the option is said to be *at-the-money*.

> **Intrinsic value (options):**
> For a call option, the excess of market value of the underlying asset over exercise price. For a put option, the excess of exercise price over market value of the underlying asset.

3.2 OPTIONS EXCHANGES AND UNDERLYING ASSETS OF TRADED OPTIONS

Domestically, these options are traded on the:

- Chicago Board of Trade (CBOT)
- Chicago Board Options Exchange (CBOE)
- Chicago Mercantile Exchange (CME)
- New York Stock Exchange (NYSE)
- American Stock Exchange (AMEX)
- New York Futures Exchange (NYFE)
- Philadelphia Stock Exchange (PHLX)

Major exchanges abroad include:

- London International Financial Futures Exchange (LIFFE)
- Singapore International Monetary Exchange (SIMEX)

Expiration dates for these contracts are generally the third Friday of the month of expiration.

The underlying assets of traded options include common stock, stock indexes, foreign currency, and futures contracts. In the case of *stock options*, the contract is usually for the right to buy or sell 100 shares of the underlying asset. These options are readily available for firms whose stock is widely traded. A *stock index option* does not have a physical underlying asset. Instead, the contract is for some multiple of the underlying index.

For example, the S&P 500 index option contract is valued in terms of 100 times the index level. The owner of the option receives the difference between the exercise price and market value without physically delivering anything. If an investor buys a call option with a strike price of 400 and the index is at 425 on the exercise date, the investor exercises the option and receives $2,500 – the difference between the market value of the index and the exercise price multiplied by 100. Likewise, an investor who exercises an S&P 500 index put option with a strike price of 460 when the index is 425 receives the difference between the exercise price and the market value multiplied by 100 – $3,500.

In addition to the S&P 500, stock index options are available on the:

- S&P 100
- NYSE composite index
- AMEX major market index
- AMEX institutional index
- AMEX computer technology index
- AMEX oil index
- PHLX value line index
- PHLX national OTC index

Currency option contracts (in which physical delivery does take place) are available in all major currencies. Contract specifics are

Currency	Denomination	Exchange
Australian dollar	A$50,000	PHLX
Canadian dollar	C$50,000	PHLX
Deutsche mark	DM 62,500	PHLX
Deutsche mark	DM 125,000	SIMEX
European currency unit (ECU)	ECU 62,500	PHLX
Eurodollar	$1,000,000	SIMEX
French franc	FFr 250,000	PHLX
Japanese yen	¥6,250,000	PHLX
Japanese yen	¥12,500,000	PHLX
British pound	£31,250	PHLX
Swiss franc	SFr 62,500	PHLX

(The use of currency options is discussed in chapter 8.)

Options on interest rate futures contracts include:

Instruments	Denominations	Exchange(s)
Treasury bonds	$100,000	CBOT, LIFFE
Treasury notes	$100,000	CBOT
Treasury bills	$1,000,000	IMM
Municipal bond index	$100,000 times index	CBOT
UK gilt (government bond)	£50,000	LIFFE
German government bond	DM 250,000	LIFFE

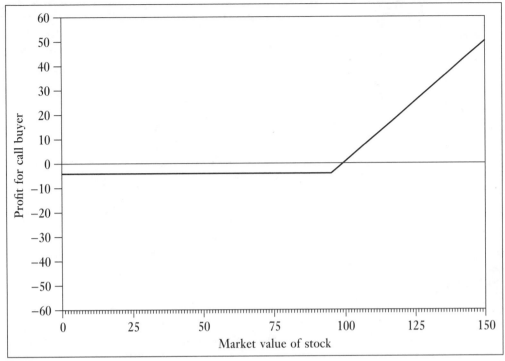

◆ **Exhibit 7.3: Buying a call option**

◆ *Notes*:   Exercise price = $95
                 Call premium = 4

3.3 RISK AND RETURN

There are four primary positions that an individual can assume in an options transaction:

- Buy a call option
- Write a call option
- Buy a put option
- Write a put option

When an investor *buys a call option*, the maximum loss exposure is the option premium. Exhibit 7.3 illustrates this point. In this case, the underlying instrument is a stock. The exercise price is $95, and the option premium $4. The maximum loss for a call option investor is the $4 premium. The option will not be exercised until the market price exceeds the exercise price. In fact, exercising the option will not be profitable until the market price exceeds the sum of the exercise price and the premium.

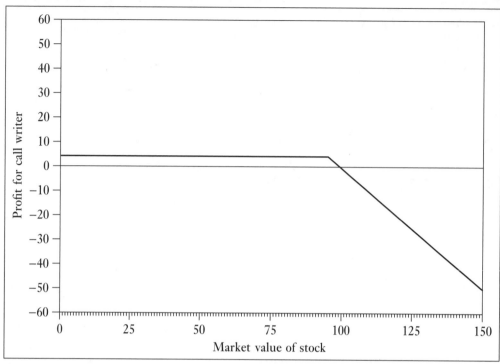

◆ **Exhibit 7.4:**   **Writing a call option**

◆ *Notes:*   Exercise price = $95
                Call premium = 4

$$\text{profit} = MV - X - C$$

where MV = market value of the underlying stock
      X = exercise price
      C = the value of the call option
        = the call premium

Substituting the values in this example:

$$\text{profit} = MV - 95 - 4$$

Notice that for any market value less than $99, profit will be negative, i.e., a loss will be sustained. A market value of $99 will exactly offset the exercise price and option premium. It will be profitable to exercise the option only when the market value exceeds $99.

The maximum loss for the owner of the call option is the $4 premium because the option will not be exercised if the market value is below the exercise price.

The party on the other side of a call option is the *call writer or seller*. Profits for this individual are the mirror image of profits for the call buyer. Exhibit 7.4 illustrates that the maximum profit for the call writer is the amount of the premium. Using the same exercise price and premium as in the example above, as long as the market value is below $95, the call owner will not exercise and the call writer keeps the $4 premium with no further obligation. As the price rises above $95, the likelihood of an exercise increases. When the market value of the stock rises above $99,

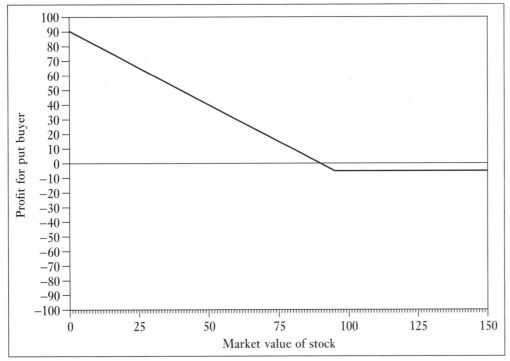

◆ **Exhibit 7.5: Buying a put option**

◆ *Notes*:　　Exercise price = $95
　　　　　　　Call premium = 4

prompting option exercise, the call writer must enter the market and purchase the stock at the going price and sell it to the call owner at $95. The profit for the call writer can be described as:

$$\text{profit} = X + C - MV$$

The call writer receives X and C but must pay MV. To the extent that the market value is not bounded, neither are the losses for a call writer.

A *owner of a put option* has the right to sell an asset at the exercise price. Exhibit 7.5 shows the profit for a put owner, assuming an exercise price of $95 and an option premium of $4. If the price of the stock higher than $95, the owner has no incentive to exercise. Assuming the put owner already owns the stock, it would be more profitable to sell in the market rather than to exercise the option and sell at $95. Assuming that the put owner does not already own the stock, the investor would be forced to buy the stock in the market at a price higher than $95 and then sell it at $95. Under no circumstances will the option be exercised when the market value exceeds $95.

As the market value drops below $95, it becomes more profitable to exercise. For example, at $94, the put owner may enter the market, purchase the stock, exercise the option, and resell it to the put writer for $95. Of course, the $1 profit is offset by the $4 premium paid for the put writer, for a net loss of $3. At a market value of $91, the put owner breaks even, paying $91 for the stock, $4 for the premium, and receiving $95 upon exercise of the option and resale of the stock. When the price declines below $91, the put owner realizes a profit. In general, the profit for the owner of a put option is:

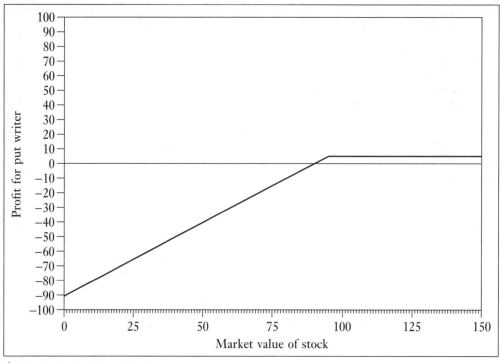

♦ **Exhibit 7.6:** **Writing a put option**

♦ *Notes:*   Exercise price = $95
                       Call premium = 4

$$\text{profit} = X - P - MV$$

where P = the value of the put option
       = the put premium

The put buyer receives the exercise price and pays the option premium and the market value of the underlying asset. In the event that the security becomes worthless, the maximum potential profit is the exercise price less the option premium or $91 in this case.

The profits of a *put option writer* are the mirror image of the profits of the put option owner (Exhibit 7.6). The put writer will gain no more than the option premium. If the price of the stock is above the exercise price, the option will not be exercised and the writer keeps the premium. As the market value declines below the exercise price, exercise becomes more likely. If the market value is $91, an exercise would mean that the put writer would purchase the stock at the $95 exercise price, retain the $4 premium, and sell the stock for $91 in the market. This is the put writer's breakeven point. If the market price is lower than $91, the put writer sustains a loss. Profits for the put writer may be described as:

$$\text{profit} = MV + P - X$$

The put writer receives the option premium and, upon exercise, the market value less the exercise price. Should the security become worthless, the maximum loss is exercise price less option premium, $91 in this case.

Swap Contracts

One of the fasting growing derivative securities is the *swap contract*. The swap contract is used to manage foreign exchange risk or interest rate risk. Thus, the commercial bank with long-term fixed-rate loans, can exchange the interest income from these loans for cash flows that vary with market conditions via an interest rate swap contract.

> **Swap contract:**
> An agreement between two parties (counterparties) to exchange assets or a series of cash flows for a specified period of time at predetermined intervals.

The forerunner of the swap contract was the "parallel loan" of the 1970s, an arrangement that helped companies to reduce their exposure to fluctuating foreign exchange rates when operating overseas. In a parallel loan, a German company, for example, makes a loan denominated in Deutsche marks to a US company operating in Germany. At the same time, the US company makes a loan of equivalent value denominated in dollars to the German company operating in the United States. The US company repays its loan in marks earned from its German operations and receives dollars; the German company repays in dollars earned from its US operations and receives marks. Each company avoids the problem of unfavorable fluctuations in foreign currencies.

Parallel loans are subject to the risk that one of the counterparties will not make its required payment(s), leaving the other still obligated to pay. This deficiency was overcome by the advent of the *currency swap*. In a currency swap, two counterparties agree to exchange currencies on one date and to reverse the transaction at some future date. In the case of the two companies noted above, the US firm receives marks and provides dollars at the inception of the swap; later, the US firm repays the marks and receives dollars. In the interim, the US firm pays fixed interest on the marks; the German firm pays fixed interest on the dollars. Should one counterparty default, the other is released from its obligation. The *currency coupon swap* is distinguished in that one stream of interest payments is fixed and the other floats with some variable market interest rate.

Soon after currency swaps were introduced, *interest rate swaps* developed. These derivative securities are denominated in one currency and are intended to provide desired cash flows from interest payments. Types of interest rate swaps are:

- coupon swaps
- basis rate swaps
- swaps with timing mismatches
- swaps with option-like payoffs

Coupon swaps exchange a fixed-rate stream of interest payments for a variable-rate stream. No principal amounts change hands; instead a *notional principal* is agreed upon for a given length of time. One party agrees to pay a fixed rate of interest on the notional principal at specified intervals, perhaps monthly or quarterly. The counterparty agrees to pay a rate that floats with a published interest rate or *basis*, perhaps the Treasury bill rate, the commercial paper rate, or LIBOR (London Interbank Offered Rate). For example, the floating rate may be specified as "six-month LIBOR plus 1," meaning one percent above LIBOR for six-month loans. Generally, the parties exchange only the difference between the two interest amounts.

The coupon swap is useful for companies with different objectives with respect to interest rates. For example, an industrial firm may have raised capital through a $50 million variable rate loan but would rather have a predictable interest payment obligation for financial planning purposes. A financial institution, on the other hand, may prefer to have variable rate liabilities (perhaps because its loans are primarily variable rate), but can raise funds competitively only through fixed-rate certificates of deposit (CDs) and other borrowings. Essentially, in a coupon swap between the two counterparties, the industrial firm agrees to pay to the financial institution a fixed rate of interest on the $50 million notional principal on a monthly basis; the financial institution uses these fixed payments to meet its CD obligations. In turn, the financial institution agrees to pay the variable rate to the industrial firm, again on a monthly basis; these payments satisfy the industrial firm's loan obligations. In practice, only the difference in the two interest payments is exchanged. For example, if the variable rate exceeds the fixed for a given month, the financial institution pays only the excess to industrial firm; the industrial firm makes no payment.

In a *basis rate swap*, both interest rates float, but the bases are different. For example, six-month LIBOR may be swapped for one-month LIBOR, or LIBOR may be swapped for the commercial paper rate. *Swaps with timing mismatches* involve counterparty payments according to different schedules. Perhaps one counterparty pays interest monthly while the other pays quarterly. A "zero" swap requires one party to pay at specified intervals throughout the term of the swap as described earlier. The other pays only at the end of the term, a "zero coupon" arrangement.

Swaps with option-like payoffs are similar to coupon swaps within specified ranges of market interest rate changes. Beyond these ranges, the terms of the swap change. For example, one party may agree to receive fixed rate interest and pay floating rate interest as long as the floating rate is within two percentage points of the current rate of 10 percent. If the market rate exceeds 12 percent, the party's obligation is then to pay the fixed rate of 12 percent. Likewise if the market rate falls below 8 percent, the party's obligation converts to a fixed rate of 8 percent. Alternatively, one party may agree to pay fixed rate interest of 10 percent as long as the market rate remains within the plus-or-minus 2 percent range. Should the market rate go beyond this range (above 12 percent or below 8 percent), the party pays a floating rate.

As these examples illustrate, swaps can be constructed in any number of ways. There are even *options on swaps*, or *swaptions*. The holder of a swaption has the right, but not the obligation, to enter into a swap contract on or before the exercise date. If the holder has the right to *receive* fixed interest payments, the instrument is a *put swaption*. On the other hand, if the holder has the right to *pay* fixed interest, it is a *call swaption*. As with other options, there is an up-front premium to pay in order to obtain the swaption.

The swap market began in order to solve problems of financial risk. In the earliest market activity, a middleman brought the two counterparties together. Since the intermediary assumed no risk in the transaction, investment banks performed the matchmaking function quite well. As the market evolved, swap contracts became more standardized and it was more important for the intermediary to be able to assume some of the risk, in much the same way, though not to the same extent, that organized exchanges assume risk in futures and options markets. For this reason, commercial banks are now significant intermediaries in the market for swaps – an efficient, high-volume business with relatively low margins (profits) for the banks.

A party can reverse or "unwind" a swap position before the end of the term of the swap by canceling the agreement and delivering a final difference payment to the counterparty. Alternatively, the party can write a "mirror" contract to exactly offset the original swap in the secondary swap market. For example, the industrial firm mentioned earlier with a $50 million variable loan originally entered a swap in which it paid fixed interest payments and received floating interest. To close this position, the firm could enter another swap contract in which it paid floating interest payments and received fixed interest. The secondary market is now so active that swap contracts for several hundred million dollars can be traded virtually 24 hours a day.

In general, derivative securities have evolved to satisfy particular needs. Specifically, futures, options, and swap contracts help investors reduce the risk associated with participation in financial markets.

 ## Summary

Derivative securities are generally not issued by corporations and government bodies. They are, instead, agreements to exchange existing financial securities at some time in the future. Futures and options contracts are traded on organized exchanges, with the largest market in the United States. This market has expanded vigorously to now include contracts on stock indexes which have no underlying security. Swap contracts, available primarily through banks, are also a growing part of US capital markets.

 ## End-of-chapter Questions

1. Why do you suppose that derivatives are sometimes referred to as "side bets"?
2. In derivative securities market trading, corporations and governments receive no additional funds for investment. Does this mean that the activity in such markets is irrelevant from a corporate financial management standpoint?
3. Buyers and sellers of futures contracts agree to accept delivery or make delivery of an underlying asset. Are most of these contracts settled in this way? Explain.
4. On which major exchanges are futures contracts traded in the United States?
5. With respect to a futures contract, differentiate *initial margin* and *variation margin*.
6. Does the buyer or seller of a futures contract face the risk of nonperformance by the other side of the trade? Explain.
7. In what significant way does a futures contract differ from an option contract?
8. With respect to options, define:
   a. strike price
   b. option premium

9. Identify the major exchanges on which options contracts are traded in the United States.

10. How does a stock option differ from a stock index option?

11. When is a call option:

    a. In-the-money

    b. At-the-money

    c. Out-of-the-money

12. When is a put option:

    a. In-the-money

    b. At-the-money

    c. Out-of-the-money

13. Referring to a recent edition of the *Wall Street Journal*, select a traded option quotation and identify the maturity date, the strike price, and the option premium.

14. When is it profitable for the buyer of a call option to exercise the option?

15. When is it profitable for the buyer of a put option to exercise the option?

16. Explain how the *parallel loan* was the forerunner of the currency swap.

17. What is the difference between a currency swap and an interest rate swap?

18. With respect to interest rate swaps, differentiate:

    a. coupon swaps

    b. basis rate swaps

    c. swaps with timing mismatches

    d. swaps with option-like payoffs

19. When might it be advisable to enter into a swap with option-like payoffs?

20. What is a swaption?

Selected References

Battley, Nick, ed. *The World's Futures & Options Markets*, Probus Publishing, Cambridge, England (now McGraw-Hill, New York), 1993.

Brown, Keith C. and Donald J. Smith. "Forward Swaps, Swap Options, and the Management of Callable Debt," *New Developments in Commercial Banking*, Donald Chew, ed., Blackwell Publishers, Cambridge, Mass., 1991, pp. 260–72.

Chicago Mercantile Exchange. *CME Futures and Options Contract Highlights*, 1994.

Cox, John C. and Mark Rubinstein. *Options Markets*, Prentice Hall, Englewood Cliffs, NJ, 1985.

Das, Satyajit. *Swap and Derivative Financing: The Global Reference to Products, Pricing, Applications and Markets*, revised, Probus Publishing, Chicago (now McGraw-Hill, New York), 1994.

Fitch, Thomas. *Dictionary of Banking Terms*, Barron's Educational Series, Hauppauge, NY, 1990.

Gibson, Rajna. *Option Valuation: Analyzing and Pricing Standardized Option Contracts*, McGraw-Hill, New York, 1991.

Howe, Donna M. *A Guide to Managing Interest-Rate Risk*, New York Institute of Finance, New York, 1992.

Hull, John. *Options, Futures, and Other Derivative Securities*, Prentice Hall, Englewood Cliffs, NJ, 1989.

Johnson, Hazel J. *The Bank Valuation Handbook: A Market-based Approach to Valuing a Bank*, revised edn, Irwin Professional Publishing, Burr Ridge, Ill. (now McGraw-Hill, New York), 1995.

Johnson, Hazel J. *Banking in Europe: Managing Change in a New Marketplace*, Lafferty Publications, Dublin, 1996.

Konishi, Atsuo and Ravi E. Dattatreya, eds. *The Handbook of Derivative Instruments*, Probus Publishing, Chicago (now McGraw-Hill, New York), 1991.

Smith, Clifford W., Charles W. Smithson, and L. Macdonald Wakeman. "The Evolving Market for Swaps," *New Dimensions in Commercial Banking*, Donald Chew, ed., Blackwell Publishers, Cambridge, Mass., 1991, pp. 213–25.

Appendix 7.1: Black–Scholes Option Pricing Model

The most widely used option pricing model is the Black–Scholes model:

$$C = (MV)N(d_1) - Xe^{-kt}N(d_2)$$

where C = value of a European call option
         MV = current market value of the underlying asset
         X = exercise price
         k = risk free rate of return
         t = time to option expiration
         $N(y)$ = the probability that an observation from a normal distribution will be less than or equal to y
         = cumulative normal probability distribution
         $d_1 = [\ln(MV/X) + (k + \sigma^2/2)(t)]/\sigma(t^{.5})$
         σ = volatility of underlying asset
         = standard deviation of rate of return of underlying asset
         $d_2 = d_1 - \sigma(t^{.5})$

The intuition of the model is based on the fact that the owner of a call option receives market value of the underlying asset less the exercise price when a call option is exercised. The first term on the right-hand side of the equation is market value, weighted by its probability of occurrence – $N(d_1)$. Notice that this probability depends on:

- the relationship of the current market value to the exercise price
- the current level of interest rates
- volatility of return
- time to maturity

The second term on the right-hand side is the continuously compounded present value of the exercise price, weighted by its probability of occurrence – $N(d_2)$.[1]

The Black–Scholes model for the value of a put option is as follows:

$$P = Xe^{-kt}N(-d_2) - (MV)N(-d_1)$$

$N(-y)$ = the probability that an observation from a normal
distribution will be less than or equal to $-y$

$$= 1 - N(y)$$

The intuition of this model is that, upon exercise, the owner of a put receives $X - MV$. The first term on the right hand side of the equation is the present value of the exercise price multiplied by its probability. The second term on the right hand side is the current market value multiplied by its probability of occurrence.

Consider the case of a stock. What are the values of put and call options on this stock if these options expire in 143 days? You are given the following information:

- $MV = 105$
- $X = 103$
- $t = 143/360 = .3972$
- The volatility of the underlying asset is the standard deviation of the rate of return, or .117117
- The risk free rate is .035

Using this information, the value of the call option is specified as:

$$C = (MV)N(d_1) - Xe^{-kt}N(d_2)$$

$$= (105)N(d_1) - (103)(e^{-(.035)(.3972)})N(d_2)$$

where $d_1 = [\ln(MV/X) + (k + \sigma^2/2)(t)]/\sigma(t^{.5})$
$\qquad = [.019231 + (.035 + .006858)(.3972)]/(.117117)(.630238)$
$\qquad = .485791$
$\quad d_2 = d_1 - \sigma(t^{.5})$
$\qquad = .485791 - (.117117)(.630238)$
$\qquad = .411979$

The values of $N(d_1)$ and $N(d_2)$ may be determined with reference to a cumulative normal distribution table (with appropriate interpolation) or to the polynomial approximation given in Exhibit 7.7. The approximation is accurate to four decimal places and facilitates a computer application of the Black–Scholes model. Using this approach for $N(d_1)$:

$$a = (.485791)^2$$

$$= .235992896$$

$$p = (1/(1+(.33267)(.485791)))$$

$$= .8608755$$

$$N(.485791) = 1 - (1/2.506628273)(.8886992)(.375499775 - .089057005 + .597996628)$$

$$= .686431134$$

For $x \geq 0$:

$$N(x) \cong 1 - (1/(2\pi)^{.5})(e^{-a/2})(b_1 p + b_2 p^2 + b_3 p^3)$$

For $x < 0$:

$$N(x) \cong 1 - N(-x)$$

where $\quad \pi = 3.14159265$
$\quad\quad a = x^2$
$\quad\quad b_1 = .4361836$
$\quad\quad b_2 = -.1201676$
$\quad\quad b_3 = .9372980$
$\quad\quad p = 1/(1 + cx)$
$\quad\quad c = .33267$
$\quad N(-x) = 1 - N(x)$

◆ **Exhibit 7.7:** Polynomial approximation of cumulative normal distribution function

Following the same procedure for $N(d_2)$:

$$a = (.411979)^2$$
$$= .169726696$$
$$p = (1/(1+(.33267)(.411979)))$$
$$= .879466439$$
$$N(.411979) = 1 - (1/2.506628273)(.918637810)(.383608837 - .092944978 + .637581202)$$
$$= .659813536$$

Substituting these values, the market value of the call option is:

$$C = 72.072 - 67.021$$
$$= 5.051$$

The value of the put option depends on $N(-d_1)$ and $N(-d_2)$.

$$N(-d_1) = 1 - N(d_1)$$
$$= 1 - .6864$$
$$= .3136$$
$$N(-d_2) = 1 - N(d_2)$$
$$= 1 - .6598$$
$$= .3402$$

The market value of the put option is:

$$P = Xe^{-kt}N(-d_2) - (MV)N(-d_1)$$

$$= (103)(e^{-(.035)(.3972)})(.3402) - (105)(.3136)$$

$$= 34.557 - 32.928$$

$$= 1.629$$

NOTE

1 It should be noted that the binomial approach is another alternative to option pricing. In this approach, the price of the underlying asset is assumed to either increase by $u\%$ or decrease by $d\%$ with some also assumed probabilities over a single period. For each subsequent period in the life of the option, these same percentage changes and probabilities apply. Each iteration produces a value for the call option, including, in some cases, zero when the call is out-of-the-money. The various values of the option are then weighted by their joint probabilities to arrive at an option value. Deficiencies of the model are:

- There are abrupt changes in option value rather than continuous changes.
- Percentage changes in the price of the underlying asset are restricted to only two values.
- Probabilities of these price changes are set arbitrarily.

Furthermore, when time to maturity is divided into an increasing number of subperiods, the binomial result converges to the Black–Scholes result. Accordingly, the Black–Scholes model is used here rather than a binomial approach.

Appendix 7.2: Black Futures Option Pricing Model

A model used to value a call option on a futures contract is the Black futures option pricing model:

$$C = e^{-kt}[(F)N(d_1) - (X)N(d_2)]$$

where F = current market value of a futures contract of the underlying asset
t = life of the option

The owner of an option on a futures contract will exercise the option if the market value of the futures contract exceeds the exercise price of the option. Upon exercise, the owner of the option receives $F - X$. The pricing model measures this difference based on the current market value of the futures contract and weights both F and X by their respective probabilities. The result is then discounted at the risk free rate.

Similarly, the value of a put option on the futures contract is:

$$P = e^{-kt}[(X)N(-d_2) - (F)N(-d_1)]$$

The owner of a put option will exercise if the exercise price is higher than the market value and will receive $X - F$. The model measures this difference, weights both X and F by their respective probabilities and discounts the result.

PART III
International Financial
Markets

Foreign Exchange Markets

chapter 8

CHAPTER OVERVIEW

This chapter:
- Explains the need for foreign currency exchange.
- Describes types of foreign currency transactions.
- Discusses the operation of foreign exchange markets.
- Illustrates methods of protecting against foreign exchange risk.

KEY TERMS

asked price
bid price
exchange rate risk
foreign currency swaps
foreign exchange futures
foreign exchange hedging
foreign exchange options
foreign exchange speculation
forward currency exchange contract
forward discount

forward exchange rate
forward forward exchange contract
forward premium
interest rate parity
long position
option–date forward contract
short position
spot currency exchange
spot exchange rate

CHAPTER OUTLINE

INTERNATIONAL COMPARISONS:
Germany
Japan
The Netherlands
New Zealand
The Philippines
Singapore
United Kingdom

 ## Introduction

Since the worldwide market turbulence in October 1987, it has been abundantly clear that price changes in the world's financial markets are, in fact, interrelated. Financial market deregulation will contribute to continuing market integration in the future.

    Financial markets that operate across national boundaries are varied both in nature and in stage of development. The oldest are currency exchange markets, which operate virtually 24 hours a day because of overlapping time zones in the United States, Asia, and Europe. These efficient markets offer buyer and seller protection against unfavorable exchange rate fluctuations. Foreign exchange swaps, futures, and options are more recent additions to traditional forward contracts. This chapter describes the products available in and the operation of foreign exchange markets. (Chapter 11 discusses factors that influence the level of exchange rates and observed exchange rate patterns. Chapter 9 describes the exchange rate mechanism of the European Community.)

 ## Foreign Currency Exchange

Foreign currency exchange is fundamental to development of any other cross-border financial markets and, in fact, foreign currency markets are the most advanced of the cross-border markets. These markets make it possible for people in two or more countries to conduct business more easily.

1.1 EXCHANGE RATE RISK EXAMPLE

Normally, a US business person who buys a piece of equipment from, for example, a German supplier must pay for the purchase in German currency – deutsche marks (Dms). At the time a contract is negotiated (December 31, for example), the cost of the equipment and the published exchange rate are both known, so the buyer can compute its cost as of the order date in US dollars.

If the cost of the equipment is Dm1,000,000 and the exchange rate is $1 = Dm1.5625, each Dm currently has a dollar value of $0.64, bringing the total cost of the equipment to $640,000.

Dm1.5625   = $1
Dm1   = $0.64
Dm1,000,000   = $640,000

Assume that delivery of the equipment is not scheduled until three months later (March 31), when payment is due.

Time Line

0	90
Order date	Delivery date

By the delivery date, the exchange rate undoubtedly will have changed and the dollar cost of the equipment may be lower or higher than that originally anticipated.

Exchange rate risk:
        The risk that changes in currency exchange rates may have an unfavorable impact on costs or revenues.

Suppose that the March 31 exchange rate is $1 = Dm1.6393. Then the dollar value of the Dm is $.61 and the cost of the equipment falls to $610,000.

Dm1.6393   = $1
Dm1   = $0.6100
Dm1,000,000   = $610,000

In this case, the decline of the dollar value of the Dm from $0.64 to $0.61 over the three-month period would save the buyer $30,000 ($640,000 − $610,000).
    On the other hand, if the March 31 exchange rate is $1 = Dm1.4802, the equipment would cost more than originally anticipated.

Dm1.4802   = $1
Dm1   = $0.6756
Dm1,000,000   = $675,600

The dollar value of the Dm would increase from $0.64 to $0.6756 and the equipment cost would increase by $35,600 ($675,600 − $640,000).

1.2 Foreign Exchange Hedging and Speculating

The US purchaser of the equipment cannot accurately predict the future spot exchange rate (the rate for immediate exchange that will be available in the future). However, the purchaser can reduce the uncertainty of the future cost of the equipment and limit the downside risk of exchange rate movements through *foreign exchange hedging*.

Foreign exchange hedging:
> Using financial contracts to protect against adverse changes in foreign exchange rates.

Hedging can be accomplished by:

1) Determining the position in cash market, that is, the actual transaction that gives rise to the exchange rate risk, and
2) Assuming the opposite position in the hedge market.

If the cash market position – the initial transaction – represents an asset or future ownership claim to foreign currency, this position is described as a *long position*. On the other hand, if the cash market position represents a liability or a future obligation to deliver foreign currency, this position is described as a *short position*. In the example above, the cash market position obligates the US business person to deliver Dm1,000,000 in three months – a short position. Each foreign exchange hedging approach illustrated below will create a long position in the hedge market.

Foreign exchange hedging must be distinguished from foreign exchange speculation. One who hedges attempts to avoid financial loss while one who speculates attempts to generate profits. The examples in this chapter are designed to illustrate hedging techniques that can be used in the example noted above. Cash market transactions occur in the spot market. Specific types of contracts that can be used for hedging include:

- Forward contracts
- Swaps
- Futures
- Options

Foreign exchange speculation:
> Buying or selling currency (or currency contracts) with the intention of producing profits by correctly predicting the direction of currency price changes.

1.3 Spot Market Exchange

An immediate exchange of dollars for Dms or other currency takes place in the *spot exchange market*. Spot transactions can be carried out through foreign exchange divisions of commercial banks or through nonbank foreign currency dealers. If a US buyer of foreign currency decides to purchase Dms through a local bank, this amounts to transferring dollars from the buyer's US bank account to the dollar-denominated bank account of the Dm seller. Dms are transferred simultaneously into a Dm account designated by the US buyer in Germany or, perhaps, London. (If the Dm account is in London, it is a Euromarket account, described in the next chapter.)

> **Spot foreign currency exchange market transaction:**
> The immediate exchange of currencies in the form of bank deposits, bank notes (money), or travelers checks. Transactions are immediate, unless they involve bank deposits, in which case both parties in the exchange have two days to deliver.

While the US business person may deal with a local bank, that bank will not necessarily be the other side of the trade. Generally, only the head offices of money center banks or large regional banks make markets in foreign currency, trading for their own account (as principals) and for their customers (as agents).

Spot market quotations have two components – the *bid price* and the *asked price*. The difference between the two prices is the dealer's profit margin or spot spread.

> **Bid price (for currency):**
> The price that a dealer is willing to pay to purchase foreign currency.

> **Asked price (for currency):**
> The price at which a dealer will sell foreign currency.

> **Spot spread (for currency trader):**
> Difference between the bid and asked quotation of a currency dealer.

If a bank gets a bid/asked quotation of 1.5645–1.5625 Dm/$, the bid price of 1.5645 Dm/$ means that the dealer will purchase Dms for $0.6392 each. (DM1.5645 = $1; DM1 = $1/1.5645 = $0.6392.) The asked price of 1.5625 Dm/$ means that the dealer will sell at the rate of $0.64 per Dm, which yields a profit of $0.0008 per Dm.

1.4 FORWARD EXCHANGE

To avoid the exposure to an increase in the dollar value of the Dm, the US business person can take a long position in the forward market. Entering a *forward contract* to buy Dms (generally through a bank) removes the uncertainty of currency fluctuations. Forward contracts usually mature 30, 60, or 90 days or 6, 9, or 12 months from the date the contract is written. At the maturity date, currencies are transferred through bank deposits in the large interbank market. (Specific instructions regarding the accounts to be credited are generally not given until time of delivery is close.)

> **Forward foreign currency exchange contract:**
> An agreement between two parties to exchange foreign currencies at a predetermined rate on a specific date in the future. Two days before the specified date, the forward contract becomes a spot contract.

1.4.1 FORWARD RATE DETERMINATION

While the advantage of a forward contract is that the purchaser can predetermine the exchange rate, a forward contract is not written at the current spot rate. A currency sells at a *premium* when the forward rate implies a dollar value of the foreign currency higher than the current spot rate. Conversely, the currency sells at a *discount* when the forward dollar value of the currency is lower than the spot rate.

Whether there will be a premium or a discount depends on relative interest rates in the two countries involved. Interest rates are important because the bank that enters the forward contract will want to "cover" its position at the time the forward contract is written so that the bank also is not exposed to adverse currency fluctuations. In the example here, the bank accomplishes this by making a short-term Dm–denominated investment (perhaps a 3-month German bank deposit) when the forward contract is written. At the end of three months, the Dm investment matures and the bank is assured of having the Dms to deliver to the US business person.

A bank that agrees in December to sell (deliver) Dm1,000,000 at the end of March will make a Dm-denominated bank deposit in December that will grow to Dm1,000,000 in three months. Since the bank prefers not to use its own working capital for such transactions, the Dm deposit is funded by borrowing US dollars now (December) and converting the dollars to Dms. The forward rate that the bank charges the customer will depend on the interest rate available on the Dm deposit, the current spot rate, the rate of interest on the dollar loan, and the bank's profit margin (which is ignored in this example).

Exhibit 8.1 shows how the forward rate is determined. Note that the bank need not borrow the full Dm1,000,000 because it earns interest on its deposit during the three-month period. Assuming that the interest rate available on a three-month Dm deposit is 3.5 percent, the bank will deposit Dm991,436.52, the present value of Dm1,000,000 at 3.5 percent for three months. In order to buy the Dms, the bank borrows the dollar equivalent on the spot market – Dm991,436.52(0.64 \$/Dm) = \$634,519.37. Thus, at the end of December, the bank has a Dm-denominated asset of Dm991,436.52 and a dollar-denominated liability of \$634,519.37.

Given:

Business person wishes to buy Dm1,000,000 from his bank in 3 months; spot rate = 1.5625 Dm/\$; $k_{US} = 0.055$; $k_G = 0.035$.

Procedure for bank to establish forward rate:

1) Determine the number of Dms necessary to invest in a German bank deposit or other short-term German investment in order to have Dm1,000,000 in three months.

$$\frac{\text{Dm}1,000,000}{(1.035)^{.25}} = \text{Dm}991,436.52$$

2) Borrow the required dollars to finance this deposit.

$$\text{Dm}1.5625 = \$1$$

$$\text{Dm}1 = \$0.64$$

$$\text{Dm}991,436.52 = \$634,519.37$$

Borrow this amount in US dollars, convert the dollars into Dms, and invest the Dms in a German bank deposit or other short-term investment.

3) Determine dollar liability (using the US interest rate) in three months.

$$\$634,519.37(1.055)^{.25} = \$643,069.63$$

4) Set dollar liability equal to Dm proceeds in three months to determine appropriate forward exchange rate.

$$Dm1,000,000 = \$643,069.63$$

$$Dm1 = \$0.6431 \quad \text{or}$$

$$Dm1.5550 = \$1$$

In general:

$$\frac{X}{(1 + k_{FC})^n} (\text{spot rate})(1 + k_{US})^n = X \, (\text{forward rate})$$

where X = foreign currency to be received

$$\frac{X}{(1 + k_{FC})^n} = \text{foreign currency borrowed}$$

spot rate, forward rate = US dollars per unit of foreign currency

k_{FC}; k_{US} = appropriate interest rates in foreign currency and US dollars, respectively

Dividing both sides by X, the foreign currency to be received, and rearranging the terms produces the relationship:

$$(\text{spot rate}) \left[\frac{(1 + k_{US})^n}{(1 + k_{FC})^n} \right] = \text{forward rate}$$

◆ **Exhibit 8.1: Forward rate determination**

At an interest rate of 5.5 percent for the dollar loan, the bank's liability in three months will be $643,069.63. The bank must receive exactly this dollar amount from its customer in three months in exchange for the Dm1,000,000 in the maturing deposit in order to fully repay the dollar loan. Setting the two amounts equal and solving, the forward rate is 0.6431 $/Dm or Dm1.5550 = $1.

At this forward rate, the cost of the German equipment for the US business person is $643,100.

Dm1   = $0.6431
Dm1,000,000   = $643,100

The cost is $3,100 higher than that implied by the current spot rate, but it is known with certainty in advance.

In this case, the forward dollar value of the Dm ($0.6431) is higher than the spot value ($0.64). The Dm is selling at a forward premium; that is, its dollar forward value exceeds its dollar spot value. The dollar is selling at a forward discount; its Dm forward value (Dm1.5550) is less than its Dm spot value (Dm1.5625). The interest-rate-dependent relationship illustrated here among forward, spot, and interest rates is called *interest rate parity*.

Interest rate parity:
> The relationship between spot and forward exchange rates that is influenced by interest rate differentials.

Referring again to Exhibit 8.1, note that the general equation reduces to:

$$(SR)\left[\frac{(1 + k_{\text{US}})^n}{(1 + k_{\text{FC}})^n}\right] = FR \tag{8.1}$$

where FR = forward rate (dollars per unit of foreign currency)
SR = spot rate (dollars per unit of foreign currency)

If interest rates in the United States and a foreign country are the same, the forward rate will equal the spot rate (again ignoring any bank fees). If the US interest rate exceeds the foreign interest rate, the forward dollar value of the foreign currency will exceed the spot dollar value. The converse is true when the interest rate relationships are reversed. If the US interest rate is less than the foreign interest rate, the forward dollar value of the foreign currency will be less than the spot dollar value.

1.4.2 OTHER FORWARD CONTRACTS

Forward currency contracts can take forms other than the standard forward contract. Two alternative forms are:

- option-date forward contracts
- forward forward contracts

For firms that are not sure when a foreign currency transaction will occur, an *option-date forward contract* may be appropriate. These contracts are similar to standard forward contracts except that the maturity date of the contract is not a specific, predetermined date. The contract gives the buyer the "option" to settle the transaction at any time within a specified period. For example, the specified period may be (1) from the date of the agreement (spot) to some future date or (2) between two future dates. The bank that writes (sells) the contract is exposed throughout the entire period, during which the spot rate will certainly fluctuate. So, the bank sets the forward rate at the least favorable level for the contract buyer.

If both the transaction for which the currency is needed (the initial cash market transaction) and the foreign currency cash flow (settlement of the cash market transaction) are in the future, a *forward forward contract* may be appropriate. This is especially true if the initial cash market position is a short position (obligation to deliver foreign currency) and the foreign currency is expected to appreciate in the future.

Suppose the business person mentioned above intends to place an equipment order two months from now (end of February, instead of end of December), with invoice payment due one month

		End of	
Dec.	Jan.	Feb.	March

Contract to buy Dm 1 mil. (long)

Contract to sell Dm 1 mil. (short)

Figure 8.1

after that (end of March). The February transaction obligates the US business person to deliver Dms, but there will be no such obligation until the end of February. If the Dm appreciates in the meantime, the buyer still is exposed to a higher dollar cost for the equipment.

To cover this exchange exposure, the buyer could arrange two forward contracts that would lock in the exchange rate only for the future one month of exposure between order placement date (end of February) and invoice due date (end of March). This arrangement reduces the cost of forward protection because it reduces the time period that is protected. To hedge exposure for the month of March:

- At the end of December, the US business person enters a forward contract to buy Dm1,000,000 three months forward, as in the forward transaction described in the section above.
- Also at the end of December, the US business person enters a forward contract to sell the same number of Dms *two* months forward. (See Figure 8.1)

The contracts will offset each other in January and February, with effectively no net open Dm position during these two months. However, exchange rate protection is maintained for the month of March.

A bank determines the two-month forward rate in much the same way as the three-month rate. The difference is that the bank agrees to buy (not sell) Dm1,000,000 from the business person at the end of February. Exhibit 8.2 shows how the two-month forward rate is determined. In this case, the bank borrows the present value of Dm1,000,000 – the amount of foreign currency that it will receive in two months. The bank converts the Dms to dollars and the dollars are invested for two months. At the end of February, the bank:

- Receives Dm1,000,000 from the business person.
- Uses the Dm1,000,000 to repay the Dm loan.
- Delivers the proceeds of the short-term dollar investment in the amount of $642,044.80 to the US business person to pay for the Dms received.

The forward forward exchange rate is $0.64204 per Dm.

A forward forward contract provides protection against adverse changes in exchange rates at less cost than a standard forward contract. The dollar value of a Dm under the standard forward contract is $0.6431. The spot value is $0.64, so the cost of the forward hedge is $0.0031 per Dm, or a total of $3,100. Under the forward forward arrangement, the cost is the difference between the three-month rate at which Dms are bought ($0.6431) and the two-month rate at which they are sold ($0.64204) – a difference of $0.00106 per Dm, which reduces total cost to only $1,060.

Given:

The bank agrees to buy Dm 1,000,000 from the business person at the end of February in exchange for dollars; spot rate = 1.5625 Dm/$; $k_{US} = 0.055$; $k_G = 0.035$.

Procedure for bank to establish the appropriate rate for the first of the two forward transactions:

1) Since the bank will receive Dms at the end of February, it borrows the present value of the Dms (in order to convert them to dollars).

$$\frac{Dm1,000,000}{(1.035)^{\frac{60}{360}}} = Dm994,282.83$$

2) The Dms are then converted to US dollars at the spot rate of $0.64 per Dm or $636,341.02.

$$(0.64 \text{ \$/Dm})(Dm994,282.83) = \$636,341.02$$

3) This dollar amount is deposited into a US dollar bank account or other short-term investment paying 5.5 precent that grows to $642,044.80 in two months.

$$\$636,341.02((1.055)^{60/360}) = \$642,044.80$$

4) At the end of February, the bank will exchange this amount for the Dm1,000,000 received from the corporate client and use the Dm1,000,000 to repay the two-month Dm loan. The projected $642,044.80 balance is set equal to Dm1,000,000.

$$Dm1,000,000 = \$642,044.80$$
$$Dm1 = \$0.64204$$
$$Dm1.5575 = \$1$$

The dollar value per Dm is $0.64204, that is, the two-month forward exchange rate is Dm1.5575 = $1.

◆ **Exhibit 8.2:** Forward forward rate determination

The business person buys Dms today at $0.64, sells them two months forward at $0.64204, and buys them three months forward at $0.6431. The cost of the Dm1,000,000 equipment is the net of these.

Buy today	<$640,000>
Sell two months forward	642,040
Buy three months forward	<643,100>
Net	<$641,060>

This is $1,060 above the current cost of the equipment.

1.5 CURRENCY SWAPS

Another way to manage foreign exchange exposure is through *currency swaps*. Like forward contracts, swaps are generally customized transactions. Multinational firms and banks use swaps to correct imbalances between their foreign currency assets and liabilities.

> **Foreign currency swap:**
> An exchange of foreign currency in the spot market with a simultaneous agreement to reverse the transaction in the forward market. Both exchange rates and timing of the forward market transaction are specified at the time of the swap.

For example, a multinational firm currently may have a German subsidiary which has a temporary shortage of Dms, but the shortage may be corrected with cash inflows in two months. If, at the same time, the parent company has a dollar surplus, it can swap its dollars for Dms with a third party for two months and lend the marks to the subsidiary. At the end of the two-month period, the subsidiary repays the Dm loan to the parent, and the parent delivers the Dms to the third party in the swap transaction – reversing the original transaction.

1.6 FOREIGN EXCHANGE FUTURES

Foreign exchange futures contracts represent a more standardized method of protection from exchange rate risk than forward contracts or swaps, which are usually individualized transactions. Like forward contracts, *foreign exchange futures* are agreements to purchase or sell currency in the future. Unlike forward contracts, futures are traded on an organized exchange. The units of underlying currency are standardized and the time of delivery likewise is set at one of four particular dates (the third Wednesday of March, June, September, or December). With contracts traded on exchanges, of course, it is possible to buy or sell a futures contract at any time. (Chapter 7 discusses the general operation of futures markets and specific contracts for interest rate and stock index futures.)

> **Foreign currency exchange futures contract:**
> A contract, traded on organized exchanges in standard units, to exchange two currencies at some specified future date. The party purchasing the contract agrees to purchase foreign currency on the specified date. The party selling the contract agrees to sell the currency on that date.

The futures market can provide the same kind of protection from adverse exchange rate fluctuations that is available through the forward market. The US buyer who needs Dm1,000,000 in three months to make an equipment purchase in Germany could buy futures contracts instead, as illustrated in Exhibit 8.3. Each exchange-traded Dm futures contract is for Dm125,000, so eight of them would be needed.[1] Assume that it is currently the end of December and that the March futures contract is selling at the three-month forward rate developed earlier – 0.6431 $/Dm – for a total purchase price of $643,100. Assume also that in the third week of March the spot

Dec. 31:

The US business person orders equipment for delivery and payment in three months, at a cost of Dm1,000,000. The spot exchange rate is Dm1.5625 = $1 (0.64 $/Dm). The price of the March futures contract is Dm1.5550 = $1 (0.6431 $/Dm), the three-month forward rate. The business person purchases eight contracts to cover the future foreign currency needs.

8 contracts × 125,000 Dm/contract × 0.6431 $/Dm

Cash market position: Short Dm1,000,000 @ $.64	$640,000
(To be delivered in three months)	
Hedge market position: Long Dm1,000,000 @ $.6431	$643,100
(To be received in three months)	

March:

The Dm has appreciated to Dm1.35 = $1 or 0.7407 $/Dm. The business person sells eight Dm futures contracts, now selling at the spot rate, to close the open futures market position. The loss in the spot market is almost completely offset by the gain in the futures market.

Cash market position:	
(December) Original estimate – Dm1,000,000 @ $.64	$640,000
(March) Actual cost – Dm1,000,000 @ $.7407	<740,700>
Loss	<100,700>
Hedge market position:	
(December) Buy Dm1,000,000 @ $.6431	<$643,100>
(March) Sell Dm1,000,000 @ $.7407	740,700
Gain	97,600

◆ **Exhibit 8.3: Futures market hedge**

rate is Dm1.35 = $1 or 0.7407 $/Dm. The futures buyer in this case can either accept delivery of the Dm1,000,000 at the spot rate or sell eight futures contracts to close the position and buy the Dms through a bank for settlement two days later (closer to the date that the currency will be needed). The economic effect is essentially the same for each method of closing the futures contracts.

Exhibit 8.3 summarizes the gains and losses for spot versus futures market transactions. The spot market loss is $100,700 and the futures market gain is $97,600. The net loss is $3,100, the same cost of using a forward hedge illustrated earlier (Exhibit 8.1).

While the two methods appear to be interchangeable, the results are the same because the three-month forward rate on December 31 and the March futures price as of December 31 were identical. If this equality had not existed, the results would have been different. Moreover, expenses associated with the two methods are not necessarily equal. Forward contract charges (bank fees) tend to be less than futures contract costs (stockbroker commissions). Lastly, the margin required for a futures contract creates an opportunity cost while funds are on deposit.

On the other hand, a futures contract provides more flexibility than the typical forward contract, because a futures contract may be closed at any time, while the forward contract is typically held until maturity. Futures contracts also are traded in relatively small denominations, so they may be more accessible for small- and medium-sized businesses than forward contracts.

1.7 FOREIGN EXCHANGE OPTIONS

Foreign exchange options are relatively new vehicles to protect against adverse exchange rate fluctuations. While the first currency futures contracts were offered in 1972 on the Chicago Mercantile Exchange, the first currency option contract was offered in 1982 on the European Options Exchange in the Netherlands and on the Philadelphia Stock Exchange in 1983.

> **Foreign exchange option:**
> A contract that confers the right to buy or sell foreign currency at a specified price through some future date. This right is exercisable at the discretion of the option buyer.

Like futures, currency options are traded on organized exchanges and are guaranteed by the exchange on which they trade. Just as in the domestic options market, a foreign currency *call option* entitles the buyer to purchase the currency and is equivalent to taking a long position. The seller (writer) is obligated to sell. A foreign currency *put option* gives the buyer the right to sell the currency (short position) while the writer must buy it. (Domestic options markets and instruments are discussed in chapter 7.)

The purchase of an option is an appropriate choice when an international transaction depends on a contingency. If a US company plans to purchase German equipment for Dm1,000,000 only if it wins a competitive bid for a contract using the equipment, its need for Dms is contingent on the outcome of the bidding. An options contract at a given strike price assures the US company that it may purchase Dms at a known price, but does not obligate it to do so. For instance, with the spot rate at 0.64 $/Dm, suppose that the buyer could purchase call option contracts of Dm62,500 each with a strike (exercise) price of 0.655 $/Dm for 0.0075 $/Dm. Sixteen contracts (representing Dm1,000,000) at $468.75 each would be required for a total of $7,500.[2]

Even if the company wins the competitive bid and orders the equipment, it would not necessarily exercise its call options. The options would be exercised only if the spot rate were to rise higher than the strike price 0.655 $/Dm (Dm1.5267 = $1), for example, to 0.67 $/Dm. Under the terms of the option contracts, the Dm1,000,000 would cost $662,500 ((Dm1,000,000 × 0.655 $/Dm) + $7,500). This is less than the $670,000 cost associated with purchasing the Dms on the spot market at 0.67 $/Dm. Of course, whether the option is exercised or not, the $7,500 call option premium has been paid.

It is also possible to purchase an *option on a foreign currency exchange futures contract*. In this case, an option buyer has the right to buy or sell a currency futures contract. Futures option contracts are denominated in the same number of currency units as the corresponding futures contracts because each futures options contract is denominated with the underlying asset of one futures contract. Also, the futures options market operates in much the same way as the regular options market. Futures options can be used to protect an actual asset or liability position against adverse currency fluctuations. For example, the firm that will need Dm1,000,000 only if it wins a contract, may purchase options on currency futures contracts.

With both regular or futures options, if favorable currency fluctuations occur instead of adverse ones, the options need not be exercised. The buyer can take advantage of the full benefit of the favorable exchange rate changes (net of the cost of the options).

The Operation of Foreign Exchange Markets

2.1 SPOT AND FORWARD MARKETS

Spot currency transactions are conducted for the most part in special divisions of major commercial banks. Small banks and local offices of major banks typically maintain lines of credit with these larger banks or with their own head office for foreign exchange. The three most actively traded currencies are the US dollar, the German mark, and the Japanese yen. Other frequently traded currencies are the British pound, the Swiss franc, and the French franc.

Currency traders are often located in one large room at a bank, where each trader has access to several telephones, video screens, and news tapes. A trader generally specializes in one or a small number of currencies, communicating with other traders at banks around the world. Interbank transactions are in wholesale denominations of $1 million or more. An unusually large currency exchange may be facilitated by a broker working on a commission basis with several banks. Long-standing business relationships and preestablished lines of credit allow both sides of a trade to make firm commitments over the telephone.

The foreign exchange market operates 24 hours a day in different time zones around the world. When the New York market closes at 5:00 p.m., the San Francisco market is still open. At 8:00 p.m., New York time, the San Francisco market closes, and the Tokyo market opens. An hour later (9:00 p.m., New York time), the Hong Kong and Singapore markets open. At 3:00 a.m. Tokyo closes, but Frankfurt opens. An hour later (4:00 a.m., New York time), Hong Kong and Singapore close, and London opens. Continuous operation and almost-instant, firm commitments via telephone make the foreign exchange market one of the most efficient in the world.

The *forward* contracts market is also primarily an interbank market. A party to a forward contract may use its line of credit, but there is usually no cash deposit required. Large and creditworthy corporations can trade for themselves in the interbank market, but it is more common for such firms to have a bank operate as agent.

2.2 SWAP MARKET

Banks are also important participants in the currency *swap* market, making markets in swaps and carrying swap inventories. In recent years, nonfinancial firms of different countries have begun to engage in swap arrangements instead of purchasing forward contracts.

In addition, issuers of bonds and other debt can raise funds in the most cost-effective currency for them – whatever that currency might be. The proceeds can then be swapped for the currency needed. Thus, the use of currency swaps has facilitated the issuance of more international bonds.

2.3 FUTURES MARKET

Commodity futures for physical assets that help assure merchants and vendors of needed supplies are the precursors of financial futures contracts. The first *currency futures* contracts were not traded in the United States until 1972. The Chicago Mercantile Exchange (CME) established the International Monetary Market (IMM), where the most broadly traded currencies are represented. Currency futures are also traded on the Mid-American Commodity Exchange in Chicago, the Philadelphia Board of Trade, and the Finex division of the New York Cotton Exchange.

Futures markets have opened in other countries including the Sydney Futures Exchange (1980), the London International Financial Futures Exchange (LIFFE, 1982), and the Singapore Monetary Exchange (SIMEX) with a link to the Chicago Mercantile Exchange (1984). The US futures market typically is the most active, with the UK and Singapore markets following. See Exhibit 8.4 for specifications for the most actively traded currency futures contracts.

Currency	Denomination	Exchange	Year[1]
Australian dollar	AUD 100,000	CME	1987
Rolling spot Australian dollar	AUD 250,000	CME	1993
Australian dollar	AUD 100,000	PBT	1987
British pound	GBP 62,500	CME	1972
Rolling spot British pound	GBP 250,000	CME	1993
British pound	GBP 62,500	MIFE	1991
British pound	GBP 12,500	MidAm	1983
British pound	GBP 62,500	PBT	1986
British pound	GBP 62,500	SIMEX	1986
British pound	GBP 500,000	LIFFE	1982
Canadian dollar	CAD 100,000	CME	1972
Rolling spot Canadian dollar	USD 250,000	CME	1993
Canadian dollar	CAD 50,000	MidAm	1983
Canadian dollar	CAD 100,000	PBT	1986
Cross-rate: DEM/JPY	DEM 125,000	CME	1991
Deutschemark	DEM 125,000	CME	1972
Rolling spot Deutschemark	USD 250,000	CME	1993
Deutschemark	DEM 62,500	MidAm	1983
Deutschemark	DEM 125,000	PBT	1986
Deutschemark	DEM 125,000	LIFFE	1982
Deutschemark	DEM 125,000	SIMEX	1984
ECU (European Currency Unit)	ECU 100,000	NYCE	1986
ECU (European Currency Unit)	ECU 125,000	PBT	1986
Euro	EUR 125,000	CME	1999
Finnish markka	GBP 20,000 or DEM 60,000 or USD 40,000	FOM	1992
French franc	FRF 500,000	CME	1993
Rolling spot French franc	USD 250,000	CME	1993
French franc	FRF 500,000	PBT	1986
Japanese yen	JPY 12,500,000	CME	1972
Rolling spot Japanese yen	USD 250,000	CME	1993
Japanese yen	JPY 6,250,000	MidAm	1983
Japanese yen	JPY 12,500,000	PBT	1986
Japanese yen	JPY 12,500,000	LIFFE	1982
Japanese yen	JPY 12,500,000	SIMEX	1984
New Zealand dollar	NZD 100,000	NZFOE	1988
Swiss franc	CHF 125,000	CME	1972
Rolling spot Swiss franc	USD 250,000	CME	1993
Swiss franc	CHF 62,500	MidAm	1983
Swiss franc	CHF 125,000	PBT	1986

Currency	Denomination	Exchange	Year[1]
Swiss franc	CHF 125,000	LIFFE	1982
Deutschemark	DEM 125,000	MIFE	1991
Japanese yen	JPY 12,500,000	MIFE	1991
US dollar/Japanese yen	USD 50,000	TIFFE	1991
US dollar/Netherlands guilder	USD 25,000	FTA	1991
US dollar/New Zealand dollar	USD 50,000	NZFOE	1985
US dollar/Philippine peso	USD 100,000	MIFE	1992
US dollar/Swiss franc	CHF 125,000	MIFE	1991

◆ **Exhibit 8.4: Currency futures contracts**

◆ *Note*:   1   Represents year during which contract was first offered or was authorized for offer.

Explanatory notes:

Rolling spot: Contracts are marked to market based on daily surveys of spot rates instead of futures contract market prices.

Currencies:
AUD   Australian dollar
CAD   Canadian dollar
CHF   Swiss franc
DEM   German deutsche mark
ECU   European Currency Unit – a GDP-weighted basket of currencies representing the members of the European Union. (See also chapter 9.)
EUR   the Euro – single European currency. (See also chapter 9.)
FRF   French franc
GBP   British pound
JPY   Japanese yen
NZD   New Zealand dollar
USD   US dollar

Exchanges:
CME   Chicago Mercantile Exchange, International Monetary Market Division
FOM   Finnish Options Market, Helsinki, Finland
FTA   Financiële Termijnmarkt Amsterdam, Netherlands
LIFFE   London International Financial Futures Exchange
MidAm   Mid-American Commodity Exchange, Chicago
MIFE   Manila International Futures Exchange, Philippines
NYCE   New York Cotton Exchange, Finex Division
NZFOE   New Zealand Futures and Options Exchange, Auckland, New Zealand
PBT   Philadelphia Board of Trade
SIMEX   Singapore International Monetary Exchange
TIFFE   Tokyo International Financial Futures Exchange, Japan

◆ *Source*:   Battley, N., ed. *The World's Futures and Options Markets*, Chicago: Probus Publishing, 1993; and Chicago Mercantile Exchange, 1999.

2.4 OPTIONS MARKET

Currency options are not a new concept, but they have not been actively traded until recently. In the 1920s there was an unsuccessful attempt to start a market, and banks have privately arranged over-the-counter (OTC) currency options for their customers since the 1940s. It was not until 1982 – when the European Options Market in Amsterdam, the Montreal Exchange, and the

Currency	Denomination	Exchange	Year[1]
Australian dollar	AUD 50,000	PHLX	1987
Cross-rate: GBP/DEM	GBP 31,250	PHLX	1992
British pound	GBP 31,250	PHLX	1982
Canadian dollar	CAD 50,000	PHLX	1983
Cross-rate: DEM/JPY	DEM 62,500	PHLX	1991
Deutschemark	DEM 62,500	PHLX	1983
ECU (European Currency Unit)	ECU 62,500	PHLX	1986
Euro	EUR 62,500	PHLX	1999
French franc	FRF 250,000	PHLX	1984
Japanese yen	JPY 6,250,000	PHLX	1983
Swiss franc	CHF 62,500	PHLX	1983
US dollar/Netherlands guilder	USD 10,000	EOE	1982
US dollar/Netherlands guilder (jumbo)	USD 100,000	EOE	1989

♦ **Exhibit 8.5:** **Currency options contracts**

♦ *Note*:   1   Represents year during which contract was first offered.

Explanatory notes:

Currencies:
AUD   Australian dollar
CAD   Canadian dollar
CHF   Swiss franc
DEM   German deutsche mark
ECU   European Currency Unit – a GDP-weighted basket of currencies representing the
       members of the European Union. (See also chapter 9.)
EUR   the Euro – single European currency. (See also chapter 9.)
FRF   French franc
GBP   British pound
JPY   Japanese yen
USD   US dollar

Exchanges:
EOE   European Options Exchange, Amsterdam, Netherlands
PHLX   Philadelphia Stock Exchange

♦ *Source*:   Battley, N., ed. *The World's Futures and Options Markets*, Chicago: Probus Publishing, 1993.

Philadelphia Exchange offered options in the five most actively traded currencies – that the currency options market began in earnest. The denomination of each contract was one-half the size of the corresponding futures contract on the International Monetary Market of the Chicago Mercantile Exchange.

While exchange-traded currency options are the American type (exercisable at any time before the expiration date), bank options are generally the European type (exercisable only at maturity). Unlike their exchange-traded counterparts, bank options are tailored to individual customer needs. Because of this lack of standardization, bank or OTC options see relatively little secondary market activity. Currency options are also traded on exchanges in London, Singapore, Bangkok, Sydney, and Vancouver. See Exhibit 8.5 for specifications of the most actively traded currency option contracts.

Currency	Denomination	Exchange	Year[1]
Australian dollar	AUD 100,000	CME	1988
Rolling spot Australian dollar	AUD 250,000	CME	1993
British pound	GBP 62,500	CME	1985
Rolling spot British pound	GBP 250,000	CME	1993
Canadian dollar	CAD 100,000	CME	1986
Rolling spot Canadian dollar	USD 250,000	CME	1993
Cross-rate: DEM/JPY	DEM 125,000	CME	1991
Deutschemark	DEM 125,000	CME	1984
Rolling spot deutschemark	USD 250,000	CME	1993
Deutschemark	DEM 125,000	SIMEX	1987
ECU (European Currency Unit)	ECU 100,000	NYCE	1992
EUR	EUR 125,000	CME	1999
Finnish markka	GBP 20,000 or DEM 60,000 or USD 40,000	FOM	1992
Rolling spot French franc	USD 250,000	CME	1993
Japanese yen	JPY 12,500,000	CME	1986
Rolling spot Japanese yen	USD 250,000	CME	1993
Japanese yen	JPY 12,500,000	SIMEX	1984
Swiss franc	CHF 125,000	CME	1985
Rolling spot Swiss franc	USD 250,000	CME	1993

◆ **Exhibit 8.6:** Options on currency futures contracts

◆ *Note*:   1   Represents year during which contract was first offered.

Explanatory notes:

Currencies:
AUD   Australian dollar
CAD   Canadian dollar
CHF   Swiss franc
DEM   German deutsche mark
ECU   European Currency Unit – a GDP-weighted basket of currencies representing the members of the European Union. (See also chapter 9.)
EUR   the Euro – single European currency. (See also chapter 9.)
GBP   British pound
JPY   Japanese yen
USD   US dollar

Exchanges:
CME   Chicago Mercantile Exchange, Index and Option Market Division
FOM   Finnish Options Market, Helsinki, Finland
NYCE   New York Cotton Exchange, Finex Division
SIMEX   Singapore International Monetary Exchange

◆ *Source*:   Battley, N., ed. *The World's Futures and Options Markets*, Chicago: Probus Publishing, 1993; and Chicago Mercantile Exchange.

In 1984, IMM (of the CME) offered the first *options* on deutsche mark *futures* contracts. Since that time, options on other major currency futures have been introduced. The United States provides, again, the most active market in these derivative securities. Exhibit 8.6 lists contract specifications for the most actively traded currency futures options contracts.

 **Summary**

Foreign currency transactions are a requirement of international trade. Changes in exchange rates can adversely affect profits from such trade, however. Instruments that allow buyers and sellers to protect against unfavorable currency exchange fluctuations include forward, swap, futures, and options contracts. Forward contracts can be customized to fit individual needs with respect to timing and denomination. Special variations of the forward contract include option-date forward contracts and forward forward contracts. Forward exchange rates are affected by spot exchange rates and differential interest rates.

A currency swap is an exchange of currencies that is reversed at a future date. Spot, swap, and forward rates are interrelated because the standard forward contract is equivalent to the combination of a spot market transaction combined with a swap.

Foreign exchange futures and options contracts, unlike forwards and swaps, are traded on organized exchanges in several countries. Holding a futures contract requires some action in order to close out the position – either the specified exchange of currencies or taking an opposite position in order the cancel the first position. The owner of an options contract has the right, but not the obligation, to take further action.

All of these markets are very efficient, especially the spot market which operates 24 hours a day. While the US dollar has historically formed the core of foreign exchange markets, other currencies have gained increased importance, especially the German mark and the Japanese yen.

 End-of-chapter Questions

1. Differentiate among spot, forward, and futures contracts for foreign currency exchange.
2. What is a currency swap?
3. Under what circumstances might an option-date forward contract be more advisable than a standard forward?
4. Differentiate between an option on a foreign exchange futures contract and a foreign exchange option.
5. Look at a recent edition of the *Wall Street Journal*. Identify the foreign currency with the greatest number of open options on futures contracts (open interest) on the International Monetary Market (IMM).
6. Describe a scenario in which the writer of a deutsche mark call option (option holder has the right to buy deutsche marks) faces potentially unbounded losses.
7. Why might an industrial firm with foreign exchange exposure prefer to hedge with an option contract rather than a forward contract?

End-of-chapter Problems

1. What equilibrium six-month forward rate is implied if the rates of interest on six-month Swiss franc and US dollar deposits are 7 percent and 5 percent, respectively? Assume the current spot rate is SFr1.6475 = $1.

2. Given your answer to question no. 1, assume now that a company wishes to purchase a SFr500,000, six-month forward contract and that the bank selling the forward contract wants to build in a $500 fee into the forward rate. Under these circumstances, what is the appropriate forward rate?

3. Assume that the spot exchange rate for Japanese yen is ¥141.65 = $1 and that the 30-day forward rate is ¥141.85 = $1. In dollar terms, is the yen selling at a forward premium or discount? On an annual basis, what is the percentage premium or discount?

4. On March 31, your firm made a sale of equipment to a British customer for £187,500 but the company will not receive the pounds until the end of June.
   a. What is the nature of the foreign exchange risk that the firm is exposed to?
   b. If you decide to protect against this risk with options, what kind of option would you buy?
   c. How many contracts should you buy?
   d. If the current exchange rate is $1.67 = £1, the option strike price is $1.65 = £1, and the option premium is 4.16 cents per £, what is the maximum potential loss for the firm after these contracts are purchased? (Ignore transactions costs.)

5. What would be the appropriate forward market hedge for the US business person in this chapter if the Dm1,000,000 was an account receivable in three months instead of an account payable. Describe appropriate actions and cash flows for the end of December and the end of March.

6. What would be the appropriate currency futures market hedge for the US business person in this chapter if the Dm1,000,000 was an account receivable in three months instead of an account payable. Describe appropriate actions and cash flows for the end of December and the end of March.

7. What would be the appropriate currency options market hedge for the US business person in this chapter if the Dm1,000,000 was an account receivable in three months instead of an account payable. Describe appropriate actions and cash flows for the end of December and the end of March.

Notes

1 Dm futures contracts are sold in contracts of Dm125,000 each on the Chicago Mercantile Exchange, the Philadelphia Board of Trade, and the Singapore International Monetary Exchange. The Mid-American Commodity Exchange (Chicago) offers Dm62,500 contracts. (See also Exhibit 8.4.)

2 $(Dm1,000,000)/(62,500 \text{ Dm/contract}) = 16$ contracts
$(62,500 \text{ Dm/contract}) \times (0.0075 \text{ \$/Dm}) =$ \$468.75/contract
$(16 \text{ contracts}) \times \$468.75/\text{contract} = \$7,500$

Selected References

Battley, N., ed. *The World's Futures and Options Markets*, Probus Publishing, Chicago (now McGraw-Hill, New York), 1993.

Brown, Brendan. *The Forward Market in Foreign Exchange: A Study of Market-making, Arbitrage, and Speculation*, St. Martin's Press, New York, 1983.

Burghardt, Galen, Terry Belton, Morton Lane, Geoffrey Luce, and Richard McVey. *Eurodollar Futures and Options: Controlling Money Market Risk*, Probus Publishing, Chicago (now McGraw-Hill, New York), 1991.

Das, Satyajit. *Swap and Derivative Financing: the Global Reference to Products, Pricing, Applications, and Markets*, revised edn, Probus Publishing, Chicago (now McGraw-Hill, New York), 1994.

Fraser, Donald R. and Peter S. Rose, eds. *Financial Institutions and Markets in a Changing World*, 3rd edn, Business Publications, Plano, Tex., 1987.

Havrilesky, Thomas M. and Robert Schweitzer, eds. *Contemporary Developments in Financial Institutions and Markets*, Harlan Davidson, Arlington Heights, Ill., 1987.

Huat, Tan Chwee. *Financial Institutions in Singapore*, Singapore University Press, Singapore, 1981.

Jones, Eric T. and Donald L. Jones. *Hedging Foreign Exchange: Converting Risk to Profit*, John Wiley and Sons, New York, 1987.

Quirk, Peter J., Graham Hacche, Viktor Schoofs, and Lothar Weniger. *Policies for Developing Forward Foreign Exchange Markets*, International Monetary Fund, Washington, DC, 1988.

chapter 9

Euromarkets and the European Union

● CHAPTER OVERVIEW

This chapter:
- Discusses the development of Euromarkets.
- Defines the instruments of Euromarkets, including deposits, bonds, commercial paper and notes, and equities.
- Discusses issues currently affecting Euromarket trading and financing.
- Describes the evolution of the European Union (EU).

● KEY TERMS

Bulldog bonds
Eurobonds
Eurocommercial paper
Eurodollars
Euroequities
Euromarkets
Euronotes
European Monetary System (EMS)
European Union

European Currency Unit (ECU)
European Community (EC)
Exchange Rate Mechanism (ERM)
Foreign bonds
Maastricht Treaty
Matador bonds
Navigator bonds
Samurai bonds
Yankee bonds

● CHAPTER OUTLINE

INTERNATIONAL COMPARISONS:
European Union
United States

 ## Introduction

Euromarkets, where home-currency instruments are traded outside national borders, continue to grow in importance, providing alternative financing vehicles and investment opportunities. Eurocurrencies, particularly Eurodollars, have proved effective in correcting international liquidity imbalances for banks, industrial firms, and sovereign governments. Eurocurrency markets that started in London are now found in other European cities, and in Singapore, Hong Kong, Tokyo, the Cayman Islands, and the Bahamas, while London is still the site of most Eurobond issues and active secondary trading. Eurocommercial paper, Euronotes, and Euroequities have all grown rapidly.

In 1992, full integration of the markets for goods and services, including financial services, was launched in the 12-nation European Community. Effective November 1993, the provisions of the Maastricht Treaty outline the remaining steps to a long-anticipated union of the currencies of the now-15 members of the European Union (with the name change signifying even greater integration of economic policies). Beginning 1999, a single European currency began to replace individual national currencies.

 ## Euromarkets

Euromarkets are financial markets that involve instruments either:

- Denominated in a currency that is not the local domestic currency,
- Denominated in the domestic currency but sold in non domestic markets, or
- Distributed by an international syndicate of investment bankers or merchant banks.

The above list describes a multitude of financial instruments and arrangements. The instruments themselves can be placed in four general classifications:

- Eurodollars
- Eurobonds
- Eurocommercial paper and Euronotes
- Euroequities

1.1 EURODOLLARS

Eurodollars form the core of international money markets transactions.

Eurodollars:
> Deposits denominated in US dollars issued by banks outside the US. Even if the bank's home office is in the US, the deposit is considered a Eurodollar deposit.

1.1.1 DEVELOPMENT OF THE EURODOLLAR MARKET

In the late 1950s and 1960s, banks in Western Europe, the Middle East, the Far East, and elsewhere began actively to trade US dollars for reasons having to do with (1) US trade deficits and (2) in response to the deficits, US legislation that discouraged the issuance of foreign securities in the United States, limited foreign lending and investment by commercial banks, and placed mandatory restrictions on direct investment by US companies.

The net effect of these developments was to put pressure on the multinational customers of US commercial banks to fund their foreign operations outside US markets. Banks' corporate customers were encouraged to seek overseas financing and foreign borrowers were discouraged. These factors combined to significantly reduce demand for bank loans.

At the same time, US commercial banks were subject to Regulation Q (Reg Q) of the Federal Reserve, which placed ceilings on deposit interest rates. When, in 1966, Reg Q ceilings for negotiable certificates of deposit (NCDs) were below market rates for short-term Treasury securities, the Treasury securities became more attractive (default-free) investments. It was apparent that banks would not be able to sell new NCDs when the outstanding issues matured. (See also chapter 3 for a discussion of NCDs.)

US banks responded by offering more competitive NCD rates in their foreign offices – offices where they were not subject to Req Q. The overseas NCDs, known as *Eurodollar CDs*, became a significant source of funds for US commercial banks (deposits included in banks' liabilities).

Investment of the proceeds from Eurodollar CD sales was, likewise, not subject to any US restrictions. Thus, Eurodollars provided banks with liquidity to finance the foreign operations of US multinational firms (loans in the asset portfolios of banks). Even after the Reg Q ceiling on domestic NCDs was removed in 1970 and the US law that restricted capital outflow was abolished in 1974, the Eurodollar market continued to flourish, primarily because of the absence of reserve requirements and deposit insurance premiums in the Eurodollar market.

1.1.2 EUROMARKET LOCATIONS

London became the most important Eurodollar financial center because of its long tradition as an international financial center with well-developed money markets. Equally important is an absence of any restrictions on non British financial institutions in foreign currency (non British-pound) transactions. Banks from other countries have been able to establish a virtually unregulated presence in London.

Paris is also a major Eurodollar market, although its transactions volume is much less than that of London. Frankfurt, Amsterdam, Zurich, Basle, Geneva, Milan, and Vienna also maintain Eurodollar operations. The Cayman Islands and the Bahamas have become major Eurodollar markets primarily because of tax advantages.

Since 1968, when the withholding tax on interest payments made to nonresidents was removed, Singapore has been an important center for US dollar deposits – an *Asiandollar* financial center. Both Hong Kong and Tokyo also have been so designated. Singapore has generally dominated Hong Kong and Tokyo, because its tax environment has been the most favorable and foreign exchange controls have been almost nonexistent. Even US dollar deposits in Asia are frequently referred to as Eurodollar deposits. In fact, the "Euro" designation applies to any transaction made outside the home country of the currency involved.

1.2 EUROBONDS AND FOREIGN BONDS

Although the Eurocurrency market is robust, growth has been even stronger in the longer-term market for Eurobonds. International bonds are either Eurobonds or foreign bonds. Eurobonds developed after the Eurocurrency markets.

> **Eurobonds:**
> Bonds issued by parties outside their domestic capital markets, underwritten by an international investment banking syndicate, placed in at least two countries, and, perhaps, issued in more than one currency.

The firms that underwrite Eurobonds generally maintain offices in New York, London, Tokyo, and other Euromarket centers. An international underwriting syndicate and multinational placement distinguish Eurobonds from other international issues. Note that Eurobond issuer and investor need not *necessarily* be in different countries. For example, a US firm may issue a Eurobond and sell part of it to a US insurance company while also selling to investors in other countries.

> **Foreign bonds:**
> Bonds issued by entities outside their own domestic capital markets in a foreign market, underwritten by a firm that is domestic to that foreign market, usually denominated in the currency of the market in which they are issued, but occasionally denominated in another currency.

In the case of foreign bonds, the country of origin of the issuer is *not* the same as that of the investor. Foreign bonds are sometimes referred to as *traditional* international bonds because they existed long before Eurobonds. Foreign bonds sometimes have specific names depending on the country of issue. Examples of these names follow.

Country	*Name of foreign bond*
United States	Yankee bond
United Kingdom	Bulldog bond
Japan	Samurai bond
Spain	Matador bond
Portugal	Navigator bond
Asia (outside Japan)	Dragon bond

A gradual decline in the relative importance of the dollar is linked to several factors. Uncertainties about the stability of the value of the dollar, over time, have contributed to the use of other currencies. Liberalization of regulations in the United Kingdom, Japan, Germany, and France have made international bond issuance easier. Lastly, the popularity of currency swaps has made it possible to issue Eurobonds in one currency and swap the proceeds for another currency. (See also chapter 7 for coverage of swap contracts.)

Global bonds are one of the newest variants of international bonds, with one *tranche* (portion of the total issue) placed in the Eurobond market and a second placed in the United States by a nonresident – a Yankee bond. The Yankee bond tranche is issued under full SEC registration. (See also chapters 5 (Capital Markets) and 6 (Investment Banking) for a description of public securities offers.) Issuers benefit because this form of security expands the number of investors that hold the bonds. Issuers also benefit from the increased liquidity of the bonds, sometimes lowering their cost of funds by as much as 0.20 percent or 20 basis points.

The market for global bonds involves investors that are financially sophisticated. Issuers in this market must be able to establish creditability on an international basis, particularly in Europe and the United States.

The growth of global bonds is indicative of the general trend of new products in the provision of cross-border financial services. This trend is supported by derivatives such as currency swaps that permit issuers to denominate their obligations in one currency but swap into another currency. Technology has also played an important role because it has facilitated trading of global bonds after issuance.

1.3 EUROCOMMERCIAL PAPER AND EURONOTES

A relatively new short-term instrument in international arena is *Eurocommercial paper*, another offshoot of the Eurocurrency markets. This instrument is one of the more recent to develop in Euromarkets. Throughout the 1970s and early 1980s, both US and foreign borrowers relied heavily on the US commercial paper market. Even though the first issue of Eurocommercial paper was in 1970 by an American firm, this form of financing did not gain widespread acceptance until 1985.

> **Eurocommercial paper:**
> Short-term unsecured notes issued by firms in markets outside their domestic markets.

Arrangements that permit an issuer to request immediate sale of the paper or that allow a securities dealer to solicit an issue when the timing is most advantageous have made the market more appealing as an alternative to short-term bank loans. Advances in communications technology have made precise timing of the issues possible. In addition, commercial paper interest rates compare favorably with other sources of financing.

Floating rate notes (FRNs) are long-term obligations with a variable interest rate. The interest rate is usually tied to LIBOR, the London Interbank Offering Rate, but most FRNs guarantee a minimum rate of return.

Euronotes are similar to Eurocommercial paper except that they include an additional agreement, a *Euronote facility* by an underwriter to place the issuer's notes, when issued, for a specified period of time. This makes a Euronote facility a medium-term credit arrangement, often referred to as a *Euro medium-term note* (EMTN). For a number of reasons, this form of financing has become popular. High-quality credits have embraced the EMTN structure enthusiastically because it favors borrowers that regularly tap the market and is a flexible method of financing. EMTNs require a standard form of documentation that has been accepted by many investors and issuers. This standardization represents a significant cost saving for the borrowers and enables borrowers to move quickly to float issues when market conditions are favorable.

Less seasoned borrowers find the EMTN market attractive, as well. EMTNs enable borrowers to evaluate the reception of the Euromarket for their paper (debt) before embarking on a full-fledged Eurobond issue. Furthermore, an initial issue of EMTNs does not lock in the borrower to relatively high interest rates. After the issuer's credit standing strengthens, subsequent notes may be issued at lower rates.

Borrowers that have had past credit problems find the instruments a good way to reintroduce their names to international capital markets, frequently through private placements with a group of sympathetic investors. (A private placement is not issued to the general public, but to a small group of investors (35 or less) who are considered to have knowledge of the markets, ussually institutional investors. Registration with the SEC is not required.)

From the investors' perspective, one negative aspect of EMTNs is that they are not as liquid as conventional Eurobonds. However, a number of issuers – anxious to maintain the market – have bought back EMTN issues that became illiquid.

1.4 EUROEQUITIES

Another segment of international financial markets that experienced rapid growth followed by contraction during the 1980s is the *Euroequities* market. Issuing equities outside the home country market is not a new practice; firms have often floated stock issues in other countries when their domestic market was too small to absorb a large issue. Firms have issued stock in London or other major capital markets.

> **Euroequities:**
> Common and preferred stocks offered outside the issuer's domestic capital market in one or more foreign markets and underwritten by an international syndicate.

Euroequities are differentiated from these more traditional international issues by the nature of the underwriting syndicate. The same network of investment firms and banks that has been active in the Eurobond market now also underwrites equity issues. To the extent that an issue or a portion of an issue is offered through such an international syndicate, it is a Euroequity issue. As is true with other Euromarkets, the home of the Euroequity market is London.

Frequently, large corporations issue two or more *tranches*, that is, groups of identical or similar securities, each offered under slightly different terms and conditions or being distributed in different ways. A multinational firm may offer domestic and international tranches, for example, with the international tranche distributed through a Euromarket syndicate, thereby qualifying as a Euroequity.

The best candidates for this form of distribution are firms that have an international product market, so that name recognition abroad will help ensure adequate investor interest. International placement helps issuing firms receive a price that is determined by worldwide market conditions and to diversify across a wider shareholder base.

The European Union

Barriers to free capital movement across national borders are being torn down. Perhaps the most significant instance of dissolution of capital barriers is the creation of a Single European Market among the countries of the European Union.

The European Economic Community (EEC) Treaty of 1957, also called the Treaty of Rome, united Belgium, France, Italy, Luxembourg, the Netherlands, and Germany for the purpose of coordinating monetary policies and actions for their mutual benefit. In 1965, the EEC joined with two other European industrial associations (the European Coal and Steel Community and the European Atomic Energy Community) and became the European Community (EC). (The European Coal and Steel Community was created by the Treaty of Paris in 1951 with the goal of transferring control of the materials of war from national governments to multilateral institutions. The founding countries were the six that signed the Treaty of Rome.)

In 1973, Denmark, the Irish Republic, and the United Kingdom joined the EC. Greece became a member in 1981, Portugal and Spain in 1986. Austria, Finland, and Sweden joined in 1995. The total number of EC members is 15 and the total population of these 15 countries is 369 million. The designation for the member countries is now the European Union (EU), signifying even closer coordination of their political and monetary policies.

2.1 DEVELOPMENT OF THE SINGLE EUROPEAN MARKET

Before 1985, the integration of Europe was to be effected through the harmonization of national rules and regulations. This meant that each EC member was to adopt identical rules and regulations – a difficult process at best. To overcome the difficulty, the Commission issued proposals in 1985 in a document entitled *Completing the Internal Market: White Paper from the Commission to the European Council.* The 1985 White Paper recommended that the concept of harmonization be replaced, in many cases, with the concept of mutual recognition. Under mutual recognition, it is not necessary for each member country to adopt exactly the same rules and regulations. Instead, each member country is required to recognize the validity of the rules and regulations of other member countries. Of course, over time, the assumption is that mutual recognition will lead to the convergence of regulatory structures, that is, harmonization. The 1985 White Paper contained a list of 300 (later reduced to 279) specific measures for implementing general principles. In 1986, the Single European Act was passed to implement the White Paper recommendations. This act created the Single European Market, effective January 1, 1992.

In February 1992, the EC Ministers met in Maastricht (the Netherlands) and signed a treaty (the Maastricht Treaty) that:

- Expanded the powers to the European Parliament (567 members elected by the EU countries).
- Allowed the European Community to form common foreign and defense policies for the first time.
- Formed the European Union.

The formation of the EU through treaties and directives (that are binding on the EU members) has had a profound effect on the banking industry and the operation of financial markets.

2.2 BANKING DIRECTIVES AND THE SINGLE PASSPORT

The First Banking Directive on Coordination of Credit Institutions (1977) was the beginning of Communitywide standards for banks. In this directive, "credit institutions" are defined as any firms that receive deposits or other repayable funds from the public and that grant credits for their own accounts. The First Banking Directive confers the right to establish a credit institution, suggests various financial ratios for such firms, and encourages the supervision of institutions (that operate in several European countries) through cooperative efforts among EU members.

The Consolidated Supervision Directive of 1983 addresses the question of supervision (regulation) of credit institutions across national borders within the EU. It stipulates that when one institution owns more than 25 percent of another, the two institutions shall be supervised on a consolidated basis. The supervisor of such institutions must review the accounts, exposure, and management of the consolidated institution at least on a yearly basis.

The Second Banking Directive on Coordination of Credit Institutions created the *single banking license*, or *single passport*. This directive, adopted in 1989 and effective January 1, 1993, builds on the First Banking Directive and the Consolidated Supervision Directive.

With a license issued in any one of the EU countries, a bank may operate throughout the EU. The activities in which a bank may engage include commercial banking, leasing, securities trading, securities underwriting, and financial advising. (See Exhibit 9.1 for a more detailed description.) If the home country of a credit institution permits these activities, the institution may provide these services throughout the EU.

Two limits are stipulated in connection with credit institutions acquiring nonfinancial businesses:

- A credit institution may not hold a stake in a nonfinancial business that exceeds 10 percent of its capital.
- The total value of all such stakes may not exceed 50 percent of the institution's capital.

In order for a credit institution from outside the EU to obtain a single passport into the EU, that firm must own or establish a subsidiary in one of the EU countries. Foreign institutions with subsidiaries that were established before the Second Banking Directive are grandfathered (permitted to continue operations) and may enjoy the full benefits of the single passport. It is also possible for a bank from a non-EU country to maintain only a branch in one of the EU members. However, such a branch will not enjoy the privileges of the single passport.

The Second Banking Directive also establishes the minimum capital required to establish a credit institution. A parent institution must have a capital base of at least Ecu5 million (about $6.2 million). (The ECU is the European Currency Unit, a basket of EU currencies. See the following section on the European Monetary Union.) However, once a parent has been established in one of the EU countries, it may branch into the other EU countries with no additional capital investment required.

The Own Funds Directive defines capital for credit institutions. The Solvency Ratios Directive incorporates the definition of capital into a minimum ratio that all credit institutions must attain. In conformity with international capital standards, the minimum ratio of capital to assets is 8 percent. (See also chatper 17 for a discussion of international capital standards.) Both these directives became effective on January 1, 1993.

1) Acceptance of:
   a) Deposits
   b) Other funds from the public that are repayable
2) Lending:
   a) Consumer credit
   b) Mortgage lending
   c) Factoring, with or without recourse
   d) Financing commercial transactions, including forfaiting
3) Financial leasing
4) Money transmission services
5) Issuing and administering means of payment:
   a) Credit cards
   b) Travellers checks
   c) Bank drafts
6) Financial guarantees and commitments
7) Trading for own account or for account of customers in:
   a) Money market instruments
   b) Foreign exchange
   c) Financial futures and options
   d) Exchange and interest rate instruments
   e) Securities
8) Participation in equity issues and the provision of services related to such share issues
9) Financial advice to clients concerning:
   a) Capital structure
   b) Industrial strategy and related questions
   c) Mergers and acquisitions
10) Portfolio management and advice
11) Safekeeping and administration of securities
12) Credit reference services
13) Safe custody services

◆ **Exhibit 9.1: Activities permitted by the Second Banking Directive**

◆ *Source*:   Golembe, Carter H. and David S. Holland. "Banking and Securities" in *Europe 1992: An American Perspective*, Gary Clyde Hufbauer, ed., Washington, DC: Brookings Institution, 1990.

2.3 ECONOMIC AND MONETARY UNION

The Second Banking Directive (and those directives related to it) moves the European Union toward harmonization of rules governing credit institutions and toward cross-border operation with minimal obstructions. In addition, the EU has taken a major step toward economic and monetary union (EMU) with the introduction of a single currency for 11 of the 15 EU members.

2.3.1 THE EUROPEAN MONETARY SYSTEM AND THE ECU

In 1979, the *European Monetary System* (EMS) was established through a resolution of the European Council. The objective was to create a zone of increasing monetary stability within Europe.

- The *European Currency Unit* (Ecu) was created. The Ecu was a GNP-weighted basket of member currencies, whose composition changed as the result of adjustments every five years.
- Some of the EC members agreed to intervene in the foreign exchange market to correct greater than agreed upon swings in individual currency values as compared to the Ecu. This new arrangement was called the *Exchange Rate Mechanism (ERM)*. Not all EU Members were members of the ERM, even though they were members of the EMS.
- The European Monetary Cooperation Fund was established to issue Ecus against member country deposits of gold and foreign exchange.

The Ecu served several functions – including the unit of account for the system and the basis for the divergence indicator. The Ecu was first used to denominate and settle central bank debts and claims of member countries. By 1989, the Ecu had become one of the top five currencies most frequently used in international transactions. Also in 1989, Luxembourg became the first EU country to encourage use of the Ecu in everyday transactions. In 1998, it was possible for private citizens to buy travellers' checks in Ecus, maintain bank accounts in Ecus, purchase Ecu-based mutual fund shares, obtain Ecu loans and mortgages, and have credit card purchases denominated in Ecus.

The maximum variation of a member country currency rate was set at plus or minus 2.25 percent of its value in terms of Ecus – the *parity limit*, with the *divergence indicator* set at 75 percent of this maximum spread. When the divergence indicator was reached, the member country was obliged to intervene in currency markets and, generally, take steps to bring its currency within the agreed upon range of values.

Parity limits defined the maximum amount by which a currency could move within the ERM. They were derived from *cross-parity rates*. Dividing one central Ecu rate by another yielded the target cross-parity rate between each pair of currencies. Divergence indicators were defined in terms of the value of a currency relative to the Ecu and were intended to reflect the overall strength within the ERM. Divergence indicators were 75 percent of the deviation that would put a currency at its limits against every currency in the Ecu.

However, divergence indicators were not simply equal to the Ecu central rates plus or minus 2.25 percent multiplied by 75 percent. Instead, they were more narrow than this simplified rule would imply because movements in each currency affect the Ecu as well. Thus, the divergence indicator for each currency was computed as follows:

$$DI_i = (0.75)(2.25\%)(1 - i)$$

where DI_i = divergence indicator for currency i
 i = weight of currency i within the Ecu

In 1988, an EC committee was asked to study the process of creating a unified European currency. The resulting *Delors Committee Report*, accepted in 1989, recommended that conversion to a totally unified currency take place in three stages:

Stage 1: A period of closer coordination and full participation of EC members in the Exchange Rate Mechanism.

Stage 2: A transition phase during which (a) the central banks (monetary authorities) of EC countries would more closely coordinate monetary policy and (b) the framework for a European central bank, a kind of "Eurofed," would be established.

Stage 3:   The final point when the "Eurofed" assumes full control of European monetary policy and a single European currency circulates in lieu of existing national currencies.

The objectives of monetary union were frustrated when the United Kingdom and Denmark withdrew from the ERM in the fall of 1992, delaying completion of Stage 2. For reasons related to the German reunification in 1990, Germany had maintained high interest rates to both attract capital and to control inflation. This caused the value of the deutsche mark to remain high *vis-à-vis* other EC currencies. The cost of maintaining agreed upon parities – in terms of both market intervention and maintenance of high interest rates – was too high and the United Kingdom and Denmark pulled out. For a period of time, currency exchange markets were in turmoil and serious doubts arose as to the feasibility of a true monetary union in Europe.

Since that time, German interest rates have fallen, easing some of the pressure on other European countries to maintain high interests to the detriment of their national economies. Also, the Exchange Rate Mechanism was "temporarily" modified in August 1993 such that most member countries were required just to maintain their currencies within 15 percent of parity (above or below). Only Germany and the Netherlands remain subject to the original fluctuation bands. This modification effectively returned the member currencies to floating rate status, but it also kept the ERM at least nominally intact.

2.3.2 THE MAASTRICHT TREATY

Effective November 1993, the Maastricht Treaty outlined an important framework for transition from *monetary system* to *monetary union*. The treaty stipulated January 1, 1994 as the date for commencement of Stage 2 of monetary union. During Stage 2, the *European Monetary Institute* (EMI) replaced the Committee of Central Bank Governors (which had presided over monetary coordination). The EMI was located in Frankfurt, Germany and, among other things:

- Took over the administration of the European Monetary Cooperation Fund (which issued Ecus) and the accompanying financing mechanisms.
- Monitored the operation of the EMS.
- Facilitated use of private Ecu.
- Oversaw development of the Ecu clearing system.
- Was consulted by national authorities on monetary policy and helped draft legislation on the eventual convergence of all currencies into one currency.

All EU central banks were members of the EMI. The organization was intended to strengthen the coordination of the member states' monetary policies in preparation for Stage 3 of monetary union. Also during Stage 2, a *European System of Central Banks* (ESCB) was formed, with the *European Central Bank* (ECB) as a the principal new monetary institution. At the beginning of Stage 3, the EMI was liquidated and the European Central Bank assumed it functions. The formation of the new system follows guidelines established by the Committee of Central Bank Governors (predecessor of the European Monetary Institute).

The European System of Central Banks and the European Central Bank assumed their full powers under Stage 3 and are responsible for issuing and managing the single currency that eventually will replace the national currencies. The United Kingdom, Denmark, and Sweden elected not to converge on January 1, 1999; that is, did not automatically join Stage 3. Greece will join upon meeting the full criteria for convergence. (The eleven converging countries on January 1,

1999, were Austria, Belgium, Finland, France, Germany, Ireland, Italy, Luxembourg, the Netherlands, Portugal, and Spain.) In order to join Stage 3, a member state must:

1) Achieve a high degree of price stability. The average one-year inflation rate before examination by EU authorities must not exceed by more than 1.5 percentage points the inflation rate of the three best performing EU members.

2) Demonstrate sustainability of its government financial position. An excessive government deficit can disqualify an EU country from convergence. Public deficits may not exceed 3 percent of GDP, while total public debt may not exceed 60 percent of GDP.

3) Observe the normal fluctuation margins provided by the Exchange Rate Mechanism for at least two years without devaluing its currency against the currency of another EU member.

4) Demonstrate adequate control of its interest rates. For one year prior to examination by EU authorities, the long-term government bond (or comparable) interest rate may not exceed by more than 2 percentage points the long-term government bond rate of the three best performing EU members.

These criteria have been established for joining Stage 3 of monetary union, but one could argue that the criteria are desirable goals in a national policy-making context. Domestic price stability, adequate control of government finance, proper management of the external value of domestic currency, and a reasonable interest rate environment are conditions in any event for which every sovereign state strives.

In December 1995, the EU heads of government met in Madrid, reaffirming January 1, 1999 as commencement of European Monetary Union. The leaders decided that the name of the new currency would be the *Euro*. Those countries that are members of the monetary union beginning in January 1999 were asked to issue their tradable, government debt in Euros to create a reasonably large pool of financial instruments denominated in the new currency. Nontradeable debt may continue to be denominated in the national currency during the transition period. Commercial banks have the option of accepting deposits and opening transactions accounts in the new currency prior to the mandatory change-over date of 2002.

Euro currency and coins will begin circulation on January 1, 2002. Until that time, national currencies will circulate but their exchange rates are irrevocably fixed in terms of other national currencies and in terms of the Euro.

 ## Summary

The Euromarkets have grown from primarily wholesale money markets to a wide array of short-term and long-term financial services and instruments. In general, growth in Eurobonds has far outpaced the growth in traditional international bonds. Eurocommercial paper and Euronote issues expanded rapidly beginning in the early 1980s. Primary issues in the international equity market were slowed considerably by the stock market crash of 1987, but secondary market trading has continued at a strong pace.

A major initiative in financial market liberalization and integration is the Single European Market. Financial firms that have been constrained by varying rules and regulations in the EU will be able to operate throughout the 15-nation region with a license from any one of them. Financial integration of Europe will be complete with an authoritative European Central Bank and a single European currency – the Euro.

End-of-chapter Questions

1. What are Eurodollars?
2. What type of financial instrument was first traded in the Euromarkets?
3. a. Where were the first Euromarkets?
   b. Where else may they be found today?
4. What other currencies are now considered Eurocurrencies?
5. Japanese banks now rank among the world's largest. Why do you think the US dollar still remains the primary Eurocurrency rather than the yen?
6. What are the advantages of offering long-term financial securities in international markets?
7. What is the difference between a Eurobond and a foreign bond?
8. Who are the major participants in the Euroequity market?
9. What are ECUs? What was the motivation for their creation?
10. What is the name of the currency that will eventually serve as the single currency for Europe?
11. Refer to a recent edition of the *Wall Street Journal*. What is the current dollar value of the ECU?
12. How have foreign currency swaps facilitated Euromarket security issuance?
13. How does Eurocommercial differ from US commercial paper?
14. Do you foresee any negative competitive implications of the Single European Market for US financial services firms?
15. a. What is monetary union?
    b. At what point did the European Community become the European Union?
16. What are the criteria for monetary convergence in the European Union?

SELECTED REFERENCES

Abrams, Richard K., Peter K. Cornelius, Per L. Hedfors, and Gunnar Tersman. *The Impact of the European Community's Internal Market on the EFTA*, International Monetary Fund, Washington, DC, December 1990.

Barber, Lionel. "EU Leaders Do the Minimum on Emu," *Financial Times*, December 18, 1995, p. 2.

Barber, Lionel and David White. "EU Backs Euro as Name for Single Currency," *Financial Times*, December 17, 1995, p. 1.

Blanden, Michael. "Target on Europe (Monetary Union)," *The Banker*, December 1995, pp. 20–5.

"Commission Prepares for the Ecu," *EC Financial Industry Monitor* in *European Banker*, June 1994, p. 6.

"The EC Single Market in Financial Services," *Bank of England Quarterly Bulletin*, February 1993, pp. 92–7.

Economic and Monetary Union, Commission of the European Communities, Luxembourg, 1990.

"Ecu-sounder," *The Economist*, April 8, 1995, p. 45.

Europe 1992: The Facts, Department of Trade and Industry and the Central Office of Information, London, 1989.

Einzig, Paul and Brian Scott Quinn. *The Eurodollar System: Practice and Theory of International Interest Rates*, 6th edn, St. Martin's Press, New York, 1977.

European Economy: One Market, One Money; An Evaluation of the Potential Benefits and Costs of Forming an Economic and Monetary Union, Commission of the European Communities, Directorate-General for Economic and Financial Affairs, Brussels, October 1990.

"European Monetary Institute Set Up," *EC Financial Industry Monitor* in *European Banker*, December 1993, p. 6.

Folkerts-Landau, David and Donald J. Mathieson. *The European Monetary System in the Context of the Integration of European Financial Markets*, International Monetary Fund, Washington, DC, October 1989.

Fraser, Donald R. and Peter S. Rose, eds. *Financial Institutions and Markets in a Changing World*, 3rd edn, Business Publications, Plano, Tex., 1987.

Havrilesky, Thomas M. and Robert Schweitzer, eds. *Contemporary Developments in Financial Institutions and Markets*, Harlan Davidson, Arlington Heights, Ill., 1987.

Huat, Tan Chwee. *Financial Institutions in Singapore*, Singapore University Press, Singapore, 1981.

International Capital Markets; Developments and Prospects, International Monetary Fund, Washington, DC, April 1989 and April 1990.

Johnson, Hazel. *Banking in Europe: Managing Change in a New Marketplace*, Lafferty Publications, Dublin, 1996.

Lee, Peter. "The Start of a Global Bulge Bracket," *Euromoney*, April 1993, pp. 28–33.

Rosenberg, Jerry M. *Dictionary of International Trade*, John Wiley & Sons, New York, 1994.

Scott, Robert Haney, K. A. Wong, and Yan Ki Ho, eds. *Hong Kong's Financial Institutions and Markets*, Oxford University Press, Hong Kong, 1986.

Task Force on the International Competitiveness of US Financial Institutions, Committee on Banking, Finance and Urban Affairs, US House of Representatives. *Report of the Subcommittee on Financial Institutions Supervision, Regulation, and Insurance*, October 1990.

Tew, Brian. *The Evolution of the International Monetary System, 1945–81*, Hutchinson & Co., London, 1982.

Ungerer, Horst, Juko J. Hauvonen, Augusto Lopez-Claros, and Thomas Mayer. *The European Monetary System: Developments and Prospectives*, International Monetary Fund, Washington, DC, November 1990.

US Securities and Exchange Commission. *Internationalization of Securities Markets: Report to the Senate Committee on Banking, Housing and Urban Affairs and the House Committee on Energy and Commerce*, Washington, DC, 1987.

PART IV
The Interest Rate
Environment

Interest Rate Fundamentals

chapter 10

INTERNATIONAL COMPARISONS:
France
Germany
Italy
Japan
United Kingdom

 Introduction

The basic commodity that financial institutions trade among themselves and with others is money and the price of money is the interest rate. Interest rates affect the value of money and capital market instruments, both domestically and internationally. Changes in interest rates have certain predictable effects on the price of fixed-income securities, or bonds.

Various theories of interest rate behavior suggest that current interest rate levels will depend on estimates of future market conditions, a basic preference to hold liquid assets, or particular preferences as to length of the investment period. Unbiased expectations theory suggests that interest rates are determined by an average of the market's estimate of future short-term rates. Liquidity preference theory adds the notion of a liquidity premium in longer-term rates. Market segmentation theory places more emphasis on the supply and demand for funds in particular maturities.

All interest rate theories include the concept of inflation, the decrease in purchasing power of money. Inflation is measured by changes in price indexes, such as consumer and wholesale price indexes and the GDP deflator.

 Interest Rate Theory

In analyzing interest rates, the *term structure of interest rates* is frequently referred to. The *yield curve* is an analytical tool that helps to describe this relationship.

Term structure of interest rates:
     The relationship between time (term) and interest rates.

Yield curve:
     A graphic description of the relationship between time to maturity and yield to maturity for a given risk class of securities.

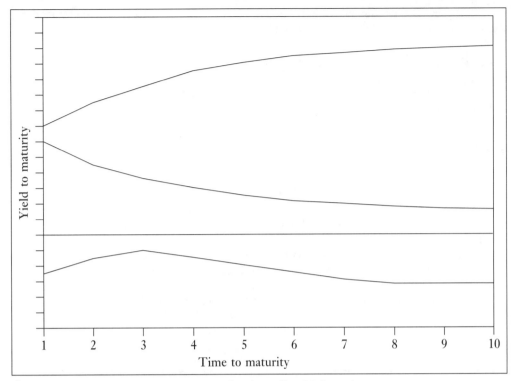

◆ **Exhibit 10.1:** Examples of yield curves: ascending, descending, flat, humped

1.1 THE YIELD CURVE

A yield curve plots the remaining time to maturity of a group of securities against yield to maturity. (The yield to maturity is the average annual rate earned by an investor who holds a security until it matures; see also chapter 4.) The unique maturity date of each security in the group is represented by a point on the curve. As the objective of the analysis is to isolate the effect of time on yield, all characteristics of the securities other than maturity are held constant.

For example, corporate bonds and US Treasury bonds would not be included in the same yield curve. Treasury bonds are considered free of default (nonrepayment) risk, corporate bonds are not. A yield curve including both types of bonds would reflect differences related to risk as well as differences related to time. Also, it would be misleading to group corporate bonds with municipal bonds, even if they are in the *same* default risk class. Corporate and municipal bonds are subject to different income tax treatment, that is, municipal bond interest usually is not taxable. A yield curve including both types of bonds would reflect differences in tax treatment as well as differences related to time to maturity.

Exhibit 10.1 illustrates four possible yield curve shapes. All four types of yield curves have been observed in the United States at one time or another. The most common curve observed in the United States has been the ascending yield curve, which describes lower short-term yields relative to long-term yields, in an environment of generally low rates.

While the shape of these curves is objectively determined – specific, observable maturity dates and yields are plotted on a graph – there are a number of differing theories that explain the reasons for the shapes. Before examining these theories, however, it is necessary to understand the relationship between bond prices and interest rates.

1.2 INTEREST RATES AND BOND PRICES

The variability of bond prices depends on market conditions and specific bond characteristics. The factors that influence bond prices and changes in bond prices are:

- The relationship between required rate of return and coupon rate
- The remaining time to maturity
- Changing interest rate levels

Consider two bonds, A and B, each with a face value of $1,000 and a coupon rate of 10 percent, paid semiannually. Bond A was issued 13 years ago with an original maturity of 15 years (remaining maturity = 2 years). Bond B also had an original maturity of 15 years, but it was issued 5 years ago (remaining maturity = 10 years).

At time of issue, assume that the market rate for bonds in this risk class was 10 percent and that the issuers set the coupon rates at 10 percent. According to the bond pricing formula, the price of each bond at issuance would be $1,000. (The bond pricing formula is Equation (1) in chapter 4.) The market value equals the maturity value because the market rate (the rate of return required by investors) and the coupon rate (the rate that determines the amount of interest to be paid) are the same. This equality typically occurs at the time of bond issuance and is the basis for the first principle of bond pricing.

Bond Theorem no. 1:

When the coupon rate equals the required rate of return, a bond will sell at par.

If the market rate for bonds in the same risk class were currently 12 percent, prices for bonds A and B would be $965.36 and $885.30. (See Appendix A at the back of the book for time value of money tables.)

$$P_0^A = 50(PVIFA_{.06,4}) + 1,000(PVIF_{.06,4})$$
$$= 50(3.4651) + 1,000(.7921)$$
$$= 965.36 \tag{10.1}$$

$$P_0^B = 50(PVIFA_{.06,20}) + 1,000(PVIF_{.06,20})$$
$$= 50(11.4699) + 1,000(.3118)$$
$$= 885.30 \tag{10.2}$$

In this case, the price of each bond is below par. Note that the coupon rate and associated interest payments do not change, but the market (required) rate frequently does. A coupon rate that is *lower* than the required return causes a bond to sell *below* its par value. The same effect works in the opposite circumstance: when the coupon rate is *higher* than the required return, a bond sells *above* par value. These relationships (caused by changing market rates of return) are described by the second principle of bond pricing.

> ### Bond Theorem no. 2:
> When the coupon rate is less than (greater than) the required rate of return, a bond sells at a discount (premium).

Note also that Bond B sells farther below its par value than Bond A. Bond A is closer to its maturity date – Bond A has two years to maturity, Bond B 10 years. The third principle of bond pricing addresses differences in time to maturity.

> ### Bond Theorem no. 3:
> All other things being equal, the price of a bond approaches its par value as its maturity date approaches.

Now assume that the general level of interest rates instantaneously increases, so that the required rate of return for these bonds is 14 percent. Again, applying the bond pricing formula yields prices for Bonds A and B of $932.26 and $788.10.

$$P_0^A = 50(PVIFA_{.07,4}) + 1,000(PVIF_{.07,4})$$
$$= 50(3.3872) + 1,000(.7629)$$
$$= 932.26 \qquad\qquad (10.1a)$$

$$P_0^B = 50(PVIFA_{.07,20}) + 1,000(PVIF_{.07,20})$$
$$= 50(10.5940) + 1,000(.2584)$$
$$= 788.10 \qquad\qquad (10.2a)$$

Both bond prices fell. If general interest rates had declined, both bond values would have risen. The fourth principle of bond pricing describes the relationship between changes in market rates and changes in bond prices.

> ### Bond Theorem no. 4:
> There is an inverse relationship between bond price movements and changes in required rate of return.

Again there is a differential effect in price that is related to the remaining maturity of the bonds. The price of Bond B fell by a larger percentage than that of Bond A.

$$A: \frac{(932.26 - 965.36)}{965.36} = -.0343$$

$$B: \frac{(788.10 - 885.30)}{885.30} = -.1098$$

The fifth principle of bond pricing explains the relative price volatility of short-term and long-term bonds. Bond B experiences a sharper price decline because it has a longer time to maturity.

This greater price sensitivity of longer-term bonds works in both directions. If market interest rates decline, the prices of both bonds increase, but Bond B's price increases by a larger percentage than Bond A's.

Bond Theorem no. 5:
>   Longer-term bonds are more price sensitive to a given change in required
>   rate of return than are shorter-term bonds.

1.3 THEORIES EXPLAINING THE TERM STRUCTURE OF INTEREST RATES

There are three basic theories explaining the term structure of interest rates:

- Unbiased expectations theory
- Liquidity preference theory
- Market segmentation theory

While there is considerable academic research testing each of these theories, none of the evidence to date is conclusive enough to dismiss any of them. Each theory contributes some insight into the behavior of interest rates and, thus, is useful in combination with the others.

1.3.1 UNBIASED EXPECTATIONS THEORY

The *unbiased expectations theory* assumes that the shape of the yield curve is explained by the market's consensus about future interest rates. That is, the yield curve is the result of both current and anticipated interest rates.

Unbiased expectations theory suggests that the short-term interest rates implied by the yield curve are *unbiased estimates* of the market consensus of future rates. Specifically, long-term rates are a geometric average of current and implied future short-term rates.

$$(1 + {}_0R_n)^n = (1 + {}_0R_1)(1 + f_2)(1 + f_3) \ldots (1 + f_n) \tag{10.3}$$

where ${}_0R_n$ = the long-term rate applicable for the period from time 0 to time n
     f_i = the implied future one-year rate for year i ($i = 2, \ldots n$)
      = unbiased estimate of s_i, the actual future one-year rate in year i

Exhibit 10.2 is a hypothetical yield curve. The ascending curve begins at 7.50 percent for one-year maturities and increases to 8.35 percent for ten-year maturities. All yields other than the one year rate, ${}_0R_1$, are averages of implied future short-term rates. The rate for a two-year security, ${}_0R_2$, is 7.80 percent and is a geometric average of ${}_0R_1$ and the one-year rate during the second year, f_2. (The second year begins one year from today and ends two years from today.)

$$(1 + {}_0R_2)^2 = (1 + {}_0R_1)(1 + f_2)$$

$$(1.0780)^2 = (1.0750)(1 + f_2)$$

$$(1.0780)^2/(1.0750) - 1 = f_2$$

$$f_2 = 0.0810 \tag{10.4}$$

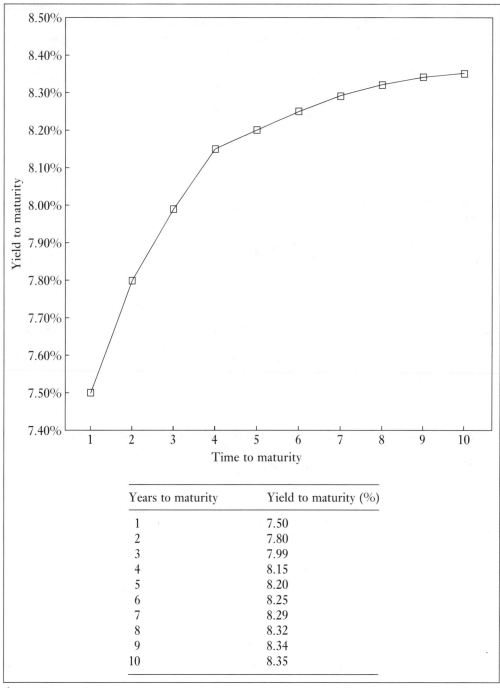

Years to maturity	Yield to maturity (%)
1	7.50
2	7.80
3	7.99
4	8.15
5	8.20
6	8.25
7	8.29
8	8.32
9	8.34
10	8.35

◆ Exhibit 10.2: Hypothetical yield curve

The implied future one-year rate for year 2, f_2, is 8.10 percent. The same procedure is followed to determine the implied one-year rate for year 3, f_3, and all the other short-term rates. (Year 3 begins two years from today and ends three years from today.) That is, increase the value of n by one year, substitute the values of known variables, and solve for f.

$$(1 + {}_0R_3)^3 = (1 + {}_0R_1)(1 + f_2)(1 + f_3)$$

$$(1.0799)^3 = (1.0750)(1.0810)(1 + f_3)$$

$$1.2594 = (1.1621)(1 + f_3)$$

$$1.2594/1.1621 - 1 = f_3$$

$$f_3 = 0.0837 \tag{10.4a}$$

To streamline the process, note that all the terms on the right-hand side of Equation (10.3) that precede $(1 + f_n)$ are equivalent to $(1 + {}_0R_{n-1})^{n-1}$.

$$(1 + {}_0R_n)^n = (1 + {}_0R_1)(1 + f_2)(1 + f_3) \ldots (1 + f_{n-1})(1 + f_n)$$

$$(1 + {}_0R_n)^n = (1 + {}_0R_{n-1})^{n-1}(1 + f_n)$$

Thus,

$$(1 + {}_0R_n)^n/(1 + {}_0R_{n-1})^{n-1} - 1 = f_n \tag{10.5}$$

To find the one-year rate implied for year 10, substitute the yields to maturity for ten- and nine-year bonds, respectively, in Equation (10.5).

$$(1.0835)^{10}/(1.0834)^9 - 1 = f_{10} = 0.0844$$

Equation (10.3) may also be used to infer yields for future multi-year periods. Suppose that the specific period of interest begins at time m and ends at time n, representing $(n - m)$ periods. Adapting Equation (10.3) to these circumstances:

$$(1 + {}_0R_n)^n = (1 + {}_0R_1)(1 + f_2) \ldots (1 + f_m)(1 + f_{m+1}) \ldots (1 + f_n) \tag{10.6}$$

where $(m + 1) < n$

Because time m is the *end* of year m, and

$$(1 + {}_0R_1)(1 + f_2) \ldots (1 + f_m) = (1 + {}_0R_m)^m \tag{10.7}$$

then

$$(1 + {}_0R_n)^n = (1 + {}_0R_m)^m(1 + {}_mR_n)^{(n-m)}$$

$$[(1 + {}_0R_n)^n/(1 + {}_0R_m)^m]^{1/(n-m)} - 1 = {}_mR_n \tag{10.8}$$

To illustrate, suppose that an investor wants to determine the yield to maturity during the four-year holding period beginning at time 6 (six years from now) and that Exhibit 10.2 describes the yield curve. In this case $m = 6$ and $(n - m) = 4$. The four-year yield implied by this curve is

$$[(1.0835)^{10}/(1.0825)^6]^{1/4} - 1 = 0.0850$$

This is the estimated yield to maturity (average annual rate of return) for the four-year period beginning at the end of period 6. It is the geometric average of the short-term rates implied by the yield curve.

Under the assumptions of unbiased expectations theory, an investor should be indifferent between holding one long-term security and holding a series of one-year securities because the terminal value is the same in either case. All long-term rates are simply averages of short-term rates. (In the real world, there are transactions costs associated with frequent buying and selling that work against true indifference.)

1.3.2 LIQUIDITY PREFERENCE THEORY

Unbiased expectations theory assumes that everyone in the market correctly anticipates interest rate changes, so that each can make appropriate portfolio adjustments. *Liquidity preference theory* suggests that investors cannot be absolutely certain about future changes in the interest rate environment. To the extent that they hold long-term securities, investors are more vulnerable to loss (Bond Theorem no. 5) and they must be compensated for exposure to this additional risk.

According to the liquidity preference theory, compensation for this greater price risk takes the form of risk premiums that increase as time to maturity increases. This means that even if actual future one-year rates, s_i, are all *equal*, the yield curve will still be upward sloping and the implied future one-year rates, f_i, will increase by the amount of the liquidity premiums.

$$(1 + {}_0R_n)^n = (1 + {}_0R_1)(1 + s_2 + L_2)(1 + s_3 + L_3) \ldots (1 + s_n + L_n) \tag{10.9}$$

where L_i = the liquidity premium applicable to period i, and $L_n > L_{n-1} > \ldots > L_2 > 0$
   $s_i + L_i = f_i$

Liquidity preference theory rests on somewhat more subjective assumptions than unbiased expectations theory because liquidity premiums are not necessarily the same for everyone. The theory does, nevertheless, predict the shape of the yield curve that has been most common in the United States – an upward sloping yield curve even if actual future rates are not expected to increase.

1.3.3 MARKET SEGMENTATION THEORY

Another approach to interest rate behavior is *market segmentation theory*, which suggests that investor time preferences involve more than price risk. That is, market participants operate essentially in one maturity band that is determined by their sources and uses of funds. For example, insurance companies and pension funds have liabilities that typically are long-term in nature. If managers of these entities invest in short-term asset portfolios, which are the least vulnerable to price risk, the company will face exposure to lower rates of return on investment that may be insufficient to service their liabilities. In other words, they face *reinvestment risk*, the potential loss of future income when short-term securities mature.

Other types of financial intermediaries (commercial banks, for example) often need assets with shorter average maturities. Their liabilities may be short-term and increases in the short-term cost of funds could quickly reduce profitability if longer-term assets are held with rates of return that are locked in at lower rates.

Market segmentation theory suggests that interest rates in a maturity band will depend on the supply of and demand for loanable funds with that maturity. Not everyone will prefer short-term securities nor will every investor prefer long-term securities.

The theory of *preferred habitat* is a compromise between market segmentation and unbiased expectations. This theory assumes that investors generally operate in the maturity class that is their preferred time horizon, that is, the maturity band in which they are most comfortable. However, sufficiently high interest rates in other maturity bands will lead them to switch.

Interest Rates and Inflation

Anticipated rates of inflation also help determine interest rate levels. *Inflation* is the loss of purchasing power of a currency. The net effect of inflation is that prices of goods and services increase, with no corresponding increase in quality or quantity.

Inflation rate:
> The percentage increase in prices of goods and services that results from the loss of purchasing power of a currency.

2.1 Price Indexes

Inflation rates are most frequently measured in terms of general price increases expressed as changes in *price indexes*.

Price index:
> The standardized value of a basket of goods and/or services.

2.1.1 TYPES OF PRICE INDEXES

Consumer price indexes measure prices of goods and services commonly purchased by individuals – food, shelter, clothing, for example. *Wholesale* price indexes refer to goods normally bought by businesses – raw materials, component parts, and finished goods. Indexes are calculated by picking a *base year* when the price of a basket, or list, of goods is set at an arbitrary number, perhaps, 100. (Technically, the aggregate price at the base year is divided by itself to form a ratio of 1 and the ratio is multiplied by 100.) If the aggregate price of the basket of goods the next year is 5 percent higher, the index value is 105. (The second-year aggregate price is divided by the first-year aggregate price and this ratio is multiplied by 100.) The inflation rate for a given year is the percentage change in a specific price index for that year. In the United States, the *Gross Domestic Product (GDP) deflator* is the most comprehensive indicator, as it includes all goods and services produced. Consumer indexes, however, are the more frequently quoted.

2.1.2 INTERNATIONAL COMPARISONS

Exhibit 10.3 shows consumer price indexes of six leading industrialized nations for the period 1980 through 1997, with 1980 as the base year.[1] Exhibit 10.4 provides the annual inflation rates

Year	US	Japan	UK	Germany	France	Italy
1980	100.0	100.0	100.0	100.0	100.0	100.0
1981	110.3	105.0	111.9	106.3	113.4	117.9
1982	117.1	107.9	121.5	111.9	126.9	137.3
1983	120.9	109.9	127.0	115.6	139.0	157.5
1984	126.1	112.4	133.4	118.4	149.4	174.5
1985	130.5	114.7	141.4	120.9	158.0	190.5
1986	133.0	115.4	146.3	120.8	161.9	201.7
1987	138.0	115.5	152.3	121.0	167.3	211.2
1988	143.5	116.3	159.8	122.6	171.9	221.9
1989	150.4	118.9	172.3	126.0	177.9	235.8
1990	158.5	122.6	188.7	129.4	183.9	251.0
1991	165.1	126.6	199.8	133.9	190.1	266.4
1992	170.2	128.8	207.2	139.2	194.7	279.9
1993	175.3	130.4	210.4	144.9	198.7	292.5
1994	179.7	131.3	215.7	149.3	202.0	304.3
1995	184.8	131.1	223.0	151.9	205.5	320.3
1996	192.1	131.6	230.0	156.4	210.3	334.8
1997	196.5	133.8	237.1	159.2	212.8	341.5

◆ **Exhibit 10.3:** Consumer price indexes, selected industrialized countries, 1980–97

◆ *Source*: Derrick Johnson of H. J. Johnson & Associates, based on data from: International Monetary Fund, *International Financial Statistics*.

Year	US	Japan	UK	Germany	France	Italy
1981	10.31%	5.05%	11.88%	6.29%	13.43%	17.90%
1982	6.15	2.73	8.60	5.23	11.84	16.48
1983	3.23	1.81	4.54	3.35	9.59	14.70
1984	4.32	2.30	5.01	2.41	7.50	10.76
1985	3.52	2.04	6.04	2.15	5.71	9.17
1986	1.90	0.60	3.40	−0.10	2.50	5.90
1987	3.73	0.10	4.16	0.20	3.32	4.72
1988	3.97	0.70	4.92	1.30	2.74	5.05
1989	4.82	2.27	7.79	2.76	3.49	6.27
1990	5.38	3.09	9.52	2.69	3.37	6.46
1991	4.19	3.26	5.89	3.47	3.35	6.14
1992	3.07	1.74	3.68	3.96	2.42	5.08
1993	2.98	1.24	1.55	4.09	2.08	4.48
1994	2.53	0.66	2.51	3.04	1.67	4.03
1995	2.82	−0.09	3.41	1.73	1.73	5.27
1996	3.95	0.37	3.13	2.98	2.33	4.54
1997	2.30	1.67	3.09	1.79	1.19	2.00

◆ **Exhibit 10.4:** Inflation rates, selected industrialized countries, 1981–97 (percentages)

◆ *Source*: Derrick Johnson of H. J. Johnson & Associates, based on data from: International Monetary Fund, *International Financial Statistics*.

implied by these index values. In 1981, the rate of inflation in the US exceeded 10 percent. Purchasing power losses were even more pronounced in Italy (17.90 percent), France (13.43 percent), and the United Kingdom (11.88 percent). A major contributing factor to the high levels of inflation during the early 1980s was significant increases in oil prices during the 1970s, reflected in both consumer and wholesale prices. Inflation rates have declined since that time, but while they persisted, market rates of interest also reached record levels.

2.2 THE FISHER EFFECT

To see the relationship between market rates of interest and inflation rates, consider a simple example. Suppose a buyer wants to purchase an item one year from today because it will not be needed until that time and storage cost in the interim is prohibitively high. Assume that the current price of the item is $110 and that the buyer decides to invest $100 now so that it will grow sufficiently in one year to cover the cost of the item. Assuming no inflation, the market interest rate that must be earned is 10 percent, that is, 10 percent is the minimum required rate of return.

Inflation will have an impact on minimum required return. If the inflation rate is expected to be 5 percent, the price of the item will be $115.50 at the end of the year [(110)(1.05) = 115.50]. The buyer now requires a higher rate of return to preserve the same amount of purchasing power. A 5 percent increase (the rate of inflation) is not sufficient because a 15 percent rate would produce only $115 at year-end, $0.50 less than the required amount. Both the original investment (principal) *and* the rate of return (interest) must increase by 5 percent to obtain the desired result.

$$100(1.10)(1.05) = 115.50 \qquad (10.10)$$

This relationship is known as the *Fisher effect*, developed by Irving Fisher. Fisher describes market rates as *nominal* rates of return, made up of elements of *real return* and *inflation premium*.

$$(1 + r^*)(1 + I) = (1 + k) \qquad (10.11)$$

where r^* = real rate of interest
$\quad I$ = expected rate of inflation
$\quad k$ = nominal (market) rate of interest

The inflation premium becomes $(I + Ir^*)$ or 0.055 in the example above.[2] The cross-term Ir^* is small (0.005 in the example), and, in practice, is usually disregarded.

The real rate of return, not the nominal rate, is important to an investor. Real rates indicate the increases in value of one's resources, the inflation premium merely restores lost purchasing power.

2.3 NOMINAL AND REAL RATES OF RETURN IN SELECTED COUNTRIES

Government securities entail minimal default risk, making them useful examples of historical real rates of return. Exhibit 10.5 shows 17 years of nominal rates of return on government securities of the six industrialized nations included in Exhibits 10.3 and 10.4.

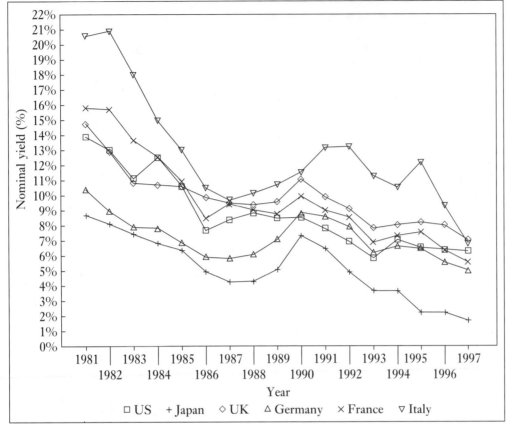

◆ **Exhibit 10.5:** Government bond nominal yields, selected industrialized countries, 1981–97

◆ *Source*:   Derrick Johnson of H. J. Johnson & Associates, based on data from: International Monetary Fund, *International Financial Statistics*.

- The highest bond yields in 1981 were offered by Italy (20.6 percent) and France (15.8 percent), the two countries with the highest inflation rates for that year (see Exhibit 10.4). The United Kingdom and the United States followed with nominal yields of 14.7 percent and 13.9 percent, respectively. Germany and Japan, with the lowest 1981 inflation rates, also had the lowest government bond yields (10.4 percent and 8.7 percent, respectively).
- Over the 17-year period, government bond nominal yields in most countries declined as inflation subsided, an illustration of the Fisher effect. A notable exception to this general trend is Italy, where long-term government bond yields reached a low of 9.68 percent in 1987, climbed to 13.3 percent in 1992, then moderated to 6.9 percent in 1997.
- Over the 17-year period, Japan had the lowest interest rates, falling to 1.7 percent in 1997.
- Until 1990, German interest rates were the second lowest among the countries shown. Beginning in 1990, German government bond rates were maintained at levels higher than those in

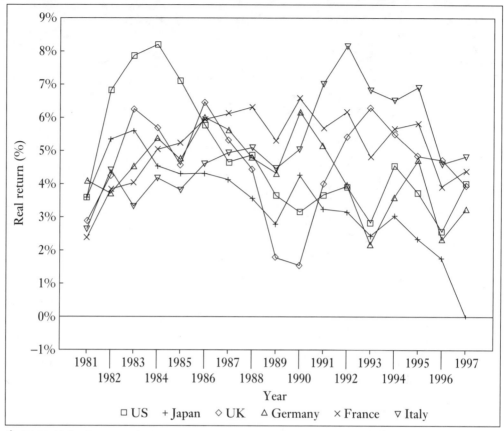

◆ **Exhibit 10.6:** Government bond real returns, selected industrialized countries, 1981–97

◆ *Source*:   Derrick Johnson of H. J. Johnson & Associates, based on data from: International Monetary Fund, *International Financial Statistics*.

the United States. This relationship was reversed in 1994. In the early 1990s, the US monetary authorities maintained an interest rate environment to stimulate a sluggish economy. At the same time German authorities sought to (1) combat inflation and (2) continue to attract capital to the newly reunified German economy. (West Germany and East Germany were reunified in October 1990.)

Contrast Exhibit 10.5 with Exhibit 10.6, which plots the approximate annual real rates of return for the same group of countries over the same period. The real rate of return, of course, is the nominal yield less the inflation rate, where the inflation rate is expressed as the percentage change in the consumer price index for the year. (Technically, the inflation premium is the *average anticipated* inflation rate for the time period that is relevant for the observed interest rate.)

From 1982 through 1985, the United States offered the highest real rate of return (from 6.8 percent in 1982 to a high of 8.2 percent in 1984). In other words, the decrease in nominal rates shown in Exhibit 10.5 was more than offset by US inflation rate declines, producing an increase in real rates in the United States. In Italy and France – the two countries in the group with the highest *nominal* yields shown in Exhibit 10.5 – 1982–5 real rates were considerably lower than in the United States.

In the second half of the 1980s, nominal yields in the United States dropped and the inflation rate increased. As a result, the US real rate of return had declined to 3.2 percent by 1990. When nominal interest rates increased in 1994, real rates of interest also increased.

In the United Kingdom nominal rates increased, as Exhibit 10.5 shows, but inflation increased even more, so that the real return dropped below 2 percent in 1989 and 1990. During the 1990s, however, real rates improved because inflation was better contained. In the late 1990s, the real rate of return on UK government bonds ranged from 4 to 5 percent.

In France, where the inflation rate stayed under 3.5 percent, nominal yields (then roughly equivalent to those in the United States) delivered real rates of return that were consistently higher than those in the United States during the second half of the decade. In 1997, US and French real government yields were roughly equivalent – 4.0 and 4.4 percent, respectively.

In the early 1990s, real rates of return on Italian government bonds were considerably higher than those in the other countries shown because nominal Italian yields were maintained at relatively high levels (Exhibit 10.5) while inflation was more controlled than in the early 1980s. In 1996 and 1997, Italian real government yields were close to those of the United Kingdom and France.

With the exception of Japan, the other countries had nominal bond yields that almost appeared to converge during the 1990s (Exhibit 10.5). However, differential inflation rates caused the real rates of return to vary considerably over the same period (Exhibit 10.6).

Controlling inflation is a critical concern for every country because only competitive *real* rates of return attract investment capital that is needed to sustain economic development. Moreover, high rates of inflation make it difficult for individual households to maintain a given standard of living and more costly for corporations to obtain needed funds for operations and investment.

 ## Summary

Evidence supports the ideas that interest rates are determined by supply and demand for money of a particular maturity (market segmentation theory), by expectations of future short-term rates (unbiased expectations theory), and by preferences to avoid the uncertainty of future investment opportunities (liquidity preference theory). These theories address the question of why interest rates have a certain pattern relative to time to maturity. The behavior of interest rates is important because the value of fixed-income securities, bonds, is closely related to this behavior. Bond prices will equal their par values only when the market rate equals a bond's coupon rate. When this is not the case, bonds sell at discounts or premiums, with bond prices moving in the opposite direction of market interest rate changes.

Expectations of changes in price levels (inflation) have a direct bearing on the magnitude of interest rate changes. Changes in price levels are measured by changes in consumer and wholesale indexes, or prices of specified baskets of goods and services. Inflation reduces the real rate of return, the difference between nominal yield and rate of inflation. When countries have difficulty controlling inflation, the lower real rates of return make their capital markets less appealing to domestic and international investors.

End-of-chapter Questions

1. What are the variables that define a yield curve? Explain their meaning.
2. What is the major difference between unbiased expectations theory and liquidity preference theory of interest rates?
3. What is the basic premise of market segmentation theory?
4. What process would you use to convert the price indexes in Exhibit 10.3 so that the 1985 value was 100?
5. Why do bond issuers attempt to estimate the rate of return required by the market for their new bonds and set this as the coupon rate?
6. Suppose that you are a bond portfolio manager. If you believe that interest rates are going to increase,
   a. What effect will this have on the value of the bond portfolio?
   b. What maturity preference do you have (short-term vs. long-term)?
7. Consider the manner in which an investment grows over time and explain why you think that interest rate theory uses the geometric mean of short-term interest rates instead of the arithmetic mean (simple average).
8. In terms of the liquidity preference theory, why should liquidity premiums increase over time?
9. If nominal interest rates increase as inflation expectations increase, why should individuals' standard of living necessarily suffer in an environment of high inflation rates?
10. During the early 1980s, the United States attracted large amounts of overseas capital despite federal budget deficits (expenditures in excess of revenues) and large trade deficits (imports in excess of exports). Why do you think this was so?

End-of-chapter Problems

1. Select a publicly traded corporate bond, determine its rating (available through business library references), and chart its default risk premium using end-of-month yields for the last two years.
2. Construct a yield curve using US Treasury securities quoted in the financial press.

3. Obtain the most recent edition of *International Financial Statistics* (published by the International Monetary Fund) in your school's library. Compute the real rates of return on government bonds for the six countries covered in this chapter and compare them to the rates in Exhibit 10.6.

4. According to unbiased expectations theory and the yield curve shown in Exhibit 10.2, calculate the estimates of:

   a. the short-term rate anticipated for the year beginning at time 3 and ending at time 4 (f_4).

   b. the rate applicable to the 3-year holding period beginning at time 3 and ending at time 6 ($_3R_6$).

5. Considering the Fisher effect, what nominal rate of return would a government security have to yield in order to provide a 2 percent real rate of return when the rate of inflation is expected to be 5 percent.

Notes

1   Together, the countries shown in Exhibit 10.3 control a large share of the world's domestic financial markets. In 1995, their stock markets represented 83 percent of stock market capitalization of all industrialized countries. (See *Emerging Stock Markets Factbook 1996*.)

2
$$(1 + r^*)(1 + I) = (1 + k)$$
$$1 + r^* + I + Ir^* = (1 + k)$$
$$r^* + I + Ir^* = k$$

Selected References

Benoit, J. Pierre V. *United States Interest Rates and the Interest Rate Dilemma for the Developing World*, Quorum Books, Westport, Conn., 1986.

Brigham, Eugene F. *Fundamentals of Financial Management*, 5th edn, Dryden Press, Hinsdale, Ill., 1989.

Cohen, Jerome B., Edward D. Zinbarg, and Arthur Zeikel. *Investment Analysis and Portfolio Management*, 5th edn, Richard D. Irwin, Homewood, Ill., 1987.

Emerging Stock Markets Factbook 1996. International Finance Corporation, Washington, DC, 1996.

Falkena, H. B., L. J. Fourie, and W. J. Kok, eds. *The Mechanics of the South African Financial System: Financial Institutions, Instruments, and Markets*, Macmillan South Africa, Johannesburg, 1984.

Havrilesky, Thomas M. and Robert Schweitzer, eds. *Contemporary Developments in Financial Institutions and Markets*, Harlan Davidson, Arlington Heights, Ill., 1987.

Homer, Sydney. *A History of Interest Rates*, 2nd edn, Rutgers University Press, New Brunswick, NJ, 1977.

International Financial Statistics, International Monetary Fund, Washington, DC, various issues.

Nelson, Charles R. *The Term Structure of Interest Rates*, Basic Books, New York, 1972.

chapter 11

Interest and Exchange Rate Patterns

⬤ CHAPTER OVERVIEW

This chapter:
- Discusses the influence of default risk on interest rates.
- Measures default risk premiums over time.
- Outlines default risk, interest rates, and other factors that affect foreign exchange rates.

⬤ KEY TERMS

balance of payments
bond rating
currency board
default risk
default risk premium

investment grade securities
purchasing power parity
real
unit of real value (URV)

⬤ CHAPTER OUTLINE

INTERNATIONAL COMPARISONS:

Argentina	Italy
Brazil	Japan
France	Mexico
Germany	United Kingdom

 ## Introduction

Chapter 10 showed that interest rates during specific periods of time depend on anticipated inflation rates and investor preferences. Interest rates also depend on the characteristics of individual borrowers. When the likelihood that a borrower will default on a financial obligation is high, the interest rate that borrower must pay will also be relatively high. These default risk premiums increase when general economic conditions are more uncertain.

Interest rates, inflation, and foreign exchange rates are all linked in markets that are becoming more integrated. A country's currency exchange rate will be influenced by a number of factors. Domestic inflation will tend to depreciate a currency. The balance of payments (difference between exports and imports) also causes exchange rates to adjust somewhat automatically when currency values are permitted to float, that is, are not fixed. All other things being equal, higher domestic interest rates attract foreign capital and increase the value of domestic currency. Capital flows can reverse quickly, however, so currency markets are volatile. Changing budget and trade circumstances will make a currency more or less attractive at a particular time.

 ## Default Risk

Default risk affects interest rates just as inflation does. While inflation is an economywide factor, default risk is specific to the borrower. Debt instruments issued by most government bodies are virtually free of default risk, but the perceived default risk of other borrowers varies.

> **Default risk:**
> The risk that a borrower may not repay principal and/or interest as originally agreed.

1.1 BOND RATINGS

Corporate debt in the United States is evaluated by rating agencies, most notably Standard & Poor's Corporation (S&P) and Moody's Investors Service. (Other rating services include Fitch Investor's Service and Duff & Phelps.) S&P bond ratings range from AAA to D.

AAA: Highest rating, suggesting extremely strong ability to pay principal and interest.

AA: High-quality issuance with very strong repayment capacity, differing from AAA only by a small degree

A: Upper medium grade with strong capacity to pay principal and interest but somewhat more susceptible to adverse economic conditions

BBB: Medium grade with adequate capacity to pay principal and interest but more susceptible to adverse economic conditions than firms in the A category

BB, B, CCC, CC, C:

Ability to pay principal and interest is to a greater or lesser degree speculative:

- BB – predominantly speculative
- B – speculative, low grade
- CCC – poor quality
- CC – high speculation
- C – highest speculation

CI: Rated debt instrument is an income bond on which interest is not being paid, lowest quality. (An income bond pays interest only if the issuing firm earns enough income.)

DDD, DD, D:

Bond is in default and principal and/or interest are in arrears:

- DDD – in default (issuer's failure to meet one or more of the contractual obligations of the bond indenture)
- DD – in arrears (bond interest due but unpaid)
- D – questionable value

Standard & Poor's also assigns + or − to ratings in order to further differentiate bond quality. Moody's ratings are similar. For example:

S&P's rating	Moody's rating
AAA	Aaa
AA+	Aa1
AA	Aa2
AA−	Aa3
A+	A1
A	A2
A−	A3
BBB+	Baa1
BBB	Baa2
BBB−	Baa3
BB+	Ba1
BB	Ba2
BB-	Ba3
B+	B1
B	B2
B−	B3
CCC+	
CCC	Caa
CCC−	
CC	Ca
C	C

Ratings are based on a number of *quantitative* and *qualitative* criteria. Basic quantitative considerations include the firm's debt and its debt servicing capacity. Structural aspects of bond issues are also evaluated – mortgage, subordination, guarantee provisions, sinking fund, and maturity – as applicable. Quantitative factors that are relevant to the firm's particular operating environment may include sales stability and unfunded pension liabilities. (See also chapter 29 for a discussion of pension fund financing.) Qualitative factors that are important to the operating environment include labor relations, resource availability, government regulatory issues, environmental issues, and political risk exposure in overseas operations.

Bonds rated AAA through BBB are considered *investment grade* securities. In the United States, many financial institutions are not allowed to invest in securities other than investment grade – commercial banks, fiduciaries (who administer investments for others), mutual savings banks, and trust companies (corporations that accept and execute trust funds). From an issuer's perspective, the higher bond ratings mean that investors will require lower rates of return. Understandably, firms are careful to protect their bond ratings.

1.2 DEFAULT RISK PREMIUMS

The *default risk premium* associated with debt issues has consistently had an inverse relationship with bond ratings. The higher the bond rating, the lower the necessary compensation to the bondholder. Higher-rated firms are subject to lower risk premiums, although the size of the premiums has varied over time.

> **Default risk premium:**
> The component of a required interest rate based on the borrower's perceived risk of default. All other things being equal, it is the difference between the bond's required rate of return and the risk-free (government security) rate.

Exhibit 11.1 graphs the yields (interest rates) for US Treasuries, Aaa-rated corporate bonds, and Baa-rated corporate bonds for the period 1961 through 1998. (The corporate ratings are by Moody's. They correspond to S&P's AAA and BBB, respectively.) Notice that rates peak in the early 1980s – a period of time associated with high inflation rates as discussed in chapter 10 (see Exhibit 10.4). Notice also that the differences between the rates, the risk premiums, are not constant. During periods of difficult economic conditions, risk premiums increase.

Exhibit 11.2, which is based on the information in Exhibit 11.1, shows for each year the difference between the corporate bond rate and the rate for US Treasuries. In 1961, both interest rates and risk premiums were low. The premium of Aaa bonds over Treasuries was 45 basis points; the Baa premium over Treasuries was 118 basis points. (A basis point is one hundredth of one percent.) Four years later in 1965, rates were at approximately the same levels, but risk premiums were even lower.

Both interest rates and risk premiums increased over time until, by 1975, the Aaa risk premium was 185 basis points and the premium for Baa bonds 363 basis points. There were also relatively high premiums during the early 1980s. Notice, too, that the risk premium of Baa bonds increased by more than the risk premium for Aaa bonds. The Baa bond premium increased from 160 basis

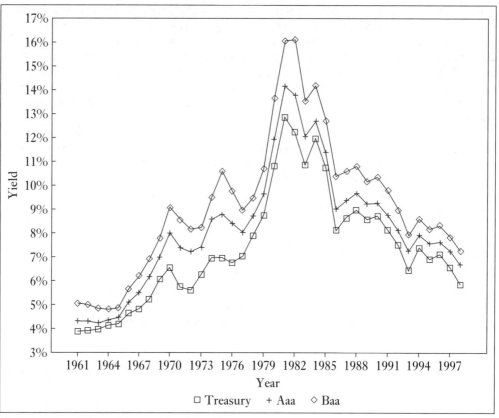

◆ **Exhibit 11.1: US bond yields by rating, 1961–98**

◆ *Source*:   Derrick Johnson of H. J. Johnson & Associates, based on data from: US Department of
              Commerce, Bureau of Economic Analysis, *Business Statistics 1961–1988* and *Survey of
              Current Business*; *Federal Reserve Bulletin*, various issues.

points in 1978 to 388 basis points by 1982 (a difference of 228 basis points). Over the same period,
the Aaa premium rose from 84 basis points to 156 basis points (a difference of only 72 basis
points).

Both the size of risk premiums and the difference in premiums (for example, Aaa risk premium
vs. Baa risk premium) are related to economic conditions. The first round of international crude
oil price increases in 1973 and 1974 caused general concern that all bond issuers would be
adversely affected by the resulting higher cost of operations and risk premiums increased. Presumably, the less creditworthy borrowers would be affected even more severely, necessitating an even
higher risk premium.

Similar concerns were raised in the early 1980s. Crude oil price increases in 1979 again affected
the cost of operations, but, in this case, the situation was complicated further by extremely high
interest rates. While the risk premium for Aaa bonds rose to almost the same level as in 1975, the
Baa premium rose even higher than its 1975 level. As interest rates eased in the 1980s, risk
premiums also dropped.

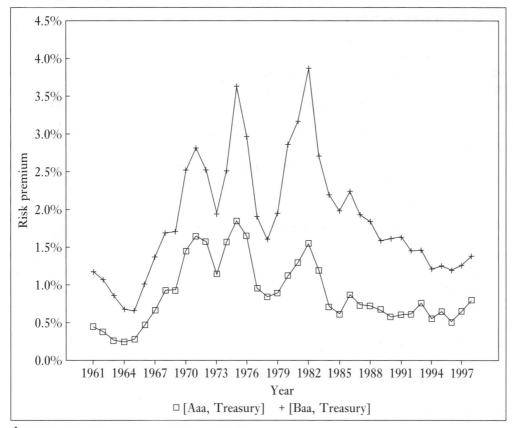

◆ **Exhibit 11.2: Risk premiums on US bonds, 1961–98**

◆ *Source*: Derrick Johnson of H. J. Johnson & Associates, based on data from: US Department of Commerce, Bureau of Economic Analysis, *Business Statistics 1961–1988* and *Survey of Current Business*; *Federal Reserve Bulletin*, various issues.

In the early 1990s, US monetary authorities maintained a generally low interest rate environment. In 1994, interest rates rose and remained higher than the 1993 levels through 1996. In 1997 and 1998, interest rates fell while risk premiums rose slightly. Essentially, in 1997 and 1998, Treasury rates fell faster than corporate bond rates.

② Factors Influencing Currency Exchange Rates

An important element of a nation's international economic well-being is how the value of its currency changes relative to others. Chapter 8 showed that interest rates influence forward currency exchange rates in a relationship referred to as *interest rate parity*. Chapter 10 showed that inflation affects domestic interest rates, thereby also affecting *forward exchange* rates through interest rate parity.

2.1 PURCHASING POWER PARITY

Spot exchange rates will also reflect inflation rate differentials, *if* exchange rates are allowed to adjust freely. High rates of inflation generally will cause a currency to lose value, all other things being equal. This concept is called *purchasing power parity*. Over the long term, purchasing power parity satisfactorily explains exchange rate changes. In the short-term, however, it is less successful.

Purchasing Power Parity:
> The concept that homogeneous goods cannot have more than one price measured in any one currency. If the price increases domestically, the domestic currency will depreciate so that the price of the goods denominated in a foreign currency remains the same. This is the *law of one price*.

The connection between theory and practice breaks down for several reasons in the short term. Technically, only goods that are traded internationally should be subject to the Law of One Price. It is also not always clear how differences in service and quality of goods are accounted for. Price increases are not necessarily uniform over all products.

2.2 OTHER FACTORS

Other fundamental factors that influence spot currency exchange rates are:

- Trade imbalances
- Capital flows
- Domestic interest rates
- Political factors

Movements of goods and services across national borders are recorded in a country's *balance of payments*, a summary of international financial activity.

Balance of payments:
> The description of financial transactions between a country and its trading partners. The categories include goods (merchandise), services, and investment capital.

Categories of merchandise and their Standard International Trade Classifications (SITCs) are:[1]

1) Food and live animals
2) Beverages and tobacco
3) Crude material excluding fuels
4) Animal and vegetable oil

5) Chemicals
6) Basic manufactures
7) Transport equipment machines

Service categories include payments for:

- Professional and other business services
- Insurance and freight
- Interest payments
- Direct investment income

Transactions that are classified as investment capital include:

- Short-term loans
- Long-term loans and other securities
- Direct investment (equity capital)

If a country receives more funds than it disburses, the country has a *surplus* for the period. If the reverse is true, a *deficit* results.

Trade (goods and services) imbalances exert fundamental pressure on exchange rates that does not reverse itself. When a country imports more than it exports, downward pressure is exerted on the domestic currency value. This is true because paying for the *imports* creates a *demand* for foreign currency to pay for the imports. On the other hand, *exports* create a *supply* of foreign currency that must be converted into the domestic currency to pay for the exports. When a nation experiences a trade deficit (imports in excess of exports), the demand for foreign currency (from imports) is only partially offset by the supply (from exports). The excess demand for foreign currency places upward pressure on foreign currency value and downward pressure on domestic currency value. A trade surplus has the opposite effect.

The effects of *capital flows* are generally reversible. When funds are borrowed abroad in a foreign currency, for example, demand for the foreign currency increases, exerting upward pressure on the foreign currency value. When the loan is repaid, the relative supply of the foreign currency increases, with the opposite effect on its value.

All other things being equal, increases in *domestic interest rates* tend to attract foreign capital and create stronger demand for domestic currency. When domestic interest rates decline, foreign capital may be reinvested in another country (and another currency), generating weaker demand for the domestic currency.

Although they may be less quantifiable than trade imbalances, capital flows, and interest rates, *political factors* also play a significant role in exchange rate fluctuations. Political stability has a favorable effect on the value of a country's currency. Stability implies that orderly markets for goods and services will prevail and that business transactions (for example, goods delivery and payments) will be completed as negotiated and contracted. Loss of stability, or even *perceived* loss of stability, depresses domestic currency value.

The value of the domestic currency can affect different market sectors in different ways. High and increasing domestic currency values benefit importing sectors, because domestic currency then has relatively more purchasing power abroad. At the same time, exporting sectors may find that their goods are not competitively priced in an international sense because the high currency value makes their products more expensive overseas in domestic currency terms.

Domestic price levels and interest rates, trade balances, international capital flows, and political factors all influence currency values and can lead to frequent changes in exchange rates.

 Recent Patterns of Currency Exchange Rates

3.1 EXCHANGE RATES DURING THE 1980s AND 1990s – SELECTED CURRENCIES

In the early 1980s, high interest rates in the United States attracted capital from industrialized and developing nations alike. Federal budget deficits rose from $79 billion in 1981 to $128 billion in 1982 and $208 billion in 1983. The US government's high demand for funds in the capital market caused government bond yields to increase.

The phenomenon of high nominal rates accompanied by low inflation is attributable in part to substantial inflows of foreign capital to the United States, a safe haven for investment dollars. This attraction became even stronger when the Tax Reform Act of 1984 eliminated the 30 percent withholding tax on new government and corporate bonds issued in the United States and sold to foreign investors. The value of the dollar reflected this inflow of capital invested in US financial instruments. As can be seen in Exhibit 11.3, the dollar value of other major currencies dropped dramatically. The dollar appreciated on the order of 30 to 40 percent against most major currencies in the early 1980s.

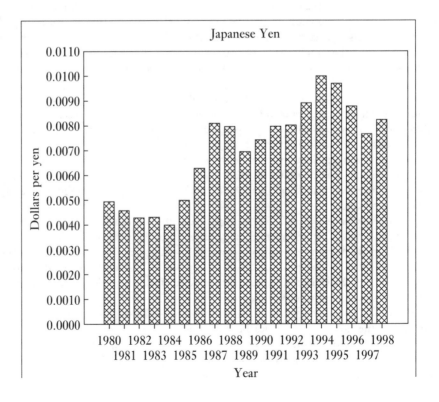

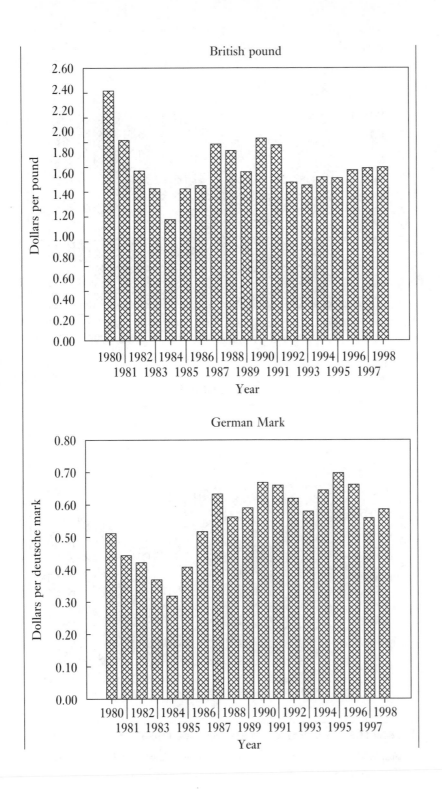

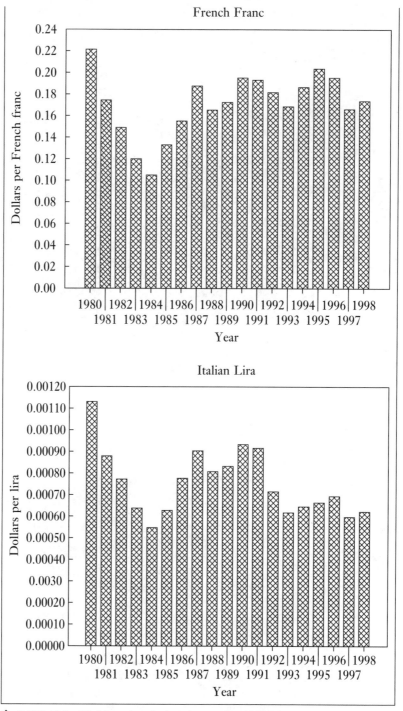

◆ **Exhibit 11.3:** US dollar value of selected currencies, 1980–98

◆ *Source*: Derrick Johnson of H. J. Johnson & Associates, based on data from: International Monetary Fund, *International Financial Statistics*.

This dramatic appreciation was possible because of the floating rate system that had been adopted in the early 1970s. The high value of the dollar, of course, was detrimental to the US manufacturing export sector and trade deficits reached alarming levels. The Federal Reserve had the unenviable task of lowering the value of the dollar while not significantly discouraging providers of foreign capital.

In September 1985, the finance ministers and central bankers of the major industrial countries met at the Plaza Hotel in New York and agreed to facilitate the orderly appreciation of non-dollar currencies. The Plaza Agreement marked the beginning of the decline in the value of the dollar. US government bond yields and associated real returns fell. The dollar value of foreign currencies increased accordingly.

However, the other currencies appreciated more than originally anticipated and central bankers in other countries attempted to stop the decline in the value of the US dollar. Despite massive dollar purchases by foreign central banks, the dollar continued to slide. At their meeting early in 1987, the financial ministers and central bankers agreed to help slow the dollar decline (the Louvre Accord). Exchange rates moderated in 1988 and 1989.

In 1990 and 1991, the low interest rate environment maintained by US monetary authorities resulted in a weaker dollar *vis-à-vis* all the currencies shown in Exhibit 11.3. This effect was compounded by the relatively high interest rates maintained in Germany to attract capital to the newly reunified country (see Exhibits 10.5 and 10.6). (In October 1990, East Germany and West Germany were reunified, having been separated at the end of the Second World War (1939–45).)

Then, in 1992, the currency markets were shocked by a crisis in the Exchange Rate Mechanism (ERM) of the European Union. (See also chapter 9.) The ERM requires its members to maintain their currency values within certain prescribed limits. As the German currency appreciated because of a strong economy and high German interest rates, other ERM members were forced (1) to keep interest rates relatively high and (2) to intervene in currency markets (buy their own currencies) to maintain domestic currency values. However, high interest rates strained the economies of other European countries and currency market intervention drained their official reserves.

In September 1992, the United Kingdom and Denmark pulled out of the ERM. The chaos which ensued in the ERM for a brief period caused the US dollar to appreciate in 1992 and 1993 against the British pound, the Italian lira, the German mark, and the French franc (higher dollar value of the currencies).

From 1993 through 1996, the dollar values of the pound and the lira were relatively stable, while the French franc and the German mark benefitted from remaining uncertainty within the ERM (higher dollar value of the currencies). During the same period, large US trade deficits with Japan were reflected in a strong yen (higher dollar value of the Japanese currency).

In 1997 and 1998, uncertainty in global financial markets began with weaknesses in Asian currencies in the summer of 1997. Sometimes referred to as the "Asian contagion," concerns over economic fundamentals affected all emerging markets during this period. International money managers sought safety in a flight to quality that generally favored the US dollar and US dollar-denominated government securities. This demand for US dollars lowered the dollar value of most currencies during 1997 and 1998. The active demand for US government securities also lowered the yields associated with them, as reflected in Exhibit 11.1.

The exchange rate volatility during the 1980s and 1990s underscores the market's sensitivity to real economic factors. Lower interest rates and persistent trade deficits in the 1980s brought the value of the US dollar down as quickly as high interest rates and tax incentives had pushed it up. In the early 1990s, economic uncertainty in the EU benefitted the "safe haven" currencies of the

US dollar and the German mark. Continued imbalance in the bilateral trade relationship between the United States and Japan resulted in a strong yen in the early 1990s. With global economic uncertainty in the late 1990s, the safe haven qualities of the US dollar again contributed to its relative value. It appears that volatility is a necessary tradeoff to avoid the financial market chaos that characterized the last days of Bretton Woods – the system of pegged exchange rates that began in 1944 and ended in 1971 when the United States abandoned the gold standard.

3.2 THE CASE OF LATIN AMERICA

Floating exchange rates will not necessarily prevent financial chaos. Latin America is a case in point.

3.2.1 EXTERNAL DEBT AND INFLATION

As crude oil prices increased in the 1970s, many developing countries found the value of their exports insufficient to cover the cost of the oil they needed, while oil-exporting countries found themselves with large trade surpluses to invest. In many cases, these surpluses were deposited in commercial banks and then loaned to oil-importing countries or *recycled* to help developing oil-importing countries cover their oil-import-driven trade deficits. As a result, external debt levels rose significantly.

From 1970 through 1980, the external debt (debt owed to foreign lenders) of all developing countries rose from $66.9 billion to $572.2 billion. Of the 1980 total, Latin American and the Caribbean countries owed $242.7 billion or 42 percent. Just two years later, the external debt of all developing countries had grown by almost $200 billion to $752.9 billion, with Latin America and the Caribbean representing $333.5 billion or 44 percent, an even higher percentage of quickly growing debt levels. In 1982, among the Latin American countries, Argentina ($43.6 billion), Brazil ($92.2 billion), and Mexico ($86.0 billion) accounted for $221.8 billion of external debt.

Mexico was actually an oil exporter, but the country borrowed heavily against future oil revenues to finance infrastructure and industrial development projects. The effect of having so much external debt was that a large proportion of export earnings went to service the debt. When the price of oil dropped precipitously, Mexico's oil export earnings could no longer cover its interest and principal payments.

In 1982, Mexico announced that it could not make its payments and the serious overburden of debt in many developing countries was recognized. Since that time, the governments and banks involved, along with international organizations such as the IMF and the World Bank, have worked to resolve the problem. (See chapter 20 for a discussion of the IMF and the World Bank.) Meanwhile, new debt was required to make the payments on old debt and the mountain of debt only continued to grow. In 1995, Argentina ($89.7 billion), Brazil ($159.1 billion), and Mexico ($165.7 billion) owed a total of $414.5 billion to foreign lenders. (See Exhibit 11.4.)

Debt payments were rescheduled (delayed) and, in the case of Mexico, some debt was forgiven. All three countries adopted austerity measures that included reducing imports, some of which would have been used for capital investment. The almost continual debt renegotiation discouraged new investment from outside the region and some of the capital already invested was moved to safer havens.

These developments caused the demand for the currencies of Argentina, Brazil, and Mexico to evaporate. Exhibit 11.5 provides a summary of the dollar values of their currencies from 1981 through 1990, reflecting the hyperinflation rates in these countries. The value of the Mexican peso went from 3.8¢ to 0.02¢. Argentina's currency value fell from the equivalent of over $1,000 to less

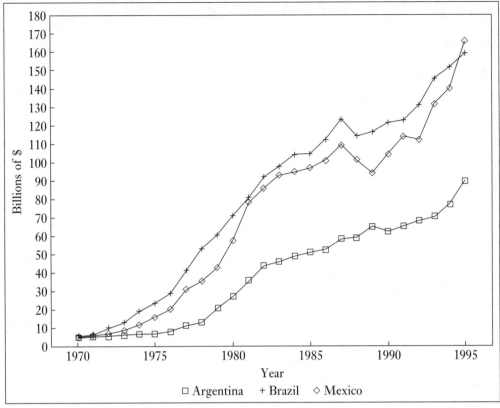

◆ **Exhibit 11.4:** External debt, Argentina, Brazil, and Mexico, 1970–95

◆ *Source*: Derrick Johnson of H. J. Johnson & Associates, based on data from: World Bank, *World Bank Debt Tables 1989–90*, *Trends in Developing Economies 1989*, *World Bank Debt Tables, 1994*, and *World Bank Debt Tables 1997*; United Nations, *Economic Survey of Latin American and the Caribbean 1988*.

Year	Argentina	Brazil	Mexico
1981	1163.960000	7682.307690	0.038168
1982	551.555000	4000.000000	0.010363
1983	43.622900	1020.408160	0.006949
1984	4.734080	314.465400	0.005192
1985	1.249624	95.328880	0.002690
1986	0.795312	67.114090	0.001083
1987	0.266670	13.840830	0.000453
1988	0.074794	1.306677	0.000438
1989	0.000557	0.088044	0.000379
1990	0.000179	0.005648	0.000239

◆ **Exhibit 11.5:** Exchange rates, Argentina, Brazil, and Mexico, 1981–90 (US dollars per unit of local currency)

◆ *Source*: Author's calculations based on data from: International Monetary Fund, *International Financial Statistics*.

than a penny. (The peso was converted to the peso Argentino in 1983. The peso Argentino was converted to the austral in 1985.) The Brazilian cruzeiro plummeted from the equivalent of over $7,000 to less than a penny.

Then in the early 1990s, each of these countries adopted economic reforms. Part of each reform package was a strategy for controlling inflation and restoring stability to the domestic currency.

3.2.2 ARGENTINA

Before 1991, Argentina suffered with 2,000 percent inflation per year, a product of its high external debt and associated inability to repay. In 1991, Argentina executed the Convertibility Plan which pegged the Argentine peso to the US dollar on a 1-to-1 basis. In addition, the plan required that the central bank hold one US dollar in reserve for every peso printed. International financial markets generally have responded favorably. Devaluation of the currency is now considered a much lower risk.

Under Argentina's currency board system, domestic money can only be issued if it is fully backed by foreign reserves. In a classic *currency board system*, there is no central bank. Instead, a monetary authority issues domestic currency at the fixed rate of exchange against foreign reserves. In the case of Argentina, there is a functioning central bank. Also in Argentina, the foreign reserves that can be used to back the Argentine peso include government bonds denominated in foreign currency to a limited extent. Argentine citizens are free to hold either dollars or pesos.

3.2.3 BRAZIL

Before 1993, Brazil operated under a number of short-lived, ill-fated plans to restore monetary order. The objective of all these plans was to curb inflation, strengthen the economy, and attract foreign investment. None of them were successful because, under the early plans, the government froze prices, unilaterally determined price changes, and confiscated financial assets. Then, in 1993, the Brazilian government instituted a comprehensive reform program that acknowledged its major contributing role to the country's inflation. The three-phase plan to restore economic stability involved the establishment of a fund to enable the federal government to satisfy its social obligations, a new unit of account for the Brazilian economy, and a new medium of exchange.

- The Emergency Social Trust was created by constitutional amendment and funded by income tax increases, a 25-basis-point tax on checks, and an increase in social security withholdings.
- The government budget was reduced from a deficit of $26 billion to $16.3 billion by cutting government payments and reducing operating expenses.
- The *URV (unit of real value)* was introduced as a daily index used for the conversion of wages and as a basis for the government to intervene in the foreign exchange markets. The URV was pegged to the value of the US dollar and became Brazil's unit of account. (See chapter 2, section 1 for a discussion of unit of account.) As such, it effectively pegged changes in Brazilian prices to dollar-based market fluctuations. The URV then became the basis of fiscal adjustment and contracts.
- The *real* then became the medium of exchange, replacing the cruzeiro. One *real* had a value equal to one URV.

Through these measures, monthly inflation was reduced from 30 percent to low single-digits. Understandably, this monetary conversion is often referred to as the Brazilian "economic miracle."

3.2.4 MEXICO

Among the Latin American countries, Mexico initially appeared to be emerging from the turbulent 1980s with the most promising economic recovery. Beginning in 1993, the *nuevo peso* (NP) began circulating in Mexico. The NP is worth 1,000 of the previous Mexican pesos. The original exchange rate between the NP and the US dollar was approximately NP3 to $1. In addition, differential inflation rates in Mexico and the United States were accounted for by an automatic devaluation of NP0.0004 per day. That is, the NP value of a dollar increased by 0.0004 each day. This automatic devaluation was intended to reduce concerns about overvaluation of the new currency.

Earlier, in 1989, the external debt of Mexico had been rescheduled through negotiations with the US Treasury Department and securitized into instruments called Brady bonds. (The Mexican debt resolution negotiations were overseen by then Secretary of the US Treasury Nicholas Brady. See also chapter 4 for a discussion of securitization.) Order had returned to the domestic government securities market as well. Inflation had declined from 160 percent in 1987 to 8 percent in 1993. Mexican government bonds became an attractive alternative for international money managers.

However, in the early 1990s, some analysts suggested that Mexico's trade and budget deficits were too high and that the automatic devaluation of 0.0004 pesos per day was insufficient. Nevertheless, Mexican officials declined to devalue the NP. To compound the situation, Mexico had several episodes of political instability which forced the Mexican monetary authorities to defend the NP by buying it in international currency markets in exchange for hard currencies. (In January 1994, a civil uprising occurred in southern Mexico. Two months later, the likely presidential successor was assassinated.) Defending the peso proved to be an expensive exercise. Foreign reserves of the Mexican treasury fell by more than $10 billion from $28 billion to $17.5 billion in the first few months of 1994.

In April 1994, Mexican officials decided to issue $5 billion in *tesobonos* – short-term, dollar-denominated Treasury bills. The reasoning was that such issuance was a better alternative than spending additional foreign reserves to buy pesos in the open market. Since *tesobonos* guaranteed investors enough pesos to compensate for any loss in the value of the peso, issuance of these instruments was considered a loan against the country's declining dollar reserves. The previously little-used instrument would become a critical source of foreign exchange exposure for Mexico. By August 1994, The amount of *tesobonos* outstanding reached $20 billion while international reserves amounted to only $17.5 billion. At this point, Mexico's promised payments in the equivalent of US dollars exceeded the country's hard currency holdings. International investors recognized the precarious position that this constituted for Mexico and the selling pressure on the peso continued.

By the end of 1994, international reserves had declined to $11 billion, roughly half the *tesobonos* exposure. Unexpectedly, a new presidential administration first undertook a 13 percent devaluation and then permitted the peso to float. This abrupt change in policy rattled the currency markets and selling pressure on the peso intensified.

By the end of January 1995, international reserves held by the Mexican government had fallen to $3.5 billion. At the same time, *tesobonos* held by foreign investors amounted to more than $20 billion. In some trading sessions, the exchange rate dipped to almost NP7 to the US dollar (as compared to NP3.5 prior to the devaluation). The Mexican stock market plunged while short-term interest rates (the *cetes* rate on 28-day Mexican Treasury bills) soared to almost 40 percent.

It was clear that assistance would be required to manage this quickly deteriorating situation. Both Standard & Poor's and Moody's Investor Service downgraded Mexico's credit rating. A failed auction of *tesobonos* in early 1995 (in which Mexico was unable to sell even half the securities offered) prompted US officials to take action to prevent a potential Mexican default. A $40 billion package of guarantees was constructed to help Mexico meet its maturing *tesobonos* (government liabilities) and its obligations with respect to dollar-denominated certificates of deposit (bank liabilities). Ultimately, the implemented rescue plan provided Mexico with $50 billion in support from the United States, Canada, other Latin American countries, the Bank for International Settlements, and the International Monetary Fund.

The financial markets of Mexico have since stabilized. However, the experience illustrates that the international balance of payments, government fiscal responsibility, and political stability can have a profound affect on exchange rates.

 ## Summary

Default risk has an effect on interest rates. The greater the perceived probability of borrower default, the greater the default risk premium that is included in interest rates. Even the highest-grade corporate bonds require a risk premium over the US Treasury bond rate and bonds with lower ratings require greater default risk premiums. Over time, default risk premiums have grown, especially during economic crises and especially for lower-rated bonds.

In a sound economy, high interest rates attract foreign investment. Demand for the currency increases, which increases its value. This linkage means that central banks can use interest rates to manage the external value of their currency, although it is a country's underlying economy that ultimately drives the value of the domestic currency.

Examples of these interrelationships have been striking in recent decades. Trade and budget deficits in the United States made other currencies more attractive. Even more graphic examples of the effects of capital flight on currency value is found in Argentina, Brazil, and Mexico.

 ## End-of-chapter Questions

1. Both anticipated inflation rates and default risk influence interest rates.
   a. How do these factors differ?
   b. How can you estimate the effect of the two factors?
2. Define default risk premiums.
3. What has been the pattern of default risk premiums for AAA corporate bonds? for BBB corporate bonds?
4. Obtain a recent edition of the *Wall Street Journal*. Calculate the approximate yield to maturity of an AT&T bond (New York Exchange Traded Bonds).
5. Using the same edition of the *Wall Street Journal*, compare your answer in no. 4 to the yield to maturity of a Treasury security of the same maturity (Treasury Bonds, Notes, and Bills). To what do you attribute the difference?
6. Describe purchasing power parity.

7. **What is the balance of payments?**
8. **Determine the current dollar value of Japanese yen, British pounds, German marks, French francs, and Italian lira. Compare these to the values shown in Exhibit 11.3.**
9. **What factors do you think have influenced your findings in no. 8?**
10. **The United States Treasury Department initiated a plan to help resolve the Latin American debt crisis that was commonly referred to as the Brady Plan. Using library resources, identify and analyze a recent Brady Plan reorganization.**

Note

1 SITCs were first adopted by the United Nations in 1950 and later revised in 1960. Member nations use these classifications in reporting foreign trade statistics.

Selected References

Adams, T. F. M. and Iwao Hoshii. *A Financial History of the New Japan*. Kodansha International, Tokyo, 1972.

Benoit, J. Pierre V. *United States Interest Rates and the Interest Rate Dilemma for the Developing World*, Quorum Books, Westport, Conn., 1986.

Comparative Economic and Financial Statistics: Japan and Other Major Countries, Bank of Japan, Tokyo, 1988.

Economic Survey of Latin America and the Caribbean 1988, United Nations, Santiago, Chile, 1989.

The European Monetary System: Developments and Perspectives, International Monetary Fund, Washington, DC, November 1990.

Foust, Dean, Susan B. Garland, Douglas Harbrecht, and Richard S. Dunham. "Anatomy of a Rescue Mission," *Business Week*, February 13, 1995, pp. 32–4.

Friedland, Jonathan. "Argentine Election Isn't Likely to Change Anti-Inflation Course Charted by Menem," *Wall Street Journal*, May 2, 1995, p. A17.

Guide to Brazil, Euromoney supplement, April 1994.

Handbook of International Trade and Development Statistics 1988, United Nations, New York, 1989.

Havrilesky, Thomas M. and Robert Schweitzer, eds. *Contemporary Developments in Financial Institutions and Markets*, Harlan Davidson, Arlington Heights, Ill., 1987.

Historical Tables; Budget of the United States Government; Fiscal Year 1990, US Office of Management and Budget, Washington, DC, 1989.

Homer, Sydney. *A History of Interest Rates*, 2nd edn, Rutgers University Press, New Brunswick, NJ, 1977.

Internationalization of the Securities Markets: Report to the Senate Committee on Banking, Housing, and Urban Affairs and the House Committee on Energy and Commerce, US Securities and Exchange Commission, Washington, DC, 1987.

Kaufman, Hugo M. *Germany's International Monetary Policy and the European Monetary System*, Brooklyn College Press, New York, 1985.

Onoh, J. K. *Money and Banking in Africa*, Longman Group, London, 1982.

Taylor, Robert. "Argentine Road to Recovery," *The Banker*, August 1995, p. 62.

Taylor, Robert. "Brazil's Tight Money Squeeze," *The Banker*, August 1995, p. 60.

Taylor, Robert. "Race of the *Real*," *The Banker*, June 1994, pp. 66–8.

Timewell, Stephen. "Call of the *Real* World," *The Banker*, January 1995, pp. 26–8.

Trends in Developing Economies 1989, World Bank, Washington, DC, 1989.

Wall Street Journal, various issues.

Wessel, David. "Clinton's Novel Move to Aid Mexico Puts Spotlight on Obscure Treasury Fund," *Wall Street Journal*, February 2, 1995, pp. A3 & A5.

Wessel, David, Paul B. Carroll, and Thomas T. Vogel, Jr. "How Mexico's Crisis Ambushed Top Minds in Officialdom, Finance," *Wall Street Journal*, July 6, 1995, pp. A1 & A3.

World Bank Debt Tables, Country Tables 1970–9, Analysis and Summary Tables 1989–90 and 1994, World Bank, Washington, DC.

Part V
The Formation of US
Bank Regulation

The Formation of US Bank Regulation and the Federal Reserve System

chapter 12

CHAPTER OVERVIEW

This chapter describes:
- The formation of the US banking system.
- Principles of central banking.
- The origin, structure, and responsibilities of the Federal Reserve System.
- The rationale for bank regulation.
- Important regulatory legislation before 1980.

KEY TERMS

bank holding companies
central bank
dual banking system
Federal Deposit Insurance Corporation
Federal Reserve System

greenbacks
lender of last resort
Office of Comptroller of the Currency
redlining
truth in lending law

CHAPTER OUTLINE

Introduction

The Federal Reserve System is one of several government organizations that play a significant role in the US banking system. As the linchpin of the banking system, its responsibilities go far beyond maintenance of an orderly banking system. This chapter explains the Fed's regulatory functions and how they relate to regulatory activities of other government institutions.

Bank regulation has evolved for close to two centuries. Both state and federal authorities oversee bank operations. A historical difference between the degree of regulatory restriction at the two levels of government encouraged the development of a dual banking system in the United States. To some extent, bank regulation represents government reaction to adverse economic conditions at the time. Both the dual banking system and the regulatory environment are best understood after considering the development of commercial banking in the United States.

 ## Early Bank Regulation

The first United States bank, the Bank of North America, was formed in 1781 by a group of patriotic merchants whose objective was to generate funds for the Continental Army. Even though it was a private financial institution, the American colonies and later the US Congress (after the US Constitution was ratified) pledged support and guaranteed depositors against loss. Operation of the bank ceased in 1791. In the interim, other state chartered banks began to operate.

By 1836, the number of state banks had grown to 600. From that date until 1863, when the National Bank Act was passed, the federal government had no role in commercial banking. In the interim, 1,600 state banks issued their own bank notes, or IOUs. Specie, generally gold or silver coins, continued to be legal tender, although the volume of notes that circulated often made guaranteed convertibility virtually impossible. Unscrupulous bankers generated large volumes of notes that could never be redeemed, or issued notes and then avoided redemption requests. Not surprisingly, then, many of these banks failed.

To finance the Civil War (1861–5), the administration of Abraham Lincoln (whose term as president coincided with the duration of the war), borrowed heavily, suspended gold convertibility of state bank notes, and issued *greenbacks*. The combination of these factors increased the money supply significantly and prices rose by 74 percent from 1861 through 1864. Institutional changes were the natural response to the need to manage both the cost of the war and the growth in the money supply.

Greenbacks:
     National paper currency printed by the federal government but not backed by gold.

1.1 THE NATIONAL BANK ACT OF 1863

The National Bank Act of 1863 brought hope of lasting relief from the lack of dependability associated with a nonuniform currency and an unregulated system. A new system of commercial banks was established – national banks. Specifically:

- National banks were to be chartered by a new Comptroller of the Currency (with reporting responsibility to the Secretary of the Treasury.
- Minimum capital requirements were set for national charters.
- National bank notes were backed by Treasury securities and printed by the Treasury to assure uniformity.
- Minimum reserves against bank notes and deposits were held by the Comptroller.
- The Comptroller imposed restrictions on the lending activities of national banks in order to ensure liquidity and safety and could examine national banks regularly for compliance.

After the Civil War, with this new banking structure in place, the government gradually retired the greenbacks from circulation and reinstated gold convertibility. The hope had been that most state banks would convert to the new national charter, which would give the federal government more control over the money supply. By 1865, there were 1,000 national banks, bringing the total number of banks to around 1,600, a lower conversion rate than Congress had anticipated.

Conversions accelerated when Congress levied a 10 percent tax on state bank notes that proved to be a powerful incentive. In 1866, fewer than 400 of the 600 state banks remained; those that survived were the strongest of the group. State bank notes virtually disappeared, replaced by deposit funds, which became a critical part of state banking. Transactions accounts grew in popularity as state banks encouraged the use and acceptance of checks, which became a mainstay of commercial banking. (See also Exhibit 12.1.)

A small group of Boston businessmen founded "The Fund at Boston in New England" in 1691, seeking to protect themselves against shortages of hard currency. The objective was to provide a ready source of coin, the only universally accepted medium of exchange at the time. To accomplish this goal, the group mortgaged their land and commodities and placed the proceeds in the fund. This enabled them to draw checks against the fund, which proved to be an idea before its time. Without a sound banking system in place, the checks were not readily accepted by other people, making the early checks an infeasible method of payment.

◆ **Exhibit 12.1:** Early checking accounts in the United States

The check was the key to state bank survival. Because state banking laws continued to be more lenient than federal ones, the number of state banks continued to grow, reaching 1,500 by 1888. From 1900 to 1920, the total number of banks expanded from 12,427 to over 30,000, with new state bank charters accounting for 76 percent of the increase.

Dual banking system:
Banking system in which a bank may obtain either a federal charter (from the Office of the Comptroller of the Currency) or a state charter (from state banking authorities).

While there was now a uniform currency printed by the Treasury, national banks and state-chartered banks operated side by side in a *dual banking system*.

1.2 THE FEDERAL RESERVE ACT

The bank created by the Federal Reserve Act in 1913 was a decentralized and independent bank, with twelve regional banks as the basis of the system. Each had authority over a specific geographic region. (Regional Federal Reserve Banks are located in New York, Boston, Philadelphia, Richmond, Va., Atlanta, Cleveland, Chicago, St. Louis, Kansas City, Minneapolis, Dallas, and San Francisco.) The regional banks were to be supervised by the Federal Reserve Board in Washington, DC.

Federal Reserve System:
> A system of twelve regional banks, coordinated by the Federal Reserve Board. It is the first system in the United States designed to perform all the traditional functions of a central bank.

Nationally chartered banks are required to be members of the Federal Reserve and state banks can elect to be members. Member banks contribute the equity capital for their respective reserve bank, receiving in return a predetermined dividend (not a share of total Federal Reserve earnings). Member banks elect six of the nine directors of their reserve bank, of whom, no more than three can be bankers. Those directors not selected by member banks are appointed by the Federal Reserve Board. The President of the United States appoints all members of the Federal Reserve Board.

The Federal Reserve System was the first to assume the full range of central banking functions (performing banking activities for the government, regulating commercial banks, maintaining orderly financial markets, acting as lender of last resort, and managing the domestic currency value – discussed below).

The initial objective of the Federal Reserve was to minimize the problems of instability of the money supply and credit availability. The reserve banks are charged with maintaining sound credit conditions and accommodating commerce, industry, and agriculture in their regions. Over time, the role of the Federal Reserve has grown beyond this initial responsibility. Specifically, regional Federal Reserve Banks:

- Were given significant note issue authority
- Became fiscal agents of the federal government
- Were given the authority to rediscount commercial notes
- Were designated to hold the required reserves of members
- Became lenders of last resort in their respective regions (supporting financial institutions experiencing financial difficulty)

The Federal Reserve Board is clearly a more governmental body than the reserve banks. In supervising the reserve banks, the Board is to regulate the relationships between and among itself, the reserve banks, and the government. While it was unclear at the time of the legislation whether the regional banks or the Board had the authority (1) to intervene in the money market through securities transactions and (2) to adjust the interest rate at which commercial notes could be rediscounted, these functions became defined as US bank regulation continued to take shape.

② Characteristics of Modern Central Banking

Central banks serve a variety of functions. "Serve" is the key word. The modern central bank is a financial institution that is not established to compete with commercial banks; profitability is not its primary objective. It serves government, banks, other financial institutions, and the public.

In any country, a compelling reason for a central bank is to inspire confidence in the nation's money. This motivation forms the basis for a central bank's relationships with government and the commercial banking system. The central bank helps manage a country's national debt. In some cases, it has enhanced the marketability of government securities by requiring that early commercial bank notes be collateralized by government securities.

As economies develop, the role of a central bank tends to expand. Stability of securities markets and other financial institutions is added to the list of objectives. Furthermore, after the early 1930s, levels of national income and employment became issues for central banks, as well as federal governments. As increasing international trade caused interest rates and price levels of one country to affect those of its trading partners, central banks became international financial intermediaries. An outgrowth of this expanded scope has been a strong alliance between central bank and Treasury authorities.

> **Central bank:**
> A financial institution that carries out the financial transactions of the federal government, controls and regulates the money supply, maintains order in financial markets, promotes favorable economic conditions, and/or acts as a lender of last resort for other financial institutions.

2.1 GOVERNMENT RELATIONS

The basic characteristic of central banks is, in one sense or another, a *close link to government*. Theoretically, there are two extreme types of relationship between a central bank and the government.

- A central bank may be merely a subdivision of the Treasury. The motivation for such an arrangement is that if government is held accountable for every facet of the economy, monetary policy and the central bank must be under government control.
- As the US Federal Reserve System typifies, a central bank may be completely independent. Independence from government influence preserves freedom from the conflict of interest involved when a single official entity both creates and spends money.

Central bank–government relationships throughout the world fall somewhere between the two extremes. A central bank generally acts in both *advisory* and *operational* capacities. Government policy decisions are made on the advice of central banks. The weight that this advice carries, of course, is a function of the institution's independence. If the Bank is strongly independent, the "advice" constitutes a policy decision because the government has little power to reverse the central bank's decision. With respect to operations, central banks handle their governments' official transactions. Domestically, this encompasses Treasury security issuance, interest payments, and redemptions. Overseas responsibilities extend to foreign currency transactions. Given these responsibilities, it is not surprising that Treasury departments and central banks tend to work in close harmony.

2.2 COMMERCIAL BANKING RESPONSIBILITIES

A second characteristic of central banks is their supportive role in *maintaining of a sound commercial banking system*. Historically, economic instability frequently arises out of *monetary* instability. Excessive bank lending can lead to inflationary pressures. Strict curtailment of loans and other forms of credit can have the opposite effect. When central banks exert some influence over the amount of available credit, it is possible to smooth the peaks and valleys of monetary and therefore economic growth. Stability is a common goal of national monetary policy and the macroeconomic justification for the commercial bank–central bank relationship.

The microeconomic rationale for the relationship has to do with the nature of commercial banks. Banks are usually major participants in the payments mechanism of a country and their demand and other deposits constitute a significant portion of the money supply. The aim of profit-seeking commercial banks, however, is to invest depositors' funds in assets that will earn bank shareholders a reasonable rate of return. As a result, bank asset portfolios are at least partially illiquid.

A sudden and unusually high level of deposit withdrawals can threaten a bank's solvency. If the demands are not met, the result has often been similar pressure on other institutions. Again, the net effect is undesirable monetary instability. When central banks act as *lender of last resort*, they mitigate this instability and help to preserve confidence in the system.

> **Lender of last resort:**
> The financial institution from which other financial institutions may ultimately receive assistance during a liquidity crisis.

If such support were to be unqualified, it might lead to excessive risk-taking by commercial bank management, so central banks often supervise and oversee commercial bank operations, including the degree of loan riskiness, the amount of bank capital, and compliance with bank laws and regulations.

2.3 ORDERLY FINANCIAL MARKETS

The lender of last resort function goes beyond commercial banking. The third function of central banking is to *provide liquidity in any financial crisis*. As savings institutions, investment funds, and other institutions offer products that are essentially transactions (checking) accounts, a nation's vulnerability to monetary instability increases. Frequently, securities purchases are financed through credit arrangements. A sudden and dramatic decline in the value of marketable securities can create the need for additional liquidity to maintain adequate collateral for securities loans. If this situation is widespread and unchecked, a systemwide liquidity crisis could result. Whatever the threat to monetary stability, a central bank must be prepared to remove it.

2.4 GENERAL ECONOMIC CONDITIONS

Since the Great Depression in the 1930s, central banks have been held at least partially responsible for *preventing adverse economic fluctuations*. In order to achieve desired advances in employment and the general standard of living, governments have relied increasingly on central banks to ensure adequate credit availability for investment and consumption. This, in turn, has led central banks to adopt monetary growth targets, whether growth in money supply or growth in outstanding credit. Income and employment goals are thus added to the goal of monetary stability.

2.5 DOMESTIC CURRENCY VALUE

Cross-border trade has increased significantly in recent decades, which means that price levels in foreign countries can have a significant impact on a domestic economy. Costs for importing raw materials and finished products will fluctuate with the value of the domestic currency *vis-à-vis* foreign currencies. Thus, the last defining characteristic of modern central banking is *management of the external value of the domestic currency*.

Actual management of the exchange value of the domestic currency can be quite complicated. If the value of the domestic currency is too low, imported goods can become prohibitively expensive. If its value is too high, imports are less expensive, but the country's exports may not be competitively priced.

Factors that influence the exchange value of the currency include domestic interest rates, international trade balance, and domestic fiscal policy. All other things being equal, high interest rates attract foreign capital and increase the value of domestic currency. International trade surpluses (exports in excess of imports) also increase demand for domestic currency, placing upward pressure on its value. Low interest rates and trade deficits depress currency value. (See also chapter 11.)

Domestic budget deficits have a negative effect on currency value. When government expenditures exceed receipts of income tax and other revenues, either more money must be created or the national debt must increase. If more money is created, the value of each unit of currency declines, that is, inflation results. This causes domestic currency value to fall below its previous level *vis-à-vis* foreign currencies. Increased national debt has roughly the same effect, as more money must be created to pay the interest expense associated with the new debt.

③ Development of Bank Regulation

The basic justification for bank regulation lies in the critical role of commercial banking in a domestic economy. Bank demand deposits are the primary component of the *money supply*, and the country's money transactions often take the form of exchanges of bank deposits. Disruption of this basic system can disrupt the entire economy.

The role of commercial banks in the economy goes beyond the payments system. Commercial banks establish a dependable payments system while investing a large percentage of deposits in illiquid assets. That is, what is not needed to maintain reserves can be invested in higher-yielding, less liquid assets. For this investment function to work well, depositors must have confidence that their money is safe; the failure of one bank should not precipitate massive deposit withdrawals, or *runs*, at other institutions. Bank regulation is intended to monitor the risk of failure in the system as a whole, to guard against a domino effect when one institution fails.

Bank regulation operates under two assumptions:

1) The *safety and soundness* of the banking system are too important to leave to chance.
2) The relative illiquidity of bank portfolios makes *confidence* in the system essential.

3.1 THE BANKING ACT OF 1933

Lenient state banking laws have frequently been blamed for the bank failures during the Great Depression. Also of concern were certain commercial banking activities linking commercial banks with investment banking. (Investment banking is the process of bringing new issues of stocks and bonds to the market for sale: see chapters 5 and 6.) In some cases, commercial banks made questionable loans to clients of their investment banking affiliates. Underwriting by investment banking divisions was not always prudent, and new issues of firms in weak financial condition could be sold to the commercial bank's trust department. At other times, doubtful bank loans could be sold to investment banking affiliates to support the stock price of the parent bank.

Senator Carter Glass of Virginia, who served in the Senate between 1920 and 1946, had fruitlessly promoted separation of commercial and investment banking before the 1930s. By the time the 1933 act was drafted, economic conditions provided Senator Glass with ample support for the idea. The Banking Act of 1933 (frequently referred to as the Glass–Steagall Act) brought an end to an era. The Act required commercial banks to divest themselves of investment banking affiliates, prohibited interest payments on demand deposits, and established government authority to regulate interest rates on time deposits. The provisions of Glass–Steagall have been debated vigorously almost since their enactment. Legislation in the early 1980s dismantled some of this law and other changes are likely to follow.

3.2 THE FDIC

The 1933 Banking Act also created the first federal deposit insurance facility in the United States with the objective of preventing the massive failures that had occurred between 1929 and 1933. Regulators were particularly concerned with protection of small depositors who had suffered when banks failed during the Depression. Prior to 1933, there had been only state insurance plans, all of which eventually failed. It was hoped that the Federal Deposit Insurance Corporation (FDIC) would be more successful. Certain factors did improve the probability of success. First, the banks covered by the plan were a more diversified group than those that any single state might assemble. Second, the banks still operating in 1933 had been strong enough in the first place to weather the Great Depression. The most important advantage of the FDIC over comparable state plans, however, was its access to federal monetary authorities. No single state insurance scheme was capable of lending such credibility to its guarantees.

Insurance premiums from subscribing banks established the FDIC fund and annual contributions added to its strength. Both national and state banks are eligible for coverage. Each account was originally insured up to $2,500. Today, the limit is $100,000 per account.

Of course, to provide this safety net, it was felt that more supervision and regulation were necessary. The 1933 Act added the FDIC to the ranks of federal bank regulators (Comptroller of the Currency and Federal Reserve) already charged with oversight responsibilities. The division of authority is as follows:

- The FDIC has primary responsibility for state banks that are not members of the Federal Reserve.
- The Federal Reserve examines state-chartered banks that are members of the Federal Reserve.
- The Comptroller examines national banks that are members of the Federal Reserve.

Exhibit 12.2 shows the number of institutions, assets controlled, and average size of the institutions under the supervision of these three federal regulators.

	Federal Regulator			Totals
	Office of the Comptroller of the Currency	Federal Reserve	FDIC	
Type of banks	national	state-chartered Fed member	insured state-chartered nonFed member	
No. of banks	2,597	992	5,554	9,143
No. of offices[1]	30,833	8,981	17,974	57,788
Assets[2]	$2,893,910	$1,231,209	$889,765	$5,014,884
Average size[2,3]	$1,114.3	$1,241.1	$160.2	$548.5

◆ **Exhibit 12.2: Federal bank regulators, 1997**

◆ *Notes*: 1 Main office plus branches
2 Millions of dollars
3 Amount of assets divided by number of banks

◆ *Source*: *Statistics on Banking 1997*, Federal Deposit Insurance Corporation, Washington, DC.

FDIC is required to examine bank financial data periodically to identify potential problems. On-site examinations enable the agency to assess a bank's operational and financial stability. When loan portfolios and/or management practices expose an institution to high potential loss, thereby threatening equity capital, the institution is designated as a "problem" bank, needing closer monitoring. Because the FDIC does not charter banks, it may not revoke a charter, but can force a bank to cease operating. Only the Comptroller or a state banking authority has revocation rights, so the FDIC must work closely with other regulators.

FDIC deposit insurance premiums were originally set at one-twelfth of one percent of total deposits or 8.3 cents for each $100 of deposits. Premiums cover FDIC operating expenses and maintain the insurance fund. Beginning in 1962, Congress required that two-thirds of these premiums be refunded to contributing banks. In 1981, Congress reduced the rebate to 60 percent of premiums paid, thereby increasing the effective premium. In 1989, the Financial Institutions Reform, Recovery, and Enforcement Act increased the premium to 12 cents per $100 of deposits for 1990 and 15 cents per $100 of deposits in 1991. (See also chapter 13 for a discussion of recent changes in FDIC funding and premiums.)

3.3 THE BANKING ACT OF 1935

The Banking Act of 1935 significantly strengthened the Federal Reserve's powers with respect to monetary policy. This legislation gave the Fed greater authority over bank reserve requirements and made interest rates paid on bank time deposits subject to Federal Reserve limits. The Comptroller of the Currency and the Secretary of the Treasury came off the Federal Reserve Board in order to give the Board more autonomy and the Board's name was changed to the Board of Governors of the Federal Reserve System (heads of the regional banks had been referred to as governors). This last change suggested the greater authority given to the Board, with the clear implication that future policy decisions would be made in Washington.

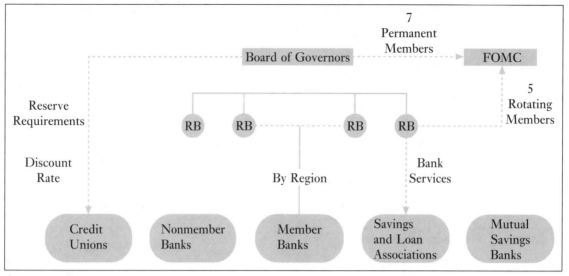

◆ **Exhibit 12.3:** **The Federal Reserve System**

◆ *Note*:   RB: Reserve Bank (total = 12)

Perhaps the most significant change accomplished by this legislation was formation of the *Federal Open Market Committee (FOMC)*. No longer would there be any question as to which agency was responsible for open-market securities transactions. The 12-member FOMC was composed of the seven members of the Board of Governors of the regional Reserve bank presidents (the former governors) with five voting on a rotating basis. The majority held by the Board of Governors ensures that, in the event of a conflict, national priorities would dominate in the setting of monetary policy. The New York Federal Reserve Bank acts as agent for the FOMC in executing open-market securities transactions. Exhibit 12.3 illustrates the organizational structure of the Federal Reserve System, including the FOMC.

The 1935 Act also gave the Comptroller more authority to make decisions about national bank charter applications. Applicants are required to show both that the proposed bank is needed and would be successful (without hurting existing banks). Making it more difficult to charter a bank was intended to help prevent bank failure.

3.4 Consumer Protection Legislation

A number of laws following this legislation in the 1930s are aimed primarily at protecting the rights of bank customers. Consumer protection law in commercial banking falls into one of three general categories:

- adequate disclosure
- access to credit
- procedures in the event of dispute

Truth in lending laws prescribe the type and method of disclosure by banks (and other financial institutions) that make loans to consumers. The 1968 Federal Consumer Protection Act (also known as the Truth in Lending Act) establishes specific consumer rights, with commercial bank disclosures monitored by the Federal Reserve. The Fed's Regulation Z stipulates that an annual percentage rate (APR) must be stated prominently, that a full accounting for all finance charges be made available to the consumer, and that other minimum disclosures be made. States have similar laws and regulations of their own.

The *Fair Credit Reporting Act* of 1970 ensures confidentiality of consumer credit information held by lenders and credit reporting agencies. Such information may not be disclosed except for specific reasons such as employment, insurance, and other legitimate circumstances. Credit agencies must provide copies of consumer credit reports upon request and methods of disputing negative information contained in the credit files.

The *Equal Credit Opportunity Act (ECOA)* of 1974 (and an amendment two years later) prohibits discrimination against borrowers because of gender, marital status, race, national origin, age, or income that is derived from public assistance.

The *Fair Credit Billing Act (FCBA)* of 1974 was enacted to protect consumers in use of credit cards. Credit card issuers must provide customers with notice of their rights and the exact procedures to follow in the event of a dispute. Lenders must correct errors within 90 days of receiving a complaint. Credit card holders are limited to $50 of liability in the event of lost or stolen credit cards. This law is also implemented by Federal Reserve Regulation Z.

The *Truth in Savings Act* was passed in 1991 and requires disclosure of a deposit's annual percentage yield, the period during which the yield is in effect, all minimum balance and time requirements to earn the advertised yield, and the minimum initial deposit.

These and other laws and regulations are applicable to consumer credit. They are intended to help ensure fair allocation of credit through complete information on rights and procedures. For lenders, the primary costs are increased administrative expense (disclosure forms and management time necessary to ensure compliance with truth in lending and FCBA) and having somewhat less information about their prospective loan customers (ECOA). (See also Exhibit 12.4.)

In the early 1980s, some suggested that US bank regulation had gone too far. (See, for example, Edward J. Kane, "Accelerating Inflation, Technological Innovation, and the Decreasing Effectiveness of Banking Regulation," *Journal of Finance*, 36, no. 2 (May 1981), pp. 355–67.) What started as an effort to ensure safety and soundness in the nation's payments system became, in some cases, an exercise in protecting special interests at the expense of the small depositor.

From the late 1960s through the 1970s, the thrift industry (savings and loan associations and savings banks), the housing industry, and construction unions helped lobby for regulation that gave thrifts a higher deposit rate ceiling than commercial banks, and raised the minimum denomination in which Treasury debt (especially the T-bill) was issued. These same interests also worked to prevent bank holding companies and nonfinancial corporations from issuing small-denomination debt (that would most likely carry interest rates close to market rates of return). At the same time, interest rate ceilings for large-denomination deposits were eliminated, allowing market rates of return to be paid on these deposits. The result was a system that discriminated against all depositors to ensure banks and thrifts of a low-cost source of funds. The interest rate a small depositor could earn on savings thus depended upon a family's wealth and financial sophistication. These circumstances discriminated, in particular, against the young, the old, and the poor. The advent in the 1970s of money market mutual funds offering market rates of return to small investors caused large-scale withdrawals from depository institutions, particularly in the thrift industry, so the "discrimination" backfired in the end.

◆ **Exhibit 12.4: Discriminatory regulation**

3.5 Community Reinvestment Act of 1977

Another significant consumer protection law that applies to commercial banks is the Community Reinvestment Act of 1977. It requires federal regulators (Comptroller, Federal Reserve, and FDIC) to encourage the banks they oversee to provide for the credit needs of the communities they serve. (Similar provisions apply for savings and loan associations.) The law mandates that regulators assess an institution's record of providing for the credit needs of the entire community, including low- and moderate-income neighborhoods. This record is to be considered when a bank seeks a new charter, acquires shares of another bank, or merges with another bank.

The objective of the Community Reinvestment Act was to discourage the practice of *redlining*. To the extent that economically deprived areas are systematically shut out from mortgage finance, loans to community organizations (churches, colleges, and professional organizations), and small businesses, their condition will continue to deteriorate. If banks wish to expand, this legislation requires that they demonstrate that they are not neglecting underserved, disadvantaged areas, although if a bank is not located to serve such an area, the law has virtually no effect on it.

Redlining:
> The systematic withholding of bank loans from low- to moderate-income communities, while still accepting deposits in them, particularly communities with a significant minority population.

The Financial Institutions Reform, Recovery, and Enforcement Act of 1989 (FIRREA) strengthened the 1977 law by requiring that regulators regularly prepare a written evaluation of each bank's community reinvestment. A portion of this evaluation that must now be made public includes the institution's rating:

- outstanding
- satisfactory
- needs to improve
- substantial noncompliance

The documentation for the rating must also made public.

3.6 Regulation of Bank Holding Companies

After the financial system contraction brought on by the Great Depression, banking activities did not grow appreciably until the Second World War had ended, when the constraints imposed by the legislation of the 1930s appeared overly restrictive. In 1945, when the war ended, loans were only 16 percent of total bank assets, compared to 63 percent in 1925. As the economy expanded in the 1950s, banks became more aggressive and competitive, with the result that the ratio of loans began to rise once again. Certificates of deposit, Eurodollars, credit cards, repurchase agreements, and renewed interest in federal funds were all born in the 1960s, all permitting greater flexibility in a more vibrant banking environment. (See chapter 3 for a discussion of certificates of deposit, federal funds, and repurchase agreements. Eurodollars and Eurodollar markets are covered in chapter 9.)

The most significant structural change in this period was the growth of *bank holding companies (BHCs)*: This organizational form was not new or unique to the post-Second World War era; the Banking Act of 1933 specifically addressed authority over BHCs that owned banks which were members of the Federal Reserve. The Fed legally can deny such a holding company the right to vote its stock in the member bank, although it also can examine the holding company and its affiliates in order to determine whether voting permission should be granted or denied. Other requirements for BHCs that own Federal Reserve member banks include publication of periodic financial statements, maintenance of reserves, and divestiture of securities businesses.

> **Bank holding company:**
> A corporation whose primary function is to own other corporations, specifically, one or more commercial banks.

Under the Bank Holding Company Act of 1956 and its subsequent amendments, BHCs are permitted a wide range of activities, which includes, but is not limited to, leasing, data processing, real estate appraisal, operation of a discount brokerage, and operation of a distressed savings and loan association. Today, bank holding companies control the vast majority of bank offices and assets.

 ## Summary

The first US banks were chartered and controlled by state authorities. National banks did not became a permanent part of the financial landscape until 1863. The Office of Comptroller of the Currency was created to charter and supervise these new national banks. While the dual system of state and national banks has continued to exist, operational differences between the two types of banks diminished.

The Federal Reserve Act of 1913 created the nation's central bank to act as lender of last resort for commercial banks and to execute monetary policy. Through major bank legislation of the earlier 1930s, its role was strengthened and it became even more independent. At the same time, the federal deposit insurance system was initiated. Other legislation followed in the 1960s and 1970s that protected consumer rights and attempted to provide equity in bank services.

 ## End-of-chapter Questions

1. There are two possible extremes with respect to the type of relationship that a central bank may have with its government. Describe them and possible justifications for them.

2. Differentiate the macroeconomic and microeconomic relationship of a central bank to the commercial banking industry.

3. Give three reasons why commercial banks should be regulated.

4. How was the Federal Reserve System reorganized in the Banking Acts of the 1930s?

5. How can a central bank influence the general economic climate of a country?

6. What is redlining?

7. If redlining is damaging to the development of individual communities, is it possible that a large presence of foreign banks in a market could present a similar problem?

8. Name the three types of consumer protection legislation and describe the scope of these laws.

9. Why do you suppose that such a large percentage of the US deposit base is controlled by bank holding companies?

10. Which banks are the primary supervisory responsibility of the Federal Reserve? the Comptroller of the Currency? the Federal Deposit Insurance Corporation?

11. Refer to Exhibit 12.2 and describe the differences you note with respect to banks regulated by the Office of the Comptroller, the Fed, and the FDIC.

SELECTED REFERENCES

Ciocca, Pierluigi, ed. *Money and the Economy: The Central Bankers' Views*, Macmillan Press, London, 1987.

Cooper, S. Kerry and Donald R. Fraser. *Banking Deregulation and the New Competition in Financial Services*, Ballinger Publishing, Cambridge, Mass., 1984.

The Federal Reserve System: Purposes and Functions, Board of Governors of the Federal Reserve System, Washington, DC, 1984.

Goodhart, Charles. *The Evolution of Central Banks*, MIT Press, Cambridge, Mass., 1988.

Greider, William. *Secrets of the Temple: How the Federal Reserve Runs the Country*, Touchstone/Simon & Schuster, New York, 1989.

Johnson, Hazel J. *Banking Regulation Today: The Markets, Players, and Issues*, Probus Publishing, Chicago (now McGraw-Hill, New York), 1994.

Spong, Kenneth. *Banking Regulation: Its Purposes, Implementation, and Effects*, Federal Reserve Bank of Kansas City, Kansas City, 1990.

Statistics on Banking 1995, Federal Deposit Insurance Corporation, Washington, DC.

Toniolo, Gianni, ed. *Central Banks' Independence in Historical Perspective*, Walter de Gruyter, Berlin, 1988.

US Monetary Policy, Deregulation, and Deposit Insurance

chapter 13

CHAPTER OVERVIEW

This chapter describes:
- Federal Reserve monetary policy.
- Bank deregulation legislation.
- Crises in federal deposit insurance.
- Restoration of the deposit insurance funds.

KEY TERMS

Depository Institutions Deregulation and Monetary Control Act of 1980
deposit insurance
discount rate
disintermediation
FDIC Improvement Act of 1991
Financial Institutions Reform, Recovery, and Enforcement Act of 1989

fiscal policy
Garn–St. Germain Depository Institutions Act of 1982
monetary base
monetary policy
open-market operations
reserve requirements
transactions account multiplier

CHAPTER OUTLINE

1 Fiscal Policy
2 Monetary Policy
  2.1 The Tools of Monetary Policy
    2.1.1 Reserve Requirements
    2.1.2 The Discount Rate
    2.1.3 Open-market Operations
  2.2 The Mechanics of Open-market Operations
    2.2.1 The Federal Reserve Balance Sheet
    2.2.2 Reserves and the Money Supply

Introduction

The Federal Reserve uses tools to manage the money supply of the United States, including reserve requirements, the discount rate, and open market operations. Of these, open market operations are the most powerful and frequently used. The objectives of Fed monetary policy are to maintain price level stability and to create an economic environment that is conducive to economic growth.

In order to compete with other financial institutions, banks and savings and loan associations were given expanded powers in the early 1980s. The combination of government safeguards and deregulatory efforts, however, made the system vulnerable in several important aspects – one of which was a threat to the US deposit insurance system. Federal legislation of 1989 and 1991 was enacted to remove the associated financial uncertainty and to restore stability to the deposit insurance system.

 ## Fiscal Policy

Bank regulation is not motivated solely by concern for the financial institutions themselves. It is part of the larger agenda of maintaining order in an economy. Generally, two broad categories of national financial policy affect an economy: *fiscal policy* and *monetary policy*.

> **Fiscal policy:**
> The policy of government with respect to government revenues and expenditures.

The legislative and executive branches of the federal government are primarily responsible for *fiscal policy*. They develop budgets of government expenditures. Tax revenues to meet these budgets may be less than, equal to, or greater than actual government expenditures. When revenues equal expenditures, the government has no impact on the aggregate level of economic activity. However, when revenues exceed expenditures, fiscal policy has the effect of dampening economic expansion. This is true because the government effectively removes purchasing power from the economy when it spends less than it collects.

When government revenues are less than government expenditures, the economy is stimulated by the incremental purchasing power that is introduced. In the United States, the federal government has run such deficits each year since 1970. In fact, between 1934 and 1969, the annual federal budget was in surplus on only eight occasions. Thus, US government financial activity historically has provided economic stimulus. In some cases, the deficits have been deliberate attempts to apply Keynesian economics.[1] In other cases, particularly in more recent years, federal budget deficits simply have been a function of increased spending that has not been offset by increased tax revenues.

Monetary Policy

Monetary policy involves control of the nation's money supply. The National Bank Act of 1863 and its subsequent amendment did not effectively eliminate money created by state banks. (See chapter 12 for a discussion of the National Bank Act of 1863 and its amendment.) While state bank notes became less prevalent, state bank checking account deposits grew more popular. As checks became readily accepted as money, state bank checking accounts became a portion of the money supply that was not subject to federal regulation. It was not until the creation of the Federal Reserve System in 1913 that the federal government gained more complete statutory power to manage the money supply.

> **Monetary policy:**
> The policy of government with respect to its money supply.

2.1 THE TOOLS OF MONETARY POLICY

The tools of monetary policy have developed over time.

- The first was the imposition of *reserve requirements* against deposits.
- When the Federal Reserve was created, the *discount rate* was used.
- The most powerful tool was later to be refined – *open market operations*.

2.1.1 RESERVE REQUIREMENTS

The National Bank Act of 1863 attempted to control the portion of the money supply that could be affected at the federal level by specifying minimum reserve requirements for the new national banks. If a policy decision to reduce the money supply were to be made, the reserve requirements could be increased, causing loanable funds to decline.

> **Reserve requirement:**
> Minimum reserve assets that, by law, a depository financial institution must maintain. (Depository institutions include commercial banks, mutual savings banks, savings and loan associations, and credit unions.) Reserve requirements are expressed in terms of a percentage of relevant bank deposits.

The imposition of reserve requirements on national banks was not completely effective, however, because state bank reserves were set at the discretion of state banking authorities. Perhaps for this reason, the use of the reserve requirement has had limited application as a tool of monetary policy. Furthermore, total national bank notes outstanding were limited to the amount of the national debt, because all such notes were required to be collateralized by government securities. As a result, there was no way for federal regulators to increase the money supply within the provisions of the National Bank Act.

2.1.2 THE DISCOUNT RATE

With creation of the Federal Reserve System in 1913, reserve banks became the lender of last resort in their respective regions, thereby giving birth to an important tool of monetary policy, the *discount rate*. Lowering the discount rate tends to encourage bank borrowing at the Fed's "discount window," all other things being equal. (The discount window is a figurative expression, not a real location.) Greater borrowing from the Federal Reserve increases the money supply, which encourages economic activity. Opposite effects should occur when the discount rate is raised – borrowing by banks is discouraged and the money supply is reduced.

Discount rate:
> The rate of interest at which a depository institution borrows from the Federal Reserve bank in its district.

2.1.3 OPEN-MARKET OPERATIONS

Although the discount rate has played a more significant role than the reserve requirement in implementation of monetary policy, neither has been as frequently used nor as effective as *open-market operations*. Open-market operations occurred to some extent in the early 1900s, but the practice was formalized and placed under the jurisdiction of the Federal Open Market Committee in 1935.

Open-market operations:
> The purchase and sale of government securities by the Federal Reserve in the public securities market.

2.2 THE MECHANICS OF OPEN-MARKET OPERATIONS

Open-market operations have a critical impact on the money supply. Buying and selling government securities is a way the Fed implements monetary policy.

2.2.1 THE FEDERAL RESERVE BALANCE SHEET

Exhibit 13.1 shows the balance sheet of the Federal Reserve as of June 30, 1998. The Fed's primary financial asset is government securities and associated repurchase agreements (85.2 percent of the total). Gold, foreign currency, and SDR certificates are the next largest component;

		Amount	%
Financial Assets			
Gold, foreign exchange, SDR certificates		$37.5	6.9%
Treasury currency		25.9	4.8
Federal Reserve float[1]		1.4	0.2
Repurchase agreements		20.5	3.8
Loans to domestic banks		1.0	0.2
Securities:			
Treasury issues	$439.8		
Government agency issues	0.5	440.3	81.4
Other assets		14.6	2.7
Total assets		$541.2	100.0%
Financial Liabilities			
Monetary base:			
Currency in circulation	$483.9		
Reserves of depository institutions[2]	23.7	$507.6	93.8%
Due to US government[2]		18.3	3.4
Due to foreign sector/rest of world[2]		0.9	0.2
Other liabilities		14.4	2.6
Total liabilities		$541.2	100.0%

◆ **Exhibit 13.1: Balance sheet of the Federal Reserve System, June 30, 1998**

◆ *Notes*: Amounts are in billions of dollars.
      1   Cash items in the process of collection (CIPC)
      2   Deposit accounts

◆ *Source*: Board of Governors of the Federal Reserve System, *Flow of Funds Accounts; Flows and Outstandings.*

they are items of international liquidity that have little impact on the domestic money supply. (SDRs are special drawing rights, a form of money created by the International Monetary Fund (IMF) and used among the sovereign governments that are members of the IMF: see chapter 20.) Next in relative importance is treasury currency (much as corporations hold treasury stock). Loans to domestic banks are generated when the Federal Reserve acts as lender of last resort for depository institutions, but the amount is small compared to government securities.

The Fed's largest liability is currency in circulation (89.4 percent of the total). Currency in circulation and reserves of depository institutions form the country's *monetary base*.

> **Monetary base:**
>   Claims against a central bank that serve as money (currency) and the reserves held by a central bank that form the basis for creation of money (reserves of depository institutions).

The reserve base is a part of the money supply that can be held only by financial institutions. Because banks are required to keep a percentage of transactions accounts on deposit with the Federal Reserve (the reserve requirement), both the amount of reserves and the reserve requirement influence aggregate transactions account balances. The exact relationship is:

$$T = mR$$

where T = aggregate transactions account balances
        m = the transactions account multiplier (the inverse of the reserve requirement)
        R = aggregate reserves of depository institutions

Changes in these parameters (Δ) will also be interrelated.

$$T + \Delta T = (m + \Delta m)(R + \Delta R)$$
$$= mR + R\Delta m + m\Delta R + \Delta m \Delta R$$

Subtracting the two equations, the change in transactions accounts balances equals the amount of reserves multiplied by the change in the multiplier plus the multiplier times the change in reserves plus the change in multiplier times the change in reserves.

$$\Delta T = R\Delta m + m\Delta R + \Delta m \Delta R$$

When the multiplier does not change, a change in reserves will have the following potential effect on transactions account balances.

$$\Delta T = m\Delta R$$

◆ **Exhibit 13.2:**   The relationship between reserves and transactions accounts

◆ *Reference*:   Smith, Paul F. *Comparative Financial Systems*, Praeger Publishers, New York, 1982.

2.2.2 RESERVES AND THE MONEY SUPPLY

Exhibit 13.2 summarizes the connection between reserves and transactions account balances, a major part of the money supply. When the Fed sells government securities, the balance of the government securities account declines. Because the transaction is settled through the banking system, reserves of depository institutions also declines. The reverse is true when the Federal Reserve purchases government securities. The balance of government securities increases, as do depository institution reserves. The effect on the money supply of either selling or buying is several times the amount of the original transaction because of the *transactions account multiplier*. If the reserve requirement for transactions accounts is 12 percent, a $1 change in reserves can change transactions accounts balances in depository institutions (part of the money supply) by $8.33 [$1(1/0.12) = $8.33].

> **Transactions account multiplier:**
>   The potential increase in transactions accounts for a $1 change in depository institution reserves – the inverse of the reserve requirement for transactions accounts.

a	Federal Reserve		Commercial banks	
	Treasury Securities +500	Due to commercial banks +500	Due from Fed +500 Securities (500)	

b	Federal Reserve		Commercial banks	
	Treasury Securities +500	Due to commercial banks +500	Due from Fed +500 Securities (500) Loans +4,165	Transactions accounts +4,165

◆ **Exhibit 13.3:** Expanding the money supply through open-market operations (millions of dollars)

◆ *Notes*:
    a) The Federal Reserve purchases government securities ($500 million).
    b) The initial government securities transaction and the eventual effect on the money supply (transactions accounts) and loans outstanding (a $4.2 billion increase).

Exhibit 13.3 illustrates this principle. In this example, the Federal Reserve purchases $500 million in government securities from commercial banks. Payment is made through the banking system so that reserve accounts (Fed liabilities) increase by the same amount. On the books of commercial banks, securities balances decline and reserves at the Fed increase. This $500 million is now excess reserves for the banking system and, assuming a 12 percent reserve requirement, can support additional transactions account balances of $4.165 billion [$500/(0.12) = $4.165 billion]. The new transactions accounts add to the money supply. This example assumes that the money supply increase is invested in loans, thereby boosting the amount of funds available for investment purposes and consumer purchases. Thus, open-market operations can be a powerful tool in managing the country's money supply.

③ Deregulation

In the 1970s, interest rates were high and volatile. As a result, commercial banks and other depository institutions found themselves at a competitive disadvantage in financial services markets. As market interest rates rose and mutual funds and securities firms began to compete with commercial banks and savings and loan associations, the flow of funds to depository institutions declined.

3.1 DISINTERMEDIATION

Money market mutual funds offer small savers market rates of interest for a substantially smaller investment than once required. The funds then pool these small investments to purchase Treasury securities, large bank certificates of deposit (not subject to interest rate ceilings after 1970), commercial paper, and banker's acceptances. Individual investors not only earned high rates of return but also received limited check writing privileges. In 1974, money market funds controlled roughly $2 billion in assets; by 1980, the total was $200 billion. (As of mid-1998, US money market funds held $1.2 trillion in assets. See chapter 28 for a description of money market funds.) The growth of these funds was one of the major motivations behind elimination of deposit interest rate regulation.

Securities firms too offered transactions accounts in direct competition with bank checking accounts. Besides earning interest on their accounts, clients received a full range of brokerage services. Competition from these two sources resulted in *disintermediation*.

Disintermediation:
The withdrawal of funds from depository institutions for the purpose of investing in other vehicles.

Consumer groups lobbied for deregulation. They argued that Regulation Q discriminated against small investors. Since 1970, the deposit rate ceilings for certificates of deposit in excess of $100,000 had been eliminated. Only rates paid to small depositors were still maintained at artificially low levels.

At the state level, mutual savings banks had won the right to offer NOW (negotiable order of withdrawal) accounts that were in fact interest-bearing checking accounts. However, such permission had been won primarily in the Northeast, the region in which mutual savings banks are concentrated; NOW accounts were not available nationwide. The US Congress had little alternative. In 1980, the first major legislative overhaul of depository institutions since the 1930s was carried out.

3.2 THE DEPOSITORY INSTITUTIONS DEREGULATION AND MONETARY CONTROL ACT OF 1980

The Depository Institutions Deregulation and Monetary Control Act, DIDMCA, provided for expanded asset and liability powers and, simultaneously, increased the authority of the Federal Reserve. (The DIDMCA is also known as the Monetary Control Act of 1980 and as the Omnibus Banking Act.) Its main features are listed below.

1) New reserve requirements for both member and nonmember commercial banks were set. (See Exhibit 13.4.)
2) The Federal Reserve was instructed to provide services to *all* depository institutions, including access to the discount window.
3) The reserve requirements applicable to commercial banks were applied to other depository institutions. Savings and loans associations, mutual savings banks, and credit unions are now subject to uniform reserve requirements.
4) The Federal Reserve was instructed to establish a schedule of fees for services. (Prior to DIDMCA, there were generally no fees.)
5) The Depository Institutions Deregulation Committee (DIDC) was created to oversee the phase-out of Regulation Q deposit interest rate ceilings over a six-year period.

Type of deposit	Percentage
Transactions Accounts	
$0 = $26.3 million[1]	3%
Over $26.3 million[2]	12
Nonpersonal time deposits[3]	
Less than 1.5 years[4]	3
1.5 years or more	0
Eurocurrency liabilities[5]	3

◆ **Exhibit 13.4: Uniform reserve requirements specified in the DIDMCA of 1980**

◆ *Notes*:

1 This amount is adjusted each year by 80% of the change in total transactions accounts for all depository institutions. Effective December 1998, the base amount was $47.8 million.

2 Effective December 1995, the reserve requirement was reduced to 10% for transactions accounts in excess of the cut-off amount – $47.8 billion in 1998.

3 By original maturity.

4 Effective December 1990, the reserve requirement for all nonpersonal time deposits was reduced to 0%.

5 Effective December 1990, the reserve requirement for Eurocurrency liabilities was reduced to 0%.

◆ *Sources*:   Cooper, S. Kerry and Donald R. Fraser, *Banking Deregulation and the New Competition in Financial Services*, 1984, p. 117; *Federal Reserve Bulletin*, various issues; Federal Reserve Bank of Minneapolis: *http://woodrow.mpls.frb.fed.us/info/policy/res-req.html*.

6) Interest-bearing transactions accounts became legal products for all depository institutions. All banks and thrifts could offer negotiable order of withdrawal (NOW) accounts. Credit unions were permitted to offer share drafts. Only individuals and nonprofit organizations, however, could take advantage of NOW accounts.

7) The limit of insurance for accounts in depository institutions was raised from $40,000 to $100,000.

8) S&Ls could now offer credit cards and were permitted to make commercial real estate loans and consumer loans, each up to 20 percent of total assets.

9) Mutual savings banks could make business loans and offer demand accounts to business clients.

10) State usury laws were effectively eliminated for mortgage, business, and agricultural loans.

With the DIDMCA, the scope of Federal Reserve authority has been expanded from state bank members to *all* depository institutions. Depository institutions are more competitive in that they may now offer interest-bearing checking accounts. The legislation mandated the phased-out elimination of all deposit interest rate ceilings and allowed S&Ls and mutual savings banks to move into more diversified and profitable, albeit more risky, lines of business. At the same time, the deposit insurance ceiling increased by 150 percent. In other words, as more potential risk was introduced into depository institutions, the government safety net expanded – a dangerous combination.

Problems in the thrift industry did not completely disappear, of course. Moreover, both commercial banks and thrifts continued to operate at a competitive disadvantage *vis-à-vis* money market mutual funds, whose rates of return to investors were not constrained in any way. Legislation in 1982 attempted to correct these deficiencies.

3.3 THE GARN–ST. GERMAIN DEPOSITORY INSTITUTIONS ACT OF 1982

The Garn–St. Germain Act of 1982 was intended to expand financial institutions' powers even more and to facilitate the rescue of failing institutions. Its major provisions are:

1) The money market deposit account (MMDA) was legalized for depository institutions. MMDAs could compete directly with money market mutual funds.
2) Federal, state, and local governments were permitted to own NOW accounts.
3) Federally chartered S&Ls were empowered to offer demand accounts to persons or organizations with whom they had business relationships.
4) The DIDC was instructed to eliminate (Regulation A) deposit rate differentials between commercial banks and thrifts.
5) Savings and loan associations were permitted to diversify asset portfolios further, up to certain percentages of total assets:
   a) commercial real estate loans   40 percent
   b) secured and unsecured commercial loans   5 percent
   c) commercial leasing   10 percent
   d) consumer loans   30 percent
6) Savings and loan associations could add state and local government revenue bonds to their asset portfolios. (Before 1982, only investments in general obligation bonds were allowed.)
7) Federal regulators received more financial and geographic flexibility for rescuing thrifts, making it possible for financial and nonfinancial firms to purchase thrifts on more favorable terms for the buyers.
8) The percentage of capital that a national bank could lend to a single borrower was increased from 10 to 15 percent, plus an additional 10 percent for loans collateralized by readily marketable assets.
9) National banks were permitted to form bank service companies and to invest in export trading firms. These provisions gave national banks more operational flexibility.
10) The transfer of assets (excluding low-quality assets) between bank holding companies and affiliated banks was substantially liberalized.
11) The Federal Deposit Insurance Corporation (FDIC), the Federal Savings and Loan Insurance Corporation (FSLIC), and the National Credit Union Administration (NCUA) were instructed to study the Federal deposit insurance system and to identify and evaluate possible alternatives.

The Garn–St. Germain Act made it easier for regulators to close failing thrift institutions. Under the Act, depository institutions can now compete directly with money market funds, by offering a similar instrument *with* deposit insurance coverage. For commercial banks, lending limits to individual customers were increased and the scope of activities expanded. S&Ls' powers were so transformed that, at least in terms of statutory powers, it became difficult to distinguish S&Ls from commercial banks.

Even these expanded powers did not bring an end to the problems in the savings and loan and commercial banking industries. In fact, the 1980s would witness bank and S&L failure rates that had not seen since the 1930s.

Deposit Insurance

In 1989, Congress was compelled to restructure the deposit insurance system and make major changes in regulatory oversight. The federal deposit insurance agencies that were created in the early 1930s have only recently been seriously challenged. During the 37 years from 1943 through 1979, only 210 banks failed. But in the six-year period ended 1985, 300 failed. Another 769 failed between 1986 and 1989. Thus, in the 1980s, over 1,000 banks failed, five times the number of failures in the previous four decades. Contraction of the savings and loan industry has been even more severe. S&Ls numbered over 5,000 in 1979. By 1989, only 3,000 remained and the number continues to decline each year.

4.1 Too Big to Fail

Not all the bank failures have been handled in the same way. When the troubled bank is large, it is more likely that all depositors and creditors will be paid by the FDIC. The controversial arrangement for large banks is attributed to the "too big to fail" theory of deposit insurance. In essence, it means that depositors in large institutions have implicit insurance on all deposits, including those with balances in excess of $100,000, and that general creditors (without the status of deposits) will also face no loss. The concept is controversial because it:

- Involves differential treatment of bank depositors by a government agency
- Discourages depositors in large banks from forcing market discipline on those banks, as the depositors remain confident that their investments are safe regardless of bank behavior
- Causes depositors to have less confidence in small banks, thereby making them less competitive
- Greatly increases the exposure of FDIC to loss, thereby indirectly exposing the US taxpayers to greater loss

The FDIC's reason for handling large troubled banks in this way is the potential effect to the banking system as a whole should a large bank fail. A large bank failure could bring systemwide instability and bank runs. The cost of this instability is thought to be greater than the cost of an unconditional bank bailout.

The first instance of this special treatment was Continental Illinois National Bank in 1984, with liabilities of $33 billion, of which only $3 billion were insured. All claims of depositors and creditors were completely guaranteed by the government. To rescue the bank, the coordinated efforts of the FDIC, the Federal Reserve, and a private bank syndicate were necessary.

4.2 The Crisis and FIRREA

In the savings and loan industry, there were no institutions that were too big too fail. In fact, most operate with relatively little regulatory oversight. The new powers of the 1980 and 1982 legislation combined with higher deposit insurance, were tailor-made for abuse in a lax regulatory climate.

Many S&Ls attracted *brokered deposits*, large certificates of deposit (CDs) sold through securities brokers. Since the CDs were completely insured as long as the deposit did not exceed $100,000, investors were confident that their money was safe and asked few questions about the soundness of the S&L that issued the CDs. The S&L had a ready source of cash then to invest in new activities permitted to it, including junk bonds, commercial loans, commercial real estate loans, and direct real estate investments. The originally conservative residential mortgage finance industry was transformed into a free-wheeling, high risk money machine, completely insured by the federal government. (See also chapter 26.)

The failure rate among S&Ls became so high that the Financial Institutions Reform, Recovery, and Enforcement Act (FIRREA) was passed in August 1989. Under the strain of widespread failures, the Federal Savings and Loan Insurance Corporation (FSLIC) was declared insolvent and absorbed by the FDIC. (The fund that insures savings and loan associations is still maintained separately from the bank insurance fund. Under the FDIC, the S&L fund is designated the Savings Association Insurance Fund (SAIF).) FDIC resources had also been strained. Bank failures had accelerated because of bank loans to Third World countries and domestic bank loans in the oil and gas and commercial real estate sectors. The Bank Insurance Fund (BIF, the renamed FDIC fund), which stood at $18 billion at the beginning of 1988, fell to $11.4 in 1990. At year-end 1991, the BIF had a deficit (negative) balance of $7 billion.

FIRREA attempted to correct some of the excesses of the early 1980s legislation by requiring higher capital levels and more prudent investment policies for thrifts, shoring up the federal insurance funds, and limiting the use of brokered deposits. Exhibit 13.5 outlines the major provisions of this legislation.

4.3 AFTER FIRREA

FIRREA also instructed the Treasury Department to conduct major studies on the issue of federal deposit insurance. In fact, the current deposit insurance system had sometimes been cited as a significant cause of the instability in the banking industry. The rationale for this argument was that the government guarantee encourages excessive risk taking by managers of financial institutions. The incentive to take risk was said to be strong because any failure of risky investments to pay off as originally anticipated does not hurt depositors; the federal government assumes the deposit liabilities. The converse is true if these risky investments *do* pay off, the bank and its managers prosper. This situation is often referred to as a *moral hazard* – investing with all the attendant benefits, but passing the costs (potential losses) along to another party.

The FDIC Assessment Act of 1990 gave the FDIC broad authority to set premiums in order to maintain desired reserves-to-deposit ratios for the BIF and the SAIF. The assessment ceilings and maximum rate increases specified in FIRREA were eliminated.

4.4 FDIC IMPROVEMENT ACT OF 1991

The FDIC Improvement Act (FDICIA) of 1991 mandated that risk-based insurance assessments be developed by FDIC no later than January 1994. According to this legislation, BIF assessments were not permitted to fall below 0.23 percent of deposits until the ratio of fund balance to insured deposits reached 1.25 percent. FDICIA required that such restoration of the BIF be achieved within 15 years of enactment of the legislation. For the SAIF, the 1.25 percent ratio was to be achieved within 20 years of enactment.

FIRREA includes provisions affecting commercial banking and savings and loan associations. Major provisions are:

1) The Federal Home Loan Bank Board (previously the primary regulator of savings and loan associations) and the Federal Savings and Loan Insurance Corporation were abolished. The Office of Thrift Supervision (within the Treasury Department), became the chief regulator and the FDIC took over the insurance function. The FDIC now maintains two funds: the Bank Insurance Fund (BIF) and the Savings Association Insurance Fund (SAIF).

2) The Resolution Funding Corporation was created to sell bonds to raise the funds necessary to complete the liquidation of failed savings and loan associations (S&Ls). The Resolution Trust Corporation (RTC) oversees the liquidations.

3) Insurance premiums increased for both S&Ls and commercial banks. S&L premiums per $100 of deposits were to increase from 20.8 cents to 23 cents in 1991, then decrease to 18 cents in 1994 and to 15 cents in 1998. Bank insurance premiums per $100 of deposits were to increase from 8.3 cents to 12 cents in 1990 and to 15 cents in 1991. FIRREA also gave FDIC the right to increase the rates in either fund, if necessary, to ensure solvency of SAIF and BIF. Premiums may not exceed 32.5 cents per $100 of deposits or be raised by more than 7.5 cents per year.

4) The Community Reinvestment Act of 1977 was amended to require public disclosure of a depository institution's regulatory rating with respect to community reinvestment. In addition, member institutions of Federal Home Loan Banks were to establish special funds to help finance home purchases, housing rehabilitation, and economic development for low- and moderate-income families.

5) For S&Ls, minimum tangible capital was set at 1.5 percent of total assets.[1] Minimum core capital was set at 3 percent of total assets. By the end of December 1992, thrifts are required to meet the same capital requirements as commercial banks (prescribed by the Office of the Comptroller of the Currency).

6) Any insured depository institution that does not meet minimum capital requirements may not accept brokered deposits.[2]

7) Savings institutions may no longer invest in bonds that are not rated investment grade. All holdings of such "junk" bonds must be sold as soon as possible, but no later than 1994.

8) The penalties for bank fraud were stiffened. The maximum fine increased from $5,000 to $1 million and the maximum prison term increased from 10 to 20 years.

◆ **Exhibit 13.5: The Financial Institutions Reform, Recovery, and Enforcement Act (FIRREA) of 1989**

◆ *Notes:*   1   Tangible capital includes common stock equity, noncumulative preferred stock, nonwithdrawable deposit accounts, pledged deposits, and minority interest in consolidated subsidiaries. Core capital is tangible capital plus qualifying intangibles, including goodwill (the premium paid by an investor when purchasing a troubled thrift institution).

                2   Brokered deposits are placed with a depository institution through a third party, typically a securities broker. The broker tries to find the highest rate of return available in an institution that is federally insured. Previously, troubled institutions could attract large amounts of brokered deposits by offering high interest rates, putting even more pressure on profits.

◆ *Reference:*   Meyer, Dianne and Sandra A. Ballard. "Issues in Lending: A Guide to FIRREA," *Journal of Commercial Bank Lending*, 72 (January 1990), pp. 11–23.

Also, FDICIA permitted the FDIC to borrow up to $70 billion from the US Treasury Department and from member banks to fund resolution of troubled institutions. However, the average BIF and SAIF assessment rates were not permitted to fall below 0.23 percent and 0.15 percent, respectively, until the 1.25 percent fund balance-to-insured deposits had been achieved and any borrowings repaid.

4.5 RESTORATION OF THE INSURANCE FUNDS

In May 1995, the BIF had repaid its borrowings (approximately $30 billion) and had achieved the 1.25 percent fund balance-to-insured deposits ratio. The SAIF achieved this status as of September 30, 1996. By first quarter 1999, the BIF and the SAIF amounted to $29.9 billion and $9.9 billion, respectively. In 1999, insurance assessments for both funds were based on capital ratios and on overall ratings of risk. (The overall ratings of risk are called CAMEL ratings and they range from 1 (best) to 5 (worst). See also chapter 15.) With the funds officially recapitalized, assessment rates were set between 0 percent and 0.27 percent. Exhibit 13.6 summarizes the risk-based assessments. The deposit insurance funds have been restored to health and the wave of failures in the industry appears to have ended.

Capital Adequacy	Risk Category		
	Low	Moderate	High
Well capitalized	0.00%	0.03%	0.17%
Adequately capitalized	0.03	0.10	0.24
Undercapitalized	0.10	0.24	0.27

◆ **Exhibit 13.6: FDIC assessment rates, second quarter, 1998**

◆ *Notes*: a) Capital adequacy is established based on three different capital ratios involving common equity, regulatory capital, total assets and risk-adjusted assets. (See also chapter 17 for a discussion of capital ratios and international capital standards.)

b) Risk categories are evaluated based on capital levels, asset quality, management of the bank, earnings, and liquidity (CAMEL).

◆ *Source*:   Federal Deposit Insurance Corporation, *FDIC Quarterly Banking Profile*, First Quarter 1999.

 **Summary**

The basic tools of monetary policy are reserve requirements, the discount rate, and open market operations. The Federal Reserve has the responsibility to conduct monetary policy so as to maintain price stability and to encourage economic growth.

After the major bank legislation of the 1930s, the structure of the commercial bank system remained virtually unchanged until 1980, when depository institutions were deregulated in order to overcome competitive disadvantages *vis-à-vis* nondepository financial institutions. Thereafter, institutions failed at rates not seen since before the 1930s legislation.

In 1989, the federal agency responsible for savings and loan insurance (FSLIC) folded and was replaced by the FDIC-supervised SAIF. Commercial banks continued to be insured by the FDIC-supervised BIF. Commercial bank failures accelerated, causing assets in the commercial bank insurance fund (FDIC) to decline for the first time since its inception. New legislation in 1991 provided new resources to FDIC in the form of borrowings and higher compulsory insurance premiums.

The low-interest-rate environment of the early 1990s helped depository institutions. By 1996, the banking and savings and loan industries had been restored to health, the FDIC had been recapitalized, and FDIC premiums had been converted to a risk-based system.

 End-of-chapter Questions

1. How were the powers of the Federal Reserve increased by the legislation of 1980?

2. Define the primary tools of monetary policy and indicate their relative importance.

3. Refer the *Federal Reserve Bulletin* in your university library.

   a. How many times in the last two years has the discount rate been changed?

   b. Why do you suppose the Fed made these changes?

4. What factors led to the "deregulation" of banks?

5. What were the major provisions of the Depository Institutions Deregulation and Monetary Control Act of 1980?

6. What were the major provisions of the Garn-St. Germain Depository Institutions Act of 1982?

7. In what ways did the Financial Institutions Reform, Recovery, and Enforcement Act of 1989 attempt to correct the excesses of the 1980s?

8. Why was federal deposit insurance a topic of debate in the early 1990s?

9. Why does deposit insurance present a moral hazard?

10. Describe the risk-based deposit insurance premiums in effect in 1998.

NOTE

1   John Maynard Keynes (1883–1946), the English economist, advocated the use of government deficit spending in order to promote employment and to maintain (or increase) national income. His theories inspired national economic policies in the United States after the Great Depression. Keynes was also an advocate for the creation of the World Bank at the Bretton Woods Conference in 1944. See chapter 2 for coverage of Bretton Woods.

Selected References

Benston, George J. and George G. Kaufman. *Risk and Solvency Regulation of Depository Institutions: Past Policies and Current Options*, Salomon Brothers Center for the Study of Financial Institutions at the Graduate School of Business Administration of New York University, New York, 1988.

Ciocca, Pierluigi, ed. *Money and the Economy: The Central Bankers' Views*, Macmillan Press, London, 1987.

Cooper, S. Kerry and Donald R. Fraser. *Banking Deregulation and the New Competition in Financial Services*, Ballinger Publishing, Cambridge, Mass, 1984.

Federal Deposit Insurance Corp. "Executive Management Report: Financial Results for the Nine Months Ending September 30, 1996," Washington, DC, 1996.

The Federal Reserve System: Purposes and Functions, Board of Governors of the Federal Reserve System, Washington, DC, 1984.

Goodfriend, Marvin. *Monetary Policy in Practice*, Federal Reserve Bank of Richmond, Richmond, Va., 1987.

Goodhart, Charles. *The Evolution of Central Banks*, MIT Press, Cambridge, Mass., 1988.

Greider, William. *Secrets of the Temple: How the Federal Reserve Runs the Country*, Touchstone/Simon and Schuster, New York, 1989.

Modernizing the Financial System: Recommendations for Safer, More Competitive Banks, US Department of the Treasury, Washington, DC, 1991.

Price Waterhouse. *A Guide to the FDIC Improvement Act*, Washington, DC, 1992.

Spong, Kenneth. *Banking Regulation: Its Purposes, Implementation, and Effects*, Federal Bank of Kansas City, Kansas City, Mo., 1990.

Toniolo, Gianni, ed. *Central Banks' Independence in Historical Perspective*, Walter de Gruyter, Berlin, 1988.

Central Banks and Regulatory Systems Outside the US

chapter 14

CHAPTER OVERVIEW

This chapter:
- Pinpoints certain trends in the evolution of financial system regulation.
- Provides an overview of the financial regulatory systems of selected developed and developing countries.

KEY TERMS

Basle Accord
Basle Committee on Banking Regulations
central bank
chaebol
European Central Bank
keiretsu

mutual recognition
North American Free Trade Agreement
universal banking
window guidance
zaibatsu

CHAPTER OUTLINE

INTERNATIONAL COMPARISONS:

Belgium	Korea
Brazil	Malaysia
Canada	Mexico
European Union	The Netherlands
Germany	Taiwan
Japan	United Kingdom

 Introduction

Chapters 12 and 13 examined the US Federal Reserve System. In this chapter, the regulatory environments of several other countries are discussed. With sometimes significant differences in orientation, one of the biggest challenges to today's central banks in industrialized countries is to manage their role in a global environment and to coordinate their activities with the rest of their counterparts.

 Regulatory Trends

1.1 Regulatory Systems

There are essentially two distinctly different forms of bank regulation. The first is a *formal regulatory system*, complete with specific requirements and guidelines for balance sheet ratios. The objective of such legal stipulation is to ensure stability of bank activity and monetary conditions. Examples of formal regulatory systems are those of the United States, Japan, and continental Europe.

The second type of system has involved much more informal control. This is not to suggest that orderliness is a lower priority under less formal systems. Instead, the difference appears to be more related to financial system infrastructure. Where a small number of banks has existed or where banks and other financial institutions have been concentrated within a limited geographical area, a *system of nonstatutory supervision* has evolved.

The geographically concentrated financial markets of the United Kingdom, Belgium, and Luxembourg are examples. Frequent interaction between senior bank management and supervisory authorities has made it possible for authorities to adequately assess bank operations and attendant risks. To the extent that such close contact has been effective, there exists little incentive to formalize the relationships.

Nevertheless, deregulation of financial services and the blurring of past lines of distinction between financial institutions has led to a trend toward *increased statutory guidelines* and even more effective oversight. The UK Banking Act of 1979 created a legislative framework for authorization of deposit-taking activity and supervision by the Bank of England. Before 1979, supervision was largely informal.

In Canada, there is a combination of informal and formal controls. The banking system there developed after its US counterpart, with the first commercial bank being chartered in 1817 and the Bank of Canada (central bank) not being created until 1934. This time difference allowed Canadians to observe some of the problems in the United States associated with having a large number of unit banks. Nationwide branching was accepted in Canada from the outset. As a result, six Canadian banks now control about 90 percent of all bank assets. This structure makes it easy to coordinate policies with fewer laws and regulations. Formal controls consist mainly of laws that mandate public disclosure and regulate permissible bank activities. Laws have also been passed to allow supervisory authorities to issue formal regulations with respect to cash and secondary reserves, capital adequacy, and liquidity levels.

1.2 INTERNATIONAL COORDINATION

Another significant worldwide trend is toward greater *international cooperation* among supervisory authorities. Until the 1970s, there was no formalized international coordination. Then the Herstatt Bank, one of Germany's largest privately held banks, failed. This $900 million bank ran up foreign currency exchange losses in June 1974 that sent it to the Bundesbank for emergency funds. The Bundesbank found that the record-keeping was so poor that it could not determine the extent of loss within a short period of time. The bank was closed at 4:00 p.m., German time. New York banks were still open but unable to complete their currency transactions with the closed Herstatt. This, of course, also exposed the US banks to loss. In the final accounting, Herstatt's losses amounted to $500 million. The growing interdependence of systems and the ease with which risk is sometimes spread across borders has led to more structured international communications.

The European Union (EU) has an ultimate goal of uniform bank regulation throughout the region. (This objective is part of the larger initiative of creating *one* economic market that is composed of the 15 member nations. See chapter 9.) The 1977 directive was the first step in this direction. Guidelines for bank licensing and supervision were to be formulated in as consistent a fashion as possible across EC members. The Banking Act of 1979 in the United Kingdom was drafted to comply with this first banking directive. To encourage the flow of information across borders, the second banking directive in 1989 is based on the concept of a single banking license. With one license, a bank has the right to operate throughout the EU. Similar provisions have been made for securities firms and insurance companies. With the so-called single passport, banks will be able to essentially engage in universal banking throughout the EU as long as there is *mutual recognition* in the home country of the bank. The list of permissible activities includes:

1) Deposit-taking and other forms of borrowing
2) Financial leasing
3) Money transmission services
4) Guarantees and commitments
5) Trading for the bank's own account in CDs, bonds, government securities, futures and options, foreign currency and securities
6) Issuance of securities
7) Money brokering
8) Portfolio management
9) Securities safekeeping services
10) Credit reference services

> **Mutual recognition:**
> In the context of the European Union, when foreign banks are licensed to operate in a host country, those banks domestic to the host country must be permitted the same scope of activities when they establish offices in the home countries of the foreign banks.

The final stage of monetary union for EU countries includes a functional European Central Bank. The central bankers within the EU differ with respect to the degree of autonomy that the members should have to determine national monetary policy. There is also debate as to the autonomy of the European Central Bank itself. On one hand, monetary policy can be considered only one part of an agenda aimed toward economic policy coordination. In this sense, it is possible that the objectives of the European Central Bank could change over time, given changing needs for employment and economic growth. On the other hand, monetary policy can be considered a cornerstone not to be disturbed, that is, price stability is an objective that would not change under differing economic conditions. Of course, the second interpretation implies a more independent European Central Bank, such as the Federal Reserve. The exact status of the European Central Bank must be developed by EU members over a number of years. But whatever its form, the European Central Bank will significantly increase international cooperation among central banks.

International cooperation extends beyond the EU. The Organization for Economic Cooperation and Development (OECD) organized the Basle Committee on Banking Regulations and Supervisory Practices to address the relevant issues of international banking. The committee's report, known as the Basle Concordat, was completed in 1975 and subsequently revised. (The Basle Accord addresses the coordination of bank capital requirements: see chapter 17, Capital and Asset/Liability Management.) It was endorsed by the regulators of the Group of Ten and Luxembourg in 1983 and subsequently endorsed by the regulators of several other countries. (The Group of Ten consists of Belguim, Canada, France, Germany, Italy, Japan, the Netherlands, Sweden, the United States, and the United Kingdom. Switzerland is an associate member.) Now referred to as the Basle Accord, this agreement is the basis for international coordination among banking authorities.

The two broad, primary principles of the Accord:

- No foreign banking institution in a given host country should be without supervision.
- Supervision should be adequate.

The Accord also outlines basic areas of responsibility for oversight, assigning some functions to host country authorities and others to parent country authorities.

Functional assignments are in the areas of *solvency*, *liquidity*, and *foreign exchange operations*. Supervision to assure solvency of foreign *branches* (offices of the parent institution) is the primary responsibility of the parent country. The solvency of foreign *subsidiaries* (separate legal entities) is assigned to the host country, while that of *joint ventures* (owned by interests from the home and the host countries) falls to the country of incorporation.

The level of liquidity of both branches and subsidiaries falls within the purview of host country supervisory bodies. Again, for joint ventures, the country of incorporation is held accountable. However, the liquidity of foreign offices can affect the liquidity of the group to which it belongs. So, parent countries are held responsible for adequacy of control systems and procedures.

Lastly, foreign exchange operations are the shared responsibility of host and parent countries. The host country monitors the foreign exchange position of those institutions operating within its territory. The parent monitors the position of the entire institution.

In general, regulators seek to coordinate their financial systems across national borders with the same objectives that operate within these borders – safety and soundness, efficiency, and competitiveness. As these systems evolve, the changing environment will require flexibility for the oversight function to keep pace with, but not constrain, the evolution.

Developed country	Stock market capitalization	
	Amount	% of all developed countries
United States	$6,857,622	43.2%
Japan	3,667,292	23.1
United Kingdom	1,407,737	8.9
Germany	577,365	3.6
France	522,053	3.3
Switzerland	433,621	2.7
Canada	366,344	2.3
The Netherlands	356,481	2.2
Others	1,703,659	10.7

Developing country	Stock market capitalization	
	Amount	% of all developing countries
Malaysia	$222,729	11.7%
Taiwan	187,206	9.9
Korea	181,955	9.6
Brazil	147,636	7.8
Thailand	141,506	7.5
India	127,199	6.7
Mexico	90,694	4.8
Others	796,784	42.0

◆ **Exhibit 14.1:** **Stock market capitalization, selected countries, 1995 (millions)**

◆ *Source*:   International Finance Corporation, *Emerging Stock Markets Factbook 1996.*

② Selected Regulatory Systems

Exhibit 14.1 contains lists of the largest financial systems in developed and developing countries in the mid-1990s. The remainder of the chapter includes highlights of central banks and financial system regulation in several of these countries.

2.1 JAPAN

The bank regulatory system of Japan has several features in common with that of the United States. Article 65, like the Glass-Steagall Act in the United States, prohibits commercial banks in Japan from underwriting corporate stock. Historically, interest rates have been closely regulated but are being liberalized. Policies of the Bank of Japan (central bank) are essentially extensions of government policy.

Before the the Second World War (1939–45), the *zaibatsu* dominated Japan. These huge industrial groups represented joint ownership of financial institutions and diverse nonfinancial firms. The banks channeled funds to the industrial firms. After the war, Allied powers dismantled the legal ties to reduce the concentration of economic power.

Zaibatsu:
> A Japanese holding company with a wide of variety of subsidiary firms, a form of business organization that existed after the Meiji Restoration of 1868 until the end of the Second World War.

After the Second World War, the close link between the banking and industrial sectors was still undeniable. The legal structure disappeared, but economic ties remained. The more loosely constructed groups, *keiretsu*, continued to function.

Keiretsu:
> A system of joint corporate ownership without a formal holding company. Each member of the group owns a small portion of stock in all the other members so that as much as 80 percent of the stock of each is held by affiliated companies.

This heritage has had a profound effect on the regulatory environment in Japan, where banks are permitted to hold large portfolios of corporate stocks. Short- and medium-term loans have historically been rolled over with the effect that they essentially became long-term loans. Using these close ties between financial and nonfinancial sectors, the Bank of Japan has given preferential loan rates to banks to fund loans specifically targeted for industries that the government has considered high priorities. Through *window guidance*, the Bank of Japan controls all aspects of commercial credit and money supply. In this way, the government indirectly influenced the post-Second World War reconstruction of Japan through its central bank.

Window guidance:
> Persuasion used by the Bank of Japan to convince commercial banks to support those industries deemed important for the country's growth and development.

One outgrowth has been high debt ratios in Japanese firms as compared to US companies. However, as Japanese capital markets have developed, corporations have begun to rely much less on their *keiretsu* banks. Today, stocks and bonds are much more common sources of corporate finance than previously has been the case.

In 1993, the Financial System Reform Act (FSRA) reversed the restriction on commercial banks in the securities industry (according to Article 65). The FSRA allows (1) banks to operate securities subsidiaries and (2) securities firms to engage in banking activities. Implementation of FSRA has been staggered.

- Long-term credit banks were allowed to enter securities business before major commercial banks were permitted to establish securities subsidiaries.
- The new subsidiaries are restricted from entering certain lines of business.
  - New trust bank subsidiaries may not engage in the management of pension funds. These are reserved for trust banks licensed prior to the FSRA.
  - New securities subsidiaries established by banks are not permitted to engage in brokerage activities or to underwrite equity securities. This provision protects pre-FSRA brokerage activities and securities firms involved in stock underwriting.

In June 1997, the Ministry of Finance (treasury department of Japan) formally announced a "blueprint" for financial deregulation that is intended to place Tokyo on equal footing with London and New York as an international financial center – the Japanese "Big Bang." The recommendations were the product of a panel of more than 100 experts from several bureaus of the Ministry of Finance. The most significant of these recommendations is that, by March 2000, banks, insurance companies, and brokerage firms will be able to enter each other's business by forming holding companies. The holding companies will also enable weaker institutions to be merged into larger firms. Also, these reforms will provide foreign firms the ability to enter the Japanese market.

Such holding companies had been banned for more than 50 years. However, the Ministry of Finance hopes that these companies will foster greater competition and shift the emphasis from traditional lending and deposit-taking business to a full range of sophisticated and varied financial services. After long negotiations, Japanese banks will be able to offer insurance and investment funds.

2.2 GERMANY

German corporations also have close relationships with their banks. As was true in Japan, these ties were instrumental in Germany's post-Second World War industrial buildup.

There is an important difference, however. The German bank system is much less regulated than that of Japan. An important manifestation of this relative freedom from regulation is the long-standing ability of West German banks to underwrite and hold corporate stocks and bonds. In fact, German banks offer such a wide range of services that they are called *universal bank*, offering these services to their customers in a competitive environment.

> **Universal bank:**
> A bank that has the legal authority to offer all financial services and may, thus, be engaged in securities and insurance underwriting as well as the full range of more traditional banking services.

While interest rate deregulation in the United States and Japan *began* in the late 1970s, West German rate deregulation *was completed* in 1976. Thus, in a legal structure emphasizing minimal government interference, German banks have been free to compete vigorously in the provision of corporate finance and other services.

2.3 CANADA

The Canadian banking system is highly concentrated, with six institutions with nationwide branches representing the vast majority of banking activities. Competition among Canadian financial institutions has increased since 1967, as a result of the Canadian Bank Act. The act removed deposit rate ceilings and granted expanded lending powers to depository institutions. Chartered (commercial) banks began to offer deposits at market rates of interest and to cultivate mortgage and consumer loan business.

Having been permitted greater powers through deregulation in the late 1980s, Canadian banks have purchased Canada's largest securities dealers, made major acquisitions in the trust industry, started insurance subsidiaries, and assumed a major role in the mutual fund industry. In this regard, the Canadian banking system may now be considered a "universal" banking system, as is the case in Germany.

Under terms of the North American Free Trade Agreement (NAFTA), rules were established to govern trade and investment in financial services in the countries involved – the United States, Canada, and Mexico. US and Mexican financial services firms (banks, securities firms, and insurance companies) have the right to establish operations in Canada under the same rules as indigenous firms. (See also chapter 19 for a discussion of NAFTA.)

Thus, the Canadian banking system is dominated by a few, large institutions with good relations with the government. As a result, Canadian banks have wide-ranging powers in the financial sector. The foreign banking sector is largely insignificant in terms of market share, but does enjoy support of bank regulators to encourage competition. Under NAFTA, US and Mexican financial services firms enjoy the same treatment as Canadian institutions.

2.4 THE NETHERLANDS

The Netherlands Bank is the central bank of the Netherlands. Founded as a private institution in 1814, The Netherlands Bank has had the sole right of note issue since 1863. The Netherlands Bank was nationalized in 1948 and is the regulatory body that is responsible for registering banks and other credit institutions. The Act on the Supervision of the Credit System of 1952 and its 1956 and 1978 amendments, gives the Netherlands Bank power to regulate banks and other institutions. These powers include carrying out audits, enforcing minimum liquidity and solvency conditions, and, when insolvency threatens, appointing a supervisor to oversee the bank's operations.

In 1980, government restrictions were imposed to prevent Dutch banks from investing in Dutch insurance companies, and vice versa. In 1990, these restrictions were removed, paving the way for formation of universal banks in the Netherlands. The banking industry is dominated by three institutions involved in universal banking. Domestic and foreign banks operate under the same rules and regulations. However, indigenous institutions have a competitive advantage based on business practice in the Netherlands, including linked directorships and long-standing financial relations.

2.5 MALAYSIA

When Malaysia became an independent state within the British Commonwealth in 1957, foreign banks controlled 89 percent of all bank offices. The government used the banking system to promote development in specific industrial sectors and to promote more equitable income distribution. The indigenous residents of Malaysia and ethnic Malays are referred to as the Bumiputra community. Bank Negara, the central bank, sets lending guidelines that target the Bumiputra community, small businesses, and low-cost residential real estate. Banks are required to extend 20 percent of loans to Bumiputras.

In 1996, there were 37 commercial banks in Malaysia. Three quarters of the assets of these institutions are held by domestically controlled banks. However, many of the domestic banks had foreign participation. The top five domestic banks controlled approximately one-half of total commercial bank assets in 1996.

The Malaysian banking authorities are concerned that the banking industry is too fragmented. Already, some consolidation has taken place. A mid-1980s recession in Malaysia revealed the severe problem of bad bank loans, attributable partially to government direction or credit allocation policies (by which the government directs the granting of loans to specific sectors of the economy). Also, there were indications that both management and supervision had been inadequate. From the mid-1980s to the mid-1990s, nearly half of all domestic and foreign banks in Malaysia changed ownership. The government is now taking steps to encourage further consolidation in the industry, especially in those institutions that offer only one type of banking such as consumer banking or corporate finance.

2.6 TAIWAN

The banking system of Taiwan is dominated by state-owned institutions that have been used to achieve the goals of economic development. These institutions continue to dominate the economy even as new private institutions have been established recently. The financial system is protected from foreign competition, although this, too, is changing. Rapid escalation of real estate values in Taiwan led to a "bubble economy" that burst in the early 1990s when real estate values declined significantly. As a result, Taiwanese banks are exposed to associated, troublesome, real estate loan losses.

The largest deposit-taking financial institution in Taiwan is the Postal Savings System (PSS). With more than 1,500 branches throughout the country, the PSS has more offices than the commercial banks. However, the PSS may not extend conventional loans. Instead, the deposits (liabilities) are redeposited (assets) with designated commercial banks.

Historically, the commercial banking system of Taiwan has been tightly controlled. Until 1991, there were 16 domestic banks, of which all but four were either government-owned or government-controlled. The four privately owned institutions accounted for less than 10 percent of total bank deposits in 1991, while the six banks owned by provincial (state) governments held more than 75 percent of total deposits. In 1991, 16 new banks were established. Each of these new banks must have a minimum capital of NT$10 billion (US$370 million) and is operated by a private conglomerate. The new banks have been permitted to operate a maximum of seven offices initially and to, subsequently, open five additional offices each year. In addition, 37 branches of foreign banks and eight banks that specialize in business loans operated in Taiwan in 1996.

2.7 KOREA

When military rule began in Korea in 1961, banks were nationalized and the central bank, the Bank of Korea, was placed under control of the Ministry of Finance and Economy. Subsequently in the 1980s, democratic rule returned to Korea. Over time, many of the banks have been privatized. However, the Bank of Korea remains under the strong influence of the Korean government. Nevertheless, independence of the central bank has increased in recent years.

Having enjoyed rapid economic growth in the 1980s and 1990s, Korea is moving from the status of a developing country to that of a developed one. Ironically, Korea is also in the position of having a high savings rate (individuals investing in financial instruments) *and* a chronic shortage of capital (shortfalls of funds for consumer finance and for business). This paradox is the result of many years of credit allocation by the government, policy loans – often to selected major companies, called *chaebol* – and no alternative for the individual and small business.

> *Chaebol:*
> A Korean system of business organization through which manufacturers, suppliers, and distributors are linked in large, diversified conglomerates. (Similar to Japanese *keiretsu*.)

For example, Korean banks are not permitted to lend to a firm involved in tourism. This is not a statutory restriction or a regulatory prohibition. Instead, it is an unwritten, understood guideline that the government wants to promote, for example, the steel industry, not tourism. Control of the government is such that many bank presidents are appointed by the government and banks may not raise funds on the Korean Stock Exchange without government permission. Banks may neither open overseas offices nor merge without government permission.

Such restrictions have led to the formation of an illegal financial market – the kerb market. It is estimated that thousands of Korean companies use these neighborhood, underground banks for financing. Local newspapers contain classified advertisements for a variety of financing including balances in alias bank accounts and the use of credit cards as an extension of financing. One may even be approached with the offer of kerb finance while walking at mid-day in Seoul (nation's capital). The interest rate is usually between 25 percent and 30 percent per year, but the credit is readily available.

For consumers and small businesses, the kerb credit is also needed. Because the government has directed credit toward targeted industries, consumer finance is virtually nonexistent within the formal commercial bank system. There are no real mortgage loans in the formal market, as banks provide loans of up to 10 percent of construction costs and only after a substantial, upfront, deposit is made. Potential home buyers must pay the remainder in cash or seek financing from family and friends. If these sources prove insufficient, many tap the kerb market.

In the 1980s, the Korean government attempted to disband these illegal activities by offering kerb institutions licenses to operate as quasi-banks. Many kerb institutions converted to short-term financing companies while others converted to formal banks and stock brokerage firms. The government is attempting to remove demand for those that remain in the kerb market by permitting the establishment of financial institutions to provide loans for purchases of big-ticket consumer durables such as automobiles. Beginning in 1996, foreign investors have been able to open consumer credit companies in joint ventures with local Korean firms.

2.8 Brazil

In Brazil, some banks are privately owned, but others are owned by the government – state banks. The state banking system of Brazil has been a destabilizing force in the economy. State-owned financial institutions are a major source of financing for state governments. In the 1980s, despite revenues from the federal level, in many cases state governments ran budget deficits. That is, state expenditures exceeded cash inflows from all sources. These shortfalls were covered by borrowings from state banks, with a result that some of the state banks have had 80 percent of their loan portfolios invested in loans to state and local governments. When these governments defaulted on their loans, it became necessary for the Central Bank of Brazil (CBC) to intervene. This became a vicious cycle in which state banks alternatively were forced to lend to state and local governments and, upon default of the loans, then forced to seek relief from the federal government. Resolution of these financial circumstances continues, but will not be resolved quickly.

On the other hand, the private-sector banks of Brazil are much more efficiently managed. For this sector of the banking industry, nonperforming loans are, on average, less than 1 percent of total loans.

The ultimate success of economic reform in Brazil will depend on the extent to which constitutional reform is implemented. In 1996, the administration, among other things, continued to negotiate with the Brazilian Congress to reform the financial system. One aspect of such reform is to convince Brazilians that an independent central bank is advisable. The concept of a central bank that is free to defend the currency without government interference is foreign to most Brazilian citizens.

2.9 MEXICO

In the 1970s, inflation in Mexico became a problem that could not be ignored. Mexico was affected by the same inflationary pressures being felt in other countries. Mexican interest rate controls and high reserve requirements that were put in place only made the situation worse for banks. There was significant disintermediation in the Mexican financial sector, particularly the country's commercial banks. (*Disintermediation* is the withdrawal of funds from deposit accounts when other financial instruments offer more competitive rates of return.) To counteract the disintermediation, new reforms were introduced in 1974 and 1975.

Restructuring within the Mexican banking system took the form of consolidating the industry and giving commercial banks powers that previously they had not enjoyed. Financial groups, or conglomerates, were constructed of different types of financial institutions – banks, brokerage houses, insurance companies, and others. In addition, banks were permitted to take equity positions (buy stock) in industrial firms.

The Mexican banking industry consolidated as a result of the 1974 Law on Credit Institutions. This law permitted merger of different types of financial institutions. The number of banks in Mexico went from 139 in 1975 down to 60 by 1982, when the banks were nationalized. In 1982, Mexico announced that debt owed by the government to external creditors – in many cases, foreign commercial banks – could not be repaid as promised. This was the beginning of the Latin American debt crisis that affected the entire region. The financial crisis weakened Mexican banks and the Mexican government took over (nationalized) all the institutions and continued the consolidation process.

After nationalization of the banks, many of the former owners of commercial banks acquired or established nonbank financial institutions. Many affiliated with brokerage firms. Others entered the insurance, leasing, or foreign exchange business. During this period, the array of nonbank financial services increased considerably. Nonbank financial institutions became the main source of financial products and services for the private sector, including commercial paper and money market mutual funds. (See chapter 3 for coverage of commercial paper and chapter 28 for money market mutual funds.) By 1987, Mexican commercial banks held less than 50 percent of the assets of the country's financial institutions, among the lowest in Latin American countries.

In the late 1980s, the Mexican government began to restructure and liberalize bank regulations. In the interest of bank soundness, new laws and regulations imposed stiff capital level requirements. Also, a new loan classification system was instituted that promptly recognized past-due loans and limited certain activities – such as lending to one client or lending to the bank's own affiliates. At the same time, more independent, market-oriented management was assigned to the banks. Deregulation eliminated interest rate ceilings on deposits, eliminated forced investment in government securities, and removed foreign exchange controls. In an environment of improving government finances and an active government securities market, the competition among the banks increased almost immediately.

Beginning in June 1991, the 18 Mexican banks that remained after nationalization were re-privatized. Within 14 months, all Mexican banks were sold to private investors. Many of the new bank owners were holding companies that also owned securities firms and insurance companies, creating universal banking in Mexico.

Under terms of the North American Free Trade Agreement (NAFTA), effective January 1994, rules were established to govern trade and investment in financial services in the countries involved – the United States, Canada, and Mexico. Essentially, US and Canadian financial services firms (banks, securities firms, and insurance companies) have the right to establish operations in Mexico under the same rules as indigenous firms. (See also chapter 19 for a discussion of NAFTA.)

Subsequently in December 1994, the Mexican *peso* collapsed in value because of the high level of US dollar-denominated liabilities of the Mexican government and the relatively low level of US dollar reserves (dollar assets). As Mexican banks also had US dollar-denominated liabilities, these institutions were significantly weakened by the currency devaluation. As Mexican interest rates rose to counteract the currency devaluation, increasing numbers of Mexican bank customers found it very difficult to pay the higher interest on loans. Thus, Mexican banks had loss exposure in both liability and asset portfolios. Once again, the banking system has been weakened and it is necessary for the Mexican government to support the industry.

 ## Summary

Increased interaction of financial markets has driven much of the change in regulatory environments. Since world trade transmits many of the characteristics of one market to those of its trading partners, increased coordination among monetary authorities has become necessary. Even within national borders, competition among different financial institutions has led to deregulation of interest rates and investment powers. Nevertheless, wider scope of activity places even heavier responsibilities on the shoulders of regulators to maintain the systems' safety and soundness.

 ## End-of-chapter Questions

1. Explain current trends with respect to bank regulation.
2. With regard to the single bank license in the EU, is it possible that US banks might not be able to take advantage of the universal banking privileges provided for in the Second Banking Directive? Explain.
3. In several countries, there is a recent trend toward more statutory regulation of the banking system.

a. Why do you think this is so?

b. What took the place of statutory regulation previously?

c. Generally, contrast these systems to the US banking system.

4. In terms of the regulation of cross-border banking activities,

 a. What are the two basic principles of the Basle Accord?

 b. What are the three functional areas that must be supervised?

5. In Japan before the Second World War,

 a. What form of business conglomerate could be observed? Please explain the nature of this form of business.

 b. What role did banks play in this business system?

 c. What role did bank regulators play in this system?

6. In Japan,

 a. What form of business conglomerate can now be observed? Please explain the nature of this form of business.

 b. Using resources in your library, determine the status of bank regulation in Japan, especially as it relates to portfolios of bad loans.

7. With respect to US and Mexican banks operating in Canada, what has been the net effect of the North American Free Trade Agreement?

8. In Malaysia, how have government policy goals impacted the commercial banking industry?

9. In Taiwan,

 a. What has been the historical role of government in the Taiwanese banking industry?

 b. How has this changed recently?

10. Using your library sources, determine the status of the banking system in South Korea in connection with the *chaebol* system.

11. Why might it be said that the Brazilian banking system is really two different banking systems?

12. In what ways has the decline in the value of the Mexican peso put pressure on the Mexican banking system?

SELECTED REFERENCES

Adams, T. F. M. and Iwao Hoshii. *A Financial History of the New Japan*, Kodansha International, Tokyo, 1972.

Binhammer, H. H. *Money, Banking, and the Canadian Financial System*, Nelson Canada, Scarborough, Ont., 1988.

Bradbury, Nicholas. "Playing Lean and Mean in Canada," *Euromoney*, November 1993, pp. 92–4.

Bronte, Stephen. *Japanese Finance: Markets and Institutions*, Euromoney Publications, London, 1982.

Bureau of Economic Analysis, US Department of Commerce. *Business Statistics 1961–1988*, Washington, DC, 1989.

"Cardoso's Next Challenge (Brazil)," *The Banker*, November 1994, p. 87.

Ciocca, Pierluigi. *Money and the Economy: Central Bankers' Views*, Macmillan Press, London 1987.

"Commercial Banks Brace for Change," *Asiamoney*, May 1995, pp. 77–89.

Cooper, S. Kerry and Donald R. Fraser. *Banking Regulation and the New Competition in Financial Services*, Ballinger Publishing, Cambridge, Mass., 1984.

Department of Trade and Industry. *Europe 1992: The Facts*, London, February 1989.

Economic Council of Canada. *Globalization and Canada's Financial Markets*, Canadian Government Publishing Centre, Ottawa, Canada, 1989.

Folkerts-landau, David and Donald J. Mathieson. *The European Monetary System in the Context of the Integration of European Financial Markets*, International Monetary Fund, 1989.

Francke, Hans–Hermann and Michael Hudson. *Banking and Finance in West Germany*, Croom Helm, London, 1984.

Friesen, Connie M. *International Bank Supervision*, Euromoney Publications, London, 1986.

Goodhart, Charles. *The Evolution of Central Banks*, MIT Press, Cambridge, Mass., 1988.

Grady, John and Martin Weale. *British Banking, 1960–85*, Macmillan Press, London, 1986.

Guide to Brazil, Euromoney supplement, April 1994.

Hay, Tony. *A Guide to European Financial Centres*, Chicago and London: St. James Press, 1990.

International Monetary Fund. *International Capital Markets; Developments and Prospects*, Washington, DC, April 1989.

International Monetary Fund. *International Financial Statistics*, Washington, DC, Yearbook 1990 and May 1991.

Johnson, Hazel. *Banking in Asia*, Lafferty Publications, Dublin, 1997.

Johnson, Hazel. *Banking in Latin America*, Lafferty Publications, Dublin, 1998.

Kaufmann, Hugo M. *Germany's International Monetary Policy and the European Monetary System*, Brooklyn College Press, New York, 1985.

Korea, Asiamoney supplement, May 1995.

Malaysia: The Tiger Comes of Age, Asiamoney supplement, September 1995.

McGill, Peter. "Bank Reforms Start to Bite (Korea)," *Euromoney*, September 1995, p. 378.

McLean, Stuart K., ed. *The European Bond Markets: An Overview and Analysis for Money Managers and Traders*, 5th edn, Probus Publishing Company, Cambridge, England and Chicago, Ill., 1993.

Mexico, Euromoney supplement, January 1993.

Mullineux, Andrew. *International Banking and Financial Systems: A Comparison*, Graham and Trotman, London, 1987.

Organization for Economic Cooperation and Development. *Regulations Affecting International Banking Operations of Banks and Non-banks*, Paris, 1981.

Pecchioli, R. M. *Prudential Supervision in Banking*, Organization for Economic Cooperation and Development, Paris, 1987.

Poole, Claire. "Trolling for Dollars," *Mexico Business*, November 1995, pp. 18–20.

Shale, Tony. "The New US$101 Billion Man (Taiwan: Central Bank)," *Asiamoney*, June 1994, pp. 10–11.

Skully, Michael T. *Financial Institutions and Markets in the Far East*, St. Martin's Press, New York, 1982.

Subcommittee on Financial Institutions Supervision, Regulation, and Insurance. *Report of the Task Force on International Competitiveness of US Financial Institutions*, US House of Representatives Committee on Banking, Finance and Urban Affairs, Washington, DC, 1990.

Taiwan, Asiamoney supplement, September 1995.

Toniolo, Gianni, ed. *Central Banks' Independence in Historical Perspective*, Walter de Gruyter, Berlin, 1988.

Torres, Craig. "Investors Ponder Mexican Peso's Future," *Wall Street Journal*, February 2, 1995, p. A10.

Ungerer, Horst, Jouko J. Hauvonen, Augusto Lopez-Claros, and Thomas Mayer. *The European Monetary System: Developments and Perspectives*, International Monetary Fund, Washington, DC, 1990.

US Department of the Treasury. *Modernizing the Financial System; Recommendations for Safer, More Competitive Banks*, Washington, DC, 1991.

US Department of the Treasury. *National Treatment Study 1994*, Washington, DC, 1994.

Warner, Alison. "Profits and Pressures (Malaysia)," *The Banker*, September 1995, pp. 65–6.

Welch, John H. and William C. Gruben. "A Brief History of the Mexican Financial System," *Financial Industry Studies* (Federal Reserve Bank of Dallas), October 1993, pp. 1–10.

Part VI
Management of
Financial Institutions

Profitability, Liquidity, and Liability Management

c h a p t e r 15

CHAPTER OVERVIEW

This chapter:
- Describes a commercial bank balance sheet.
- Explains a bank's income statement and measures of profitability.
- Discusses bank liquidity.
- Compares liquidity and liability mix in selected countries.

KEY TERMS

cost of funding earning assets
cost of funds
equity multiplier
equity ratio
interest rate spread (net interest margin)
liquidity
net interest income

net interest yield
net margin after tax
return on assets
return on equity
taxable-equivalent rate
yield on earning assets

CHAPTER OUTLINE

INTERNATIONAL COMPARISONS:

Australia	Luxembourg
Austria	Mexico
Belgium	Netherlands
Canada	Norway
Denmark	Portugal
Finland	Spain
France	Sweden
Germany	Switzerland
Greece	Turkey
Italy	United Kingdom
Japan	

 Introduction

The banking system is vital to every country's economic well-being and financial stability. One of the important challenges to the US banking system has been the volatility of interest rates. When interest rates change, the cost of bank funds can change virtually overnight. If a bank is to maintain adequate profitability, asset portfolios must reflect such changes. The analysis of bank profitability necessarily begins by examining the balance sheet, the income statement, and related ratios.

In recent years, perhaps the most dramatic changes in bank balance sheets have occurred in the liabilities section. The *mix* of liabilities has changed to offer depositors interest rates that are more competitive with other financial institutions, such as money market mutual funds. The *use* of liabilities has changed to afford commercial bank managers more flexibility in managing liquidity needs and in raising funds for investment. At the same time, the increased flexibility of liability management can also add to instability of profits or sources of funds. This paradox is an important issue in bank management today.

 Bank Profitability

Banks realize profits as long as interest earned on assets exceeds interest paid on interest-bearing liabilities. (In addition, fee income is an important feature of bank operations. However, this section concentrates on the more traditional determinants of bank profitability.) Other noninterest income and expense items also effect bank profits.

$$P = II - IE + NIIE - T \qquad (15.1)$$

where P = bank profits
II = interest income and fees
IE = interest expense
$NIIE$ = net noninterest income and expense
T = income taxes

By far, the most important categories are interest income on assets and interest expense on liabilities. Over time, asset and liability combinations have changed significantly. The asset portfolio that was once dominated by short-term commercial loans now includes more real estate and consumer loans. These and other asset categories have enhanced interest income but, at the same time, have contributed to reduced *bank liquidity*.

> **Bank liquidity:**
> The ability of a bank to meet its current obligations for cash outflow and to respond to changes in customer demand for loans and cash withdrawals *without* selling assets at a substantial loss. Bank assets are liquid to the extent that they may be easily converted into cash without loss.

On the other hand, a significant portion of low-cost demand and time deposits has been replaced by certificates of deposit, subordinated debentures, Eurocurrency deposits, and commercial paper. These instruments have helped banks have more control over access to funds, that is, increased liquidity. However, they have also increased interest expense because interest paid on them is higher.

1.1 BANK ASSETS

Exhibit 15.1 is the balance sheet of First National Bank, a hypothetical bank, as of December 31, 1999. Notice that assets are composed of liquid assets, investment securities, loans, and other assets.

ASSETS		
Cash and due from banks	$2,491	7.6%
Interest-bearing time deposits in other banks	1,103	3.4
Federal funds sold and securities purchased under agreement to resell	1,063	3.2
Investment securities:		
US Treasury and government agencies	$2,192	6.7
Obligations of states and political subdivisions	696	2.1
Other securities	1,261	3.8
Total investment securities	4,149	12.6
Loans:		
Commercial, financial and agricultural	$9,168	27.9
Real estate – construction	4,762	14.5
Real estate – mortgage	1,838	5.6

Credit card	2,793	8.5
Installment	2,407	7.3
Lease financing	975	2.9
Foreign	479	1.4
Unearned income	<245>	<0.7>
Total loans, net of unearned income	22,177	67.4
Reserve for possible credit losses	<460>	<1.4>
Net loans	21,717	66.0
Customers' liability on acceptances outstanding	105	0.3
Investments in subsidiaries	632	1.9
Premises and equipment	420	1.3
Other assets	1,212	3.7
TOTAL ASSETS	$32,892	100.0%

LIABILITIES AND STOCKHOLDERS' EQUITY

Domestic deposits:

Noninterest-bearing demand	$4,544	13.8%
Interest-bearing transactions accounts	1,539	4.7
Money market deposit accounts	4,889	14.9
Time, $100,000 or more	6,847	20.8
Other time	3,189	9.7
Savings	1,622	4.9
Total domestic deposits	$22,630	68.8
Foreign deposits	1,737	5.3
Total deposits	24,367	74.1

Short-term borrowings:

Federal funds purchased and securities under agreements to repurchase	$3,411	10.3
Commercial paper	388	1.2
Other	954	2.9
Total short-term borrowings	4,753	14.4
Long-term borrowings	395	1.2
Bank acceptances outstanding	104	0.3
Other liabilities	724	2.2
Total liabilities	30,343	92.2
Common stock	$150	0.5
Capital surplus	359	1.1
Retained earnings	2,040	6.2
Total equity	2,549	7.8
TOTAL LIABILITIES AND STOCKHOLDERS' EQUITY	$32,892	100.0%

◆ **Exhibit 15.1:** First National Bank balance sheet (in millions), December 31, 1999

	1964	1969	1974	1979	1984	1989	1994	1998
Financial assets ($billions)	$312	$472	$836	$1,356	$2,106	$2,954	$4,164	$5,405
Cash:								
Vault cash and due from banks	1.5%	1.6%	1.5%	1.5%	1.3%	0.9%	1.0%	0.8%
Reserves at FRBs[1]	5.7	4.7	3.1	2.2	1.0	1.3	0.7	0.4
Total cash	7.2	6.3	4.6	3.7	2.3	2.2	1.7	1.2
Commercial paper and BAs[2]	2.1	2.6	3.3	3.5	4.0	2.3	0.7	0.3
Securities	33.3	26.9	23.6	21.6	21.6	20.6	22.1	20.7
Loans	56.3	61.6	63.0	63.6	61.1	63.3	57.4	58.4
Investments in subs:[3]	–	0.8	4.4	6.3	7.5	8.2	8.7	10.3
Misc. assets	1.1	1.8	1.1	1.3	3.5	3.4	9.4	9.1
Total	100.0%	100.0%	100.0%	100.0%	100.0%	100.0%	100.0%	100.0%

◆ **Exhibit 15.2:** Financial assets of domestic and foreign commercial banks in the United States, 1964–98 (percentages)

◆ *Notes:*   1   Federal Reserve Bank
2   Banker's acceptances
3   Investments in bank and nonbank subsidiaries by bank holding companies

◆ *Source:*   Board of Governors of the Federal Reserve System, *Flow of Funds; Financial Assets and Liabilities.*

1.2 BANK INDUSTRY ASSETS

Exhibit 15.2 shows the composition of bank industry assets from 1964 through 1998. In 1964, commercial banks held 7.2 percent of financial assets as cash and much of that with Federal Reserve banks. These percentages have consistently grown smaller so that by 1998, only 1.2 percent of financial assets was cash. Securities have declined even more – from 33.3 percent of assets in 1964 to 20.7 percent by 1998. These changes help to underscore the reduced liquidity in the system as a whole.

1.3 BANK LIABILITIES AND CAPITAL

As shown in Exhibit 15.1, the largest classification of liabilities for a bank is its deposits. Borrowed funds and capital make up the remaining categories.

Note that the *equity ratio* is only 7.8 percent of total assets.

$$ER = \frac{TE}{TA} \tag{15.2}$$

where ER = equity ratio
TE = total equity (common stock, capital surplus, and retained earnings)
TA = total assets

	1964	1969	1974	1979	1984	1989	1994	1998
Liabilities ($billions)[1]	$290	$447	$822	$1,344	$2,092	$2,924	$4,049	$5,254
Checkable deposits	52.1%	45.7%	28.8%	25.1%	15.5%	16.5%	18.5%	12.2%
Small time and savings deposits	35.4	37.1	32.1	31.9	39.0	37.2	33.7	34.6
Large time deposits	8.7	6.8	19.7	16.8	15.3	15.0	8.0	11.5
Total US deposits	96.2	89.6	80.6	73.8	69.8	68.7	60.2	58.3
Deposits of banks in US possessions	0.4	0.7	0.6	0.7	0.4	0.4	0.6	0.6
Federal funds and security repos	0.2	2.0	3.4	7.0	7.4	8.6	9.7	11.2
Commercial paper	–	1.0	1.0	1.5	2.1	1.6	0.8	1.3
Total short-term borrowings	0.2	3.0	4.4	8.5	9.5	10.2	10.5	12.5
Banker's acceptances	1.2	1.2	2.3	2.5	3.6	2.1	0.6	0.3
Taxes payable	0.2	0.1	0.1	0.1	(¹)	(²)	0.1	0.1
Bonds	0.3	0.4	1.3	1.6	2.5	2.7	3.5	4.0
Equity in subsidiaries	–	1.8	7.9	8.9	10.6	9.6	8.4	9.1
Misc. liabilities	1.5	3.2	2.8	3.9	3.6	6.3	16.1	15.1
Total financial liabilities	100.0%	100.0%	100.0%	100.0%	100.0%	100.0%	100.0%	100.0%

◆ **Exhibit 15.3: Liabilities of domestic and foreign commercial banks in the United States, 1964–98 (percentages)**

◆ *Notes:* 1 Includes net interbank claims
2 Less than 0.1%

◆ *Source:* Board of Governors of the Federal Reserve System, *Flow of Funds; Financial Assets and Liabilities.*

This is typical for commercial banks. Compared to nonfinancial corporations, with closer to 50 percent equity financing, commercial banks are thinly capitalized. All other things being equal, a relatively small equity base improves the rate of return on equity. Of course, the combination of low capital ratios and illiquid loan portfolios can threaten bank safety and liquidity. If a significant number of loans is not repaid, the resulting losses can amount to more than the sum of all capital accounts. When this happens, liabilities exceed assets and the bank becomes insolvent, that is, the bank fails.

1.4 BANKING INDUSTRY LIABILITIES

Exhibit 15.3 shows the changes that occurred in US commercial bank liability structure from 1964 through 1998. In 1964, deposits were 96.2 percent of liabilities, with checkable (or transactions) accounts constituting over one half of total liabilities. By 1998, deposits were only 58.3 percent of liabilities and low-cost checkable deposits 12.2 percent. These changes have had a significant impact on commercial bank profits.

1.5 INCOME AND EXPENSE

A commercial bank income statement does not follow the same format as that of a nonfinancial firm. Instead, interest income and expense are the first two classifications, reflecting their importance to the bank. The difference between interest income and interest expense is *net interest income*. All other income and expense items follow net interest income.

Net interest income:
>   The difference between (1) interest earned on time deposits, investment
>   securities, loans, and other earning assets and (2) interest paid on deposits
>   and other interest-bearing liabilities.

1.5.1 FIRST NATIONAL

Exhibit 15.4 is First National's income statement for the year ended December 31, 1999. Since loans are the most important assets, *interest and fees on loans* is listed first. *Interest on investment securities* is next, with interest from taxable investments shown separately from tax-exempt interest. *Interest on time deposits and interest on federal funds sold* follow.

Interest expense includes the major categories of *interest on deposits* and on *short-term* and *long-term borrowings*. With total interest income and expense of $3.010 billion and $1.874 billion, respectively, First National's net interest income is $1.136 billion. The bank's provision for credit losses is an amount set aside in the current year to cover future uncollectible loans. The cumulative provision is a contra-asset account (see the balance sheet). Deducting the 1999 provision of $280 million brings the after-provision net interest income to $856 million.

Noninterest expense for the year ($1.118 billion) exceeds noninterest income ($762 million) by $356 million. This reduces taxable income to $500 million. After deducting taxes, net income is $384 million. Thus, First National earned, $384 million on a year-end asset base of $32.892 billion in 1999.

INTEREST INCOME	
Interest and fees on loans	$2,417
Interest on investment securities	
Taxable	$331
Exempt from federal income taxes	66
Total	397
Interest on time deposits in other banks	128
Interest on funds sold and repurchase agreements	68
Total interest income	$3,010
INTEREST EXPENSE	
Interest on deposits	1,374
Interest on short-term borrowings	462
Interest on long-term borrowings	38
Total interest expense	<1,874>
NET INTEREST INCOME	1,136
Provision for possible credit losses	<280>
Net interest income after provision for possible credit losses	856
OTHER OPERATING INCOME	
Trust department income	53
Service charges on deposit accounts	97
Credit card fees	222
Other service charges and fees	63
Servicing fees from asset sales	151
Investment securities gains (losses)	<3>
Other income	179
Total other operating income	762
OTHER OPERATING EXPENSES	
Salaries and employee benefits	506
Occupancy expense of premises	74
Equipment expense	61
Other expense	477
Total other operating expense	<1,118>
Income before income taxes	500
Applicable income taxes	<116>
NET INCOME	$384

◆ **Exhibit 15.4: First National Bank income statement, 1999 (in millions)**

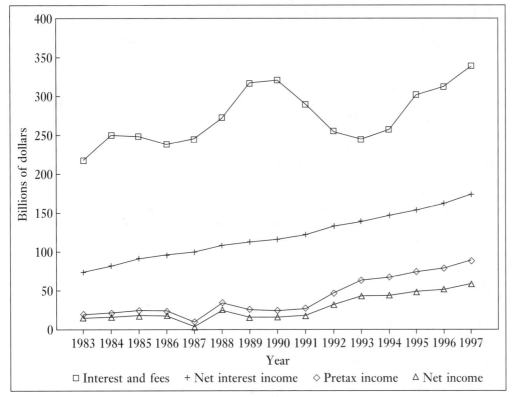

◆ **Exhibit 15.5: Income of insured commercial banks, 1983–97**

◆ *Source*:   Author's graphic, based on data from: Federal Deposit Insurance Corporation, *Statistics on Banking*, various issues.

1.5.2 BANKING INDUSTRY

Exhibit 15.5 illustrates industry revenues and profits for the years 1983 through 1997. Revenues (gross interest and fees) grew from $217 billion in 1983 to $320 in 1990. However, in the early 1990s, three factors caused the industry's gross income to decline.

- The number of US commercial banks declined from 14,496 at the end of 1984 to 12,347 at the end of 1990, approximately a 15 percent decline. Industry consolidation through mergers and acquisitions often led to a reduction in the number of physical locations to increase efficiency. This industry consolidation continued after 1990. By mid-1998, the number of US commercial banks had fallen to 8,984, a decline of 27 percent.
- The introduction of new capital standards (see chapter 17) encouraged banks to have smaller balance sheets and to focus more on fee-income-generating activities that were not tied to the balance sheet categories of securities and loans.
- Market interest rates, including rates on securities and loans, declined significantly. (See also chapters 1, 10, and 11 for a discussion of interest rates.)

During 1994, market interest rates began to rise and revenues on loans and securities increased significantly to $340 billion in 1997.

While gross interest income was relatively volatile from 1983 to 1997, net interest income for the industry showed a more stable, increasing trend over time. This suggests that interest expense (the distance between interest income – the first line of Exhibit 15.5 – and net interest income – the second line) also changed over time with a resulting smooth, upward trend in net interest income. From 1983 to 1997, net interest grew from $73 billion to $175 billion.

The third line of Exhibit 15.5 is pretax income. The difference between net interest income and pretax income is net noninterest income and expense – the distance between the second and third lines. The net has been consistently negative and was a larger negative in 1997 than in 1983.

The fourth line of Exhibit 15.5 is net income. Income tax is represented by the distance between the third and fourth lines. Essentially, even though bank revenues virtually mushroomed by $100 billion from 1983 through 1989, interest expense, net noninterest expense, and taxes almost exactly kept pace. Industry net income in 1983 was $14.9 billion. The corresponding amount in 1989 was only marginally higher – $15.6 billion. However, the 1990s brought substantial increases in industry profitability. By 1997, industry net income was $59 billion.

This exhibit illustrates the profit pressures under which banks sometimes operate. However, the analysis is not complete without reviewing *rates* of return which give an even clearer picture of the bank profitability.

1.6 RATES EARNED AND PAID

1.6.1 FIRST NATIONAL

When computing rates of return and interest rates paid, both income statement and balance sheet items are used. However, year-end balance sheet totals can give misleading results, particularly if account balances have changed significantly during the year. Average balances are preferable because they capture these changes and are a better match for the income and expense stream for the year. Since most bank accounting systems are now automated, average balances are relatively easy to generate. Exhibit 15.6 shows average balances of the accounts of First National Bank. They are computed as follows.

$$\bar{A}_i = \frac{\left(\sum_{t=1}^{n} A_{it}\right)}{n} \tag{15.3}$$

where $\bar{A}_i$ = average balance of asset or liability account i
n = total number of dates used to calculate the average balance
A_{it} = balance of account i at time t

Banks commonly generate monthly financial statements. However, this section discusses the rates for First National Bank for the entire year of 1999. The balance sheet amounts shown in Exhibit 15.6 should be thought of as the average of either twelve month-end balances or 360 daily balances. (Twelve 30-day months produce a 360-day year.)

In addition to average balances, Exhibit 15.6 also contains details of interest income and expense. Rates earned or paid are simply the relevant interest amounts divided by the average balances.

$$r_i = \left(\frac{I_i}{\bar{A}_i}\right)\left(\frac{360}{N}\right) \tag{15.4}$$

	Income or expense (in millions)	Average balance[1] (in millions)	Rate[2] (percentage)
ASSETS			
Time deposits in other banks	128	1,391	9.20%
Federal funds sold and repurchase agreements	68	895	7.60
Investment securities			
Taxable	331	3,917	8.45
Tax-exempt	100[3]	962	10.40
	431	4,879	8.83
Loans			
Commercial, financial, agricultural	896	8,699	10.30
Real estate – construction	386	3,509	11.00
Real estate – mortgage	184	1,688	10.90
Credit card	430	3,071	14.00
Installment	353	2,942	12.00
Lease financing	109	1,147	9.50
Foreign	59	567	10.41
Total loans	2,417	21,623	11.18
Total interest earning assets	3,044	28,788	10.57
Cash and due from banks		2,252	
Other assets		2,107	
Reserve for possible credit losses		<408>	
Total assets		32,739	
LIABILITIES			
Deposits:			
Interest-bearing transaction accounts	78	1,500	5.20
Money market deposit accounts	319	4,984	6.40
Time, $100,000 or more	517	6,544	7.90
Other time	240	3,004	7.99
Savings	92	1,720	5.35
Foreign – time	128	1,753	7.30
Total interest-bearing deposits	1,374	19,505	7.04
Short-term borrowings:			
Federal funds purchased	276	3,603	7.66
Commercial paper	112	1,503	7.45
Other short-term	74	931	7.95
Long-term borrowings:	38	386	9.84
Total funds borrowed	500	6,423	7.78
Total interest-bearing liabilities	1,874	25,928	7.23
Demand deposits		3,695	
Other liabilities		759	
Total liabilities		30,382	
		2,357	
STOCKHOLDERS' EQUITY			
Total liabilities and stockholders' equity		32,739	
Net interest income and interest rate spread	1,170		3.34
Net interest income as % of earnings assets			4.06

◆ **Exhibit 15.6:** First National Bank, detail of interest income and expense with rates earned and paid, 1999

◆ *Notes*:   1   Average balances are computed using Equation (15.1)
               2   Rate is computed using Equation (15.2)
               3   Interest income has been adjusted to its taxable-equivalent amount. See Equation (15.3).

where r_i = interest rate earned or paid on account i (annual basis)
    I_i = interest income or expense associated with asset or liability account i during the period
    N = number of days in the period

Equation (15.4) explains the computation of all rates in Exhibit 15.6, with one exception. The rate earned on tax-exempt investment securities is based on interest income of $100 million (Exhibit 15.6), instead of the $66 million recorded in the income statement (Exhibit 15.4). All other sources of income are taxable and have been recorded on a before-tax basis. Since municipal bond interest is not taxable, the income of $66 million is also the after-tax amount. In order to compare municipal interest income (after-tax) to other taxable income (before-tax), municipal bond interest has been increased to a *taxable-equivalent amount*.

Taxable-equivalent amount:
    The amount of before-tax income from taxable source that is equivalent to a corresponding amount of tax-exempt income, once applicable taxes have been considered.

To determine a taxable-equivalent amount, the relationship between before- and after-tax amounts must be identified. Beginning with the definition that an after-tax amount equals the corresponding before-tax amount less taxes, the following relationship develops.

$$AT = BT - tax$$
$$AT = BT - BT(t)$$
$$AT = BT(1 - t)$$
$$\frac{AT}{(1 - t)} = BT \tag{15.5}$$

where AT = after-tax amount
    BT = before-tax amount
    t = tax rate

In the case of First National, assume that the marginal tax rate is 34 percent. Thus, the amount of taxable income that is equivalent to $66 million, after-tax, is $100 million (($66 million)/ (1 − .34) = $100 million). The resulting rate of return is the *equivalent* of 10.40 percent from a taxable source. Note that this compares favorably to the bank's rate of return on taxable securities (US Treasury securities, government agency securities, and corporate bonds) of 8.45 percent. All other things being equal, the municipal bond taxable-equivalent yield varies positively with the tax rate, that is, higher tax rates result in higher taxable-equivalent yields.

The rates of return associated with loan categories range from a low of 9.50 percent for lease financing to a high of 14.0 percent for credit card loans. Generally speaking, loans are higher yielding assets than time deposits in other banks and investment securities. The average rate of return on First National's investment securities was 8.83 percent (($431 mil./$4,879 mil.)(360/360) = 0.0883), while the average return on the loan portfolio was 11.18 percent (($2,417 mil./$21,623 mil.) (360/360) = 0.1118). More specifically, consumer and real estate loans are two of the highest yielding categories. (It should also be noted that real estate loans are risky in that they are exposed to the cyclical nature of the real estate industry.)

Total interest income for the year is $3.044 billion and the average balance of all earning assets was $21.623 billion. The *yield on earning assets* was, therefore, 10.57 percent.

$$k_{EA} = II/EA \qquad (15.6)$$

where k_{EA} = yield on earning assets
II = total interest income and fees
EA = average balance of earning assets

Interest rates paid on interest-bearing deposits range from 5.20 percent for interest-bearing transactions accounts to 7.99 percent for time deposits. Note that transactions and regular savings accounts carry lower rates of interest than time deposits. Note also that the relatively high level of time deposits as a percentage of total deposits causes the average rate paid on interest-bearing deposits to be slightly over 7.0 percent.

The cost of other borrowings is, in every case, well over 7 percent. Long-term borrowings (bonds) cost First National almost 10 percent. Total interest expense for the year totaled $1.874 billion. On an average liability base of $25.928 billion, the *average rate paid on interest-bearing liabilities* was 7.23 percent.

$$k_{IBL} = IE/IBL \qquad (15.7)$$

where k_{IBL} = average rate paid on interest-bearing liabilities
IE = total interest expense
IBL = average balance of interest-bearing liabilities

The *interest rate spread* or *net interest margin* is the difference between the yield on earning assets and the average rate paid on interest-bearing liabilities.

$$IS = k_{EA} - k_{IBL} \qquad (15.8)$$

where IS = interest rate spread

Spread measures the rate of return per dollar invested in earning assets less the rate paid per dollar of borrowed funds. First National's spread was 3.34 percent (10.57 percent – 7.23 percent).

Another measure of the cost of funds for a commercial bank is the *cost of funding earning assets*. This is essentially the interest expense per dollar of earning assets.

$$k_{FEA} = IE/EA \qquad (15.9)$$

where k_{FEA} = cost of funding earning assets

For 1996, this cost was 6.51 percent ($1.874 billion/$28.788 billion) for First National.

Net interest income measures bank profits that are linked to interest-sensitive assets and liabilities. First National's net interest income is $1.17 billion, that is, $3.044 billion of interest income less $1.874 billion of interest expense.

Net interest yield is net interest income as a percentage of earning assets, that is, a measure of return on those assets that are devoted to a bank's primary activities of borrowing and reinvesting funds. Alternatively, net interest yield can be calculated as the difference between yield on earning assets and the cost of funding earning assets.

$$NIY = NII/EA \qquad (15.10)$$

$$NIY = k_{EA} - k_{FEA} \qquad (15.11)$$

First National's net interest income and average earning assets of $1.17 billion and $28.788 billion, respectively, provide a 4.06 percent net interest yield on earning assets. Alternatively, applying Equation (15.11) gives the same result (10.57 percent – 6.51 percent = 4.06 percent).

Recently, competition for deposits from money-market funds and transactions accounts offered through brokerage firms has led to deregulation of interest rates, as explained in chapter 13. Deposit interest rate deregulation, in turn, has meant that banks rely more on interest-sensitive deposits and other borrowings, placing significant pressure on interest rate spreads. As a result, emphasis on higher-yielding assets has increased.

Another trend in commercial banking is increasing lines of business that generate fee income. Included here are longer-term commercial loans with origination fees that are paid at the beginning of the term of the loan. Mortgage loans also generate "up-front" fees in the form of points, or percentages of the loan amount (usually between 1 percent and 5 percent) that are paid at the time the loan is disbursed.

Still another major activity that brings fee income to the bank credit card issuance to both consumer and business clients. As shown in Exhibit 15.4, First National realized $222 million during the year from these annual charges to credit card holders. This amount was almost 30 percent of the bank's noninterest income for the year. These fees are in addition to the $430 million earned as interest on credit card loans, reflected in Exhibit 15.6.

When *all* categories of income and expense are considered, the bank's net income is $384 million (Exhibit 15.4). A bank's profit margin is called the *net margin after tax* and is net income as a percentage of total revenues.

$$NMAT = NI/(II + GNI) \qquad (15.12)$$

where $NMAT$ = net margin after tax
$\qquad NI$ = net income
$\qquad II$ = interest income and fees
$\qquad GNI$ = gross noninterest income

First National's profit margin after tax was 10.09 percent ($384 mil./($3.044 bil. + $762 mil.)).
Return on assets and *return on equity* are also based on net income.

$$ROA = NI/TA \qquad (15.13)$$

$$ROE = NI/TE \qquad (15.14)$$

First National's return on assets and return on equity were 1.17 percent (($384 mil.)/($32,739 mil.) = .0117) and 16.29 percent (($384 mil.)/($2,357 mil.) = .1629), respectively. Each of these ratios measures the amount of net income per dollar invested.

ROA and ROE are related to each other through the *equity multiplier*, the inverse of the equity ratio.

$$EM = TA/TE \qquad (15.15)$$

The equity multiplier is the number of asset dollars supported by each dollar of equity. As the equity multiplier increases, the amount of equity supporting each asset dollar declines. In addition, *ROE* is the product of *ROA* and the multiplier.

$$ROE = (NI/TA)(TA/TE)$$
$$= (ROA)(EM) \tag{15.16}$$

Applying Equations (15.15) and (15.16) to First National, the equity multiplier is 13.8901 times ($32.739 bil./$2.357 bil.) and *ROE* is 16.29 percent ((0.011729)(13.8901)), as before.

Bank regulators recently have placed considerable emphasis on increasing capital ratios (equity capital as a percentage of total assets) in order to enhance the safety of the banking system. Obviously, increasing profits improves *ROA*, *ROE*, and capital ratios. However, decreasing total assets, all other things being equal, has the same effect. (When earning assets are sold, interest income also declines. However, if the forgone interest income can be replaced by fee income (not related to asset holdings), income can be maintained while reducing balance-sheet investment.)

Securitization of loans allows a bank to sell some of the loans on its balance sheet. While proceeds of asset sales can be used to fund new loans, a bank may also reduce the size of its balance sheet by retiring debt with the proceeds. (See also "Securitization" in chapter 4.)

Even after the sale of securitized assets, a bank may continue to service the loans, that is, maintain records, send account statements, and collect payments. Compensation for these services takes the form of additional fee income. These incremental fees on loans that no longer appear on the balance sheet improve earnings and boost *ROE*. First National has adopted the practice of securitizing its credit card loans. Servicing fees appear as "servicing fees from asset sales" in the other operating income section of the bank's income statement (Exhibit 15.4). In 1999, these fees amounted to $151 million, just under 20 percent of other operating income for First National, and helped to offset the cost of interest-sensitive deposits.

1.6.2 BANKING INDUSTRY RATES

Generally, industry profitability ratios in the late 1980s reflected a considerable profit squeeze attributable to high interest costs and noninterest expense. The pressure was partially relieved by asset securitization and other fee-generating activities. Low and stable interest rates in the early 1990s brought higher profitability to the industry.

Exhibit 15.7 provides ratios for the US banking industry as a whole for 1988 through 1997. The yield on earning assets increased and then decreased over the period as interest rates rose and then fell. However, the cost of funding earning assets decreased faster so that the net interest yield (the difference between yield on earning assets and cost of funding earning assets) was fairly stable. Increased emphasis on fee income and on securitization resulted in much improved returns on assets and equity for the industry.

These industry ratios are not necessarily representative of every type of bank. The size of an institution can significantly affect profit performance.

Exhibit 15.8 shows a breakdown by four size groups for 1988, 1991, 1994, and 1997. Larger banks can earn as much or more on asset portfolios as smaller banks, but must also rely more on borrowed funds and large CDs – both of which are quite sensitive to market conditions. That is, the cost of funding earning assets is often higher. The net effect is that net interest yield is consistently lower for larger banks. In the early 1990s, as suggested by the 1991 results, the returns on assets and equity for larger institutions were also often lower than smaller banks' returns.

Ratio	1988	1989	1990	1991	1992	1993	1994	1995	1996	1997
YEA	9.84%	11.44%	11.06%	9.91%	8.64%	7.82%	7.74%	8.42%	8.20%	8.19%
CFEA	5.96	7.40	7.07	5.73	4.12	3.37	3.28	4.13	3.93	3.48
NIY	3.88	4.05	3.99	4.18	4.51	4.45	4.46	4.29	4.27	4.21
ROA	0.86	0.50	0.50	0.56	0.96	1.23	1.21	1.17	1.19	1.23
ROE	10.03	7.82	7.73	8.32	13.35	15.72	15.35	14.68	14.46	14.70

◆ **Exhibit 15.7:** **Selected industry rates in the United States, 1988–97**

◆ *Notes*:   YEA   Yield on earning assets
                    CFEA   Cost of funding earning assets
                    NIY   Net interest yield
                    ROA   Return on assets
                    ROE   Return on equity

◆ *Source*:   Federal Deposit Insurance Corporation, *Quarterly Banking Profile*, various issues.

However, by the mid-1990s, as suggested in the 1994 and 1997 charts, larger banks benefited from the generally favorable banking environment and, in many cases, the increased use of securitization.

② Liquidity Management

Since a bank can realize higher profits from assets that are relatively illiquid, there is a natural tradeoff between profitability and liquidity. Commercial banks must invest as profitably as possible within reasonable limits of liquidity. Because of this potential conflict, regulators in a number of countries have established certain minimum liquidity requirements.

2.1 REGULATING LIQUIDITY

2.1.1 REGULATORY ISSUES

The adequacy of bank liquidity is tied to solvency of the banking system. From a regulatory perspective, liquidity means a bank's ability to meet its obligations – deposits and borrowed funds – when they are due. Before the widespread use of liability management, liquidity was more easily measured. Maintaining high-quality, liquid assets assured both the public and the regulators.

The ability to convert these assets into cash meant that even heavy deposit withdrawal could be met. In turn, this situation led to confidence in the bank's solvency, so that "runs" were unlikely. However, it is not always possible to exactly assess the liquidity of certain assets. Municipal bonds are a good example. Large sales of municipals can depress their market value since secondary markets for municipals are not as well developed as markets for Treasury securities. Nevertheless, municipal bond yields frequently compare favorably with government bond yields. From the bank's perspective, then, the less liquid municipal bonds may be preferable.

Another shortcoming of attempting to measure liquidity based on asset holdings is that this approach does not consider the dynamic aspect of banking. Examining asset holdings does not address the issue of pending maturity of short-term liabilities that must be refunded. That is, the balance sheet alone does not reflect the ease or difficulty that a bank might have in refinancing maturing deposits or other liabilities.

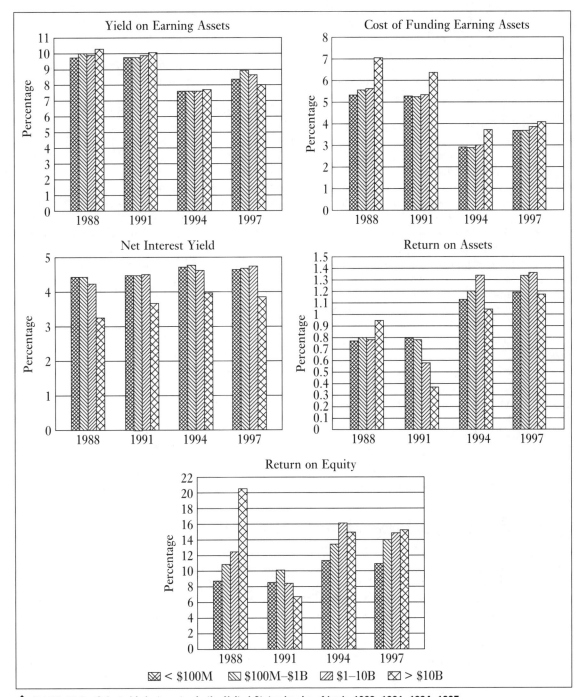

◆ **Exhibit 15.8:** Selected industry rates in the United States by size of bank, 1988, 1991, 1994, 1997

◆ *Source*: Author's graphic, based on data from: Federal Deposit Insurance Corporation, *Quarterly Banking Profile*, various issues.

2.1.2 REGULATORY APPROACHES IN SELECTED COUNTRIES IN THE OECD

Because of these considerations, many regulators have moved more to a *cash-flow* approach in assessing bank liquidity. In general, cash-flow techniques attempt to measure any mismatch in the maturity structure of asset and liability portfolios.

The specific regulatory approach varies by OECD country (OECD is an acronym for the Organization for Economic Cooperation and Development.). Continental European countries still apply variations of specific liquidity measures. Denmark has maintained a liquid assets to liabilities ratio. The Netherlands and Switzerland vary required liquidity coefficients (coverage percentages) for specific balance sheet accounts (liabilities) based upon type and maturity.

In Germany, guidelines are established by law for maintenance of liquidity. However, regulators reserve the right to impose stricter or more lenient ratios or guidelines as conditions warrant.

Some countries have fewer formal requirements. Instead, liquidity review is a part of the regular oversight process. In Canada, this is accomplished through informal monitoring of maturity mismatching. In the United Kingdom, cash flow over the next 12 months is routinely reviewed.

The approach in the United States is a combination of fixed ratio maintenance and cash-flow analysis. Smaller banks are evaluated primarily on the basis of liquid asset levels. Larger banks, considered to have greater access to money and capital markets, are assessed on the basis of (1) projected cash flow or (2) maturity mismatches in assets vs. liabilities.

The CAMEL rating system is used in the United States. The specific qualities that are considered are:

C   Capital adequacy
A   Asset quality
M   Management and administrative ability
E   Earnings level and quality
L   Liquidity level

Each bank is scored between 1 (best) and 5 (worst). Banks with poor results are examined more frequently by federal regulators.

2.2 OBSERVED LIQUIDITY LEVELS IN SELECTED COUNTRIES

Actual liquid asset holdings vary significantly. Exhibit 15.9 highlights the range of variation from one country to another. In 1994, among members of the OECD, US banks held less than 8 percent of total assets as cash, deposits at the central bank, and interbank deposits. Canadian and Japanese banks held approximately the same percentage in liquid assets. Mexican banks held a considerably lower 2.4 percent. Banks in the United Kingdom were considerably more liquid with a liquidity-to-assets ratio of roughly 16 percent.

Several banking systems reflect significantly higher levels of liquidity and, with the exception of Greece, the high levels of liquidity are associated with interbank deposits. These banking systems are actively involved in money market activities in these countries. That is, these banks focus a large share of assets in short-term, wholesale transactions. Banking systems with 20 percent or more in liquid assets, primarily interbank deposits, include Austria, Belgium, Denmark, France, Germany, Luxembourg, the Netherlands, Portugal, Spain, and Turkey.

Country (institutions)	Cash[1]	Interbank deposits	Total liquid assets
Australia (all banks)	1.02%	5.28%	6.30%
Austria (all banks)	1.84	28.99	30.83
Belgium (all banks)	0.18	27.58	27.76
Canada (domestic banks)	0.61	7.44	8.05
Denmark (banks and savings banks)	3.64	19.39	23.03
Finland (commercial banks)	1.59	0.84	2.43
France (commercial banks)	0.23	41.04	41.27
Germany (commercial banks)	1.31	22.45	23.76
Greece (large commercial banks)	19.00	8.45	27.45
Italy (all banks)	3.77	6.71	10.48
Japan (commercial banks)[2]	–	9.86	9.86
Luxembourg (commercial banks)	0.34	60.05	60.39
Mexico (commercial banks)	1.31	1.05	2.36
Netherlands (all banks)	2.66	18.72	21.38
Norway (commercial banks)	0.56	6.19	6.75
Portugal (all banks)	1.66	31.32	32.98
Spain (commercial banks)	3.06	16.75	19.81
Sweden (commercial banks)	0.56	9.90	10.46
Switzerland (large banks)	0.72	16.35	17.07
Turkey (commercial banks)	5.66	17.07	22.73
United Kingdom (commercial banks)	0.71	15.71	16.42
United States (commercial banks)	4.34	3.25	7.59

◆ **Exhibit 15.9:** Liquid assets as a percentage of total assets for selected countries, 1994

◆ *Notes*:   1   Includes deposits at central bank
            2   Cash included in interbank deposits

◆ *Source*:   Organization for Economic Cooperation and Development, *Bank Profitability, Financial Statements of Banks, 1985–94*, Paris, 1996.

③ Liability Management

With the advent of negotiable certificates of deposits, commercial banks became much more active participants in money market transactions and far less dependent on traditional deposit-taking activity.

3.1 LIABILITY MIX AND COST OF FUNDS

From the perspective of bank management, the mix of liabilities will materially affect profitability. Recall that First National Bank's average cost of funds on interest-bearing liabilities was 7.23 percent (see Exhibit 15.6). In general, the average cost of funds is:

$$k_{IBL} = \sum_{i=1}^{n} w_i r_i \qquad (15.17)$$

	[1] Weight[1]	[2] Cost[2]	[3] Weighted Cost[3]
DEPOSITS			
Interest-bearing transaction accounts	0.058	5.20%	0.3016
Money market deposit accounts	0.192	6.40	1.2288
Time deposits ≥ $100,000	0.252	8.50	2.1420
Other time	0.116	8.59	0.9964
Savings	0.066	5.35	0.3531
Foreign-time	0.068	7.90	0.5372
SHORT-TERM BORROWINGS			
Federal funds purchased	0.139	8.16	1.1342
Commercial paper	0.058	7.95	0.4611
Other	0.036	8.45	0.3042
LONG-TERM BORROWINGS	0.015	9.84	0.1476
Total	1.000		7.6062%

◆ **Exhibit 15.10:** First National Bank, cost of funds

◆ *Notes*:   1   Percentage of total interest-bearing liabilities
              2   Interest rate after change
              3   Column [1] times column [2]

where k_{IBL} = cost of interest-bearing liabilities or the weighted average cost of funds
   w_i = weight of liability i as a percentage of total interest-bearing liabilities
   r_i = average interest rate associated liability i
   n = total number of interest-bearing liabilities

Equation (15.17) makes it possible to change the assumptions of liability mix and/or the cost of specific interest-bearing liabilities. Of particular importance is the effect of changes for liabilities that carry market rates of interest. Assume that money market participants considered First National's asset mix to be somewhat riskier than originally assessed.

Such an assessment might stem from the bank's investments in real estate and consumer loans. Note from Exhibit 15.6 that, on average, almost 40 percent of First National's earning assets were invested in these categories. The average balances in the categories of real estate-construction, real estate-mortgage, credit card, and installment total $11.21 billion or 38.9 percent of the average balance of total interest earning assets of $28.788 billion.

Referring again to Exhibit 15.6, assume further that the perceived higher risk affects the cost of time deposits and short-term borrowings. If the rates paid on time deposits and short-term borrowings each increased by 60 and 50 basis points, respectively, the average rate paid on interest-bearing liabilities would also increase from its present level of 7.23 percent. (A basis point is one hundredth of one percent.)

Exhibit 15.10 includes the new higher rates for the three time deposit accounts and the three short-term borrowing accounts. The exhibit also includes the weight of each average balance for interest-bearing liabilities given in Exhibit 15.6. Applying Equation (15.17), the revised average rate paid is 7.6062 percent, approximately 38 basis points higher, or less than one-half of one percent greater than the original average cost.

As small as this change may seem (a 5 percent increase in the average cost), it translates into a larger effect on bank profitability. A revised interest expense amount is implied by the new rate on interest-bearing liabilities. Note that it is also possible to apply Equation (15.7) to arrive at total interest expense. Substituting the revised cost of funds of 7.6062 percent and the average interest-bearing liability balance of $25.928 billion (Exhibit 15.6), implied interest expense for the year becomes $1.972 billion.

As a result, taxable-equivalent net interest income drops from $1.170 billion to $1.072 billion, an 8.4 percent decline.

Interest income	$3.044 billion
Interest expense	<1.972 billion>
Net interest income	1.072 billion

Net interest income as a percentage of earning assets declines at the same rate to 3.72 percent (($1.072 billion)/($28.788 billion) = 0.0372). The increase in the rate paid on liabilities reduces the interest rate spread by the same 38 basis points to 2.96 percent. Note, however, that the 5 percent increase in cost of funds (from 7.23 to 7.61 percent) produces an 11.4 percent drop in interest rate spread (from 3.34 to 2.96 percent). Thus, changes in the cost of funds can produce more than proportional changes in net interest income and interest rate spread.

Of course, First National's net income will also be adversely affected. The $98 million increase in interest expense ($1.972 billion – $1.874 billion = $98 million) reduces reported income before taxes to $402 million (see Exhibit 15.4). Applying the bank's average tax rate (t), net income for the year is revised downward to $309 million.

$$t = \frac{\text{income taxes}}{\text{income before taxes}}$$

$$= \frac{\$116 \text{ million}}{\$500 \text{ million}}$$

$$= .232 \tag{15.18}$$

$$NI = \$402 \text{ million } (1 - .232)$$

$$= \$308.736 \text{ million} \tag{15.19}$$

This represents an almost *20 percent reduction* in net income (from $384 million to $309 million), return on assets (from 1.17 percent to 0.94 percent), and return on equity (from 16.29 percent to 13.10 percent).

$$ROA = \frac{\$308.739 \text{ million}}{\$32,739 \text{ million}}$$

$$= .0094 \tag{15.20}$$

$$ROE = \frac{\$308.739 \text{ million}}{\$2,356 \text{ million}}$$

$$= .1310 \tag{15.21}$$

As this example shows, seemingly small changes in interest rates paid on liabilities can have *significant* impact on bank profitability. To prevent this, it is critical that adjustments in asset portfolios be made in an attempt to compensate for increases in the cost of funds.

Under these circumstances, it is not surprising that bank regulators have begun to emphasize the cash-flow approach of liquidity review, particularly with respect to banks that are active participants in money markets. Of particular importance are maturity mismatches of assets and liabilities. (Chapter 17 discusses the application of asset/liability management techniques.)

3.2 Observed Liability Mix in Selected Countries

For the most part, US banks rely on individual and nonbank corporate customers for deposit funds. And, despite the fact that it is more common now than in the past, bond financing is less frequently used by banks in the United States than in other countries. Exhibit 15.11 shows that

Country (institutions)	Interbank deposits	Nonbank deposits	Bonds	Total
Australia (all banks)	7.09%	57.78%	–	64.87%
Austria (all banks)	28.99	44.74	16.70%	90.43
Belgium (all banks)	32.91	34.73	17.85	85.49
Canada (domestic banks)	13.50	66.57	2.24	82.31
Denmark (banks and savings banks)	21.64	58.30	–	79.94
Finland (commercial banks)	3.93	50.11	9.98	64.02
France (commercial banks)	44.19	22.01	21.72	87.92
Germany (commercial banks)	28.52	44.40	12.35	85.27
Greece (large commercial banks)	6.43	75.37	0.95	82.75
Italy (all banks)	6.76	37.44	8.80	53.00
Japan (commercial banks)[1]	–	78.32	0.85	79.17
Luxembourg (commercial banks)	45.23	42.37	4.89	92.49
Mexico (commercial banks)[2]	14.32	65.93	–	80.25
Netherlands (all banks)	23.11	44.44	15.53	83.08
Norway (commercial banks)	9.30	63.10	14.04	86.44
Portugal (all banks)	19.00	56.15	1.25	76.40
Spain (commercial banks)	21.91	43.28	3.28	68.47
Sweden (commercial banks)	21.93	54.43	7.99	84.35
Switzerland (large banks)	23.49	54.01	8.44	85.94
Turkey (commercial banks)	2.71	66.05	0.90	69.66
United Kingdom (commercial banks)[1]	–	69.67	11.44	81.11
United States (commercial banks)	4.28	67.26	1.02	72.56

◆ **Exhibit 15.11:** Liabilities as a percentage of total assets for selected countries, 1994

◆ *Notes*:   1 Interbank deposits included in nonbank deposits
          2 Bonds included in capital

◆ *Source*:   Organization for Economic Cooperation and Development, *Bank Profitability, Financial Statements of Banks, 1985–94*, Paris, 1996.

67 percent of total US bank assets in 1994 were financed with nonbank deposits, that is, deposits by companies and individuals. Other bank systems in 1994 that funded 50 percent or more of assets with nonbank deposits are Australia, Canada, Denmark, Finland, Greece, Mexico, Norway, Portugal, Sweden, Switzerland, Turkey, and the United Kingdom.

In contrast, banks in Austria, Belgium, France, and Luxembourg relied much more on *interbank* deposits and *bonds*, with more than 45 percent in these categories in 1994. At the same time, these sources contributed only 5 percent to US bank resources. Notice, too, that within these European banking systems, approximately 30 percent or more of total liabilities and capital is in the form of interbank deposits alone. As noted above, banks in these countries also concentrate more on wholesale banking activities in the asset portfolio, involving large transactions at market interest rates.

Small changes in market interest rates can have a major impact on profits, particularly if a significant proportion of liabilities is sensitive to market rates. To reduce this exposure, a large percentage of assets should also be rate-sensitive. Referring to Exhibit 15.9, we find that this is the case in Austria, Belgium, France, and Luxembourg. In each of the three instances, no less than 29 percent of total assets has been invested in interbank deposits, whereas US banks invested less than 4 percent of assets in this way.

The typical banking activities in a country will be reflected in the industry's balance sheet composition. However, the fundamental principles of rate sensitivity and maturity matching are applicable in every instance.

 ## Summary

Bank profitability, liquidity, and liability management are interrelated. There is a tradeoff between bank profitability and liquidity. This is especially true in the United States and other countries in which deposit interest rates vary with market interest rates. Profitability, in terms of net interest margin, interest rate spread, and returns on assets and equity, is quite sensitive to changes in rates paid on interest-bearing liabilities.

There is, then, an incentive to invest in more profitable asset categories, notably loans. However, loans are usually illiquid and provide little or no protection against unanticipated deposit withdrawals. As a result, access to money markets has become important in accommodating liquidity needs. Especially for larger banks, liquidity is now *less* a function of the existing balance sheet and *more* a function of the ability to issue large-denomination time deposits, to purchase federal funds and repos, and to issue commercial paper.

Nevertheless, the actual mix of liquidity and liabilities depends on primary banking activities. In countries where money market activity dominates, a relatively large percentage of assets and liabilities will be composed of interbank balances. In countries where banks are more involved in consumer and industrial finance, balance sheets reflect less reliance on interbank transactions. Regardless of the composition of banking business, however, the principles of maturity matching and interest sensitivity apply.

End-of-chapter Questions

1. In the United States, what are the major assets and liabilities of commercial banks?
2. Under what circumstances can a bank be considered illiquid even when liquid asset holdings appear adequate?
3. Define net interest income and interest rate spread.
4. a. Why might it be said that a bank's balance sheet can be used to estimate some of the parameters of its income statement such as major income categories?
    b. What parameters of income might not be estimated by reference to a bank's balance sheet?
5. To what other financial institutions might the concepts of profitability, liquidity, and liability management in this chapter apply?
6. Obtain an annual report of a local bank. In which fee generating (noninterest income generating) activities is the local bank engaged?
7. Which type of banks – regionals or money center banks – would you expect to have a higher proportion of small time and savings deposits? Why?
8. Obtain an annual report of a nonfinancial corporation. Compare the liabilities and equity of the corporation to that of First National bank in this chapter.
9. How did the liability mix of US commercial banks change from 1964 to 1998? What were some of the primary contributing factors in this change?
10. Contrast the levels of interbank balances in Austria, Belgium, France, and Luxembourg to those of the United States. Explain any observed difference.

End-of-chapter Problems

1. a. Calculate the annual interest rate earned from an investment security with an average balance of $125,000 for which $5,312.50 of income is received each month.
    b. Now, calculate the taxable-equivalent annual interest rate, assuming that this investment is a municipal bond and that the marginal tax rate is 34 percent.
2. Refer to Exhibits 15.6 and 15.10. Recall that certain rates paid on liabilities were assumed to increase in Exhibit 15.10. Now assume that rates earned on certain assets also increase by 50 basis points. The assets categories that are affected are:

- • Time deposits in other banks
- • Federal funds sold and repurchase agreements
- • Commercial, financial, and agricultural loans
- • Construction (real estate) loans
  a. Recompute annual interest earned for each asset category and in total.
  b. Recompute the ratios in Equations (15.6) through (15.14).
3. Obtain an annual report from a local bank in your area. Compare the local bank's profitability and equity levels to First National Bank's in this chapter.

SELECTED REFERENCES

Board of Governors of the Federal Reserve System. *Flow of Funds Accounts, Financial Assets and Liabilities*, Washington, DC, various issues.

Calomiris, Charles W. and Charles M. Kahn. "The Role of Demandable Debt in Structuring Optimal Banking Arrangements," *American Economic Review*, 81, no. 3 (June 1991), pp. 497–513.

Federal Deposit Insurance Corporation. *Statistics on Banking*, Washington, DC, 1988 and 1989.

Federal Deposit Insurance Corporation. *Quarterly Banking Profile*, various issues.

International Bank for Reconstruction and Development/ The World Bank. *The World Bank Atlas 1988*, Washington, DC, 1988.

Jacklin, Charles J. and Sudipto Bhattacharya. "Distinguishing Panics and Information-Based Bank Runs: Welfare and Policy Implications," *Journal of Political Economy*, 96, no. 3 (June 1988), pp. 568–92.

Organization for Economic Cooperation and Development. *Bank Profitability, Statistical Supplement, Financial Statements of Banks, 1985–1994*, Paris, 1996.

Pecchioli, R. M. *Prudential Supervision in Banking*, Organization for Economic Cooperation and Development, Paris, 1987.

Spong, Kenneth. *Banking Regulation: Its Purposes, Implementation, and Effects*, 3rd edn, Federal Reserve Bank of Kansas, 1990.

Wallace, Neil. "Another Attempt to Explain an Illiquid Banking System: the Diamond and Dybvig Model with Sequential Service Taken Seriously," *Federal Reserve Bank of Minneapolis Quarterly Review*, Fall 1988, pp. 3–16.

Whalen, Gary. "Concentration and Profitability in Non-MSA Banking Markets," *Economic Review*, Federal Reserve Bank of Cleveland, first quarter 1987, pp. 2–9.

Williamson, Stephen D. "Liquidity, Banking, and Bank Failures," *International Economic Review*, 29 (February 1988), pp. 25–43.

Wilson, J. S. *Banking Policy and Structure: A Comparative Analysis*, Croom Helm, London, 1986.

Investment and Loan Portfolio Management

INTERNATIONAL COMPARISONS:

Australia	Luxembourg
Austria	Mexico
Belgium	Netherlands
Canada	Norway
Denmark	Portugal
Finland	Spain
France	Sweden
Germany	Switzerland
Greece	Turkey
Italy	United Kingdom
Japan	United States

 ## Introduction

The primary earning assets for commercial banks are investment securities and loans. In the United States, these two categories account for over 80 percent of banking industry assets. But the dramatic change in bank liabilities that was discussed in chapter 13 has forced adjustments in bank asset portfolios as well. The increasing cost of funds has led to a smaller proportion of assets in the form of safe and liquid Treasury securities. The trend in blue-chip corporate America toward direct financing through instruments such as commercial paper has meant that commercial banks have had to look to other areas for high yielding loans. But these changes have not come without risk. Corporate bonds and real estate loans are subject to risk that must be properly managed in order to maintain profitability and solvency.

 ## Investment Securities

Commercial banks hold many of the debt securities described in chapter 4, including Treasury issues, government agency bonds, municipal bonds, and corporate securities with the exception of Federal Reserve Bank stock, stock in subsidiaries, and stock held temporarily as collateral on defaulted loans. While the debt securities that are permitted are quite liquid, they do not merely satisfy the bank's liquidity needs. The *composition* of the investment portfolio will also depend on yield considerations and expectations of future interest rates. Profitability is a much more important decision variable in the management of securities than in the management of bank liquidity.

Loan demand will determine the *amount* of securities held. When loan demand is weak, securities are the next best investment alternative for a bank. Conversely, when loan demand is strong, security balances can be reduced in order to provide the liquidity that is necessary to meet loan demand. In this sense, the securities portfolio is the *residual* of loan demand.

1.1 Liquidity Considerations

Treasury issues are the most liquid securities a bank can hold. An extensive secondary market in Treasury securities helps to assure the quick sale of Treasury bills and bonds at the going market price. Even large sales will not tend to depress the price.

Asset liquidity:
> The extent to which an asset may quickly be converted to cash without realizing a loss on the transaction.

Government agency securities are almost as liquid as Treasury issues. Government securities firms (described in chapter 3) regularly trade both Treasury and government agency obligations. Agency securities include those issued by the Federal National Mortgage Association (Fannie Mae) and the Federal Home Loan Mortgage Corporation (Freddie Mac). (See chapter 4 for a description of Treasury and government agency bonds and other capital market instruments, including municipal and corporate bonds.)

Municipal bonds are significantly less liquid than Treasury and government agency securities. State and local governments have issued approximately 81 percent of municipals. Another 10 percent have been issued by nonfinancial corporations to fund local projects that qualify for tax-exempt treatment (industrial revenue bonds). Because of this, municipal bond trading tends to be concentrated in more narrow geographical regions than Treasury and government agency securities trading.

Corporate bonds are also not as liquid as government securities. But, when issued by major firms, they may be actively traded on organized exchanges and, thus, reasonably liquid. At the same time, significant, unexpected developments may have an adverse effect on their market value. For example, an announcement that the issuing firm plans to initiate a highly leveraged takeover (financed with debt) of another firm can produce uncertainty about the quality of already existing bonds and drive down their market price.

1.2 Yield Considerations

As deposits (liabilities of financial institutions) have become increasingly interest rate sensitive, the yield on investment securities (assets) has become even more critical. Corporate bonds are attractive because they have relatively high yields.

Government agency debt issues share many of the attributes of Treasury securities. They are readily marketable and are backed by at least an implicit guarantee by the federal government. However, since they are not direct liabilities of the Treasury, they yield a slightly higher return to compensate for the higher risk. Also, many agency securities are pass-through certificates backed by mortgage loan pools. Since mortgage loan rates are substantially higher than Treasury rates, these pass-through certificates enjoy a competitive advantage in terms of rate.

The competitiveness of municipal bonds will depend not only on the bond's coupon rate but also on the bank's marginal tax rate. Recall that the taxable-equivalent yield of a municipal bond may be calculated as follows (see chapter 15).

$$k_{TE} = k_M/(1 - t) \qquad\qquad (16.1)$$

where k_{TE} = taxable-equivalent yield
$\quad k_M$ = municipal bond yield
$\quad\ t$ = marginal tax rate

If a municipal bond has a yield of 7 percent and the bank's marginal tax rate is 46 percent, the bond's taxable-equivalent yield is 12.96 percent (k_{TE} = 7.0 percent/(1 − .46) = 12.96 percent). At this tax rate, this relatively low yielding municipal bond is equivalent to a much higher yielding corporate bond.

However, if the marginal tax rate is lowered, the same municipal security is less attractive. For example, a marginal tax rate of 34 percent, reduces the taxable-equivalent yield to 10.61 percent. Thus, tax rate structure is a fundamental determinant in investment portfolio composition.

Investment Securities Management

2.1 INTEREST RATE RISK

Since it is difficult to predict the direction and magnitude of interest rate changes, investment portfolios can be exposed to significant *interest rate risk*.

> **Interest rate risk:**
> Risk associated with fixed income securities because of changing interest rates.

Any investment in a fixed-income instrument creates interest rate risk. At this point, the discussion of interest rate risk will be focused on investment securities. However, in chapter 17 it is shown that the principles also apply generally to portfolios of assets and liabilities of financial institutions.

Two types of interest rate risk are relevant for portfolio managers, *price risk* and *reinvestment risk*. Recall the bond price behavior theorems in chapter 10. Longer-term bonds will be subject to greater price risk. Similarly, short-term securities present more reinvestment risk.

> **Price risk:**
> The risk that the market value of a fixed-income security will decline when interest rates increase.

> **Reinvestment risk:**
> The risk that it may not be possible to reinvest the proceeds of maturing fixed-income securities at rates equivalent to those of the maturing securities because of generally declining interest rates.

2.2 Managing Interest Rate Risk

2.2.1 PASSIVE MANAGEMENT

Actual management of interest rate risk may take several forms. *Passive management* involves purchasing long-term securities with the intention of holding them until they mature. As long as a financial institution does not need the funds to meet loan or other liquidity demands, this strategy may work reasonably well. Since the yield curve is usually upward sloping, longer maturities will produce higher yields, all other things being equal.

However, should interest rates increase significantly, holding the long-term bonds at the previous, lower rates can result in a substantial opportunity cost for a financial institution. The institution cannot earn the higher rates that are available. Selling the bonds in order to reinvest at now higher market rate presents another problem. The higher rate environment has reduced the market value of the current portfolio. Selling will produce "losses on securities transactions" that must be reported in the financial statements, reducing, for example, a bank's net income for the period. Thus, the passive management approach has a built-in incentive to avoid recognizing losses in market value by simply holding the securities until maturity. A hidden cost is that opportunities for enhanced cash flow from higher market yields may be forgone.

2.2.2 LADDERED MATURITY APPROACH

The *laddered maturity approach* for investments provides such flexibility. This approach spreads investment dollars evenly over several maturities. For example, if management decided that a 10-year investment horizon was appropriate, one-tenth of the portfolio would be invested in securities maturing in one year. Another one-tenth would be invested in bonds maturing in two years. This process continues until the final one-tenth is invested in bonds with ten years to maturity.

If the institution needs additional liquidity at any point, it may sell securities with the shortest time to maturity. These can be sold at prices close to par, producing little or no loss upon sale. Medium- to long-term securities continue to earn, presumably, higher returns. To maintain the "ladder," proceeds of maturing issues are reinvested into the longest term of the investment horizon. Using the example above, funds from maturing issues would be reinvested in 10-year bonds. This approach assures regular liquidity infusions from short-term maturities while also allowing relatively higher rates of return from longer-term investments.

2.2.3 BARBELL MATURITY APPROACH

Another approach that is geared for even greater liquidity and high-yield potential is the *barbell maturity approach*. Here, a large portion of the portfolio is invested short-term, perhaps five years or fewer. The remaining is invested in long-term securities, perhaps 15 years or more. For example, 40 percent may be invested in securities with one to four years until maturity, perhaps with 10 percent in each of the four maturity classes. These investments provide a continual supply of liquidity and a reserve in the event of additional liquidity needs.

The remaining 60 percent can be spread over maturities from 15 to 25 years, yielding maximum available rates in a normal (upward sloping) yield curve environment. As long as the yield curve slopes upward, it could even be possible to sell the longer term bonds at a capital gain when 12 to 13 years remain until maturity. As before, proceeds are reinvested in the longest term on the investment horizon.

Both the laddered maturity approach and the barbell maturity approach provide liquidity and income-earning capability and are superior to the passive approach (which does not consider price or reinvestment risk). With its greater concentration in the longer maturities, the barbell maturity approach provides even more income than the laddered maturity approach.

2.3 Trends in Bank Holdings of Investment Securities

In 1964, fully one-third of bank financial assets were held as securities. Referring to Exhibit 16.1, notice that Treasury securities dominated at 20 percent. Next in importance were tax-exempt securities, 11 percent of financial assets. Government agency and corporate bonds together represented approximately 2 percent.

Over time, the relatively low returns available on Treasury securities have caused bank managers to shift away from them in favor of other higher yielding investment alternatives. Government agency bonds, with the next lowest default risk grew from less than 2 percent of assets to approximately 11 percent in 1998. At the same time, Treasury issues had fallen to 5 percent. The 1998 share of corporate bond holdings (2.9 percent) was much higher than the corresponding number in 1964 (0.4 percent). The share of tax-exempt securities declined from 10.8 percent of financial assets in 1964 to 1.9 percent in 1998.

Overall, these changes mirror the trend toward more interest-sensitive liabilities. As such liabilities increase, the cost of funds increases. In response, there have been adjustments in the pool of highest yielding assets – loans.

③ Loan Portfolio Management

3.1 Trends in Loan Portfolio Composition

The diversification noted above and generalized profit pressures have had significant impact on US loan portfolios. Over time, loans have represented between 56 and 64 percent of banks' financial assets. Exhibit 16.2 shows some of the changes within the loan portfolio.

Business loans increased somewhat and then declined, with the most significant growth in noncorporate business loans from 1.9 to 5.8 percent in 1989 and then declining to about 4.3 percent in 1998. For the industry as a whole, all business loans represented 18.9 percent of 1998 financial assets.

The largest increase, however, is attributable to *mortgage loans*. Home (one- to four-family residence), multifamily, and commercial mortgage loans have all shown significant increases in their proportions of bank assets. The farm mortgage percentage has essentially been stable over the 34-year period shown in Exhibit 16.2. In 1964, total mortgage loans were only 14 percent of financial assets, 6 percent less than business loans. By 1998, mortgages comprised almost 24 percent versus the 19 percent associated with business loans. During the early 1990s, this increased exposure led to loan losses (particularly in the Northeast section of the country) because of an oversupply of housing and commercial real estate. The oversupply hampered the efforts of bank customers to sell or lease the projects involved and made repayment less likely. These factors led to a retrenchment in the mortgage market to correct the excesses. By 1998, the correction was complete.

Household and *consumer* loans are the third largest category of bank loans and have consistently represented 10 to 15 percent of financial assets over the period shown. *Foreign loans*, *loans to financial institutions*, and *loans to finance securities* complete bank loan portfolios, usually making up 10 percent or less.

	1964	1969	1974	1979	1984	1989	1994	1998
Financial assets (billions)	$311.5	$471.6	$836.4	$1,335.9	$2,105.8	$2,954.4	$4,163.7	$5,405.1
Securities as a % of financial assets:								
Treasury	20.4%	11.8%	6.7%	7.3%	8.8%	6.9%	7.0%	5.0%
Government agency	1.7	2.1	4.0	3.8	3.7	5.9	10.3	10.9
Tax-exempt	10.8	12.6	12.1	10.0	8.3	5.1	2.3	1.9
Corporate & foreign	0.4	0.4	0.8	0.5	0.8	2.7	2.5	2.9
	33.3%	26.9%	23.6%	21.6%	21.6%	20.6%	22.1%	20.7%

◆ **Exhibit 16.1: Investment securities, US banks, 1964–98**

Source: Board of Governors of the Federal Reserve System, *Flow of Funds Accounts, Financial Assets and Liabilities*, various issues.

	1964	1969	1974	1979	1984	1989	1994	1998
Financial assets (billions)	$311.5	$471.6	$836.4	$1,355.9	$2,105.8	$2,954.4	$4,163.7	$5,405.1
Loans as a %:								
Business								
Corporate	16.1%	20.9%	19.1%	15.1%	16.7%	16.0%	12.7%	13.8%
Noncorp, nonfarm	1.9	2.6	4.3	5.4	5.9	5.8	3.6	4.3
Farm	2.3	2.2	2.2	2.3	1.9	1.0	0.9	0.8
	20.3	25.7	25.6	22.8	24.5	22.8	17.2	18.9
Foreign	2.1	1.3	2.1	3.9	1.5	0.7	0.6	1.0
Financial institutions	3.2	2.4	3.8	2.0	1.4	1.1	1.3	1.7
Mortgages								
Home	8.7	8.8	8.9	11.0	9.3	10.7	14.8	14.5
Multifamily	0.5	0.7	0.9	0.8	1.0	1.2	0.9	1.0
Commercial	4.0	4.7	5.2	5.6	7.3	10.8	8.0	7.7
Farm	0.8	0.8	0.7	0.6	0.5	0.6	0.5	0.5
	14.0	15.0	15.7	18.0	18.1	23.3	24.2	23.7
Household and consumer	13.7	14.8	14.2	15.4	13.9	14.0	11.8	10.5
Security credit	3.0	2.4	1.6	1.5	1.7	1.4	2.3	2.6
	56.3%	61.6%	63.0%	63.6%	61.1%	63.3%	57.4%	58.4%

◆ **Exhibit 16.2: US bank loans, 1964–98**

Source: Board of Governors of the Federal Reserve System, *Flow of Funds Accounts, Financial Assets and Liabilities*, various issues.

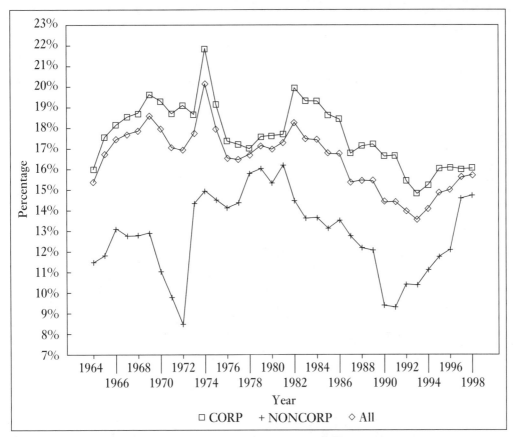

♦ **Exhibit 16.3:** Commercial bank loans as a percentage of business liabilities, 1964–98

♦ *Notes*:   CORP   Corporate
                         NONCORP   Noncorporate
                         ALL   Corporate and noncorporate

♦ *Source*:   Author's graphic, based on data from: Board of Governors of the Federal Reserve System,
                         Flow of Funds Accounts Financial Assets and Liabilities, various issues.

3.2 COMMERCIAL BANK MARKET SHARES

Exhibit 16.3 helps to illustrate the trend of more direct financing by US businesses. While bank loans made to nonfarm business more than tripled from $277 billion in 1979 to $977 billion in 1998, the percentage that these loans represented of total business liabilities dropped from 17 percent in 1979 to 13.5 percent in 1993 and then recovered somewhat to 15.7 percent by 1998. Commercial paper and long-term debt instruments have become much more important sources of finance for businesses.

   However, what has been lost in the business sector has been gained in the mortgage market. In 1979, bank mortgage loans amounted to $245 billion or 18.5 percent of all mortgages as shown in

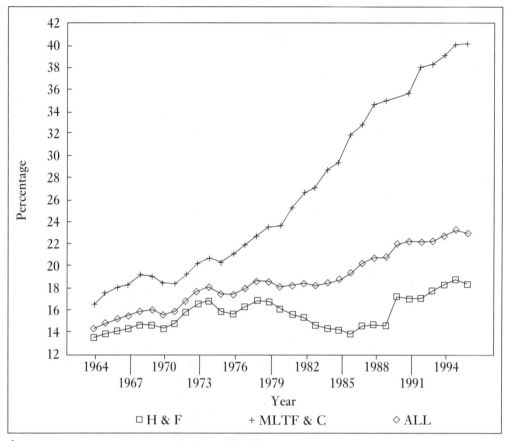

◆ **Exhibit 16.4:**   **Commercial bank share of mortgage loans**

◆ *Notes*:   H & F   Home and farm
                MLTF & C   Multifamily and commercial
                ALL   Home, farm, multifamily, and commercial

◆ *Source*:   Author's graphic based on data from: Board of Governors of the Federal Reserve System,
                Flow of Funds Accounts Financial Assets and Liabilities, various issues.

Exhibit 16.4. By 1996, commercial bank mortgages loans were $1.28 trillion or 23 percent of all mortgages outstanding. Within the general category of total mortgages, multifamily and commercial mortgages have grown even faster. In 1979, banks held 23.5 percent of this subset, by 1998 38 percent even after retrenching from the highs in the mid-1990s.

In the consumer sector, as Exhibit 16.5 shows, the share has been more consistent, although on a downward trend during the 1990s. Commercial banks provided 53 percent of all consumer credit in 1979, 40 percent by 1998.

Banks are important providers of finance in all three markets. A substantial amount of consumer credit is through commercial banks, but market share of banks is being eroded by competing credit cards offered by nonbank financial institutions. Mortgage lending continues to be a growth sector. Banks are attempting to recover market share in the business sector.

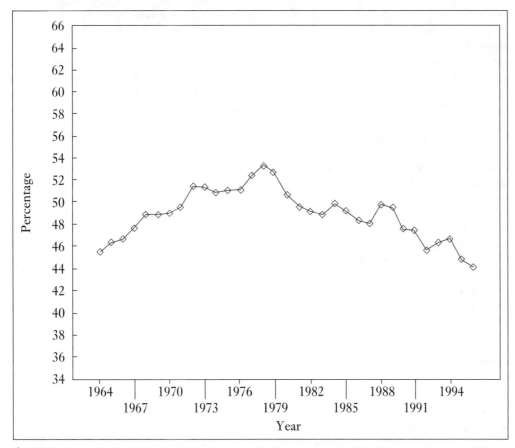

◆ **Exhibit 16.5:** **Commercial bank loans as a percentage of consumer credit, 1964–98**

◆ *Source*:   Author's graphic based on data from: Board of Governors of the Federal Reserve System,
                 Flow of Funds Accounts Financial Assets and Liabilities, various issues.

3.3 CREDIT ANALYSIS

The evaluation of a prospective borrower's loan request for credit risk is crucial to maintain the soundness of the loan portfolio. The criteria for this analysis are frequently referred to as the "three Cs" of credit, *character*, *capacity*, and *collateral*.

Assessing the borrower's *character* includes an evaluation of past performance. If the request is for a commercial loan, managerial experience and proficiency are important. If it is a consumer loan request, payment history and other accounts should be examined. In a sense, evaluation of character is an evaluation of *willingness* to repay the loan.

Capacity is a measure of *ability* to repay. For business loans, capacity will depend upon the type of loan. As noted above, short-term loans are repaid from liquidity, long-term loans from profits. Ratio analysis of a firm's financial statements is often helpful to arrive at succinct descriptive variables of the firm's financial position. Comparisons of these data to industry statistics can help to highlight any major deviations from industry norms for further investigation. In addition, any present or anticipated conditions that may have a significant impact on future cash flows should also be a part of the analysis.

Consumer credit decisions can usually be made in a more objective way. A consumer's income relative to existing debt is, perhaps, the best measure of capacity. If the bank analyzes the profile of its individual customers over time, the characteristics that have been associated with timely loan repayment will help the bank identify the best potential customers in the future. This process is called *credit scoring*.

Collateral is of particular importance for asset-based loans, since loan repayment is directly tied to the assets' cash flow potential. The bank should obtain every reasonable assurance that the collateral is adequate. For other types of loans, the bank should attempt to anticipate fluctuations in market value of the securing property so that the loan does not become seriously under-collateralized. For example, an automobile loan whose unpaid balance declines at a slower rate than the value of the auto can leave the loan under-secured. In addition, the borrower then owes a loan balance that exceeds the value of the property, providing him with a disincentive to repay the obligation.

Of course, general economic conditions will have an impact on credit analysis. In strong economies, corporations are better able to service debt because sales volume is more predictable. Individuals are less likely to have their employment interrupted and, therefore, better able to repay loans. In expanding economies, relatively strong demand for real estate will support the value of property that is used as loan collateral.

3.4 Loan Pricing

Banks may offer loans at either *fixed* or *variable* rates of interest. A fixed rate loan removes uncertainty for the borrower, particularly with respect to commercial term loans and residential mortgage loans. Should interest rates increase, the borrower's debt-servicing cash flow is un-affected. However, the lending institution sustains an opportunity cost because it is unable to reinvest at the higher rates. At the same time, for competitive reasons, banks permit more timely adjustments of deposit interest rates. These conditions can have significant adverse implications for bank profitability.

Variable rate loans relieve this pressure for lending institutions. Still, the pressure is not eliminated, it is simply shifted to the borrower. As a result, borrowers are willing to pay a higher interest rate for fixed rate loans than for their variable rate counterparts, particularly if interest rates are expected to increase.

In terms of consumer loans, residential mortgages have been issued in significant numbers with variable rates attached. The differential between variable and fixed rates may be as much as 3 percent. Interest rate caps for variable rate loans are commonly established to limit both the amount of rate increase for a given *year* (annual cap) and over the *term* of the mortgage (lifetime cap). The rate itself is tied to either a quoted interest rate or the bank's average cost of funds.

Floating rate commercial loans are more common than are consumer variable rate loans. Furthermore, many that are technically fixed are short-term enough so as to expose the bank to minimal interest rate risk. If interest rates increase over the term of the loan, the bank can reprice the loan (increase the interest rate) at the end of the relatively short time to maturity. The bank's CD rate or average cost of funds may serve as a *base rate* or *reference rate*. Alternatively, the London Interbank Offered Rate (LIBOR) may be the base rate. The contractual (loan) rate equals the base rate plus a *spread*.

Pricing a specific loan requires consideration of the cost of debt funds, default risk and term premiums (for fixed rate long-term loans), and expected administrative expense. The cost of funds is the marginal or incremental cost of borrowing rather than the historical cost. To illustrate, consider First National Bank from chapter 15 once again. According to Exhibit 15.6, 60 percent of average assets were financed with interest-bearing deposits, 20 percent borrowed funds, 11 percent demand deposits, 2 percent other liabilities, and 7 percent equity.

Assume that these *proportions* will be constant in the future but:

- The *cost* of interest-bearing deposits will increase to 7.25 percent (from the current 7.04 percent).
- The *cost* of borrowed funds will increase to 7.85 percent (from 7.78 percent).

Note that demand deposits and other liabilities have no explicit cost associated with them. (Technically, required reserves impose an implicit cost on transactions accounts. The opportunity cost is the reserve requirement percentage multiplied by the earning rate that is forgone.) If the target return on equity is 17.5 percent (up from 16.3 percent), the weighted cost of debt funds is expected to be 7.15 percent ($(0.60)(0.0725) + (0.20)(0.0785) + (0.07)(0.175) = 0.07145$). If default risk and term premiums are 1 percent each and administrative expense is expected to be 0.5 percent of the loan amount, the loan is appropriately priced at 9.65 percent.

In general,

$$k_L = \left(\sum_{i=1}^{n} w_i r_i \right) + DRP + TP + A \tag{16.2}$$

where k_L = loan rate

$\sum_{i=1}^{n} w_i r_i$ = cost of interest-sensitive liabilities (debt funds)

DRP = default risk premium
TP = term premium
A = administrative expense

Alternatively, compensating balances may be required in connection with a lower stated rate. For example, suppose that First National wishes to earn an effective rate of 9.65 percent while quoting an 8.65 percent loan rate. The compensating balance that is required causes 8.65 percent of the gross loan to equal 9.65 percent of the net funds.

$$k_L = k_E(1 - x) \tag{16.3}$$

where k_E = effective rate of the loan
       x = compensating balance as a percent of the gross loan

Substituting the specifics of our example, $x = 0.1036$, that is, a 10.36 percent compensating balance will bring the effective rate to 9.65 percent. Intuitively, if a bank client pays 8.65 percent of the loan amount as interest, but can actually use only 89.64 percent of the loan ($1 - .1036$), the effective interest rate is 9.65 percent (8.65/89.64).

Whatever approach is taken, it is important to consider all relevant factors. Not only are cost considerations crucial, but competitive factors play a role in the loan pricing decision. An institution must offer its client a package that meets his needs for efficient service and, at the same time, provides depositors and investors a reasonable rate of return. Otherwise, bank customers may elect the alternatives to commercial bank services, such as commercial paper, that are increasingly available.

④ Observed Combinations of Securities and Loans in the OECD

As can be observed from Exhibit 16.6, US banks held high percentages of 1994 assets as securities (22.84 percent) and loans (61.25 percent), or a total of approximately 84 percent. Other countries with loan portfolios representing 60 percent or more of total assets include Australia, Canada, Japan, Mexico, the Netherlands, and Norway. However, among these countries, securities portfolios constituted 15 percent or less in Australia, Japan, the Netherlands, and Norway.

However, loans contributed less than 40 percent to total banking assets in Belgium (39 percent), France (33 percent), Greece (23 percent), Luxembourg (18 percent), Portugal (32 percent), and

Country (institutions)	Securities	Loans
Australia (all banks)	8.22%	61.06%
Austria (all banks)	12.58	50.45
Belgium (all banks)	29.24	38.73
Canada (domestic banks)	18.68	69.31
Denmark (banks and savings banks)	26.59	45.87
Finland (commercial banks)	28.75	49.19
France (commercial banks)	18.68	33.02
Germany (commercial banks)	16.48	57.76
Greece (large commercial banks)	39.33	23.31
Italy (all banks)	15.65	42.16
Japan (commercial banks)	14.28	65.62
Luxembourg (commercial banks)	17.42	18.43
Mexico (commercial banks)	21.08	61.12
Netherlands (all banks)	13.12	63.02
Norway (commercial banks)	10.22	77.15
Portugal (all banks)	22.66	32.18
Spain (commercial banks)	18.87	41.55
Sweden (commercial banks)	36.19	47.93
Switzerland (large banks)	17.61	58.30
Turkey (commercial banks)	11.80	37.37
United Kingdom (commercial banks)	17.46	51.99
United States (commercial banks)	22.84	61.25

◆ **Exhibit 16.6:** Securities and loans as a percentage of total assets for selected countries, 1994

◆ *Source*:   Organization for Economic Cooperation and Development, *Bank Profitability, Financial Statements of Banks 1985–94*, Paris, 1996.

Country (institutions)	Gross income
Australia (all banks)	6.22%
Austria (all banks)	6.39
Belgium (all banks)	9.36
Canada (domestic banks)	6.53
Denmark (banks and savings banks)	7.76
Finland (commercial banks)	5.60
France (commercial banks)	5.47
Germany (commercial banks)	6.65
Greece (large commercial banks)	11.85
Italy (all banks)	7.06
Japan (commercial banks)	4.08
Luxembourg (commercial banks)	6.98
Mexico (commercial banks)	16.85
Netherlands (all banks)	6.85
Norway (commercial banks)	7.48
Portugal (all banks)	9.16
Spain (commercial banks)	8.32
Sweden (commercial banks)	7.37
Switzerland (large banks)	4.87
Turkey (commercial banks)	36.36
United Kingdom (commercial banks)	6.09
United States (commercial banks)	6.66

◆ **Exhibit 16.7:** **Gross interest income as a percentage of total assets for selected countries, 1994**

◆ *Source*:   Organization for Economic Cooperation and Development, *Bank Profitability, Financial Statements of Banks 1985–94*, Paris, 1996.

Turkey (38 percent). Recall from Exhibit 15.9, that these countries held from 23 to 60 percent of total assets as liquid assets (cash and interbank deposits), while US banks held less than 8 percent in such liquid assets. As a result, these European banks are less involved in providing finance to businesses and individuals, more involved in wholesale interbank transactions and the securities market.

Exhibit 16.7 shows gross interest income for OECD countries in 1994. Notice that the return in Japan (4.08 percent) was lower than in the United States (6.66 percent). This is because of lower interest rate levels in Japan during the year analyzed. On the other hand, higher interest rate environments in other countries are reflected in the gross earnings of their commercial banks, notably Greece (11.85 percent), Mexico (16.85 percent), and Turkey (36.36 percent). These rates are also measures of the cost of obtaining loans in the respective countries. It should be remembered that, as nonfinancial US firms compete with Japanese companies in world export markets, the cost of bank loans historically has been lower, giving these firms a certain competitive advantage. At a minimum, this rate differential encourages US firms to look for alternatives to traditional bank financing.

 **Summary**

Securities and loan portfolios represent as much as 80 percent of bank assets in the US. Management of these portfolios is interrelated. Strong loan demand may necessitate partial liquidation of securities portfolios in order to generate required liquidity. Generally, the share of bank assets represented by investment securities has declined, as commercial banks have focused more on higher yielding loans.

Management of investment securities should incorporate considerations of both liquidity and profitability. When the yield curve slopes upward, long-term fixed-income securities provide the highest yields, but also expose a portfolio to maximum price volatility. Laddered and barbell approaches to securities management afford both liquidity and high yield potential.

Considerations of character, capacity, and collateral of respective borrowers are the basic priciples of effective loan portfolio management. Interest rates, default risk, and administrative expense also are factored into loan pricing.

 End-of-chapter Questions

1. What are the major categories in bank investment securities portfolios? Are these securities held primarily to provide the bank with liquidity?

2. Of the types of securities described in this chapter, which are the most liquid? Why do you suppose this is true?

3. Refer to a recent edition of the *Wall Street Journal*.
   a. Compare the yields of a government agency security to that of a Treasury issue with the same time to maturity.
   b. To what do you attribute the observed difference in yield?

4. a. Describe interest rate risk.
   b. Differentiate price risk and reinvestment risk.

5. Management of the securities portfolio is somewhat simplified by easily determined market values of the instruments. Why do you think that the market value of loans is more difficult to determine?

6. Differentiate the laddered approach of securities management from the barbell approach.

7. What are the deficiencies associated with the passive management approach of securities?

8. What are the primary components of credit analysis?

9. Frequently, it is said that lending is an increasingly competitive business. Describe bank industry trends that might support this assertion.

End-of-chapter Problems

1. Suppose that a bank may invest in either qualified municipal bonds that pay 7.5 percent interest or taxable bonds that pay 11 percent interest. Suppose further that the marginal tax rate and cost of funds are 34 percent and 8 percent, respectively. Which bonds provide the higher after-tax yield?

2. Recompute the appropriate loan rate for the example presented in section 3.4, "Loan Pricing," assuming a funding mix of 40 percent interest-bearing deposits and borrowed funds each.

3. Suppose that bank management priced a loan at 11.5 percent, but also required a 15 percent compensating balance. What would be the effective interest rate?

SELECTED REFERENCES

Board of Governors of the Federal Reserve System. *Flow of Funds Accounts, Financial Assets and Liabilities*, various issues.

Johnson, Frank P. and Richard D. Johnson. *Commercial Bank Management*, Dryden Press, Hinsdale, Ill., 1985.

Koch, Timothy W. *Bank Management*, Dryden Press, Hinsdale, Ill., 1988.

Organization for Economic Cooperation and Development. *Bank Profitability, Financial Statements of Banks 1985–1994*, Paris, 1996.

Wilson, J. S .G. *Banking Policy and Structure: A Comparative Analysis*, Croom Helm, London, 1986.

Capital and Asset/Liability Management

CHAPTER OVERVIEW

This chapter:
- Describes bank capital.
- Examines the need for bank capital.
- Highlights international coordination of capital standards.
- Explores the impact of interest rate risk on bank assets, liabilities, and capital.
- Illustrates duration analysis.
- Describes the use of interest rate futures, options on futures, and swaps to reduce interest rate risk.
- Discusses market value accounting.

KEY TERMS

allowance for loan loss
bank capital
Basle Accord
capital ratio
common stock
direct charge-off
duration
hedging
interest rate futures
interest rate options

interest rate swaps
market value accounting
net worth
preferred stock
provision for loan loss
risk-based capital
risk-weighted assets
solvency
subordinated debt

CHAPTER OUTLINE

1 Bank Capital
    1.1 Equity and Nonequity Capital
    1.2 The Need for Bank Capital

Introduction

The challenge for managers of financial institutions is to maximize shareholder wealth while maintaining solvency and adequate liquidity. As illustrated in chapters 15 and 16, profitability is closely linked to the composition of the balance sheet. Bank regulators must encourage both profitability and soundness. The proper management of capital is central to all of these objectives. However, a philosophical tug of war often results when bank managers and regulators address the issue of the "right" level of capital. If the level is too high, the resulting cost of funds can put the bank at a competitive disadvantage. If the level is too low, the bank will be in danger of insolvency.

The right level of bank capital is a difficult issue at the domestic level. It is even more complicated at the international level. Nevertheless, the central bankers of the industrialized West have designed a uniform set of capital standards to help place banks in international circles to compete on a more level playing field.

Volatile interest rates can threaten the capital base of a financial institution. Equity is the difference between assets and liabilities, that is, net assets. Whenever the market value of assets and/or liabilities changes, the market value of equity also changes. The use of derivative securities, such as interest rate futures, options, and swaps can be useful in protecting bank equity from the adverse effects of interest rate volatility.

Interest rate changes can have a significant impact on any firm with large portfolios of interest-sensitive financial assets and liabilities. While the discussions in this chapter focus on commercial banks, the principles can be applied to a wide range of financial institutions.

Bank Capital

1.1 EQUITY AND NONEQUITY CAPITAL

Common equity capital includes *preferred and common stock, paid-in surplus (or paid-in capital), and undivided profits (or retained earnings)*. *Preferred stock* is another form of equity capital. These categories are included in capital according to generally accepted accounting principles (GAAP).

Bank regulators also include other items that are not normally regarded as capital in nonfinancial corporations. This is a major difference between GAAP and regulatory accounting principles (RAP). Nonequity capital includes:

- Allowance for loan loss
- Subordinated notes and debentures

According to RAP, the *allowance for loan loss* (or allowance for credit loss) is also considered capital. The allowance is an asset valuation account associated with loans, that is, a contra-asset account. A contra-asset account is one that has a credit balance but is recorded in the asset section with accounts that have a debit balance. The net effect of this arrangement is that the asset balance is lower than it would be otherwise. (A common example of a contra-asset account is accumulated depreciation, recorded in the fixed assets section of the balance sheet. Gross fixed assets less accumulated depreciation equals net fixed assets.)

Each year (or, in some cases, each month), bank management estimates the amount of loss that should be recorded for the period. This amount is not usually *actual* loss. Instead, it is an amount considered necessary to cover anticipated *future* loss and to maintain an adequate allowance. The amount is recorded as *provision for loan loss* (or provision for credit loss), an expense for the period. The offsetting entry is to allowance for loan loss. For example, suppose that the management of a $500 million bank (total assets) estimates that $10 million is an appropriate provision given current economic conditions and the specific loans in its portfolio. The accounting entry is as follows (in millions of dollars).

	DR	CR
Provision for loan loss	$10	
Allowance for loan loss		$10

The provision reduces income before taxes by $10 million and ultimately reduces capital. The allowance entry reduces the carrying value of loans by the same amount. Ignoring taxes, the size of the bank is reduced to $490 million. An important advantage of the allowance method is that provisions can be structured to smooth the impact on earnings over time. The alternative, *direct charge-off* method, requires recognition of loss in the amount and the period of actual loan write-off.

Under the *allowance method*, when loans are actually written off, the allowance (not operating income) is reduced. For example, if bank management determines that an $8 million loan is uncollectible, the following entry is made (in millions of dollars).

	DR	CR
Allowance for loan loss	$8	
Loans		$8

While the appropriate amount of provision for loan loss is a subjective determination by individual bank management, the aggregate provision for all US commercial banks in recent years has ranged from 1 to 2 percent of total loans.

In addition to the allowance for loan loss, *subordinated notes and debentures* are also considered bank capital for regulatory purposes. Before 1962, regulators did not permit a bank to classify these debt instruments as capital unless the institution was in financial distress. The Comptroller of the Currency allowed the classification for all national banks in 1962. Thereafter, state banking authorities modified state regulations to conform with the change. As noted in Exhibit 15.3, these long-term debt instruments grew from 0.3 percent of systemwide liabilities in 1964 to 3.7 percent in 1996.

The features of subordinated debt make it an attractive source of long-term financing. Unlike stock dividends, interest payments are tax-deductible. To the extent that the rate of return on earning assets exceeds the after-tax interest cost, the difference accrues to equity investors. In other words, subordinated debt provides important leverage effects.

However, the fixed nature of interest payments can present cash flow problems. When interest income slumps, fixed interest payments can adversely affect net income. Any sinking fund requirements (money that must be set aside before the obligations mature) magnify this effect. Any failure to repay interest and/or principal constitutes default and can lead to the bank's liquidation.

In order to *qualify* as bank capital, debt instruments must meet certain criteria. The claim of debt holders must be subordinated to *all* depositors, insured and uninsured. In addition, only debt issues with a weighted average original maturity of five years or more qualify, according to regulations of the FDIC and the Comptroller's office.

1.2 THE NEED FOR BANK CAPITAL

Bank capital serves much the same functions as capital in a nonfinancial firm. It provides a *buffer for temporary operating losses*. Capital absorbs these losses until profitability is restored so that the firm remains *solvent*.

> **Solvency:**
> The financial condition of a bank in which the book value of its assets exceeds the book values of liabilities.

Theoretically, the solvency of a bank should be determined by *market value* of assets and liabilities rather than *book value*. Regulators increasingly are moving toward more market valuation. However, the book value of equity still determines solvency and the ability to absorb operating losses.

Perceived capital adequacy increases *public confidence* in an institution. If public confidence is maintained, management can avoid unexpectedly high deposit withdrawals (bank runs). On the surface, bank runs may not appear to present a risk of insolvency since, presumably, the value of liquidated assets equals the value of deposits and other liabilities to be satisfied. However, when large quantities of assets must be sold quickly, the bank may realize less than asset carrying values, that is, sustain losses upon sale. These losses deplete capital just as operating losses do.

Even if asset liquidation is not necessary, a loss of public confidence can increase the bank's cost of funds. If the increase is significant enough, profitability will be hurt, once again putting pressure on an already thinly capitalized institution. Thus, capital adequacy can help preserve public confidence and avoid bank runs and higher costs of doing business.

From a regulatory perspective, bank capital places *constraints on bank growth*. In this sense, minimum capital requirements prevent unlimited deposit taking and lending (or other investment activities). With a given capital ratio, dividend payout ratio, and rate of return on equity, a bank can expect to grow in the normal course of operating profitably.

$$\Delta TA = (ROE)(E)(b)(EM) \tag{17.1}$$

where ΔTA = change in the asset base for one year
ROE = return on equity (net income as a percentage of equity)
E = equity (dollar amount)
b = retention ratio (percentage of net income not paid as dividends)
EM = equity multiplier (total assets to equity)

$(ROE)(E)(b)$ is the change in retained earnings that can be projected. This addition to retained earnings forms a new equity layer that will support asset growth. When the equity multiplier is high (or the capital ratio is low), the bank's asset base can grow relatively faster. All other things being equal, regulators usually prefer to see a lower equity multiplier (higher capital ratio) because it implies a greater buffer against loss. Of course, regulators must seriously consider the impact of minimum capital requirements on bank profitability and competitiveness.

1.3 REGULATION OF BANK CAPITAL

1.3.1 UNITED STATES

Until recently, bank regulators established capital guidelines by reference to peer groups. Banks were classified by size and banks within a given size category were expected to maintain minimum *capital ratios*. In addition to these minimum ratios, regulators established target, or desirable, capital ratios within each size category.

Capital ratio:
   Capital as a percentage of bank assets.

Generally, larger banks maintained lower capital ratios. This disparity was justified by the shorter-term, more commercially oriented loan portfolios of large banks. In addition, larger banks held more diversified (therefore, less risky) loan portfolios. Nevertheless, this system did not prevent significant erosion of bank capital ratios over time. The aggregate ratio of total capital to assets of all insured US banks fell from 12 percent in 1935 to 6.5 percent by 1990.

1.3.2 INTERNATIONAL COORDINATION

In December 1987, the Cooke Committee (Committee on Banking Regulation and Supervisory Practices of the Bank for International Settlements, also known as the Basle Committee) announced agreement on international convergence of capital standards – the *Basle Accord*. The definition of capital under the Basle Accord includes Tier I and Tier II capital.

Tier I (core) capital:

- Shareholders' equity
- Perpetual preferred stock, net of goodwill

Tier II (supplemental) capital:

- Perpetual and term subordinated debt
- Mandatory convertible debt (into common stock)
- Asset revaluation reserves (associated with assets that have increased in market value)
- Other supplementary items at the discretion of individual countries

---

Tier II capital is limited to 100 percent of Tier I capital. According to the Accord, beginning January 1993, international banks must maintain both Tier I and Tier II capital equal to 4 percent of risk-weighted assets for a total capital ratio of 8 percent.

Risk-weighted assets:
Assets adjusted for risk by applying capital standards to 100 percent of the riskiest assets while applying the standards to 0 percent of the least risky assets. Other assets are assigned weights less than 100 percent and greater than 0 percent .

Germany and Japan are permitted to use 45 percent of unrealized gains on equities held as investments toward the Tier II capital requirement. (In late 1991 and early 1992, the value of Japanese equites fell dramatically because of a collapse in real estate prices and a general recession. As much as half of the unrealized gains that had been available were eliminated in the sharp market decline, creating a threat to the ability of Japanese banks to comply with the Basle Accord.)

Exhibit 17.1 shows the risk weights and capital definitions that have been adopted in the United States. Essentially, cash and cash equivalents have no capital requirements. Less liquid assets have weights that range from 20 to 100 percent. Risk-weighted asset totals are computed by multiplying balances in accounts and contingent liabilities by the appropriate weight. When these are aggregated, the result is the asset base used for the 4 percent guidelines.

RISK WEIGHTING

0 percent risk weighting
- Cash
- Balances due from Federal Reserve banks
- Balances due from OECD central and commercial banks in immediately available funds
- US Treasury and government agency securities
- All direct claims (securities and loans) on OECD governments
- Non-US-dollar claims (assets) unconditionally guaranteed by OECD governments, to the extent that they are offset by the bank's liabilities

20 percent risk weighting
- Cash items in the process of collection
- Short-term claims (including transactions account balances) on US depository institutions and foreign banks (both OECD and non-OECD)
- Long-term claims on US and OECD-based banks
- Claims conditionally guaranteed by OECD central governments and by US government agencies
- Non-US-dollar claims (assets) conditionally guaranteed by non-OECD governments, to the extent that they are offset by the bank's liabilities
- Claims guaranteed by US government-sponsored agencies, the World Bank, the International Finance Corporation, the Inter-American Development Bank, the Asian Development Bank, the African Development Bank, the European Investment Bank, the European Bank for Reconstruction and Development, the Nordic Investment Bank, and other multilateral lending institutions in which the US government is a shareholder or member
- General obligation claims guaranteed by the full faith and credit of states or political subdivisions of the United States and of OECD countries
- Claims collateralized by securities issued or guaranteed (1) by US government-sponsored agencies or (2) by multilateral or regional lending institutions in which the US government is a shareholder or member

50 percent risk weighting
- Loans secured by first liens on one- to four-family residential properties that are no more than 90 days past due
- Loans secured by first liens on multifamily residential properties (1) with original maturities from seven to 30 years, (2) that are no more than 90 days past due, and (3) for which principal and interest payments have been made on time for at least the year preceding placement in the 50 percent weight category
- Privately issued mortgage-backed securities with underlying collateral loans that meet one of the two above sets of criteria for individual mortgage loans

100 percent risk weighting
- All claims on non-OECD central governments
- Long-term claims on US bank holding companies and on non-OECD banks
- All claims on non-OECD central governments
- Claims on the domestic and foreign private sector entities, including nondepository financial institutions and bank holding companies
- Premises and other real estate
- All other assets that do not qualify for 0 percent, 20 percent, or 50 percent risk weighting

Off-balance-sheet categories weighted according to the obligor or guarantor

- 100 percent of general guarantees or direct credit substitutes, such as (1) standby letters of credit that guarantee payment of another party's obligation and (2) general commercial letters of credit
- 50 percent of transaction-related contingencies, such as (1) performance bonds and standby letters of credit backing nonfinancial performance of other parties; (2) unused portions of commitments with original maturities greater than one year; and (3) note issuance facilities
- 20 percent of short-term, self-liquidating, trade-related trade commitments

CAPITAL GUIDELINES

	Required ratio to risk-weighted assets
Tier I capital	
Common stockholders' equity (dominant portion of Tier I capital) Noncumulative perpetual preferred stock (with minor role in Tier I capital) Minority interest in consolidated subsidiaries	4%
Tier II capital (up to 100% of Tier I capital)	
Allowance for loan loss (up to 1.25% of risk-weighted assets) Perpetual preferred stock (no limits) Mandatory convertible debt (converting to common stock, no limits) Subordinated debt (subordinated to depositors and general creditors) and limited-life preferred stock with original maturities of at least five years (up to 50% of Tier I capital)	4%

◆ **Exhibit 17.1: Risk-based capital guidelines**

◆ *Source*:   Board of Governors of the Federal Reserve System, *Commercial Bank Examination System*, 1998.

1.4 Capital Ratios in the United States

For the industry as a whole, the equity capital to total assets has recently ranged between 6 and 8 percent. Since equity capital is part of the Tier I category, these rates indicate that US banks have little difficulty complying with the Basle Accord. However, Exhibit 17.2 shows that capital ratios vary by bank size.

Banks with assets under $100 million are well capitalized with average equity of 9–10 percent of assets. For banks with assets between $100 million and $1 billion, the range drops to 7.7–9.1 per-

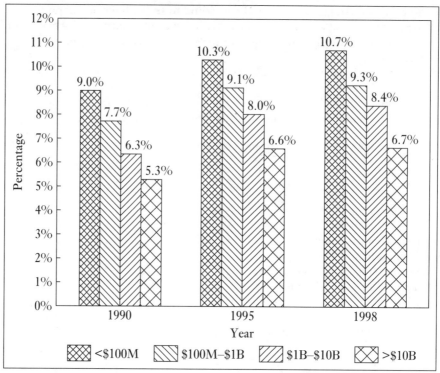

◆ Exhibit 17.2: **US bank capital ratios by size, 1990, 1995, and 1998**

◆ *Source*: Author's graphic, based on data from: Federal Deposit Insurance Corporation, *Quarterly Banking Profile*, various issues.

cent. The range for those banks with assets between $1 billion and $10 billion is between 6.3 and 8.0 percent. For the largest banks (assets over $10 billion) the range shown is 5.3–6.6 percent.

Mid-1998, there were 5,647 banks in the first size group, but only 2,963 in the second. The third group represented 310 banks, while the largest size category contained only 64 institutions. Thus, the vast majority of US banks easily comply with the Basle Accord standards, as the ratios noted above are equity (Tier I) capital to total assets (not risk-weighted assets). If risk-weighted assets were used the denominator of the capital ratio would be smaller and, thus, the capital ratio would be larger.

Exhibit 17.2 also highlights another recent trend in capital management in the US banking industry. Strong profits in the early 1990s are reflected in higher capital ratios in all size categories.

1.5 CAPITAL MANAGEMENT OUTSIDE THE UNITED STATES

On average, the capital levels in the United States are similar to those in several other countries. Exhibit 17.3 compares the average capital ratios of selected OECD members in 1994. The variation of these ratios has important implications for the competitiveness of these banking systems. The leverage effects translate directly into income effects for bank shareholders.

Country (institutions)	Capital/assets[1]
Australia (all banks)	10.47%
Austria (all banks)	5.19
Belgium (all banks)	4.04
Canada (domestic banks)	5.34
Denmark (banks and savings banks)	6.58
Finland (commercial banks)	4.89
France (commercial banks)	3.46
Germany (commercial banks)	5.54
Greece (large commercial banks)	4.69
Italy (all banks)	8.89
Japan (commercial banks)	3.75
Luxembourg (commercial banks)	2.40
Mexico (commercial banks)	5.50
Netherlands (all banks)	4.26
Norway (commercial banks)	6.25
Portugal (all banks)	10.03
Spain (commercial banks)	9.43
Sweden (commercial banks)	5.39
Switzerland (large banks)	6.80
Turkey (commercial banks)	4.51
United Kingdom (commercial banks)	4.09
United States (commercial banks)	7.80

◆ **Exhibit 17.3:** Capital as a percentage of total assets for selected countries, 1994

◆ *Note*: 1 Capital includes reserves but excludes bonds

◆ *Source*: Organization for Economic Cooperation and Development, *Bank Profitability, Financial Statements of Banks, 1985–94*, Paris, 1996.

1.6 INCOME EFFECTS

All other things being equal, low capital ratios improve rate of return on equity (ROE). Recall from Chapter 15, Equation (15.16), that ROE is the product of the return on assets (ROA) and the equity multiplier (EM).

$$ROE = (ROA)(EM) \qquad (17.2)$$

Notice that a higher ROE can be achieved by increasing ROA *or* increasing the EM.

Exhibit 17.4 shows this relationship for the same group of OECD nations. Among these countries, the highest ROE in 1994 was in Turkey at 99.33 percent. Turkey's 1994 ROA was approximately twice that of the United States. In addition, Turkey's EM was also approximately twice that of the US banks. As a result, ROE of the Turkish banking system was four times that of the US system.

Country (institutions)	Equity multiplier[1]	ROA	ROE[2]
Australia (all banks)	9.55%	1.62%	15.47%
Austria (all banks)	19.27	0.93	17.92
Belgium (all banks)	24.75	0.50	12.38
Canada (domestic banks)	18.73	2.36	44.19
Denmark (banks and savings banks)	15.20	0.90	13.68
Finland (commercial banks)[3]	20.45	−1.17	−23.93
France (commercial banks)	28.90	0.24	6.94
Germany (commercial banks)	18.05	1.06	19.13
Greece (large commercial banks)	21.32	1.59	33.90
Italy (all banks)	11.25	1.21	13.61
Japan (commercial banks)	26.67	0.30	8.00
Luxembourg (commercial banks)	41.67	0.61	25.42
Mexico (commercial banks)	18.18	2.32	42.18
Netherlands (all banks)	23.47	0.89	20.89
Norway (commercial banks)	16.00	1.43	22.88
Portugal (all banks)	9.97	1.60	15.95
Spain (commercial banks)	10.60	1.44	15.27
Sweden (commercial banks)	18.55	0.77	14.29
Switzerland (large banks)	14.71	1.37	20.15
Turkey (commercial banks)	22.17	4.48	99.33
United Kingdom (commercial banks)	24.45	1.48	36.19
United States (commercial banks)	12.82	2.02	25.90

♦ **Exhibit 17.4:   Equity multiplier, ROA, and ROE for selected countries, 1994**

♦ *Notes*:   1   Inverse of the capital ratio.
            2   Equity multiplier multiplied by ROA.
            3   Finland's banking system sustained considerable losses in the early 1990s as the result of economic declines when Finnish trade collapsed because of the dissolution of the former Soviet Union. Between 1990 and 1994, Finnish gross domestic product (GDP) fell by 14%. Finnish banks suffered losses on problem loans and required support by the Finnish government.
            ROA   Return on assets
            ROE   Return on equity

♦ *Source*:   ROA – Organization for Economic Cooperation and Development, *Bank Profitability, Financial Statements of Banks, 1985–94*, Paris, 1996; Equity multiplier and ROE – author's calculations based on data from ibid.

On the other hand, the 1994 ROEs for the United States (25.90 percent) and Luxembourg (25.42 percent) were quite comparable. This is true despite the fact that the ROA for US banks was 2.02 percent, while ROA for banks in Luxembourg was only 0.61 percent. The counterbalancing effect was the EM – 12.82 times for US banks, but 41.67 times for banks in Luxembourg.

The ROAs for Canadian banks (2.36 percent) and Mexican banks (2.32 percent) were slightly better than the ROA for US banks (2.02 percent). However, because the EMs for Canadian banks and Mexican banks were 18.73 times and 18.18 times, respectively, the 1994 ROEs for Canada

(44.19 percent) and Mexico (42.18 percent) were much higher than the ROE for the United States (25.90 percent).[1]

These examples illustrate the importance of the capital ratio in international banking. If a bank can operate with less capital than the competition, it can afford to realize a lower ROA and still produce a strong ROE. Alternatively, a comparable ROA will be translated into a superior ROE. This means that higher EMs enable banks to offer services with thinner profit margins (which lower ROA) and but still be more competitive in the international market place.

However, operating with low capital ratios has definite drawbacks. The bank's capital base will be even more susceptible to the adverse effects of volatile interest rates.

② Interest Rate Risk and Bank Capital Changes

2.1 INTEREST RATE CHANGES AND NET WORTH

Changes in interest rates can have an adverse affect on the net worth of a financial institution. The simple example in Exhibit 17.5 will help to illustrate. Suppose that two banks, A and B, each have total assets of $100 million, liabilities of $95 million, and net worth of $5 million.

> **Net worth:** The difference between the *market values* of assets and liabilities. In this context, net worth is to be distinguished from GAAP-defined share-holders' equity and from RAP-defined capital.

	Year				
	1	2	3	4	5
Bank A					
Loans	12	12	12	12	112
Certificates of deposit	0	0	0	0	<152.998>
Bank B					
Loans	0	0	0	0	176.234
Certificates of deposit	0	0	0	0	<152.998>

Bank	*Instrument*	Value at Rate	*year zero*
A and B	Loans	12%	$100
A and B	CDs	10%	$95
A	Loans	11.5%	$101.82
B	Loans	11.5%	$102.26
A and B	CDs	9.5%	$ 97.19

◆ Exhibit 17.5: Anticipated cash flows, Banks A and B ($ Millions)

Each bank holds fixed rate loans that mature in five years on the same date. Liabilities consist of five-year certificates of deposit that mature on the same date as the loans. The only difference in the portfolios of Banks A and B is the type of loans held. Bank A's loans pay 12 percent interest each year on the face amounts, with principal due at maturity. Bank A plans to receive $12 million per year until the maturity date, at which time the last interest payment and principal repayment will be received.

Bank B's 12 percent loans, however, will be completely repaid in year 5. The bank will receive no cash flows until maturity, at which time its customers will repay all accrued interest and principal. (We assume that both banks assessed loan origination fees sufficient to cover all operating expenses during the 5-year period.) Given these terms, loan repayments for Bank B will total $176.234 million ($100 mil. $(1.12)^5$ = $176.234 mil.).

The 10 percent certificates of deposit (CDs) are identical. At the end of five years, each bank will pay a total of $152.998 million to depositors ($95 mil. $(1.10)^5$ = $152.998 mil.). Notice that at required loan and CD rates of 12 percent and 10 percent, respectively, the present values are also identical. Loans are valued at $100 million, CDs, $95 million. Net worth, of course, is $5 million.

Now, assume that interest rates decline by 50 basis points across-the-board. Loan and CD rates fall to 11.5 percent and 9.5 percent, respectively. Anticipated cash flows will not change, but the present values of the cash flows will change. Since there is an inverse relationship between interest rate changes and changes in market value, present values increase. (See chapter 10 for a discussion of bond price behavior. These principles apply to any fixed-income instrument, including loans and CDs.)

The present value of CDs increases to $97.19 million for both banks. However, changes in loan market values are not equal. Bank B loans increase more in value than those held by Bank A. After the rate change, loan portfolios of Banks A and B are worth $101.82 million and $102.26 million, respectively. Bank B's loan portfolio value increases more because of the time pattern of its cash flows. All cash flows occur in year 5. As noted in chapter 10, longer term instruments are more price sensitive to changes in yield. Bank B's loan portfolio will be more rate sensitive since Bank A receives a portion of its cash flows in the interim years 1 through 4.

Note, too, that these different changes in asset values cause net worth of the two banks to also differ after interest rates decline. (In the discussion of duration, net worth and capital ratio refer to the market value concept of these terms. Neither GAAP-reported capital nor RAP-defined capital change.) The market value of equity drops from $5 million to $4.63 million for Bank A ($101.82 mil. − 97.19 mil.) and increases to $5.07 million for Bank B ($102.26 mil. − 97.19 mil.). Gap analysis does not satisfactorily explain this phenomenon because the technique does not consider the time value of money.

2.2 Duration

Duration is a concept that measures a financial instrument's *average life* or the *weighted average time of cash receipt*. The time of each cash receipt is weighted by the proportion of total present value which that cash flow represents.

$$D = \frac{\sum_{t=1}^{n}\left[\dfrac{CF_t t}{(1+k)^t}\right]}{\sum_{t=1}^{n}\left[\dfrac{CF_t}{(1+k)^t}\right]} \tag{17.3}$$

(1) Instrument	(2) Bank	(3) Year	(4) CF	(5) PVCF	(6) (3) × (5)	(7) Duration (years)
Loan (12%)	A	1	$12	$10.71	10.71	
		2	12	9.57	19.14	
		3	12	8.54	25.62	
		4	12	7.63	30.52	
		5	112	63.55	317.75	
				100.00	403.74	4.0374
Loan (12%)	B	1	0	0	0	
		2	0	0	0	
		3	0	0	0	
		4	0	0	0	
		5	176.234	100	500	
				100	100	5.0
CD (10%)	A&B	1	0	0	0	
		2	0	0	0	
		3	0	0	0	
		4	0	0	0	
		5	153.998	95	475	
				95	475	5.0

◆ **Exhibit 17.6:** Duration analysis, Banks A and B ($ Millions)

◆ *Note:*   Duration equals the total of column (6) divided by the total of column (5).

where D = duration
   CF_t = cash flow in time t
   t = number of periods before CF_t occurs
   k = appropriate discount rate for the instrument
   n = number of periods before instrument matures

To the extent that the duration of two financial instruments differs, their price sensitivity to interest rate changes will differ. Exhibit 17.6 illustrates duration calculations for Banks A and B. Bank A will receive interest payments prior to year 5. So the weighted average time of cash receipt, duration, is less than 5 years. On the other hand, Bank B loans generate no interim cash flows and, as a direct result, these loans have a duration of exactly 5 years. The same is true for both banks' CDs.

Just as the stated maturity of a financial instrument suggests its degree of price sensitivity to yield changes, duration also helps to describe price sensitivity. The following formula uses duration to estimate the percentage price change that will be associated with a particular change in rates.

$$\frac{\Delta P}{P} = -D\left[\frac{\Delta k}{(1 + k)}\right] \tag{17.4}$$

where P = market value of financial instrument
   ΔP = change in market value of financial instrument
   D = duration
   k = appropriate discount rate
   Δk = change in discount rate

The algebraic sign of the percentage change in market value is inversely related to the algebraic sign of the change in rates, that is, the relationship between price and rate changes is inverse. Note, too, that the greater an instrument's duration, the greater will be the *absolute value* of its change in market value for a given change in rate. This is consistent with the concept of greater price volatility for longer-term instruments. Equation (17.4) works well for relatively small changes in rates.[2]

Referring again to Banks A and B, the durations of their loan portfolios are 4.0374 years and 5 years, respectively. For Bank A, Equation (17.4) predicts a positive 1.802 percent change in price:

$$\frac{\Delta P}{P} = -4.0374\left(\frac{-.005}{1.12}\right)$$

$$= .018024$$

The actual change was 1.820 percent. Similarly, the predicted change for Bank B's loan portfolio is 2.232 percent:

$$\frac{\Delta P}{P} = -5\left(\frac{-.005}{1.12}\right)$$

$$= .022321$$

The actual change was 2.260 percent.

In general, when rates decline, the predicted price increase is less than the actual increase. When rates increase, Equation (17.4) will predict a greater percentage price decline than will actually occur. However, for very small rate changes, the error will also be small.

2.3 DURATION AND NET WORTH

The most significant implication of duration analysis is that asset and liability portfolios with the same duration will have similar market value sensitivity to interest rate changes. The process of matching durations of asset and liability portfolios can significantly *reduce* interest rate risk. However, this matching will not necessarily *eliminate* the risk.

Notice that, when interest rates declined, the net worth of Bank A declined from $5 million to $4.63 million and that the capital ratio fell from 5 to 4.55 percent (4.63/101.82 = 0.04547). However, the corresponding results for Bank B were less severe. After the rate change, net worth was $5.07 million and the capital ratio only fell to 4.96 percent (5.07/102.26 = 0.04958). That is, the interest rate risk to net worth was reduced by matching the duration of assets and liabilities, but not eliminated.

When the durations of two instruments are equal *and* the instruments are discounted by the same rate, Equation (17.4) suggests that a given change in interest rate would produce equivalent percentage changes in their respective values. Furthermore, the difference between the values of the two instruments should change by the same percentage. If *both* conditions had existed, the net worth of Bank B would have increased by this same percentage.

However, we note that for Bank B this was not the case. This result is attributable to the differential rates at which loans and CDs were discounted. The 0.5 percent decline in rates represented a larger percentage change in deposit rates than in loan rates. In essence, the present value of the liabilities changed by a greater percentage than the present value of loans.

Notice from Equation (17.4) that the percentage change in market value has an inverse relationship with rate level prior to any change in rates. Thus, a 50 basis point decline will produce a greater proportional change for a 10 percent financial instrument than a 12 percent instrument. Bank B's CDs increased by 2.30 percent, loans by only 2.26 percent. Thus, the capital ratio declined by 0.4 percent.

The case of Bank A is further complicated by the unmatched durations of loans and CDs. Bank A's aggregate CD value also increased by 2.30 percent, but loan values only increased by 1.82 percent because the duration of the loan portfolio was just over 4 years. The combination of shorter asset duration and differential discount rates resulted in a larger decline in net worth than would have been true if durations were matched and both assets and liabilities discounted at more similar rates.

Certain points should be remembered when applying duration analysis:

- Unless the instrument involved is a zero-coupon instrument (no cash flows until maturity), duration will not equal time to maturity.
- Duration changes as time passes and as market interest rates change.
- If the instruments have any embedded options that may alter the future cash flows, the objective of duration analysis can be frustrated. An example of such an embedded option is a mortgage prepayment option which can severely shorten the future cash flow stream of a mortgage loan.
- If interest rate changes for assets do not equal interest rate changes for liabilities, matched durations will not help at all.

③ Hedging Financial Portfolios

It is possible to use external means to *hedge* financial portfolios. In particular, *interest rate futures*, *futures options*, and *swaps* can be used effectively. The mechanics of futures, options, and swap markets are discussed in chapters 7 and 8 in the context of domestic securities and foreign currency transactions. This section extends these principles to other segments of financial institution balance sheets.

> **Hedging:**
> Using one or more financial innovations to protect the market value of specific assets and liabilities (microhedge) or of equity (macrohedge) from adverse effects of interest rate changes.

3.1 Interest Rate Futures

Interest rate futures are contracts to buy or sell fixed-income financial securities at some future specified date. Exhibit 17.7 provides a description of the most common interest rate futures contracts. Treasury bond and Treasury bill futures have historically been the most actively traded.

	Instruments	Denominations	Exchange(s)
Futures	Treasury bonds	$100,000	CBT, LIFFE
	Treasury bonds	$ 50,000	MCE
	5-yr Treasury notes	$100,000	CBT, FINEX
	2-yr Treasury notes	$200,000	FINEX
	13-week Treasury bills	$1 million	IMM
	1-yr Treasury bills	$500,000	IMM
	Municipal bond index	$1,000 times Bond Buyer MBI	CBT
	3-month Eurodollar	$1,000,000	IMM
	3-month Euromark	$1,000,000	IMM
	1-month LIBOR	$3,000,000	IMM
Options on futures	Treasury bonds	$100,000	CBT
	Treasury notes	$100,000	CBT
	13-week Treasury bills	$1 million	IMM
	1-yr Treasury bills	$500,000	IMM
	Municipal bond index	$100,000	CBT
	3-month Eurodollar	$1,000,000	IMM
	3-month Euromark	$1,000,000	IMM
	1-month LIBOR	$3,000,000	IMM

◆ **Exhibit 17.7:**   Interest rate derivatives

◆ *Notes*:
     CBT   Chicago Board of Trade
     FINEX   Financial Instrument Exchange, a division of the New York Cotton Exchange
     IMM   International Monetary Market at Chicago Mercantile Exchange
     LIFFE   London International Financial Futures Exchange
     MCE   MidAmerica Commodity Exchange

◆ *Sources*:   *Wall Street Journal*; Chicago Mercantile Exchange, International Monetary Market, *CME Futures and Options Contract Highlights*, 1994.

A futures contract entitles the buyer to purchase the underlying asset at a future date at a specific price. If in the interim, the value of the underlying asset increases, the value of the futures contract also increases. If the purchaser chose to sell the contract instead of taking delivery of the underlying asset, he would realize a profit. This is the basic principle that makes the use of futures a viable method of hedging against portfolio loss.

A securities portfolio manager holding Treasury bonds may be concerned that the value of the portfolio will decline if rates increase. The appropriate hedge would be to take the opposite position in the futures markets. Since the institution holds Treasury bonds, it is said to have a "long position" in bonds in the cash market (asset). Accordingly, the portfolio manager would take a "short position" in the futures market by selling Treasury bond futures contracts for subsequent delivery (liability).

If rates do, indeed, increase, the long portfolio will decline in value. However, the futures position can be closed by buying an offsetting contract (settling the liability) at a now lower price. The profit in the futures market will work to offset the loss in the cash market.

To the extent that the cash market asset is similar to the underlying asset in the futures market, profits in one market will be close to the amount of losses in the other market. Financial assets do

	Cash market	Futures market
Jan. 1	Bank makes $1,000,000, 5-yr, fixed rate loan at 10 percent.	Bank sells 10 Treasury note futures contracts for delivery in 6 months at 95-10[1]
June 30	Loan rates have increased such that the average rate for the 6 month period was 11.0 percent. Opportunity cost = 0.01 (1,000,000)(.5) = 5,000	Treasury notes are now selling at 94-20. Bank buys 10 Treasury note futures contracts to close its position.[2] Price = $946,250
Gain<loss>	$<5,000>	$6,875

◆ **Exhibit 17.8: Hedging a fixed rate loan in the futures market**

◆ *Notes:*   1   95-10 means that Treasury bonds are selling at 95 and 10/32 percent of face value, i.e., $95.3125 for every $100 face value. One $100,000 futures contract would, therefore, cost $95,312.50.
2   $1,000,000/$95,312.50 = 10.49. The bank buys 10 contracts.

not always match futures contract underlying assets. As a result, hedges can be subject to *basis risk*, the risk that changes in the price of cash market assets will not exactly coincide with price changes in the futures market.

Nevertheless, futures hedging can reduce potential loss. When cash market and futures market instruments are not the same, the transaction is considered a *cross-hedge*. Exhibit 17.8 illustrates a cross-hedge using Treasury note futures contracts. On January 1, management of a financial institution makes a 5-year loan to a valued customer at a fixed rate of 10 percent. If interest rates increase, the institution could incur a significant opportunity cost in interest income.

Management decides to construct a cross-hedge with intermediate-term Treasury note contracts. Ten of the $100,000 contracts costs $953,125 on January 1. A short position (liability) in the futures market hedges a long position (asset) in the cash market. When the futures contract expires in six months, rates have increased. The institution has sustained an opportunity cost of $5,000 in interest income, but the $6,875 in futures market profits more than offset the loss.

It should be noted that if interest rates had declined, the loss in the futures market would have more than offset the bank's interest income "windfall." Thus, hedging activities will prevent the realization of gains that might otherwise be possible.

To purchase or sell a futures contract, an initial deposit, or *margin*, is required. Margin ranges from 3 percent to 10 percent of the initial price. At the end of each trading day, however, contracts are marked to market by the futures exchange (that is, effectively the "other side" of the transaction). The change in value of the contract is recorded in the bank's account. If losses are sustained, the institution must add additional funds to the account.

3.2 OPTIONS ON FUTURES CONTRACTS

Options on futures contracts can be used in much the same way as futures contracts themselves in terms of constructing the hedge. The primary differences are cost and related obligations.

A futures contract purchaser (seller) must accept delivery of (deliver) the underlying asset or sell (purchase) an offsetting contract to close his position. The purchaser of a call or put option may allow the option to expire without taking any action at all. After an option is purchased, the buyer has *no obligation* to do anything further. This is in contrast to a futures contract in which some later action must be taken to close the contract. A call option for a futures contract entitles the purchaser to buy the underlying futures contract at the specified price. A put option entitles the purchaser to sell the contract.

The prices of options are paid in full at the time of purchase. Prices are quoted in full points (percentage of face value) plus fractional points (64ths). For example, a quotation of 2−42 on a Treasury note contract ($100,000 face value) means 2 and 42/64 percentage of face value, or $2,656.25. Often, option prices are lower than the required initial margin for a futures contract. Thus, a financial institution may put in place an options hedge for considerably less expense than a futures hedge. In addition, maximum loss is limited to the price of the option.

That is, the maximum loss is limited to the price of the option as long as the institution purchases the option. Selling, or writing, an option exposes the writer, in some cases, to unlimited risk. (See also chapter 7.)

3.3 Interest Rate Swaps

Interest rate swaps do not involve purchasing financial market instruments. Instead, the rights to future cash flows are exchanged. Alternatively, the obligations to pay future cash may be exchanged. The fundamental concept is to exchange a fixed rate cash flow stream with a floating rate stream.

While parties design swaps in any number of combinations, the most basic interest rate swap is a *coupon swap* in which a floating rate is exchanged for a fixed rate. For example, a financial institution may hold a large portfolio of fixed rate loans (assets) while most of its deposits (liabilities) are floating rate CDs. Another bank may hold considerable variable rate investments (assets) with fixed rate obligations (liabilities). To minimize interest rate risk, the two institutions agree to swap interest payments on liabilities.

They agree on a *notional principal*, or the amount of liabilities for which interest rates will be swapped. The maturity of the swap and the frequency of payments are also established. For example, Bank C may enter into an agreement that stipulates:

- $10 million notional amount
- Four-year term for the swap
- Semiannual payments

If the fixed rate is 9 percent for Bank C, it may agree to swap a fixed 9 percent for a floating rate of the "Treasury bill plus 1," meaning 1 percent above the Treasury bill rate. When paid to the other party in the swap (the counterparty), recorded interest expense on the notional amount is the same as would otherwise be the case every six months (in thousands).

	DR	CR
Interest expense	$450	
Cash		$450

In addition, the bank records the interest rate swap when the floating rate payment is received. If Treasury bill plus 1 is 8.5 percent, the bank has saved 0.5 percent on an annual basis for this six-month period. When the payment is received, the following entry is made (in thousands).

	DR	CR
Cash	$25	
Interest expense		$25

The one-half of one percent difference for six months on $10 million is $25,000. Bank C receives this payment from the counterparty in the swap and its own net interest expense is reduced.

Because the success of this arrangement depends on the creditworthiness of the two counterparties, the role of intermediary has become increasingly important. In the early days of the interest rate swap market, large US money center banks and investment banks acted primarily as brokers. Currently, these institutions frequently act as principals in offsetting swaps, providing more credit assurance for all involved.

In addition, interest rate swaps enable commercial banks to offer loans and deposits with competitive features. Even if these products expose the bank's balance sheet to undesirable interest rate risk, an interest rate swap may be constructed to reduce the risk to a more acceptable level while still offering its clients a full range of banking services.

 Summary

Bank capital protects depositors by absorbing temporary losses, inspiring public confidence, and placing reasonable constraints on asset growth. Capital consists primarily of equity (common and preferred stock) and subordinated debt. Over time, capital ratios declined worldwide. In some cases, this has placed US banks at competitive disadvantages. Competing banking systems have benefitted from lower capital ratios by being able to offer bank services at discount prices. At the same time, rates of return on equity in a number of competing banking systems have remained relatively strong because of the effect of high equity multipliers. The Basle Accord attempts to level the playing field among international banks by prescribing uniform capital standards among OECD countries. In recognition of the difference among banking systems, central banks are given some discretion in terms of how these standards are administered.

Changes in the market value of equity can occur when cash flow streams from assets are substantially different from the cash flow streams for liabilities. Duration captures the difference in cash flow timing. It is a more theoretically sound approach, but it is also more difficult to apply practically.

External hedging approaches can help compensate for these theoretical and practical difficulties. Futures contracts, options on futures contracts, and interest swaps can be used to significantly reduce interest rate risk.

 End-of-chapter Questions

1. List the elements in bank capital. Differentiate GAAP-defined capital from RAP-defined capital.
2. In your opinion, do you think that the Basle Accord will reverse the international trends in returns on equity noted in Exhibit 17.4? Why or why not?
3. What are the three functions of bank capital?

4. a. What are risk-weighted assets?

   b. What are the capital guidelines according to the Basle Accord?

5. What is the difference between a futures contract and an options contract?

6. a. What is duration?

   b. Under what circumstances is the duration of a financial instrument the same as its maturity?

7. In general, how can a financial institution use the concept of duration to protect the market value of its equity?

8. Explain the basic rationale in using futures or options contracts to protect the balance sheet of a financial institution from interest rate risk.

9. Name the advantages and disadvantages of using futures and options hedges.

10. a. What is an interest rate swap?

   b. How can an interest rate swap be used to protect against interest rate risk?

End-of-chapter Problems

1. Your bank has accepted a $1,000,000 deposit in the form of a certificate of deposit (CD) at 8 percent. Interest rates are high and expected to decline soon. Your customer bought this CD in order to lock this rate. But this also means that your bank will be paying higher than market rates on the CD when rates decline. Construct an appropriate hedge using six-month futures contracts on two-year Treasury notes assuming that the price is 98–14.

2. Referring to problem 1, assume that interest rates fell during the six-month period that the hedge was in place. Shortly after issuing the CD, the rate on these instruments fell to 6.5 percent. Upon expiration of futures contract, the price of 2-year Treasury notes is 99–7. Compute the profit and loss in cash and futures markets when the bank closes out its position.

3. Refer to Exhibit 17.6. Calculate the duration for Bank A's loan portfolio if the appropriate market rate is 10 percent. (Note that future cash flows do not change.)

NOTES

1 Chapters 15 and 16 discuss the asset and liability mix of these OECD countries. Specific information is found in the following exhibits:

Item	Exhibit
Liquid assets	15.9
Liabilities	15.11
Securities and loans	16.6
Gross income	16.7

2 Equation (17.4) is an approximation formula specifying that percentage price changes are a linear function of rate changes. The actual relationship is nonlinear. This means that for small changes in rate the approximation will give a fairly accurate result. However, the larger the change in rate, the less accurate the approximation.

SELECTED REFERENCES

Bank for International Settlements, Basel, Switzerland. *Recent Innovations in International Banking*, April 1986.

Bierwag, Gerald O. *Duration Analysis: Managing Interest Rate Risk*, Ballinger Publishing Cambridge, Mass., 1987.

Chicago Board of Trade. *CBOT Financial Instruments Guide*, Chicago, 1987.

Economic Council of Canada. *Globalization and Canada's Financial Markets*, Ottawa, 1990.

Fraser, Donald R. and Peter S. Rose. *Financial Institutions and Markets in a Changing World*, 3rd edn, Business Publications, Plano, Tex., 1987.

Grumball, Clive. *Managing Interest Rate Risk*, Quorum Books, Westport, Conn., 1987.

International Monetary Fund. *International Capital Markets: Developments and Prospects*, Washington, DC, April 1989.

Johnson, Hazel J. *Bank Asset/Liability Management: The Concepts and Tools*, Probus Publishing, Chicago (now McGraw-Hill, New York), 1994.

Johnson, Hazel J. *The Bank Valuation Handbook: A Market-based Approach to Valuing a Bank*, revised edn, Irwin Professional Publishing, Burr Ridge, Ill. (now McGraw-Hill, New York), 1995.

Koch, Timothy W. *Bank Management*, Dryden Press, Hinsdale, Ill., 1988.

Mitchell, Karlyn. "Interest Rate Risk at Commercial Banks: An Empirical Investigation," *Financial Review*, 24, no. 3 (August 1989), pp. 431–55.

Organization for Economic Cooperation and Development. *Bank Profitability, Financial Statements of Banks, 1985–1994*, Paris, 1996.

Pecchioli, R. M. *Prudential Supervision in Banking*, Organization for Economic Cooperation and Development, Paris, 1987.

Sprenkle, Case M. "Liability and Asset Uncertainty for Banks," *Journal of Banking and Finance* (Netherlands), 11, no. 1 (March 1987), pp. 147–59.

Subcommittee on Financial Institutions Supervision, Regulation, and Insurance. *Report of the Task Force on the International Competitiveness of US Financial Institutions*, Committee on Banking, Finance, and Urban Affairs, Washington, DC, October 1990.

US Department of the Treasury. *Modernizing the Financial System: Recommendations for Safer, More Competitive Banks*, Washington, DC, February 1991.

Appendix 17.1:
Market Value Accounting

This chapter has illustrated the sensitivity of bank performance to interest rate changes. Historically, this interest rate sensitivity is perhaps best illustrated by the distress of the savings and loan industry during the 1970s and early 1980s. During this time, the market value of long-term, low-interest, fixed-rate mortgage loans held by these thrifts declined dramatically as interest rates soared. At the same time, the value of short-term, high-interest deposits did not decline. The economic reality was that, in all too many cases, the value of assets was lower than the value of liabilities, that is, many thrifts were insolvent in market value terms. This economic reality was not recognized in the financial statements of these institutions, however, because of the GAAP practice of recording assets at historical cost, not current market value, until the assets were actually sold or otherwise disposed of.

Before the 1970s, this GAAP practice presented no real problems because interest rates were stable and most deposit interest rates were regulated. The volatile interest rates of the late 1970s and early 1980s and the attendant problems in the financial services industry led to a reevaluation of reporting practices. The Financial Institutions Reform, Recovery, and Enforcement Act of 1989 (FIRREA) directed the US Treasury Department to examine the question of *market value accounting* for depository institutions. In 1991, the Treasury concluded that increased market value disclosure was desirable, but not comprehensive market value accounting (marking all assets and liabilities to market).

Even before Congressional action in 1989, the Financial Accounting Standards Board (FASB), the body that is responsible for defining generally accepted accounting principles, began to examine the question. For some time, GAAP has required banks to report (1) securities held for short-term trading purposes and (2) interest and foreign exchange contracts at market values. In addition, estimates of the market value of other investment securities have been required for supplemental (footnote) disclosure.

The FASB and the Securities and Exchange Commission (SEC) became strong advocates for increased market value accounting (MVA). There are several benefits of increasing MVA:

- The capital of each depository institution can be better estimated.
- Regulators will be better able to identify those institutions that are capital impaired.

- The accountability of management for its decisions will be facilitated by the more transparent measurement of economic performance.
- Transactions motivated strictly by accounting considerations will be discouraged. An example is "gains trading" in which securities that have appreciated in value are sold to reflect the gain in current operations and securities that have depreciated are not sold to avoid recognizing the loss. Under MVA both gains and losses would be recognized, eliminating the incentive to gains trade.

FINANCIAL ASSETS AND LIABILITIES

As a step in the direction of full MVA, in 1992 the FASB issued the Statement of Financial Accounting Standards no. 107 (SFAS no. 107) that requires disclosure of the market value of all financial instruments, including loans and deposits for banks. Each firm must disclose the fair value of financial assets and liabilities either in the body of the financial statements or in the accompanying notes. In addition, the methods and assumptions used to arrive at these values must be disclosed.

SECURITIES

SFAS no. 115, Accounting for Certain Investments in Debt and Equity Securities, was issued in May 1993 (effective after December 15, 1993). Basically, SFAS no. 115 requires distinctions in the securities portfolio between:

- Investment portfolio – held-to-maturity
- Trading portfolio
- Available-for-sale portfolio

The new classification of held-to-maturity (HTM) is the category in which most investment securities historically have been recorded. Under SFAS no. 115, in order to classify securities as held-to-maturity, banks must have positive intent and the ability to hold to maturity. This classification of securities is not marked-to-market, instead the securities are recorded at amortized cost. Only realized gains and losses are recorded (upon sale), with recognition in the income statement.

The trading portfolio is unchanged in its interpretation. This is the portfolio of securities that is actively traded with the objective of generating profits on short-term price changes. While there is no predetermined classification for particular classes of securities, mortgage-backed securities held for sale in connection with mortgage banking activities must be reported in the trading portfolio. Trading securities are marked-to-market, with unrealized gains and losses being recorded in the income statement for the period.

The available-for-sale (AFS) portfolio contains all securities that cannot be classified as either part of the HTM or trading portfolios. AFS securities are marked-to-market, with unrealized gains and losses *not* recorded in income, but reflected in a separate component of stockholders' equity.

IMPAIRED LOANS

Also in May 1993, market value accounting (MVA) was expanded to certain elements of the loan portfolio through SFAS no. 114, Accounting by Creditors for Impairment of a Loan (effective after December 15, 1994). In October 1994, SFAS no. 114 was amended by SFAS no. 118, Accounting by Creditors for Impairment of a Loan – Income Recognition and Disclosure (also effective after December 15, 1994).

The two statements apply to all categories of loans with the following exceptions:

- Large groups of smaller-balance homogeneous loans
- Loans recorded at fair value or at lower-of-cost-or-market
- Leases
- Debt securities

The statement does not provide guidance with respect to the identification of impaired loans. Instead, an institution is expected for follow its normal credit review procedures. Also, the normal provisions for loan loss are not affected by the statement.

The definition of impairment revolves around changes in the cash flows as originally contracted. There has been impairment if:

- It is probable that all payments of principal and interest will not be collected.
- There are delays in timing of the collection of all payments of principal and interest.

"Probable" is interpreted to mean likely to occur. Insignificant differences in either payments or timing of payments do not create an impairment.

The present value of future cash flows is used to arrive at the "measurement value." This value is based on the best estimate of the amount and timing of future cash flows, under reasonable and supportable assumptions. These cash flows are then discounted at a rate that is the contractual rate adjusted for premiums, discounts, deferred fees, or other considerations. Alternatively, the measurement value may be the (1) observable market price of the loan or (2) fair value of collateral in the case of collateral-dependent loans. (A collateral-dependent loan is defined as one for which repayment is generated solely from sale or operation of the collateral.) In the event that foreclosure is probable, measurement value must be set at the fair value of collateral.

Loan impairment is measured as the excess of the amount of recorded investment over the measurement value. The loan impairment is provided for as bad debt expense for the period.

THE TREND TOWARD MVA

Other SFASs have been issued for derivative securities (SFAS no. 119) and mortgage servicing rights (SFAS no. 122). SFAS no. 119 requires the market valuation of derivatives held for trading purposes. Under provisions of SFAS no. 122, mortgage servicing rights (rights to collect payments and keep records for securitized mortgages) must be carried at market value, with impairment reflected in a valuation account. The regulatory focus on market value accounting is significant and growing. The composition of asset and liability portfolios and associated exposure to interest rate risk make a strong sense of market valuation concepts a prerequisite for assessing a financial institution.

Bank Valuation

chapter 18

Introduction

High and volatile interest rates of the late 1970s and early 1980s demonstrated beyond question the need for market valuation of financial institutions. The classic example of the valuation deficiency is the experience of savings and loan associations. In this beleaguered industry during the 1970s, the true economic value of large portfolios of low-yielding, fixed-rate mortgage loans declined to such an extent that many S&Ls were fundamentally insolvent. At the same time, their financial statements did not suggest financial distress. Market valuation technique helps to correct this deficiency.

Regulatory agencies now stress the need for market valuation of financial assets and liabilities. Beginning with fiscal years ended after December 15, 1995, all institutions (financial and nonfinancial) must include disclosures with respect to the "fair value" of financial assets and liabilities. (For institutions with at least $150 million in assets, the effective date of this disclosure requirement was for fiscal years ending after December 15, 1992.) Other market valuation requirements affect the securities portfolio, the loan portfolio, off-balance-sheet items, and fee-generating activities. (See the the appendix to chapter 17 for coverage of Financial Accounting Standards Board disclosure requirements with respect to market value accounting.) Market valuation concepts have long been a part of the securities industry and other financial services industries, but are a relatively recent phenomenon in banking circles.

 ## The Debate over Market Value vs. Book Value

Despite the trend toward market valuation in the banking industry, some observers believe that full market value accounting (MVA) is either not necessary or may in fact destabilize the banking industry.

> **Market value accounting:**
> Reporting assets and liabilities at market values in public financial statements rather than historical cost or replacement cost.

For example, a bank loan portfolio contains financial assets for which there is, at best, a thin market. For these MVA opponents argue that historical cost is preferable for several reasons:

- MVA ignores the situation in which a financial institution has an *intent to hold an asset until maturity* – thus necessitating the reporting of interim, periodic gains and losses in value that have no real economic meaning since the asset is held to maturity and the financial institution receives the maturity value in any event.
- MVA understates the value of an illiquid asset as compared to the asset's value to a *going concern*. Selling an illiquid asset may generate a loss on sale while the value of the asset, if held, may be substantially higher.
- The periodic gains and losses associated with MVA may not be well understood by the public, causing depositors and investors in the bank to lose confidence in the financial institution. Such reactions could endanger the bank's *financial stability*.

On the other hand, proponents of MVA point to the following as support for greater emphasis on market valuation:

- *Intent to hold an asset until maturity*. During the early 1980s, high market interest rates caused the economic value of the loan portfolios of many S&Ls to decline below the value of the institutions' liabilities, rendering the S&Ls economically insolvent. (See chapter 26 for a description of the S&L crisis.) Under these circumstances, the institutions themselves were so weak that they did not have the *ability* to hold the assets until maturity. Also, some bank managers are evaluated on the basis of their management of the securities portfolio on an MVA basis. In this context, intent to hold an asset until maturity has little relevance.
- *Transactions value vs. going concern value*. Proponents of MVA acknowledge the illiquidity of some assets held in bank portfolios. When transactions prices are either not available or not relevant, the better alternative is to use discounted cash flow methods. Referring again to the S&L example, if discounted cash flow accounting had been used for the mortgage loan portfolios, the severity of the crisis within the industry would have been recognized sooner and billions of taxpayer dollars could have been saved. Also, the markets for securitized assets have developed to such an extent that the parameters for market valuation are now much more readily available. For example, mortgage-backed securities trade in a healthy secondary market and securities backed by credit card loans and automobile loans have also emerged. (Chapter 5 discusses the securitization process.)
- *Financial stability*. MVA proponents note that the federal deposit insurance system is in place to prevent any "bank runs" and that the Federal Reserve System as lender of last resort would act to shore up the system if necessary. Moreover, those institutions that are known to be sound on an MVA basis will generate even more confidence on the part of depositors and investors. Indeed, the market discipline that would result from MVA could, in the long run, reduce the "moral hazard" associated with the investment of federally insured deposits.

> **Moral hazard:**
>> The incentive for bank managers to invest insured deposits in risky assets, realizing any benefit associated with high returns of such investments, but avoiding necessary repayment of deposits should such investments fail.

Market Valuation Models for the Balance Sheet

All market valuation models for bank assets and liabilities are based on time value of money concepts.[1] The exact specifications of a model, however, will depend on the characteristics of the particular financial instrument. (See chapter 15 for a description of bank assets and liabilities.) The market value of some instruments is reliably approximated by book value. For a few categories, professional appraisals are the best estimates.

In general, the major parameters of market valuation models are:

- Future cash flows
- Time to maturity
- Appropriate discount rate

The basic model is:

$$MV = \sum_{t=1}^{n} \frac{CF_t}{(1 + k)^t}$$

where MV = Market value
CF_t = Cash flow in year t
n = number of periods in the term of a fixed-income instrument
k = appropriate discount rate

The market value of a bank's equity is the difference between the market value of assets and the market value of liabilities.

$$MV_E = MV_A - MV_L$$

where MV_E = Market value of equity
MV_A = Market value of assets
MV_L = Market value of liabilities

Future cash flows should be determined for major classifications of assets and liabilities. The group of US Treasury bonds, for example, is a homogeneous group of assets, as is the classification of consumer automobile loans. Financial instruments should be grouped in order to determine the total balance, the *contractual* rate, and the average maturity. (This valuation approach is consistent with Statement of Financial Accounting Standards Board no. 107.) The contractual rate will be called one of the following:

- Coupon rate – temporary investments, investment securities, and long-term debt
- Loan rate – commercial loans, consumer loans, real estate loans
- Deposit rate – short-term and long-term deposits

> **Contractual interest rate:**
>> The rate of interest that is determined by the specific arrangement associated with a financial instrument, that is, the rate of interest to be paid by the borrower to the investor.

The *interest rate used for discounting the cash flow stream* will *not* be the contractual rate. The appropriate discount rate will depend on market conditions at the time of valuation and the issuers' credit risk.

2.1 Cash

Cash includes the categories of:

- Vault cash
- Due from other banks
- Due from the Federal Reserve
- Cash items in collection

The balances in these accounts are funds that are available on a same-day or next day basis. There is no difference between book value and market value for these assets.

2.2 Temporary Investments

Temporary investments are:

- Interest-bearing time deposits in other banks
- Federal funds sold
- Term federal funds sold
- Securities purchased under agreement to resell

These are short-term instruments whose coupon (earning) rates and discount (market) rates will be similar. Thus, market value will be quite close to book value.

2.2.1 INTEREST-BEARING DEPOSITS IN OTHER BANKS

The valuation model of these deposits is:

$$MV = \frac{D(1 + k_c)^n}{(1 + k)^n}$$

where D = deposit amount
k_c = contractual (coupon) rate
k = appropriate discount rate
n = fraction of the year remaining before maturity

Consider the following example in which the discount rate exceeds the contractual rate: $D = \$100,000$; $k_c = .05$; $k = .055$; $n = .5$.

$$MV = 100,000(1.05)^{.5}/(1.055)^{.5}$$
$$= 100,000(1.024695)/(1.027132)$$
$$= 99,762.74$$

The market value is only slightly lower than book because the time to maturity is relatively short.

2.2.2 FEDERAL FUNDS SOLD

The valuation model for federal funds follows the same format as that for time deposits.

$$MV = \frac{FF(1 + k_c)^n}{(1 + k)^n}$$

where FF = amount of funds loaned

The most typical case is an overnight transaction for which there is no difference between contractual and market rates.

Even if there is a significant difference in rates, the short duration of an overnight transaction forces the market value to be close to book value. For example, if $FF = 1,000,000$; $k_c = .04$; $k = .06$; $n = 1/365$:

$$MV = 1,000,000(1.04)^{1/365}/(1.06)^{1/365}$$
$$= 1,000,000(1.000107)/(1.000160)$$
$$= 999,947.01$$

This is an extreme example with an unrealistic difference in rates. However, it illustrates the point – there is only a $53 difference in book vs. market value because of the short time to maturity.

2.2.3. TERM FEDERAL FUNDS SOLD

Term federal funds sold (and securities purchased under agreement to resell) are slightly longer term investments. Thus, the rate used to discount the cash flows will have a more significant impact on market value. Term federal funds sold are valued by the same model used for overnight transactions.

2.2.4 SECURITIES PURCHASED UNDER AGREEMENT TO RESELL

The valuation model for these investments assumes that interest is earned on the securities while held by the bank.

$$MV = \sum_{t=1}^{n} \frac{CP_t}{\left(1 + \dfrac{k}{m}\right)^t} + \frac{SP}{\left(1 + \dfrac{k}{m}\right)^t}$$

where CP_t = coupon payment that the bank receives before resale
      = $CR(M)/m$
  CR = coupon rate of securities purchased
  M = maturity value of securities purchased
  SP = selling price specified in resale agreement
  n = number of periods before resale
  k = appropriate discount rate

Consider the following example: SP = \$1,050,000; k = .045; n = one six-month period; m = 2; M = 1,000,000; CR = .05.

$$CP_t = .05(1,000,000)/2$$

$$= 25,000$$

$$MV = 25,000/(1.0225) + 1,050,000/(1.0225)$$

$$= 24,449.88 + 1,026,894.87$$

$$= 1,051,344.75$$

In this case, the earned interest increases the market value of the investment.

2.3 INVESTMENT SECURITIES

Investment securities can have much longer maturities than temporary investments. For example, a bank may hold Treasury securities with maturities up to 30 years. Categories of investment securities include:

- Treasury bills
- Treasury notes and bonds
- Government agency securities
- Municipal bonds

2.3.1 TREASURY BILLS

The market value of Treasury bills (T-bills) is easily obtained through market quotation because of the depth of the Treasury market. Original maturity will never exceed one year. The T-bill pricing model follows.

$$MV = M - M(k)\left(\frac{N}{360}\right)$$

$$= M - D$$

where M = maturity or face value

k = annual discount rate

N = number of days until maturity

D = discount from face value

$= M(k)(N/360)$

Because T-bills are issued on a discounted basis, the market value will always be less than face value (minimum denomination $10,000).

This example is a T-bill with an original maturity of six months purchased 82 days ago, that is, with 100 days to maturity: $M = 10,000$; $k = .04$; $N = 100$.

$$MV = 10,000 - 10,000(.04)(100/360)$$

$$= 10,000 - 111.11$$

$$= 9,888.89$$

2.3.2 TREASURY NOTES AND BONDS

Like Treasury bills, Treasury notes (T-notes) and Treasury bonds (T-bonds) are traded in a well developed market. In contrast to T-bills, T-notes have original maturities that range from two to ten years, specifically 2, 3, 5, and 10 years. T-bonds have an original maturity of 10 to 30 years, with only 30-year original maturities issued effective 1998. Another difference between T-bills with respect to T-notes and T-bonds is that the vast majority of the latter securities pay interest on a semiannual basis. The model values both the annuity of interest payments and the maturity value (minimum denomination of $1,000).

$$MV = \sum_{t=1}^{n} \frac{\left(\frac{(M)(CR)}{m} \right)}{\left(1 + \frac{k}{m} \right)^t} + \frac{M}{\left(1 + \frac{k}{m} \right)^n}$$

where

M = maturity or face value

CR = coupon rate

m = number of times per year interest is paid

$= 2$

$(M)(CR)/m$ = periodic (semiannual) interest payments

n = number of (semiannual) periods before maturity

k = annual discount rate

Suppose that a bank holds Treasury notes with the following characteristics: $M = 100,000$; $CR = .05$; $m = 2$; $k = .04$; $n = 6$ (3 years). The cash flows for these notes are shown in Exhibit 18.1. Notice that the maturity date of January 1, 2003 is exactly three years from the point of valuation, January 1, 2000.

Date						
Jan. 1 2000	July 1 2000	Jan. 1 2001	July 1 2001	Jan. 1 2002	July 1 2002	Jan. 1 2003
Time Line						
	2,500	2,500	2,500	2,500	2,500	2,500

◆ **Exhibit 18.1: Three-year US treasury notes**

◆ *Note*: Time line describes $100,000 in 5% US Treasury notes that pay interest semiannually and mature in exactly 3 years (6 semiannual periods).

$$MV = \left[\sum_{t=1}^{6} \frac{\left(\frac{(100,000)(.05)}{2} \right)}{(1.02)^t} \right] + \frac{100,000}{(1.02)^6}$$

$$= \left[\sum_{t=1}^{6} \frac{2,500}{(1.02)^t} \right] + \frac{100,000}{(1.02)^6}$$

$$= 2,500 \left[\sum_{t=1}^{6} \frac{1}{(1.02)^t} \right] + \frac{100,000}{(1.02)^6}$$

$$= 2,500(PVIFA_{.02,6}) + \frac{100,000}{1.126162}$$

$$PVIFA_{.02,6} = \left(\frac{1}{.02} \right)\left(1 - \frac{1}{(1.02)^6} \right)$$

$$= 5.601431$$

$$MV = 2,500(5.601431) + 88,797.17$$

$$= 14,003.58 + 88,797.17$$

$$= 102,800.75$$

The market value of these notes is $102,800.75. However, the market quotation will not be this exact amount because prices are stated as dollars and 32nds of a dollar per $100 of face value. Thus, the market quotation for these notes will be between 102:25 or $102,781.25 (25/36 = .78125) and 102:26 or $102,812.50 (26/32 = .8125). Notice too that market value is higher than par value because the coupon rate exceeds the required return. (See chapter 10 for bond theorems that relate bond prices to interest rates.)

Treasury bonds are valued using these same principles. The primary differences are that original maturities are greater and, typically, the required market rate of return is higher.

2.3.3 MUNICIPAL BONDS

Municipal bonds are also valued in the same manner as Treasury bonds. One important difference, however, is the required rate of return. Because the interest income from municipal bonds is exempt from federal taxation, the required return for high-quality municipals is lower than for Treasury bonds.

Another important feature is that some municipal bonds are callable, that is, can be redeemed by the issuer prior to the original maturity date. The call feature is essentially an option owned by the bond issuer. This section describes the valuation of:

- Noncallable bonds
- Bonds for which there has already been an advance refunding

Callable bonds:
> Bonds that contain a provision in the indenture that permits the issuer to redeem all or part of the issue prior to maturity.

The model for a noncallable bond is the same as for Treasury notes and bonds.

$$MV = \sum_{t=1}^{n} \frac{\left(\frac{(M)(CR)}{m}\right)}{\left(1 + \frac{k}{m}\right)^t} + \frac{M}{\left(1 + \frac{k}{m}\right)^n}$$

Assume that municipal bonds issued five years go have 15 years remaining to maturity: $M = 50,000$; $CR = .07$; $m = 4$; $k = .05$; $n = 60$.

$$MV = \sum_{t=1}^{60} \{(50,000)(.07)/4\}/(1.0125)^t + [50,000/(1.0125)^{60}]$$

$$= 875 \, (PVIFA_{.0125,60}) + 50,000/2.107181$$

$$PVIFA_{.0125,60} = (1/.0125)(1 - \{1/(1.0125)^{60}\})$$

$$= 42.03459179$$

$$MV = 875(42.03459179) + 23,728.38$$

$$= 36,780.27 + 23,728.38 = 60,508.65$$

Now assume that the municipal bonds that were issued 5 years ago are callable and that the bonds have call protection for a total of 10 years or another 5 years from now – year 0. If called in year 6, the bonds will be redeemed at 103, that is, for par value plus a call premium of 3.

Call protection:
> The provision of an indenture for a callable bond that prohibits redemption by the issuer for a specified period of time, often 10 years for municipal and corporate bonds.

> **Call premium:**
> The amount above par that must be paid by the issuer if bonds are called.
> Often decreases as the bonds approach maturity.

Assume that, because market interest rates are low, the bond issuers have structured an advance refunding, whereby new bonds have already been issued and the proceeds placed in trust until the first call date 5 years from now.

> **Advance refunding (municipal bonds):**
> Sale of new bonds prior to the first call date of previously issued bonds.
>
> - New bonds are sold at market rates of interest.
> - The proceeds of the sale are placed with a trustee.
> - The trustee invests the proceeds in Treasury securities or other high-quality debt that matures at the first call date of the original bonds.
> - On the first call date, the trustee redeems the original bonds.

The valuation model reflects these circumstances.

$$MV = \sum_{t=1}^{c} \frac{\left(\frac{(M)(CR)}{m}\right)}{\left(1+\frac{k}{m}\right)^{t}} + \frac{CP}{\left(1+\frac{k}{m}\right)^{c}}$$

where c = number of periods before the first call date
CP = call price on first call date

Given: $M = 50{,}000$; $CR = .07$; $m = 4$; $k = .05$; $n = 60$; $c = 20$; $CP = 51{,}500$ (103 percent of face value):

$$MV = \sum_{t=1}^{20} \{(50{,}000)(.07)/4\}/(1.0125)^{t} + [51{,}500/(1.0125)^{20}]$$

$$= 875 \, (PVIFA_{.0125,20}) + 51{,}500/1.282037$$

$$PVIFA_{.0125,40} = (1/.0125)(1 - \{1/1.0125)^{20}\})$$

$$= 17.599316$$

$$MV = 875(17.599316) + 40{,}170.45$$

$$= 55{,}569.85$$

Under an advance refunding, the market value of municipal bonds is generally lower than it would be otherwise ($60,508.65). As shown in this example, this is true even when the bonds will be called at a premium.

2.4 LOANS

The investment securities portfolio contains financial instruments that have readily accessible market quotations. The loan portfolio is even more significant in terms of bank investment, but has much less readily available market information. Market valuation models are discussed below for:

- Commercial loans
- Mortgage loans
- Consumer installment loans
- Lease financing

2.4.1 COMMERCIAL LOANS

Anticipated cash flows for commercial loans are contractually set and these form the basis for market valuation. The discount rate should be based on current interest rates, the time to maturity, and the risk characteristics of the borrowers in the pool of loans being valued.

Prime rate:
> The interest rate that banks use in pricing short term commercial loans to their most creditworthy corporate clients.

The prime rate is the rate that banks charge their best, most creditworthy commercial customers, although loans are sometimes made at rates below prime. Prime also acts as the basis for pricing other commercial loans to smaller businesses.

The terms of commercial loans can vary significantly but most can be described as one of the following general classifications:

- Bullet loans
- Working capital lines of credit
- Term loans

Bullet Loans

Bullet loans require no payment of interest or principal until the loan matures. The market value of these loans is the present value of the future payoff of interest and principal.

$$MV = \frac{L\left(1 + \dfrac{k_L}{m}\right)^n}{\left(1 + \dfrac{k}{m}\right)^n}$$

where L = loan amount
k_L = loan rate
n = number of periods before loan matures
m = number of times per year interest is compounded

This example assumes quarterly interest compounding: $L = 250,000$; $k_L = .075$; $m = 4$; $k = .08$; $n = 20$ (five years).

$$MV = 250,000(1 + .075/4)^{20}/(1 + .08/4)^{20}$$
$$= 250,000(1.449948)/(1.485947)$$
$$= 243,943.42$$

Working Capital Lines of Credit

Working capital lines of credit involve a loan amount that will change. A line of credit involves a maximum amount of credit authorized for a specified period of time. The borrower draws down amounts as needed. At any given point in time, the value of the portfolio of lines of credit must be based on actual borrowings outstanding and an estimate of when these balances will be repaid. These estimates are most appropriately based on past experience with these loans. In addition to normal interest payments, commitment fees are assessed on unused portions of the lines. These fees are usually stated in terms of percent per annum as are interest rates. The valuation model considers both the borrowings and the unused portion of the line.

$$MV = \frac{A(1 + k_{LC})^n + (MX - A)((1 + k_{CF})^n - 1)}{(1 + k)^n}$$

where A = actual borrowings to date
MX = maximum credit available
k_{LC} = interest rate on borrowings
k_{CF} = commitment fee
n = average maturity of lines of credit or average time before they are paid off

Consider a portfolio of credit lines that have an average maturity of nine months: $A = 2,000,000$; $MX = 5,000,000$; $k_{LC} = .10$; $k_{CF} = .01$; $k = .105$; $n = .75$

$$MV = [2,000,000(1.10)^{.75} + (5,000,000 - 2,000,000)((1.01)^{.75} - 1)]/(1.105)^{.75}$$
$$= [(2,000,000)(1.0740995) + (3,000,000)(.0074907)]/(1.0777591)$$
$$= 2,014,059.64$$

Term Loans

Term loans are extended for periods of time in excess of one year. They are generally structured in one of two formats:

- Installment loans
- Interest-only loans

The market value of an *installment loan* is the present value of the payment annuity. The amount of the payment for a given loan is determined by the contractual loan rate and time to maturity.

$$MV = \left(\frac{L}{PVIFA_{\left(\frac{k_L}{m},n\right)}}\right)\left(PVIFA_{\left(\frac{k}{m},n\right)}\right)$$

where

L = loan amount

m = number of times per year that payments are made

n = number of periods before maturity

$L/PVIFA_{k/m,n}$ = periodic loan payment

Consider a three-year loan with quarterly payments: $L = 1,000,000$; $k_L = .11$; $k = .105$; $m = 4$; $n = 12$.

$$MV = [1,000,000/PVIFA_{.11/4,12}][PVIFA_{.105/4,12}]$$

$$PVIFA_{.11/4,12} = (1/(.11/4))(1 - \{1/(1 + .11/4)^{12}\})$$

$$= (36.363636)(1 - .7221344)$$

$$= 10.10420354$$

$$PVIFA_{.105/4,12} = (1/(.105/4))(1 - \{1/(1 + .105/4)^{12}\})$$

$$= (38.0952381)(1 - .732760345)$$

$$= 10.18055829$$

$$MV = [1,000,000/10.10420354][10.18055829]$$

$$= 1,007,556.73$$

The market value of an *interest-only loan* is the value of the interest payments and the payoff the end of the term. In this sense, this type of loan is valued in the same way as an interest-paying bond.

$$MV = L\left(\frac{k_L}{m}\right)\left(PVIFA_{\left(\frac{k}{m},n\right)}\right) + \frac{L}{\left(1 + \frac{k}{m}\right)^n}$$

where $L(k_L/m)$ = periodic interest payment

Consider a three-year loan that compounds interest semiannually: $L = 1,000,000$; $k_L = .11$; $k = .105$; $m = 2$; $n = 6$.

$$MV = [1,000,000(.11/2)(PVIFA_{.105/2,6})] + [1,000,000/(1 + .105/2)^6]$$

$$PVIFA_{.105/2,6} = (1/(.105/2))(1 - \{1/(1 + .105/2)^6\})$$

$$= (19.047619)(1 - .73564345)$$

$$= 5.0353628$$

$$MV = [(55,000)(5.0353628)] + 735,643.45$$

$$= 1,012,588.40$$

2.4.2 MORTGAGE LOANS

Mortgage loans are long-term loans secured by real estate. Both residential and commercial mortgage loans will be governed by the same principles of market valuation. However, the two types of mortgages should be kept separate in the valuation process because they have significantly different risk profiles which will affect the selection of discount rate. Within each of the two categories, subgrouping should include loans with common characteristics. Three appropriate subgroups are:

- Fixed-rate mortgages
- Adjustable rate mortgages (ARMs)
- Balloon mortgages

Fixed-rate Mortgages

The traditional home mortgage is a *fixed-rate* instrument with an original maturity of 25 to 30 years. The market value of a portfolio of such loans will depend on the implied periodic (usually monthly) payment and the average time to maturity.

$$MV = \left(\frac{L}{PVIFA_{\left(\frac{k_L}{m},n\right)}}\right)\left(PVIFA_{\left(\frac{k}{m},n\right)}\right)$$

where $L/PVIFA_{k/m,n}$ = implied periodic payment based on the loan amount (L) and the contractual mortgage rate

Note that this is the same valuation formula as that used for commercial loans of the installment type.

Adjustable Rate Mortgages

The loan rates for *adjustable rate mortgages (ARMs)* will vary with market interest rates. The rate adjustments are often made twice a year. As a result, the market value of a portfolio of ARMs will be close to book value because the loan (coupon) rate will be close to the market (required) rate.

These rate adjustments cause ARMs to be less subject to prepayments that are motivated by interest rate changes. However, if the loan contract includes interest rate caps (ceiling – maximum rate, floor – minimum rate; or collar – cap and floor), these provisions constitute options owned either by the borrower or the bank.

Balloon Mortgages

Balloon Mortgages are shorter term loans that require a large payment at the end of the term of the loan. They are generally of two types:

- Interest-only loans
- Amortized loans

Interest-only loans are similar to bonds that pay interest during the life of the loan and the entire principal at the end of the term.

$$MV = \frac{(L)\left(\frac{k_m}{m}\right)}{PVIFA_{\left(\frac{k_L}{m},n\right)}} + \frac{L}{\left(1 + \frac{k}{m}\right)^n}$$

where L = loan amount
        $(L)(k_m/m)$ = periodic interest payment

An example of annual interest payments illustrates this application: $L = 100{,}000$; $k_m = .09$; $k = .095$; $m = 1$; $n = 5$.

$$MV = 100{,}000(.09)(PVIFA_{.095,5}) + 100{,}000(1/(1.095)^5)$$
$$= 9{,}000(3.839709) + 100{,}000(.6352277)$$
$$= 34{,}557.38 + 63{,}522.77$$
$$= 98{,}080.15$$

On the other hand, the payments for an *amortizing balloon mortgage* are established as if the loan will be repaid over a longer period of time, perhaps 30 years, while the balance is due after a shorter period of time.

$$MV = \left(\frac{L}{PVIFA_{\left(\frac{k_L}{m},n\right)}}\right)\left(PVIFA_{\left(\frac{k}{m},b\right)}\right) + \frac{B}{\left(1 + \frac{k}{m}\right)^b}$$

where n = number of periods over which the interim payments are set up
        $(L/PVIFA_{k/m,n})$ = periodic payment of interest and principal
                b = number of periods that will elapse before the date of the balloon payment
                B = amount of the balloon payment
                = $(L/PVIFA_{k/m,n})(PVIFA_{k/m,n-b})$
                = value of the remaining payments

In some cases, the loan rate may be set below market for this type of loan because of the early payoff. The market value of the loan will be the present value of the periodic payments and the balloon payment.

Consider a loan that is to be amortized over 30 years with a balloon payment after year 5: $L = 100{,}000$; $k_m = .07$; $k = .095$; $n = 360$; $b = 60$.

$$\text{Monthly payment} = 100{,}000/PVIFA_{.07/12,360}$$
$$= 100{,}000/150.307568$$
$$= 665.30$$
$$PV \text{ of payments} = 665.30(PVIFA_{.095/12,60})$$
$$= 665.30(47.614827)$$
$$= 31{,}678.14$$

$$B = 665.30(PVIFA_{.07/12,300})$$

$$= 665.30(141.486903)$$

$$= 94,131.24$$

$$PV \text{ of } B = 94,131.24/(1/(1 + .095/12)^{60})$$

$$= 94,131.24(.6230493)$$

$$= 58,648.40$$

$$MV = 31,678.14 + 58,648.40$$

$$= 90,326.54$$

When valuing a portfolio of balloon mortgages, it is necessary to determine the total loan amount, the average loan (coupon) rate, and the average loan term over which the payments have been set up. This information will form the basis of the estimate of the periodic payment. These implied payments will be received until the average date of balloon payment.

2.4.3 CONSUMER INSTALLMENT LOANS

The most common type of consumer installment loan is an automobile loan. These loans are valued as annuities in the same way as installment commercial loans and fixed-rate mortgage loans. The valuation model is as follows:

$$MV = \left(\frac{L}{PVIFA_{\left(\frac{k_L}{m},n\right)}}\right)\left(PVIFA_{\left(\frac{k}{m},n\right)}\right)$$

2.4.4 LEASE FINANCING

In terms of cash flows, lease financing is similar to purchase financing with the exception that the borrower must pay a residual value at the end of the term of the lease to obtain ownership of the asset. Commercial leases should be separated from consumer leases for purposes of market valuation because the collateral and risk profiles of portfolios may be quite different. Once separated, however, the principles of market valuation are the same.

The residual value is similar to a balloon payment in a mortgage. The difference is that the residual is not a legal obligation of the borrower. At the end of the lease, the borrower may elect not to pay the residual and relinquish possession of the asset. Because the bank would then sell the asset, it is vital that the residual used for valuation purposes be a realistic estimate of the fair market value at the end of the lease term.

The market value of a lease is the present value of lease payments plus the present value of the residual.

$$MV = \left(\frac{L}{PVIFA_{\left(\frac{k_L}{m},n\right)}}\right)\left(PVIFA_{\left(\frac{k}{m},n\right)}\right) + \frac{R}{\left(1 + \frac{k}{m}\right)^n}$$

where
$$L = \text{loan amount}$$
$$= \text{amount to be amortized}$$
$$(L/PVIFA_{k/m,n}) = \text{periodic payment of interest and principal}$$
$$R = \text{residual value}$$

Consider the lease for a major piece of equipment to be leased over five years: $L = 1,000,000$; $R = 500,000$; $k_L = .12$; $k = .10$; $n = 60$.

$$MV = (1,000,000/PVIFA_{.12/12,60})(PVIFA_{.10/12,60}) + 500,000(1/(1 + .10/12)^{60})$$

$$= (1,000,000/44.955038)(47.065369) + 500,000(.6077886)$$

$$= 1,046,943.15 + 303,894.30$$

$$= 1,350,837.45$$

This example is for a commercial lease. Most consumer leases are for automobiles and their terms can vary with respect to the amount to be amortized relative to the original value of the asset. The key to appropriate market valuation of leases is the estimate of average residual value.

2.5 OTHER ASSETS

Bank premises and equipment do not lend themselves to a present value analysis because they are not financial assets that yield measurable cash flows. Their market valuation is best estimated by professional appraisals. *Other real estate owned* is another category of assets that should be valued via up-to-date appraisal.

Investments in subsidiaries can be evaluated using present value analysis. It is necessary to first value the assets and liabilities of the subsidiary at market. In this way, an implied (market value) equity of the subsidiary may be established. The parent bank's asset is then the proportional share of the implied equity of the subsidiary.

2.6 LIABILITIES

The market value of bank liabilities will be closer to the book value as compared to bank assets because most liabilities are relatively short-term and some are due on demand. The largest divergence of market value from book value will be in long-term borrowings. The major categories of liabilities are:

- Deposits due on demand, including transactions and savings accounts
- Time deposits
- Short-term borrowings
- Long-term borrowings

2.6.1 TRANSACTIONS AND SAVINGS ACCOUNTS

Transactions accounts are legally due on demand at book value; savings accounts are effectively due on demand at book value because the notification requirement is generally waived. The market value of these liabilities is equivalent to book value.

2.6.2 TIME DEPOSITS

Time deposits include both small and large time deposits with maturities from seven days to seven years or more. The market value will depend on the face amount of the deposit, the deposit rate, the time to maturity, and the appropriate discount rate.

$$MV = \frac{D\left(1 + \dfrac{k_D}{m}\right)^n}{\left(1 + \dfrac{k}{m}\right)^n}$$

where D = deposit amount
k_D = deposit rate
m = number of times per year interest is paid or compounded

This valuation model is equivalent to that used for the asset category, *time deposits in other banks.*

2.6.3 SHORT-TERM BORROWINGS

Short-term borrowings include *federal funds purchased* (overnight), *term federal funds purchased*, and *securities sold under agreement to repurchase*. These are liabilities with a maturity of well under one year. As a result, the difference between book value and market value will be small. The actual models for valuation are the same as for the corresponding asset categories.

   Commercial paper is a short-term liability of a bank-holding company that is usually sold on a discount basis. The original maturity is no more than 270 days and the market valuation model is similar to that for Treasury bills.

$$MV = M - M(k)\left(\frac{N}{360}\right)$$

where M = maturity value
N = number of days before maturity

2.6.4 LONG-TERM BORROWINGS

Long-term borrowings usually take the form of *subordinated notes and debentures.* In order for these instruments to qualify as regulatory capital, the instruments must be long-term and subordinated to deposits. These liabilities are valued using the same models developed for debt securities held as assets.

 Summary

All of the models discussed in this chapter for the market valuation of commercial bank assets will yield close approximations. They will be especially useful for assets with little secondary market price information. In the cases for which there is ample market data, the models also will be useful in predicting changes in the market value of assets when interest rates change.

End-of-chapter Questions

1. Why are some bank financial assets and liabilities difficult to assess in terms of market value?

2. Summarize:

   a. The three arguments often presented against market valuation in the banking industry.

   b. The responses to these arguments by market value proponents.

3. Why is it true that the book value of cash items is an appropriate measure of market value?

4. Why is it true that market values of investment securities can vary substantially from book values, while there is usually little difference between market and book values for temporary investments?

5. Is the valuation approach for federal funds sold different from that of term federal funds sold? Explain.

6. What factor differentiates the valuation of repurchase agreements from that of other temporary investments?

7. How does the valuation of T-bills differ from the valuation of T-notes and T-bonds?

8. Why are the required returns for municipal bonds often lower than Treasury yields?

9. What other financial instrument is similar to an interest only loan? Why?

10. In valuing financial assets and liabilities, what is the difference between the contractual rate and the required rate?

11. Generally, what is the relationship between book value and market value for variable rate loans (such as adjustable rate mortgages)? Why?

12. Are differences between market value and book value likely to be greater for bank assets or bank liabilities? Why?

13. Obtain a copy of the most recent annual report for a local bank.

    a. Identify the market value disclosures in the footnotes of the financial statements.

    b. By how much do market values differ from book values? What explanations are given for these differences?

Note

1   In some cases, assets and liabilities may have embedded options. In these cases, option pricing models are appropriate. See the Appendices in chapter 7 for the Black–Scholes option pricing model and Black futures option pricing model.

Selected References

Cox, John C. and Mark Rubinstein. *Options Markets*, Prentice Hall, Englewood Cliffs, NJ. 1985.

Fabozzi, Frank J. *Fixed Income Mathematics*, Probus Publishing Company, Chicago, 1988.

Gibson, Rajna. *Option Valuation: Analyzing and Pricing Standardized Option Contracts*, McGraw-Hill, New York, 1991.

Howe, Donna M. *A Guide to Managing Interest-Rate Risk*, New York Institute of Finance, New York, 1992.

Hull, John. *Options, Futures, and Other Derivative Securities*, Prentice Hall, Englewood Cliffs, NJ, 1989.

Johnson, Hazel J. *The Bank Valuation Handbook: A Market-based Approach to Valuing a Bank*, revised edn, Irwin Professional Publishing, Burr Ridge, Ill. (now McGraw-Hill, New York), 1995.

Appendix 18.1: Summary of Valuation Concepts

Category	Market valuation model
Interest-bearing time deposits in other banks	$D(1 + k_c)^n/(1 + k)^n$
Federal funds sold	$FF(1 + k_c)^n/(1 + k)^n$
Securities purchased U/A to resell	$\left[\sum_{t=1}^{n} CP_t/((1 + k/m)^t)\right] + SP/(1 + k/m)^n$
Treasury bills	$M - M(k)(N/360)$
Treasury notes & bonds	$\left[\sum_{t=1}^{n} \{(M)(CR)/m\}/((1 + k/m)^t)\right] + [M/(1 + k/m)^n]$
Government agency:	
Pass-throughs	$\sum_{t=1}^{n} CF_t/((1 + k/m)^t)$
Mortgage-backed	$\left[\sum_{t=1}^{n} \{(M)(CR)/m\}/((1 + k/m)^t)\right] + [M/(1 + k/m)^n]$
Municipal:	
Noncallable	$\left[\sum_{t=1}^{n} \{(M)(CR)/m\}/((1 + k/m)^t)\right] + [M/((1 + k/m)^n)]$

Advance refunding	$\left[\sum_{t=1}^{c}\{(M)(CR)/m\}/((1+k/m)^{t})\right] + [CP/((1+k/m)^{c})]$
Zero-coupon bonds	$M/((1+k)^{n})$
Commercial loans:	
Bullet	$L((1+k_{L}/m)^{n})/((1+k/m)^{n})$
Line of credit	$[A((1+k_{LC})^{n}) + (MX - A)((1+k_{CF})^{n} - 1)]/(1+k)^{n}$
Term:	
Installment	$[L/PVIFA_{k/m,n}][PVIFA_{k/m,n}]$
Interest only	$[L(k_{L}/m)(PVIFA_{k/m,n})] + [L/((1+k/m)^{n})]$
Mortgage loans:	
Fixed-rate	$(L/PVIFA_{k/m,n})(PVIFA_{k/m,n})$
Graduated pymt (GPM)	$\left[\sum_{t=1}^{g}\{(L/PVIFA_{k/m,n}) - PR_{t}\}/(1+k/m)^{t}\right] +$ $\left\{\left[(L/PVIFA_{k/m,n})(PVIFA_{k/m,n-g}) + \sum_{t=1}^{g}PR_{t}\right]\right.$ $\left./PVIFA_{k/m,n-g}\right\}(PVIFA_{k/m,n-g})(1/((1+k/m)^{g}))$
Balloon:	
Interest only	$\left[\sum_{t=1}^{n}(L)(k_{m}/m)/((1+k)^{t})\right] + L/((1+k/m)^{t})$
Amortizing	$(L/PVIFA_{k/m,n})(PVIFA_{k/m,b}) + B/((1+k/m)^{b})$
Consumer installment loans	$(L/PVIFA_{k/m,n})(PVIFA_{k/m,n})$
Lease financing	$(L/PVIFA_{k/m,n})(PVIFA_{k/m,n}) + R(1/((1+k/m)^{n}))$
Nonaccrual loans	$\left[\sum_{t=1}^{n}CF_{t}/((1+k)^{t})\right]$
Time deposits	$D(1+k_{D})^{n}/((1+k)^{n})$

Short-term borrowings:

Fed funds purchased	$FF(1 + k_c)^n/(1 + k)^n$
Securities sold U/A to repurchase	$\left[\sum_{t=1}^{n} CP_t/((1 + k/m)^t)\right] + SP/(1 + k/m)^n$
Commercial paper	$M - M(k)(N/360)$
Long-term borrowings	$\left[\sum_{t=1}^{n}\{(M)(CR/m)\}/((1 + k/m)^t)\right] + [M/(1 + k/m)^n]$

Notes:

For the following loan categories, the loan amount (L) is divided by *PVIFA* computed with the loan (contractual) interest rate and then multiplied by *PVIFA* computed with the required rate of return:

- commercial – term installment
- mortgages – fixed rate, graduated payment, and amortizing balloon
- consumer installment
- lease financing

A	actual borrowings for line of credit
b	number of periods before balloon payment
B	amount of balloon payment
c	number of periods before first call date of a bond
CF_t	cash flow in period t
CP	call price
CP_t	coupon payment in period t
CR	coupon rate
D	deposit
FF	federal funds
g	number of periods with graduated payments (GPM)
k	discount rate
k_c	contractual (coupon) rate
k_{CF}	commitment fee for line of credit
k_D	deposit rate
k_L	loan rate
k_{LC}	interest rate for line of credit
k_m	mortgage rate
L	loan amount
m	number of times per year interest is either paid or compounded
M	maturity value
MX	maximum credit available for line of credit
n	number of periods before maturity
N	number of days before maturity
PR_t	payment reduction in period t
R	residual value in lease financing

Regional Trade Agreements and Financial Services

 chapter 19

INTERNATIONAL COMPARISONS

Argentina	Mexico
Bolivia	Paraguay
Brazil	Peru
Canada	Uruguay
Colombia	Venezuela
Ecuador	

 Introduction

Trade agreements typically focus primarily on trade in merchandise. Trade in services is often negotiated after the negotiations for merchandise trade. Trade in financial services has been addressed in global discussions such as the General Agreement on Tariffs and Trade and the World Trade Organization.

    Bilateral and regional trade discussions also routinely address the issues that will affect the provision of financial services among the signatories of the agreements. In addition to the European Union (discussed in chapter 9), the Asia-Pacific Economic Cooperation (APEC) Forum, the North American Free Trade Agreement (NAFTA), and several Latin American regional trade pacts have implications for cross-border financial services – perhaps none more than NAFTA which establishes an explicit, formal framework for the foreign acquisition and operation of Mexican financial institutions for the first time in recent history.

 GATT: The Foundation for Regional Trade

The provisions of the General Agreement on Tariffs and Trade (GATT) are points of reference for virtually every trade agreement in force or in negotiation.

General Agreement on Tariffs and Trade (GATT):
       Multilateral trade treaty, signed January 1948, with commercial rights
       and obligations intended to expand and liberalize world trade.

    GATT sets the worldwide standards for managing tariff and nontariff barriers to international trade. In so doing, GATT also sets the foundation for international financial services.

1.1 THE MOTIVATION FOR GATT

In the nineteenth century, international trade was governed by two basic principles:

- The greater the economic differences between two countries, the greater their propensity to trade.
- The benefits of such trade are maximized under conditions of free trade.

In a sense, two countries with different economies could complement each other in a free trade environment. The two assumptions under which free trade yielded the greatest benefits were:

- Market imperfections, such as monopolies or restrictive tariffs, did not exist.
- No country could possibly improve its access to other markets by restricting its own imports from these markets.

The United Kingdom was the pioneer of free trade principles in 1846 when it unilaterally abolished its restrictions on the trading of corn. By the 1870s, this philosophy had resulted in the formation of a multitude of bilateral trade agreements in Europe. Each of these pacts had a common feature – the unconditional most-favored-nation (MFN) clause. This clause stipulated that each of the two countries in a bilateral agreement must offer the other any trade privilege that it granted to a third party. Because there were so many bilateral agreements in Europe, effectively they created a multilateral trade agreement. Under this system of liberalization, cross-border trade expanded rapidly.

> **Most favored nation:**
> The concept of extending to other nations any advantage, favor, privilege, or immunity that is granted to the trade of a nation receiving the most favorable treatment.

However, this nineteenth-century spirit of trade liberalization was severely dampened by the protectionist legislation and practices that followed the Stock Market Crash of 1929. During the depression years of 1929 to 1932, the volume of world output declined by 20 percent and the volume of world trade fell at the even faster rate of 40 percent. The framers of GATT sought to reverse these effects.

1.2 THE BASIC PRINCIPLES OF GATT

During and after the Second World War (1939–45), the British and the Americans led the initiative to restore to the world trade arena the principles of *comparative advantage*, *multilateralism*, and *nondiscrimination*.

- The theory of *comparative advantage* suggests that nations should (1) export those products that they can produce more efficiently than other nations and (2) import those products for which they are relative high-cost producers.
- *Multilateralism* is a policy that seeks to permit international trade without restrictive bilateral arrangements that may prevent trading partners from fully realizing their comparative advantage. That is, bilateral trade agreements should not discourage trade with other, third-party countries.

- *Nondiscrimination* prevents nations from applying treatment to either imports or exports that favors one nation at the expense of another.

On January 1, 1948, GATT was signed by over 80 fully participating countries and by almost 30 that signed special arrangements. GATT addressed reciprocal commercial rights and spelled out obligations of the signatories, explicitly including the concept of MFN treatment. Through GATT, common regulations and a framework for negotiating trade-liberalizing agreements were established.

Because of GATT, since the end of the Second World War, world trade has expanded faster than world output. The average worldwide tariff declined from 40 percent in 1947 to approximately 5 percent in the mid-1990s. This process has been facilitated by "rounds" of trade talks. The most recent round, the *Uruguay Round* (1986–94) was the most difficult to conclude. From the outset, there was an ambitious agenda that broached the most sensitive issues involving the trade of goods and services.

1.3 THE FINAL ACT OF THE URUGUAY ROUND

Early in 1994, the Uruguay Round was completed, including the resolution of some of the most difficult issues and the creation of a new trade organization. The Final Act of the Uruguay Round contained a number of agreements, including agreements on agriculture, intellectual property, textiles, and import licensing procedures.

Also, among the issues addressed in the Final Act of the Uruguay Round was a General Agreement on Trade in Services (Services Agreement). The Services Agreement is composed of three parts:

- The *Framework Agreement* contains the basic obligations that apply to all member countries.
- *National schedules* contain specific commitments by individual countries to continue to liberalize the services sectors of their economies.
- *The annexes* address special situations of the services sectors.

The Services Agreement covers a broad range of activities in which services are supplied from the territory of one party (member country) to the territory of another party:

- Services supplied in the territory of one party to the consumers of any other (for example, tourism)
- Services provided by nationals of one party in the territory of any other (for example, construction projects or consulting)
- Services provided through the presence of service-providing entities of one party in the territory of another (for example, banking)

In all of these situations, each member country must "accord immediately and unconditionally to services and service providers of any other Party, treatment no less favorable than that it accords to like services and service providers of any other country." ("General Agreement on Trade in Services," *A Summary of the Final Act of the Uruguay Round*, http://www.wto.org). That is, member countries must accord MFN status in services as well as merchandise trade. In those cases in which MFN status is not possible, that is, when MFN exemptions exist, such exceptions must be specified in an annex and the annex must indicate the specific MFN exemption that is relevant.

However, these exemptions must be reviewed after five years and normally may not exceed 10 years in duration.

In addition, the national schedules of individual member countries contain commitments for *market access* and *national treatment*. With respect to foreign service providers, market access provisions eliminate limitations on:

- Numbers of service providers
- Total value of service transactions
- Total number of service operations
- Total number of people employed
- Foreign investment
- Level of foreign participation

National treatment:
        Extending to foreign or imported goods and services the same treatment accorded to domestic goods and services.

National treatment provisions require a member country to treat service providers of other countries in the same way in which domestic service providers are treated. That is, the conditions of competition cannot be modified to favor domestic service providers.

One of the annexes addresses financial services, primarily banking and insurance. Member countries are entitled to take prudential measures, that is, to regulate financial services, for the protection of investors, bank deposit holders, and insurance policy holders. The annex also recognizes the need to maintain the integrity and stability of the financial system. With respect to *market access*, the annex addresses the responsibility of each member country not to impede insurance policy writing, financial data processing, financial data transfer, establishment or expansion of a commercial presence, and the temporary entry of personnel. In terms of *national treatment*, the annex specifies that there must be access to payments and clearing systems operated by public entities (such as the Federal Reserve System) and to official funding and refinancing facilities (such as the sale of US Treasury securities). National treatment must also be accorded in the areas of membership, or participation, in self-regulatory bodies (such as the US National Association of Securities Dealers), securities exchanges (such as the New York Stock Exchange), futures exchanges (such as the Chicago Mercantile Exchange), and clearing agencies (such as the Federal Reserve System).

② The World Trade Organization

The Final Act of the Uruguay Round also contained the Agreement Establishing the World Trade Organization (WTO), which began operations in early 1995. The WTO is a single institutional framework that encompasses the GATT, as modified by the Uruguay Round, all GATT agreements and all GATT arrangements.

2.1 OBJECTIVES AND FUNCTIONS

The objective of the WTO is to help its members conduct their trade and economic relations in order to:

- Raise standards of living
- Ensure full employment
- Steadily increase incomes and demand for goods and services
- Expand production and trade in goods and services

Functionally, the WTO:

- Administers and implements multilateral trade agreements
- Acts as a forum for multilateral trade negotiations
- Seeks to resolve trade disputes
- Oversees national trade policies
- Cooperates with other international institutions (such as the International Monetary Fund and the World Bank) that are involved in economic policy-making

Based in Geneva, Switzerland, the WTO is governed through Ministerial Conference meetings that occur at least once every two years. The General Council oversees implementation of the agreements and ministerial decisions. The General Council is also a Dispute Settlement Body and a Trade Policy Review Mechanism. The General Council delegates responsibilities to three other bodies:

- Council for Trade in Goods
- Council for Trade in Services
- Council for Trade-Related Aspects of Intellectual Property Rights

In 1997, 131 governments were members of the WTO.

2.2 REGIONAL TRADE AGREEMENTS UNDER THE WTO

Over time, and especially during the Uruguay Round of GATT, there has been some frustration with operating solely under the provisions of GATT. For example, preferential treatment is permitted by GATT for developing countries. However, as the developing countries have become "newly industrializing," there has been pressure on some of them to more fully adopt the free-trade principles of GATT and now the WTO. Also, some trade issues, such as intellectual property rights, have been difficult to manage under GATT and the WTO. Finally, geographical proximities of countries to neighboring nations sometimes make it more efficient to address specific issues through bilateral or regional agreements. Thus, there has been a growing tendency for regional trade agreements. (See also chapter 9 for a discussion of the European Union.)

The WTO maintains the primacy, or priority, of the multilateral trading system. At the same time, the WTO established a new Committee on Regional Trade Agreements to coordinate the processes of global and regional trade liberalization.

 **NAFTA**

The North American Free Trade Agreement (NAFTA) is an agreement between the United Sates, Canada, and Mexico. As shown in Exhibit 19.1, these three countries, represent approximately nearly 400 million residents and almost $9 trillion in gross domestic product.

Member country	Population[1]	Gross domestic product	
		Total[2]	Per capita
United States	268,700	$7,920,000	$29,475
Canada	30,600	633,200	20,693
Mexico	97,100	324,700	3,344
	396,400	$8,877,900	$22,396

◆ **Exhibit 19.1: Members of the North American Free Trade Agreement**

◆ *Notes*:   1   Represents 1997 population in thousands
                2   Represents projected 1997 GDP in millions of US dollars

◆ *Source*:   *The World in 1997*, The Economist Group, London, 1996.

3.1 NAFTA PROVISIONS FOR FINANCIAL SERVICES

The NAFTA treaty had significant implications for financial services. Specific areas addressed by the treaty include:

- Establishment of financial institutions. Each NAFTA member allows the other two members to establish financial institutions and to expand geographically.
- Cross-border trade. No member may restrict cross-border trade in financial services.
- National treatment. No NAFTA member may accord treatment to investors or financial institutions of another member that is less favorable than that which it accords its own investors and financial institutions.
- Most-favored-nation treatment. Each NAFTA member must treat the institutions of another member no less favorably than it treats the institutions of a third member or a nonmember.
- New financial services and data processing. One NAFTA member, as host country, may not prohibit the financial institution of another member from fully participating in any sort of deregulation or expansion of powers that occurs within the host member country.
- Senior management and boards of directors. No NAFTA member may insist that the senior management of the financial institution be of any particular nationality.
- Transparency. The decision-making process with respect to permission to operate within a NAFTA member must be easily determined and understood, that is, not be cloaked in secrecy.
- Financial Services Committee. The Financial Services Committee supervises implementation of rules for financial services, participates in dispute settlement procedures, and is composed of officials of the Department of Finance of Canada (Canada), Secretaría de Hacienda y Crédito Público (Mexico), the Department of the Treasury (US banking), and the Department of Commerce (US insurance).
- Dispute settlement. A 15-member arbitral panel considers disputes that arise in the provision of financial services in connection with NAFTA members.
- Investment transfers. Each NAFTA member must permit the transfer of profits, dividends, interest, capital gains, royalty payments, management fees, technical assistance fees, loan payments, proceeds from sale of investment (partial or complete), and other payments in freely usable currency at the market rate of exchange prevailing on the date of transfer.

- Expropriation and compensation. Any expropriation must be done in accordance with due process and must be compensated at the fair market value of expropriated investment immediately before the expropriation takes place. Furthermore, the compensation must be made in a G-7 currency and include interest at a commercially reasonable rate for that currency from date of expropriation until date of actual payment.

> **Expropriation:**
> Taking property from its owner, especially, taking property for public use or control.

G-7 is an acronym for the Group of 7 – the group of industrialized countries including the United States, Canada, Japan, Germany, France, Great Britain, and Italy.

3.2 THE MEXICAN BANKING SYSTEM BEFORE NAFTA

For the first time, NAFTA – an international treaty – protected investors in Mexico. Commercial banks had been nationalized in 1982 and were not reprivatized until 1991.

> **Nationalization:**
> Government takeover of private property.

Under the administration of President Carlos Salinas de Gortari (elected in 1988), the government began to restructure and liberalize bank regulations. In the interest of bank soundness, new laws and regulations imposed stiff capital level requirements. Also, a new loan classification system was instituted that promptly recognized past-due loans and limited certain activities, such as lending to one client or lending to the bank's own affiliates. At the same time, more independent, market-oriented management was assigned to the banks. Deregulation eliminated interest rate ceilings on deposits, eliminated forced investment in government securities, and removed foreign exchange controls.

In an environment of improving government finances and an active government securities market, the competition among the banks increased almost immediately. This process culminated with the privatization of the 18 remaining commercial banks that had been nationalized in 1982. Starting in June 1991, the privatization process was completed in an impressive 14-month period.

3.3 NAFTA AND THE MEXICAN BANKING SYSTEM

Under NAFTA, for the first time since 1982 (when Mexican banks were nationalized), foreign investors could own 100 percent of Mexican banks and other financial institutions. Limits on the total amount of financial industry capital that could be controlled by an individual or by all foreign investors were established, to be phased out by the year 2004 entirely.

Exhibit 19.2 outlines the specific financial service industries and the limits established by NAFTA. For example, in the case of commercial banks, a 1.5 percent limit of total Mexican banking capital is imposed for individual foreign investors. This means that no individual investor may own banking interests (capital) that exceed 1.5 percent of all Mexican bank capital. After 1999,

	US and Canadian ownership limitations			US and Canadian ownership limitations	
	Individual[1]	Aggregate[2]		Individual[1]	Aggregate[2]
Banks			*Factors and Leasing Companies*		
Before NAFTA	5%[3]	30%[4]	Before NAFTA	–	49%[4]
After NAFTA:			After NAFTA:		
1994	1.5	8	1994	None	10
1999	1.5	15	1999	None	20
After 1999	4[5]	None[6]	After 1999	None	None
Securities Firms			*Limited-Scope Finance Companies*		
Before NAFTA	10%[3]	30%[4]	Before NAFTA	–	49%[4]
After NAFTA:			After NAFTA:		
1994	4	10	1994	None	3%[8]
1999	4	20	1999	None	3%[8]
After 1999	None	None[7]	After 1999	None	None
Insurance Companies					
Before NAFTA	–	49%[4]			
After NAFTA:					
1994	1.5	6			
1999	1.5	12			
After 1999	None	None			

◆ **Exhibit 19.2:** Liberalization of financial services investment in Mexico under NAFTA

◆ *Notes*:

1   Represents the limit of US and Canadian ownership by *an individual investor* in a specific type of financial institution as a percentage of total applicable industry capital, unless otherwise noted.

2   Represents the limit of foreign ownership of *all Mexican institutions* as a percentage of total applicable industry capital, unless otherwise noted.

3   Represents the limit for *an individual foreign investor* in *an individual institution* as a percentage of the individual institution's total capital.

4   Represents the limit for *all foreign investors*, including US and Canadian investors, in *an individual institution* as a percentage of the individual institution's total capital.

5   After 1999, acquisitions by US and Canadian investors are subject to approval by the Mexican government and will be granted only if capital of the acquired bank and that of all other Mexican banks owned by the acquiring investor is less than 4% of all Mexican bank capital.

6   Mexico has the one-time right to freeze, for no more than 3 years, ownership of Mexican banks by foreign investors if their aggregate investment reaches *25%* or more. This option is available only until January 1, 2004.

7   Mexico has the one-time right to freeze, for no more than 3 years, ownership of Mexican securities firms by foreign investors if their aggregate investment reaches *30%* or more. This option is available only until January 1, 2004.

8   Represents the limit of *aggregate assets* of limited-scope finance companies as a percentage of the *aggregate assets* of all commercial banks and limited scope finance companies in Mexico.

◆ *Sources*:   *North American Free Trade Agreement*, chapter 14; Sczudlo, Raymond S. "NAFTA: Opportunities Abound for US and Canadian Financial Institution," *The Bankers Magazine*, July/August 1993, pp. 28–33.

this limit is raised to 4 percent under NAFTA provisions. The limit that applies to aggregate foreign investment, that is, all foreign investors, is 8 percent in 1994, increasing to 15 percent by 1999, with no limit thereafter. This phased-in approach to foreign investment is intended to give Mexican financial institutions ample time to prepare to compete efficiently and effectively with foreign institutions.

The provisions of NAFTA in the securities and insurance markets are similar to those in the banking sector. Restrictions for factors, leasing companies, and limited-scope finance companies are generally more lenient.

The Mexican peso devaluation occurred almost one year after the effective date of NAFTA. (See also chapter 11 for a description of the Mexican peso devaluation of late 1994 and early 1995 – the section entitled "Mexico.") The collapse of the Mexican peso led to significant economic distress and a revision of Mexico's position with respect to foreign investment in Mexican financial institutions. After this crisis, the Mexican government relaxed the limits and allowed foreign financial institutions to purchase controlling interests in any commercial bank with a market share of up to 6 percent – four times the limit for individual foreign investment established by NAFTA. This effectively permits foreign control of all Mexican banks with the exception of the big three – Banamex, Bancomer, and Banca Serfin.

 Regional Integration in Latin America

4.1 THE STAGES OF REGIONAL INTEGRATION

The process of regional integration has been classified in five stages. (These stages were developed by Bela Balassa and are the most frequently cited. See Goto, Irie, and Soyama (1990). Each successive stage implies closer economic integration between the member countries than the preceding stage.

- Free Trade Area
- Customs Union
- Common Market
- Economic Union
- Complete Economic Integration

In a *free trade area*, tariffs and quantitative restrictions between the member countries are eliminated. However, trade policy of each member country *vis-à-vis* countries outside the free trade area is left to the discretion of each member country. A *customs union* is a free trade area in which the member countries also jointly determine the level of tariffs on goods from outside the free trade area. In a *common market*, not only tariffs and duties on goods are eliminated, but also factors of production (labor and capital) may flow freely between the member countries. When countries are part of an *economic union*, the common market member countries coordinate national economic policies (to a greater or lesser extent). When there is *complete economic integration* between the member countries, national economic policies are completely coordinated. The member countries virtually become one new country with the formation of supranational entities and a single monetary system.

The North American Free Trade Agreement represents the first stage of regional integration – a free trade area. On the other hand, the 15 member countries of the European Union have progressed from the stage of free trade area through common market and are now in the economic union stage. The ultimate goal of the EU is effectively to reach the fifth stage of complete economic integration with a European central bank and a single currency by the year 2000. (See also chapter 9 for a discussion of the European Union.)

4.2 LATIN AMERICAN REGIONAL PACTS

4.2.1 MERCOSUR

Mercosur (Mercado Común del Sur) was created as a result of the Southern Cone Common Market Treaty, also known as the Treaty of Asunción. This treaty was modelled after the Treaty of Rome that led to the creation of the European Union. Members are Brazil (Latin America's largest economy), Argentina (Latin America's third largest economy), and two of the region's smallest countries – Paraguay and Uruguay. (Mexico is Latin America's second largest economy.) (See Exhibit 19.3.)

Mercosur is dismantling trade barriers and encouraging cross-border investment and joint projects. Provisions in the treaty allow for the admission of other countries. By January 1996, Mercosur had abolished tariffs on goods accounting for 90 percent of the trade among its member countries, with the remaining 10 percent scheduled to decline to zero by the year 2000. Also in the latter 1990s, Mercosur plans to introduce a single customs document to complete the customs union.

An important linkage for Mercosur is with the European Union (EU). The EU has been the largest trading partner of the four Mercosur members since 1986. One quarter of Mercosur's imports originate from Europe and the EU accepts more than one quarter of exports originating within Mercosur. The EU is also the principal foreign direct investor in Mercosur, representing 40 percent of the foreign banks operating in the region. In addition, large multinational corporations from the EU represent 50 percent of such foreign multinationals (as of 1996). At a December 1994 summit held in Essen, Germany, the EU committed to further political and economic coordination with Mercosur. Approved by the European Parliament, negotiations opened in 1995

Member country	Population[1]	Gross Domestic Product	
		Total[2]	Per capita
Argentina	35,000	$296,600	$8,474
Brazil	166,800	908,800	5,448
Paraguay[3]	4,800	7,584	1,580
Uruguay[3]	3,200	14,912	4,660
	209,800	$1,227,896	$5,853

◆ **Exhibit 19.3: Members of Mercosur**

◆ *Notes*: 1 Represents 1997 population in thousands
2 Represents projected 1997 GDP in millions of US dollars
3 Information is for 1994 and represents Gross National Product. (Source: World Bank, *World Development Report 1996*.)

Mercosur was formed in 1991.

◆ *Source*: *The World in 1997*, The Economist Group, London, 1996.

Member country	Population[1]	Gross Domestic Product	
		Total[2]	Per capita
Bolivia[3] (1969)	7,200	$5,544	$770
Colombia (1969)	38,300	89,100	2,326
Ecuador[3] (1969)	11,200	14,336	1,280
Peru[3] (1969)	23,200	48,952	2,110
Venezuela (1973)	22,300	65,900	2,955
	102,200	$223,832	$2,190

◆ **Exhibit 19.4: Members of the Andean Group**

◆ *Notes*:
1 Represents 1997 population in thousands
2 Represents projected 1997 GDP in millions of US dollars
3 Information is for 1994 and represents Gross National Product. (Source: World Bank, *World Development Report 1996*.)

The year noted in parentheses after the name of a country designates the year in which that country joined the Andean Group (which was formed in 1969). Chile was one of the founding members of the Andean Group but left the Group in 1976. The Andean Group was relaunched in 1990.

◆ *Source*: *The World in 1997*, The Economist Group, London, 1996.

to pursue a strategy whose final objective is a political and economic interregional association between the EU and Mercosur.

In order to qualify truly as a common market, however, Mercosur must open trade in services, especially financial services. The central banks of the Mercosur countries have discussed harmonizing or coordinating bank regulatory systems and finance officials have discussed harmonizing tax systems. However, the differences are considerable. For example, Uruguay has a large off-shore financial business and liberal corporate tax provisions. At the same time, Brazil has not yet eliminated its currency exchange controls.

4.2.2 THE ANDEAN GROUP

The Andean Group was formed in 1969 to pursue import substitution and to keep out investment by foreign multinationals. (Import substitution is adopted by many developing countries and involves reducing imports through local manufacture of specific items.) The original members were Bolivia, Colombia, Ecuador, and Peru. (Chile was one of the founding members of the Andean Group, but left the Group in 1976.) Venezuela joined in 1973. (See Exhibit 19.4.) Members believed that comprehensive coordination of industrial planning was necessary to accomplish their stated goals. However, as market reforms increasingly were adopted, it became clear that the restriction of foreign capital to 50 percent of a domestic industry and prohibitive tariffs would stagnate economic growth.

On January 1, 1992, the Andean Free Trade Zone was formally launched, with the five members agreeing to eliminate all mutual tariffs that remained. As of January 1, 1995, the five countries formed a customs union, adopting common external tariffs averaging approximately 14 percent.

In June 1995, initial steps were taken to negotiate a free trade agreement between the Andean Free Trade Zone and Mercosur.

The core of the Andean Group is the economic relationship between Colombia and Venezuela. In 1992, the stock markets of these two countries were electronically linked. The Venezuelan government has successfully floated bond issues on the Colombian stock market.

The Andes Development Corporation (Corporacion Andino de Fomento), based in Caracas, Venezuela is the financial arm of the Andean Group. The objective of this organization is to encourage integration and economic growth within the region.

4.3 CROSS-BORDER FINANCIAL SERVICES

Already, cross-border investments in Latin American financial services are accelerating. One example of this is the investment in Mexican financial institutions. Since the relative stabilization of the Mexican peso crisis in late 1994, the pace of investment has quickened. Foreign banks are targeting the 50 largest blue-chip companies in Mexico with a product range focused primarily on capital markets, trade finance, and derivatives. At the same time, there are signs that the presence of foreign financial institutions in Mexico is becoming diversified.

- Citibank has begun to market its services to 700 medium-sized companies in Mexico.
- First Chicago is marketing its services to Mexican companies that have investment plans for the United States, such as physical manufacturing plants.
- Bank of America Mexico SA opened a wholly owned subsidiary bank in Mexico City in May 1995, upgrading the representative office (contact only) which it had maintained for 45 years. Services now include commercial banking, capital markets services in pesos and dollars, securities and foreign exchange trading, clearing for peso futures contracts on the Chicago Mercantile Exchange, and leasing and capital equipment financial services (through Arrendadora Bank America SA).
- NationsBank de Mexico SA and Republic Bank (New York) opened offices in 1996.
- Bank of Boston upgraded its representative office to the wholly owned Bank de Boston SA in September 1995. Bank de Boston SA caters to local and multinational corporations, as well as other financial institutions. The bank is particularly active in trade services and trade financing. This includes financing foreign trade through local banks by setting up lines of credit for these banks or confirming their letters of credit.

Summary

The impact of regional trade agreements on financial services is as profound as the impact on trade in goods. Issues related to the provision of cross-border services typically are more difficult to resolve, but increasingly are being addressed. The Final Act of the Uruguay Round of GATT established clear principles for free trade in services. Regional trade agreements embody these principles – most notably, the North American Free Trade Agreement (NAFTA). The provisions of NAFTA have established a model for the reconciliation of differences in financial systems without requiring changes in national law, as with the European Union. As economic liberalization continues in Latin America, this model will be useful in facilitating the free flow of capital throughout the region.

End-of-chapter Questions

1. What are the two principles that governed international trade in the nineteenth century?
2. What are the three principles upon which GATT is based?
3. With respect to the Final Act of the Uruguay Round,
   a. Describe *market access* guidelines.
   b. Explain *national treatment*.
4. How is GATT related to the WTO?
5. Using facilities at your university, visit the Internet website of the WTO at http://www.wto.org
   a. When did your country join the WTO?
   b. Review the summary of the most recent meeting and determine the outcome of discussions in the area of trade in services.
6. Of the three countries that are signatories of NAFTA, which country initiated early discussion of this arrangement? Why did this country initiate such discussion?
7. List and briefly describe the 11 issues addressed by NAFTA that relate to financial services.
8. How did NAFTA change the rules concerning foreign investment in Mexican banks?
9. Which other financial services sectors were affected by NAFTA?
10. What was the impact of the Mexican peso collapse of late 1994 and early 1995 on the NAFTA guidelines for foreign participation in the Mexican financial system?
11. List and briefly describe the five steps of regional economic integration.
12. Which of the Latin American trade agreements has thus far had the most impact on trade in that region?

SELECTED REFERENCES

Byrne, Eileen. "Trade in the Americas: Liberalization Throughout the Hemisphere," *Business Mexico*, Special Edition 1994, pp. 80–3.

Edwards, Sebastian. "Latin American Economic Integration: A New Perspective on an Old Dream," *The World Economy*, July 1993, pp. 317–38.

Goto, Fumihiro, Kazutomo Irie, and Akihiko Soyama. *The Current Situation and Prospects for Regional Integration: Asia-Pacific Free Trade Area Proposals and Japan's Choice*, Tokyo: Research Institute of International Trade and Industry, Ministry of International Trade and Industry, 1990.

Harbracht, Douglas, Owen Ullmann, Bill Javetski, and Geri Smith. "Finally, GATT May Fly," *Business Week*, December 20, 1993, pp. 36–7.

International Financial Statistics, International Monetary Fund, Washington, DC, April 1997.

Jackson, John H. "Regional Trade Blocs and the GATT," *The World Economy*, March 1993, pp. 121–32.

Johnson, Hazel J. *Banking in Latin America: Competing and Winning in a New Era*, Lafferty Publications, Dublin, 1998.

Latin American Trade Finance 1995–1996, *Latin Finance* supplement, September 1995.

"NAFTA is Not Alone," *The Economist*, June 18, 1994, pp. 47–8.

North American Free Trade Agreement, chapter 14, US Printing Office, Washington, 1993.

Pilling, David. "The Joys of a Banking Crisis," *Euromoney*, March 1996, pp. 47–53.

Quiñones, Sam. "A Win–Lose Situation (NAFTA)," *Mexico Business*, March 1996, pp. 10–11.

"The Road to a Single Market (Mercosur)," *The Economist*, October 12, 1996, pp. 24–7.

Rosenberg, Jerry M. *Dictionary of International Trade*, John Wiley & Sons, New York, 1994.

Sczudlo, Raymond S. "NAFTA: Opportunities Abound for US and Canadian Financial Institutions," *The Bankers Magazine*, July/August 1993, pp. 28–33.

Seib, Gerald F. "Debate on GATT Recalls NAFTA Battle In Many Ways, but the Passion Is Gone," *Wall Street Journal*, July 14, 1994, p. A12.

The World Bank Atlas 1994, The World Bank, Washington, DC, 1994.

The World in 1997, The Economist Group, London, 1996.

PART VII
Bank Operations

Commercial and Noncommercial Banks

chapter 20

Introduction

Commercial banks are common in all industrialized countries. Yet the scope of activities of banks in other countries differs considerably from that in the United States. In general, US banks are prohibited from several important activities that are permitted for banks in major trading partners of the United States.

Outside the commercial banking realm, several international institutions affect financial operations in a global sense. Central bankers coordinate their activities through the Bank for International Settlements. The International Monetary Fund and the World Bank Group help smooth international liquidity imbalances and promote economic expansion in less developed countries.

 Commercial Banks

The national/regional distribution of the world's top largest 1,000 banks in 1998 appears in Exhibit 20.1. In terms of number of banks, bank assets, and capital, the largest concentration is in the European Union, followed by Asia and the United States.

Country or region	Number of banks	Assets ($ billion)	Tier I capital[1] ($ billion)
United States	154	$4,317	$283
European Union	325	14,613	580
Japan	118	6,974	253
Asia excluding Japan	162	3,321	164
Rest of Europe	89	1,661	74
Latin America	62	664	44
Middle East	60	332	30
Rest of the world	30	1,329	60
Total	1,000	$33,211	$1,488

◆ **Exhibit 20.1:** **The world's top 1,000 banks by location, 1998**

◆ *Note*:   1   See chapter 17 for a definition of Tier I capital

◆ *Source*:   Author's calculations based on data from *The Banker*, July 1998, p. 122.

	Among top 1,000, percentage of:		
Banks in	*Institutions*	*Assets*	*Capital*
European Union	33%	44%	39%
Asia	28	31	28
United States	15	12	18

Because the most significant banking activity occurs in these regions, the commercial banks of the United States, the United Kingdom, Canada (with its close proximity to the United States), Germany, France, Switzerland, and Japan are discussed in this chapter. In each case, commercial bank development and industry structure are analyzed.

1.1 UNITED STATES

The United States has a large number of both state-chartered and national commercial banks. While New York is often described as the US money center because the country's largest banks are headquartered there, the structure of the US banking system has historically been a diverse collection of institutions with limited geographical service areas. Among industrialized countries, the United States is unusual in this regard. Even regional banks in other countries often constitute a strong system of institutions that branch nationwide. (See chapter 25 for a discussion of the Riegle–Neal Act and nationwide banking in the United States.) In addition, commercial banks in other countries typically have had a wider range of permissible activities in the securities industry. (See also chapter 21 for a discussion of domestic operations and chapter 24 for coverage of commercial bank involvement in the securities markets.)

Exhibit 20.2 shows the growth of US bank assets from 1981 through 1994. In 1981, US bank assets totaled $2 trillion. By 1989, the total stood at $3.3 trillion, representing an annual increase of 6.2 percent. The assets of commercial banks expanded rapidly during the 1980s because of a general expansion in the US money supply. Capital levels, however, did not keep pace and, by the early 1990s, expansion of bank assets slowed as bank regulators placed more emphasis on building

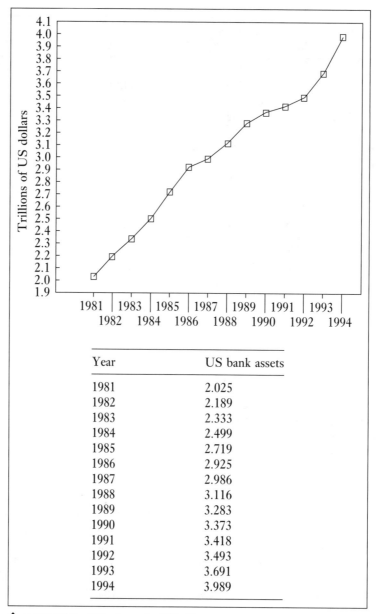

Year	US bank assets
1981	2.025
1982	2.189
1983	2.333
1984	2.499
1985	2.719
1986	2.925
1987	2.986
1988	3.116
1989	3.283
1990	3.373
1991	3.418
1992	3.493
1993	3.691
1994	3.989

◆ **Exhibit 20.2: US bank assets, 1981–94**

◆ *Sources*: Author's calculations and graphic based on data from: *Bank Profitability: Statistical Supplement; Financial Statements of Banks 1981–9* and *Bank Profitability: Financial Statements of Banks 1985–94*, Organization for Economic Cooperation and Development, 1991 and 1996. *International Financial Statistics*, International Monetary Fund, various issues.

Rank	US bank	Capital ($ million)
1	Chase Manhattan Corp. (New York, NY)	$22,594
2	Citicorp (New York, NY)[1]	21,211
3	BankAmerica Corp. (San Francisco, CA)	17,292
4	NationsBank (Charlotte, NC)	13,599
5	J. P. Morgan & Co. (New York, NY)11	11,854
6	First Union Corp. (Charlotte, NC)[2]	10,203
7	Banc One Corp. (Columbus, OH)	8,909
8	First Chicago NBD Corp. (Chicago, IL)	8,540
9	Bankers Trust New York Corp. (New York, NY)	6,431
10	Fleet Financial (Providence, RI)	6,159
11	Wells Fargo & Co. (San Francisco, CA)	6,126
12	Norwest Corp. (Minneapolis, MN)	5,498
13	Wachovia Corporation (Winston Salem, NC)	5,469
14	PNC Corp. (Pittsburgh, PA)	5,108
15	US Bancorp (Minneapolis, MN)	5,028
16	BankBoston (Boston, MA)	4,971
17	Bank of New York (New York, NY)	4,507
18	KeyCorp (Albany, NY)	4,504
19	National City Corp. (Cleveland, OH)	4,095
20	CoreStates Financial (Philadelphia, PA)	3,757

♦ **Exhibit 20.3: Top 20 US banks ranked by Tier I capital, 1998**

♦ *Notes*: 1 Merger with Travelers Group announced in 1998
2 First Union acquired CoreStates Financial in April 1998

Capital is as of December 31, 1997.

♦ *Source*: *The Banker*, July 1998.

capital levels, a policy position observed in many industrialized countries. (See chapter 17 for a discussion of the Basle Accord on international capital standards.) From 1989 to 1992, assets increased from $3.3 trillion to $3.5 trillion – only 2 percent per year. By 1993, capital levels had improved and a low interest rate environment provided banks with low-cost funds, gains on government securities holdings, and strong profits, with industry return on assets exceeding 1 percent for the first time in recent history. (See chapter 15 for an analysis of bank profitability and Exhibit 15.7 for ROA statistics.) As a result, industry assets also grew from $3.5 trillion in 1992 to $4.0 trillion in 1994 – an average of 6.9 percent per year. Exhibit 20.3 shows the top 20 US banks ranked by capital ratio in 1998.

1.2 THE UNITED KINGDOM

The center of the UK financial system is London. In fact, prior to 1914, London was recognized as the world's center for international finance. The pound sterling was the major currency of the world because London has historically provided significant amounts of long-term investment capital and short-term trade finance. Furthermore, the government of the United Kingdom has a long tradition of facilitating domestic and international trade.

Clearing banks in the United Kingdom perform the same functions as commercial banks in the United States. In particular, clearing banks provide the nation's primary payments mechanism (checks and other forms of payment) and short-term liquidity to industrial firms through extensive overdrafts.

Overdraft:
> A check written for which there are insufficient funds but which the bank honors, effectively granting the check writer a short-term loan.

Unlike US banks, British clearing banks have always branched nationwide. This system has resulted in a relatively small number of clearing banks that process 80 percent of all check and credit card transactions. Among these, the largest are HSBC Holdings (holding company that owns Midland Bank), Barclays, National Westminster, and Lloyds.

Secondary banks, also known as merchant banks, offer primarily time, rather than demand, deposits. (See chapter 5 for a discussion of merchant banks.) Competition among secondary banks is aggressive and the banks use interest rates to attract large, wholesale deposits. To match the average maturity of deposits and loans, secondary banks generally make longer-term loans, frequently to non British enterprises.

Exhibit 20.4 shows the growth in assets of the 47 clearing and secondary banks in the United Kingdom. From slightly over $300 billion in 1981, the total assets of UK banks increased at an average rate of 11 percent per year to reach $731 billion by 1989. The significant increase in UK bank assets in US dollar terms in 1990 is primarily attributable to the appreciation of the British currency. (See chapter 11, Exhibit 11.3.) By 1994, UK had reached $1.1 trillion.

1.3 CANADA

The Canadian banking system is a blend of the US and UK systems. Structurally, it resembles the UK system in that banks branch nationwide, but its monetary policy implementation is similar to that of the United States with the Canadian central bank having direct relations with the commercial banks.

Generally, there has been a good relationship between government and the banking industry. Canadian banks have been permitted to expand lending powers as desired and have enjoyed virtually complete freedom to offer a variety of deposits. This contrasts with the US experience in which expansion of banking powers has been permitted primarily by bank regulators rather than by legislators because of the reluctance of legislators to pass further bank liberalization laws.

The Canadian equivalent of commercial banks is *chartered banks*. Between 1820 and 1970, 157 charters were granted. Sixty of these, however, were never used; 45 banks either failed or ceased operation for some other reason, and there were a number of bank mergers. These factors have caused the number of Canadian banks to be much smaller than the number of US banks. Five chartered banks control roughly 90 percent of Canadian bank assets: the Royal Bank of Canada, Canadian Imperial Bank of Commerce, the Bank of Nova Scotia, the Bank of Montreal, and Toronto-Dominion Bank. Unlike US money-center banks, these five operate branching networks throughout Canada, a practice prohibited for US banks until recently.

Exhibit 20.5 shows total Canadian bank assets in US dollars from 1981 through 1994, over which period assets increased from $281 billion to $516 billion. On average, the increase in assets

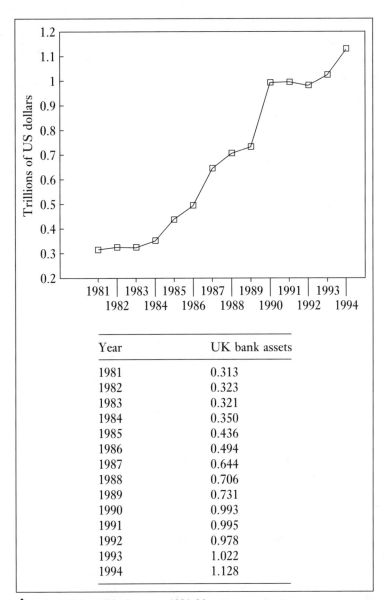

Year	UK bank assets
1981	0.313
1982	0.323
1983	0.321
1984	0.350
1985	0.436
1986	0.494
1987	0.644
1988	0.706
1989	0.731
1990	0.993
1991	0.995
1992	0.978
1993	1.022
1994	1.128

◆ **Exhibit 20.4: UK bank assets, 1981–94**

◆ *Sources*:   Author's calculations and graphic based on data from: *Bank Profitability: Statistical Supplement; Financial Statements of Banks 1981–9* and *Bank Profitability: Financial Statements of Banks 1985–94*, Organization for Economic Cooperation and Development, 1991 and 1996. *International Financial Statistics*, International Monetary Fund, various issues.

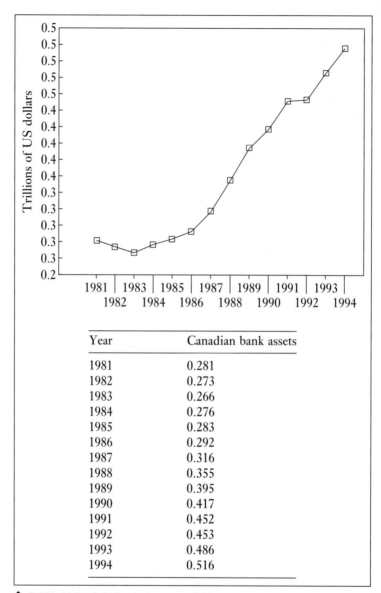

Year	Canadian bank assets
1981	0.281
1982	0.273
1983	0.266
1984	0.276
1985	0.283
1986	0.292
1987	0.316
1988	0.355
1989	0.395
1990	0.417
1991	0.452
1992	0.453
1993	0.486
1994	0.516

◆ **Exhibit 20.5:** Canadian bank assets, 1981–94

◆ *Sources*: Author's calculations and graphic based on data from: *Bank Profitability: Statistical Supplement; Financial Statements of Banks 1981–9* and *Bank Profitability: Financial Statements of Banks 1985–94*, Organization for Economic Cooperation and Development, 1991 and 1996. *International Financial Statistics*, International Monetary Fund, various issues.

was 4.8 percent per year. The slump in growth in the early 1980s is attributable primarily to the strength of the US dollar versus the Canadian dollar at that time.

1.4 GERMANY

Commercial banks in Germany have even greater operational freedom than Canadian banks. Individual states in Germany have a long history of regional strength and independence from the central government, resulting in several cities with significant economic influence. Hamburg is the country's largest city and busiest port; Dusseldorf is a major manufacturing site; and Frankfurt is the financial center. In this respect, German banking is comparable to US banking, with a large number of state and regional banks.

In contrast to the US system, however, German banking authorities do not restrict the scope of bank activities. German banks offer corporate underwriting services and hold the common stock of their clients as investments. Because of this wide range of bank services, German banks are called *universal* banks. The German banking system has operated in this way since shortly after the Second World War (1939–45).

In addition to the state and regional banks, there are three big banks in Germany – Deutsche Bank, Dresdner Bank, and Commerzbank. In 1994, these banks controlled 45 percent of all German commercial bank assets and 50 percent of bank branches. Like Canadian banks, the "big three" German banks operate nationwide.

Exhibit 20.6 shows the strong growth in total German banking assets. From $271 billion in 1981, total assets increased at an annual rate of 12 percent annually to reach $1.236 trillion in 1994. Part of this is attributable to the depreciation of the US dollar after 1984, but even in marks, assets of German banks increased at an average rate of 9 percent per year over the 13-year period.

1.5 FRANCE

Prior to the First World War, Paris was second only to London as an international financial center. The Banking Law of 1984 embraced the concept of universality (as in Germany), removing all distinctions among bank categories. A new designation – *établissement de crédit* – was applied and broad bank functions were defined. French banks offer a full line of financial services, including short- and medium-term loans, demand and time deposits, and securities dealing and underwriting.

Like Germany, France has a number of large banks that dominate the industry. The top five French banks controlled 82 percent of all French commercial bank deposits in 1994. The largest French banks are Crédit Agricole, Banque Paribas, Banque Nationale de Paris, Société Générale, and Crédit Lyonnais.

Exhibit 20.7 shows asset growth of the five big banks of France. Assets of these French banks increased at an average rate of 8.6 percent from $410 billion in 1981 to $1.2 trillion in 1994. (Fluctuations in the value of the French franc played little role in the increase, as there was an 8 percent increase in French bank assets in franc terms over the same period.)

1.6 SWITZERLAND

Swiss commercial banks operate in an environment of privacy that is unmatched in the rest of the world. The 1934 Banking Law, the country's first federal banking law, contained provisions that protected depositors in Swiss banks. Banks are prohibited from revealing details of financial

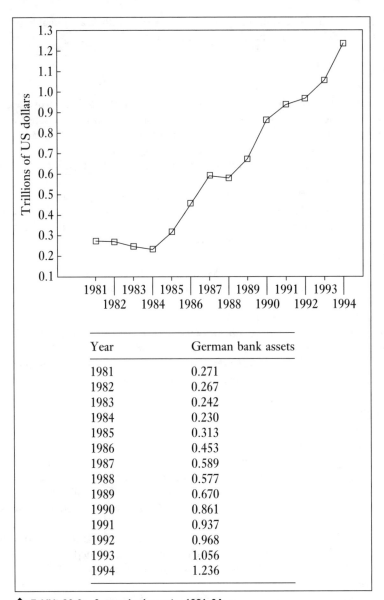

Year	German bank assets
1981	0.271
1982	0.267
1983	0.242
1984	0.230
1985	0.313
1986	0.453
1987	0.589
1988	0.577
1989	0.670
1990	0.861
1991	0.937
1992	0.968
1993	1.056
1994	1.236

◆ **Exhibit 20.6:** German bank assets, 1981–94

◆ *Sources*:   Author's calculations and graphic based on data from: *Bank Profitability: Statistical Supplement; Financial Statements of Banks 1981–9* and *Bank Profitability: Financial Statements of Banks 1985–94*, Organization for Economic Cooperation and Development, 1991 and 1996. *International Financial Statistics*, International Monetary Fund, various issues.

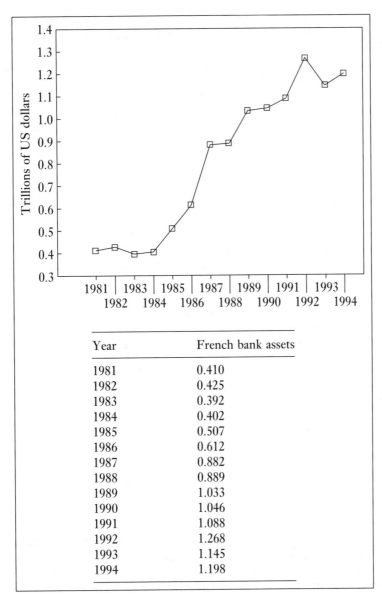

Year	French bank assets
1981	0.410
1982	0.425
1983	0.392
1984	0.402
1985	0.507
1986	0.612
1987	0.882
1988	0.889
1989	1.033
1990	1.046
1991	1.088
1992	1.268
1993	1.145
1994	1.198

◆ **Exhibit 20.7: French bank assets, 1981–94**

◆ *Sources*: Author's calculations and graphic based on data from: *Bank Profitability: Statistical Supplement; Financial Statements of Banks 1981–9* and *Bank Profitability: Financial Statements of Banks 1985–94*, Organization for Economic Cooperation and Development, 1991 and 1996. *International Financial Statistics*, International Monetary Fund, various issues.

transactions to outsiders unless an illegal act, according to Swiss law, is involved. This secrecy provision was partially motivated by attempts of agents of Nazi Germany to determine the nature and amount of Swiss deposits owned by German citizens. The bank secrecy law protected private citizens from the whims of government by allowing depositors to use accounts identified with numbers only, the so-called "numbered accounts," and by preventing transactions disclosure.

Switzerland has had a favorable financial climate for other reasons. The Swiss people themselves have long been ardent savers, with the result that the country has consistently been a net exporter of capital. Consistent with its respect for privacy, Switzerland has remained politically neutral, avoiding burdensome expenses of war. Stability of the Swiss franc and the Swiss banking system after the First World War contributed to its reputation as a safe haven for funds. As a result, during the 1920s and 1930s, the country's commercial banks received large deposits, primarily from Germany.

Over time, Switzerland's economic stability, political neutrality, and bank secrecy law have attracted capital worldwide. Foreign banks have likewise been attracted to Switzerland's stable financial markets.

Like German banks, the major banks in Switzerland are also universal banks. In 1994, the four largest institutions controlled 58 percent of Swiss commercial bank assets. The "big three" are Union Bank of Switzerland, Credit Suisse Group, and the Swiss Bank Corporation. (In late 1997, Union Bank of Switzerland and Swiss Bank Corporation announced their intentions to merge.) As compared to even German and French banks, Swiss banks are more involved in capital markets and equity investments in industrial firms.

Cantonal banks are publicly owned and restricted to the geographical areas in which they are located. While these 27 institutions are considered banks, they tend to specialize in savings deposits and mortgage loans. Controlling 24 percent of bank assets in 1994, cantonal banks are the second most important group of banks. Zürchur Kantonalbank is one of the four large banks in Switzerland, is authorized to conduct business internationally, and is quite active in international markets.

Exhibit 20.8 shows the assets of big banks and cantonal banks from 1981 through 1994. Growing at an average rate of 9 percent a year, Swiss bank assets totaled $672 billion by 1994. The volatility of asset growth is attributable to the volatility of the Swiss franc. In Swiss franc terms, Swiss bank assets grew at the average rate of 6.4 percent per year. (See also Exhibit 20.9.)

1.7 JAPAN

Japan accounts for many of the world's largest banks primarily because of its large trade surpluses and strengthening of the Japanese yen over time. Japanese banks are either *city banks* or *regional banks*. City banks are large, nationwide organizations that target major industrial firms, while regional banks cater to the needs of smaller businesses and individuals. The activities of regional banks are typically limited to one prefecture or state.

Prior to the Second World War (1939–45), Japanese banks were often members of large industrial combinations called *zaibatsu*. Through this mechanism, strong ties between banks and industrial firms were formed with the largest *zaibatsu* banks, Sumitomo, Mitsui, and Mitsubishi being particularly instrumental in Japan's economic development.

After the Second World War, *zaibatsu* were dismantled and *keiretsu*, or industrial groups with interlocking ownership, formed. (See also chapter 14 for a discussion of *zaibatsu and keiretsu*.) Former *zaibatsu* banks still provided the majority of debt financing to their *keiretsu* affiliates. Although the regional banks channeled their savings deposits to the *keiretsu* city banks through interbank loans, until the 1970s city banks were consistently overloaned.

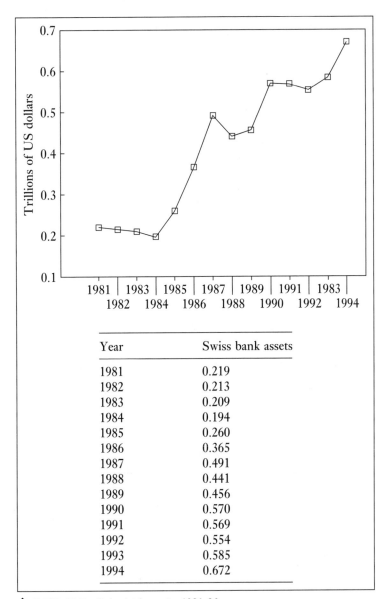

Year	Swiss bank assets
1981	0.219
1982	0.213
1983	0.209
1984	0.194
1985	0.260
1986	0.365
1987	0.491
1988	0.441
1989	0.456
1990	0.570
1991	0.569
1992	0.554
1993	0.585
1994	0.672

◆ **Exhibit 20.8: Swiss bank assets, 1981–94**

◆ *Sources*: Author's calculations and graphic based on data from: *Bank Profitability: Statistical Supplement; Financial Statements of Banks 1981–9* and *Bank Profitability: Financial Statements of Banks 1985–94*, Organization for Economic Cooperation and Development, 1991 and 1996. *International Financial Statistics*, International Monetary Fund, various issues.

Rank by capital	European bank	Capital ($ million)
1	HSBC Holdings (London, UK)	$27,392
2	Crédit Agricole (Paris, France)	22,280
3	Deutsche Bank (Frankfurt, Germany)	17,371
4	ABN-Amro Bank (Amsterdam, Netherlands)	15,864
5	Union Bank of Switzerland (Zurich, Switzerland)[1]	13,570
6	Barclays Bank (London, UK)	13,020
7	Credit Suisse Group (Zurich, Switzerland)	12,984
8	Rabobank Nederland (Utrecht, Netherlands)	12,680
9	National Westminster Bank (London, UK)	12,342
10	Halifax (West Yorkshire, UK)	11,955

Rank by assets	European bank	Assets ($ million)
1	Deutsche Bank (Frankfurt, Germany)	$581,979
2	Credit Suisse Group (Zurich, Switzerland)	473,832
3	HSBC Holdings (London, UK)	473,608
4	Société Générale (Paris, France)	441,115
5	Crédit Agricole (Paris, France)	419,980
6	ABN-Amro Bank (Amsterdam, Netherlands)	414,654
7	Union Bank of Switzerland (Zurich, Switzerland)[1]	396,878
8	Barclays Bank (London, UK)	388,055
9	Dresdner Bank (Frankfurt, Germany)	372,594
10	Banque Nationale de Paris (Paris, France)	339,819

◆ **Exhibit 20.9: Europe's top 10 banks ranked by capital and asset size, 1998**

◆ *Notes*:   1   In late 1997, Union Bank of Switzerland and Swiss Bank Corporation announced that they would merge. This merger creates an institution with capital of $20 billion and assets of $698 billion.

Assets and capital are as of December 31, 1997.

◆ *Source*:   *The Banker*, July 1998.

Overlending:
      The situation in which a bank's loan demand consistently exceeds available deposits and capital.

The Bank of Japan relieved the overlending by making loans to the city banks. The Bank of Japan encouraged loans to high priority industries by offering its loans to city banks at favorable interest rates, which were then reflected in favorable interest rates to industrial firms. Overlending ended after the 1970s when Japan became a net capital exporter because of large trade surpluses. While industrial firms are now less dependent on their *keiretsu* banks, they still maintain close relationships.

City banks hold over 50 percent of total Japanese commercial bank assets and more than 20 percent of all bank offices. The largest include Bank of Tokyo–Mitsubishi, Sumitomo, Dai-Ichi Kangyo, Fuji, Sanwa, and Sakura.

Exhibit 20.10 illustrates the rapid growth of assets for all Japanese commercial banks. From a total of $1.2 trillion dollars in 1981 Japanese bank assets increased at the rate of 14 percent a year in dollar terms to reach $6.9 trillion in 1994, 1.7 times as large as the total assets of all US banks. Part of this increase is attributable to the appreciation of the Japanese yen. In yen terms, the Japanese banking system grew at almost 14 percent per year during the 1980s.

However, the real estate and stock market expansion of the 1980s came an abrupt end in the early 1990s and the banking system has become crippled by huge bad loan portfolios. As a result, Japanese banking assets (in yen terms) declined each year after 1989. Nevertheless, there is no question that Japanese trade surpluses and the strong yen have moved these banks to the forefront of international finance as indicated in Exhibit 20.11.

1.8 A Cross-country Comparison

When the banking system of the United States is compared to the systems in other industrialized countries, the contrasts are striking. Several points are clear:

- The amount of total assets in the US banking system is smaller than the Japanese but larger than the others in the comparison.
- The average bank size in the United States is smaller than in any other country analyzed.

1.8.1 TOTAL ASSETS

Exhibit 20.12 shows the relative proportions of bank assets in 1994 in the seven countries discussed above. Japanese bank assets alone are 44 percent of the total and the United States represents over 25 percent. The other shares range from 3.3 percent to 7.9 percent. Taken in the aggregate, the US banking system is the second largest banking system in the world.

1.8.2 AVERAGE SIZE

Even with a large share of total banking assets, US banks operate at a competitive disadvantage because their average size is so much smaller. Consider the following breakdown of average bank size for these countries in 1994.

	No. of banks	*Average assets ($ billions)*
United States	10,489	$0.38
United Kingdom	37	30.49
Canada	11	46.92
Germany	273	4.53
France	421	2.85
Switzerland	230	2.92
Japan	140	49.33

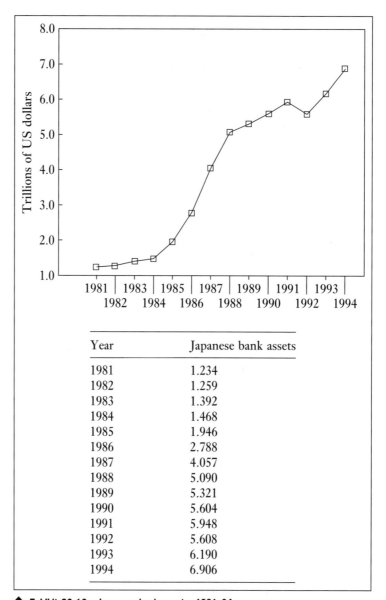

Year	Japanese bank assets
1981	1.234
1982	1.259
1983	1.392
1984	1.468
1985	1.946
1986	2.788
1987	4.057
1988	5.090
1989	5.321
1990	5.604
1991	5.948
1992	5.608
1993	6.190
1994	6.906

◆ **Exhibit 20.10: Japanese bank assets, 1981–94**

◆ *Sources*: Author's calculations and graphic based on data from: *Bank Profitability: Statistical Supplement; Financial Statements of Banks 1981–9* and *Bank Profitability: Financial Statements of Banks 1985–94*, Organization for Economic Cooperation and Development, 1991 and 1996. *International Financial Statistics*, International Monetary Fund, various issues.

Rank by capital	Bank	Capital ($ million)
1	HSBC Holdings (London, UK)	$27,392
2	Chase Manhattan Corp. (New York, NY)	22,594
3	Crédit Agricole (Paris, France)	22,280
4	Citicorp (New York, NY)	21,211
5	Bank of Tokyo-Mitsubishi (Tokyo, Japan)	18,585
6	Deutsche Bank (Frankfurt, Germany)	17,371
7	BankAmerica (San Francisco, CA)	17,292
8	ABN-AMRO Bank (Amsterdam, Netherlands)	15,864
9	Sumitomo Bank (Osaka, Japan)	14,757
10	Dai-Ichi Kangyo Bank (Tokyo, Japan)	14,458

Rank by assets	Bank	Assets ($ million)
1	Bank of Tokyo-Mitsubishi	$653,408
2	Deutsche Bank (Frankfurt, Germany)	581,979
3	Industrial & Commercial Bank of China (Beijing, China)	489,012
4	Credit Suisse Group (Zurich, Switzerland)	473,832
5	HSBC Holdings (London, UK)	473,608
6	Sumitomo Bank (Osaka, Japan)	468,962
7	Société Générale (Paris, France)	441,115
8	Crédit Agricole (Paris, France)	419,980
9	Dai-Ichi Kangyo Bank (Tokyo, Japan)	419,101
10	Sanwa Bank (Osaka, Japan)	415,887

♦ **Exhibit 20.11:** The world's top 10 banks ranked by capital and by asset size, 1998

♦ *Note*:   Assets and capital are as of December 31, 1997

♦ *Source*:   *The Banker*, July 1998.

The average size of US banks is much smaller than the average in the other countries shown. This significant size difference is important because a growing share of banks operating in the United States are foreign banks and compete directly with US domestic banks. To the extent that US banks are smaller and less able to offer a full range of services, domestic banks will continue to lose market share on their own turf. (See chapter 1 for a description of the increasing trend of foreign bank loans as a percentage of total bank loans in the United States.)

The size difference is important also because industrial firms operate increasingly in a global environment. The future international competitiveness of the United States will depend in large measure on the ability of small- and medium-size firms to sell their goods and services abroad. Just as the large *zaibatsu* banks helped Japanese industrial firms to compete and to expand internationally, so too US banks can assist US firms. However, this assistance might be limited by

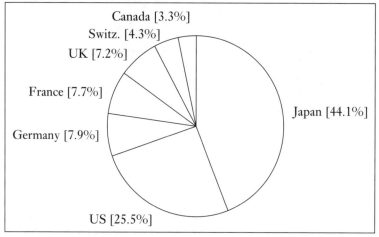

◆ **Exhibit 20.12:** **Bank assets of selected industrialized countries, 1994**

◆ *Sources*:   Author's calculations and graphic based on data from:
Bank Profitability: Financial Statements of Banks 1985–94,
Organization for Economic Cooperation and Development,
1996. *International Financial Statistics*, International Monetary
Fund, Yearbook 1996.

the size of the bank because a smaller bank's loan portfolio can more easily become overly concentrated in one industry. Furthermore, it is not certain that foreign banks will have the same kind of commitment to US firms that US banks have.

1.8.3 POPULATION PER BANK

The relative small size of US banks is not tied to the lack of banking assets in this country, but to the large number of banks. The number of banks in the United States is much greater than the other countries analyzed. Admittedly, the populations of these countries are smaller than the US population – but not so much as to reconcile the difference in number of banks. Exhibit 20.13 shows that the population per bank in the United States in 1994 was 25,000 people. This statistic indicates a relatively high number of banks – one bank for every 25,000 residents. Switzerland had the next smallest population per bank at 30,000. The United Kingdom had the highest such statistic – 1.568 million residents per bank or 63 times the US statistic.

Exhibit 20.13 also shows that availability of banking services has not necessarily been compromised by the smaller number of banks in other countries. The population per bank branch among the six countries shown is remarkably similar. In the United States, France, the United Kingdom, and Switzerland, the population per bank branch is between 4,500 and 6,000 people. In Japan and Germany, the number is no more than twice this level. Thus, the convenience and availability of banking services need not be compromised in a banking system of larger institutions.

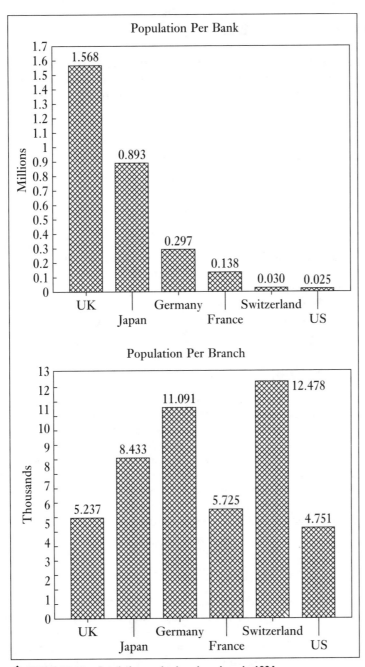

◆ **Exhibit 20.13:** **Population per bank and per branch, 1994**

◆ *Sources*: *Bank Profitability: Financial Statements of Banks 1985–94*, Organization for Economic Cooperation and Development, 1996. *International Financial Statistics*, International Monetary Fund, Yearbook 1996.

Noncommercial Banks

Commercial banks perform intermediation functions that are vital to an individual country's economic growth and development. In an international context, there are banks that focus on the development and economic coordination of a number of countries. Three examples of such banks are:

- The Bank for International Settlements
- The International Monetary Fund
- The World Bank

2.1 BANK FOR INTERNATIONAL SETTLEMENTS

The Bank for International Settlements (BIS) in Basle, Switzerland, is a central bank for central banks. It is technically a commercial bank with a Swiss license, but has immunity from government interference in its operations through an international treaty. Its depositors are central bankers, who meet privately ten times a year to discuss monetary issues and policies in the major industrialized countries of the world. The Committee on Banking Regulations and Supervisory Practices of the BIS issued the recommendation for international coordination of capital standards that was implemented in 1993.

2.1.1 ORIGIN AND OBJECTIVES

There had been little coordination among central banks prior to 1914. After the First World War (1914–18), however, central banks began to work together on an ad-hoc (as needed) basis to stabilize the value of major currencies and to make settlements of payments used for post-war reconstruction. Also, the war reparations of Germany were transformed into less political payments through the Young Plan of 1929, which specified that Germany would make loans abroad to satisfy its remaining obligation. The loans would be repaid over a period of time on a normal commercial loan basis. An official bank was needed to channel these loans and to accept the repayments.

To accommodate these needs, the Bank for International Settlements was organized in 1930. Thus, the first role of the BIS was as agent for the Young Plan to handle the German war reparations.

2.1.2 STRUCTURE AND MEMBERSHIP

The BIS was established as a commercial bank with special international recognition. This form prevented the Bank from being subjected to political forces and allowed it to maintain its independence. The original shareholders of the bank were the central banks of Belgium, France, Germany, Great Britain, Italy, and Japan, and a financial group from the United States that was composed of J. P. Morgan and Company, First National Bank of the city of New York (now Citibank), and First National Bank of Chicago. Belgium, France, Germany, Italy, and the United Kingdom hold over 50 percent of the outstanding shares.

The US allocation of shares was sold to the public, but Citibank of New York is designated to exercise the voting rights of these shares. The Federal Reserve System did not purchase shares because it wanted to avoid any conflict of interest that may result from owning a private bank, but the Fed does participate actively as a member of BIS committees. Almost all European central banks, as well as those of the United States, Canada, Japan, Australia, and South Africa, participate in, or are closely associated with, the activities of the BIS.

The BIS can perform almost any financial service for central banks. Deposits of gold, currency, and securities are held at the central banks that are its correspondent banks. The Federal Reserve Bank of New York is the correspondent for the BIS in the United States market. Also, since 1986, the BIS has performed the functions of agent for the private European Currency Unit (Ecu) clearing system.

However, the BIS must not create money in the way that a conventional bank might nor act in the capacity of an industrial financier. It is also not permitted to directly finance government operations or to facilitate government payments except in special cases of international settlements.

2.1.3 OPERATIONS

Although the BIS followed the guidelines of its original mission, questions arose as to the role of the Bank in its dealings with the German central bank during the Second World War. Prior to the war, the customary practice was that European countries paid interest on the Young Plan loans by making deposits in the BIS to be transferred to Germany's account. The allegations of wrongdoing involve a suspected pro-German sentiment on the part of the BIS and knowing acceptance by BIS of looted gold from countries that Germany occupied, gold that had been stolen rather than being paid in the normal course of business.

After the war, the origins of all such gold transfers were investigated. The amount of gold illegally transferred was identified as 3,740 kilograms or 120,244 troy ounces, valued at $4.2 million at that time or $36 million at today's price. (At the time, gold was valued at $35 per ounce; today the price is closer to $300 per ounce.) Because of this controversy, the United States advocated disbanding the BIS but Western European governments did not agree. The BIS made the gold available to the countries from which it had been illegally seized and then resumed operations as before the war. The stigma of this episode, however, stayed with the BIS and prevented it from being accepted as a dominant international financial institution.

Despite reservations about the operations of the BIS on the part of the Treasuries of Western governments, the central banks of the same countries have consistently used the BIS as a forum to resolve issues concerning the world's money supply, currency values, and interest rates. At their meetings in Basle, held once a month for ten months of the year, the central bankers exchange information on their countries' problems and the international monetary situation. A central bank governor who is contemplating a policy change can discuss it confidentially with the others and get their reaction to it. The meetings are essentially free of formal documentation either public or private. Instead, "gentlemen's agreements" are reached and each is bound by his word to the others.

On a daily basis, the foreign exchange officers of central banks and BIS officers communicate in multilateral conversations via telephone to discuss the currency markets. The BIS provides the central banks with a cloak of anonymity in that their deposits are pooled and then invested in currencies and loans on behalf of the BIS without any particular national identity being associated with them.

2.2 INTERNATIONAL MONETARY FUND

The International Monetary Fund (IMF) is an organization conceived by the Treasuries of the United States and the United Kingdom during the Second World War. The objectives were to assure free convertibility of currencies in trade and to avoid currency devaluations (to make exports more price competitive) that brought chaos to currency markets. While the Bank for International Settlements was formed by central banks, the International Monetary Fund was formed through the cooperation of national Treasuries.

2.2.1 OBJECTIVES

The fund was to involve a finite pool of funds that could be drawn upon by countries experiencing balance of payments deficits, that is, imports in excess of exports. The assets of the fund would be composed of gold and currencies. Each member country would contribute a specified amount of its own currency and gold, to be determined based on that country's general economic strength. Forty-four countries reached agreement in 1944 at Bretton Woods, New Hampshire to create the International Monetary Fund. There are now over 150 members.

The IMF seeks to help member countries manage their external trade situation. With resources available to cover balance of payments deficits and assistance to correct these imbalances, member countries could avoid international monetary crises.

2.2.2 STRUCTURE AND QUOTAS

The IMF is composed of two main departments: the General Department and the Special Drawing Rights (SDR) Department. The SDR is the first reserve asset (that is, money) to be created by international decision. Membership in the IMF confers the right to participate in the SDR Department.

Within the General Department, each member has a General Resource Account (GRA). Each member deposits in its GRA the *quota* that it is assessed. The sum of these quotas forms the pool of funds available to members as needed. A country's quota is based on several economic factors, including gross domestic product, international reserves (gold and foreign exchange), international payments and receipts, and the variability of international payments.

Quota (IMF):
> The minimum subscription (contribution) that a country must pay in order to become a member of the International Monetary Fund.

A member satisfies its quota subscription by depositing (1) freely usable (convertible) currencies and/or SDRs and (2) its own currency. At least 25 percent of the subscription must be in freely usable currencies and/or SDRs, on which the IMF pays remuneration or interest. Quotas are reviewed at least once every five years.

The aggregate of quota subscriptions is available to other members as needed. When a member experiences a balance of payments deficit, it essentially faces a shortage of currencies other than its own. It may then tap the resources of the IMF, with the first resource being its *reserve tranche*. When a country first joins the IMF, its reserve tranche is 25 percent of the quota, that is, the portion contributed in SDRs and other freely usable currencies. A member can use its reserve tranche to satisfy a balance of payments deficit by exchanging its own currency for the freely usable currencies. There is no obligation to reverse this transaction, that is, to repurchase its own currency because the reserve tranche is considered the member's own international liquidity.

> **Reserve tranche (IMF):**
> The excess of a country's quota over the holdings by the International Monetary Fund of its own currency.

If the reserve tranche is insufficient to satisfy the need, *credit tranches* may be obtained. These tranches are denominated in four increments, each equal to one quarter of the member's quota. As long as the member is making efforts to correct its balance of payments deficit, the first tranche is liberally available and subject to few terms and conditions other than repurchase, that is, repayment of the loan. Subsequent tranches, called *upper credit tranches*, are subject to increased scrutiny and conditionality. The IMF has also instituted a number of special programs to assist members that find themselves in chronic balance of payments difficulties.

2.2.3 SPECIAL DRAWING RIGHTS

SDRs are a form of money created by the IMF that may be used only by monetary authorities and other official agencies. A member obtains SDRs by participating in the SDR Department and SDRs allocated to the member entitle it to obtain freely usable currencies from other IMF members. A participant in the SDR Department agrees to accept SDRs from any other participant designated by the IMF and to provide the designated participant with an equivalent amount of freely usable currency. The allocation of SDRs is in proportion to a member's quota. The IMF may periodically add to or subtract from the SDRs outstanding depending upon economic conditions.

The value of the SDR is tied to the value of specified units of five major currencies. Currently the currencies and units are:

Currency	*No. of units*
US dollar	0.582
Euro (Germany)	0.228
Japanese yen	27.2
Euro (France)	0.1239
British pound	0.105

The components of the SDR are determined once every five years. These five countries had the largest amount of exports among IMF members from 1991 through 1995 and the units reflect the relative magnitude of their exports. The value of the SDR will be determined by the above-mentioned units of these currencies for the period 1996 through 2000. In mid-1999, the dollar value of the SDR was $1.33.

2.2.4 BALANCE SHEET

Exhibit 20.14 shows the balance sheet of the General Department of the IMF for fiscal 1998. Assets totaled SDR 152 billion, with 95 percent invested in currencies and securities. SDR holdings, gold, loans, and receivables are the other major categories. The liabilities of the IMF are primarily member quotas which constitute almost 96 percent of the total.

	Millions of SDRs	%
Assets		
Currencies and securities	SDR144,639	95.3%
SDR holdings	764	0.5
Gold holdings	3,625	2.4
Structural adjustment loans	928	0.6
Receivables[1]	1,586	1.0
Other	264	0.2
	SDR151,806	100.0%
Liabilities		
Quotas	SDR145,321	95.7%
Reserves	4,940	3.3
Unearned income	923	0.6
Payables[2]	434	0.3
Other	188	0.1
	SDR151,806	100.0%

◆ **Exhibit 20.14:** **International Monetary Fund balance sheet, 1998**

◆ *Notes*:   1   Interest income
            2   Interest expense

Balance sheet date is April 30, 1998, at which time the dollar value of an SDR was approximately SDR1 = $1.35.

◆ *Source*:   Author's calculations based on data from *International Monetary Fund 1998 Annual Report*.

2.3 THE WORLD BANK GROUP

The World Bank Group is composed of four affiliates:

- The International Bank for Reconstruction and Development (IBRD, also frequently called the World Bank)
- The International Development Association (IDA)
- The International Finance Corporation (IFC)
- The Multilateral Investment Guarantee Agency (MIGA)

The common objective of all these organizations is to help raise the standard of living in developing countries by channeling financial resources from developed countries to developing regions.

2.3.1 INTERNATIONAL BANK FOR RECONSTRUCTION AND DEVELOPMENT

The IBRD or World Bank was created at the same time as the IMF during the Bretton Woods conference in 1944. While the IMF concentrates primarily on short-term financial difficulties, the World Bank is concerned with long-term development. The two organizations generally hold their annual meetings jointly, and a prerequisite for membership in the World Bank is membership in the IMF. Currently there are over 150 World Bank members.

According to its charter, the World Bank must lend for productive purposes and must stimulate economic growth in the developing countries in which it lends. World Bank loans must be made to governments with all due consideration to assure repayment and be guaranteed by that government. In this way, IBRD loans are not considered concessional loans, that is, containing some form of grant assistance. The loans are generally repayable in 15 to 20 years and the purposes for the loans include:

- agriculture and rural development
- education
- energy
- education
- transportation
- urban development

Exhibit 20.15 shows the balance sheet of the World Bank in 1998. Of the total $205 billion in assets, $103 billion, or 50 percent, was devoted to loans to member countries. Bank capital was 13 percent of total liabilities and capital. Medium- and long-term borrowings constituted 47 percent. Unlike the IMF which is funded primarily through member quotas, or contributions, the IBRD issues debt instruments in money and capital markets to fund the largest share of its loans to member countries.

In fact, the World Bank has been at the forefront of innovation in the international bond markets. In 1993, the World Bank was the first issuer to float a *global bond*. The World Bank is a seasoned participant in international financial markets.

Global bond:
An international bond issued in the Eurobond and Yankee bond (US) markets simultaneously. The Yankee bond tranche is issued under full SEC registration.

2.3.2 INTERNATIONAL DEVELOPMENT ASSOCIATION

The International Development Association (IDA) is the concessional affiliate of the World Bank Group. Its loans, for similar purposes as IBRD loans, are made to the poorest member countries – those not able to qualify for IBRD loans. The wealthier members contribute to IDA, which then makes interest-free loans, called credits, repayable in 35 to 40 years.

Exhibit 20.16 shows the breakdown of external debt to developing countries by region in 1994. While the amount of external debt varies, the contribution of the IBRD and IDA has been significant in each case. Between 5 percent and 8 percent of total financing for developing countries in Europe and Central Asia; Latin America; and North Africa and the Middle East has been derived from these organizations. East Asia (11 percent), Sub-Saharan Africa (20 percent), and South Asia (30 percent) have depended on the World Bank and IDA for even more of their external financing. Both organizations perform an extremely important function in terms of development assistance in the countries that are recipients of their services.

	US dollars (millions)	%
Assets		
Cash: Due from banks	$767	0.4%
Government securities	27,413	13.4
Other investments[1]	466	0.2
Receivables[2]	70,973	34.6
Loans	103,336	50.4
Other	2,016	1.0
Total assets	$204,971	100.0%
Liabilities and capital Liabilities		
Payables[3]	$72,878	35.5%
Short-term borrowings	6,729	3.3
Medium- and long-term borrowings	96,860	47.3
Other liabilities	1,990	1.0
Total liabilities	178,457	87.1
Capital		
Capital stock	11,288	5.5
Reserves[4]	<1,507>	<0.8>
Retained earnings	16,733	8.2
Total capital	26,514	12.9
Total liabilities and capital	$204,971	100.0%

◆ **Exhibit 20.15:** **World Bank balance sheet, 1998**

◆ *Notes*:   1   Securities purchased under resale agreements.
2   Currency swaps, securities sold, accrued interest income on loans and securities, demand obligations for subscribed capital.
3   Currency swaps, securities purchased, accrued interest expense on borrowings.
4   Primarily cumulative foreign currency translation adjustment.

Balance sheet date is June 30, 1998.

◆ *Source*:   Author's calculations based on *The World Bank Annual Report 1998*.

2.3.3 INTERNATIONAL FINANCE CORPORATION

The International Finance Corporation (IFC) makes private sector investments, rather than loans to governments. It was established in 1956 and its capital is provided by 170 member countries.

The operations of the IFC are unique within the World Bank group with respect to its assistance in development of financial markets. The organization advises governments on the fiscal, legal, and regulatory frameworks that are required for healthy, market-oriented financial sectors. When it gives financial and technical assistance to local financial institutions, it is often the first such assistance in the host country. The IFC attracts international investors to host country securities markets by sponsoring, underwriting, and distributing the shares of both individual host country companies and funds that invest in host country securities.

Like IBRD, IFC relies heavily on capital markets for its funding. Also, the IFC has been an aggressive participant in the privatization initiatives launched by many developing countries to

	Sub-saharan Africa	East Asia and Pacific	Europe & Central Asia	Latin America	North Africa & Middle East	South Asia
Total ($ mil.)	$165,048	$327,993	$283,346	$443,649	$159,394	$143,140
Official creditors:						
Concessional credit:						
IDA	15.2%	2.7%	0.1%	0.4%	1.2%	19.9%
Other	27.8	29.6	10.1	12.9	32.6	44.7
Nonconcessional credit:						
IBRD	4.9	8.7	5.0	8.0	6.3	9.9
Other	28.0	8.6	26.8	17.4	21.6	5.1
Total Official	75.9	49.6	42.0	38.7	61.7	79.6
Private creditors:						
Bonds	1.8	15.0	21.1	42.1	0.8	3.8
Commercial banks	10.4	23.5	22.9	16.2	12.8	13.9
Other	11.9	11.9	14.0	3.0	24.7	2.7
Total private	24.1	50.4	58.0	61.3	38.3	20.4
Grand total	100.0%	100.0%	100.0%	100.0%	100.0%	100.0%

◆ **Exhibit 20.16: Developing country external debt by region, 1994**

◆ *Source:* *World Bank Debt Tables 1994: External Debt of Developing Countries,* 1996.

transfer control of state-owned enterprises to the private sector. (See also chapter 5 for a discussion of privatization.)

2.3.4 MULTILATERAL INVESTMENT GUARANTEE AGENCY

The Multilateral Investment Guarantee Agency (MIGA) is the newest member of the World Bank Group, beginning operations in 1988. MIGA was formed by 42 World Bank member countries but membership had expanded to 158 members by the late 1990s. MIGA guarantees foreign investors against the risk associated with noncommercial risk and, in conjunction with the International Finance Corporation, provides policy and advisory services to promote the flow of foreign investments to developing countries and to assist developing countries in creating an attractive and hospitable investment climate.

The Guarantee Program provides insurance protection for foreign investors that might otherwise avoid long-term commitments in developing countries because of perceived political risks. MIGA guarantees projects against specific risks for typically a 15-year period. Guarantees are provided against *currency transfer risk*, that is, the risk that conditions for converting and repatriating currency (transferring it to home country of foreign investor) will deteriorate. Investors are also protected against *expropriation risk*, or the risk of being unwillingly deprived of the investment or the benefits from the investment. *Risk of war, revolution, and civil disturbance* is covered in that the investor will be compensated for loss of physical assets and business interruption from a military action or civil disturbance in the host country. If the host country denies the investor justice in contractual matters, the investor will be compensated under the *breach of contract* coverage.

MIGA may insure:

- For equity investments, up to 90 percent of the investment contribution, plus an additional 450 percent of the investment contribution to cover earnings attributable to the investment.
- For loans and loan guarantees, up to 90 percent of the principal amount, plus an additional 135 percent of the principal to cover interest that will accrue over the life of the loan.

In the late 1990s, maximum coverage was $50 million and the limit of coverage for a single country was $225 million. There is no minimum amount of coverage. For each guarantee contract (insurance policy), an application fee of between $5,000 and $10,000 is assessed. In the case of environmentally sensitive projects, an additional processing fee of $25,000 is assessed to cover the cost of outside advisers. Annual premiums range from 0.25 to 1.25 percent of the investment or loan.

By mid-1989, one year after its formation, MIGA had received 69 applications for project insurance coverage in 24 member countries. By the mid-1990s, 223 guarantee contracts had been issued covering investments of $15 billion. MIGA is an important addition to the World Bank Group in terms of promoting more foreign investment from the private sector.

 Summary

Commercial banks are an integral part of the economy in all industrialized countries. In the United States, commercial banks serve a relatively small geographic area because nationwide branching has not been permitted until recently. In other major trading partners of the United States, there is no such prohibition. One of the consequences of this is that US banks are on average much smaller than banks in other industrialized countries. Furthermore, the large trade surpluses of Japan have led to that country's banks dominating the ranks of the world's largest, despite the country's recent financial distress. The competitive position of US banks will be improved as the number of banks was reduced through consolidation and nationwide branching is effected.

Several international, noncommercial banks have special roles in international finance. The Bank for International Settlements serves the central bankers of the world. Through it, coordinated monetary policy is implemented and monetary crises averted. The International Monetary Fund helps countries alleviate balance of payments problems by making pooled resources available to its members and by issuing a unique form of money, called Special Drawing Rights. The World Bank Group concerns itself with the long-term development issues of its members by providing long-term loans, equity investments, advice concerning capital market formation, and insurance to protect against political risk. The members of the World Bank Group are the International Bank for Reconstruction and Development, the International Development Association, the International Finance Corporation, and the Multilateral Investment Guarantee Agency.

End-of-chapter Questions

1. Does it appear that commercial banking systems must follow a particular format with respect to structure and branching in order for an industrial economy to thrive? Why or why not?

2. Discuss the contributory factors in the emergence of Japanese banks as the world's largest.

3. In what ways has the Canadian banking system been more deregulated than the US system?

4. Name a factor that is common to both German and Japanese banks with respect to industrial firms.

5. Among the commercial bank systems discussed in this chapter, in which system(s) has nationwide branching not been permitted?

6. In what ways is the Canadian banking system a blend of both the UK and the US systems?

7. Explain the bank secrecy law in Switzerland.

8. Compare the commercial banks of Germany to those of the United States.

9. Compare the total banking assets of the United States to those of the other countries included in this chapter.

10. a. Which country in this chapter has the largest average bank asset base?
    b. How does this compare to the United States average?

11. In what ways are the founders of the Bank for International Settlements different from the those of the International Monetary Fund?

12. What is a special drawing right?

13. Why does the BIS not have an equivalent to the IMF's special drawing right?

14. What kinds of financial assistance does the IMF offer its members?

15. How is the financial assistance offered by the IMF different from that offered by the International Bank for Reconstruction and Development?

16. Why would a country that can obtain loans from the International Development Association not qualify for loans from the IBRD?

17. How do the sources of funds of the IMF differ from those of the World Bank (IBRD)?

18. Why did the BIS not take over the major international monetary functions in 1944?

19. How do the operations of the International Finance Corporation differ from those of the IBRD?

20. How does the Multilateral Investment Guarantee Agency encourage foreign investment in developing countries?

SELECTED REFERENCES

Auboin, Roger. *Bank for International Settlements 1980–1955*, International Finance Section, Department of Economics and Sociology, Princeton University, Princeton, NJ, 1955.

Bank Profitability, Financial Statements of Banks 1985–1994, Organization for Economic Cooperation and Development, Paris, 1996.

Financial Organization and Operations of the IMF, International Monetary Fund, Washington, DC, 1990.

Grady, John and Martin Weale. *British Banking: 1960–85*, St. Martin's Press, New York, 1986.

Horne, James. *Japan's Financial Markets*, George Allen and Unwin, North Sydney, Australia, 1985.

How the World Bank Works with Nongovernmental Organizations, The World Bank, Washington, DC, 1990.

International Finance Corporation Annual Report, International Finance Corporation, Washington, DC.

International Financial Statistics, International Monetary Fund, Washington, DC, various issues.

International Monetary Fund 1998 Annual Report, International Monetary Fund, Washington, DC.

MIGA Annual Report, Multilateral Investment Guarantee Agency, Washington, DC.

Neufeld, E. P. *The Financial System of Canada*, Macmillan Company of Canada, Toronto, 1972.

Revell, Jack. *The British Financial System*, Macmillan Press, London, 1973.

Schloss, Henry. *The Bank for International Settlements*, New York University, Graduate School of Business Administration, New York, 1970.

Skully, Michael T. *Financial Institutions and Markets in the Far East: A Study of China, Hong Kong, Japan, South Korea, and Taiwan*, St. Martin's Press, New York, 1982.

Suzuki, Yoshio. *Money and Banking in Contemporary Japan*, Yale University Press, London, 1980.

Viner, Aron. *Inside Japanese Financial Markets*, Dow Jones-Irwin, Homewood, Ill., 1988.

World Bank Annual Report 1998, The World Bank, Washington, DC.

World Debt Tables 1994; External Debt of Developing Countries, The World Bank, Washington, DC, 1996.

The Domestic Operations of Commercial Banks

chapter 21

CHAPTER OVERVIEW

This chapter:
- Highlights characteristics of corporate and retail banking.
- Surveys changes in corporate services in the US banking system.
- Covers some of the most prevalent interbank services.
- Discusses the emergence of bank discount brokerages.
- Analyzes the issue of US bank participation in the insurance industry.
- Outlines basis tenets of Socialist and Islamic banking.

KEY TERMS

corporate banking
correspondent bank
discount brokerage
Islamic banking
leveraged buyout

off-balance-sheet activity
respondent bank
retail banking
socialist banking

CHAPTER OUTLINE

1 Corporate vs. Retail Services
2 Corporate Services
   2.1 Large Corporations
   2.2 Small- and Medium-sized Corporations
   2.3 Leveraged Buyouts
   2.4 Commercial Real Estate Loans
   2.5 Off-balance-sheet Activities
3 Bank Clients
4 Discount Brokerage
5 Insurance

6   Other Banking Systems
   6.1   Socialist Banking
   6.2   Islamic Banking

INTERNATIONAL COMPARISONS:
Canada
China
Germany
Japan
Poland
The former Soviet Union
United Kingdom

 Introduction

Banking services in the United States have evolved from an early emphasis on deposit-taking (primarily demand deposits and savings accounts) and short-term loans into a much wider range of deposits and loans. As banking clientele has become more financially sophisticated, so have bank operations. Large corporate clients are now more financially independent and have substituted direct financing (via commercial paper, for example) for previous bank loans. This has led banks to look more to fee-generating services for large corporations (letters of credit to back commercial paper, for example) and increasingly to small- and medium-size firms.

At the same time, bank entry into many fee-generating activities (securities underwriting and insurance, for example) has been frustrated by federal law that prohibits these activities. There are numerous issues. How can the banks remain profitable when large corporate business continues to offer thinning margins? How can income be augmented when fee-generating activities are restricted? How can the risk in banking be contained when banks must turn increasingly to smaller, *more risky* clients to boost profit margin? How can banks maintain their market share if competitors may provide bank-like services, but banks may not expand their product offerings?

 Corporate vs. Retail Services

In the past, US commercial banks fostered relationships with corporate clients such that one bank provided a number of services for a given firm. Loan pricing was a function of all the other services and their respective profitability. Recently, however, surplus corporate cash is more frequently invested in money market instruments, instead of bank deposits. Corporate loan pricing must now be competitive with commercial paper rates for large, creditworthy clients. Thus, while this relationship for banking is still an important concept, performance and profitability measurement of individual services is critical.

> **Corporate banking:**
> Providing services to businesses, including checking accounts, loans, foreign exchange, trade finance (for imports and exports), and other financial support.

Because of the diversity of clients, corporate services are often custom-tailored. In fact, banks engage in corporate banking to varying degrees.

Retail banking:
>   Providing services to individuals, including checking accounts, installment loans, credit cards, mortgage loans, and other financial products. (Also referred to as consumer banking.)

On the other hand, retail banking can be offered through more standardized procedures, frequently supplemented with automated services. Whatever the degree of emphasis on corporate services, certain trends are undeniable. Historically, commercial banks have earned substantial spreads by assuming credit risk of their corporate clients and financing these loans with relatively inexpensive deposit funds (demand or savings deposits). Deposit funds are now more expensive. Furthermore, larger corporations more frequently use commercial paper (direct) financing at lower interest rates. Thus, traditional spreads are no longer available on loans to major corporations.

One consequence of this situation is that medium-sized firms represent a market segment with significant future growth potential. Because these corporations have relatively less access to money and capital markets, they must necessarily depend more heavily on commercial banks and other financial intermediaries.

Another consequence of the thinner spreads available on traditional corporate loans is that fee income has become a much more important part of bank profitability. Thus, conventional services such as checking accounts and associated activities (e.g., stop payment orders and items returned for insufficient funds) are now important fee income generators.

② Corporate Services

2.1 LARGE CORPORATIONS

In addition to loans and deposits, bank services for large corporations include foreign exchange or treasury operations. Multinational clients with domestic and international telecommunications networks can contract with the bank for worldwide cash flow information. With the assistance of the bank, receipts and disbursements can be more readily offset, often reducing the required number of foreign currency transactions. The bank performs all the required transactions, sometimes including risk management techniques that compensate for the multinationals' total exposure in specific currencies. To the extent that bank cash management techniques and technology are more advanced than those of its client, the client is more likely to contract with its bank.

2.2 SMALL- AND MEDIUM-SIZED CORPORATIONS

Smaller corporate clients will not usually require foreign exchange and risk management. Instead, payroll or general ledger maintenance may be appealing and appropriate services, in addition to loans and deposits. This arrangement generally involves little or no incremental cost for the bank but enables it to sell unused time on its computer system. Since the bank already has cash flow details in connection with its clients' deposit and loan accounts, it has a comparative advantage over other data processing services.

2.3 LEVERAGED BUYOUTS

Banks also have also become involved in *leveraged buyouts* (*LBOs*), beginning primarily in the 1980s.

> **Leveraged buyout (LBO):**
> The purchase of the common stock of a firm with borrowed funds.

The objective for an LBO is to gain control of the company. Presumably, the group that gains control will be able to manage the firm more effectively than was the case before the LBO. The assets of the firm form the basis for the transaction and are sometimes at least partially sold to repay the borrowing. When bonds are used to raise the money to buy the stock, they are often referred to as "junk bonds" because the credit rating is not investment grade. When bank loans are used to raise the money, these loans are referred to as *highly leveraged transactions (HLTs)*.

HLTs carry an attractive interest rate for the lending institutions, but they are also risky. In an economic downturn, companies have difficulty paying the high rates of interest on relatively large amounts of debt. This, of course, puts the lender at risk of default.

2.4 COMMERCIAL REAL ESTATE LOANS

Commercial real estate loans have also offered attractive returns to help replace the blue-chip commercial borrowers that have turned to the commercial paper market. But this market is also risky. In 1998, commercial real estate loans totaled $415 billion, or 13 percent of total bank loans.

2.5 OFF-BALANCE-SHEET ACTIVITIES

The high interest rates of the 1980s presented banks with real profit pressures. The high cost of deposits and borrowed funds motivated banks to search for high-yielding loans and sources of fee income. Many *off-balance-sheet* activities are good sources of fee income.

> **Off-balance-sheet activity:**
> An activity or service that does not appear on the bank's financial statements, that is, a contingent obligation or an obligation to provide service in the future.

Examples of off-balance-sheet activities include:

- Commitments to make or purchase loans
- Futures and forward contracts
- Letters of credit
- Standby letters of credit (bank pays only if customer defaults on an obligation to a third party)
- Open lines on credit cards
- Loans sold with recourse (purchaser may collect from the bank if the original borrower defaults)

- Commitments to purchase foreign currencies
- Interest rate swaps
- Interest rate and foreign exchange options written by the bank

In 1984, the dollar value of these contingencies and commitments was just under 60 percent of those liabilities recorded on the balance sheet. By 1997, this percentage had grown to 498 percent or $22.9 trillion. The growth in these activities is clear evidence of the emphasis on fee income.

 Bank Clients

The relationship between large banks and smaller banks is not new. Respondents have long relied on correspondents for investment advice and securities safekeeping. Because lending limits are sometimes binding constraints for smaller banks, larger banks often purchase the excess amounts of particular loans, the "overlines."

> **Correspondent bank:**
> A bank that holds deposits owned by other banks and performs banking services, such as check clearing, for banks in other cities.

> **Respondent bank:**
> A smaller bank that relies on a larger bank for services, such as check clearing, foreign exchange, or derivatives market access.

Enhanced technology has also made it possible for larger institutions to clear checks for respondents on a scale that was previously not possible. Even when respondents are members of the Federal Reserve, these arrangements are often faster than the federal clearing service. For example, many larger banks have established clearing facilities at airports to eliminate the time required to transport the items into the city and back again. Some of these operations run two or three work shifts per day to provide the fastest possible turnaround. Foreign items are also handled and immediate credit is given for cash items. It is estimated that several thousand banks are still processing their own checks. Centralized, third-party check clearing systems offered by correspondents provide important efficiencies.

 Discount Brokerage

In 1983, the Federal Reserve Board permitted BankAmerica Corporation to purchase Charles Schwab Corporation. Since then, more than 2,000 banks and bank holding companies in the US have begun to offer discount brokerage services.

During the early 1980s, stock market participation by individual investors increased significantly, largely because of strong, broadly based stock price increases. The increased interest by individuals is also attributable to demographic factors. As the "baby boom" generation ages, its members (born shortly after the Second World War) have more time to analyze their investments, that is, will be less dependent on the *advice* of brokers. For these investors, convenient, low-cost transactions are an appealing alternative.

Beyond demographic considerations, individual investors are becoming more sophisticated with respect to investment opportunities. A consequence of this heightened awareness is interest rate and price sensitivity – including the price of financial services.

The securities industries, both corporate services and retail brokerage, have substantial growth potential for commercial banks. As the conventional intermediation functions of accepting deposits and making loans continue to be challenged by nonbank competition and shrinking spreads, banks will seek these and other avenues to diversify their product mix.

 Insurance

The insurance industry also holds promise. The National Bank Act (1863) permits national banks to engage only in underwriting and brokerage of insurance that is incidental to banking. This includes credit life, accident and health insurance. The Bank Holding Company Act (1956) and the Garn–St. Germain Act (1982) prohibit bank holding companies (companies that own banks) from engaging in *any* insurance activity. However, existing insurance operations were grandfathered (permitted to continue) when the legislation was passed. Also, national banks and bank holding companies in towns of fewer than 5,000 persons are exempted from the prohibitions.

Federal regulators have attempted to liberalize national bank powers. The Office of the Comptroller of the Currency (which charters national banks) has given permission to national banks to underwrite and sell title insurance (protecting the buyer of real estate property from ownership claims of previous owners) and property insurance related to loan collateral. National banks have also been granted the right to broker fixed-rate annuities (insurance policies that pay a stream of fixed payments rather than a lump-sum).

Federal regulators have attempted to liberalize bank powers within the framework of existing federal law that relates to national banks, state banks that are members of the Federal Reserve, and banking holding companies. Only US Congressional action can change the federal law.

In 1998, a bill was introduced in the US House of Representatives (HR 10) that would permit the formation of a holding company that had subsidiaries in the three main financial services sectors:

- Banking
- Securities
- Insurance

The bill passed in the House and appeared to have good possibilities for full passage. However, at year-end 1998, the bill had not completed the legislative process.

In some ways, HR 10 tried to capture and structure the market forces that had gained considerable momentum with the early-1998 announcement of a merger between Citicorp (banking) and Travelers (insurance). The new firm is Citigroup and has probably done more to change the thinking about the combination of banking and insurance than any other single event in US history.

 Other Banking Systems

Not all banking systems follow the Western model. Particularly noteworthy in this regard are socialist and Islamic systems.

6.1 SOCIALIST BANKING

Even though the US seems overly regulated when compared to other Western systems, it appears relatively free of regulation when compared to socialist banking systems. In the early 1930s, the former Soviet Union restructured its system in accordance with doctrines that were later to be followed by most socialist countries. Initially, all parties (state, collective, and private enterprises) were required to deposit all funds with the state bank. This step accomplished three objectives.

1) The government wished to gain control of private sector activities in order to limit future development, monitor funds use, and to exercise monetary control over such enterprises.
2) State banks sought to orchestrate economic and industrial development in public sector enterprises.
3) Control of any private sector surpluses would facilitate their reallocation to the public sector.

As socialist systems developed, the need for specialized attention in several areas arose. As a result, *foreign trade*, *agricultural*, *industrial*, and *savings* banks appeared.

The state bank has always acted as a buffer between the domestic and foreign sectors through its *foreign-trade* bank branch. A typical arrangement involves both a foreign-trade enterprise and a domestic enterprise. Using metal ore as an example, a domestic enterprise wishing to sell ore overseas first sells it to a state-owned foreign-trade enterprise, receiving a predetermined price in local currency. The foreign-trade enterprise, in turn, sells the iron ore to a foreign buyer in exchange for foreign currency. The foreign-trade enterprise exchanges the foreign currency for local currency at the foreign-trade bank. The original domestic enterprise is thus insulated from world commodity price fluctuations. Furthermore, the difference between the local currency purchase and sale prices indicates the efficiency of the transaction and the industry's contribution to centralized plans for the national economy.

While foreign-trade banks are somewhat uniform from one socialist country to another, *agricultural banks* tend to vary more. In all socialist societies, considerable time was required to bring about land reform, that is, to dismantle large estates, distribute land to peasants, and to help the newly endowed peasants to increase agricultural output.

In the former German Democratic Republic (before reunification with the Federal Republic of Germany), capitalist farmers were permitted to retain 20 to 100 hectares of land and to employ workers. (A hectare is an area equal to 10,000 square meters or 2.471 acres. The capitalist farmers could, therefore, retain approximately 50 to 250 acres.) However, the government required these farmers to deposit their funds in the agricultural cooperative bank. Furthermore, capitalist farmers were not eligible for long-term financing. Instead, peasants holding 6 to 10 hectares of land received interest-free loans that they did not, in some cases, have to repay. Subsequently, the government encouraged small landowners to form cooperatives in order to better afford more farm equipment, which could then be financed through the state.

In the People's Republic of China, a less centralized approach to agricultural finance was adopted. While a state-level agricultural bank was formed in 1951 (two years after the Communists gained government control), the state encouraged a certain amount of self-help on the part of peasant farmers. In addition to state financing, the government encouraged formation of rural credit cooperatives, largely funded by short-term deposits made by the peasants themselves. By 1955, there were 130,000 such cooperatives. In 1958, they became credit departments of the communes being formed, acting as local offices of the People's Bank, the state bank.

Initially, in the areas of *industry* and *commerce*, state bank branches usually made only short-term loans. Separate, specialized banks financed long-term, capital projects. Over time, the separation of state and investment bank functions has been reduced in order to provide more financing flexibility. Nevertheless, industrial and commercial enterprises generally must still maintain their accounts in a specific state bank branch so that the state can monitor productivity.

Savings banks hold the deposits of individuals. To encourage saving, a low interest rate (approximately 3 percent) is offered. With almost no other investment opportunities, a 3 percent rate is apparently felt to be sufficient to attract savings. Housing loans are generally also available.

The monetary and banking systems of the former Soviet Union and of Eastern Europe are undergoing changes to make them more compatible with their western counterparts. Russia has formed over 2,000 private commercial banks. However, only 50 offer customer service that is comparable to a Western institution. Many of the others have been formed by newly privatized enterprises, but do not have the staff or technological support common in the West.

On the other hand, Poland has completed an initially painful transition to a market economy, overcoming high inflation and scarcity of goods. The Polish currency (the zloty) is now pegged to a basket of five currencies (the US dollar, the German mark, the British pound, the French franc and the Swiss franc). Banks in Poland have benefited from this transition by attracting a higher percentage of Polish savings and helping to prepare for eventual privatization of Polish banks.

6.2 ISLAMIC BANKING

As some socialist banking systems attempt to become more similar to Western institutions, other non-Western systems attempt to distinguish themselves from Western banks. Islamic banks are good examples.

The Koran is the Islamic equivalent of the Christian Bible. Unlike the Bible, however, the Koran addresses specific economic issues including inheritance, hoarding, usury, and the use of financial resources. *Interest* and *profit* are considered fundamentally different forms of compensation. The objective of trade-related activities should be profit. In fact, Islam encourages its followers to invest productively. The investment function should, of course, include a determination of the proper distribution of any resulting profit (or loss). Since ultimate proceeds cannot be known with certainty at the time of the investment, final distributions also cannot be known with certainty.

Interest or *riba* is considered exploitative since its fixed nature ignores the possibility that ultimate proceeds of the investment may be inadequate to repay both interest and principal. Thus, Islamic banks accept deposits but do not guarantee the amount to be repaid. Similarly, bank loans are granted with the same understanding.

However, most of the *first* commercial banks established in the Muslim world were European branches or subsidiaries. At least initially, most governments were content to overlook the violations of Islamic principles in exchange for economic and technical advancements. When religious fundamentalists gained more influence, these religious issues began to be raised.

The first Islamic bank was formed in rural Pakistan in the 1950s. Deposited funds were loaned after deducting only a small, permissible administrative fee to cover the bank's operating expense. However, new deposit funds did not materialize and trained personnel was scarce. The bank effectively self-liquidated during the early 1960s.

The Nasser Social Bank, the oldest existing Islamic bank, was formed in 1972, with over $2 million of capital invested by the Egyptian government. Currently, over 60 Islamic institutions operate worldwide, most having been established by private Muslim citizens. Pakistan and Iran are the only countries that have implemented nationwide Islamic banking. (See also Exhibit 21.1.)

In addition to a prohibition against interest, among other things, Muslim law prescribes segregation of the genders in matters of finance. This implies no joint bank accounts for spouses.

Name	Date founded
Nassar Social Bank (Egypt)	1972
Islamic Development Bank (Saudi Arabia)	1974
Dubai Islamic Bank	1975
Faisal Islamic Bank of Egypt	1977
Faisal Islamic Bank of Sudan	1977
Kuwait Finance House	1977
Jordan Islamic Bank for Finance and Investment	1978
Bahrain Islamic Bank	1979
Iran Islamic Bank	1979
Islamic Investment Company (Nassan)	1979
Islamic Investment Trust (Geneva)	1980
Dar Al-Maal Al-Islami (Bahamas, Geneva)	1980
Bank Islam Berhad (Malaysia)	1983
Muslim Commercial Bank	(1)
National Investment Trust	(1)
Investment Corporation of Pakistan	(1)
House Building Finance Corporation	(1)

◆ **Exhibit 21.1: Selected Islamic banks**

◆ *Note*: 1 These Pakistani banks were nationalized in 1974 and converted to Islamic institutions in 1984.

Inheritance law dictates that a wife inherits one-quarter of her husband's estate. If the wife is deceased before the husband, he inherits half the wife's estate. Children receive the remainder with distributions to sons being twice as large as distributions to daughters. Through this system, many women accumulate substantial fortunes.

Conservative Islamic women may hesitate to frequent male-dominated banks or to comingle funds in their spouses' accounts. In response to these dynamics, Saudi Arabia has initiated banks operated by women for women, with the first beginning operations in 1979. As more Saudi women enter the work force, it is expected that these institutions will increase in economic significance.

As Muslim economies have grown, greater observance of Islamic principles has been called for. As Islamic women gained more financial resources, the demand for banking services for women has grown. Likewise, in the United States, as population demographics have changed, the manner in which banking services are offered has been affected by these changes.

 Summary

Universal functions of commercial banks are accepting deposits and making loans. Greater access to money and capital markets by large corporate bank clients has meant thinner margins in corporate lending activities. As a result, banks have turned increasingly to fee-generating services and to the middle segment of the corporate market. Cash management, data processing, commercial paper underwriting, and provision of discount brokerage facilities are some of the services being emphasized.

Political and cultural differences can alter the nature of the domestic operations of commercial banks, however. Socialist economies have much more centralized and regulated banking systems than these observed in the West. In the Muslim world, Islamic banks have emerged in an attempt to reconcile modern finance and fundamentalist principle.

End-of-chapter Questions

1. Why is the middle-market corporate sector considered to have high growth potential for commercial banks?

2. With respect to socialist banking:

   a. Discuss the reasons why all parties were required to deposit funds with the state bank in the early years of socialist banking.

   b. Instead of the state bank providing loans based on the central planning budget, how should bank funds be allocated as the systems are reformed?

3. Why is interest prohibited in Islamic banking? What is the alternative?

4. Banks often sell "overlines," the portion of loans that is in excess of their legal lending limit, to other banks. To what activity in the securities industry is this similar?

5. In your opinion, what competitive strengths can banks bring to the securities industry?

6. What are the potential dangers of banks being involved in the securities industry?

7. In your opinion, how has technology changed the services banks offer?

8. Review your most recent bank statement. Identify the type and amount of bank fees accessed in that statement.

9. Why do commercial banks have an interest in offering to larger, corporate customers services such as cash management facilities and interest rate swaps?

10. Obtain the most recent annual report for a local bank. Which of the services discussed in this chapter are offered by the bank?

11. Using the Internet, research the status of recent US federal legislation in the area of financial services reform, beginning with HR 10 in 1998.

12. Research the status of Citigroup (the merger between Citicorp and Travelers).

    a. Have there been any issues raised or discussed concerning the combined management of the two predecessor firms?

    b. What regulatory issues have been raised concerning the combination of insurance and commercial banking?

Selected References

Abdeen, Adnan M. and Dale N. Shook. *The Saudi Financial System: in the Context of Western and Islamic Finance*, John Wiley and Sons, New York, 1984.

Allen, Paul H. *Reengineering the Bank: A Blueprint for Survival and Success*, Probus Publishing, Chicago (now McGraw-Hill, New York), 1994.

Bayliss, B. T. and A. A. S. Butt Philip. *Capital Markets and Industrial Investment in Germany and France: Lessons for the UK*, Saxon House, Westmead, England, 1980.

Boreham, Gordon F. "Canadian and US Banking Systems: Some Comparisons," *Canadian Banker*, 94, no. 3 (1987), pp. 6–14.

Bronte, Stephen. *Japanese France: Markets and Institutions*, Germany Publications, London, 1982.

Brown, Albert J. *The High Performance Bank*, Probus, Chicago, 1994.

Chew, Donald, ed. *New Developments in Commercial Banking*, Blackwell Publishers, Malden, Mass., 1991.

Coler, Mark and Ellis Ratner. *Financial Services: Insiders' Views of the Future*, New York Institute of Finance, New York, 1988.

Johnson, Hazel J. *Dispelling the Myth of Globalization: The Case for Regionalization*, Praeger Publishers, New York, 1991.

Lee, Peter. "Can Citigroup Get in Step?" *Euromoney*, May 1998, pp. 27–32.

McCoy, John B., Larry A. Frieder, and Robert B. Hedges, Jr *BottomLine Banking: Meeting the Challenges for Survival and Success*, Probus, Chicago, 1994.

McRae, Hamish and Frances Cairncross. *Capital City: London as a Financial Centre*, Methuen, London, 1984.

Miller, Richard B. *Citicorp: The Story of a Bank in Crisis*, McGraw-Hill, New York, 1993.

Mullineux, A. W. *UK Banking After Deregulation*, Croom Helm, London, 1987.

Raghavan, Anita and Paul Beckett. "How Jamie Dimon Became a Casualty of Citigroup's Travails," *Wall Street Journal*, November 3, 1998, pp. A1 & A14.

Rogers, David. *The Future of American Banking: Managing for Change*, McGraw-Hill, New York, 1993.

Seznec, Jean-François. *The Financial Markets of the Arabian Gulf*, Croom Helm, London, 1987.

Smith, Roy C. *Comeback: The Restoration of American Banking Power in the New World Economy*, Harvard Business School Press, Boston, 1993.

Spong, Kenneth. *Banking Regulation; Its Purposes, Implementation, and Effects*, 3rd edn, Federal Reserve Bank of Kansas City, 1990.

Subcommittee on Financial Institutions Supervision, Regulation and Insurance. *Report of the Task Force on the International Competitiveness of US Financial Institutions*, Committee on Banking, Finance and Urban Affairs, US House of Representatives, Washington, DC, 1991.

Suzuki, Yoshio. *The Japanese Financial System*, Oxford University Press, New York, 1987.

US Department of the Treasury. *Modernizing the Financial System: Recommendations for Safer, More Competitive Banks*, Washington, DC, 1991.

Wilson, Rodney. *Banking and Finance in the Arab Middle East*, St. Martin's Press, New York, 1983.

Wohlers-Scharf, Traute. *Arab and Islamic Banks: New Business Partners for Developing Countries*, Development Centre of the Organization for Economic Cooperation and Development, Paris, 1983.

chapter **22**

The International Operations of Commercial Banks

CHAPTER OVERVIEW

This chapter:
- Explains the motivations for entering international banking markets.
- Describes the organizational forms of international banking.
- Outlines international banking services.
- Discusses risk in international banking.

KEY TERMS

agency
agreement corporation
branch
country risk
LIBOR
Edge Act corporation

note-issuance facility
offshore center
representative office
subsidiary
syndicated loan

CHAPTER OUTLINE

INTERNATIONAL COMPARISONS:

Bahamas	Iran
Bermuda	Netherlands Antilles
Cayman Islands	Singapore
China	United Kingdom
Hong Kong	

 Introduction

International financial transactions date back to ancient times when Egyptians and Sumerians wrote letters of credit on papyrus and "checks" on clay tablets to finance cross-border trade. Merchants in Babylonia and Assyria used bills of exchange to achieve the same objective.

In more recent times, the Medicis of Florence operated branches in Rome, Venice, Milan, Paris, Avignon, Bruges, London, and Geneva. The Baring Brothers of London established extensive correspondent relationships with other banks, including a representative office in the United States. Other London-based merchant banks maintained substantial Latin American and South African branch networks. By the 1860s, British bank branches in California and the Far East were not uncommon.

In the twentieth century, international banking become even more widespread. As industrial firms have found that their growth markets are often overseas, their banks have followed them to these new markets. US banks have been international market pioneers in many respects, having engineered such innovations, for example, as the Eurodollar certificate of deposit.

 Reasons for International Expansion

There are three main reasons that banks begin to operate internationally. Banks seek to:

- Penetrate local markets
- Serve domestic clients
- Participate in the Euromarkets

1.1 PENETRATING LOCAL MARKETS

A primary motivating factor for international expansion is to gain direct access to the *host country's markets*. Perhaps, indigenous (host country) banks are not competitive in *lending* activities, either in terms of loan pricing or servicing. Alternatively, host country banks may not realize their full potential in *deposit-taking*.

If a bank can offer lower loan rates, higher deposit rates, and/or better service, expansion into a foreign market can be profitable. When indigenous banks react to the foreign presence by improving their own product offerings, host country residents clearly benefit from this heightened competition. (See also Exhibit 22.1.)

Travel and entertainment cards have been available in Europe for some time. However, bank credit cards are a recent innovation. With widespread acceptance and issuance of bank cards in the United States, American banks have turned to Europe for possible market expansion. In Germany, where bankers rely heavily upon their clients' presence in bank offices to cross-sell a number of products, the bank credit card received a cool reception.

To the displeasure of German banks, American Express purchased a Frankfurt bank through which insurance and other services were sold via credit card. Attempts to block this activity with regulatory intervention and with agreements among German banks for nonparticipation in the card venture proved unsuccessful. Unable to stop the introduction of the bank card, German banks joined with their own version, the Eurocard. In 1987, retailers announced plans to issue their own cards.

The introduction of credit cards by American firms facilitated market expansion. As a result, German residents enjoy a broader range of financial services.

♦ **Exhibit 22.1: Credit cards in Germany**

The target market may be nonfinancial corporations, other banks, government, or individuals. The government and banking sectors are generally most easily penetrated. Corporate and individual clients may be more difficult to lure away from local institutions. Also, availability of sufficient information needed to evaluate corporate and individual credit worthiness initially may be limited.

However, just as many US banks have sought to expand their retail markets domestically, a number have also found that some overseas consumer markets have not been fully exploited. This appears to be particularly true in countries with a highly concentrated banking structure. A relatively small number of indigenous banks may not feel significant competitive pressure to innovate products and services.

1.1.1 CHINA

China is a useful example of local market potential because the country represents a huge market in which "free market forces" have only recently been introduced. (See also chapter 21, section 6.1, "Socialist Banking.") Foreign businesses in China are restricted by the government to only specific locations. In 1979, Special Economic Zones or SEZs were opened to foreign business, trade, and technology – Shenzhen, Zhuhai, Hainan, Xiamen, and Shantou. In 1992, China liberalized the permissible locations for foreign bank branches. In addition to the five SEZs, another eight cities may now be the home of foreign banks:

- Shanghai
- Dalian
- Tianjing
- Qingdao
- Nanjing
- Ningbo
- Fuzhou
- Guangzhou

At the end of 1995, 102 representative offices (contact offices) of foreign institutions operated in China. In addition, a number of foreign bank branches have been opened. Shanghai alone had

42 foreign bank branches in mid-1996. However, foreign banks have not been permitted to loan or trade in the local Chinese currency, called *renminbi* or *yuan*.

Despite restrictions on their ability to trade in renminbi, foreign banks are having a significant impact on the Chinese market. The introduction of bank cards likely will lead to an international-style network for the acceptance of bank cards in China. Currently, stores and restaurants accept only those cards issued by the banks with which they do business. Government authorities have issued directives to build interbank networks in 12 cities that will authorize and settle card transactions. Both Visa and MasterCard of the United States are vying to help develop this initiative. Involvement by foreign banks will be in the best interest of the Chinese financial system as China is plagued by chronic shortages of currency and a mounting problem with counterfeiting.

Chinese authorities also hope that foreign institutions will help develop Shanghai into the financial center of Asia. Specifically, the People's Bank of China (PBOC, central bank) has permitted nine foreign banks to conduct business in renminbi on a limited basis beginning in late 1996. Permissible renminbi business includes deposits, loans, payment settlements, security for loans (loan guarantees), bonds issued by the government, and other business individually authorized by the PBOC. The condition for doing so is opening subbranches in the Pudong development district of Shanghai or in the cities of Tianjin, Dalian, and Guangzhou. Pudong is slated to be the new financial district of Shanghai. Early in 1997, Fuji Bank of Japan became the first foreign bank to open an office there.

The Chinese government recognizes the benefit of foreign institutions. Through foreign competition with indigenous institutions, modernization will be facilitated in the Chinese banking system.

1.1.2 RELEVANT ISSUES FOR INTERNATIONAL BANKS

Several issues are important for banks expanding into local markets abroad:

- Foreign bank entry is often encouraged by government authorities to improve efficiencies in indigenous banking markets.
- The ability to enter foreign markets may be affected by the extent to which the home market is open to banks from other countries (reciprocity).
- Successful banks that expand abroad must understand the culture of business in the host countries. (See also Exhibit 22.2.)
- Bank regulations in a host country may differentiate between indigenous and foreign institutions in such a way as to create a competitive disadvantage for the foreign bank.

1.2 SERVING DOMESTIC CUSTOMERS

1.2.1 CORPORATE CLIENTS

Banks also begin operating abroad in order to serve corporate clients that expand internationally. In the 1960s and 1970s, US multinational corporations greatly increased worldwide operations. As these firms established facilities in Canada and Western Europe, their banks followed them. Foreign direct investment trends shifted toward the United States in the 1970s and 1980s. Likewise, European, Canadian, and Japanese banks followed their clients to the United States.

However, serving corporate clients in this way can be complicated. As noted above, host country governments may impose restrictions on foreign bank entry or operations. Also, as noted earlier, indigenous banks will generally compete to maintain or expand their own market shares.

In the late 1980s, the Flushing area of Queens, New York had few Asian residents. By 1991, more than 140,000 Chinese and Korean immigrants resided there. Asian banks are, likewise, an important element of the economy. The oldest Chinese-American bank in Flushing is Asia Bank. Others include Amerasia Bank and Hong Kong-Shanghai Banking Corporation.

One of the entrants in the early 1990s was China Trust, the largest private bank in Taiwan. In its first two weeks of operation, China Trust took in $6 million from 400 depositors. American banks compete aggressively for Oriental deposits. For example, ATMs in Flushing offer transactions in three languages and the employees in Citibank's Asian Banking Center speak Korean, Mandarin, and Cantonese. Nevertheless, the Asian banks have certain competitive advantages:

- Deposit interest rates are higher than at American banks.
- Weekend banking hours are maintained.
- In some cases, free parking (a rare commodity) is provided.
- The reputations and past records of customers from the home country are considered in credit evaluations.
- Gifts are often distributed during Chinese New Year.

The success of Asian banks in Flushing is not an accident. Competitive pricing, a high level of service, and cultural links all contribute.

◆ **Exhibit 22.2:   Asian culture in the suburbs of New York**

◆ *Source*:   Lorch, Donatella, "Banks Follow Immigrants to Flushing," *New York Times*, Aug. 7, 1991.

Once a bank has expanded internationally, it is even possible for conflicts between bank and customer to arise. The US multinational is most likely a very creditworthy firm that can command the most competitive loan rates and fees for bank services. On the other hand, local industrial firms may be associated with more credit risk and, therefore, larger spreads and increased bank profitability. If the overseas bank operation neglects its US multinational client to develop local client relationships, relations between the parent firm and the parent bank can become strained.

Notwithstanding these potential complications, attempts by banks to continue to provide services to their domestic corporate clients account for a significant portion of international expansion.

1.2.2 CONSUMERS – THE CASE OF THE BANK OF CHINA

China presents a particularly interesting case of following consumer clients through international bank operations. Chinese who live outside mainland China, called overseas Chinese, and residents of Hong Kong and Macao, called compatriots, regularly remit funds to family members in mainland China. This remittance of funds has taken place since the People's Republic of China was established in 1949. The government encourages these payments because they improve the country's balance of payments.

Bank of China overseas branches and branches in mainland regions from which large numbers of Chinese citizens have immigrated facilitate this process. Funds sent through the banking system are denominated in foreign currency. Once the foreign currency is received, the recipient must deposit it in exchange for *renminbi* (Chinese local currency).

1.3 PARTICIPATING IN EUROMARKETS

Recent developments in money and capital markets have also provided impetus for overseas operations. As discussed in chapter 9, Euromarkets began to develop in the 1960s. Initially, interest rate ceilings in the United States threatened to severely constrict new negotiable certificates of deposit (CDs) as market interest rates climbed above the Federal Reserve Regulation Q limits on deposit interest rates. However, these ceilings did not apply to deposits offered in overseas offices of US banks. Large money center institutions were the primary issuers of the new instruments and they responded by offering CDs with competitive rates in offices located in Europe, especially London.

Thus, an important funding source, the negotiable CD, was protected from noncompetitive interest rate ceilings. As a further consequence of the relative freedom from regulatory oversight, overseas operations avoided reserve requirements and federal deposit insurance premiums. Without these added costs of doing business, Eurocurrency loan rates were set below the rates that were feasible domestically.

At the same time, growing deficits in the United States balance of payments (trade and capital flow deficits) prompted the Federal Reserve to restrict further overseas investment. This effectively prevented multinational banks from repatriating profits earned abroad and subsequently redeploying them overseas. As a result, these offshore profits became new bank capital – invested outside the United States. This higher capital base supported even more deposit-gathering abroad.

In the 1970s, unprecedented crude oil price increases generated correspondingly high international trade surpluses for oil-exporting countries. The Eurocurrency market provided an efficient mechanism for the absorption of resulting liquidity. Investment of the OPEC surpluses within the domestic financial markets of the United States and other industrialized countries sometimes met with governmental resistance because such large infusions of liquidity complicated the efforts of monetary authorities to control money supply and inflation. But investing OPEC (Organization of Petroleum Exporting Countries) funds in the unregulated Eurocurrency markets posed no such problem.

Historically, the primary participants in the Eurodollar market have been larger banking institutions. For example, in the 1970s only 20 institutions held over 90 percent of all foreign-branch assets of US banks. By the early 1980s, Citicorp attributed 80 percent of earnings to overseas operations, in which 50 percent of its total assets were invested. Even after retrenchment associated with the 1980s Latin American debt crisis, Citicorp has a large share of revenues generated overseas. (See chapter 11 for a discussion of the Latin American debt crisis.) In 1997, 43 percent of Citigroup retail banking revenues were attributed to markets outside North America (United States and Canada) and fully two-thirds of corporate banking revenues were generated outside North America.

As other countries relaxed banking regulations and tax laws, they too became prime locations for Euromarket activity. The prestige and the potential for job creation associated with the Euromarkets appear to have had some bearing on bank regulatory changes in Belgium, Luxembourg, and the Netherlands. Outside of Europe, Singapore, Hong Kong, and the Caribbean have attracted considerable "Euromarket" activity.

② **Organizational Forms for International Banking**

Various forms of international banking have existed in the United States before Euromarkets, some as early as the 19th century. However, a specific institutional framework for international operations for national banks was created through amendments to the Federal Reserve Act, the *Edge Act corporation*. The state bank equivalent is the *agreement corporation*. Both types of corporations operate in the United States. In terms of overseas locations, banks may establish *representative offices*, *agencies*, *branches*, or *subsidiaries*. When an overseas location is chosen because of tax advantages or greater freedom from regulation, the location is called an *offshore center*.

2.1 Edge Act and Agreement Corporations

A 1916 amendment of the Federal Reserve Act empowered national banks (with $1 million of capital) to invest up to 10 percent of capital in state-chartered banks or corporations that were to be engaged primarily in international banking. A condition of such an arrangement was that the state-chartered corporation enter into an "agreement" to conduct its business subject to limitations and restrictions imposed by the Federal Reserve Board. These institutions have come to be referred to as *agreement corporations*.

However, this increased flexibility to operate an agreement corporation under more lenient state laws did not stimulate the interest that had been anticipated. In the next three years, only three agreement corporations applied for and received charters. In 1919, the Edge Act created a *federally* chartered institution for foreign transactions through another amendment of the Federal Reserve Act.

In some ways, an *Edge Act corporation* was subject to more restrictions than an agreement corporation. For example:

- All Edge Act corporation directors must be US citizens.
- Ten percent of all domestic deposits must be held in reserve.
- Total liabilities must never exceed 10 times the sum of capital plus surplus.

However, Edge Act corporations were permitted to invest in nonbank financial institutions – investments *not* explicitly permissible for agreement corporations.

Early Edge Act corporations were established primarily to engage in nonbanking enterprises. Later, banks used this framework in order to open facilities outside the home state. Edge Act corporations now compete with the foreign banks in the United States. (See also Exhibit 22.3.)

	Agreement	Edge Act
Date of authorization	1916	1919
Charter	State	Federal
Minimum capital	No federally mandated minimum	$2 million
Nationality restrictions for ownership	None	Directors: US citizens
Authority to invest conferred by	Federal Reserve Board	Statute
Powers	International banking	International banking and investment in nonbank financial institutions engaged in international operations
Reserve requirements	None	10 percent on all deposits accepted in the US
Restrictions on debt issuance	None	Total liabilities must not exceed 10 times the sum of capital and surplus

◆ **Exhibit 22.3: Comparison of Edge Act and agreement corporations**

2.2 LOCATIONS ABROAD

There are four general forms of business organizations through which a bank may conduct overseas operations. The *representative office* is the most restricted of the four. Representative offices may *not* accept deposits, make loans, or conduct any banking services. They are simply points of contact between parent banks and their clients.

Agencies have somewhat more authority. They may accept predetermined payments in connection with international trade or deliver undisbursed portions of loans made by the parent bank. However, deposit-taking or fiduciary activities (such as portfolio management) are strictly prohibited. Essentially, no credit decisions are made by agencies. Agencies may execute only credit decisions made by the parent.

Branches and *subsidiaries* perform all normal banking functions. In the United States, a foreign *branch* must be licensed by either the state in which it is located or by the federal government. Technically, the results of operations are not distinguished from those of the parent bank. As a result, its lending limits are tied to the capital and surplus of the parent. Laws and regulations of the home country govern branch activities.

Subsidiaries are separate legal entities, incorporated by the government of the country in which they operate. Each has its own capital base. However, it is not uncommon for the parent bank to own 100 percent of the subsidiary's stock. Generally, laws of the host country govern the operation of overseas subsidiaries.

The choice of organizational form will depend upon a number of circumstances. If the bank has a large number of clients in the overseas location or a small number of major clients, a full service bank (branch or subsidiary) may be preferable. On the other hand, a representative office is a cost-effective way to explore a new geographical market before setting up more extensive operations. In fact, in some cases tax and other advantages associated with a foreign market may be exploited without a substantial investment in physical facilities or personnel.

2.3 OFFSHORE CENTERS

An *offshore center* is a site (country or city) that has made special provisions to attract international banking business. *International banking* can be broadly defined in one of three ways from the perspective of a commercial bank.

> **International banking:**
> Transactions with (1) domestic clients denominated in foreign currency, (2) foreign clients denominated in foreign or domestic currency, or (3) domestic clients denominated in domestic currency but *recorded* or "*booked*" in another country.

Notice that the first two definitions describe situations that are easily classified as "international," whether the transactions are recorded in the home country or abroad. However, the third definition requires that the transactions be recorded in a location other than the home country in order for them to be considered international transactions.

The third type of transaction will only be cost-effective when the foreign location offers an incentive. An offshore banking center has a tax or regulatory advantage that makes the third type of transaction an attractive arrangement. Of course, once the center has attracted a sufficient number of institutions, it may encourage a wider range of services and evolve into a full-scale international banking center.

As explained earlier in this chapter and in chapter 9, London was the site of early offshore activity by US banks. Dollar-denominated transactions took place between US banks and other US residents – but were carried out in London. Nonresident transactions in London were free from reserve requirements and deposit insurance premiums, while also receiving favorable tax treatment. Indeed, London continues to be the largest offshore market. Interestingly, because of its already considerable stature as an international financial center, London is not usually *classified* as an offshore center.

The term is usually reserved for cost-effective locations whose money and capital markets are relatively new and whose laws and regulations have been intentionally designed to attract financial firms. Examples are the Bahamas, the Cayman Islands, Bahrain, Hong Kong, Luxembourg, Panama, and Singapore.

Offshore centers may be either *paper* or *functional* centers. Paper centers are merely locations of record with little actual banking activity in the country.

The Bahamas is an example of a paper center. Over 250 financial institutions are licensed to do business in the Bahamas, but only 50 or so actually have employees in the Bahamas. The rest transact business through a post office address. No clients are seen and no financial decisions are made in the Bahamas.

Functional centers develop other related financial markets. Singapore and Hong Kong are good examples of functional centers where Eurobonds are issued and traded. Also, the stock markets of both countries are considered important emerging markets. Singapore is an important financial intermediary in the region. For example, in the early 1980s, over $13 billion in crude-oil related surpluses of oil-exporting countries was deposited in Singapore banks and channeled to other Asian countries.

Because of its limited offering of financial services, a paper center will be more vulnerable to increases in its own tax structure. Banks make minimal capital investments in paper centers because their primary advantage is a favorable tax environment. In functional centers, banks derive additional benefit from related services and other advantages associated with the location. Many functional centers have increased taxes without seriously damaging their market share of world financial transactions. (See also Exhibit 22.4.)

Tax haven provisions	Bermuda	Bahamas	Caymans	Netherlands Antilles
No tax	✗	✗	✗	
Low tax				✗
Best for				
1) Trusts	✗	✗	✗	
2) Holding Companies				✗
No tax treaties	✗	✗	✗	
US tax treaty				✗
Bank secrecy		✗	✗	
Numbered bank accounts		✗		
Bearer shares		✗	✗	✗

◆ **Exhibit 22.4:** **Features of Caribbean offshore centers**

◆ *Note*:   These provisions are applicable to nonresident companies and trusts

◆ *Source*:   Johns, Richard Anthony. *Tax Havens and Offshore Finance: A Study of Transactional Economic Development*, 1983, p. 193.

International Lending

In terms of the services offered by banks to their international clients, many of these products have been discussed in previous chapters. Examples include:

Services	*Chapter*
Bankers' acceptances	3
Letters of credit to back commercial paper	3
Negotiable certificates of deposit	3
Interest rate swap contracts	7
Currency forward, option, and swap contracts	8

In addition to these, there are two other important services in international banking: *syndicated loans* and *note issuance facilities*.

3.1 SYNDICATED LOANS

A *syndicated loan* differs from a conventional commercial loan in that a number of banks provide credit instead of one institution. The model for the syndicated loan in Euromarkets was the multibank, floating-rate loan that was developed and refined in the United States. The vehicle has been particularly useful for governments and major corporations. The reasons for its development were:

1) Increasingly larger individual loans.
2) A desire by international bankers to diversify risk.
3) Fee income potential for management of the loan.
4) Favorable public visibility for participating banks.
5) Enhanced working relationships with other banks.

The interest rate associated with a Euromarket syndicated loan is usually quoted as a spread over LIBOR, the London Interbank Offered Rate. For example, "LIBOR plus 1" is 1 percent over LIBOR. A lead bank or syndicate manager negotiates this interest rate and all other terms and conditions of the loan with the borrower, documenting them in the loan agreement. Participating banks then each purchase some portion of the total loan.

> **LIBOR:**
> The rate of interest at which short-term funds are exchanged between banks in London.

London has historically served as the primary location for international loan syndications. Other sites that have developed include Singapore, Hong Kong, Bahrain, Luxembourg, and the Caribbean.

The participating banks will expect that the normal, necessary conditions of prudent lending be satisfied. The borrower should be creditworthy, the interest rate competitive, and appropriate restrictive covenants incorporated into the loan agreement. In addition, participating banks expect the lead manager to perform in a way that is consistent with their own financial interests. Ultimately, however, participating banks accept the full credit risk of the borrower for their respective parts of the loan. The syndication process enables regional banks to take part in large international transactions that might, otherwise, be unavailable to them.

3.2 NOTE ISSUANCE FACILITIES

In recent years, the heightened regulatory emphasis on capital adequacy has, in part, led to greater securitization in capital markets. (See chapter 4 for a discusion of securitization.) *Note issuance facilities (NIFs)* provide financing for highly creditworthy borrowers through securities, rather than through bank loans.

NIFs are structured to permit the borrower to issue a series of short-term notes ("Euro-notes") over a medium-term. Like the syndicated loan, an NIF is a legal commitment between the borrower and the banks(s). *Unlike* a syndicated loan, however, an NIF commitment does not appear on bank balance sheets. The NIF arranger establishes a mechanism in which *other investors* provide funds as needed by purchasing its client's short-term notes, as issued.

The NIF arranger acts as an underwriter, by either purchasing only those notes that the issuer is unable to sell or providing standby credit to back the notes. The standby credit is similar to letters of credit that are issued to support commercial paper domestically. The underwriting commitment does not appear on the balance sheet of the NIF arranger *unless* the bank actually purchases notes (or pays them in the event of borrower default). However, the 1992 international capital standards (Basle Accord) require that standby credit be included in the computation of risk-weighted assets. (See chapter 17 for a discussion of international capital standards.)

In the cases of both syndicated loans and NIFs, credit evaluation is extremely important. However, this process is decidedly more complex because of the nature of the underlying transactions.

3.3 RISK IN INTERNATIONAL LENDING

To the extent that international lending is denominated in a foreign currency, commercial banks will be exposed to *foreign exchange risk*. Forward contracts, currency swaps, foreign exchange futures and options on futures are useful in the management of this form of risk. (See chapter 8 for a description of these management techniques.)

Commercial banks also face *country risk* when they expand into overseas markets. In the evaluation of country risk, historical data with respect to the economic and financial profile of the country is vital. Commonly, a weighted system is used. Specific variables are weighted according to their historical behavior. Variables typically include inflation rate, balance-of-payments deficits, international reserve positions, GNP growth rates, and international debt service payments. Qualitative factors such as political and social stability are also considered. Exhibit 22.5 is an example of some of these factors.

> **Country risk:**
> Risk associated with the creditworthiness of a borrower with residence outside the home country of the lending institution.

Dynamic	Developmental
Growth in real GNP per capita	GNP per capita
Export growth	GNP
Share of manufactured goods in total exports	Ratio of agriculture, investment, savings to GNP
Debt-service ratio	
Ratio of reserves to imports	
Rate of inflation	

◆ **Exhibit 22.5:** Dynamic and developmental country risk factors

◆ *Source*: Mathis, F. John, ed. *Offshore Lending by US Commercial Banks*, 2nd edn, 1981, pp. 50–5.

Unfortunately, *political risk* is difficult, if not impossible, to assess in an objective sense. However, when the quantitative variables suggest a favorable lending environment, the bank must next consider the probability that these conditions will persist. In a developing country, this is equivalent to the probability that the fundamental political system will *not* change.

The less developed is the country, in general, the higher the probability of disruptive political change. Important variables to consider are the extent to which the government is a collective process (reflecting the wishes of a broad spectrum of citizens), the likelihood that actions of a strong leader may anger another powerful group in the country (such as the military), the depth of leadership talent (should the government change), and the existing mechanism for a smooth transition in government. (See also Exhibit 22.6.)

Summary

Commercial banks enter international markets for a variety of reasons. However, penetrating local markets, following domestic clients, and participating in Euromarkets have been dominant reasons for doing so.

The organizational structure of overseas operations will usually take the form of a representative office, an agency, a branch, or a subsidiary. In the US, Edge Act and agreement corporations have been designed and authorized by Congress in order to promote international trade and/or banking.

In the international arena, banks offer syndicated loans and note issuance facilities. Syndicated loans spread the risk among lenders in large financings. Note issuance facilities provide flexibility of financing to bank clients.

During the last years of the Pahlavi dynasty in Iran, Chase Manhattan acted as syndicate manager or co-manager in eleven syndicated loans to Iran. While other US, German, British, Canadian, and Japanese banks were also active in Iran, Chase Manhattan was, by far, the most involved bank in the region. The Shah had agreed to have all payments for Iranian oil flow through the National Iranian Oil Company (NIOC) account at Chase. Before the government transition, Chase Manhattan had been able to depend on deposit flow from Iran of up to $15 billion per year.

After the Shah was forced to leave the country, the new Iranian government no longer permitted oil revenues to flow through the NIOC account because it was suspected that the Shah had used the account to misappropriate funds. Up to this time, Chase had maintained Iranian loans in amounts roughly equivalent to Iranian deposits. However, most of the deposits were quite short-term, while loans were longer-term with maturities up to several years.

To make matters worse, several of the syndicated loans had not been approved by the National Consultative Assembly, that is, the parliament. With the Shah deposed, enforceability of the loans became questionable. Further, since Chase Manhattan had acted as syndicate manager, the bank might also be liable for losses by participating banks. Chase had been aware of the nonapproval, but had *not* advised participating banks of this omission.

When Iranian deposits (and other holdings) in the United States were frozen by the US government, Chase declared the Iranian loans in default. Thus, the bank maintained both the loans and deposits until Iranian assets were released. The Iranians agreed to allow the right of offset. Thus, the $4.7 billion in syndicated loans was satisfied when Iranian deposits of $5.5 billion were released, netting Iran $800 million.

◆ **Exhibit 22.6:**   **Chase Manhattan and the Shah of Iran**

◆   *Source*:   Hulbert, Mark. *Interlock: The Untold Story of American Banks, Oil Interests, the Shah's Money, Debts and the Astounding Connections Between Them*, Richardson and Snyder, New York, 1982.

End-of-chapter Questions

1. Describe three possible reasons for entering international banking markets.
2. What is an Edge Act corporation? How does it differ from an agreement corporation?
3. Differentiate between an international bank branch and a subsidiary.
4. What advantages may be attributed to offshore centers? Are they generally all alike?
5. At a local bank, inquire whether and where the institution has the following international facilities:
   a. Edge Act or agreement corporation
   b. Representative office
   c. Agency

d. Branch

e. Subsidiary

Now, evaluate the types of service that this bank is likely to be able to offer a local company that expands operations internationally.

6. Do you believe there is a connection between the competitive strength of multinational industrial firms and international banks? Why or why not?

7. For what reasons did syndicated loans become widely used on Euromarkets?

8. In what ways are note issuance facilities (NIFs) preferable to syndicated loans.

9. Obtain a copy of the most recent annual report for a local bank. Determine the extent to which the bank is involved in international lending.

   a. What amount and percentage of loans are attributable to international transactions?

   b. To what extent has the bank offered international NIFs?

10. From the Board of Governors of the Federal Reserve System, obtain the most recent *Country Exposure Lending Survey*.

   a. Analyze the amounts and percentages of total US bank loans by country.

   b. Which US banks have extended the greatest amount of outstanding international loans?

SELECTED REFERENCES

Dale, Richard. *The Regulation of International Banking*, Prentice-Hall, Englewood Cliffs, NJ, 1986.

Hulbert, Mark. *Interlock: The Untold Story of American Banks, Oil Interests, the Shah's Money, Debts, and the Astounding Connections Between Them*, Richardson and Snyder, New York, 1982.

Johns, Richard Anthony. *Tax Havens and Offshore Finance*, St. Martin's Press, New York, 1983.

Johnson, Hazel J. *Banking in Europe: Managing Change in a New Marketplace*, Lafferty Publications, Dublin and London, 1996.

Johnson, Hazel J. *Banking in Asia*, Lafferty Publications, Dublin and London, 1997.

Johnson, Hazel J. *Banking in Latin America: Competing and Winning in a New Era*, Lafferty Publications, Dublin and London, 1998.

Jones, Frank J. and Frank J. Fabozzi. *The International Government Bond Markets*, Probus, Chicago (now McGraw-Hill, New York), 1992.

Kim, Seung H. and Steven W. Miller. *Competitive Structure of the International Banking Industry*, Lexington Books, Lexington, Mass., 1983.

Kraar, Louis. "How Americans Win in Asia," *Fortune*, 124, no. 8 (October 7, 1991), p. 140.

Lorch, Donatella. "Banks Follow Immigrants to Flushing," *New York Times*, August 7, 1991, pp. B1–B2.

Mathis, F. John, ed. *Offshore Lending by US Commercial Banks*, 2nd edn, Bankers' Association for Foreign Trade, Washington, DC, and Robert Morris Associates, Philadelphia, 1981.

Mullineux, Andrew. *International Banking and Financial Systems: A Comparison*, Graham and Trotman, London, 1987.

Park, Keith K. H. and Antoine W. Van Agtmael. *The World's Emerging Stock Markets*, Probus, Chicago, 1993.

Pastré, Oliver. *Multinationals: Bank and Corporation Relationships*, JAI Press, Greenwich, Conn., 1981.

Reynolds, Paul D. *China's International Banking and Financial System*, Praeger Publishers, New York, 1982.

Spendlei, J. Andrew. *The Politics of International Credit: Private Finance and Foreign Policy in Germany and Japan*, The Brookings Institution, Washington, DC, 1984.

Stone, Charles, Anne Zissu, and Jess Lederman, eds. *The Global Asset Backed Securities Market*, Probus, Chicago, 1993.

Subcommittee on Financial Institutions Supervision, Regulation and Insurance. *Task Force Report on the International Competitiveness of US Financial Institutions*, Committee on Banking, Finance and Urban Affairs, US House of Representatives, Washington, DC, 1990.

United Nations Centre on Transnational Corporations. *International Income Taxation and Developing Countries*, United Nations, New York, 1988.

Walter, Ingo. *Global Competition in Financial Services: Liberalization*, Ballinger Publishing Company, Cambridge, Mass., 1988.

The Impact of Technological Change

chapter 23

CHAPTER OVERVIEW

This chapter:
- Examines the development of payment systems in the context of technology.
- Identifies several ways in which technology has changed the way commercial banks provide services.
- Outlines the impact that technology has had on the securities industry.
- Briefly describes financial services on the Internet.

KEY TERMS

automated teller machine
back-office operations
check float
credit card annual fee
credit card draft
credit card discount
credit cards
debit card
e-cash
electronic check presentment
expert system
giro system
house check

inference engine
Internet
knowledge base
magnetic ink character recognition (MICR)
on-us check
payment mechanisms
point-of-sale transaction
private clearing house
proof of deposit
smart card
truncation
user interface
wire transfer

CHAPTER OUTLINE

Introduction

Banking services in the United States have evolved from an early emphasis on deposit-taking (primarily demand deposits and savings accounts) and short-term loans into a much wider range of deposits and loans. As banking clientele has become more financially sophisticated, so have bank operations. Commercial banks have always played a vital role in the country's payments system. Now that role is more highly automated in order to expand capacity and to provide more convenient, round-the-clock service to retail customers.

The evolution of technology in corporate banking services has been just as profound. Banks now have direct links between their systems and those of their clients. These applications have been made possible in large part by the development of client–server architecture which allows the sharing of files, programs, and data by multiple users. Electronic data interchange (EDI) enables corporate bank clients to request funds, monitor their accounts, and execute certain transactions automatically.

Technology has virtually revolutionized the provision of financial services in the securities industry. During the 1970s, paper-dependent activities that documented securities trades became such a processing problem that the industry was almost paralyzed by high transaction volume. Technology has simplified this process. Through technological innovations in the securities industry, on-line financial information is available and actual securities trades are possible.

The Internet is the frontier of financial services provision. Its impact has only begun to be felt. Yet already a new form of money – e-cash – and a full array of banking services are being offered.

 Payments Mechanisms

Commercial banks historically played a central role in the payment systems in the United States and other countries. Until the Federal Reserve System was formed in 1913, commercial banks issued notes that circulated as money. After the Federal Reserve took over note issuance responsibilities, banks continued to play a major role in payments because checks became a widely accepted means of payment. Over time, the acceptance of checks has created a massive and expensive check clearing requirement. New methods of managing the check clearing process use technology to reduce this cost. In addition, other payment methods – such as credit cards, wire transfers, automated teller machines, debit cards, and smart cards – reduce the need for the paper check.

1.1 CHECK CLEARING

After cash, *checks* are the most preferred method of payment in the Unites States. Worldwide, it has been estimated that the daily settlement of checking account balances in the United States and abroad amount to $2 trillion. In the United States alone, approximately two billion checks are written each day.

1.1.1 THE CHECK CLEARING PROCESS

When a check is drawn on the same bank in which it is deposited, it is referred to as an *on-us* check or *house* check and is cleared by the next day. At the end of the day, on-us checks are separated from on-others checks (those drawn on other banks) by a reader/sorter that reads the *magnetic ink character recognition (MICR)* line at the bottom of each check.

> **On-us or house check:**
> Check payable from funds on deposit at the same bank where it is presented for collection.

> **Magnetic ink character recognition (MICR) line:**
> Machine readable characters used to encode checks so that they can be read electronically by a reader/sorter. MICR information includes the identifying number of the bank on which the check is drawn, routing information, and the serial number of the check.

The second step in check clearing is the *proof of deposit* process in which the check amounts are verified.

> **Proof of deposit:**
> The process of verifying the dollar amount on a check that has been deposited. This is done by comparing the amount written on the check with the amount on the deposit slip.

The third step in the check clearing process depends on whether the check is drawn on a local bank or on a bank in another city. If the payor (writer of the check) and the payee (depositor of the check) are in the same city, their banks may clear these transactions directly. On the initial day of check processing, the bank into which the check has been deposited (Bank B) records an increase in the deposit balance (bank's liability) of the payee and an increase in a temporary cash account. After the check has cleared (often the next day):

- The bank on which the check was drawn (Bank A) records a reduction in deposits (liability) and cash (asset).
- Bank B reclassifies the amount to a permanent cash account – Due from Bank A (or Due from the local clearing house).

For a $100 check, the accounting entries are:

Bank	DR	CR
(Day of deposit)		
B Cash Items in Collection	100	
Deposits (Payee)		100
(After clearing)		
A Deposits (Payor)	100	
Due from Bank B		100
B Due from Bank A	100	
Cash Items in Collection		100

One of the consequences of this system is that payors benefit from *check float*. Float exists because a check is technically not paid until the payor's bank receives it and verifies sufficiency of available funds. The greater the distance between payee and payor, the greater the float will be. In the interim, the payor's balance is not reduced and any applicable interest continues to accrue – creating *payor float*. This situation favors payors (who receive credit for the payments as soon as the payees receive the checks) at the expense of payees (who must wait until checks clear before funds are available to them). Furthermore, the payee's banks may not prevent the payee from having access to the deposited funds beyond a reasonable period of time that is stipulated by law.

> **Check float:**
> The time that elapses between the payee's receipt of a check and the corresponding reduction in the payor's account.

Checks often cross state lines in the clearing process. In these cases, the Federal Reserve System facilitates the check-clearing process.

First Tennessee Bank operates a particularly interesting private clearing service. First Tennessee is head-quartered in Memphis, also the headquarters of Federal Express Corporation, the overnight delivery company. Federal Express packages are shipped to Memphis, where they are sorted and then shipped to their final destinations. First Express, the service offered by First Tennessee Bank, operates on the same principle. Each night, banks send their checks to Memphis via Federal Express or other overnight courier. The checks are processed at the Federal Express hub within three hours – run through reader/sorters and sorted by city and bank. By 8 a.m. the following morning, all checks have been shipped to the cities of the banks on which they have been drawn.

First Tennessee plays an important role because small banks do not have the resources to develop a high-speed and highly efficient clearing facility. In the mid-1990s, it was estimated that more than 8,000 banks were still processing their own checks. Further advances in alternative means of check presentment will likely lead to a decline in the number of paper checks being handled and a corresponding over capacity in check processing departments of many banks. In turn, a centralized, third-party check clearing system can offer important efficiencies.

◆ **Exhibit 23.1:** **The high-speed clearing services of First Tennessee Bank**

◆ *Source*:   Murphy, Patricia A., "Using Imaging to Increase Check Shop Productivity," *Bank Management*, October 1993, pp. 54–5.

1.1.2 PRIVATE CHECK CLEARING SERVICES

In addition to the check clearing services provided by the Federal Reserve System, a significant number of checks are processed in *private clearing houses* operated by depository institutions that agree to a common set of rules.

> **Private clearing house:**
> A central collection location where banks and other depository institutions exchange checks and other payments.

Private clearing houses keep track of the value of checks presented by their members and, at a cutoff time, determine the net position of each. Those members that have more funds credited to their accounts (received) than debited (paid), receive payment from the clearing house. On the other hand, those that have more funds debited (paid) than credited (received) make payments to the clearing house. (See also Exhibit 23.1.)

1.1.3 CANADA, EUROPE, AND JAPAN

The check-writing habit is also well developed in Canada, but the clearing function is much different. Five major banks control approximately 90 percent of total bank assets: the Royal Bank of Canada, the Canadian Imperial Bank of Commerce, Scotiabank (the Bank of Nova Scotia), the Bank of Montreal, and the Toronto Dominion Bank. Reciprocal agreements among them have all but eliminated check float. Consumer checks are paid on a same-day basis, despite the fact that actual settlement occurs the next day. Writers of checks in denominations of $50,000 or more (business transactions) are assessed any float costs that accrue. This system is possible because there is a high degree of concentration in the Canadian banking system. In addition, nationwide branching of the five major banks has resulted in well distributed locations and market shares.

In Europe, most countries have a *giro system* that performs the function of checking accounts in the US. Because payments are effected at a centralized location, there is no payor float. The bank transaction in the US that is most similar to a giro transfer is the "on-us" check, as described above.

Giro system:
> A nonbank payments system (frequently at the post office) that transfers funds from one account to another on a same-day basis.

Interestingly, the giro system of the United Kingdom is not used as frequently as its continental European counterparts. This is partially because the UK Post Office Giro system was not introduced until 1968. More fundamentally, however, British clearing banks have long emphasized personal banking services – branching nationwide and encouraging the use of checks. The four major UK banks dominate the retail banking market, controlling 80 percent of all personal bank accounts. They are HSBC Holdings, National Westminster, Barclays Bank, and Lloyds Bank.

In contrast, in Japan, checks and giro transactions originate almost exclusively in the business sector. Japanese payments are much more frequently in the form of cash or electronic transfer. The Japanese postal savings system has no parallel in the United States. This system accumulates savings from individuals and small businesses. The postal savings system is the largest savings bank in the world and, in the mid-1990s, represented approximately 17 percent of total assets of the banking system of Japan. It is a popular outlet for savings because the interest income was tax-exempt for deposits up to ¥3 million until 1988 and because there are over 20,000 locations, compared to approximately 10,000 bank branches.

Currently, Japanese postal savings accounts may be maintained with balances up to ¥5 million. While interest income on these accounts is no longer tax-exempt, the interest rate is attractive as compared to other alternatives. Also, the postal system is extremely convenient. Through the postal savings system, wire transfers are easily done. (This and other forms of electronic payment are discussed in the following sections entitled "Wire Transfers" and "Other Retail Electronic Payments.") Transfers are possible not only to all domestic locations, but also to 82 other countries that have agreements between their postal authorities and that of Japan.

1.1.4 ELECTRONIC CHECK PRESENTMENT

Through *electronic check presentment (ECP)*, information on a check may be shared electronically much faster than the physical check can be cleared.

Electronic check presentment (ECP):
> Process of clearing checks in which information from the MICR line is exchanged rather than the physical checks.

With ECP, the payee bank (bank in which the check has been deposited) scans the MICR line. This information is wired to the payor bank (bank upon which the check has been written). If there are insufficient funds for the check, the check is flagged overnight instead of several days, or even a week, later.

ECP standards and practices are being developed through the Electronic Check Clearing House Organization (ECCHO), with some of the larger member banks including:

- Citicorp
- Bank of America
- Chase Manhattan
- Chemical Bank
- NationsBank

In the mid-1990s, a total of more than 60 banks were members of ECCHO and the ECP procedure was being tested in Michigan and California. During the same period, it was estimated that as many as 1,000 banks had the computer capacity to receive some sort of electronic check information.

The Federal Reserve System is also examining the ECP technology. In a pilot program including several banks, the Federal Reserve sends and receives ECP information of the participating institutions.

1.1.5 CHECK TRUNCATION

The Federal Reserve has long been a champion of further efficiencies in the payments system, actively encouraging *truncation* – the ultimate efficiency in check processing. Checks can either be truncated at the bank of first deposit or by a Federal Reserve bank. Excluding canceled checks from customer statements saves the payor bank at least $1 per account per month. Given the thousands of accounts maintained by most banks, the savings can be substantial.

> **Truncation:**
> Bank service in which canceled checks are held by the payor's bank or by another bank in the check clearing process, rather than being returned in the account statement.

Under the electronic check clearing program of the Federal Reserve – available in all 12 Federal Reserve Bank districts – paper checks may follow the electronic exchange of payment data. However, if the bank requests, the Federal Reserve Bank will not forward the paper checks, but instead record microfilm copies or other images of the checks for later access by banks or their customers.

1.1.6 IMAGING TECHNOLOGY

Employing *imaging technology* in check clearing means that a bank would receive graphical images of the checks drawn against it instead of the actual paper check. The Federal Reserve also has much interest in this technology because it can provide backup support for truncating. Using images can assist the payor bank in such areas as pay-or-no-pay decisions and signature verifications. (Such systems are being developed by technology companies such as IBM, Unisys, NCR, and Banctec Systems.)

> **Imaging technology (check clearing):**
> Creating and transmitting an electronic picture (image) of a check during the check clearing process instead of shipping the physical check.

The biggest technical challenge in imaging the check clearing process is the correct interpretation of the written check amounts. *Character amount recognition* or *character amount read (CAR)* means that personnel need not manually read the numerals written in the courtesy amount boxes of checks. The challenge is that there are as many as 30 different ways that checks are written. The problems with CAR tend to center around three factors:

- The condition or readability of the physical checks
- The various ways that customers write checks
- The variety of locations for the courtesy amount box on the checks

Imaging technology significantly improves the work environment in the check processing area. Typically, in this fast-paced operational area, two people who want to speak to each other must shout to be heard. With imaging technology, the same people may whisper and still hear each other. At the same time, the speed of processing has dramatically increases over conventional systems. An average, conventional check-clearing operation can clear about 1,400 checks per hour. An imaging system clears more than 20,000 per hour.

1.2 CREDIT CARDS

1.2.1 THE UNITED STATES

Credit cards are a relatively new means of payment that has become extremely popular. The first cards were introduced in the 1950s, at which time, card payees manually telephoned to receive authorization for each transaction. The current technology most often uses plastic cards with magnetic stripes on the back. The magnetic stripe enables payees to verify cards electronically before accepting them as payment. This verification is via a communications network set up over telephone lines. Credit cards are convenient and reduce the need to carry cash. Because card verification is now so streamlined, many retail establishments frequently accept credit cards more readily than checks.

For banks, credit cards are a profitable product line. Income is realized in several ways. In every case, the payee accepting the credit card for payment does not receive the full amount shown on the *credit card draft*. The draft is an instruction by the payor to the credit card issuer to pay the amount shown to the payee. However, when the draft is presented to the credit card issuer, it is discounted by 3 to 5 percent. The *discount* is a source of income for commercial banks that issue credit cards.

Credit card draft:
   The sales slip created in a credit card transaction, showing amount, payee, payor, credit card issuer, and payor signature.

If the bank charges an *annual fee* to cardholders (usually $25 to $50), these fees are also income for the bank. The payor receives a monthly statement from the bank that lists the transactions for that month. If the cardholder pays the bank for these transactions before the specified due date, no interest is charged. If not, the bank earns *interest income* on unpaid balances. The interest rate on credit cards loans is higher than other forms of consumer lending, often in excess of 18 percent.

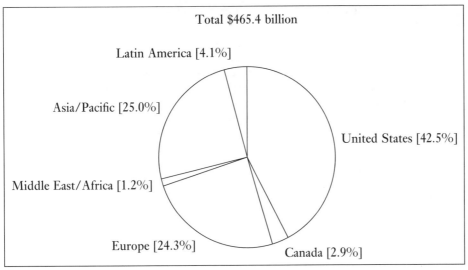

Total $465.4 billion

Latin America [4.1%]

Asia/Pacific [25.0%]

Middle East/Africa [1.2%]

Europe [24.3%]

Canada [2.9%]

United States [42.5%]

◆ **Exhibit 23.2:** **Worldwide credit card sales, 1995**

◆ *Source*: Author's graphic based on data from: Frank, John N. "MasterCard Prepares for a Makeover," *Credit Card Management*, May 1996, p. 61.

Because of this high rate, the discounts, and annual fees, credit card operations can be quite profitable.

Of course, there is also a relatively higher probability of uncollectible loans since the majority of credit cards are unsecured. This was particularly true in the mid-1990s when banks competed vigorously to attract consumer credit card customers.

Credit cards are offered primarily through two member associations:

- MasterCard
- Visa

Major retailers in the United States also offer credit cards that are honored in their retail establishments. Many smaller retailers avoid the expense of stand-alone credit card programs by issuing private-label cards that are managed by credit card banks or finance companies. Sears has issued a competing card called the Discover card which is accepted at establishments not associated with any Sears affiliate.

A *travel and entertainment* credit card is used only for 30-day credit cycles. The entire balance is due before the end of the 30–day cycle that follows the customer billing. The first such card was issued in 1950 by Diners Club (now owned by Citicorp). The most common travel and entertainment card is American Express, first issued in 1958.

1.2.2 JAPAN

Bank credit cards also have gained prominence outside the United States. Exhibit 23.2 shows the relative volume of credit card sales in 1995. After the United States (42.5 percent), Asia was the second largest credit card market in 1995. Japan is the largest Asian market.

In general, consumer banking services have been slower to evolve in Japan than in the United States. This is primarily because the larger city banks have historically focused on large corporate clients. The regional banks that catered to individuals had neither comparable nationwide networks nor management. However, at the urging of the Ministry of Finance (the equivalent of the US Treasury Department) and certain political factions, city banks began to issue credit cards in the 1960s. The regulators did not permit Japanese banks to issue the cards directly. Instead, they are issued by bank affiliates. Another difference is that Japanese regulators do not permit bank cards to be repaid in installments. Thus, Japanese bank credit cards are similar to US travel and entertainment cards – the balance must paid in total each month.

The Japan Credit Bureau (JCB) card is the most widely distributed with 40 percent of the Japanese credit card market in the mid-1990s. Other major issuers are Sumitomo Credit Service, and Union Credit Company.

It should be noted that there may still be considerable payor float involved with credit card transactions. In this case, the float is the time necessary to process, invoice, and collect the sales drafts. In essence, card-issuing banks are compensated for this sometimes considerable float through the discount.

Telecommunications technology has enhanced the use of bank credits as a part of the payments system in the United States and abroad. In a similar way, the use of direct electronic payments has increased.

1.3 WIRE TRANSFERS

Wire transfers eliminate the need for magnetic tapes and are more direct electronic links. Through Fedwire (Federal Reserve), CHIPS (Clearing House Interbank Payments System, New York), or SWIFT (Society for Worldwide Interbank Financial Telecommunications), large interbank transactions are settled on a same-day basis. Wire transfers are an extension of the special handling for important transactions such as money market purchases or sales. Currently, immediately available funds can be transferred to any other party almost instantaneously.

Fedwire is a high-speed electronic communications network (operated by the Federal Reserve Bank of New York) that links banks with the Federal Reserve Board of Governors, the 12 Federal Reserve District Banks and their 24 branches, the US Treasury Department, and other federal agencies. Depository institutions use Fedwire to transfer funds on their own behalf or on behalf of their customers in connection with federal funds sold and purchased, other interbank transactions, purchases and sales of securities, and other time-sensitive payments.

The authorization of each transaction is ensured through appropriate internal controls. While some transactions are still initiated by telephone, most are now done via terminal or personal computer. Because a depository institution may be unable to predict the flow of payments through Fedwire in its account with the Federal Reserve, there may be insufficient funds to cover all payments when they are processed. The Federal Reserve sets limits on the amount of credit that it provides to an institution. That is, the Federal Reserve limits *intra-day* loans by requiring collateral or assessing fees. Fedwire is the largest dedicated network in operation.

CHIPS, owned and operated by the New York Clearing House Association, transfers large amounts for interbank settlements for institutions with offices in New York City. This computerized funds transfer system links 140 depository institutions and is used primarily for international dollar payments, accounting for 90 percent of the interbank payments relating to international trade. Settlement is accomplished at the close of business each day through special accounts at the Federal Reserve Bank of New York.

SWIFT (the Society for Worldwide Interbank Financial Telecommunications) is a nonprofit, cooperative organization that facilitates the exchange of payments messages, but not the payments, between more than 1,000 financial institutions in the North America, Europe, Latin America, Africa, Asia, and Australia. SWIFT was developed as a more efficient alternative to telex or mail. Today, it is a widely used system for the secure transmittal of financial data.

SWIFT began operations in 1977, providing a framework for an international communications system among financial institutions using common terminals and standard communication techniques. In 1988, access to the SWIFT network was expanded to securities firms and securities broker-dealers. At that time, securities transfers were added to the menu of SWIFT services.

A SWIFT transaction is not a payment, but instead is an advice or instruction to transfer funds of a specified amount at another financial institution. The actual exchange of funds takes place on the domestic clearing system. In the United States, SWIFT interbank transfers of funds are completed via Fedwire or CHIPS.

1.4 OTHER RETAIL ELECTRONIC PAYMENTS

Other technological advances in consumer payments are an off-shoot of the use of cards and innovations in corporate payments systems. As noted in Exhibit 23.3, these include:

Method	Description
Cash dispenser (CD) or automated teller machine (ATM)	CDs are unmanned facilities that may be accessed with plastic cards with magnetic stripes. Cash withdrawals reduce the balance of the relevant account (checking, savings, etc.).
	ATMs dispense cash and provide other services such as transfers among the individual's accounts, routine bill payments, balance verification, and deposits.
Debit card or point-of-sale (POS) transaction	Bank card that withdraws funds from a bank account instead of a line of bank credit. Purchases are charged directly to a checking or savings account.
	A transaction-specific transfer of funds that immediately reduces the payor's bank account balance and increases the payee's. Transfer is completed before payor leaves the retail establishment.
Smart card	Bank card containing a computer chip for identification, special purpose processing, and data storage. The computer chip has the ability to validate the cardholder's personal identification number, authorize retail purchases, and store personal records.

◆ **Exhibit 23.3: Other retail electronic payments**

- Automated teller machines (ATMs)
- Debit cards
- Smart cards

1.4.1 ATMs

The United States

Cash dispensers (CDs) were the first applications of automation in retail banking. These early machines usually dispensed a fixed amount of currency in a single denomination and most were off-line. Fairly rapid advances made it possible to receive larger amounts of currency and to perform other functions, such as loan payments, deposits, transfers between accounts owned by the customer, and payments to third parties. The later generations are referred to as *automated teller machines (ATMs)*.

Some ATMs are positioned in an outside wall of the bank building to provide 24-hour access to bank services. Others are located in the lobby of the bank or in separate, adjoining lobbies. The enclosed ATMs provide greater customer security while using the machine. Increasingly, ATMs are on-line operations, particularly in the United States.

Shared ATMs away from bank branches enable several banks to establish a "branch" in high density areas such as factories, hospitals, universities, and airports. Generally, banks have been reluctant to share ATMs that are located on their own premises. Banks in various geographical regions have agreed to sharing arrangements in order to provide convenient service for their traveling customers.

The functions of the ATM have only begun to be explored. Other financial functions that are possible with ATM technology include:

- High-speed dispensing stamps, coupons, tickets, traveler's checks
- Printing and dispensing checkbooks
- Check imaging and cashing
- Printing and dispensing cashier's checks and money orders
- Printing mini account statements
- Advertising and selling mutual funds

It is clear that the use of this technology will be greatly expanded in the future.

Canada and Mexico

The networks in Canada are as well defined and developed as those in the United States. In fact, since the Canadian banking system is composed of relatively few banks *vis-à-vis* that of the United States, the Canadian ATM system complements its nationwide system of branches and is perhaps even more efficient than that in the United States. On the other hand, in Mexico 70 percent of the ATMs are controlled by just two banks – Banamex (30 percent) and Bancomer (40 percent). The Mexican retailing banking market has not yet been developed to its full potential.

1.4.2 DEBIT CARDS

Point of sale (POS) electronic links theoretically accomplish the same objective as wire transfers. However, while wire transfers typically involve large denominations, POS is geared to the smaller-denomination, high-volume retail market, for example, grocery stores and service stations. In this context, *convenience* and *cost* are important considerations.

In order to be convenient, a standardized system with adequate distribution is necessary. Standardization is achieved with plastic *debit cards* with magnetic strips that contain information about the payor's account. Telecommunications equipment that connects the records of participating banks makes it possible to simultaneously reduce the account balance of the payor by the amount of the retail transaction and increase the balance of the retailer.

Debit card:
A card whose use results in reduction of the payor's bank account balance, that is, a "debit" to the deposit account of the payor. The offsetting "credit" is to the payee's deposit account, or, alternatively, to the deposit account of the payee's bank.

There are two basic types of debit cards:

- Bank-issued ATM cards
- National debit cards

The bank-issued ATM cards were first used by customers as access cards to their bank accounts for cash withdrawals. Over time, these cards have been converted to general purpose transactions cards, that is, substitutes for checks in retail establishments.

The national debit cards were designed, from the outset, for retail purchases. The Visa version is Interlink and the MasterCard national debit card is called Maestro.

By the mid-1990s, the POS and debit card technologies had been accepted both by banks and the consuming public. For the banks, debit transactions are much cheaper to process than checks – by about one half. Also, debit cards represent a source of bank fee income – annual fees (often from $12 to $15) and per-transaction fees (from $0.25 to $2.00). Banks earn a discount – from the merchants – that is comparable to a credit card discount. Consumers consider the on-line debit card (with personal identification number, PIN) as a secure alternative to checks or off-line arrangements.

1.4.3 SMART CARDS

Smart cards are the next generation of alternatives to cash and checks. The computer chip in a smart card can validate a user's personal identification number (PIN), authorize retail purchases, verify account balances, and store personal records. The chip memory can also hold information on the user's relationship with, for example, a bank, a securities firm, or an insurance company. Each time the card is used, the personal database is updated.

Smart card:
A card containing a computer chip for identification, special purpose processing, and data storage. Also called a *chip card* or a *memory card*.

Technically, a smart card contains a computer chip instead of a magnetic strip. However, the first generation of smart cards were *prepaid* cards with magnetic strips, also called *electronic purses* or *stored-value* cards. The two most common uses of such prepaid cards have been prepaid transit cards and prepaid telephone cards. Transit authorities in New York City and Washington, DC use these smart cards to eliminate the use of tokens and to charge different fares for different routes. Telephone cards, representing a $1 billion in sales in 1996, are issued by MCI, AT&T, and GTE.

From the perspective of financial institutions, smart cards with magnetic strips represent less of a shift in technology than smart cards with computer chips. Retailers with whom the banks cooperate in POS facilities have invested heavily in magnetic strip technology. Examples of these retailers include oil companies (service stations), national food chains, and national department store chains. A move to chip cards will represent significant costs for a large-scale transition.

Another issue for financial institutions and the development of smart card technology is Regulation E (Reg E), the Federal Reserve regulation that sets rules, liabilities, and procedures for electronic funds transfers (EFT). Reg E also establishes consumer protections in EFTs. One of these protections is that receipts are generally required to document EFTs. This provision must be addressed before smart cards can be used to, for example, transfer funds between bank and securities accounts or settle insurance claims.

Lastly, the financial services industry must address the issue of consumer acceptance of smart cards. In the mid-1990s, few US residents had been presented the opportunity to use a smart card. Thus, the level of consumer acceptance remained uncertain.

② Direct Banking

The need for increased efficiency in the banking industry means that many services will be offered without the intervention of a human teller – *direct banking*. Direct banking can be offered through telephone access or computer access. Typically, direct banking permits customers to make account inquiries, to pay utility bills, to transfer funds between checking and savings accounts, and, in some cases, to purchase mutual fund shares. However, the cost of offering such a service is high in terms of software, hardware, personnel training, and building customer awareness/acceptance.

MasterBanking is offered by MasterCard to provide home banking and electronic bill payment. A strategic alliance between MasterCard and Independent Bankers Association of America (IBAA) makes it possible for smaller banks to provide these services to their customers and earn fee income in the process.

MasterBanking is a nationwide service that permits depositors to make payments at any time and from any location. The system will support personal computers, screen phones (special equipment), or conventional telephones. Customers give instructions via one of these media and receives a confirmation number when the transaction is complete. Should the customer have any questions about the transaction, he or she may telephone to confirm the details. Other services include intrabank transfers, balance inquiries, and paid and cleared checks. Ultimately, MasterBanking will provide access to investment brokerage, yellow pages, and news retrieval services.

In general, bank customers are more likely to contact the bank via telephone than by any other means besides a branch visit. As a result, *call centers* built and operated by individual banks have grown rapidly in importance. In each case, a voice-response system is available for balance inquiries and other routine transactions. In addition, many banks now use the call center in connection with a human operator to accept loan applications. Because the applications are subject to standardized underwriting criteria, that is, standard rules for loan approval, response to the loan applications is sometimes possible within 30 minutes. Technology supports both the application process and the approval process.

The Securities Industry and Technology

Fully electronic transmission and storage of trading information began in the 1960s. Quotation devices were first attached to ticker circuits to provide bid and ask quotations and prices. This system evolved into the Central Certificate Service, a subsidiary of the New York Stock Exchange, that computerized the transfer of securities ownership and reduced the paper required to record the transfer. (See also chapter 5 for a discussion of securities exchanges.) In 1973, this service became the Depository Trust Company. In 1971, the over-the-counter market was computerized by NASDAQ – National Association of Securities Dealers Automated Quotations.

3.1 Back-office Operations and Order Execution

Technology has been particularly helpful in relieving pressures in the back-office operations of securities firms. In the 1960s, a severe back-office paperwork crisis occurred. Brokerage houses were unable to maintain timely processing of the required paperwork associated with high volume. Finally, in April 1968, the crisis became so acute that exchange trading was halted so that the back-offices could bring the paper processing up to date. This led to the development of automated systems for back-office processing. In 1972, the New York Stock Exchange and the American Stock Exchange formed the Securities Industry Automation Corporation (SIAC) to coordinate development of data processing. SIAC introduced three major innovations in the 1970s:

> **Back-office operations (securities):**
> The area of a securities exchange or firm in which orders are processed, customer accounts are updated, trade confirmations are prepared, and payments are made and received.

- Market Data System (MDS) to provide price information, including last-trade prices.
- Designated Order Turnaround System (DOT) to automate the delivery of small orders (fewer than 199 shares) from member firms to exchange floors.
- Common Message Switch (CMS) to allow member firms to communicate with other SIAC firms.

In 1969, the Pacific Stock Exchange (PSE) automated a portion of its trade execution. Unless interrupted by a specialist, trades were completed by a computer without human intervention. This system, the first of its kind, was called COMEX. In 1979, the PSE introduced an improved version of this system, called Securities Communication Order Routing and Execution (SCOREX). The process of order execution is as follows:

- When an order reaches SCOREX from a member firm of the PSE, the current Intermarket Trading Price (ITS) is determined, that is, its market price.
- Both the order and the ITS are displayed on the specialist's computer.

- For a market order, that is, an order that is to be filled at the ITS, the specialist has 15 seconds to modify the order (for a more favorable price) before the order is executed.
- For a limit order, that is, an order for a buy or sell only when the price of the security reaches a specified "limit," the specialist has 15 seconds to (1) reject or (2) accept and hold the order in his or her electronic "book."
  - If the order is rejected, it is returned to the member firm that originated the order.
  - Otherwise, the order is held until the specified market price coincides with the ITS.

Most exchanges now have systems that operate in a similar way as SCOREX. There are also systems for small orders in option contracts and in NASDAQ for small orders of over-the-counter stocks. The Cincinnati Stock Exchange and the London International Stock Exchange have no physical trading floors but operate through computer rooms only. The London International Stock Exchange and NASDAQ combine computer-screen-based quotation systems with telephone negotiation. In Toronto, Madrid, Brussels, Copenhagen, Zurich, and Frankfurt, exchanges are virtually "floorless" and operate primarily through technology applications.

3.2 FINANCIAL INFORMATION SERVICES

As early as 1850, Paul Julius Reuter first used carrier pigeons to fly stock market quotations between Brussels (Belgium) and Aachen (Germany). Shortly thereafter, when an underwater telegraph cable was installed between Dover (England) and Calais (France), Reuter began delivering financial news and market quotations from London to continental Europe. Today, Reuters Holdings PLC continues to be one of the dominant providers of financial information. Reuters maintains a vast international communications network and is a market leader in foreign exchange, international bonds, and other debt issues. In foreign exchange and fixed-income securities (bond) markets, there is no central exchange. Thus, price information is provided by banks and securities firms to financial information vendors.

However, growing links between the equities, futures, fixed-income, and foreign-exchange markets have led to diversification among information vendors who have traditionally specialized in one market.

- Dow Jones & Co., Inc. has a dominant role in providing information concerning the US equity markets.
- Telerate, owned by Dow Jones, enjoys a near monopoly in the market for US government securities price quotes.

Telerate electronically distributes bids, offers, and last-trade information to both primary government securities dealers and retail customers. This is done under an exclusive agreement with a securities broker that provides information gathered from all government securities dealers. In a move toward diversification, Telerate acquired the leading stock quote provider in Canada and entered the equity market.

Some companies provide information gathered from only one broker/dealer. For example, Bloomberg (partially owned by Merrill Lynch) is another important provider of government securities pricing information via electronic media – primarily computer screen-based applications. Data fed to subscribers of the service is obtained from the primary dealers of Merrill Lynch.

Other information vendors provide information concerning equity and commodity price information. Using either dedicated telephone lines or satellite technology, quotations are sent from the vendor to their customers. Among these are ADP, Dow Jones, Knight-Ridder, and PC Quote.

3.3 INSTINET

Instinet Corporation is a subsidiary of Reuters Holdings PLC and a broker/dealer registered with the US Securities and Exchange Commission (SEC). Its offices are in New York, London, Frankfurt, Paris, Zurich, Hong Kong, Tokyo, and Toronto. Instinet's brokerage service is provided to securities industry professionals. These services are provided primarily through computer and communications technology.

Customer orders that are entered into an Instinet terminal are displayed on the computer screens of all users of the worldwide service simultaneously. Traders execute their own orders, reducing transactions costs and ensuring more control over the actual trades. Approximately 85 percent of Instinet activity is concentrated in the NASDAQ market.

3.4 EXPERT SYSTEMS

In addition to providing back-office support, financial information, and on-line trading, technology also is making it possible to partially replace the decision-making process surrounding a financial transaction. Expert systems interpret defined parameters of market conditions and arrive at buy and sell decisions.

Expert system:
>   A computer software program that imitates human decision-making in the context of securities trading.

The first component of an expert system is the *experiential knowledge*, that is, a set of rules and facts or if/then statements. This is also referred to as the system's *knowledge base*.

The second component of an expert system is an *inference engine*. This part of the software program analyzes the knowledge to interpret which parts of it are relevant.

The third component of an expert system is the *user interface* that permits the operator of the system to review the output and decide which rules apply.

In constructing an expert system, programmers interview traders to determine the information used by them to make investment decisions. Once the computer code is written to imitate this process, the system must be reviewed to verify that the system interprets the external data in the same way that the human trader interprets it. To date, such systems have been used to assist traders, but not to replace them. The primary advantage of expert systems appears to be that they relieve traders of repetitive data interpretation.

4 The Internet

The Internet is a worldwide system of computers that are connected primarily through telephone lines. These computers are part of the *World Wide Web (WWW)*. Almost anyone with a computer, a modem, and a telephone line may tap into or "log onto" the Internet. Web sites are locations that may be visited on computers that are a part of the WWW. Commercial firms and educational institutions have *home pages* that provide information about their operations to the public. Government and other data is available on the Internet and may be *downloaded* or printed.

Increasingly, the Internet is being using for commercial transactions. Goods of all varieties may be purchased via the Internet. The method of payment is most often a credit card. Companies selling goods on the Internet establish security measures to prevent the misuse of credit card information.

In addition, *e-cash* is a new type of money that exists only in electronic form. One example of e-cash is offered by CyberCash, a company founded in 1994. This company focuses on providing secure financial transactions over the Internet. As a part of these services, CyberCash offers a security system for credit card transactions.

Also, CyberCash offers a CyberCash wallet that can be used to make purchases over the Internet. The CyberCash Internet wallet is a software program for installation on personal computers that makes it possible to make purchases directly from merchants on the Web. The CyberCoin service is the PC-based equivalent of a debit card for small transactions – between $0.25 and $10.00. Larger transactions can be completed with credit card information.

Financial transactions on the Internet are not limited to purchases of goods. Security First Network Bank (SFNB) is the first bank that operates completely over the Internet. Services provided include basic checking accounts, interest-bearing checking accounts, credit cards, savings accounts, money market deposit accounts, and certificates of deposit. While SFNB has a home page that is accessible to the public, access to the "banking lobby" is strictly controlled by access codes and a kind of electronic buffer between the banking system and the Internet.

Now, virtually every large bank offers Internet services and many smaller ones as well. Online services include checking accounts, mortgages, investment products and other, nonproprietary products. In some cases, bank customers have the alternatives of (1) completing online applications or (2) providing a telephone number so that a bank employee can call and facilitate the application by telephone.

There are strong motivations for banks to offer Internet services. An electronic check costs approximately $0.10 to process while the paper-based counterpart costs $1.25. Furthermore, as the consuming public becomes more comfortable with online services and payments, institutions that do not participate in Internet banking may face a loss of deposits – or disintermediation.

 Summary

The pace at which technology is changing the provision of financial services is quickly accelerating. Technological advances have led to changes in both the delivery and form of payments services. Check clearing is increasingly done with electronic support and likely will be associated with an eventual elimination of the paper document. Credit cards and debit cards have been accepted as substitutes for checks. Without technology, such alternatives would not be possible.

Technology is changing:

- The methods through which banks provide service to clients
- The distribution of information in the securities industry
- Trading and decisions about trading in the securities industry
- The actual location of commercial and financial transactions through the Internet

End-of-chapter Questions

1. a. What is payor float?
   b. How is payor float reduced in Canada?
2. a. Describe a European giro system.
   b. How does a giro system differ from the Japanese postal system?
3. What are some of the contributing factors to the widespread acceptance and use of credit cards in the United States?
4. Differentiate a credit card and a debit card.
5. What is the motivation for eliminating paper in payments processes?
6. What is the difference between electronic check presentment and imaging technology in the check clearing process?
7. What additional services may be provided through smart cards that are not available through debit cards?
8. a. What is direct banking?
   b. What advantages do banks realize from direct banking?
   c. What advantages do customers realize from direct banking?
9. In your opinion, what demographic factors may contribute to the increased use of available technology in financial services?
10. What were the early motivations for introducing technology into the securities industry?
11. Through what technologies/service-providers is it currently possible to obtain financial information?
12. a. What is Instinet?
    b. Who are the primary users of Instinet?
13. a. What is an expert system?
    b. How do expert systems help securities traders?
14. Why is it necessary to devise methods of payment over the Internet?
15. Use the facilities at your university to "log onto" the Internet. Visit the web site of First Security Network Bank. Determine the security measures used to separate the bank from the Internet.
16. Use the facilities at your university to "log onto" the Internet. Visit the website of your bank or another local bank and determine the range of services offered by the institution.

Selected References

Crone, Richard K. "Internet Bill Presentment and Payment: Billers and Bankers Empowering Each Other," *Journal of Retail Banking Services*, Summer 1998, pp. 55–63.

England, Robert Stowe. "Payoff Deferred (Online banking)," *Banking Strategies*, March/April 1998, pp. 41–7.

"Fed: Extra Day Needed to Clear Local Checks," *America's Community Banker*, October 1996, p. 11.

The Federal Reserve System: Purposes and Functions, 8th edn, Washington, DC, 1994.

Frank, John N. "MasterCard Prepares for a Makeover," *Credit Card Management*, May 1996, pp. 60–1.

Lawrence, Colin and Robert P. Shay. *Technological Innovation, Regulations, and the Monetary Economy*, Ballinger Publishing Company, Cambridge, Mass., 1986.

Mitchell, Richard. "Beyond the Basics with ATMs," *Credit Card Management*, pp. 57–62.

Murphy, Patricia A., "Using Imaging to Increase Check Shop Productivity," *Bank Management*, October 1993, pp. 54–5.

US Congress, Office of Technology Assessment, *Electronic Bulls and Bears: US Securities Markets and Information Technology*, Washington, DC, US Government Printing Office, 1990.

Wall Street and Technology, various issues.

Zack, Jeffrey. "As Call Centers Become Profit Centers, Will They Make Banks Seem Too Remote?", Management Strategies, *American Banker* supplement, August 5, 1996.

Commercial Banks and the Securities Markets

chapter 24

Introduction

Since 1933, commercial banks in the United States have been precluded by federal law from engaging in securities activities. The Glass–Steagall Act separated commercial banking from investment banking. However, beginning in the late 1980s, this barrier has been eroded. Banks have long been permitted to engage in the underwriting of government securities and certain municipal securities. By special permission of the Federal Reserve, a small number of banks now operate so-called Section 20 subsidiaries. Offshore, US commercial banks have begun to make their presence felt in underwriting syndicates. Domestically, serious debate continues to chip away Glass-Steagall barriers. It is clear that commercial banks must turn increasingly to lines of business that will supplement shrinking lending margins.

 The Separation of Commercial Banking and Securities Activities

The US banking industry unjustly has been held responsible for a number of economic problems that the country has experienced. Unfortunately, many of the legal and regulatory constraints to a more effective banking system are based on these misconceptions. One misconception is that large money center banks were responsible for money panics that destabilized the financial system. Another is that commercial banks were primarily responsible for the financial devastation of the Great Depression. Neither of these is true. In fact, the banking system was prevented from developing in ways that would avoid some of the money panics. Moreover, it was the Federal Reserve System, not the commercial banking system that prolonged the agony of the Great Depression.

1.1 Early US Money Panics

Before the Federal Reserve System (1914) or the Federal Insurance Corporation (1933), money panics occurred when depositors lost faith that a bank could meet its obligations. (See also chapters 12 and 13 for a discussion of US bank regulation and monetary policy.) When this faith was lost, virtually all bank depositors requested repayment. Under these circumstances, even sound banks could be driven to insolvency because loans and securities could not be liquidated fast enough to satisfy all requests for cash. Essentially, smaller banks were more susceptible to these crises of confidence than larger institutions.

The evolution of US bank regulation almost guaranteed that the country would be subject to money panic episodes because a system of strong, nationwide banks was not permitted to develop. Federal regulation of the early 1900s permitted a nationally chartered bank to branch only to the extent that its home state allowed. (See also chapter 25 for a discussion of bank branching.) As a result, banks had narrowly defined geographic markets which precluded any significant geographic diversification. Such problems were not the result of large money center banks, but instead restrictions on bank operations.

1.2 The Great Depression – Whose Responsibility?

One of the instructions contained in the 1913 Federal Reserve Act was that the reserve banks should maintain credit conditions that accommodated commerce and business. The Fed is charged with maintaining adequate access to credit by expansion of the money supply, if necessary. At the same time, the Fed is responsible for not allowing inflationary spirals to develop as a result of excessive growth in money supply. There is clearly a tradeoff between ensuring adequate money supply and avoiding excess money supply. The early choices made by the Federal Reserve concerning these two opposing objectives had more influence over economic conditions in the United States than did the structure of the banking system.

1.2.1 THE RECESSION OF 1920–1

One of the first important decisions by the Federal Reserve occurred after the end of the First World War (1914–18). To finance the war, the national debt had risen from $1 billion to $27 billion. By the fall of 1919, prices rose at an annual rate of 15 percent. The Federal Reserve decided to stop the inflationary spiral. The discount rate (the rate that banks pay to borrow from the Fed) rose from 4 to 7 percent over the course of a few months and was maintained at this level for 18 months. Other interest rates followed suit. In other words, the price of money nearly doubled.

The economic consequences were dramatic. Commodity prices declined by 50 percent from their 1920 peak and US farmers found themselves in financial crisis. In general, business activity declined precipitously. Specifically:

- Manufacturing output fell 42 percent.
- The unemployment rate increased by a factor of five to almost 12 percent.
- In 1919, 63 banks had failed; in 1921, the number was 506.

1.2.2 THE ROARING TWENTIES

The economy began to recover in 1921, although it was plagued by two milder recessions during the decade (1923 and 1926). New technologies led to a 63 percent increase in output per hour of labor. Mass markets for goods developed, such as automobiles, refrigerators, and radios. New factories were built and manufacturing production increased. The stock market reached new heights. This was the "roaring twenties." The promises of the Federal Reserve appeared to have been fulfilled.

However, signs of trouble also began to develop. Farmers did not recover from the recession of 1920–21. There was a glut of agricultural commodities and commodity prices remained deflated. In 1920, farm families represented 15 percent of gross national product. By 1928, their share was down to nine percent. Even factory laborers were being affected. Some of the productivity gains came from laborers working longer hours for the same pay. Other productivity gains came from improvements in technology that required fewer workers, creating a labor surplus.

In the financial markets, individual loans to purchase stock increased rapidly. The public was eager to buy equities and credit was easy to obtain. Leveraged investment trusts – a new form of financial institution – were formed with a little capital and a lot of borrowed money for the purpose of investing in stocks. Both banks and investors engaged in stock speculation and stock prices rose dramatically as a result. By the summer of 1928, the Federal Reserve was concerned about the level of speculative financial activity.

1.2.3 THE CRASH AND THE DEPRESSION

The bubble burst on October 24, 1929. Within a few days, the value of the stock market declined by one-third. Of the order of $7 billion in bank loans for stock purchases became worthless. The money panic psychology threatened to resurface. But surely the same sort of panic would be averted, because the Federal Reserve could ease the contracted money supply by exercising the powers conferred upon it by Congress. The Fed could lower interest rates and inject liquidity into the economy to stabilize the decline.

The Federal Reserve neither lowered interest rates nor consistently pumped money into the economy. In fact, the position of the Fed was that the stock market declines were a natural consequence of the speculative activities in which the market had engaged. By mid-1930, the decision was made to *increase* interest rates to stop the flow of gold to Europe as concerned overseas investors converted US dollars to gold. The higher interest rates only served to exacerbate depressionary conditions in the United States.

Meanwhile, in a misguided attempt to protect American farmers and producers from lower prices for their products because of foreign competition, the Hawley-Smoot Tariff Act was passed in mid-1930 to increase the price of imported goods. In some cases, these tariffs accounted for 50 percent of the price of imported products. In retaliation, two dozen countries raised their own tariffs and drastically reduced their imports of US goods. The reduced demand for US output added to the country's economic woes.

The combination of difficult financial and economic conditions was devastating. Billions of dollars of bank loans were liquidated through defaults and bankruptcies by farmers and businessmen. Money disappeared on a massive scale, with the money supply shrinking by more than one-third from 1929 to 1933. Almost 10,000 commercial banks failed during the same period.

Later, the commercial banking system would be punished for the excesses of the 1920s. It is true that commercial banks became involved in speculative activities of the decade by lending money for stock with inflated prices. It is also a fact that commercial bankers foreclosed on defaulted loans during the Great Depression that followed the 1929 Stock Market Crash. It is a myth, however, that the banking system was responsible for the severity and the length of the depression. Instead, inappropriate action by the Federal Reserve and ill-advised tariff legislation prolonged the misery of this difficult period in US history.

1.3 THE GLASS–STEAGALL ACT

Under the administration of President Franklin Roosevelt sweeping reforms of the banking industry were initiated. The Glass–Steagall Act of 1933 was intended to rein in the practices of the 1920s and restore the banking industry to a more mundane level of activity. The principle measures in the act that pertained to commercial banks included restrictions on deposit interest rates, deposit insurance, and the separation of commercial and investment banking. While these measures may appear reasonable on the surface, they have had serious negative implications over time.

The Banking Act of 1933 represented major legislative reform of the US banking system at the federal level. Through this act (and the Banking Act of 1935), the Federal Deposit Insurance Corporation (FDIC) and the Federal Open Market Committee were created. Control of monetary policy was placed in the hands of the Federal Reserve Board of Governors. In addition, Sections 16, 20, 21, and 32 separated the commercial banking and investment banking industries in what is commonly referred to as the Glass–Steagall Act.[1]

- Section 16 prohibits Federal Reserve member banks from owning equity securities. This section also prohibits member banks from underwriting and dealing in any securities with the exception of US Treasury Securities, federal agency Securities, and general obligation securities of states and municipal governments.

- Section 20 prohibits Federal Reserve member banks from affiliating with firms that are engaged principally in underwriting and selling corporate bonds and equity securities.
- Section 21 is aimed at securities firms, specifically underwriters of corporate securities. Such institutions may not accept deposits.
- Section 32 separates the control of banks and securities firms. Under this section, there may be no interlocking directorates between member banks and securities firms.

Thus, since Glass–Steagall, US banks have been restricted with respect to investment banking activities. Commercial banks that offered investment banking services were required to divest themselves of such affiliates. While Glass–Steagall permitted Federal Reserve member banks to buy and sell securities without recourse as agents for their customers, subsequent rulings by the Comptroller of the Currency *prohibited commercial banks from engaging in any brokerage activities.*

At the time that the Glass–Steagall Act was enacted, many observers felt that bankers were prone to excessive competition when they paid interest on checking accounts. Paying interest on their deposits led bankers to make more risky loans to cover the cost of interest expense. Then, according to this logic, during difficult economic conditions, the banks forced liquidation on their loan customers. Accordingly, the Glass–Steagall Act *prohibited the payment of interest on checking accounts.* Also, *rates paid on time deposits would be regulated* by Federal Reserve System. The logic was that once banks were assured a much lower cost of funds, they would be more careful in their lending practices and more tolerant of delinquent borrowers when economic conditions worsened. Certain Congressional members that aligned themselves with the interests of the small depositor included deposit insurance in the act. As a result, the *Federal Deposit Insurance Corporation also was established.* (See chapter 13 for a discussion of interest rate deregulation during the 1980s and the FDIC.)

Upon closer examination, the removal of investment banking privileges by Glass–Steagall appears to be basically a punishment, not a true testament that commercial banks cannot or should not engage in the activity. Under the act, national banks and state banks (that were members of the Federal Reserve) were still permitted to underwrite US government securities and general obligations of states and political subdivisions. (General obligations of states and political subdivisions are those which are backed by the full taxing authority of the issuer. See also chapter 4, for a discussion of municipal bonds; and chapter 6, for coverage of municipal bond underwriting.) They were prohibited from the same activities with respect to corporate securities.

However, two important factors were ignored in the analysis of the separation of commercial and investment banking:

1) The banks that failed during the Depression were not large banks, but small banks. The larger banks with securities operations withstood the economic crisis much better than the smaller ones without such operations.
2) The securities houses that were *not* subsidiaries of commercial banks were just as involved in the speculative frenzy of the 1920s as those which were bank-affiliates. There is no evidence that the episode would have been avoided even if Glass–Steagall had been enacted twenty years before.

1.4 The Effects of Glass–Steagall

The 1933 Glass-Steagall Act did not correct the basic structural problems of the banking industry. Before Glass-Steagall was enacted, the US banking system was a fragmented collection of approximately 15,000 institutions governed by differing rules and regulations at the state *vis-à-vis* the federal level. After Glass–Steagall, the only change in the system was that it then was deprived of one of its most important functions – the ability to underwrite corporate stocks and bonds.

One might argue that the Act produced stability in the banking system that lasted for more than 40 years. After all, it was not until the 1980s that the system seemed to come under competitive pressure once again. Bank failures numbered less than 20 per year from the end of the Second World War through 1979. This number rose to over 200 in the late 1980s.

The argument that the reforms worked is only partially correct. Indeed, the number of bank failures was drastically reduced. However, the banking system itself was unable to remain competitive. Under Regulation Q (the Federal Reserve regulation that governed deposit interest rate ceilings), banks were less able to compete effectively for deposits when interest rates rose beginning in the 1970s. Checking accounts that paid no interest and savings accounts that paid five percent interest were not attractive when the rate of inflation reached double-digit proportions and safe, short-term Treasury bills yielded as much as 14 percent. (See chapters 10 and 11 for coverage of interest rates and interest rate patterns.)

Money market mutual funds filled the gap created by these interest rate disparities by providing a means of investing in a pool of safe, short-term instruments that yield market rates. Consider the growth in these funds since 1974, when assets under management of money market mutual funds amounted to approximately $2 billion. By the mid-1990s, assets under management were well in excess of $800 billion. (See chapter 28, especially Exhibit 28.6.) Despite the fact that, starting in 1980, bank deposit interest rates were deregulated, money market mutual funds have captured market share that the banks will probably never regain.

In addition, the inability of banks to offer a full-range of corporate services has led to loss of business in the corporate sector. Corporate treasurers are now more likely to invest temporarily excess liquidity in various money market instruments (assets) rather than in bank deposits. For the largest, most creditworthy industrial firms, issuing commercial paper (liability) is a less expensive alternative to short-term bank loans. With the exception of providing a standby letter of credit to support commercial paper, commercial banks may not participate in the issuance of commercial paper under the provisions of Glass–Steagall. Moreover, Glass–Steagall has prevented banks from actively participating in the long-term financing of industrial America.

② Relaxation of the Glass–Steagall Barrier

The general prohibition for banks to operate in the securities industry has been relaxed through:

- Regulatory exceptions for overseas operations
- Special subsidiaries permitted by the Federal Reserve, called Section 20 subsidiaries

In the absence of legislative measures, that is, changes in federal law, US bank regulators have granted expanded powers with respect to securities activities. During the 1980s and 1990s, the Federal Reserve Board and the Comptroller of the Currency permitted bank holding companies and national banks to:

1) Underwrite commercial paper, mortgage-backed securities, municipal revenue bonds, and consumer-related receivables through subsidiaries that underwrite US government securities.
2) Place commercial paper without recourse for the account of customers.
3) Transfer the commercial paper to a holding company subsidiary.

4) Issue, underwrite, and deal in collateralized mortgage obligations through finance subsidiaries.
5) Offer securities brokerage and investment advisory services to institutions.
6) Offer and sell units in a unit investment trust solely on the order and for the account of the bank's customer through a bank or bank holding company subsidiary.
7) Make limited investments in an investment bank.
8) Create and sell interests in a publicly offered common trust fund for individual retirement account assets.

2.1 OVERSEAS AND FOREIGN EXCEPTIONS

Full-scale underwriting activities by US banks are permitted in overseas markets. The net result of this regulatory difference is that only those banks that are large enough to maintain substantial overseas operations have been able to enter the securities business to any meaningful extent. At least in this respect, small- to medium-sized banks have found themselves at a competitive disadvantage as compared to larger institutions.

While federal law does not permit US commercial banks to engage in securities underwriting in the United States, foreign banks have long been permitted to do so because, before 1978, foreign banks operating in the United States were not subject to Glass–Steagall. The *International Banking Act of 1978* had the effect of prohibiting foreign banks from engaging in securities underwriting. However, 17 foreign banks were grandfathered, that is, permitted to continue to operate existing securities affiliates in the United States. Among these are eight German firms, three French, three Swiss, and one Japanese. Of course, the ability of these firms to engage in securities underwriting places domestic firms at a competitive disadvantage.[2]

Federal legislators have thus far not been responsive to these apparent competitive inequities. While recent banking laws have served to remove interest rate ceilings and to provide for more attractive deposit instruments (e.g., NOW accounts, small-saver certificates and money market deposit accounts), they have *not* thus far relaxed prohibitions against securities operations. (See chapter 13, especially section 3, "Deregulation.")

2.2 REGULATORY EFFORTS TO REPEAL GLASS–STEAGALL

In 1991, the Secretary of the Treasury Department proposed, among other things, that commercial banks in sound financial condition, be permitted to engage in securities transactions through a separate affiliate. No legislative action followed this recommendation.

In 1997, the Comptroller of the Currency presented to Congress a Financial Modernization proposal by the Treasury Department. The proposal was intended to repeal Glass–Steagall and to permit diversified financial activities by financial institutions. Notably, such diversified services would be permitted in either separate bank holding company affiliates or in direct subsidiaries of banks.

By mid-1999, the US Senate and the US House of Representatives had passed separate bills for the repeal of Glass–Steagall.

2.3 SECTION 20 SUBSIDIARIES

Beginning in 1987, the Federal Reserve interpreted the Glass–Steagall Act in such a way as to permit banks to engage *indirectly* in securities activities. The Federal Reserve interpreted section 20 as permitting a bank to affiliate with a firm engaged in securities transactions as long as securities transactions are not the principal business of the firm. (Section 16 prohibits a bank from participating in these activities *directly*.)

In 1987, the Federal Reserve Board ruled that bank "affiliates" could underwrite commercial paper, revenue bonds, and other securities. This ruling was challenged in federal court by the securities industry in *Securities Industry Association v. Board of Governors*. However, the position of the Federal Reserve was upheld by the US Supreme Court in 1988. This permission was granted under section 20 of the Glass–Steagall Act. Specifically, the act prohibits any member of the Federal Reserve from affiliating "with any corporation, association, business trust, or other similar organization engaged principally in the issue, flotation, underwriting, public sale, or distribution at wholesale or retail or through syndicate participation of stocks, bonds, debentures, notes or other securities."

The Federal Reserve interpreted section 20 to permit affiliating with a securities firm as long as that firm was not "principally engaged" in the prohibited securities activities. In 1989, revenues from underwriting the otherwise prohibited securities was capped at 10 percent of revenue of the securities affiliate. In 1996, the limit was increased to 25 percent. Because of this restriction, most banks with section 20 subsidiaries have consolidated all of their securities activities (unrestricted and restricted) into one affiliate of their respective holding companies. The Federal Reserve is careful to ensure that there is a proper separation between the commercial banking business and the securities business within the holding company. This separation is referred to as a *firewall*. One part of the approval process is an on-site examination of the physical premises. The Federal Reserve examiners audit to ensure:

1) That section 20 subsidiaries are not funded by deposits or bank holding company debt, and
2) That firewalls have been constructed that appropriately restrict transactions between the commercial bank affiliate and the section 20 subsidiary.

Over time, various federal laws have been considered that would repeal Glass–Steagall. While no such law has been passed, most bills that have been considered require establishment of a separate subsidiary for securities activities. Thus, the section 20 subsidiary likely will continue to be a relevant structure for securities operations by US commercial banks. (At the end of 1996, the Office of the Comptroller of the Currency modified the regulations for, among other things, the *operating subsidiaries* of national banks, referred to as "Part 5." Previously, the scope of activity of operating subsidiaries coincided with those activities permitted for the parent national bank. The new regulation expanded the possible scope to activities different from those permissible for the parent bank, but part of or incidental to the business of banking. It is anticipated that future operating subsidiaries of national banks will be granted powers similar to those of section 20 subsidiaries of bank holding companies.)

A section 20 subsidiary may receive three levels of underwriting powers:

• Municipal revenue bonds, mortgage-related securities, commercial paper, and consumer-receivable related securities.
• Corporate debt.
• Corporate debt and equity.

Exhibit 24.1 contains a list of the section 20 subsidiaries. Of these 51 institutions, 32 are US banks and 19 are foreign banks. The foreign banks are concentrated in the New York, Chicago, and San Francisco districts of the Federal Reserve. Among the section 20 subsidiaries are both money center banks (New York–based) and large regionals. The number of section 20 subsidiaries

Parent organization	Section 20 subsidiary	Date of approval
BOSTON DISTRICT		
BancBoston Corporation	BancBoston Robertson Stephens, Inc.	11/96
Fleet Financial Group	Fleet Securities, Inc.	10/88
NEW YORK DISTRICT		
Banco Bilbao Vizcaya SA	BBV Latinvest Securities, Inc.	3/98
Bank of New York Co., Inc.	BNY Capital Markets, Inc.	6/96
Banco Santander, SA	Santander Investment Securities, Inc.	3/95
The Bank of Nova Scotia	Scotia Capital Markets (USA), Inc.	4/90
Bankers Trust NY Corp.	BT Alex Brown, Inc.	4/87
Barclays Bank PLC	Barclays Captial, Inc.	1/90
Canadian Imperial Bank of Commerce	CIBC Oppenheimer Corp.	1/90
Chase Manhattan Corp.	Chase Securities, Inc.	5/87
Citigroup	Citicorp Securities, Inc.	4/87
Citigroup	Salomon Smith Barney, Inc.	9/98
Citigroup	Robinson Humphrey Company LLC	9/98
Deutsche Bank AG	Deutsche Bank Securities Corp.	12/92
Dresdner Bank AG	Dresdner Kleinwort Benson North America LLC	7/96
HSBC Holdings PLC	HSBC Securities	2/96
J. P. Morgan & Co.	J. P. Morgan Securities, Inc.	4/87
National Westminster Bank PLC	Greenwich Capital Markets, Inc.	9/96
The Royal Bank of Canada	RBC Dominion Securities Corp.	1/90
Saban/Republic New York Corp.	Republic NY Securities Corp.	1/94
Société Générale	SG Cowen Securities Corp.	6/98
The Toronto Dominion Bank	TD Securities (USA), Inc.	5/90
Union Bank of Switzerland	Warburg Dillon Reed LLC	6/98
PHILADELPHIA DISTRICT		
Commerce Bancorp., Inc.	Commerce Capital Markets, Inc.	3/98
CLEVELAND DISTRICT		
Fifth Third Bancorp.	Fifth Third Securities	6/98
Huntington Bancshares, Inc.	Huntington Capital Corp.	12/92
KeyCorp	McDonald Key Investments, Inc.	2/96
Mellon Bank Corporation	Mellon Financial Markets, Inc.	4/95
National City Corporation	NatCity Investments, Inc.	2/94
PNC Bank Corp.	PNC Capital Markets, Inc.	7/87
RICHMOND DISTRICT		
Allied Irish Banks PLC	Hopper Soliday & Co., Inc.	5/97
BankAmerica Corp.	NationsBanc Montgomery Securities, LLC	5/89
BB&T Corporation	Craigie Incorporated	9/97
Crestar Financial Corp.	Crestar Securities Corp.	4/97
First Union Corp.	Wheat First Securities	11/97
First Union Corp.	CoreStates Securities	4/98
Wachovia Corporation	Wachovia Capital Markets, Inc.	5/98

Parent organization	Section 20 subsidiary	Date of approval
ATLANTA DISTRICT		
SouthTrust Corp.	SouthTrust Securities, Inc.	7/89
SunTrust Banks, Inc.	SunTrust Equitable Securities Corp.	8/94
CHICAGO DISTRICT		
ABN AMRO Bank NV	ABN AMRO Securities (USA), Inc.	6/90
Banc One Corp.	Banc One Capital Corp.	7/90
Banc One Corp.	First Chicago Capital Markets, Inc.	8/88
Bank of Montreal	Nesbitt Burns Securities, Inc.	5/88
Bank of Montreal	Nesbitt Burns Chicago, Inc.	2/96
KANSAS DISTRICT		
BOK Financial Corp.	BOSC, Inc.	4/97
MINNEAPOLIS DISTRICT		
US Bancorp	US Bancorp Investments, Inc.	11/97
US Bancorp	Piper Jaffray, Inc.	4/98
SAN FRANCISCO DISTRICT		
Dai-Ichi Kangyo Bank Ltd.	DKB Securities Corp.	1/91
First Security Corporation	First Security Capital Markets, Inc.	12/97
The Sanwa Bank, Ltd.	Sanwa Securities (USA) Co., LP	5/90
Wells Fargo & Company	Norwest Investment Services	12/89

◆ **Exhibit 24.1:**   Section 20 subsidiaries

◆ *Note*:   As of November 17, 1998

◆ *Source*:   Board of Governors of the Federal Reserve System.

has increased over time. In 1990, there were 29 such affiliates; by 1993, 31; and by 1995, 37. In 1998, the total was 51. All of the section 20 subs listed in Exhibit 24.1 have the first level of powers granted under section 20 of the Glass–Steagall Act. In addition, Barclays PLC Bank has corporate debt securities powers. Most of the institutions with section 20 subsidiaries have equity powers as well as corporate debt powers. Only the following 10 subsidiaries *do not* have both debt and equity powers:

- BOSC, Inc.
- Crestar Securities Corporation
- DKB Securities (USA) Corp.
- First Security Capital Markets, Inc.
- Greenwich Capital Markets, Inc.
- Huntington Capital Corp.
- Mellon Financial Markets, Inc.
- Sanwa Securities (USA) Co., L.P.
- SunTrust Securities, Inc.
- Wachovia Capital Markets, Inc.

Summary

For commercial banks, participation in the securities industry is a vital step in remaining a competitive force in financial services. The legal separation of commercial banking and investment banking in the United States (as a result of the Glass–Steagall Act of 1933) is being eroded through regulatory intervention. The increased competition implied by increased commercial bank involvement in the securities markets ultimately will result in more readily available capital for US business and industry.

End-of-chapter Questions

1. How did the structure of the US banking system contribute to money panics in the nineteenth century?

2. After the First World War, what action on the part of the Federal Reserve contributed to the economic recession of 1920 and 1921?

3. What factors during the "Roaring Twenties" indicated underlying weakness in the US economy, despite rapidly escalating stock prices?

4. Generally, what action was taken by the Federal Reserve after the Stock Market Crash of 1929?

5. List and describe briefly the four sections of the Banking Act of 1933 that are referred to as the Glass–Steagall Act.

6. a.   What appeared to be the underlying reasons for passage of the Glass–Steagall Act?

    b.   What two factors were overlooked that tend to contradict the appropriateness of separating commercial banking and securities activities?

7. What other restrictions were placed on commercial banks through the Banking Act of 1933?

8. In hindsight, what have been the consequences of the restrictions placed on commercial banks during the 1930s?

9. In the late 1990s, Glass–Steagall had not been repealed. Nevertheless, US commercial banks were actively involved in securities activities. To what can this apparent contradiction be attributed?

10. What is a section 20 subsidiary?

11. For a section 20 subsidiary, what is the limitation for revenue from otherwise nonpermissible underwriting of securities?

12. What is the function of a firewall in a section 20 subsidiary?

13. In the approval process for a section 20 subsidiary, what two criteria outlined in the Bank Holding Company Act must be met to the satisfaction of the Federal Reserve?

Notes

1 The full description of the corporate powers of national banks in contained in Title LXII of the Revised Statutes of the United States (entitled "National Banks"), chapter 1, section 5136. National banks may own and underwrite certain securities. To the extent permitted by the Comptroller of the Currency, national banks may own investment securities – bonds, notes and/or bonds. Banks may deal in, underwrite, and purchase for its own account only debt securities issued by the US Treasury, government agencies, political subdivisions, and multinational organizations.

2 According to the International Banking Act, after 1985, the Board of Governors of the Federal Reserve System may revoke the grandfathered rights to engage in securities activities if it is determined that there is an undue concentration of resources, decreased or unfair competition, a conflict of interest, or unsound banking practice. This provision has had the effect of limiting the acquisition of other US banks by those foreign banks with securities powers.

SELECTED REFERENCES

Committee on Banking, Finance, and Urban Affairs, *Compilation of Basic Banking Laws*, US Government Printing Office, Washington, DC, 1992.

Developments in the Word's Equity and Bond Markets: Volume 1, Europe and Asia, Euromoney Publications, London, 1995.

Johnson, Hazel J. *The Banker's Guide to Investment Banking: Securities and Underwriting Activities in Commercial Banking*, Irwin Professional Publishing, Chicago (now McGraw–Hill, New York), 1996.

Nationwide Banking and the Riegle–Neal Act

chapter 25

CHAPTER OVERVIEW

This chapter:
- Examines structural changes in the banking industry in the context of the consolidation trend.
- Reviews state provisions for expansion within state boundaries.
- Describes the Riegle–Neal Act and its implications for nationwide banking in the United States.

KEY TERMS

bank holding company
Bank Holding Company Act
Douglas Amendment
de novo bank or branch
interstate bank agency
interstate banking

intrastate bank branching
McFadden Act
multibank holding company
reciprocity
Riegle–Neal Interstate Banking and Branching
Efficiency Act of 1994

CHAPTER OUTLINE

Introduction

NationsBank Chairman Hugh McColl called it "a victory for bank customers everywhere" (NationsBank News Release, September 13, 1994). McColl was referring to the passage of the Riegle–Neal Interstate Banking and Branching Efficiency Act of 1994. For the first time, the act ushers in the right to operate nationwide for all US commercial banks. Bank customers are able to conduct banking business at any location of their bank, without regard to state boundaries. A direct effect of this new federal legislation will be to sustain the already strong momentum of the consolidation trend in the US banking industry.

 Structural Changes in the Industry

As recently as 1975, US banks numbered over 14,000. The number of banks was relatively stable even in light of the difficult economic conditions produced by the hyperinflation of the early 1980s. However, as illustrated in Exhibit 25.1, the number began to decline precipitously in the mid-1980s. By 1998, the number of US banks was down to 8,984. Early consolidation in the industry resulted primarily from bank failures that rose from less than 20 per year in the 1940-to-1980 period to over 200 per year by the late 1980s. Since that time, the failure rate has declined significantly to 72 in 1992, 42 in 1993, 11 in 1994, six in 1995, five in 1996, one in 1997, and one in the first two quarters of 1998. In fact, the banking industry posted new record profits each year between 1992 and 1997. Before 1992, the US commercial bank industry realized record profits in 1988 in the amount of $24.8 billion. From 1989 through 1991, profits ranged from $15.6 billion to $18.0 billion. After 1991, bank profits were:

Year	Profits (billions)
1992	$32.0
1993	43.1
1994	44.7
1995	48.8
1996	52.4
1997	59.2

Nevertheless, the industry continues to shrink. Exhibit 25.2 shows that the level of merger activity has increased from less than 100 in 1975 to a high of 800 in 1988 to between 500 and 600 per year. (The 237 mergers for 1998 are for the first two quarters only.) It has been projected that this merger and acquisition trend will end only when the number of US banks is closer to 5,000.

As the industry consolidates, fewer banks serve the country's banking needs. This implies coverage of wider geographic areas for each institution – branching within state boundaries and across state lines.

 State Laws

The process of consolidation has also been facilitated by individual state laws. Gradually, intrastate bank branching and interstate banking laws at the state level have been liberalized.

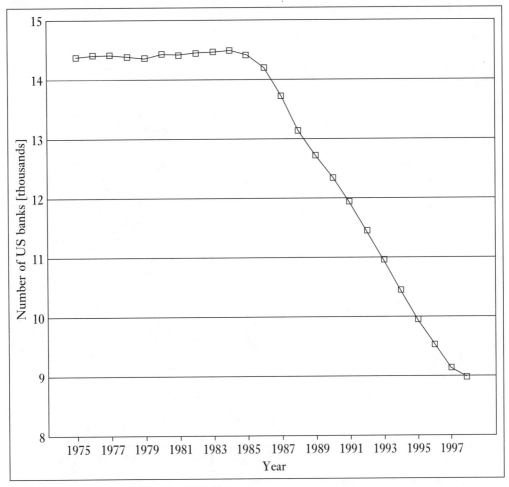

◆ **Exhibit 25.1:** **Number of US banks, 1975–98**

◆ *Note*:   Number of banks for 1998 as of June 30

◆ *Source*:   H. J. Johnson & Associates, based on data from *FDIC Statistics on Banking*, various years.

Intrastate bank branching:
Operating bank branches within the boundaries of a state.

Interstate banking:
Operating bank branches or subsidiaries across state lines.

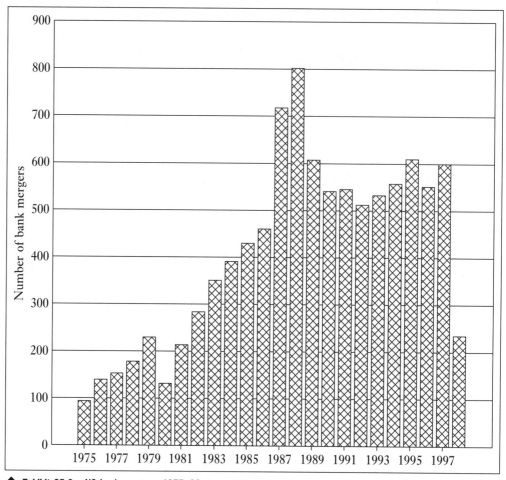

◆ **Exhibit 25.2: US bank mergers, 1975–98**

◆ *Note*: Mergers for 1998 through of June 30

◆ *Source*: H. J. Johnson & Associates, based on data from *FDIC Statistics on Banking*, various years.

2.1 INTRASTATE BANK BRANCHING LAWS

The federal *McFadden Act of 1927* gives national banks the right to branch within the state to the same extent that state banks are permitted to branch. There are generally three categories of branching powers:

- *Unit-banking* states permit no branching whatsoever.
- *Statewide branching* states permit branching throughout the state.
- *Limited branching* states permit some branching, but not statewide branching.

Unit (0)			
None			
Limited (4)			
Kentucky[1]	Montana[2]	Oklahoma[3]	Wyoming[4]
Statewide (47)			
Alabama	Idaho	Missouri	Rhode Island
Alaska	Illinois	Nebraska[6]	South Carolina
Arizona	Indiana	Nevada	South Dakota
Arkansas[5]	Iowa[6]	New Hampshire	Tennessee
California	Kansas[6]	New Jersey	Texas
Colorado	Louisiana	New Mexico	Utah
Connecticut	Maine	New York	Vermont
Delaware	Maryland	North Carolina	Virginia
District of Columbia	Massachusetts	North Dakota	Washington
Florida	Michigan	Ohio	West Virginia
Georgia[6,7]	Minnesota	Oregon	Wisconsin
Hawaii	Mississippi	Pennsylvania	

◆ **Exhibit 25.3:   Intrastate bank branching laws**

◆ *Notes*:
1 Branching permitted within home county.
2 Branching permitted within home and contiguous counties and into unbanked communities.
3 Must be within corporate city limits or within 25 miles of main branch.
4 Branching permitted within the county of bank or branch.
5 After December 31, 1998.
6 Statewide branching by merger or acquisition.
7 Statewide, unconditionally, after July 1, 1998.

◆ *Source*:   Conference of State Bank Supervisors, "Intrastate Bank Branching," *1996 Profile of State-Chartered Banking*, 1996.

Exhibit 25.3 classifies each state and the District of Columbia according to these guidelines. There are no remaining unit banking states. Four states permit limited branching, while the remaining states permit statewide branching. In some cases, statewide branching is permissible only through mergers or acquisitions.

2.2 INTERSTATE BANKING LAWS

Until enactment of the Riegle–Neal Interstate Banking and Branching Efficiency Act of 1994, state law dictated the extent to which bank holding companies could expand across state lines. The bank holding company structure has been instrumental in effecting interstate banking since the mid-1950s, when interstate banking was discouraged by federal legislation.

> **Bank holding company:**
> Company owning or controlling one or more banks, often identifiable by the word *Bancorp* or *Bancshares* in the corporate name. Any company (1) owning 25 percent or more of a bank or (2) controlling a majority of a bank's directors must register as a banking holding company with the Federal Reserve Board of Governors.

The federal *Bank Holding Company Act of 1956*:

- Required registration with the Federal Reserve Board of Governors by any company that owned a bank (25 percent of stock or control of directors).
- Made it unlawful for any holding company to acquire more than 5 percent of the shares of a bank without approval by the Federal Reserve Board.
- Made it unlawful for any bank holding company to own or operate a nonbank company unless the activity of the subsidiary was closely related to banking or had a public benefit.
- Prohibited nonbank companies from owning a bank.

The Bank Holding Company Act also stipulates that states may impose limits on holding company acquisitions of banks within state boundaries. All states permit multibank holding companies. Limitations of bank holding company acquisitions take various forms, including specific geographic restrictions, a maximum share of state deposits, or a maximum number of acquisitions for a specified period of time. However, some states place no limits on holding company acquisitions of banks. Since, until now, state and federal laws have prohibited banks themselves from branching across state lines, interstate acquisitions of banks have been accomplished largely through acquisitions by the bank holding companies.

The *Douglas Amendment* (adopted in the 1960s) of the Bank Holding Company Act prohibits interstate acquisition of banks by multibank holding companies unless specifically authorized by the laws of the state in which the acquired bank is located.

> **Multibank holding company:**
> Bank holding company owning more than one bank.

The 19 multistate banking organizations in existence at the time of the Douglas Amendment were grandfathered, that is, permitted to retain their multistate holdings. Most of these were small, with four holding companies representing 86 percent of the assets of the 19 institutions. At the time of the Douglas Amendment, no state had any such laws and cross-border acquisitions were effectively halted. Also, the Bank Holding Company Act was amended in 1970 to encompass one-bank holding companies.

Over time, however, the impact of the Bank Holding Company Act and its amendments has been eroded because of several factors:

- While the Act limited nonbank subsidiaries of bank holding companies to product lines "closely related" to banking, there was no limitation on the location of these permissible nonbank subsidiaries. Thus, wider geographic scope was possible by operating:

1) Nonbranch offices that were often called "nonbank banks" because they deleted either demand deposits or commercial loans from their product line, both of which were necessary to be considered a bank.
2) Limited purpose agency offices.
3) Off-premises electronic delivery systems.

- Beginning in 1981, the federal prohibitions concerning cross-border acquisitions were relaxed to accommodate the need to salvage the savings and loan industry. Acquisitions of failing thrifts by large out-of-state banks (permitted by federal regulators) demonstrated to consumers the often superior service and pricing that could be offered by the larger institutions.
- State legislatures began to enact laws that permitted out-of-state bank holding companies to acquire banks in their states, often on a reciprocal basis.

> **Reciprocity (bank holding companies):**
> One host state permitting bank holding companies domiciled in a second state to own banks located within the host state boundaries, as long as banks domiciled in the host state are permitted to own banks in the second state.

③ The Riegle–Neal Interstate Banking and Branching Efficiency Act of 1994

The Riegle–Neal Interstate Banking and Branching Efficiency Act of 1994 was passed after many earlier versions of this legislation had been defeated. The major activities addressed in the act are outlined in Exhibit 25.4.

> - Interstate Bank Holding Company Acquisitions
> - Interstate Bank Mergers
> - *De novo* Interstate Bank Branching
> - Foreign Bank Interstate Branching
> - Interstate Bank Agency

◆ **Exhibit 25.4:** Provisions of the Riegle–Neal Interstate Banking and Branching Efficiency Act of 1994

◆ *Source*:   Stock, Stuart C. and Peter L. Flanagan. "Riegle–Neal Interstate Banking and Branching Efficiency Act of 1994: Summary," Board of Governors of the Federal Reserve System, Washington, DC.

3.1 INTERSTATE BANK HOLDING COMPANY ACQUISITIONS

Beginning in September 1995, a bank holding company (BHC) may acquire banks located in any state. This amounts to a repeal of the Douglas Amendment of the Bank Holding Company Act.

States may not prohibit or "opt-out" of these interstate BHC acquisitions. However, individual states may establish a minimum age of local banks (up to 5 years) that are subject to interstate acquisition by out-of-state BHCs. (For purposes of this provision, the home state of a BHC is the state in which its banking subsidiaries have the largest amount of deposits as of the later of July 1, 1966 or the date on which the company became a BHC.)

This provision did not have a material impact on all states. In fact, only Hawaii (no interstate banking law) and the 15 states that participated in regional reciprocal pacts realized significant change in the ability of out-of-state BHCs to banks within their state boundaries.

In order to qualify for such acquisitions, the acquiring BHC must be adequately capitalized and managed. Even if the BHC is qualified for the acquisition, the Federal Reserve Board (FRB) may not approve the acquisition if:

- After the acquisition, the BHC will control more than 10 percent of total US insured depository institution deposits, or
- The BHC already has a depository institution affiliate in the host state *and*, after the acquisition, the acquiring BHC will control 30 percent or more of the insured depository institution deposits of the host state.

Even if the 30 percent limitation is exceeded, the FRB may approve the acquisition if the host state has established a higher limit. At the same time, a state may limit the share of deposits held within the state by any bank or BHC as long as the limitation does not discriminate against out-of-state banking organizations.

The FRB will also consider the extent of compliance with the CRA. Notwithstanding these stipulations, the act gives the FRB the authority to approve an acquisition if the target bank is in default (or in danger of default) or if the FDIC is providing assistance for the acquisition.

3.2 INTERSTATE BANK MERGERS

Beginning June 1997, national and state banks may merge across state lines, thus creating interstate branches. However, such mergers may not take place if the home state of one of the banks, prior to June 1997, enacted legislation that prohibits or "opts-out" of interstate bank mergers. Any such law does not affect mergers approved prior to the effective date of the opt-out legislation. Only Texas and Montana enacted opt-out legislation in connection with interstate bank mergers or interstate branches.

States were also permitted to "opt-in" prior to June 1997 and establish a minimum age (up to 5 years) of local banks that are permitted to participate in interstate mergers. In order to take advantage of this provision, both home states of the merging banks must have adopted early opt-in legislation. A host state may not discriminate against out-of-state banking organizations in this legislation with the exception of establishing a nationwide reciprocity rule. That is, a host state may not favor the banks of (1) one state or (2) a group of states to the disadvantage of banks of other states. Prior to June 1997, every state other than Montana and Texas either:

- Enacted early "opt-in" legislation;
- Enacted interstate branching legislation prior to Riegle–Neal (Alaska); or
- Enacted interstate branching legislation that did not expressly authorize interstate branching, but did establish requirements for and restrictions on interstate branch operation (Colorado, Iowa, and Louisiana).

Such interstate mergers can be undertaken by both affiliate banks and independent banks. Mergers may also involve the acquisition of individual branches of a bank, instead of the entire bank, only if the state in which the branches are located permits such acquisitions by statute. (The states that permit acquisition of a branch only, are Connecticut, District of Columbia, Indiana, Maine, Maryland, Massachusetts, Michigan, Nevada (in counties with a population of less than 100,000), New Jersey, New York, North Carolina, Oregon, Rhode Island, Utah, Vermont, Virginia, and West Virginia.)

Also applicable in interstate bank mergers are the provisions that are specified in connection with interstate bank holding company acquisitions:

- 10 and 30 percent concentration limitations
- Higher limits permitted by state law
- Different limits that do not discriminate against out-of-state banking organizations
- CRA compliance (CRA is an acronym for the Community Reinvestment Act, which requires banks to invest in all of the communities from which they receive deposits)
- Approval of mergers involving a troubled institution

In reviewing potential mergers, the appropriate federal regulators must determine that each participating bank is adequately capitalized and that the resultant bank will be adequately capitalized and well managed. Furthermore, nothing in the act affects the applicability of antitrust laws or the ability of states to charter, supervise, regulate, and examine banks within their state boundaries.

After the merger is complete, the resultant bank may continue to operate those offices that had been in operation prior to the merger. The resultant institution also may acquire additional branches in any location where the acquired bank previously could have established and acquired branches.

The branches of an out-of-state bank will be subject to the host state laws, whether the out-of-state bank has a national charter or a state charter. If the out-of-state bank is a national bank, the Office of the Comptroller will enforce applicable state laws for national banks in the host state. If the out-of-state bank is a state-chartered bank, the branches will be subject to the same laws as other state banks in the host state. However, the branches of an out-of-state state-chartered bank may not engage in any activity not permissible for a bank that is chartered in the host state.

3.3 DE NOVO INTERSTATE BANK BRANCHING

A national or state bank may, with appropriate federal approval, establish a *de novo* branch in a state outside its home state in which it previously has not maintained a branch. However, the host state must have enacted legislation that applies to all banks and specifically permits all out-of-state banks to branch *de novo* into the host state. (The states that enacted legislation to permit *de novo* interstate bank branching did so on a reciprocal basis; they are Colorado, District of Columbia, Indiana, Maine, Maryland (unrestricted after June 1997), Massachusetts, Michigan, Nevada (in counties with populations less than 100,000), North Carolina (unrestricted after June 1997), Pennsylvania, Rhode Island, Virginia, and West Virginia.) All state and federal laws that apply to a existing branch also apply to a *de novo* branch.

De novo **bank or branch:**
      A newly chartered bank or branch, as opposed to an existing office acquired through acquisition.

3.4 FOREIGN BANK INTERSTATE BRANCHING

Essentially, foreign banks are permitted to engage in interstate bank mergers and establish *de novo* interstate branches to the same extent and on the same conditions as national and state banks. However, Federal regulators may require a foreign bank to establish a US subsidiary to branch interstate if the regulators determine that they can verify the foreign bank's compliance with capital adequacy guidelines only through the use of a separate subsidiary. Also, any branch of a foreign bank will continue to be subject to CRA requirements unless the branch receives only deposits that are permissible for an Edge Act Corporation. (An Edge Act Corporation is chartered by the Federal Reserve, owned by state or national banks, may operate interstate branches, accepts deposits outside the United States, and invests in non US firms. The Edge Act subsidiary buys and sells notes, drafts, and bills of exchange, complementing the international banking activities of the parent bank. See also chapter 22, especially section 2.1.)

3.5 INTERSTATE BANK AGENCY

According to Riegle–Neal, effective September 1995, a bank may receive deposits, renew time deposits, close loans, service loans, and receive payments on loans and other obligations as agent for any bank or thrift affiliate, whether the affiliate is located in the same state or a different state than the agent bank. However, a depository institution may neither conduct, as agent, an activity that it is prohibited from conducting as a principal – nor have an agent conduct for it any activity that the depository institution is prohibited from conducting as principal. Also, if an out-of-state bank is not prohibited from operating a branch in a host state (because of an opt-out statute), a savings institution affiliate located in the host state may act as agent for the bank.

The significance of this provision of Riegle–Neal is that the definition of a branch, according to federal statutes, is revised. A bank affiliate can perform virtually all the functions that a retail branch performs. This represents an alternative way to achieve the efficiencies that may be realized by merging the separate entities across state lines to form a network of interstate branches as discussed above (in section 3.2).

 Summary

Taken together, the provisions of the Interstate Banking Act provide a framework for a more efficient US banking system. The industry's continued consolidation will lead to more convenient access for bank customers, more technological advancements, and better diversification of bank portfolios.

As many as 60 million Americans live in metropolitan areas that represent more than one state. It has been estimated that four million people commute across state lines. For these citizens, it will no longer be necessary to maintain multiple bank accounts or to wait several days before their deposits are recorded.

From the banks' perspective, the ability to eliminate separate corporations in each state – each with a board of directors and support staff – can significantly reduce the cost of doing business. Interstate information networks and uniform marketing campaigns can also help banks realize cost efficiencies. Thus, larger banks can lower the cost of funds, service credit cards more efficiently, offer better mortgage services, and stream administrative costs. The Riegle–Neal Act enables banks to diversify geographic markets in a number of ways. Specifically, banks may:

- Purchase a separately incorporated bank or bank holding company
- Merge separately incorporated banks in multiple states to form an interstate branch network
- Open *de novo* branches in those states in which such activity is permitted
- Use affiliates – even thrift affiliates – to process a wide range of interstate banking transactions.

However, banks that expand their geographic scope must be careful not to sacrifice credit availability and customer service. When creditworthiness is evaluated from a central location, character and other more qualitative factors can be overlooked. For example, if higher bank fees are charged in a community because a new parent bank routinely charges higher fees in other markets, the consuming public will be disadvantaged.

At the same time, merging banks will realize substantial diversification benefits. Banks that operate nationwide are less susceptible to economic crises in specific areas. Such diversification will enhance the safety and soundness of the US banking system.

 End-of-chapter Questions

1. a. Differentiate unit, limited, and statewide intrastate branching powers.
   b. Which of these branching powers is most prevalent within individual states?
2. What is a bank holding company?
3. What two criteria have been established to determine whether a holding company controls a bank?
4. Why did the bank holding company become such a dominant form of business organization in the US banking system?
5. What were the major provisions of the Banking Holding Company Act of 1956?
6. Of what significance was the Douglas Amendment of the Bank Holding Company Act?
7. Over time, what trends have diluted the impact of the Banking Holding Company Act and its amendments?
8. What the major impact of the Riegle–Neal Interstate Banking and Branching Efficiency Act of 1994?
9. Through what organizational forms may US commercial banks create nationwide operations?
10. For foreign banks, what is the impact of the Riegle–Neal Interstate Banking and Branching Efficiency Act of 1994?
11. What benefits may be associated with nationwide bank operations?

SELECTED REFERENCES

Conference of State Bank Supervisors. "Intrastate Bank Branching," *1996 Profile of State-Chartered Banking*, Washington, DC, 1996.

Conference of State Bank Supervisors. "Status of Interstate Branching Legislation in the States," Washington, DC, 1997.

Eisenbeis, Robert A. "Regulation: Eliminating Special Antitrust Treatment for Banking," *Journal of Retail Banking Services*, 18, no. 1 (Spring 1996), pp. 65–9.

Federal Deposit Insurance Corporation. "FDIC Statement of Policy: Bank Merger Transactions," Washington, DC, December 31, 1989.

Fitch, Thomas. *Dictionary of Banking Terms*, Barron's Educational Series, Hauppauge, NY, 1990.

Kane, Edward J. "DeJure Interstate Banking: Why Only Now?" *Journal of Money, Credit, and Banking*, 28, no. 2 (May 1996), pp. 142–61.

Knecht, G. Bruce. "Nationwide Banking is Around the Corner, But Obstacles Remain," *Wall Street Journal*, July 26, 1994, pp. A1 & A8.

LaWare, John P., Member, Board of Governors of the Federal Reserve System. Statement Before the Committee on Banking, Housing and Urban Affairs; United States Senate, October 5, 1993.

Lohse, Deborah. "Interstate Banking Promises Conveniences – And Costs," *Wall Street Journal*, August 3, 1994, pp. C1 & C11.

Stock, Stuart C. and Peter L. Flanagan. "Riegle–Neal Interstate Banking and Branching Efficiency Act of 1994: Summary," Covington & Burling, Washington, DC, September 16, 1994 (through the Legal Division of the Board of Governors of the Federal Reserve System, Washington, DC).

PART VIII
Nonbank Financial
Institutions

Savings and Loan Associations and Mutual Savings Banks

chapter 26

CHAPTER OVERVIEW

This chapter:
- Traces the origins of savings and loan associations and mutual savings banks.
- Identifies the regulatory restrictions under which thrifts operated originally.
- Lists the recent expansion of thrift powers.
- Discusses the causes of thrift industry distress.
- Highlights changes in asset and liability mix over time.
- Discusses thrifts in selected countries.

KEY TERMS

brokered deposit
building Society
Federal Home Loan banks
FIRREA
jusen
mutual savings bank
Mutual depository organization

net worth certificate
savings and loan association
Savings Association Insurance Fund (SAIF)
terminating building society
thrift institution
US League of Savings Institutions

CHAPTER OUTLINE

Introduction

The thrift industry in the United States is composed of savings and loan associations and mutual savings banks. These institutions were originally intended to provide residential mortgage financing and consumer loans. They also provided a safe investment for small savers. What started as an industry to serve the American family turned into one of the worst financial scandals in US history. Thrifts failed at record rates. Federal deposit insurance guarantees exposed the US government and, ultimately, US taxpayers to bailout costs in the range of $500 billion. This is roughly $2,000 for every man, woman, and child in the United States. In addition, the enormous inventory of foreclosed real estate that once belonged to the failed thrifts seriously weakened the real estate market. Thus, the crisis in the thrift industry has already negatively affected individual families and financial institutions (such as banks and insurance companies) that have substantial investments in real estate or real-estate-based loans.

The causes of the crisis are varied. One of the primary causes is the historical mismatch of asset and liability maturities. The consequence of this mismatch became painfully obvious during the 1970s and early 1980s when long-term, low-yielding mortgage loans failed to produce sufficient income to offset the rising cost of deposits and short-term borrowings. Deregulation gave thrifts the power to invest in higher yielding assets. But regulatory oversight of these expanded powers was grossly inadequate. This situation was further complicated by a lack of commitment on the part of the US Congress to maintain safety and soundness within the industry. The net effect was virtually a death blow to the thrift industry in the United States.

Origins of the Thrift Industry

1.1 SAVINGS AND LOAN ASSOCIATIONS

1.1.1 THE UNITED STATES

The first thrift in the United States was formed in 1831 in Frankfort, Pennsylvania. The objective of the Oxford Provident Building Association was to enable its shareholders to secure housing finance. Most shareholders worked in the textile industry as wage earners. The amounts that wage earners contributed were not deposits, but, instead, equity investments. Thus, the first thrift was a *mutual organization* and the precursor of modern savings and loan associations.

> **Mutual depository organization:**
> Noncorporate financial institution in which individual contributions are considered equity investments even though they closely resemble deposits in most other aspects (stated interest rate, variability of amount invested, and ease of withdrawal, relative to other equity investments.)

Each shareholder was entitled to a loan. However, no loan could be used to build a home more than five miles away from Frankfort. Oxford Provident, and other associations similar to Oxford, provided loans to buy land and to build homes and were called *building societies*.

> **Building society:**
> A mutual organization that uses its financial resources to make loans for the purpose of buying land and constructing homes.

Later, shareholders borrowed money to build on land that they already owned and to purchase existing homes. At this point, the organizations became *building and loan societies*. Originally, the societies *terminated* when each shareholder had obtained a loan and all loans had been repaid.

> **Terminating building society:**
> A mutual organization with the purpose of providing each member with a loan to construct a home. When each member has received and repaid his loan, the society ceases operations.

These early organizations served two purposes:

- providing mortgage loans
- providing investment vehicles for small-balance powers.

If shareholders wished to withdraw their savings, they were required to give a month's notice. Early withdrawal resulted in a penalty. With this structure, the societies promoted thrift, savings, and mortgage financing for residential property. The thrifts' balance sheets reflected large amounts of mortgage loan investments that were funded by savings shares.

> **Thrift institution:**
> A financial institution that encourages moderate-income workers to save money on a regular basis. Likewise, the institution invests in loans to these savers, especially mortgage loans. In the United States, savings and loan associations and mutual savings banks are classified as thrift institutions.

At the time, building societies were necessary because commercial banks did not actively seek small savings deposits or solicit mortgage loan business. As the US manufacturing sector grew, the population of cities in which these enterprises were located also grew. However, since the new wage earners spent most of their time working, little time remained to build their own homes. Building societies helped wage earners to have their homes constructed by others.

1.1.2 THE UNITED KINGDOM

Building societies were patterned after the same institution in Britain. The Industrial Revolution in England led to an unsatisfied demand for housing comparable to that which later developed in the United States. The first documented building society originated in 1781 in Birmingham, England.

The Birmingham Building Society was a mutual organization with overseers who were elected from within the ranks of the society and served without compensation. Each member was required to make a monthly contribution until all members had received a loan. The society terminated when all outstanding loans had been repaid.

Building societies spread throughout continental Europe and, later, to the United States, Canada, Australia, New Zealand, and other countries. The form of the building society evolved from a terminating plan to a permanent plan, that is, one that was not self-liquidating. Under a permanent plan, it was not necessary for all members to obtain a mortgage loan. Instead, the savings by those who did not wish to purchase homes were pooled to provide loans for members who *did* desire mortgage financing. An added advantage was that shares could be purchased in any amount at any time with no withdrawal penalties. Building societies and their successors have provided an important service in many countries.

1.2 Mutual Savings Banks

While the precursors of savings and loan associations were cooperative organizations of middle-class wage earners, mutual savings banks were motivated by philanthropic concerns. Just as commercial banks of the eighteenth century did not satisfy the needs for residential mortgage finance, they also did not provide depository services for wage earners. Mutual savings banks filled this gap.

The first prototype of a mutual savings bank was formed in Hamburg, Germany in 1765. However, the first institution that was structurally similar to the modern savings bank began operations in Ruthwell, Scotland in 1810. Unlike building societies, early mutual savings banks were not financed entirely by wage earner contributions. The early institutions were benevolent organizations in the sense that wealthy individuals contributed necessary capital to establish them. The mutual banks then accepted small deposits from laborers. The founders' objective was to encourage thrift, virtue, industriousness, and prosperity.

The first US savings bank, the Philadelphia Savings Fund Society started in 1816 as a voluntary association and was not chartered until 1819. The Provident Institution for Savings in Boston was the first to be incorporated, receiving its charter in 1816. These early institutions frequently used the term "society" or "institution" in their titles because of the early distrust of banks in the United States.

Mutual savings banks had no stockholders. In this sense, they were similar to early savings and loan associations. Depositors owned the assets and any profits from operation were credited to their accounts. Bank trustees were not allowed to profit from the banks or to accept any form of compensation. However, as the banks successfully expanded, it became necessary for trustees to appoint salaried management personnel.

Also, like early savings and loan associations, mutual savings banks were largely funded by savings deposits. However, unlike S&Ls, savings banks invested in consumer loans as well as mortgage loans. Also, savings banks gave depositors more flexibility in terms of denomination, maturity, and withdrawal.

② Evolution of the Thrift Industry

After the first thrift was established in the United States, the movement enjoyed considerable growth. Savings and loan associations appeared next in New York in 1836 and in South Carolina in 1843. By 1890, S&Ls could be found in every state. Until the late 1880s, all S&Ls had purely local operations. A brief experiment with nationwide fund raising and lending ended in failure for most of the associations that were involved (see Exhibit 26.1).

The Great Depression of the 1930s led to a number of failures in the thrift industry, primarily savings and loan associations, as shown in Exhibit 26.2. From 1930 through 1939, 1,700 S&Ls, or 14 percent of all savings and loans in existence in 1925, failed. Consolidations within the industry explain the remaining reduction in numbers. By 1940, S&Ls and mutual savings banks numbered 7,521 and 542 respectively.

In the post-Depression era, the number of thrift institutions continued to decline primarily through industry consolidation. At the same time, total assets grew substantially and S&Ls, in particular, began to control a greater percentage of total financial assets.

In the late 1880s, "Nationals," or National Building and Loan Associations, appeared. These organizations solicited contributions nationwide and made loans through the mail. In an environment of widespread speculative investments, some nationals became "get rich quick" schemes for their organizers. Others made questionable loans over widely dispersed geographic areas. A sharply depressed real estate market during the 1890s, together with poor business practices and more restrictive legislation that followed later caused most nationals to fail.

As early as the turn of the century, the savings and loan industry experienced the consequences of investment. As is true today, the well publicized experiences of these "high-flying" associations hurt the public acceptance of safer, more conservatively run local associations.

◆ **Exhibit 26.1: The National Building and Loan Associations**

◆ *Reference*: Ornstein, Franklin H. *Savings Banking, An Industry in Change*, Reston Publishing, Reston, Va., 1985, p. 10.

Year	S&Ls		MSBs	
	Institutions[1]	Assets[2]	Institutions[1]	Assets[2]
1900	5,356	$ 571	626	$ 2,328
1905	5,264	629	615	2,969
1910	5,869	932	637	3,598
1915	6,806	1,484	627	4,257
1920	8,633	2,520	618	5,586
1925	12,403	5,509	610	7,831
1930	11,777	8,829	594	10,164
1935	10,266	5,875	559	11,046
1940	7,521	5,733	542	11,925
1945	6,149	8,747	534	15,924
1950	5,992	16,893	530	22,252
1955	6,071	37,656	528	30,383
1960	5,320	71,476	516	39,598
1965	6,185	129,580	505	56,383
1970	5,669	176,183	497	76,373
1975	4,931	338,200	476	121,100
1980	4,594	620,626	460	171,564
1985	3,535	1,070,012	394	216,776
1986	3,488	1,163,851	472	236,862
1987	3,408	1,250,855	484	261,843
1988	2,949	1,350,500	492	284,194
1989	2,878	1,251,697	489	279,931
1990	2,359	1,036,222	454	230,117
1991	2,111	901,966	446	217,705
1992	1,870	816,913	517	218,037
1993	1,669	774,813	593	226,169
1994	1,542	744,124	610	234,521

◆ **Exhibit 26.2:   Number of institutions and assets of the thrift industry in the United States, 1900–94**

◆ *Notes*:   Last edition of *Savings Institution Sourcebook* was published for 1994. The FDIC does not report separate statistics for S&Ls and MSBs.
1   Includes insured and uninsured institutions
2   Millions of dollars

◆ *Sources*:   Brumbaugh, R. Dan, Jr. *Thrifts Under Siege: Restoring Order to American Banking*, 1988, p. 7. US League of Savings Institutions, *Savings Institutions Sourcebook*, 1994.

However, high and volatile interest rates of the late 1970s placed considerable pressure on the thrift industry because of its substantial investment in residential mortgages. While the relatively short-term cost of funds climbed, the yield on much longer-term assets lagged behind.

Exhibit 26.3 shows selected yields from 1976 through 1989, the year in which the Financial Institutions Reform, Recovery, and Enforcement Act (FIRREA) was passed. (See also chapter 13 for a discussion of FIRREA.) Referring to this exhibit, notice that, in 1976, the Treasury bill rate averaged approximately 5 percent and that new mortgages yielded just over 9 percent. Both

Year	Rate on new mortgages	3-month T-bills	Yields			
			S&Ls		MSBs	
			Assets	Funds	Assets	Funds
1976	9.10%	4.99%	8.18%	6.38%	7.23%	5.98%
1977	9.02	5.27	8.44	6.44	7.43	6.03
1978	9.61	7.22	8.73	6.67	7.73	6.14
1979	10.89	10.04	9.29	7.47	8.26	6.80
1980	12.90	11.51	9.72	8.94	8.79	7.96
1981	15.00	14.08	10.11	10.92	9.42	9.48
1982	15.38	10.69	10.82	11.38	9.71	9.64
1983	12.57	8.62	10.99	8.82	10.04	7.31
1984	12.38	9.57	11.34	9.08	10.62	7.57
1985	11.55	7.49	11.46	8.60	11.17	6.83
1986	10.17	5.97	10.54	7.51	11.08	6.77
1987	9.31	5.83	9.53	6.69	10.57	6.38
1988	9.19	6.67	9.31	6.90	10.44	6.60
1989	10.13	8.11	11.14	8.40	11.39	7.60

◆ **Exhibit 26.3: Selected yields, 1976–89 (passage of FIRREA)**

◆ *Sources*: Carron, Andrew S. *The Rescue of the Thrift Industry*, 1983, p. 5; Author's calculations based on data from: US League of Savings Institutions, *Savings Institutions Sourcebook*, 1990, p. 11; International Monetary Fund, *International Financial Statistics*, Yearbook 1990, p. 731.

savings and loan associations and mutual savings banks enjoyed a relatively comfortable spread between asset yield and cost of funds.

In the six years after 1976, Treasury and new mortgage yields both increased by approximately 6 percent. As a result of these rising market rates, the costs of funds for savings and loan associations and mutual savings banks grew by 5.0 percent and 3.7 percent, respectively. At the same time, the asset yields of the thrifts only increased by 2.6 percent and 2.5 percent, respectively.

In 1981, the cost of funds for S&Ls exceeded asset yields by 81 basis points (10.92 percent vs. 10.11 percent). The following year, the difference was 56 basis points (11.38 percent vs. 10.82 percent). Thus, it is not surprising that the industry sustained substantial losses during this period. (FSLIC-insured thrifts lost over $4 billion per year in 1981 and 1982.) Nor should it be surprising that 252 S&Ls failed during 1982. In fact, from 1980 through 1984, a total of 511 S&Ls failed.

These early-1980s failures were attributable to a severely mismatched balance sheet for the industry as a whole. A heavy concentration of fixed-rate mortgage loans left little opportunity to adjust asset portfolios in response to the rising cost of funds. To further complicate the situation, traditional savings deposits were being withdrawn in massive waves of disintermediation to be reinvested in more attractively priced money market mutual funds.

To remedy these structural problems in the industry, laws were enacted both to give thrifts greater investment flexibility and to make it easier for other healthy firms to acquire ailing institutions. Some of this legislative relief was misused, bringing the industry even more financial difficulty than it experienced in the early 1980s.

Regulation and Deregulation

3.1 BEFORE THE GREAT DEPRESSION

With the creation and failure of a number of national thrifts, local thrifts in 1892 formed the US League of Local Building and Loan Associations (later the US League of Savings Institutions, and currently America's Community Bankers). The League lobbied state legislatures for laws restricting nationals (see Exhibit 26.1). The measures that resulted helped to protect the locals from territorial infringement by their peers (other local associations) and other competitors.

However, rising income levels brought the thrift and banking industries into direct competition. In the early 1900s, national banks were permitted to offer savings deposits and the Federal Reserve placed lower reserve requirements on these deposits than on demand deposits. (See chapters 12 and 13 for coverage of the Federal Reserve and monetary policy, including reserve requirements.) Nevertheless, thrifts retained a competitive advantage in that they were exempt from federal income taxation.

3.2 FEDERAL REGULATION SINCE THE 1930s

3.2.1 FEDERAL CHARTERS

Widespread bank and thrift failures of the Great Depression attracted the attention of the federal government. After the Great Depression, the federal government began to also regulate the savings and loan industry.

The Federal Home Loan Bank Board was established in 1932 to charter federal S&Ls and to provide advances to members. State S&Ls were entitled to join; federal S&Ls were obligated to do so. So as not to compete unfairly with their state-chartered counterparts, federal S&Ls were to be chartered only when the number of existing state institutions was insufficient to adequately service the community. Furthermore, federal S&Ls were to be mutual organizations with a local focus.

3.2.2 DEPOSIT INSURANCE

Federal Savings and Loan Insurance Corporation (FSLIC) was established in 1934 to provide deposit insurance to Federal Home Loan Bank members. For many years, insurance premiums were the same as for FDIC-insured institutions, one-twelfth of a percent. Beginning in 1985, a special assessment of one-eighth percent was levied to help cover large and mounting costs of the thrift industry bailout. This brought the total assessment to $0.2083 per $100 deposit. At the same time, the assessment for banks was only one-twelfth percent, or $0.083 per $100 deposit. The higher cost of doing business motivated some S&Ls to convert to bank charters in order to avoid the special assessment. Exhibit 26.2 reflects the impact of these conversions. The number of mutual savings banks stopped its previous decline and grew in six of the nine years after 1985. Over the same period, the number of savings and loan associations continued to decline.

The Financial Institutions Reform, Recovery, and Enforcement Act (FIRREA) of 1989 increased the premiums even more. FSLIC was dissolved and FDIC took over responsibility for federally insured thrifts with the Saving Association Insurance Fund (SAIF), while banks were covered by a separate Bank Insurance Fund (BIF). (FIRREA also replaced the Federal Home Loan Bank Board with the Office of Thrift Supervision – a division of the US Treasury Department.) FIRREA specified that insurance premiums would increase to $0.23 per $100 deposit. FDIC was also given the power to increase the premiums for either SAIF or BIF. The maximum was set at $0.325 per $100 deposit.

The FDIC Improvement Act (FDICIA) of 1991 mandated that risk-based insurance assessments be developed by FDIC no later than January 1994. With respect to SAIF, FDICIA stipulated that BIF assessments were not permitted to fall below $0.23 per $100 deposit until the ratio of fund balance to insured deposits reached 1.25 percent – a level to be achieved within 20 years of the law's enactment.

Also, FDICIA permitted the FDIC to borrow up to $70 billion from the US Treasury Department and from member banks to fund resolution of troubled institutions. However, the average SAIF assessment rate was not permitted to fall below $0.15 per $100 deposit until the 1.25 percent fund balance-to-insured deposits had been achieved and any borrowings repaid. The SAIF achieved this status as of September 30, 1996. Also, as of this date, the SAIF amounted to $4.2 billion. Insurance assessments for the SAIF were based on capital ratios and on overall ratings of risk. (The overall ratings of risk are called CAMEL ratings and they range from 1 (best) to 5 (worst). See also chapter 15, section 2.1.) With the funds officially recapitalized, assessment rates were set between $0.00 and $0.27 per $100 deposit. The following summarizes the assessment rates. The SAIF has been restored to health.

Capital adequacy	Risk category		
	Low	Moderate	High
Well capitalized	0.00%	0.03%	0.17%
Adequately capitalized	0.03	0.10	0.24
Undercapitalized	0.10	0.24	0.27

Capital adequacy is established based on three different capital ratios involving common equity, regulatory capital, total assets and risk-adjusted assets. (See also chapter 17 for a discussion of capital ratios and international capital standards.) Risk categories are evaluated based on capital levels, asset quality, management of the bank, earnings, and liquidity (CAMEL).

3.3 Deregulation of the 1970s and 1980s

3.3.1 DEPOSITS

The high interest rates of the 1970s and early 1980s, noted in Exhibit 26.3, led to substantial growth in money market mutual funds. Thrift accounts became unattractive alternatives for small investors. Federal regulators responded in 1978 by authorizing *money market certificate accounts* with minimum denominations of $10,000. These instruments offered competitive, market rates of interest. While the new deposits halted the threat of massive disintermediation, money market certificates also placed significant pressure on thrift profitability.

The *NOW account*, first introduced in Massachusetts in 1972, became another interest-bearing deposit – in large measure replacing the interest-free demand deposit account after its nationwide legalization in 1980. However, these and other liability innovations were not sufficient to stem the flow of funds out of savings and loan associations and mutual savings banks. Specifically, in 1981 and 1982, deposit withdrawals exceeded new deposits by $32 billion. Nevertheless, because of interest credited to those accounts that *did* remain, deposit balances actually increased by $52 billion.

3.3.2 ASSETS

It was apparent that the historical purpose of thrift institutions had been, at least partially, compromised by competition for savings deposits from banks and nonbanks. The regulatory reaction to this phenomenon was to relieve thrifts of many of their historical *investment* restrictions. The logic was that greater asset powers should augment earnings and help offset the higher cost of funds. New powers were conferred by both regulators and legislators.

Exhibit 26.4 highlights the most significant regulatory changes in the thrift industry between 1980 and 1984 – the years of thrift deregulation. Thrift regulators and federal law gave these institutions the power to invest in a wide variety of enterprises in which they had never engaged – commercial real estate, business loans, and corporate bonds. They were even allowed to engage in financial options trading. The intention was that thrifts would be able to "grow" their way out

Year	Regulatory Changes
1980	Federal associations may open branch offices and operate mobile facilities statewide (100 mile restriction dropped).
	FSLIC members may borrow up to 50% of *assets* (was 50% of *savings*) and increase liabilities maturing in 90 days or less.
	FSLIC members may offer real estate loans for property in any geographic location, and a loan for one-to-four-family residential property may exceed 90% of property value.
	Reserve requirement is reduced from 5 to 4%.
1981	Federal Home Loan Bank Board liberalizes the regulations with respect to conversion from a mutual form of business organization to a stock form.
	Adjustable rate mortgages are authorized.
	Federal association service corporations receive permission to conduct a broader range of activities without prior approval, to serve a broader range of customers, and borrow (nondeposit funds) with even fewer restrictions.
1982	FSLIC members permitted to buy financial options and write call options without limitation, to write put options up to specified limit.
1983	California legislative passes a law permitting state-chartered thrifts to broaden their investment activities.
	State savings banks that convert to federal savings institution charters may retain the powers they had under state law.
	Thrifts permitted to make loans nationwide.
1984	Federal associations may operate finance subsidiaries to issue securities for the parent.

Year	Federal Legislative Changes

1980   Depository Institutions Deregulation and Monetary Control Act:

  1) Federal Savings and loan associations given expanded asset powers.
     a) Credit card issuance.
     b) Trustee service and trust departments.
     c) Up to 20% of assets in consumer loans, commercial paper, and corporate debt.
     d) Up to 3% of assets in service corporations.
     e) Up to 20% of assets in commercial real estate loans.
  2) Federal mutual savings banks permitted to:
     a) Make business loans.
     b) Accept demand deposits from business clients.
  3) Authorized all depository institutions offer checking account services and to pay interest on individual transactions accounts.
  4) Deposit insurance limit raised from $40,000 to $100,000.

1982   Garn–St. Germain Depository Institutions Act:

  1) Federal savings and loan associations given expanded asset and liability powers:
     a) Up to 55% of assets in commercial loans (up to 5% secured or unsecured, up to 10% of lease financing, and up to 40% secured by commercial real estate).
     b) Up to 30% of assets in consumer loans (up from 20%), including inventory and floor-planning loans.
     c) Investment in state and local revenue bonds (had been only general obligation bonds).
     d) Demand deposits permitted from persons or organizations that have a business loan relationship with the association or that wish to receive payments from nonbusiness clients.
  2) All depository institutions allowed to offer money market deposit accounts with no interest rate ceiling and to offer interest-bearing transactions accounts to federal, state, and local governments.

◆ **Exhibit 26.4: Deregulation of the thrift industry**

◆ *Sources*:   Brumbaugh, R. Dan, Jr. *Thrifts Under Siege: Restoring Order to American Banking*, 1988, pp. 152–53, 196; Cooper, S. Kerry and Donald R. Fraser. *Banking Deregulation and the New Competition in Financial Services*, 1984, pp. 134–6, 116–19; Kane, Edward J. *The S&L Insurance Mess: How Did It Happen?*, 1989, pp. 34–47.

of industry collapse. The new activities would generate income at higher rates of return to help offset the high and increasing cost of funds. To take full advantage of these new powers, thrifts were permitted to make loans nationwide.

3.3.3 REGULATORY EXCESSES

The move toward deregulation went too far. At the same time that federal deposit insurance increased from $40,000 to $100,000 (1980), the safeguards that limited exposure to excessive risks were being dismantled.

Savings and loan associations – that in 1979 had 68 percent of financial assets invested in home mortgages and derived 82 percent of financial liabilities from small time and savings deposits – were permitted to engage in much riskier activities during the 1980s:

- Mutual fund investments
- Futures and options trading
- Retail securities repurchase agreements without limit
- Mortgage loans without restrictions as to the value of underlying collateral
- Security issuance for parent company through a finance subsidiary
- Commercial loans up to 55 percent of assets
- Corporate bonds up to 20 percent of assets

At the same time, deposit interest rates were deregulated and the deposit insurance limit was raised to $100,000 per account. In essence, funds could be attracted easily by raising the rate on certificates of deposit (CDs) of $100,000 or more. These deposits then could be marketed through securities brokers to become *brokered deposits*.

Brokered deposits:
> Deposits placed with an institution through a securities broker, who, in turn, earns a commission on the sale. Such deposits were most often sold in $100,000 increments to retain full federal deposit insurance.

Before FIRREA (1989) restricted their issuance, brokered deposits enabled an S&L to raise funds easily. In some cases, these deposits were invested in high-yielding corporate bonds of less than investment grade, that is, junk bonds. These bonds provided a positive spread over the high cost of brokered funds. Brokered deposits assured the institution of a steady inflow of funds even if the institution was financially unsound.

Regulatory excesses went further. To encourage the purchase of dying thrifts, the ownership criteria were relaxed.

- Instead of 400 owners with no one owner holding more than 25 percent of ownership interest, a single owner could purchase a thrift.
- Instead of investing cash to obtain ownership interest, land and other noncash assets were accepted.

Thus, a land developer with idle land could invest the land in exchange for control of a savings and loan association. Using brokered deposits, funds could then be attracted to invest in almost anything. This was particularly true for state-chartered S&Ls. In California, for example, a law enacted in 1983 allowed almost anyone to own a thrift, attract as much in brokered deposits as desired, and invest the proceeds in almost anything. Of course, the operation was fully backed by the federal government.

3.3.4 US CONGRESSIONAL ACTION

Savings and loan association fraud occurred frequently, especially in those states with liberalized thrift laws. The industry became even more unstable. Capital adequacy became a real concern.

But because of the enormity of the problem and the lack of resources in the federal insurance fund, the 1982 Garn–St. Germain Act also included a measure to conceal the degree of capital inadequacy. Those institutions with insufficient capital were permitted to issue *net worth certificates*. The net worth certificates were then exchanged for promissory notes issued by FSLIC. The FSLIC promissory were included in the computation of regulatory capital. Of course, the true capital of the institution was not enhanced by these exchanges because FSLIC itself would soon be declared insolvent.

> **Net worth certificate:**
> A claim issued by a capital-deficit S&L for the purpose of increasing regulatory capital. Its issuance is *not* accompanied by the infusion of real capital.

It was not until 1989 when FIRREA was enacted that many of these excesses were corrected. Specifically, FIRREA:

- Prohibited state-chartered, federally insured savings institutions from engaging in any activity not permitted for federally chartered institutions.
- Prohibited all savings associations from investing in junk bonds and required divestment of existing junk bond portfolios no later than 1994.
- Required thrifts to invest 70 percent (up from 60 percent) of assets in residential mortgage assets.
- Prohibited any depository institution with insufficient capital from accepting brokered deposits.
- Established a federal subcommittee to monitor and oversee real estate appraisal practices.
- Increased criminal and civil penalties for fraudulent practices.
- Required that savings associations meet the same risk-based capital requirement as national commercial banks by 1992.

The turmoil of the 1970s and 1980s has left the thrift industry very much transformed. Many institutions are converting to bank charters and many others are being purchased by commercial banks. Furthermore, the role of these institutions in the financial services industry is being redefined.

Thrift Assets and Liabilities

4.1 Financial Assets

As shown in Exhibit 26.5, financial assets of thrifts (savings and loan associations and mutual savings banks) grew at an average annual rate of 9.4 percent to $1.6 trillion during the 25 years ended 1989. By 1996, this total was down to $1 trillion, reflecting contraction in the industry. From 1964 to 1989, home mortgages declined from 67.1 percent of thrift assets to 41.7 percent, with the greatest decline noted after 1979, that is, after the major deregulatory movement of the early 1980s. By 1998, the home mortgage share of thrift assets had increased to 49.7 percent.

Government agency securities and corporate and foreign bonds constituted only 2.6 percent of financial assets in 1964 but 20.6 percent by 1998. Over the same period, Treasury issues declined

	1964	1969	1974	1979	1984	1989	1994	1998
Financial assets ($billions)	$172.1	$234.2	$401.4	$732.7	$1,194.3	$1,621.1	$1,013.5	$1,047.3
Checkable deposits and currency	2.1%	1.0%	0.5%	0.4%	0.7%	1.1%	1.7%	1.7%
Time deposits	0.1	0.1	1.1	0.7	0.9	0.4	0.1	0.1
Federal funds and security repos	–	0.1	1.5	2.0	2.8	2.0	0.6	1.4
Investment securities:								
Treasury	7.4	4.9	1.1	1.1	2.9	1.3	2.7	1.2
Government agency	0.8	1.7	4.4	6.2	12.1	15.1	15.8	14.4
Tax-exempt	0.2	0.2	0.4	0.6	0.2	0.2	0.2	0.2
Corporate & foreign bonds	1.8	3.0	3.5	2.8	3.0	4.2	8.6	6.2
Corporate equities	1.2	0.9	0.5	0.3	0.2	0.5	1.0	2.6
Total securities	11.4	10.7	9.9	11.0	18.4	21.3	28.3	24.6
Loans:								
Mortgages:								
Home	67.1	66.9	61.4	61.6	44.5	41.7	47.1	49.7
Multifamily	7.4	8.2	9.2	7.4	6.3	6.8	6.4	5.6
Commercial	6.5	7.6	9.3	8.2	8.7	8.5	5.3	4.8
Farm	0.1	0.1	(1)	(1)	(1)	–	(1)	(1)
Total mortgages	81.1	82.8	79.9	77.2	59.5	57.0	58.8	60.1
Consumer:								
Installment	0.5	0.8	1.5	1.5	3.1	4.0	3.8	4.6
Noninstallment	1.1	1.0	1.0	1.0	0.7	0.3	–	–
Business	–	–	–	–	1.0	1.6	–	–
Total loans	82.7	84.6	82.4	79.7	64.3	62.9	62.6	64.7
Commercial paper and banker's acceptances	0.1	0.3	0.6	0.8	2.0	2.9	(1)	(1)
Miscellaneous	3.6	3.2	4.0	5.4	10.9	9.4	6.7	7.5
	100.0%	100.0%	100.0%	100.0%	100.0%	100.0%	100.0%	100.0%

◆ **Exhibit 26.5: Financial assets of savings institutions, 1964–98 (percentages)**

◆ *Note:*   (1) Less than 0.1%

◆ *Sources:*   Board of Governors of the Federal Reserve System, *Flow of Funds Accounts, Financial Assets and Liabilities*, various issues.

from 7.4 to 1.2 percent. The greater emphasis on government agency securities and corporate bonds is primarily attributable to the relatively higher yields available on these securities *vis-à-vis* Treasuries. While mutual savings banks held corporate bonds over the entire period included in Exhibit 26.5, these investments have been permissible for federal S&Ls only since 1980.

4.2 LIABILITIES

Financial liabilities of thrifts (S&Ls and MSBs) grew from $159 billion in 1964 at an average annual rate of 9.6 percent to $1.6 trillion in 1989, representing a growth rate roughly equivalent to that of thrift assets (Exhibit 26.6). However, by 1998, liabilities declined substantially to $1.0 trillion. Also, similar to the observed trend of home mortgages on the asset side, small time and savings deposits contributed 94.6 percent to liabilities in 1964, but only 41 percent in 1998. Most of the difference is explained by greater use of (1) large time deposits (from 0 percent in 1964 to 10.2 percent in 1998), (2) Federal Home Loan Bank loans (from 3.3 percent in 1964 to 14.2 percent in 1998), and (3) federal funds purchased and repurchase agreements (from 0 percent in 1964 to 4.7 percent in 1998). Nevertheless, since FIRREA, large time deposits and fed funds/ repos provide much less funding for the thrift industry.

4.3 SHARE OF THE MORTGAGE LOAN MARKET

Exhibit 26.7 underscores a threat to the thrift industry. These institutions developed primarily to provide mortgage finance. As recently as 1964, almost half (45.7 percent) of all mortgages were held by thrifts. This share was maintained through 1977 (45.9 percent). Thereafter, the share declined substantially. By 1998, savings and loan associations and mutual savings banks held only 11.4 percent of all mortgages.

This is the dilemma. Because of the excesses of the 1980s, regulators expect thrifts to concentrate more of their assets in mortgages. At the same time, thrifts are losing ground in the mortgage market. There is a real question as to whether the industry can compete with other financial services firms. When the high failure rates of the 1980s also are considered, in combination with continuing consolidation of the industry, the answer appears to be negative. Perhaps thrifts, as originally conceived, are no longer necessary.

⑤ Thrifts in Other Countries

There is a sharp contrast between the thrift industry in the United States and those in other countries. Examples from the United Kingdom, the European Union, Canada, and Japan follow.

5.1 THE UNITED KINGDOM

Building societies in the United Kingdom are a subset of the general classification of European savings banks. Thrifts in the United Kingdom also face competitive pressure from clearing (commercial) banks, but are nowhere near the point of extinction. In fact, United Kingdom building societies hold more deposits than the banks and are second only to insurance companies and pension funds.

	1964	1969	1974	1979	1984	1989	1994	1998
Financial liabilities ($billions)	$159.0	$217.2	$375.5	$688.7	$1,159.3	$1,561.3	$998.3	$1,015.6
Deposits:								
Checkable	0.2%	0.2%	0.2%	0.6%	2.2%	4.6%	8.3%	16.4%
Small time & savings	94.6	93.1	89.4	84.3	68.4	58.8	58.1	41.4
Large time	–	–	1.4	4.6	12.9	11.2	7.1	10.2
Total deposits	94.8	93.3	91.0	89.5	83.5	74.6	73.5	68.0
Federal funds and security repos	–	–	0.8	1.2	4.2	6.9	4.5	4.7
Federal home loan bank loans	3.3	4.3	5.8	6.3	6.7	11.5	10.0	14.2
Bonds	–	–	–	0.6	0.4	1.1	0.3	0.3
Other bank loans	0.2	0.2	0.4	0.7	1.2	3.2	0.9	2.3
Taxes payable	0.1	(1)	(1)	(1)	–	(1)	0.1	0.2
Miscellaneous	1.6	2.2	2.0	1.7	4.0	2.7	10.7	10.3
	100.0%	100.0%	100.0%	100.0%	100.0%	100.0%	100.0%	100.0%

◆ **Exhibit 26.6: Financial liabilities of savings institutions, 1964–98 (percentages)**

◆ *Note:*   (1) Less than 0.1%

◆ *Sources:*   Board of Governors of the Federal Reserve System, *Flow of Funds Accounts, Financial Assets and Liabilities*, various issues.

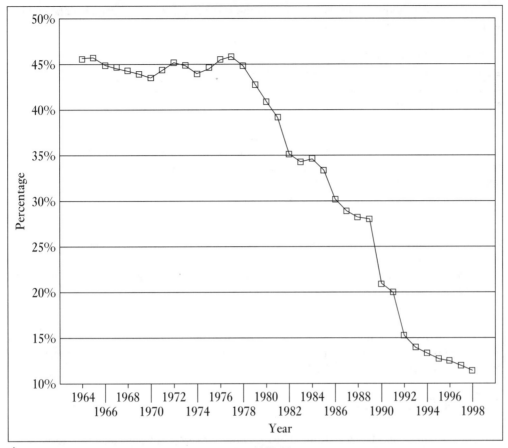

◆ **Exhibit 26.7:** **Thrifts' share of the mortgage market, 1964–98**

◆ *Source*:   Author's graphic based on data from: Board of Governors of the Federal Reserve System, *Flow of Funds Accounts; Financial Assets and Liabilities*, various issues.

Part of the reason for the strength of the UK market is that building societies are still nonprofit organizations and there is trust in the management. As a result, deposits and mutual shares remain on deposit with the institution. Thus, disintermediation has not been a significant problem in the United Kingdom.

Nevertheless, the lines of demarcation between banks and building societies are blurring as is true in the United States. Also, the industry is consolidating as in the United States. There are over 80 such institutions in the United Kingdom and the top 10 represent over 80 percent of the industry's total assets. However, the future is much brighter for UK building societies than for US counterparts.

The traditional structure of a building society is a mutual organization that uses its financial resources to make loans for the purpose of buying land and constructing homes. However, the UK building society industry is undergoing significant change. The more ambitious societies feel their powers are unnecessary constrained, limiting their growth. Many would like more wholesale banking powers so that they could tap the relatively cheap wholesale money markets.

After rapid expansion in the 1980s, growth in the 1990s has slowed considerably. The building societies still retain certain advantages:

- Established local franchises
- In some cases, an established international franchise
- Public confidence
- Strong capital base

Nevertheless, banks are increasingly infringing on the territory of UK building societies. During the early 1990s, the share of new mortgage lending by banks increased from 25 percent of the total to 33 percent. When the effect of repayments is removed, the new lending of banks actually exceeded that of building societies by 1993.

To counteract these trends, there appear to be several options available to a British building society:

- Become a bank. A building society can *demutualize*, that is, become a stockholding company
- Buy a bank
- Merge. There is apparent need for industry consolidation and consolidations make it possible to reduce operating costs
- Sell the society to a bank

The most frequent question is the one being asked in the United States. Does this form of institution bring enough benefit to the financial system to justify the cost of separate rules, separate regulation, and separate charters? Or has the building society outlived its *raison d'être*?

5.2 THE EUROPEAN COMMUNITY

In the Single European Market, UK building societies have certain advantages. The UK mortgage market is more active than in other EC countries. For example, the German real estate market is much more oriented toward rental property. Even affluent Germans often do not seek home ownership until they are close to retirement. In contrast, the UK rental market is not as well developed and most residences are owner-occupied. As UK businesses relocate workers throughout the Single European Market, the demand for a wide variety of mortgages will increase. UK building societies are being positioned for expansion.

In Germany, the savings banks are more similar to commercial banks. In fact, they conduct universal banking business, with strong participation in lending to domestic businesses and individuals. Westdeutsche Landesbank (WestLB) is the largest German savings bank and the third largest German financial institution overall. WestLB is a liquidity manager for local savings banks and, increasingly, an international commercial and investment bank. The German institution has branches in the United Kingdom, France, Luxembourg, and Switzerland. In 1989, WestLB acquired a 50 percent stake in the merchant-banking operations of Standard Chartered (United Kingdom) and operates the affiliate as a wholly owned subsidiary under the name West Merchant Bank. With a specialty in emerging market debt, West Merchant Bank is one of the most profitable merchant banks in London.

One of the largest savings banks in the world is the Italian Cariplo. In Italy, as elsewhere, savings banks concentrate on areas that have historically been neglected by commercial banks, especially mortgages. However, Italian savings banks are also merging to better compete in the

Single European Market. Cariplo is positioning itself as a major international bank. With branches in London, New York, and Hong Kong, it already has the capability to operate on a 24-hour basis because of overlapping time zones.

5.3 CANADA

In Canada, building societies have evolved into mortgage loan companies. Many are wholly owned subsidiaries of chartered (commercial) banks. Like the UK system, the Canadian system is highly concentrated. Furthermore, the chartered bank subsidiaries represent the largest share of mortgage loan company assets (over 50 percent).

Unlike the UK system, however, Canadian mortgage loan companies are for-profit operations. The problem of mismatched maturity of assets and liabilities is not solved through public trust and stable deposits. Instead, the term of mortgage loans is shorter. Prior to 1969, the average term of a mortgage loan was 25 years. However, in 1969 federal legislation was passed that introduced a five-year renewable mortgage. This permitted institutions to better match the maturities of loans to term (long-term) deposits. Since the late 1970s, open mortgages have allowed borrowers to repay mortgages before maturity with no penalty. Three-year, one-year, and six-month renewable mortgage loans are now available.

5.4 JAPAN

In Japan, the Housing Loan Corporation is the major provider of mortgage, holding over 35 percent of all mortgage loans. This government agency is financed primarily by postal savings deposits and by operating surpluses of other government agencies.

Ordinary (commercial) banks and insurance companies have also provided mortgage finance. However, until 1971, there were no private companies that were geared specifically to mortgage borrowers. There are now private housing finance companies, or *jusen*, that are funded by banks as encouraged by the Ministry of Finance (comparable to the US Treasury Department). *Jusen* are specialized housing lenders – and now a particularly problematic sector because of bad loans that constitute the majority of jusen loan portfolios. In addition to holding mortgage loans, the *jusen* also act as lending agents for private insurance companies and the public Housing Loan Corporation.

In Japan, specialized financial institutions include associations and cooperatives with either a specific clientele or special functions. For example, there are approximately 2,700 agricultural cooperatives (agricultural savings associations) that are financed with deposits and have significant exposure in real estate loans. In addition, agricultural cooperatives own Norinchukin Bank which acts as their central bank. In turn, Norinchukin Bank is the single largest lender to the jusen. As a result, the agricultural cooperative sector currently is deeply involved in resolving a major part of bad loan portfolios in the Japanese financial system.

 ## Summary

The thrift industry in the United States filled a vital need in housing finance in its early years. Also, there was no outlet for small savings at the time. As long as both asset and liability portfolios conformed with this initial arrangement, thrifts were viable institutions. However, competition from commercial banks was but the first attack on the industry.

The inflation that began in the 1960s was a particularly troublesome development for thrifts. Except for a brief period of "national" thrifts, these institutions served a limited geographic region. Thus, overseas operations and Euomarket participation were not viable alternatives, as they were for commercial banks. Deregulation of the 1970s and 1980s opened the floodgates of innovation. The powers of thrifts were expanded to make them more competitive. However, regulatory overseers failed to monitor the thrifts for evidence of power abuse, and Congress was slow to react.

In 1989, FIRREA was enacted. The legislation took major steps to reverse the abuses and clean up the industry. A much smaller but healthier thrift industry now operates in a very competitive environment.

End-of-chapter Questions

1. The Federal Home Loan Bank System was designed in the 1930s to be roughly comparable to the Federal Reserve System. The Federal Savings and Loan Insurance Corporation was similarly intended to parallel the Federal Deposit Insurance Corporation. Explain how this thrift regulatory structure was dismantled by legislation in 1989.

2. How did early building societies differ from commercial banks?

3. What is a mutual depository organization?

4. What factors contributed to the need for thrifts in the 1800s?

5. How did the early mutual savings banks differ from savings and loan associations (building societies)?

6. Explain the effect of rising interest rates on the profitability of thrifts in the late 1970s and early 1980s. Be specific.

7. Summarize the scope of activities that were permitted for thrifts during the 1980s.

8. In previous years, thrifts relied heavily on savings deposits as a source of funds. Currently, how has the mix of liabilities changed?

9. In light of recent losses in the thrift industry and the consolidation trend, assess the prospect of future viability of thrifts, in particular with respect to their original justification for existence.

10. If thrifts cease to exist, would you have any concerns about the mortgage services available to consumers?

11. What were the major mistakes that were made in regulating the thrift industry during the 1980s?

SELECTED REFERENCES

Binhammer, H. H. *Money, Banking, and the Canadian Banking System*, 4th edn, Methuen Publications, Agincourt, Ontario, 1982.

Board of Governors of the Federal Reserve System, *Flow of Funds Accounts, Financial Assets and Liabilities*, various issues.

Brumbaugh, R. Dan, Jr. *Thrifts Under Siege; Restoring Order to American Banking*, Ballinger Publishing Company, Cambridge, Mass., 1988.

Carron, Andrew S. *The Rescue of the Thrift Industry*, The Brookings Institution, Washington, DC, 1983.

Carter, H. and I. Partington. *Applied Economics in Banking and Finance*, 3rd edn, Oxford University Press, Oxford, UK, 1984.

Chant, John F. *The Market for Financial Services; Deposit-Taking Institutions*, The Fraser Institute, Vancouver, 1988.

Cooper, S. Kerry and Donald R. Fraser. *Banking Deregulation and the New Competition in Financial Services*, Ballinger Publishing Company, Cambridge, Mass., 1984.

Johnson, Hazel J. *Banking in Asia*, Lafferty Publications, Dublin, 1997.

Johnson, Hazel J. *Banking in Europe: Managing Change in a New Marketplace*, Lafferty Publications, Dublin, 1996.

Kane, Edward J. *The S&L Insurance Mess: How Did It Happen?*, The Urban Institute Press, Washington, DC, 1989.

Meyer, Dianne A. and Sandra A. Ballard. "Issues in Lending: A Practical Guide to FIRREA," *Journal of Commercial Bank Lending*, 72 (Jan 1990), pp. 11–23.

Office of Thrift Supervision, Washington, DC, unpublished quarterly data.

Ornstein, Franklin H. *Savings Banking: An Industry in Change*, Reston Publishing, Reston, Va., 1985.

Pizzo, Stephen, Mary Fricker, and Paul Muolo. *Inside Job: The Looting of America's Savings and Loans*, Harper Perennial, New York, 1991.

Sizilo, Yoshio. *The Japanese Financial System*, Clarendon Press, Oxford, UK, 1987.

US League of Savings Institutions. *Savings Institutions Sourcebook*, Washington, DC, 1990 and 1994.

Credit Unions

CHAPTER OVERVIEW

This chapter:
- Compares and contrasts credit unions and thrifts.
- Highlights the important role that trade associations have played in the industry's development.
- Describes credit union regulation.
- Studies the industry balance sheet.
- Illustrates structural aspects of credit unions in other regions of the world.

KEY TERMS

Central Liquidity Facility (CLF)
common bond
Credit Union National Association (CUNA)
CUNA Mutual Insurance Group
CUNA Service Group

field of membership
Financial Institutions Reform Act of 1978
share account
US Central Credit Union
World Council of Credit Unions

CHAPTER OUTLINE

1 Credit Unions as Compared to Thrifts
2 Unique Characteristics
   2.1 The Common Bond
   2.2 Other Characteristics
3 Development of Credit Unions
   3.1 Trade Associations
   3.2 Credit Union Growth
4 Credit Union Regulation
5 Assets and Liabilities
   5.1 Assets
   5.2 Liabilities
6 Credit Unions Around the World

INTERNATIONAL COMPARISONS:
Africa
Asia
Canada
Europe
Latin America and the Caribbean

 ## Introduction

Credit unions grew from the same spirit that motivated thrift institutions. Through a credit union formed on the basis of a common bond, members were able to obtain consumer financing that was not available from commercial banks. But while thrifts evolved into profit-seeking enterprises, credit unions never departed from their self-help, volunteer-worker mode of operation. As such, they have maintained their tax-free status.

At the same time, credit unions *have evolved* in terms of service. At one time, credit unions were funded almost exclusively by savings accounts (liabilities) and offered consumer loans (assets). Today, credit unions also offer transactions accounts, credit cards, and home mortgages. Deposits are federally insured and members have access to their accounts through automated teller machines (ATMs). A modern credit union offers consumers the same types of service available from a commercial bank. In fact, credit unions are so much like commercial banks that commercial banks often point to credit unions' exemption from income taxation as an unfair competitive advantage. This debate will continue as long as credit unions evolve more and more into bank-like financial institutions.

 ## Credit Unions as Compared to Thrifts

The primary difference between credit unions and other depository institutions is their emphasis on service. They are neither profit-oriented nor motivated by philanthropy. In fact, the industry motto has been:

Not for profit,
Not for charity,
But for service.

In terms of business structure, credit unions are tax-exempt, *mutual organizations* in which deposits are considered *shares* and interest paid is considered *dividend payment*. With the exception of the treasurer, most of the officers of credit unions are unpaid volunteers. While savings and loans and savings banks are also frequently mutual organizations, they *may* convert to a corporate form. Since credit unions *may not* convert to a corporate form, they represent the best example of a cooperative financial institution in the United States.

> **Credit union share account:**
> An ownership claim on a credit union, similar in form to a common stock interest. Payments to owners are called dividend payments. In substance, share accounts are equivalent to deposits.

More specifically, there are three other characteristics that distinguish credit unions from thrifts.

1) Mutual savings banks were first established to encourage *thrift* among members. The original savings and loan associations restricted operations to the provision of *mortgage finance* for members. Credit unions originated to provide reasonably priced *consumer finance*.

2) Early savings banks were started by wealthy individuals out of a sense of *philanthropy*. Credit unions are based on the concept of *self-help*. While early S&Ls also espoused a self-help philosophy, modern associations are more often *profit-oriented* than not.

3) Credit union members share a *common bond* that has never applied to savings banks. In the case of savings and loan associations, the only common characteristic originally shared by members was that property purchased with loan proceeds was restricted to a given geographical area. In a modern context, S&L loans are restricted neither to a specific geographic area nor to the association members (or depositors).

② Unique Characteristics

2.1 THE COMMON BOND

From the start, credit union members have shared a *common bond*. Common bonds are either *associational, occupational,* or *residential*. Examples of associational bonds are religious, fraternal, professional, and labor union groups. Occupational bonds most often describe a common employer. Residential bonds describe a common geographical location and have been less important in quantitative terms than associational and occupational bonds.

> **Common bond:**
> An attribute that describes all members of a credit union. The common bond distinguishes credit unions from all other mutual financial institutions.

Credit unions with a residential common bond have recently accounted for less than 5 percent of all US organizations; associational credit unions represent between 15 percent and 20 percent. By far, the largest category is occupational.

Common bonds define a credit union's *field of membership*. Over time, bonds have been loosely interpreted in many cases. For example, it is not unusual for the immediate family of a member to also be eligible for membership. When permitted by state law, those who leave the field of membership may retain their credit union membership. In some cases, the common bond defines a nontraditional field – for example, owners of Arabian horses.

> **Field of membership:**
> The group of people who have a particular common bond and may join a particular credit union.

2.2 OTHER CHARACTERISTICS

The common bond and other features give credit unions certain advantages.

- Members of occupational (job-related) credit unions often make *contributions through payroll deduction*. This process streamlines operations and reduces default risk of loans.
- Credit union income is *exempt from income taxation*. This reduces the cost of funds.
- Many of the employees of credit unions are *volunteer personnel*. This feature reduces the operating expense.

These cost advantages make it easier for credit unions to offer competitively priced loans. However, before interest rate deregulation, these cost advantages were partially offset by the higher interest rates that could be paid on share accounts. Federal Reserve Regulation Q (which controlled deposit interest rate ceilings for banks and thrifts until the 1980s) did not apply to credit unions.

③ Development of Credit Unions

The credit union industry was established on a basic underlying principle – People should pool their money and make loans to each other. The movement started in Germany and then moved to North America and other regions of the world. The first credit unions in the United States were formed in Massachusetts in 1910.

3.1 TRADE ASSOCIATIONS

To stimulate the formation of more associations, the Massachusetts Credit Union (MCU) was established in 1914. While the MCU was a functioning credit union, its objectives also included encouraging the formation of additional associations and providing support for individual credit unions and the industry as a whole. Through its activities, the MCU evolved into a kind of central facility.

The original MCU was eventually reorganized as the *Credit Union National Extension Bureau* (*CUNEB*) in 1921. The CUNEB would promote the movement on a national scale, while the Massachusetts Credit Union League would represent associations within the state.

CUNEB worked to have credit union laws passed in every state. Virginia and Kentucky enacted credit union legislation in 1922, followed by Tennessee and Indiana in 1923. While a number of states subsequently enacted credit union legislation, advocates sometimes faced strong opposition by banking and savings and loan representatives that did not welcome the competition. In spite of this resistance and the Great Depression, by 1933 only 10 states had failed to enact credit union legislation. Those states that had credit union laws represented 80 percent of the nation's population.

The *Credit Union National Association* (*CUNA*) replaced the CUNEB in 1935. The new structure was intended to serve state *leagues* that elected to affiliate with it. In turn, CUNA encouraged individual credit unions to affiliate with their state leagues. Membership dues, rather than outside financing, fund CUNA operations.

As early as the first meeting of CUNA's board of directors, the issue of mutual life insurance arose. *CUNA Mutual Insurance Group* also began operation in 1935 to provide credit life insurance. In the event of death of a borrower prior to full repayment, CUNA Mutual guaranteed repayment. A small number of companies (not owned by CUNA) constitute CUNA Mutual.

The *CUNA Service Group* is a profit-making affiliate that plays a support role and supplies new products to credit unions. CUNA Service Group is owned by CUNA and by credit union leagues.

Members of the group provide specific services. *CUNA Supply, Inc.* makes wholesale purchases of operational and promotional supplies for distribution to CUNA members. The CUNA Supply Print Center produces and distributes to members forms, stationery, business cards, as well as newsletters and other publications. *CUNA Internet* makes it possible for individual credit unions to be linked to an on-line telecommunications network. Through CUNA's website on the Internet, consumers receive league telephone numbers, information on joining or organizing a credit union, and consumer tips on purchasing homes and automobiles – at the rate of 30,000 downloaded files per month in the mid-1990s. *Credit Union Products and Services* provides US government securities investment vehicles, automated payment mechanisms, and Individual Retirement Account/Keogh Account plans. *Card Services* provides support for credit unions to offer debit and credit cards – printing monthly statements and offering telephone customer support. In the mid-1990s, Card Services managed five million individual accounts for 2,300 credit unions.

CUNA Mortgage Corporation is jointly owned by CUNA Service Group and by CUNA Mutual Insurance Group. This mortgage corporation provides a liquidity facility for mortgage lending by purchasing mortgage loans that have been originated by credit unions, packaging them into mortgage pools, and selling the securitized mortgages on the secondary market. Taken together, the research and development activities of the Service Group help member credit unions realize economies of scale and maintain competitiveness in the provision of financial services.

In 1974, the *US Central Credit Union* began operations. The corporation, capitalized at 1 percent of assets by member credit unions, acts as a *credit union for credit unions.* It is a private liquidity facility and provider of investment advice, settlement, and payment services. Its operations are funded with commercial paper issuances that have historically earned high ratings from rating services.

US Central Credit Union and the state corporate credit unions form the *CUNA Corporate Credit Union Network.* Through the Network, individual credit unions may invest in a large portfolio of securities managed by US Central and obtain services normally available only through correspondent relationship with commercial banks. These services include wire transfers, share draft settlements, provision of currency and coin, and federal funds trading.

The organizational structure of the US credit union system is described in Exhibit 27.1.

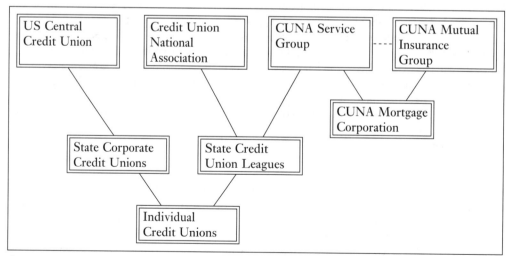

◆ **Exhibit 27.1:   US credit union system**

Year	Active		Membership	
	Credit Unions	% Change	Thousands	% Change
1929	974		264.9	
1933	2,016	107.0%	359.6	35.9%
1936	5,241	160.0	1,170.4	225.5
1939	7,964	52.0	2,309.2	97.3
1942	9,767	22.6	3,144.6	36.2
1945	8,683	<11.1>	2,842.9	<9.6>
1948	9,924	14.3	4,090.7	43.9
1951	11,279	13.7	5,169.4	26.4
1954	15,041	33.4	7,355.6	43.3
1957	18,198	21.0	9,861.5	34.1
1960	20,148	10.7	12,059.2	22.3
1963	21,382	6.1	14,579.3	20.9
1966	22,684	6.1	17,922.6	22.9
1969	23,776	4.8	21,628.3	20.7
1972	23,070	<3.0>	25,690.3	18.8
1975	22,611	<2.0>	31,262.8	21.7
1978	22,202	<1.8>	40,720.0	30.3
1981	20,784	<6.4>	45,187.9	11.0
1984	18,375	<11.6>	49,210.3	8.9
1987	16,274	<11.4>	56,468.2	14.7
1990	14,549	<10.6>	61,611.0	9.1
1993	12,960	<10.9>	65,459.1	6.2
1995	12,230	<5.6>	69,305.9	5.9

◆ **Exhibit 27.2:** Growth in numbers and membership of US credit unions, 1929–95

◆ *Sources*: Pugh, Olin S. and F. Jerry Ingram, *Credit Unions: A Movement Becomes An Industry*, pp. 8–9; World Council of Credit Unions, *1995 Statistical Report*; Author's calculations based on previous sources.

3.2 CREDIT UNION GROWTH

After the 1909 Massachusetts credit union legislation, the number of associations grew rapidly, especially in the early 1930s. Despite the adversity of the Great Depression, the number of credit unions grew 107 percent between 1929 and 1933, as shown in Exhibit 27.2. Over the same period, membership grew 35.9 percent. In 1933, 359,600 members belonged to 2,016 associations. Credit unions prospered because of reduced confidence in the banking system.

State laws, federal credit union legislation in 1934, and restructuring of the national association provided a strong push for the industry. During the three years ended 1936, membership and the number of organizations more than doubled.

This trend reversed in 1941 when the United States became involved in the Second World War (1941–5). The uncertainties of war resulted in more reductions in membership than had been witnessed during the Great Depression. After the war, membership gains resumed and remained strong. However, the growth in the number of associations has been mixed. From 1945 through 1960, there was double-digit growth in each three-year period. From 1960, growth in the number of credit unions slowed to 5 percent or 6 percent during the next few three-year periods. At 23,776 credit unions in 1969, the industry reached its peak. Thereafter, numbers began to decline.

Liquidations and *mergers* have been responsible for most of the reduction. Liquidations most often occur in connection with smaller credit unions. From 1970 through the early 1980s, less than 15 percent of liquidating associations controlled more than $100,000 each in savings. Frequently, the organization was affiliated with a manufacturing plant that had been closed. In this respect, the credit union industry has been affected by the strong consolidation trend evident in other areas of financial services. The consolidation in the credit union industry during the 1970s, 1980s, and 1990s has resulted in fewer institutions that control more financial resources, that is, larger credit unions.

④ Credit Union Regulation

Since 1934, federal charters for credit unions have been permitted. The Federal Credit Union Act of that year contained the following provisions:

- At least seven persons were required as founding members.
- Funds were to be invested only for provident (prudent) and productive purposes.
- Credit unions formed under the Act were exempt from income taxation.
- Charters would be granted by the Farm Credit Administration.[1]

(See also Exhibit 27.3.)

Ray Burgengren (head of the predecessor of CUNA) helped draft the Federal Credit Union Act early in 1934. However, he knew that he needed the support of President Franklin Roosevelt (1933–45) and of the Chairman of the House Banking Committee Henry Steagall, co-author of the major banking legislation of 1933.

In early June 1934, the President endorsed the bill and encouraged Steagall to see to it that the legislation moved quickly through his committee before Congress adjourned near the middle of the month. On June 13, Burgengren and a close associate were called to Steagall's office to defend the measure. Satisfied that the legislation was sound, Steagall presided the next day when the Banking Committee rendered a favorable report.

At that point, adjournment seemed imminent. On the morning of June 16, predictions were that Congress would adjourn that evening. After 7:00 p.m., Steagall asked that the bill be considered. Only thirty minutes were allotted for debate. Chairman Steagall persuasively argued that the bill had received unanimous support in the Senate and in the House Banking Committee and that the President had endorsed it.

There was no opposition to the creation of federally chartered, tax-exempt credit unions that would later compete vigorously with the country's commercial banks. Even before the allotted 30 minutes had elapsed, the House passed the Federal Credit Union Act with only two dissenting votes.

◆ **Exhibit 27.3: Congressman Steagall and the Federal Credit Union Act**

◆ *Source*: Moody, J. Carroll and Gilbert C. Fite, *The Credit Union Movement, Origins and Development, 1850–1970*, 1971, pp. 160–5.

The Federal Credit Union Act was amended in 1970 to create the *National Credit Union Administration (NCUA)* and the *National Credit Union Share Insurance Fund (NCUSIF)*, to be controlled by the Administrator of NCUA. The NCUA is organized into six regions. (The six regions have headquarters in Albany, NY; Washington, DC; Atlanta, GA; Itasca, IL; Austin, TX; and Concord, CA.) Since 1970, NCUA has acted as the primary federal regulator of credit unions, issuing charters, supervising operations, conducting examinations, and insuring shares and deposits.

From 1970 through the early 1980s, the NCUSIF insurance premium paid by member credit unions was 1/12 of 1 percent or 8.3 cents per $100 of share account balance. The high interest rates of the early 1980s, together with numerous industrial plant closings, drained the insurance fund. Premiums were increased to 17 cents per $100 of share account balance to rebuild the fund. In 1984, the US Congress authorized the recapitalization of NCUSIF. As a result of this legislation, member credit unions must place 1 percent of insured share balances on deposit at NCUSIF. This amount is not expensed, but is recorded as an asset on the books of member credit unions. Income earned on these funds is used by NCUSIF to cover losses. An annual insurance premium up to one-twelfth of 1 percent may be assessed if necessary.

The investment and lending powers of federal credit unions were liberalized in the 1977 amendment of the Federal Credit Union Act. The amendment:

- Allowed federal credit unions to offer 30-year residential mortgages and 15-year mobile home and home-improvement loans
- Extended the maximum maturity for nonresidential loans from 10 years to 12 years
- Permitted other new product offerings such as government-insured loans, lines of credit, and share certificates (similar to certificates of deposit)

The *Financial Institutions Reform Act of 1978* reorganized the NCUA and helped make the shrinking numbers of credit unions more competitive financial institutions. A three-member board, appointed by the President and confirmed by the Senate, replaced the Administrator and the credit union board. Members of the new board served staggered six-year terms. In addition, the separate fees assessed for chartering, supervision, and examination were replaced by one fee.

Also, permissible products and activities were expanded to include:

- Six-month, $10,000 share certificates
- Shares certificates in excess of $100,000 to carry market interest rates
- Small share certificates with interest rates up to 8 percent
- Sale of mortgages to Federal National Mortgage Association, Federal Home Loan Mortgage Corporation, and Government National Mortgage Association

The 1978 Act also created a federal source of liquidity or lender-of-last-resort. The *Central Liquidity Facility (CLF)* was formed to fulfill this function for credit unions as the Federal Reserve did for commercial banks. By subscribing 0.5 percent of capital, federal- and state-chartered associations may join the CLF and receive short-term loans for temporary liquidity needs. The National Credit Union Share Insurance Fund may now also borrow from the CLF. Most of the funds of the CLF are borrowed from the federal government.

The *Depository Institutions Deregulation and Monetary Control Act (DIDMCA) of 1980* legalized share drafts (interest-bearing transactions accounts) and other interest-bearing transactions accounts. Credit unions were also brought under the control of the Federal Reserve System, along with thrifts (savings and loan associations and mutual savings banks) with respect to a uniform system of reserve requirements. As is true for other depository institutions, DIDMCA raised the federal insurance limit to $100,000, deregulated deposit interest rates, and superseded state usury laws. The previous credit union loan interest rate ceiling of 1 percent per month (12 percent per year) was increased to 15 percent per year. Subsequently, the NCUA gave individual credit union boards rate-setting authority.

The Garn–St. Germain Act of 1982 gave credit unions additional flexibility. Federal credit unions were allowed to determine both the par value of shares and internal organizational structure. Provisions also included further liberalization of mortgage lending. Limits on the size and maturity of mortgage loans were lifted, first mortgages were allowed to be refinanced, and the limit on maturity of second mortgages was expanded. The suspension of reserve requirements for the first $2 million in reservable deposits exempted virtually all credit unions from reserve requirements since the account balances of the typical association fall well below this cutoff point.

Assets and Liabilities

5.1 ASSETS

Compared to banks and thrifts, the balance sheet of credit unions is relatively simple. Member loans, government securities, and time deposits dominate the asset portfolio, as can be seen in Exhibit 27.4. From 1964 through 1998, financial assets of credit unions increased from $9.9 billion to $376.6 billion, or at an average annual rate of 11.3 percent.

In the credit union industry, the $376.6 billion in assets in 1998 was held by approximately 11,000 institutions. As a result, the average credit union in 1996 was a relatively small $34 million institution. Thus, the amount of assets under management by the typical credit union is much smaller than that of other firms in the financial services industry.

The mix of assets has changed over time, as is true of other depository institutions. In 1964, over 22 percent was invested in time deposits, 5 percent in checkable deposits and currency, and only 3 percent in securities. Consumer loans represented over 64 percent, while home mortgages were only 5 percent of total financial assets. Essentially, credit unions were highly liquid with almost 28 percent of assets in cash or cash equivalents. Consistent with the original purpose, consumer installment credit absorbed well over half of investable funds.

The emphasis on consumer credit was sustained through 1979. After federal credit unions were permitted to offer residential mortgages in 1977, mortgage loans became an increasingly important component of the industry's balance sheet. As noted above, the 1982 Garn–St. Germain Act again enhanced mortgage market participation. By 1998, mortgage loans represented over 25 percent of the asset portfolio, as compared to 5 percent in 1964.

By 1998, time deposits and cash represented only 4.9 percent of assets as the industry has become much less liquid. The reduction in liquid assets (17 percentage points) has been largely offset by higher proportional investments in money and capital market instruments. Combined, (1) federal funds and repurchase agreements and (2) investment securities constituted 21.7 percent in 1998, as compared to 3.1 percent in 1964. In this respect, credit union asset portfolio changes have mirrored those in the thrift industry, that is, (1) lower investments in liquid assets and (2) higher investments in securities.

	1964	1969	1974	1979	1984	1989	1994	1998
Financial assets ($billions)	$9.9	$16.1	$31.1	$63.1	$113.0	$200.5	$292.9	$376.6
Checkable deposits and currency	5.1%	3.8%	3.2%	1.7%	2.3%	2.6%	2.2%	2.3%
Time Deposits:								
At banks	11.2	5.1	6.1	4.0	7.1	6.1	3.1	(1)
At S&Ls	11.2	5.0	6.1	3.3	6.1	5.4	2.6	4.9
Total time deposits	22.4	10.1	12.2	7.3	13.2	11.5	7.9	4.9
Federal funds sold and repos	–	–	–	–	4.1	5.1	2.1	2.7
Investment securities:								
US Treasury	3.1	3.1	2.6	1.0	3.0	7.1	7.5	3.7
Agency	–	3.1	6.8	4.3	5.2	3.7	14.0	15.3
Total securities	3.1	6.2	9.4	5.3	8.2	10.8	21.5	19.0
Loans:								
Consumer	64.3	75.5	70.4	73.7	58.6	43.6	40.8	39.7
Home Mortgages	5.1	4.4	4.8	6.3	8.2	20.2	21.2	25.2
Total loans	69.4	79.9	75.2	80.0	66.8	63.8	62.0	64.9
Miscellaneous	–	–	–	5.7	5.4	6.2	6.5	6.2
	100.0%	100.0%	100.0%	100.0%	100.0%	100.0%	100.0%	100.0%

◆ Exhibit 27.4: Financial assets of US credit unions, 1964–98 (percentages)

◈ *Note:* (1) Bank and S&L time deposits not reported separately

◈ *Source:* Board of Governors of the Federal Reserve System, *Flow of Funds Accounts, Financial Assets and Liabilities,* various issues.

	1964	1969	1974	1979	1984	1989	1994	1998
Financial liabilities ($billions)	$9.9	$16.1	$31.1	$63.1	$113.0	$200.5	$270.3	$342.1
Shares and deposits:								
Checkable	–	–	0.3%	2.4%	8.4%	9.6%	10.7%	11.3%
Small time and Savings	82.8%	85.6%	88.2%	88.1%	81.7%	80.0%	84.1%	82.2
Large Time	–	–	–	0.5	0.7	1.3	2.7	4.8
Total shares/deposits	82.8	85.6	88.5	91.0	90.8	90.9	97.5	98.3
Miscellaneous	17.2	14.4	11.5	9.0	9.2	9.1	2.5	1.7
	100.0%	100.0%	100.0%	100.0%	100.0%	100.0%	100.0%	100.0%

◆ **Exhibit 27.5: Liabilities of US credit unions, 1964–98 (percentages)**

◈ *Source:*   Board of Governors of the Federal Reserve System, *Flow of Funds Accounts, Financial Assets and Liabilities*, various issues.

5.2 LIABILITIES

The liability section of the credit union industry balance sheet (Exhibit 27.5) has also reflected significant changes, though not as marked as those in the asset section. Unlike thrifts, credit unions still have relatively little reliance on large time deposits. The most notable change is the increase in checkable shares and deposits making up 11.3 percent of the total in 1998 (there were no such facilities in 1964).

A *share account* is an equity claim on the assets of the credit union. However, the dividends paid on a share account are a stated percentage of the value of the account. Thus, a share account is more similar to a deposit than to a typical equity investment. In fact, according to generally accepted accounting principles (GAAP), share accounts are classified as liabilities and the Internal Revenue Service considers share dividends received as interest income.

Small time and savings accounts have not declined as dramatically in the credit union industry as in the thrift industry. In 1964, thrifts (chapter 26, Exhibit 26.6) funded 95 percent of operations with small time and savings accounts. By 1998, this proportion was down to 41 percent. On the other hand, credit unions have managed to finance more than 80 percent of operations with small time and savings deposits for the years shown in Exhibit 27.5. Furthermore, reliance on small time and savings accounts does not appear to have hampered the growth of the industry.

 ## Credit Unions Around the World

The credit union movement has reached every part of the world since inception. Consider the data for 1995 in Exhibit 27.6, describing the World Council of Credit Unions (led by CUNA).

In 1995, over 37,286 CUNA-affiliated credit unions operated worldwide with 85 million members. Since the affiliation is with a US-based organization, most of these members were in the United States. However, the number of credit unions in Asia was higher than the number in the United States. In fact, India (in Asia) accounts for roughly 75 percent of all credit unions, including those not affiliated with CUNA. As shown in Exhibit 27.7, US credit unions within the World Council accounted for approximately 80 percent of all shares and deposits, as well as assets in 1995.

 ## Summary

The credit union is a financial institution that began as a service organization for members, not unlike savings and loan associations and mutual savings banks. Over time, the latter have evolved into financial institutions that closely resemble commercial banks. They make business loans and invest in corporate securities. They market large time deposits in order to attract funds.

In contrast, credit unions have retained their service orientation and are the best example of cooperative banking in the United States. Their balance sheets are relatively simple and small share accounts still dominate as the primary source of funds.

The competition between credit unions and banks is intensifying because credit unions now offer consumers a wide variety of services including transactions accounts, retirement accounts, and mortgage loans. At the same time, credit unions have retained their volunteer work force and tax-exempt status which has given them a significant cost advantage over commercial banks.

Region/country	Credit unions		Membership	
	Number	%	Thousands	%
Asia	14,508	38.9%	6,125	7.2%
United States	12,230	32.8	62,200	73.3
Europe	1,070	2.9	2,649	3.1
Canada	952	2.6	4,140	4.9
Africa	5,493	14.7	2,910	3.4
Latin America and the Caribbean	2,621	7.0	3,778	4.6
Australia, New Zealand and Fiji	412	1.1	2,990	3.5
	37,286	100.0%	84,792	100.0%

◆ **Exhibit 27.6:** **Membership of the World Council of Credit Unions, worldwide, 1995**

◆ *Source*: World Council of Credit Unions, Inc., *1995 Statistical Report.*

Region/country	Shares/deposits		Loans		Total assets	
		%		%		%
Asia	$14,180.9	4.7%	$12,504.9	5.5%	$18,631.4	5.10
United States	248,100.0	81.4	176,800.0	78.2	300,783.0	82.1
Europe	2,689.7	0.9	2,131.5	0.9	3,083.0	0.9
Canada	28,161.4	9.2	23,441.3	10.4	31,101.7	8.5
Africa	451.7	0.1	262.2	0.1	88.1	(1)
Latin America and the Caribbean	2,764.5	0.9	3,534.6	1.6	3,063.7	0.8
Australia, New Zealand and Fiji	8,388.6	2.8	7,487.5	3.3	9,563.5	2.6
	$304,736.8	100.0%	$266,162.0	100.0%	$366,314.4	100.0%

◆ **Exhibit 27.7:** **Credit union shares, loans, and total assets of the World Council of Credit Unions, worldwide, 1995 ($millions)**

◆ *Note*: (1) Less than 0.1%

◆ *Source*: World Council of Credit Unions, Inc., *1995 Statistical Report.*

End-of-chapter Questions

1. What is a common bond? In general, what are the three types of common bonds?
2. How do credit unions differ from savings and loan associations and mutual savings banks?

3. Federal regulation of credit unions began in 1934, but there was no independent federal credit agency until 1970. Describe the private trade organizations that organized credit unions on a national basis in the face of this relative lack of federal involvement.

4. Compare the effects of the Great Depression on the credit union industry with those on the thrift industry. (Hint: refer also to chapter 26.)

5. In what ways did the federal legislation of 1980 and 1982 affect credit union operations?

6. Over time, credit unions have changed least among all depository institutions. Describe those changes that have occurred in the industry balance sheet.

7. Within the World Council of Credit Unions, where is the greatest concentration of resources held by credit unions?

8. Where are the largest credit unions in terms of average membership? (Hint: refer to Exhibit 27.6.)

9. Present arguments for and against the continued exemption of credit unions from federal income taxation. Answer this question from the perspective first of the credit unions and then commercial banks.

10. In your opinion, why do you believe credit unions have enjoyed such a steady increase in membership over the years?

NOTE

1   In 1942, the Federal Credit Union Program was transferred to the Federal Deposit Insurance Corporation as the Credit Union Section. Six years later, the Federal Security Agency assumed responsibility. When this agency was liquidated in 1953, a newly reorganized Bureau of Federal Credit Unions was assigned to the Department of Health, Education and Welfare.

SELECTED REFERENCES

Board of Governors of the Federal Reserve System. *Flow of Funds Accounts, Financial Assets and Liabilities*, various issues.

Credit Union National Association Annual Report 1995, Madison, Wis.

Dublin, Jack and Selma M. Dublin. *Credit Unions in a Changing World: The Tanzania–Kenya Experience*, Wayne State University Press, Detroit, 1983.

Flannery, Mark J. *An Economic Evaluation of Credit Unions in the United States*, Federal Reserve Bank of Boston, 1974.

Friars, Eileen M. And Robert N. Gogel, eds. *The Financial Services Handbook; Executive Insights and Solutions*, John Wiley and Sons, New York, 1987.

Havrilesky, Thomas and Robert Schweitzer, eds. *Contemporary Developments in Financial Institutions and Markets*, 2nd edn, Harlan Davidson, Arlington Heights, Ill., 1987.

Moody, J. Carroll and Gilbert C. Fite. *The Credit Union Movement, Origins and Development, 1850–1970*, University of Nebraska Press, Lincoln, 1971.

Pugh, Olin S. and F. Jerry Ingram. *Credit Unions: A Movement Becomes an Industry*, Reston Publishing Company, Reston, Va., 1984.

US Department of the Treasury. *Modernizing the Financial System; Recommendations for Safer, More Competitive Banks*, Washington, DC, 1991.

World Council of Credit Unions. *1995 Statistical Report*, Madison, Wis., 1996.

chapter 28

Investment Companies

○ CHAPTER OVERVIEW

This chapter:
- Compares and contrasts different forms of investment companies.
- Describes investment company organizational structure.
- Outlines regulatory issues.
- Examines investment company asset composition.

○ KEY TERMS

capital shares
closed-end fund
dual-purpose investment company
growth funds
income funds
income shares
investment adviser
investment company
investment company distributor

investment philosophy
money market mutual fund
mutual fund
net asset value
prospectus
real estate investment trust
sales charge
securities broker

○ CHAPTER OUTLINE

1   The Nature of Investment Companies
    1.1   Closed-end Funds
    1.2   Mutual Funds
    1.3   Money Market Mutual Funds
    1.4   Growth of Mutual Funds
2   Investment Company Organization
    2.1   Financial Management
    2.2   Investors

INTERNATIONAL COMPARISONS:
Germany
France
Japan
Luxembourg
Single European Market
United Kingdom

Introduction

Investment companies accept money (often small denominations) from individuals and others and invest these funds according to the company's investment philosophy. After management and other fees have been deducted, profits from investing are passed through to the company's shareholders. During the 1970s and early 1980s, market rates of return increased sharply. These returns were passed through to owners of investment company shares, primarily money market mutual fund shares. During the same period, commercial banks and thrift institutions, were unable to offer their small depositors the same market rates of return because of regulated deposit interest rate ceilings. Banks and thrifts suffered massive disintermediation. Assets of investment companies grew from $48 billion in 1969 to $4.6 trillion in 1998 – more than 95 times the 1969 level.

The Nature of Investment Companies

An *investment company* is an organization through which individual investors purchase ownership interest in a well diversified portfolio of securities. When an individual considers investing in the capital markets, there are several potential problems:

- The individual's knowledge of stocks and bonds may be limited.
- The amount of investable funds may be relatively small, enabling the investor to purchase relatively few issues.
- Each subsequent investment may require reevaluation of holdings to ensure an appropriate mix.

> **Investment company:**
>   A firm that is organized and operated for the exclusive purpose of purchasing the debt and/or equity of other business organizations, government securities, municipal securities, or some combination of these.

To a large extent, investment companies offer viable solutions to these problems. An investment company portfolio is managed by professional investment advisers, who decide which securities to hold and in what proportions. Of course, these decisions must be consistent with the company's stated *investment philosophy*.

> **Investment philosophy:**
> An investment company's approach to investing in terms of types of securities, risk tolerance, average maturity of the portfolio, and emphasis on current income (interest or dividend income) or capital gains yield (change in market value of the securities).

Investors need not be concerned with day-to-day operations. Also, minimum investments may be as low as $250; that is, large amounts of investable funds are not necessary.

1.1 Closed-end Funds

The shares of a *closed-end fund* are issued and exchanged much like the shares of other firms. That is, once issued, shares of a closed-end fund trade on secondary markets (where existing securities are exchanged among investors) at prices that are determined by factors of supply and demand.

> **Closed-end fund:**
> An investment company that issues a fixed number of ownership claims, or shares. After these shares have been sold initially, investors who wish to purchase shares must buy them from other investors who own them.

A few closed-end funds are *dual-purpose* companies in that one class of shares is entitled to all interest and dividend income of the portfolio and the other class of shares earns only capital gains. The former are *income shares* and the latter, *capital shares*.

> **Income shares:**
> Shares of a closed-end investment company that receive only the interest and dividend income from the fund's asset investments.

> **Capital shares:**
> Shares of a closed-end investment company that receive only the increase (or decrease) in market value of the fund's asset investments.

Income shares are comparable to preferred stock, with a minimum, cumulative dividend. Income shares are also entitled to any income that the portfolio earns (for example, premiums earned if the fund sells options on its securities). But income shares are callable after a number of years and, thus, have a limited life. The capital shares of dual-purpose funds benefit from the use of leverage (fixed-rate debt), because the amount paid to debt holders does not increase even if assets earn a higher rate. However, capital shareholders must rely on increases in the market value of the portfolio for return.

Managers of closed-end funds must make necessary adjustments within the essentially fixed portfolios to accommodate changing market conditions, required dividend payments, and other distributions to shareholders.

A *real estate investment trust (REIT)* is a special type of closed-end fund that invests in real estate loans or in physical real estate. Shareholders in REITs receive the income attributable to these investments – interest or rental income. These investment companies originated during the late 1960s and controlled $54 billion in financial assets by 1998.

1.2 Mutual Funds

An investment company that makes new shares available on a continuous basis *and redeems* (buys back) outstanding shares at any time is an *open-end* investment company or a *mutual fund*.

Mutual fund:
> An open-end investment company, that is, one which issues new shares whenever investors wish to buy them. Likewise, a mutual fund redeems shares whenever investors wish to sell them.

Because of this arrangement, the capital of a mutual fund is not fixed. Instead, total capital will increase if more new shares are purchased than redeemed. Conversely, total capital declines when shareholders surrender more shares than are newly issued within a given period of time.

Even though easy redemption provides liquidity to an investor, a mutual fund investment should not be viewed as a bank deposit. As is also true with closed-end funds, there is no *guarantee* that the principal investment in a mutual fund will not decrease or that current income (interest and/or dividends) will be earned at a specified level. (This statement excludes income shares of dual-purpose funds discussed in the previous section.)

Investment philosophy varies from one fund to another. However, there are certain broad categories into which most funds can be placed.

Growth funds concentrate on appreciation of the value of the fund's portfolio. At the other end of the spectrum, *income funds* emphasize security investments with high periodic interest and dividend payments. Even within these categories, the investment philosophy can differ.

Some growth funds may seek *maximum capital gains* with little or no current income. Others may target *long-term price appreciation* with a *secondary focus* on periodic payments. The greater the emphasis on capital gains, however, the more risky the fund's investments are likely to be.

Income funds may invest primarily in stocks *or* bonds. Corporate stocks with consistent records of high dividend payments are selected for *common stock income funds. Senior securities income funds* invest in corporate bonds and preferred stock. If the income fund is permitted to invest in *either* stock or bonds, it is a *flexible income fund*.

Balanced funds hold roughly equivalent proportions of stocks and bonds. The rationale for a balanced fund is that shareholders may realize gains during periods of both economic expansion (good for stocks) and contraction (good for bonds).

Specialized mutual funds may target a particular sector for investment. For example, some hold only public utility stocks, others, only high technology stocks. International funds often select only

Type	Objective(s)/composition	Number
Aggressive growth	Maximum capital gains	352
Balanced	1) Conserve initial principal	210
	2) Pay current income	
	3) Promote long-term growth of principal and income	
Corporate bond	High income from corporate bonds	98
Flexible portfolio	Respond to economic conditions with no restrictions on investment	94
GNMA (Ginnie Mae)	Mortgage-backed securities	88
Global bond	Debt securities worldwide	145
Global equity	Equity securities worldwide	167
Growth	Common stock of well-established firm's	699
Growth and income	Combining capital gains and current income	481
High-yield bond	At least two-thirds of portfolio in below-investment-grade corporate bonds	99
Income-bond	Obtain high income from a combination of corporate and government bonds	312
Income-equity	Obtain high income by investing in equities that provide a high dividend yield	112
Income-mixed	Obtain high income by investing in corporate bonds, government bonds, and high-dividend-equities	165
International	At least two-thirds of the portfolio must be invested in equities of companies outside the United States	367
Long-term municipal bond	Long-term bonds issued by states and other political subdivisions for public purposes (interest income exempt from federal income taxation)	306
Money market	Investments in short-term, stable, money market instruments	672
Precious metals/gold	At least two-thirds in securities associated with gold, silver, and other precious metals	33
Short-term municipal bond	Short-term municipal securities, also called tax exempt money market funds	158
State municipal bond (long-term)	Same as long-term municipal bond except that securities are issued by one state only	704
State municipal bond (short-term)	Same as short-term municipal bond except that securities are issued by one state only	167
US government income	Combination of US Treasury and government agency securities	332
		5,761

◆ **Exhibit 28.1:**   Types and number of mutual funds, 1995

◆ *Source*:   Investment Company Institute, *Mutual Fund Factbook 1996*, Washington DC, 1997.

the highest quality stocks and bonds in the countries covered. Several specialized funds hold only US government securities or tax-exempt bonds.

Exhibit 28.1 contains 21 classifications of mutual funds and the number of each in 1995.

From management's perspective, a mutual fund portfolio is a more fluid pool of funds than a closed-end investment company. The size of a mutual fund is determined by shareholder purchases and redemptions. Management must invest large cash inflows as quickly as possible in a way that is consistent with the fund's investment philosophy. At the same time, the fund must always be liquid enough to meet unanticipated redemption requests.

1.3 MONEY MARKET MUTUAL FUNDS

Money market mutual funds are a subset of the broader category of open-end investment companies or mutual funds. Several factors distinguish money market funds from other mutual funds:

- Average maturity of the asset portfolio.
- Lower risk of the asset portfolio.
- The relative importance of denomination intermediation in the growth of money market funds.
- The rate of growth of money market mutual funds.

> **Money market mutual fund:**
> An open-end investment company whose assets consist primarily of Treasury bills, negotiable certificates of deposit, Eurodollar deposits, commercial paper, and banker's acceptances.

The average *maturity* of the investment portfolio is short. Money market fund assets are invested in short-term, highly liquid securities.

Because these funds invest only in short-term, high-quality instruments, risk to shareholders is considerably lower as compared to common stock and long-term bond funds. This second distinguishing characteristic, *lower risk*, makes money market mutual funds a close substitute for bank deposits. While they are not federally insured, typical fund investments have historically low default rates.

Of course, individuals can invest directly in Treasury bills and other short-term instruments. However, the minimum denomination for a Treasury bill investment is $10,000 and that of a negotiable certificate of deposit $100,000. Thus, *denomination intermediation* provided by money market funds is a particularly valuable attribute. (See chapter 1 for a discussion of intermediation functions.)

Money market fund balances can usually be withdrawn via check. Minimum check amounts are often $500 to discourage using the account as a transactions account. Nevertheless, the combination of convenient use, relatively safe fund investments, and high-yield when compared to bank deposits led to the fourth distinguishing characteristic. The money market fund industry has experienced phenomenal *growth* in recent years.

In fact, there was no money market mutual fund industry before the 1970s. Even in 1974, only $2.4 billion in assets were held in these investment companies. High and volatile market rates of interest during the late 1970s and early 1980s, together with low, regulated bank deposit interest rates, created enormous demand for small denomination, higher yielding investments. Before the 1980 Depository Institutions Deregulation and Monetary Control Act, small depositors could earn only 5 percent on savings, with *no interest* payable on demand deposits. As noted above, a minimum of $100,000 was necessary in order to earn higher rates available on jumbo CDs.

At the same time, money market rates averaged 16 percent in 1981. Not surprisingly, investors poured billions of dollars into money market mutual funds. By 1982, industry assets totaled more than $200 billion. Legalization of the bank money market deposit account (with interest rates tied to money market rates) in 1982 attracted many investors back to commercial banks and money market fund balances dropped below $200 billion. However, this was only a temporary setback. By 1998, total assets in money market mutual funds amounted to more than $1.2 trillion.

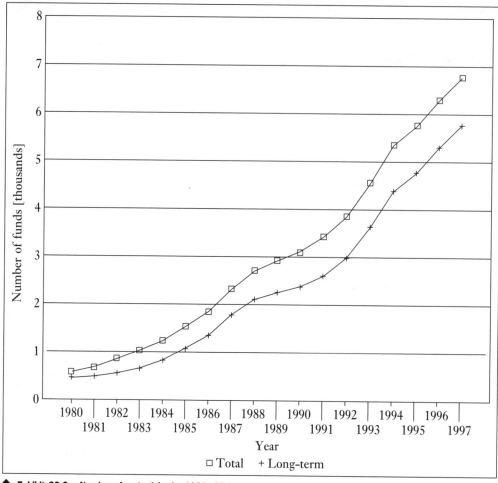

◆ **Exhibit 28.2: Number of mutual funds, 1980–97**

◆ *Notes*:   Total   Money market funds, short-term municipal bond funds, and stock, bond, and
                                    income funds
                  Long-term   Stock, bond, and income funds

◆ *Source*:   Author's graphic based on data from: Investment Company Institute, *Mutual Fund
                  Factbook 1998.*

1.4 CROWTH OF MUTUAL FUNDS

While the commercial bank, thrift, and credit union industries are consolidating in terms of the number of institutions, the number of mutual funds grew substantially during the 1980s and 1990s. Exhibit 28.2 shows that the total number of funds grew from 564 in 1980 to 6,778 by 1997. The majority of these are long-term funds, that is, stock, bond, and income funds and they increased from 458 to 5,765 over the period shown in Exhibit 28.2. Short-term funds include regular money market funds and tax-exempt money market funds (short-term municipal bond). The number of short-term funds grew as rapidly, from 106 (564 − 458) in 1980 to 1,013 (6,778 − 5,765) in 1997.

No other financial institution has experienced these rates of growth. This trend reflects:

- More reliance on nonbank financial institutions by the investing public.
- Increased sophistication of investors in terms of their knowledge of and appreciation for alternatives to commercial bank services.

As investors continue to become more involved in financial planning, they will continue to search for the combination of product and service that best suits their individual needs. As the mutual fund industry continues to develop varied financial alternatives, it becomes even more attractive. Furthermore, as retirement savings continue to be invested in mutual funds, the industry will enjoy a steady flow of contributions.

② Investment Company Organization

Every investment company has an *investment adviser*. *Securities brokers* execute purchases and sales as directed by the investment adviser. *Investment company distributors* sell new shares to the public, in the case of open-end companies. *Shareholders* invest in the stock of the investment company.

2.1 FINANCIAL MANAGEMENT

Investment advisers may be individuals, partnerships, or corporations. An investment company is typically owned by a large number of shareholders with relatively little ownership control. The *adviser*, on the other hand, is likely to be a more closely held organization with significant ownership control. In addition, it is not uncommon for an adviser to provide physical facilities, clerical support, and bookkeeping service to its client investment company. Investment advisers are professional money managers.

> **Investment adviser:**
> The party which makes asset investment decisions for an investment company. These decisions must conform with the company's stated investment philosophy.

> **Securities broker (investment company):**
> The party that executes the securities trades (purchases and sales) that have been initiated by the investment adviser.

Often, the *broker* selected to execute investment portfolio transactions is affiliated with the adviser. A bank or trust company is usually selected as custodian for portfolio securities.

Distribution of new shares may be the responsibility of a separate organization or may be accomplished by the investment company itself. In general, larger investment companies employ

	1964	1969	1974	1979	1984	1989	1994	1998
Mutual fund financial liabilities (shares in $billion)	$29.1	$47.6	$35.2	$51.8	$136.7	$486.3	$1,477.3	$3,456.0
Investors:								
Households	97.6%	95.8%	90.6%	86.3%	86.1%	86.7%	85.4%	78.1%
Nonfinancial corporations	1.0	1.5	2.3	2.1	5.3	3.7	2.1	2.7
Life insurance companies	0.4	1.2	1.7	1.8	2.2	2.9	0.5	1.9
Commercial banks	–	–	–	–	–	–	0.1	0.2
State and local government	–	–	–	–	–	–	–	1.3
Credit unions	–	–	–	–	–	–	–	0.1
Private pension plans	1.0	1.5	5.4	9.8	6.4	6.7	11.9	15.7
	100.0%	100.0%	100.0%	100.0%	100.0%	100.0%	100.0%	100.0%

◆ **Exhibit 28.3: Investors in US mutual funds, 1964–98 (percentages)[1]**

◆ *Note:* 1 Excludes money market mutual funds

◆ *Source:* Board of Governors of the Federal Reserve System, *Flow of Funds Accounts, Financial Assets and Liabilities*, various issues.

their own sales force for new share distribution. Such a sales force is a *captive* or *dedicated* sales force. Alternatively, the investment may employ *no distributor* and advertise directly to the public through direct mail or other means. Most often, however, shares are distributed through *securities brokers* and *dealers* as are other securities. Distribution is a critical function since the sale of new shares is the primary source of asset growth for an open-end company.

> **Investment company distributor:**
> The party that markets the shares of an investment company to the public.

2.2 INVESTORS

Initially, individuals owned virtually all mutual fund shares. As can be seen in Exhibits 28.3 and 28.4, individuals still account for the vast majority of mutual fund holdings. Nevertheless, nonfinancial corporations, life insurance companies, banks, state and local government, credit unions, and private pension plans held over 21 percent of nonmoney-market mutual fund shares in 1998, or $757 billion. In addition, firms held money market mutual fund investments amounting to 36.3 percent of 1998 industry shares, or $419 billion.

	1974	1979	1984	1989	1994	1998
Money market fund financial liabilities (shares in $billion)	$2.4	$45.2	$233.6	$363.8	$602.9	$1,153.7
Investors:						
Households	100.0%	88.5%	86.6%	89.5%	63.4%	63.7%
Funding corporations	–	–	–	–	19.5	15.9
Nonfinancial business	–	6.6	6.9	5.9	9.3	10.1
Life insurance companies	–	2.2	3.0	2.1	2.6	5.8
Private pension funds	–	2.7	3.5	2.5	5.2	4.5
	100.0%	100.0%	100.0%	100.0%	100.0%	100.0%

◆ **Exhibit 28.4:** Investors in US money market mutual funds, 1974–98 (percentages)[1]

◆ *Note*:   1   Prior to the 1970s, money market mutual funds did not exist

◆ *Source*:   Board of Governors of the Federal Reserve System, *Flow of Funds Accounts, Financial Assets and Liabilities*, various issues..

③ **Share Pricing**

3.1 OPEN-END FUNDS

3.1.1 NET ASSET VALUE

In an open-end investment company, the price of a share is dictated by the value of the investment portfolio. The *net asset value per share* is the basis for pricing.

> **Net asset value per share (NAV):**
> Market value of investment company assets less liabilities (net assets) divided by the number of shares outstanding.

Since asset market values change daily, so does the NAV. An investor who purchases (or redeems) shares pays (or receives) the NAV next computed after his order is received. Price determination occurs at least once a day – at the time that the New York Stock Exchange closes.

Price quotations are the *bid* and *asked* prices. The bid is the price at which shares may be redeemed and is usually the NAV. In some cases, a fund may charge a small redemption fee, which is reflected in the bid price. The asked, or purchase, price is the maximum amount that an investor would be required to pay for a mutual fund share.

3.1.2 SALES CHARGES

The asked price includes a *sales charge* or *load*. The load compensates the national distributor, the local firm, and the salesperson who executes the investor's order. Generally, this sales charge, or front-end load, ranges from 3 to 8.5 percent.

> **Sales charge (load):**
> A sales commission that is paid by purchasers of mutual fund shares.

Also, some funds assess on *annual distribution fee*. This is called a 12b-1 fee, named for the Securities and Exchange Commission (SEC) rule that permits it. The 12b-1 fee is 1.25 percent or less of the assets under management, spread proportionately among shareholders. This fee is used to pay for advertising or may substitute for the front-end load.

In addition, a *contingent deferred sales charge* may apply. Assessment of this sales charge occurs only if the investor redeems shares before a specified period elapses. Often, the contingent sales charge gradually declines after the specified period so that no fee is assessed for redemptions after a substantially longer period of time.

There are exceptions to these general rules. One exception is the group of investment companies that do not maintain a sales force and, therefore, assess little or no sales charge. Another exception is the practice of providing a quantity discount to investors for large purchases.

3.1.3 MANAGEMENT FEES

In addition to sales charges when shares are purchased initially or redeemed, pricing is affected by *management fees*. A management fee compensates the funds' adviser for making appropriate investment decisions, providing clerical and administrative support, and, generally, operating the company. The basis of the management fee is total net asset value. The typical fee is 1 percent or less of average net asset value per year. Management fees and other expenses are deducted from investment portfolio income before distributions are made to shareholder accounts.

> **Management fee:**
> A annual fee charged to an investment company buy its investment adviser for services rendered.

3.2 Closed-end Funds

Prices of closed-end investment companies can trade above or below net asset value, since market forces of supply and demand determine price movement. However, more often than not, closed-end shares sell below NAV, that is, at a discount.

$$D = \frac{(NAV - MV)}{NAV} \qquad (28.1)$$

where D = discount from NAV
NAV = net asset value per share
MV = market value per share

Several possible reasons why closed-end investment company shares frequently sell at a discount have been proposed. They include:

- If the company were liquidated, substantial costs would be incurred, including severance packages for officers and market value dilution in the event of large asset sales.
- Management fees and expenses must be satisfied before investment income can be distributed to shareholders.
- The market for closed-end company shares may not be as large as the market for shares of the underlying companies.

While closed-end investment company shares *may* sell at a premium, *discounts* of 5 to 20 percent are not uncommon.

4 Investment Company Regulation

Investment companies are regulated at both state and federal levels. An investment company is incorporated at the state level. While a few companies are business trusts, most are corporations. However, as long as an investment company distributes at least 90 percent of its income during the year to shareholders, it is not subject to corporate income tax.

"Blue sky" state laws often require that the securities of investment companies be registered with the state. Also, state laws protect investors who believe that they have received insufficient or inaccurate information with regard to a specific company. In some states, laws and regulations govern share pricing and commissions. These laws pertain to investment companies that operate within state borders.

The federal *Securities Act of 1933* governs the initial sales of securities to the public, including investment company shares. This law was enacted because of industry abuses during the 1920s that contributed to the stock market crash of 1929, which was then followed by the Great

Depression. The Securities and Exchange Commission (SEC) reviews the *registration statement* for accuracy and completeness. The registration statement details all pertinent management and financial data with respect to the securities offering. The SEC does not rule on the desirability of the new securities, but determines the adequacy of disclosure. The *prospectus* is a shorter version of the registration statement and must be made available to every prospective purchaser. If it is later found that any material information was omitted or misrepresented, injured parties may pursue legal means to recover financial damages.

The *Investment Company Act of 1940* was enacted to further protect investors. The specific provisions cover the following aspects of investment company operation:

- Persons not affiliated with the company adviser must be included on the board of directors.
- Financial transactions between the investment company and advisers/managers (as principals) must be approved by the SEC.
- Shareholders must approve any change in the company's basic investment philosophy.
- Management contracts (for investment adviser, securities broker, and distributor) must be approved by a majority of shareholders and the initial term of such contract may not exceed two years. Thereafter, the board of directors or a majority of shareholders must approve annual contract renewals.
- Redeemable shares must be sold at the price indicated in the prospectus.

The *1970 amendment to the Investment Company Act* addressed the fairness of management fees and sales charges. Prior to 1970, a shareholder claim of excessive fees could not be upheld unless the amount was so large that it amounted to *corporate waste*. The 1970 amendment relaxed this criterion to *breach of fiduciary duty*. This change was motivated by a belief on the part of lawmakers that the normal one-half of 1 percent of net assets constituted excessive compensation, particularly in light of the rapid growth of the industry and the average size of the funds themselves.

Mutual Fund Assets

Exhibits 28.5 and 28.6 show the mix of mutual fund assets over the period from 1964 through 1998. Nonmoney-market mutual funds (Exhibit 28.5) held primarily corporate equities in 1964, with the percentage of total financial assets so invested approaching 90 percent. Treasury and corporate bonds made up another 10 percent. Over time, the equities share declined to 40 percent in 1989. Strong performance in US stock markets increased the relative value of equities in mutual fund portfolios as well as encouraging more investor interest in stock funds. By 1998, corporate equities were 70 percent of financial assets.

Exhibit 28.6 contains similar information for money market funds, beginning in 1974. (Before the mid-1970s, there were no such funds.) The early money market funds relied heavily on bank time deposits. Even before small deposit interest rate deregulation of the 1980s, the rate ceiling on large time deposit (CDs over $100,000) had been removed (since 1970). It was through these CDs (67 percent of the industry's assets in 1974) and through commercial paper and banker's acceptances (25 percent) that money market rates were first passed through to fund shareholders in 1974. As reflected in the 1998 balance sheet, the industry asset mix is a well diversified blend of short-term, liquid assets.

The US mutual fund market is the largest in the world. Other large mutual fund markets include France, Luxembourg, and Germany. (See also Exhibit 28.7.)

	1964	1969	1974	1979	1984	1989	1994	1998
Financial assets ($billion)	$29.1	$47.6	$35.2	$51.8	$136.7	$486.3	$1,477.3	$3,456.0
Demand deposits and currency	1.4%	1.5%	1.4%	1.4%	1.5%	1.5%	–	–
Security repos	–	–	–	–	–	–	2.9%	1.6%
Corporate equities	88.3	85.9	74.9	68.5	59.0	40.0	48.0	70.2
Debt instruments:								
US Govt securities:								
Treasury issues	2.8	1.5	3.1	2.9	8.4	16.7	13.1	6.9
Agency issues	–	–	–	–	0.3	6.7	6.9	3.9
Total US Govt securities	2.8	1.5	3.1	2.9	8.7	23.4	20.0	10.8
Tax-exempt	–	–	–	7.7	14.0	16.9	14.0	6.6
Corporate and foreign bonds	7.2	6.1	14.0	13.9	12.1	13.9	11.7	9.1
Commercial paper and bankers' acceptances	0.3	5.0	6.6	5.6	4.7	4.3	2.9	1.5
Total debt instruments	10.3	12.6	23.7	30.1	39.5	58.5	48.6	28.0
Miscellaneous	–	–	–	–	–	–	0.5	0.2
	100.0%	100.0%	100.0%	100.0%	100.0%	100.0%	100.0%	100.0%

◆ **Exhibit 28.5: Financial assets of US mutual funds, 1964–98 (percentages)[1]**

◆ *Note:*   1   Excludes money market mutual funds

◆ *Source:*   Board of Governors of the Federal Reserve System, *Flow of Funds Accounts, Financial Assets and Liabilities*, various issues.

	1974	1979	1984	1989	1994	1998
Financial assets ($billion)	$2.4	$45.2	$233.6	$363.8	$602.9	$1,153.7
Demand deposits and currency	–	0.2%	<0.5>%[2]	<0.5>%[2]	<0.4>%[2]	–[3]
Time deposits (domestic)	66.6%	26.5	10.1	9.7	5.2	9.3
Foreign deposits	–	1.3	9.1	8.0	2.6	1.9
Total currency and deposits	66.6	38.0	18.7	17.2	7.4	11.2
Security repos	4.2	5.3	9.8	13.1	11.4	12.4
Investment securities:						
US Govt securities:						
Treasury issues	4.2	3.5	10.8	3.5	11.0	7.0
Agency issues	–	8.9	7.3	3.8	12.8	8.1
Total US Govt	4.2	12.4	18.1	7.3	23.8	15.1
Tax-exempt	–	–	10.2	18.6	18.8	15.4
Corporate and foreign bonds	–	–	–	–	2.5	5.9
Commercial paper and banker's acceptances	25.0	42.7	41.9	41.1	31.0	34.3
Total investment securities	29.2	55.1	70.2	67.0	76.1	70.7
Miscellaneous	–	1.6	1.3	2.7	5.1	5.7
	100.0%	100.0%	100.0%	100.0%	100.0%	100.0%

◆ Exhibit 28.6: Financial assets of US money market mutual funds, 1974–98 (percentages)[1]

◆ *Notes:* 1 Prior to the 1970s, money market mutual funds did not exist
2 Aggressive cash management may involve considerable payor float, i.e., outstanding check disbursements that exceed actual bank balances. See also chapter 23 for a description of payor float
3 Less than 0.1%

◆ *Source:* Board of Governors of the Federal Reserve System, *Flow of Funds Accounts, Financial Assets and Liabilities*, various issues.

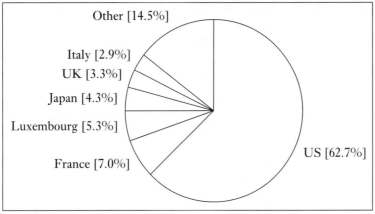

◆ **Exhibit 28.7:** International comparison of mutual fund assets, 1997

◆ *Other*:   Canada (2.8%), Spain (2.5%), Brazil (1.5%), Netherlands (0.9%), Hong Kong (0.8%), Australia (0.7%), Switzerland (0.7%), Austria (0.6%), Sweden (0.6%), all others (3.4%).

◆ *Source*:   Author's graphic based on data from: Investment Company Institute, *Mutual Fund Factbook 1998*.

 International Operations

Unlike commercial bank branches, investment companies have not spread across national boundaries to a great extent. The primary impediment has been securities laws that differ from one country to another. In the United States, a foreign company must obtain an "order" from the SEC permitting sale of the shares. However, before an order can be issued, the SEC must satisfy itself that it can enforce regulations with respect to the foreign company. Since US laws usually require more disclosure and investor protections, the laws of the two countries are often incompatible. The advice of the SEC is frequently for the foreign entity to establish a "mirror fund", that is, an identical US company.

The Single European Market enables US investment companies to more easily market their products abroad. The EC directive, Undertakings for Collective Investment in Transferable Securities, requires that registration in one EC country be recognized in the other EC countries. This eliminates the need for duplicate registrations.

From the perspective of the US investor, buying shares of an investment company with international investments is becoming easier. In 1983, only 21 US mutual funds held foreign securities. By 1995, 679 mutual funds were specifically designated as global or international funds (see Exhibit 28.1).

Summary

Investment companies have enjoyed the most rapid growth among US financial institutions during the last decade. This is particularly true of money market mutual funds. High and volatile interest rates of the 1970s and 1980s pushed up the yield on Treasury securities (minimum denomination of $10,000) and on large bank deposits (minimum $100,000) to over 13 percent. Small investors could do no better than 5 percent at commercial banks. When money market mutual funds offered market rates of interest to these small investors, the industry experienced explosive growth.

Now a wide variety of funds is available to investors. Some emphasize capital gains (increase in the market value of the fund's assets). Others concentrate more on current income (interest and dividend income). Still others combine the two objectives. Others specialize in tax-exempt securities or international investments.

Generally, these companies are not heavily regulated. Federal and state laws protect investors by requiring adequate disclosure of the funds' asset portfolio, management team, and operating expenses. Shares in these companies are attractive investments because of their variety, convenience, and competitive rates of return.

End-of-chapter Questions

1. How does an investment company differ from an industrial firm? From a depository institution?
2. What comparative disadvantages of a small investor are at least partially offset through mutual fund investment?
3. What is the difference between a closed-end fund and an open-end (mutual) fund?
4. Name the investment objectives that an investment company may adopt.
5. Describe a money market mutual fund.
6. What are the normal responsibilities of an investment company adviser/manager and how is he compensated?
7. What is net asset value? Of what relevance is net asset value to an open-end company? A closed-end company?
8. What shareholder protections are incorporated into the Investment Company Act of 1940?
9. Obtain a recent edition of the *Wall Street Journal*. Compare the 12-month rate of return on the S&P500 to that of mutual funds also contained in that issue. Summarize your observations as to type of fund and rate of return variability among the funds.
10. Obtain the prospectus for a mutual fund. Pinpoint the sections of the prospectus that specify:
    a. The fund management/investment adviser
    b. The securities broker
    c. The distributor
    d. The fee arrangements
    e. The investment philosophy

f. Total fund assets

g. Fund performance over the last five years.

11. Suppose that you were contemplating the purchase of mutual fund shares. What characteristics would you look for if you were:

a. Twenty-five years from retirement?

b. Five years from retirement?

12. Refer to a recent edition of the *Wall Street Journal* (*WSJ*).

a. Identify closed-end funds in the *WSJ* price quotations?

b. On what exchanges are they listed?

SELECTED REFERENCES

Board of Governors of the Federal Reserve System. *Flow of Funds Accounts; Financial Assets and Liabilities*, Washington, DC, various issues.

Friars, Eileen M. and Robert N. Gogel. *The Financial Services Handbook: Executive Insights and Solutions*, John Wiley and Sons, New York, 1987.

Investment Company Institute. *Mutual Fund Factbook 1996*, Washington, DC, 1997.

Investment Company Institute. *Reading the Mutual Fund Prospectus*, Washington, DC, 1990.

Matatko, John and David Stafford. *Key Developments in Personal Finance*, Blackwell, Oxford, UK, 1985.

Pension Funds

Introduction

During their working years, pension fund participants accumulate savings through employer and employee contributions. These savings then sustain participants during retirement. Today, pension funds control a large share of individual savings. In the process, pension funds have also become major investors in financial markets.

As the pension fund industry grows in terms of assets under management, it is also changing in form and character. The employer-managed pension fund with relatively little set aside to meet future obligations (partially funded defined benefit pension plan) is decreasing in importance. The employee-managed pension fund with current contributions (fully funded defined contribution pension plan) is now becoming the industry standard. In the second type of pension plan, employees accept more risk in terms of future benefit payments because retirement income depends on the investment performance of the fund during the pre-retirement saving years. At the same time, the second type of plan often provides more control and greater freedom of choice.

 Types of Pension Plans

Pension funds are asset pools that are accumulated over the working life of a participant for distribution at the time of or during retirement. A *pension plan* governs the operation of each pension fund. Pension plans may be classified by sponsor or by defined attribute.

> **Pension fund:**
> A separate entity to which periodic (or, in some cases, lump-sum) contributions are made by or on behalf of covered participants. At the time of retirement, each participant receives a distribution from the fund in the form of an annuity or lump-sum payment.

1.1 CLASSIFICATION BY SPONSOR

Governments sponsor *public* pension plans. Individual corporations oversee *private* pension plans, while life insurance companies offer *insured* plans.

Public pension plan:
> Pension plan sponsored by the federal government and by state and local governments.

At the federal level, the social security system covers virtually all nonfederal government employees. Other federal plans provide retirement benefits for federal civil and military personnel and for railroad employees. State and local governments sponsor similar pension plans for their employees. In 1998, the reserves (amounts set aside for pensions) held by (1) federal and (2) state and local government pension funds were $2.8 trillion. (See Exhibit 29.1.)

	Total amount ($billions)	% of total
Private reserves:		
Private pension funds	$4,006.4*	49.5%
Life insurance companies	1,324.1	16.4
Total private reserves	5,330.5	65.9
Public reserves:		
US government	453.9	5.6
State and Local government	2,309.4	28.5
Total public reserves	2,763.3	34.1
Total pension reserves	$8,093.8	100.0%

◆ **Exhibit 29.1: US pension fund reserves, 1998**

◆ *Note*:   *Includes Federal Employees Retirement System Shrift Savings Plan.

◆ *Source*:   Fred Herrera of H. J. Johnson & Associates, using data from: Board of Governors of the Federal Reserve System. *Flow of Funds Accounts, Financial Assets and Liabilities.*

Private corporations may either administer their retirement programs or have a life insurance company perform this function.

Private pension plan:
> Pension plan sponsored and administered by a private corporation.

> **Insured pension plan:**
> Pension plan sponsored by a private corporation but administered by an insurance company.

An *insured* pension plan has no separate pool of assets. Instead, plan assets are held in the *general accounts* of a life insurance company. The portion of the life insurance company's assets that is devoted to pension plans appears as *pension fund reserves* in the liability section of the balance sheet. In 1998, these reserves totaled $1.3 trillion.

> **General accounts:**
> The investment (asset) accounts of a life insurance company that appear in the firm's balance sheet.

Private pension plans have separate legal entities, *private pension funds*, associated with them. An insurance company may manage the private pension fund as a *separate account*.

> **Separate account:**
> Assets managed by an insurance company that do not appear on the insurance company balance sheet.

Alternatively, a bank trust department or an investment firm may manage and administer the fund. In other cases, large corporations maintain internal departments to oversee fund investments, participant accounting, and distributions. In 1998, the financial assets of all private pension funds amounted to $4.0 trillion.

1.2 CLASSIFICATION BY DEFINED ATTRIBUTE

1.2.1 DEFINED BENEFIT PLAN

A pension plan is either a *defined benefit plan* or *defined contribution plan*. A *defined benefit pension plan* fixes the level of retirement cash flow. It is a contract to provide future benefits. Since retirement benefits are based on factors such as salary and years of service, plan sponsors must manage the uncertainty of pension fund asset returns. Whether investment returns are strong or weak does not alter the level of retirement cash flows that are promised.

> **Defined benefit plan:**
> A pension plan that entitles its participants, upon retirement, to specified cash *distributions*, based upon a formula that considers a number of variables, including years of service and salary during employment.

The method of providing these future payments varies.

> **Pension plan funding:**
> The extent to which assets are set aside currently to meet future pension plan obligations.

- If assets are currently set aside in amounts equal to the *present value* of estimated retirement benefits, the plan is *fully funded*.
- If *no* assets are set aside currently, the plan is *unfunded*.
- If only some portion of the present value of future retirement benefits is funded, the plan is *partially funded*.

In addition to the formula for benefit determination, the present value of future benefits will also depend upon the plan's *vesting* provisions. For example, if the pension plan provides for 10-year vesting, the plan sponsor is not obligated to provide retirement income to those participants who have less than 10 years of service. Any participant who leaves the plan (perhaps changes place of employment) before accumulating 10 years of service is not vested.

> **Vesting:**
> The process through which the right to receive cash distributions during retirement becomes a nonforfeitable right.

To the extent that participants *are* vested, the present value of their estimated future benefits is a *pension liability* for the plan sponsor. It is this vested pension liability that is either fully funded, partially funded, or unfunded, as discussed above. Unfunded pension liabilities of corporate plan sponsors can be substantial and the amounts are disclosed in corporate financial statements.

> **Pension liability:**
> The amount of vested (nonforfeitable) pension benefits that a corporation or government organization is obligated to pay its current and retired employees.

1.2.2 DEFINED CONTRIBUTION PLAN

In the case of *defined contribution pension plans*, the plan sponsor does *not* commit to provide participants a specified *retirement income*. Instead, the sponsor pays a specified *current amount* into a pension fund. The eventual retirement income of participants depends on the nature of the pension fund. If it is a *fixed income* fund, a minimum rate of return is guaranteed with the possibility of higher returns if fund assets earn a return above the guaranteed minimum. A *variable income* fund passes along to participants all investment income (or loss) in proportion to their holdings in the fund. (In principal, a variable income pension fund operates like an investment company: see chapter 28.) Often, participants have the option of choosing some combination of fixed and variable accounts. Because employers make the contributions to these plans currently, defined contribution plans are most often fully funded.

Defined contribution plan:
A pension plan that entitles its participants, during employment, to specified cash *contributions* to a pension fund.

Upon retirement, a participant in a defined contribution plan receives benefits equal to the accumulated value in the account. The uncertainty of pension fund asset performance during the saving years is not managed by the fund sponsor, but is assumed by the plan participant. The actual distribution may take the form of an annuity, as in a defined benefit plan. Alternatively, the participant may elect a lump-sum payment, an option almost universally available in defined contribution plans.

② Government Pensions

2.1 SOCIAL SECURITY

2.1.1 COVERAGE AND CONTRIBUTIONS

In the United States, almost everyone is insured by the federal social security system, the Old Age, Survivors, Disability, and Hospital Insurance program (OASDHI). Exceptions are federal civilian employees and some employees of (1) state and local governments and (2) nonprofit organizations. After working and paying social security contributions for 40 quarters (three-month periods), an individual is insured for life. Contributions are a specified percentage of gross employee income, with matching employer contributions. In 1998, the percentage was 7.65 percent – 6.20 percent of earnings up to $68,400 for social security and 1.45 percent of all earnings for Medicare. Retirement benefits provide a "floor" for retirement income to assure recipients of at least a subsistence standard of living.

Employees contribute through payroll deduction. Self-employed individuals make quarterly payments, with an annual accounting in the federal income tax return.

In fact, the contributions themselves are commonly referred as social security "tax" payments. Both the contribution percentages and the assessable income have increased over time in order to finance benefit payments to those already retired. Essentially, the social security pension system operates on a pay-as-you-go basis. This means that contributions collected from today's working population are the source of benefits for workers that have retired.

2.1.2 TRUST FUND ASSETS AND PAYMENTS

Referring to Exhibit 29.2, note that the trust funds for the Old Age, Survivors, and Disability Insurance (OASDI) programs exceeded the $31.9 billion in disbursements (benefit payments) by only $6.2 billion in 1970. Without current contributions ($34.7 billion in 1970), the trust funds would soon be depleted. Thus, both the contribution rate (tax rate) and the amount of assessable income has increased over time in order to offset higher benefit payments.

Year	Trust fund assets[a]	OASDI[b]	Rate HI[c]	Total	Max. tax. earnings[d]	Total[e]	Disbursements[f]
1970	$38.1	4.20%	0.60%	4.80%	$7,800	$34.7	$31.9
1975	44.3	4.95	0.90	5.85	14,100	64.3	67.0
1980	26.5	5.08	1.05	6.13	25,900	116.7	120.6
1985	42.20	5.70	1.35	7.05	39,600	197.6	186.1
1990	225.20	6.20	1.45	7.65	51,300	301.7	247.8
1991	280.70	6.20	1.45	7.65	53,400	307.8	268.2
1992	331.50	6.20	1.45	7.65	55,500	317.2	286.0
1993	378.30	6.20	1.45	7.65	57,600	327.7	302.4
1994	436.40	6.20	1.45	7.65	60,600	350.1	316.8
1995	496.10	6.20	1.45	7.65	61,200	364.9	332.6
1996	n/a	6.20	1.45	7.65	62,700	422.0	356.1

◆ **Exhibit 29.2:** The US social security system: trust fund assets, contributions and disbursements, 1970–96

◆ *Notes*:
a) Represents the assets of two social security trust funds, i.e., Old Age and Survivors Insurance and Disability Insurance trust funds, in billions of dollars
b) Old Age, Survivors, and Disability Insurance
c) Hospital Insurance
d) Maximum taxable earnings per employee or self-employed person, per year
e) Represents contributions to the Old Age and Survivors Insurance and the Disability Insurance trust funds, in billions of dollars
f) Represents benefit payments under the Old Age, Survivors, and Disability Insurance programs, in billions of dollars

n/a   not available.

◆ *Sources*:   Fred Herrera of H. J. Johnson & Associates, using data from: *Historical Tables Fiscal Year 1996, Budget of the US Government and Actuarial Analysis*; US Department of Commerce Bureau of the Census, *Statistical Abstract of the United States 1996*, 116th edn, Washington, DC, 1996, p. 373; Social Security Administration, *Annual Statistical Supplement, 1996, to the Social Security Bulletin*, Washington, DC, p. 180.

Required contributions have become increasingly burdensome for the average contributor. Referring to Exhibit 29.3, note that disbursements increased at an average annual rate of 9.8 percent from 1970 through 1995 (($332,554 million/$31,884 million)$^{1/25}$ − 1 = 0.09833). Over the same period, the number of contributors only grew by 1.7 percent per year ((132.9 million/88.2 million)$^{1/25}$ − 1 = 0.01653). Income of contributors (not shown in Exhibit 29.3) increased faster than the number of contributors, but not as fast as social security disbursements. From 1970 to 1995, wages, salaries, other labor income, and self-employment income increased from $531.6 billion to $3,357.1 billion – an average annual growth rate of 7.7 percent (($3,357.1 billion/$531.6 billion)$^{1/25}$ − 1 = 0.07650). Thus, income grew at the rate of 7.7 percent while social security disbursements increased at the rate of 9.8 percent.

The result is that every contributor supports a higher average disbursement of OASDI benefits each year. As also shown in Exhibit 29.3, the average disbursement per contributor in 1970

Year	Disbursements[1]	Contributors[2]	Ratio[3]
1970	$31,884	88.2	$361.50
1975	67,020	94.9	706.22
1980	120,598	107.2	1,124.98
1985	186,075	113.1	1,645.23
1990	247,816	126.1	1,965.23
1991	268,162	125.2	2,141.87
1992	285,995	126.0	2,269.80
1993	302,368	128.2	2,358.56
1994	316,812	130.8	2,422.11
1995	332,554	132.9	2,502.29

◆ **Exhibit 29.3:**   **The US social security system: disbursements and contributors, 1970–95**

◆ *Notes*:   1   Represents benefit payments under the Old Age, Survivors, and Disability Insurance programs, in millions of dollars
2   Represents employed workers under the social security system, in millions of workers
3   Represents average benefit payments per employed worker

◆ *Source*:   Fred Herrera of H. J. Johnson & Associates, with data from: Social Security Administration, *Annual Statistical Supplement, 1996, to the Social Security Bulletin*, Washington, DC, pp. 180, 185.

was $361.50. By 1995, it had reached $2,502.29 – implying an 8.0 percent average annual increase in per capita disbursements over a period associated with 5.9 percent annual growth in per capita income.[1]

Furthermore, as the "baby boom" generation (those US citizens born during the years immediately following 1945, the end of the Second World War) continues to mature, the average age of the US population increases. As members of this generation retire, required contributions by those still in the work force will be even more burdensome. The added burden could be serious enough to threaten the continued existence of the social security system.

2.2 STATE AND LOCAL GOVERNMENT PENSIONS

State and local governments sponsor pension plans that cover over 12 million full-time employees and pay benefits to almost six million retirees. Because of their funding arrangements (largely pay-as-you-go), most federal government pension systems are defined benefit plans. Defined benefit plans also dominate in the state and local government category.

State and local governments have the option of not participating in the federal social security system. Furthermore, the government of any political subdivision that *has* elected to participate in the social security system may give written notice of intent to withdraw after participating in social security for five years. Actual withdrawal is possible two years after the written notice.

In 1998, state and local pension funds held financial assets of $2.3 trillion. Earnings on these investments constitute approximately 60 percent of annual fund receipts, with the remainder composed of government and employee contributions.

③ Private Pension Plans

3.1 DEFINED BENEFIT PLANS

As noted earlier, defined benefit plans promise a certain level of retirement income based upon the plan formula. The formula generally falls into one of two broad categories: *unit-benefit* or *flat-benefit* formulas.

3.1.1 UNIT-BENEFIT FORMULA

Unit-benefit formulas give beneficiaries a specified number of benefit units depending upon length of service with the plan sponsor. In those cases in which employees are paid on an hourly basis and there is little variation among wage rates, a set dollar amount of benefit often may be earned for each year of service. For example, an employee may earn $500 of annual retirement income for each year of service.

A more common unit-benefit formula is to award 1 percent to 2 percent of specified compensation for each year of service. For example, an employee who retires with 20 years of service may receive 40 percent of *specified compensation* as annual retirement income. The specified compensation may be average annual compensation over the participant's career or over the final years of the career. The final-average formula is, of course, the more generous of the two techniques because earnings are typically highest in the last years of a career.

3.1.2 FLAT-BENEFIT FORMULA

Flat-benefit formulas award a percentage of specified compensation that does not vary with length of service. The flat benefit usually ranges from 20 to 40 percent and specified compensation may be either a career average or a final average. Generally, a minimum of 15 years of service is required in order to qualify for full benefits. Participants with insufficient years of service may receive a reduced level of benefits.

3.2 DEFINED CONTRIBUTION PLANS

Defined contribution plans are essentially tax deferred savings plans and, thus, are much simpler to administer than defined benefit plans. The actual pension fund to which contributions are made may be (1) an investment company with the objective of long-term growth or (2) a family of funds with the option of transferring monies among them (see chapter 28).

Alternatively, the pension fund may be a guaranteed investment contract(s) with an insurance company. A conservative minimum rate of return is guaranteed by the insurance company. Contributions are placed either in the insurance company's general fund or in a separate account (separate legal entity). In turn, the insurance company invests in mortgages, private placements, or other long-term fixed-income securities. (See chapter 4 for a description of bonds and mortgages; and chapter 6 for private placements.)

From the participants' perspective, most defined contribution plans offer *portability*. When benefits are portable, they are not lost when the participant changes employment. Often, there is immediate vesting and the plan sponsor (employer) has little or no involvement after the contributions are made.

> **Portability:**
> The right of an employee to retain the vested benefits of a pension plan when changing place of employment. The employee either receives a lump-sum distribution or transfers the amount to another pension fund.[2]

3.3 OTHER PRIVATE PENSION PLANS

In addition to defined benefit and defined contribution plans, individuals may also participate in *401(k)* plans, *individual retirement accounts (IRAs)*, and *Keogh* accounts. The first is an employer sponsored plan, the second and third are not sponsored by employers.

3.3.1 401(K) PLANS

401(k) plans are employer-sponsored arrangements that:

- Are permitted by the Internal Revenue Service
- Allow deferral of income tax until retirement

> **401(k) plan:**
> A tax-deferred savings plan that sometimes supplements the basic retirement plan and allows both employer and employee contributions.

The most common 401(k) plans are profit-sharing or thrift-savings arrangements. (Profit-sharing plans involve contributions in cash based on sponsor profits.) In profit-sharing plans, employees may accept the profit-sharing distribution as taxable income in the current year or have it set aside in a 401(k) account. The Tax Reform Act of 1986 placed some limitations on the amounts that may be tax-deferred. However, the plan remains a popular vehicle for tax-deferred saving. (For employees of nonprofit organizations, a 403(b) offers similar features.)

3.3.2 INDIVIDUAL RETIREMENT ACCOUNTS (IRAs)

In 1981, individual retirement accounts (IRAs) were made available to all wage-earners in addition to employer-sponsored retirement plans. Each worker could contribute up to $2,000 to an IRA per year on a tax-deferred basis. The earnings on this account also accumulate tax-deferred.

> **Individual retirement account:**
> An individually funded, self-directed retirement account that may be established by employees that are also covered by employer-sponsored pension plans.

In 1986, tax-deferred contributions to IRAs were limited for higher income employees. Only employees (1) not covered by employer-sponsored pension plans (whose spouses are also not covered) or (2) earning adjusted gross income of $25,000 or less ($40,000 for married, filing joint tax returns) may contribute the full $2,000 on a tax-deferred basis. Above this income level for covered employees, the permissible amount is reduced and then completely eliminated for incomes in excess of $35,000 ($50,000 for married, filing joint). However, in all cases, the investment income on the account may accrue tax-deferred.

3.3.3 KEOGH ACCOUNTS

Keogh accounts are retirement accounts for the self-employed. Keogh plans are treated for tax purposes as corporate pension plans. Thus, the form of the plan may be either a regular pension or a profit-sharing plan. However, because tax laws discourage plans that favor high-income employees at the expense of lower-income employees, there are limitations on contributions. The maximum annual contribution to a Keogh account is $30,000 per year or 25 percent of self-employment income, whichever is less.

> **Keogh account:**
> A retirement account maintained by a self-employed individual. Contributions and investment income are tax-deferred until distributions are received by the individual after retirement.

 # **Regulation**

Even with the mandatory pensions of France and Switzerland, the US pension system is the most regulated pension system among industrialized countries. The Employee Retirement Security Act of 1974 (ERISA) is the major regulatory framework for private pension plans.

ERISA created the Pension Benefit Guaranty Corporation (PBGC). PBGC insures defined benefit pension plans. Premiums are based on the number of participants.

Within certain limits, pension payments are guaranteed to each participant. In the event of plan termination *and* inadequate pension assets to provide benefits, PBGC may assess the plan sponsor (employer) for the lesser of the deficiency or 30 percent of the sponsor's net worth.

In addition to the creation of PBGC, the overall objective of ERISA is to ensure that pension benefits will be paid as promised. The specific areas addressed to accomplish this goal are pension plan *funding*, *vesting* of benefits, and *fiduciary responsibility*.

4.1 FUNDING

Before 1974, there was no statutory requirement that sponsors of defined benefit pension plans adequately fund the plans. (A 1946 IRS ruling required plan sponsors to fund plans in such a way that unfunded pension liabilities did not increase over time. However, this ruling was a regulation, rather than a law.) ERISA mandated a *minimum funding* arrangement and established a *penalty* for funding *deficiencies*. The penalty is a 5 percent excise tax on accumulated funding deficiencies (or 100 percent if not corrected promptly).

Minimum funding requirements for a given year involve both *normal cost* and *past service liabilities*. Plan sponsors must fund 100 percent of normal cost each year. ERISA permitted amortization of past service cost, however. For plans in existence in 1974, past service cost attributable to years before 1974 was amortizable (could be written off) over 40 years. If plans were upgraded after 1974 and additional past service liabilities generated as a result of such liberalization, these were amortizable over 30 years. Should investment or mortality experience create unanticipated gains or losses, these differences were to be amortized over 15 years.

> **Normal cost:**
> The present value of vested pension benefits earned by participants during the current year.

> **Past service liabilities:**
> The present value of vested pension benefits earned by participants before (1) 1974 or (2) plan adoption, whichever is later.

In 1987, the US Congress updated ERISA funding requirements in order to prevent plan sponsors from inadequately funding their plans. *Minimum* funding for a given year became the sum of:

- normal cost
- investment and mortality experience gains and losses – amortized over five years
- liabilities attributable to changes in actuarial assumptions – amortized over 10 years
- required reduction of past funding deficits, as applicable

4.2 Vesting and Coverage

While pension benefits begin to accumulate (or accrue) as soon as an individual is eligible to participate, benefits might not be *vested* until some minimum period of time elapses. Whenever an *employee* contributes to the plan, associated pension benefits are immediately vested. Frequently, *employer* contributions to defined contribution plans are also immediately vested.

In 1974, ERISA provided a number of alternatives for employers in terms of vesting. The Tax Reform Act of 1986 reduced these alternatives to essentially two:

- 100 percent vesting after five years of service, with no vesting prior to five years service.
- Gradual vesting during a seven-year period:
  a. 20 percent after three years
  b. 20 percent per year for years 4 through 7

Multi-employer pension plans (such as the Teamsters Union) are also still permitted to use 100 percent vesting after 10 years.

Class-year pension plans in which each year's contribution vests separately are subject to a 100 percent vesting requirement after five years of service. Examples of these plans include defined contribution plans such as profit-sharing, stock bonus, and money purchase plans. (Profit-sharing plans involve contributions in cash based on sponsor profits. Stock bonus plans are similar except that contributions are in the form of the sponsor's (employer's) stock. Money purchase plans require cash contributions, usually a percentage of participant salary.) In addition to direct participant benefits, ERISA requires all pension plans to pay pension payments (survivor benefits) to surviving spouses when the participant dies.

Generally, all employees must be covered by a sponsor's primary pension plan. ERISA requires eligibility for any employee, age 25 or older, after one year of service. A year of service is twelve consecutive months involving not less than 1,000 hours of paid employment. New employees close to retirement age under the pension plan may be excluded. An employee who begins work within five years of retirement age need not be covered under a defined benefit plan. However, no such exclusion is possible under a defined contribution plan.

4.3 FIDUCIARY RESPONSIBILITY

Each pension plan must provide for one or more persons with the authority to control the operation of the plan. Either the plan sponsor, participants, or both, appoint these *fiduciaries*. The duties of a fiduciary may involve management of the plan or of pension fund assets. Accordingly, the designation applies to directors, officers, members of the investment committee, consultants, and advisers. In addition, any person that is designated by a fiduciary to fulfill some of the latter's responsibilities also becomes a fiduciary.

ERISA established an ethical standard for the conduct of a fiduciary. The "prudent man" rule, long used in the management of investment trusts, was applied. Under this standard, a fiduciary must act with the same diligence, skill, and prudence of a "prudent man" in like circumstances.

Subsequent rulings by the US Department of Labor have interpreted the prudent man rule in terms of total return. That is, every investment is not necessarily held to the prudent man standard. Rather, the entire portfolio is considered. Relevant factors are diversification, short-term liquidity needs, and income requirements in order to satisfy plan obligations.

There are certain activities that are strictly prohibited. A fiduciary may not:

- Manage the assets of the plan in order to benefit the fiduciary.
- Accept compensation from any party that is involved in transactions that also involve plan assets.
- Act on behalf of any party with interests that conflict with those of the plan or its participants.
- Invest in assets that are not under the jurisdiction of US district courts.

In general, a fiduciary is expected to fulfill responsibilities to the plan in a way that neither compromises the interests of participants nor serves to promote the personal interests of the fiduciary. Plan assets are to be managed with the sole objective of providing benefits for participants and their beneficiaries. Those who perform plan asset transactions must be bonded (insured) for 10 percent of the aggregate dollar amount involved, with the maximum bond being $500,000. Lastly, each fiduciary must operate in accordance with the documents governing the plan.

Pension Fund Assets

As indicated in Exhibits 29.4 and 29.5, financial assets of (1) private and (2) state and local pension funds grew by 13.1 percent and 13.5 percent per year respectively, from 1964 through 1998 (private plans: ($3,981.5 bil./$64.9 bil.)$^{1/34} - 1 = 0.1306$; state and local government: ($2,284.8 bil./$30.6 bil.)$^{1/34} - 1 = 0.1353$). This rapid pace of asset growth is responsible for the increased market share of pension funds noted in chapter 1 (see Exhibit 1.6). In 1964, pension funds represented 11 percent of the financial assets of all financial institutions (including banks, thrifts, investment companies, insurance companies and finance companies). By 1998, the share had increased to 26 percent.

Over time, the mix of pension fund assets has changed in some respects. Time deposits represented a substantial percentage of fund assets in 1989 – 8.1 percent in the case of private pension funds and 3.3 percent in the case of state and local government funds. These percentages had declined during the early 1990s, but pension funds were still large purchasers of these instruments. (It should be noted that these instruments were not available in high-yielding, negotiable form – negotiable CDs – until after 1960.)

Corporate stock (excluding mutual fund shares) constituted over 50 percent of private pension fund assets in 1964, but only 6.5 percent of state and local government funds. In 1998, the percentages were 53 percent and 66 percent, respectively. In the market for corporate equities (Exhibit 29.6), this translates into a significant presence. Pension funds held less than 6 percent of corporate stock in 1964. Their combined 25 percent share in 1998 made pension funds the largest institutional investor in the stock market. Over the same period, the percentage held by individuals declined from almost 85 percent to 44 percent. In a real sense, institutional investing on behalf of individuals now substitutes for previously direct stock market involvement. (Of course, the same can be said to a lesser extent about mutual funds.)

US Treasury and government agency securities hold prominent positions in pension fund portfolios. As Exhibits 29.7 and 29.8 show, the role of pension funds in the government securities market has *expanded* as a result. In 1998, these institutions held 15 percent and 9 percent of all US Treasury and government agency securities, respectively.

The net effect of these changes is that pension funds are major participants in today's money and capital markets. With the current growth in pension plans, particularly defined contribution plans, the role of pension funds in financial markets will not soon diminish.

 Summary

Pension plans grew in importance as personal income levels increased. The defined benefit plan was the most frequently adopted type of pension initially, especially among the larger plans. In recent years, however, far more defined contribution plans have been formed than defined benefit. In addition, virtually all workers in the United States are protected by the social security system, a pay-as-you-go minimum income maintenance arrangement.

In addition to basic employer-sponsored pension plans, individuals may save for retirement through 401(k) plans, individual retirement accounts, and Keogh accounts. Many of these accounts are invested in investment company shares (mutual funds).

With its large number of plans, both public and private, US pension funds controlled over $6 trillion in 1998. As a result, these funds are currently the most important institutional investors in a number of US financial markets.

	1964	1969	1974	1979	1984	1989	1994	1998
Financial assets ($billions)	$64.9	$103.8	$158.7	$386.1	$713.9	$1,205.6	$2,263.7	$3,981.5
Checkable deposits and currency	1.4%	0.9%	2.2%	1.3%	0.7%	1.0%	0.1%	0.1%
Time Deposits	—	0.6	2.5	6.5	6.2	8.1	2.8	0.5
Security repos	—	—	—	—	—	—	2.3	1.0
Money market fund shares	—	—	—	0.3	1.1	0.8	1.4	1.3
Cash & cash equivalents	1.4	1.5	4.7	8.1	8.0	9.9	6.6	2.9
Equity investments:								
Mutual fund shares	0.5	0.7	1.2	1.3	1.2	2.7	7.8	13.6
Other corporate equities	51.9	59.2	47.1	45.4	43.2	45.2	40.7	52.5
Total equities	52.4	59.9	48.3	46.7	44.4	47.9	48.5	66.1
Debt instruments:								
Government:								
Treasury issues	4.1	2.1	5.4	6.7	7.4	7.8	11.0	8.5
Agency issues	0.8	0.6	2.7	3.3	6.1	4.5	5.0	4.2
Total government	4.9	2.7	8.1	10.0	13.5	12.3	16.0	12.7
Corporate and foreign bonds	32.7	26.6	22.0	16.5	15.5	15.4	10.3	7.6
Mortgages:								
Home	2.0	1.7	0.5	0.3	0.4	0.1	0.2	0.1
Multifamily	1.2	1.2	0.3	0.1	0.1	0.1	(1)	(1)
Commercial	1.1	1.2	0.7	0.4	0.5	0.3	0.5	0.5
Total mortgages	4.3	4.1	1.5	0.8	1.0	0.5	0.7	0.6
Commercial paper & banker's acceptances	—	—	3.4	4.0	5.9	8.1	2.3	1.1
Total debt instruments	41.9	33.4	35.0	31.3	35.9	36.3	29.3	22.0
Miscellaneous	4.3	5.2	12.0	13.9	11.7	5.9	5.6	9.0
	100.0%	100.0%	100.0%	100.0%	100.0%	100.0%	100.0%	100.0%

◆ **Exhibit 29.4: Financial assets of US private pension funds, 1964–98 (percentages)**

◆ *Note:*   1 Less than .1%

◆ *Source:*   Fred Herrera of H. J. Johnson & Associates, with data from: Board of Governors of the Federal Reserve System, *Flow of Funds Accounts, Financial Assets and Liabilities.*

	1964	1969	1974	1979	1984	1989	1994	1998
Financial assets ($billions)	$30.6	$53.2	$88.0	$169.7	$356.6	$633.4	$1,145.7	$2,284.8
Checkable deposits and currency	1.0%	0.6%	0.4%	0.3%	0.6%	0.4%	0.5%	0.2%
Security repos	–	–	–	–	–	–	2.3	1.4
Time deposits	–	0.4	1.7	2.1	3.4	3.3	0.5	0.1
Cash & cash equivalents	1.0	1.0	2.1	2.4	4.0	3.7	3.3	1.7
Corporate equities	6.5	13.7	18.7	21.8	27.1	37.6	44.3	65.9
Debt instruments:								
US Govt:								
Treasury issues	22.9	10.1	1.8	8.7	19.0	21.8	16.1	9.4
Agency issues	1.3	3.0	5.2	9.1	12.1	9.3	6.7	5.0
Total US Govt	24.2	13.1	7.0	17.8	31.1	31.1	22.8	14.4
Tax-exempt	9.5	4.3	1.1	2.3	0.4	0.1	–	0.1
Corporate and foreign bonds	48.7	57.3	62.5	50.1	33.1	25.0	14.2	9.8
Mortgages:								
Home	5.2	5.2	3.6	1.8	1.1	0.5	0.3	0.2
Multifamily	3.3	3.5	2.5	1.9	1.7	0.9	0.4	0.2
Commercial	1.3	1.3	2.3	1.9	1.5	1.1	0.6	0.3
Farm	0.3	0.6	0.2	–	–	–	–	–
Total mortgages	10.1	10.6	8.6	5.6	4.3	2.5	1.3	0.7
Commercial paper & banker's acceptances	–	–	–	–	–	–	2.3	1.4
Total debt instruments	92.5	85.3	79.2	75.8	68.9	58.7	40.6	26.4
Miscellaneous	–	–	–	–	–	–	11.8	6.0
	100.0%	100.0%	100.0%	100.0%	100.0%	100.0%	100.0%	100.0%

◆ **Exhibit 29.5:** **Financial assets of state and local government pension funds in the United States, 1964–98 (percentages)**

◆ *Source:*   Fred Herrera of H. J. Johnson & Associates, with data from: Board of Governors of the Federal Reserve System, *Flow of Funds Accounts, Financial Assets and Liabilities.*

	1964	1969	1974	1979	1984	1989	1994	1998
Corporate equities[1] ($billions)	$633.0	$866.4	$641.7	$1,179.5	$2,021.5	$3,246.0	$6,293.4	$14,556.1
Households	84.7%	80.7%	71.7%	68.9%	65.4%	57.3%	52.9%	43.9%
Foreign sector	2.2	3.1	3.8	4.1	4.7	6.3	5.9	7.4
State and local govt	–	–	–	–	–	–	–	0.5
Mutual savings banks	0.3	0.3	0.6	0.4	0.2	0.3	0.2	0.2
Pension funds:								
Private	5.3	7.1	11.6	14.9	15.3	16.8	14.6	14.4
State and local govt	0.3	0.9	2.6	3.1	4.8	7.3	8.1	10.3
Total pension funds	5.6	8.0	14.2	18.0	20.1	24.1	22.7	24.7
Insurance companies:								
Life insurance	1.2	1.5	3.3	3.3	3.0	3.2	4.4	4.4
Other insurance	1.8	1.5	2.0	2.1	2.2	2.4	1.8	1.4
Total insurance:	3.0	3.0	5.3	5.4	5.2	5.6	6.2	5.8
Mutual funds[2]	4.1	4.7	4.1	3.0	4.0	6.0	11.3	16.7
Closed-end funds	–	–	–	–	–	–	0.5	0.4
Brokers & dealers	0.1	0.2	0.3	0.2	0.4	0.4	0.3	0.4
Totals:	100.0%	100.0%	100.0%	100.0%	100.0%	100.0%	100.0%	100.0%

◆ **Exhibit 29.6: Investors in corporate equities in the United States, 1964–98 (percentages)**

◆ *Notes:*   1   Represents market value of corporate equities excluding mutual fund shares
         2   Excludes money market mutual funds

◆ *Source:*   Fred Herrera of H. J. Johnson & Associates, with data from: Board of Governors of the Federal Reserve System, *Flow of Funds Accounts, Financial Assets and Liabilities.*

	1964	1969	1974	1979	1984	1989	1994	1998
Treasury issues ($billions)[1]	$256.6	$278.4	$351.5	$658.0	$1,373.4	$2,133.4	$3,465.6	$3,723.4
Sponsored credit agencies[2]	0.7%	0.7%	0.4%	0.2%	0.3%	1.2%	1.5%	0.4%
Monetary authority[2]	14.2	20.5	22.8	17.7	11.6	10.7	10.5	11.8
Households	29.5	34.2	28.7	30.8	31.1	26.5	22.1	9.9
Business sector	5.6	2.2	1.0	2.2	4.1	4.0	2.5	1.7
State and local govt	5.9	7.9	7.3	6.8	5.1	8.8	8.6	6.8
Foreign sector	5.2	3.6	16.6	17.7	14.1	17.0	19.0	34.0
Depository institutions:								
Commercial banks	24.8	19.9	16.0	15.1	13.5	9.5	8.4	7.0
Savings & loan assoc.	2.7	3.4	0.5	0.5	1.8	0.5	0.8	0.3
Mutual savings banks	2.3	1.1	0.7	0.7	0.7	0.4	–	–
Credit unions	0.1	0.2	0.2	0.1	0.2	0.7	0.6	0.4
Total depository institutions	29.9	24.6	17.4	16.4	16.2	11.1	9.8	7.7
Pension funds:								
Private	1.1	0.8	2.5	4.0	3.9	4.4	7.2	9.1
State and local govt	2.7	1.9	0.5	2.2	4.9	6.5	5.3	5.7
Total pension funds	3.8	2.7	3.0	6.2	8.8	10.9	12.5	14.8
Insurance companies:								
Life insurance	2.2	1.5	1.0	0.8	3.0	2.9	3.1	2.5
Other insurance	2.2	1.2	0.8	1.6	1.7	2.4	3.8	2.5
Total insurance	4.4	2.7	1.8	2.4	4.7	5.3	6.9	5.0
Investment companies:								
Mutual funds[3]	0.3	0.3	0.3	0.2	0.8	3.8	5.6	6.4
Closed-end funds	–	–	–	–	–	–	0.2	0.3
Money market funds	0	0	0	0.3	1.9	0.6	1.9	2.2
Total investment companies	0.3	0.3	0.3	0.5	2.7	4.4	7.7	8.9
Brokers and dealers	0.5	0.6	0.7	<0.9>*	1.3	0.1	–1.1*	–1.0*
Totals:	100.0%	100.0%	100.0%	100.0%	100.0%	100.0%	100.0%	100.0%

◆ **Exhibit 29.7: Investors in US Treasury securities, 1964–98 (percentages)**

◆ *Notes:* 1 Includes Federal Home Loan Banks, Federal National Mortgage Association, Federal Home Loan Mortgage Corporation, Student Loan Marketing Association, Federal Land Banks, Federal Intermediate Credit Banks, Banks for Cooperatives, and the Financing Corporation (see chapters 4 and 5)

2 Federal Reserve System

3 Excludes money market mutual funds

*Represents security repurchase agreements, net (see chapter 3)

◆ *Source:* Fred Herrera of H. J. Johnson & Associates, with data from: Board of Governors of the Federal Reserve System, *Flow of Funds Accounts, Financial Assets and Liabilities.*

	1964	1969	1974	1979	1984	1989	1994	1998
Government agency issues ($billions)	$14.8	$42.9	$106.1	$235.2	$529.4	$1,226.3	$2,199.5	$3,006.8
Sponsored credit agencies[1]	0.7%	0.5%	0.4%	0.3%	0.1%	–	0.2%	11.9%
Monetary authority[2]	–	–	4.4	3.5	1.6	0.6	–	–
Households	11.4	27.5	13.8	15.0	10.2	20.9	12.5	13.0
Business sector	6.7	4.0	2.8	0.6	0.3	0.1	1.3	0.8
State and local govt	19.5	17.7	14.2	14.9	10.4	7.3	11.2	4.3
Foreign sector	6.7	6.3	2.6	3.3	2.3	3.1	6.2	9.5
Depository institutions:								
Commercial banks	34.9	23.5	31.3	21.7	14.7	14.3	19.5	19.6
Thrifts	10.1	9.6	16.6	19.5	27.5	20.0	7.3	5.0
Credit unions	–	1.2	2.0	1.1	1.1	0.6	1.9	1.9
Total depository institutions	45.0	34.3	49.9	42.3	43.3	34.9	28.7	26.5
Pension funds:								
Private	3.3	1.4	4.1	5.4	8.2	4.5	5.2	5.6
State and local govt	2.7	3.7	4.3	6.5	8.2	4.8	3.5	3.8
Total pension funds	6.0	5.1	8.4	11.9	16.4	9.3	8.7	9.4
Insurance companies:								
Life insurance	0.7	0.9	1.0	4.0	7.0	6.2	10.6	8.0
Other insurance	3.3	3.7	2.5	2.5	2.6	2.5	2.1	2.4
Total insurance	4.0	4.6	3.5	6.5	9.6	8.7	12.7	10.4
Investment companies:								
Mutual funds[3]	–	–	–	–	0.1	2.7	4.6	4.5
Money market funds	–	–	–	0.17	3.2	1.1	3.5	3.1
Total investment companies	–	–	–	1.7	3.3	3.8	8.1	7.6
CMOs[4]	–	–	–	–	2.5	11.3	5.8	2.9
Brokers and dealers	–	–	–	–	–	–	–	–
ABS issuers[5]	–	–	–	–	–	–	4.6	3.7
Totals:	100.0%	100.0%	100.0%	100.0%	100.0%	100.0%	100.0%	100.0%

◆ **Exhibit 29.8:** Investors in US government agency securities, 1964–98 (percentages)

◆ *Notes:*

1 Includes Federal Home Loan Banks, Federal National Mortgage Association, Federal Home Loan Mortgage Corporation, Student Loan Marketing Association, Federal Land Banks, Federal Intermediate Credit Banks, Banks for Cooperatives, and the Financing Corporation (see chapters 4 and 5)

2 Federal Reserve System

3 Excludes money market mutual funds

4 Collateralized mortgage obligations (see chapters 4 and 5)

5 Asset-backed securities – federally related mortgage pool that back privately issued CMOs

◆ *Source:* Fred Herrera of H. J. Johnson & Associates, with data from: Board of Governors of the Federal Reserve System, *Flow of Funds Accounts, Financial Assets and Liabilities.*

End-of-chapter Questions

1. Differentiate public, private, and insured pension plans in general terms.
2. What distinguishes a defined benefit pension plan from a defined contribution plan?
3. Why are social security contributions commonly considered taxes rather than pension contributions?
4. With respect to defined benefit plans, what is the difference between unit-benefit and flat-benefit formulas?
5. Summarize the regulatory provisions of ERISA in the areas of pension funding, vesting of benefits, and fiduciary responsibility, in general terms.
6. More specifically, enumerate the vesting options available to plan sponsors under ERISA.
7. Relate the "prudent man" rule to the responsibilities of a pension plan asset manager.
8. In which financial markets have pension funds become particularly important? Be specific in your answer.
9. Investigate the provisions of the pension plan to which you (or a member of your family) belong(s).
   a. Is it a defined benefit or defined contribution plan?
   b. What are the vesting requirements?
10. Contributions to the social security system in the United States are counted as revenues in the federal fiscal budget. The current excess of contributions over disbursements reduces the federal budget deficit. What will be the effect of this accounting when the "baby boomers" begin to retire?
11. As corporate America restructures and downsizes, what type of pension plan will best protect workers?
12. If an overfunded defined benefit pension plan is terminated, converted to a defined contribution plan, and the vested pension liability satisfied by purchasing pension annuity contracts from an insurance company, what risk is faced by the pension plan participants?
13. In what ways is the exposure of Pension Benefit Guaranty Corporation similar to that of the Federal Deposit Insurance Corporation?

NOTES

1 Disbursements per contributor:
   $(\$2,502.29/\$361.50)^{1/25} - 1 = 0.08046$
   Personal income per contributor:
   1970: $531.6 bil./0.0882 bil. = $6,027.21
   1987: $3,357.1 bil./0.1329 bil. = $25,260.35
   $(\$25,260.35/\$6,027.21)^{1/25} - 1 = 0.05899$

2 Lump-sum distributions before the age of 59.5 that are not reinvested in a qualified pension plan are subject to the normal income tax plus a 10 percent penalty.

SELECTED REFERENCES

Board of Governors of the Federal Reserve System. *Flow of Funds Accounts, Financial Assets and Liabilities*, various issues.

Coleman, Barbara J. *Primer on ERISA*, the Bureau of National Affairs, Washington, DC, 1985.

Investment Company Institute. *Mutual Fund Factbook 1996*, Washington, DC, 1996.

Ippolito, Richard A. *Pensions, Economics, and Public Policy*, Dow Jones-Irwin, Homewood, Ill., 1986.

Office of Management and Budget, Executive Office of the President of the United States. *Historical Tables; Budget of the United States Government; Fiscal Year 1990*, Washington, DC, 1996.

Social Security Administration. *Annual Statistical Supplement, 1996, to the Social Security Bulletin*, Washington, DC.

US Department of Commerce, Bureau of the Census. *Statistical Abstract of the United States, 1989, 109th Edition*, Washington, DC, 1996.

Insurance Companies

chapter 30

◯ CHAPTER OVERVIEW

This chapter:
- Defines the concepts and classifications of insurance.
- Examines components and trends of industry profitability.
- Discusses regulation of insurance companies.
- Analyzes investment trends of insurance companies.

◯ KEY TERMS

benefit payments
general accounts
insurance agent
insurance broker
insurance premiums
insurance underwriter

life insurance
policy reserves
principles of insurance
property and casualty insurance
separate account

◯ CHAPTER OUTLINE

Introduction

Insuring risks is an activity that is almost as old as commercial banking. Insurance companies offer a wide range of products including life, health, property, and liability insurance. In addition, pension products are an increasingly important segment of the insurance industry.

 ## The Nature of Insurance

Confidence in the insurance industry is of utmost importance because *insurance policies* protect individuals and businesses from the effects of unfavorable events. To obtain this protection, the insured pays *insurance premiums*.

Insurance policy:
     A contract that provides a party (the insured) with protection against the financial loss associated with an undesirable event.

Insurance premiums:
     Either periodic or lump sum payments to an insurer in exchange for protection against a specified risk.

Should the undesirable event occur, the insured receives monetary compensation from the insurer in accordance with the contract between the two parties. By purchasing the protection, the insured reduces exposure to potential loss. Should no claim arise, that is, should the undesirable event not occur, the insurer earns profits according to the following formula:

Profits = premiums collected
        + income from the investment of premiums
        − operating expenses

An insurer cannot be certain whether an undesirable event will occur in connection with a particular insured party. However, by selling insurance policies to a large number of parties, the insurer maintains a fund from which future losses –claims – are paid. The amount of an individual premium will depend on:

- The insurer's past experience
- The probability of loss
- The amount of compensation that is contractually agreed upon in the event of loss

1.1 INSURANCE CLASSIFICATIONS

Insurance coverage is classified by the type of undesirable event against which the insured seeks protection. The two main classifications are *life* insurance and *property and casualty* insurance.

1.1.1 LIFE INSURANCE

If the undesirable event is premature loss of life, the insurance contract is a *long-term* arrangement. The uncertainty for the insured is *when* loss of life occurs. *Life insurance* protects the beneficiary of the insured from an *unexpected* loss of income. Unless the policy is for a specified period of time (term) and the insured outlives that period, a claim is eventually paid. Thus, a life insurance policy is a kind of savings vehicle with protection against an unanticipated event. Over time, life insurance companies have begun to offer additional products that provide benefits to the insured after his or her productive years. Functionally, the newer products are similar to pension funds.

Life insurers set premiums that are based on:

- Age of the insured
- Average life expectancy
- Anticipated investment returns on the insurance fund
- Operating expenses
- A reasonable profit margin

Within a large group of policyholders, the percentage that will give rise to claims within a particular year may be estimated fairly accurately. Operating expenses are also reasonably predictable. Thus, life insurers must carefully evaluate their investment income assumptions in setting appropriate premiums.

1.1.2 PROPERTY AND CASUALTY INSURANCE

When the undesirable event is *not* associated with unexpected loss of life or livelihood, the insurance is referred to as *property and casualty insurance*. Examples are automobile, fire, homeowner's, and liability insurance. While these policies cover a wide variety of risks, they also share certain common features. First, the policies are essentially *short-term* contracts, subject to frequent renewal; that is, the insurer may cancel coverage after a relatively brief period of time. Secondly, there is *no savings component* associated with property and casualty insurance. If the event against which protection is provided does not occur, the insured is not entitled to cash payment. Lastly, because of the first two factors, a property and casualty insurer must rely more on *risk evaluation* in setting premiums than a life insurer.

1.2 Basic Principles of Insurance

A few basic concepts are helpful in order to understand the nature of the products that insurance companies offer and operation of the firms themselves.

- *Insurable Interest.* There must be a relationship between the insured and the subject covered by the insurance. Furthermore, potential harm to the subject must represent a corresponding financial loss for the insured.
- *Utmost Good Faith.* Full disclosures on both sides of the transactions is expected. The insurer must inform the insured of all contractual terms. The insured must provide all information that is relevant for the assessment of risk.
- *Indemnity.* The insured is entitled to recover the amount of actual loss in connection with a property and casualty insurance claim, but may not profit as a result.
- *Right of Subrogation.* If the insured receives remedy for a loss from a third party – responsible for the loss – the insurer is entitled to be reimbursed up to the amount of the claim actually paid by insurer.
- *Contribution.* With respect to indemnity policy, if more than one insurer is involved, the insurer that actually pays a claim may collect a proportional share of such payment from the remaining insurers.

These principles are designed to maintain the integrity of the insurance process. The insurable interest principle is intended to discourage "gambling": for example, buying life insurance policies that cover strangers or well-known personalities with whom the insured has no financial relationship. The principle of utmost good faith protects both sides of the insurance transaction. The remaining concepts of indemnity, subrogation, and contribution essentially protect insurance companies from overpayment of claims.

② Insurance Companies

In terms of organizational form, insurance companies may be *mutual* or *stock* companies. The former are owned by policyholders, the latter by stockholders. In the United States, the largest and oldest insurers maintain the mutual form of business organization. Firms that have been established more recently have adopted the stock form. In 1996, there were approximately 1,700 life insurance companies and 3,400 property and casualty insurance companies in the United States.

2.1 Income and Expense

The primary sources of income for an insurance company are *premiums* and *investment earnings*. The level of premiums depends on the policies that are written, or *underwriting* activities. (The following sections explain the underwriting function and participants in the process.) Investment earnings are tied to the management of insurance fund assets. Of these two sources, premium income accounts for the largest share of total income.

Benefit payments are the largest expense for an insurance company. In addition, life insurance companies deduct *additions to policy reserves* to cover future payments to policyholders. *Commissions* and *administrative expense* apply to both life and property and casualty companies.

> **Benefit payments:**
> Payments by insurers to insureds that satisfy the terms of an insurance contract.

> **Policy reserves:**
> Profits set aside by insurance companies to enable them to make future benefit payments. These are the equivalent of capital or retained earnings in other industries.

2.1.1 LIFE INSURANCE COMPANIES

As shown in Exhibit 30.1, total US life insurance premiums in 1970 exceeded benefit payments by $20 billion, resulting in a net underwriting gain before administrative expense and commissions. After deducting these, there was still a positive underwriting cash flow of $10 billion. (Administrative expenses, commissions, and additions to policy reserves are not shown in Exhibit 30.1) In addition, the industry earned $10.1 billion in investment income. Thus, a total positive cash flow of $20.1 billion was realized in 1970. A $9.3 noncash addition to policy reserves resulted in net income before taxes of $10.8 billion before taxes. (The addition to policy reserves is a noncash expense. At least in this respect, it is similar to depreciation expense or provision for possible loan loss.)

Since 1970, premium income has exceeded benefit payments, causing the industry to realize gains in underwriting income over the 25-year period ended 1995. In addition, investment income grew considerably faster than premiums from 1970 through 1985. Thus, the life insurance industry has maintained a strong earnings pattern in recent years. This is not to suggest that life insurance companies have been unaffected by the forces of change observed in the commercial

	1970	1975	1980	1985	1990	1995
Premiums	$36.8	$58.6	$92.6	$155.8	$264.0	$339.2
		(9.8%)	(9.6%)	(11.0%)	(11.1%)	(5.1%)
Investment income	10.1	16.5	33.9	68.0	111.9	140.1
		(10.3%)	(15.5%)	(14.9%)	(10.5%)	(4.6%)
Benefit payments	16.4	22.5	38.0	66.5	88.4	165.7
		(6.5%)	(11.1%)	(11.8%)	(5.9%)	(13.4%)

◆ **Exhibit 30.1:** US life insurance company premiums, investment income, and benefit payments, 1970–95

◆ *Note*: Amounts are in billions of dollars.
The numbers in parentheses are average annual growth rates over each five-year period.
Investment income is net of investment expenses.

◆ *Source*: Fred Herrera of H. J. Johnson & Associates, based on data from: American Council of Life Insurance, *1996 Life Insurance Fact Book*, pp. 42 & 68.

	1970	1975	1980	1985	1990	1995
Premiums	$32.9	$50.0	$95.6	$144.2	$217.8	$250.7
		(8.7%)	(13.8%)	(8.6%)	(8.6%)	(3.6%)
Investment income	2.0	4.2	11.1	19.5	32.9	33.7
		(16.0%)	(21.5%)	(11.9%)	(11.0%)	(0.6%)
Benefit payments and administrative expenses	32.8	53.0	97.3	166.8	234.7	263.4
		(10.3%)	(12.3%)	(11.4%)	(7.1%)	(2.9%)

◆ **Exhibit 30.2:** **US property and casualty insurance company premiums, investment income, and total expense, 1970–94**

◆ *Notes*: Amounts are in billions of dollars.
The numbers in parentheses are average annual growth rates over each respective five-year period.

◆ *Source*: US Dept of Commerce, Bureau of the Census, *Statistical Abstract of the United States, 1989*, p. 510; US Dept of Commerce, Bureau of the Census, *Statistical Abstract of the United States, 1996*, p. 529; author's calculations based on the above sources.

banking, thrift, and investment company industries. Those companies that invested in lower-quality corporate bonds – "junk bonds" – saw the value of their asset portfolios decline precipitously after the collapse of the junk bond market in the late 1980s.

2.1.2 PROPERTY AND CASUALTY INSURANCE COMPANIES

Exhibit 30.2 provides information for property and casualty insurance companies. In 1970, premium income exceeded the sum of benefit payments and administrative expense by only $100 million ($32.9 billion – $32.8 billion). Over time, benefit payments and administrative expense grew as fast or faster than premium income. As a result, by 1985, the nonlife insurance industry sustained a pretax underwriting loss of $22.6 billion ($144.2 billion – $166.8 billion).

Even though investment income growth outpaced increases in premiums and in benefits through 1990, investment income was not sufficient to prevent net operating losses in the mid-1980s. The industry lost $9 billion, pretax, over the two-year period ended 1985 (not shown). It was not until the late 1980s that investment income was sufficient to offset underwriting losses that continued even then.

The factors leading to these results have been both social and economic circumstances. Litigation in US courts has resulted in large settlements in liability cases in recent years. As new car prices have increased, the cost of repairs has risen with them. These and other factors led to higher benefit payments and to underwriting losses in the property and casualty insurance industry.

2.2 INSURANCE INDUSTRY PARTICIPANTS

Insurance policies are written by *underwriters*. In most cases, insurance companies fill the role of underwriters. (See also Exhibit 30.3.)

Almost 5,000 years ago, Chinese merchants insured each other's cargo shipments by sharing the risk among themselves. Instead of each merchant placing his cargo exclusively on his own boat, he distributed his goods among the boats of his collaborators. They, in turn, did the same. In the event that one boat sank, no one merchant lost his entire shipment.

However, it was not until 1688 that insurance contracts were constructed in monetary terms. Once again, cargo shipments were the subject of the arrangement. At that time, England enjoyed prosperous commercial activity. Most of the goods involved were transported by sea. Lloyd's Coffee House in London became the primarily location for intelligence gathering with regard to the safe passage of specific vessels.

Since some merchants chose not to insure their ships until they were late in arriving back in London, most insurance activity began to gravitate to Lloyd's where the most up-to-date information was available.

For each insured voyage, the name of the ship was written on a piece of paper, together with all relevant details about the shipment. A person wishing to partially insure the vessel and cargo wrote his name and the portion of the risk that he was willing to assume under the details. These insurers, therefore, became known as *underwriters*. The coffee house was later known as Lloyd's of London.

◆ **Exhibit 30.3: Early insurance underwriters**

◆ *Sources*:   Falkena, H. B., L. J. Fourie, and W. J. Kok, *The Mechanics of the South African Financial System: Financial Institutions, Instruments, and Markets*, Johannesburg, Macmillan South Africa, 1984, p. 121; Davison, Ian Hay, *A View of the Room: Lloyds: Change and Disclosure*, New York, St. Martin's Press, 1987, pp. 20–1.

> **Insurance underwriter:**
> The party that assumes the risk associated with an insurance contract and agrees to pay claims arising from the policy.

The companies employ *insurance agents* to solicit business. An agent may have the authority to bind the insurance policy, that is, to legally commit the company to provide insurance coverage. He or she may also be permitted to accept premium payments and issue receipts for these payments. Generally, agents receive commissions – a percentage of premiums – as compensation for their services.

> **Insurance agent:**
> A party who conducts transactions on behalf of an insurance underwriter, but takes no personal responsibility to honor the insurance contract.

An *insurance broker* is self-employed and acts as a middleman between the insured and the insurer. A broker generally negotiates on behalf of the insured to obtain the most competitively priced insurance product. However, the broker's compensation is, again, a commission that is paid by the insurer.

> **Insurance broker:**
> A party who conducts insurance transactions as an independent third party who brings to together the insurer and the insured.

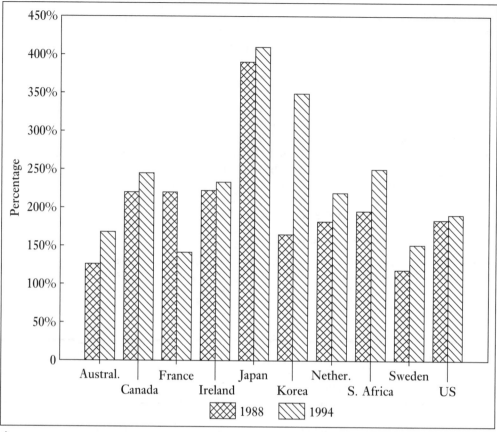

◆ **Exhibit 30.4: Life insurance in force as a percentage of GNP, selected countries,
1988 and 1994**

◆ *Notes*:   Data for France and Sweden are for 1989 and 1994.
                 Data for Japan are for 1988 and 1989.

◆ *Source*:   Author's graphic based on data from: American Council of Life Insurance,
                 1996 Life Insurance Fact Book, p. 124.

2.3 LIFE INSURANCE IN FORCE IN SELECTED COUNTRIES

A measure of the relative impact of the insurance industry in a country is the relationship between insurance in force (value of insurance policies) and the country's gross national product (GNP). Exhibit 30.4 contains information for the ten countries with the largest ratio of life insurance in force to GNP. The most notable among these is Japan where life insurance in force is almost 400 percent of GNP because of the high savings rate in that country. In contrast, the US ratio is less than 200 percent. Also, with the exception of France, the ratio increased from 1988 to 1994. This suggests a general trend of growth associated with the life insurance industry worldwide.

2.4 REGULATION

2.4.1 THE UNITED STATES

As compared to commercial banks, thrift institutions, investment companies, and pension funds, insurance companies are subject to relatively little federal regulation in the United States. The Internal Revenue Service (IRS) is the industry's primary federal regulator.

In general, special taxation rules apply to *life insurance* companies. While an insurance company's taxable income is currently defined as gross income less deductions, an additional deduction of 20 percent of taxable income is permitted. This provision was granted in the 1984 Tax Reform Act to effectively exclude investment income from taxation. The rationale is that life insurance investment income is income primarily from policyholder savings and, therefore, should no be taxed at the corporate level. (Investment companies that distribute the majority of investment earnings to shareholders receive similar tax relief.) This provision does not apply to *property and casualty* companies.

Most insurance company regulation occurs at the state level. The focus of most of this regulation is to protect policyholders from company insolvency. Accordingly, asset portfolio composition is regulated as well as the premium-to-capital ratio. Regulators attempt to guard against companies writing extensive amounts of coverage without adequate capital to absorb possible underwriting losses. In addition, states stipulate minimum absolute capital requirements in order to be permitted to conduct insurance business.

For example, regulators in the state of New York have adopted a rule of thumb that *nonlife* insurance premiums should not exceed an amount equal to twice the company's surplus (paid in capital). Limiting the amount of premiums that can be accepted is intended to ensure adequate resources for claims that may arise. In all US states, it is common for *life* insurance company investments in common stock to be limited in some way. Such provisions attempt to protect policyholder savings from extreme volatility associated with equity securities.

Life insurance firms have been able to avoid a certain amount of restriction with respect to asset composition, however. In most states, *separate accounts* have fewer investment guidelines than *general accounts*. Separate accounts are functionally similar to investment companies and are commonly offered as retirement savings vehicles, managed by a sponsoring insurance company. General accounts are legally assets of the insurance company, as well as associated liabilities.

Insurance companies are also exempted from antitrust law at the federal level. This means that insurance companies have the legal right to share information about their loss experience and to cooperate with other companies to set their premium rates. This is essentially legalized price fixing. The McCarran–Ferguson Act of 1945 permitted this practice in order to avoid premium wars that would lead, it was felt, to the failure of many insurance companies. The only restriction in the law is that companies are prohibited from setting excessive, inadequate, or unfairly discriminatory rates.

2.4.2 CANADA, LATIN AMERICA, EUROPE, AND JAPAN

Canadian insurance companies are licensed or "registered" at the federal or the provincial (state) level. However, federally registered firms dominate the life and nonlife insurance industries. In 1996, 175 Canadian life insurance companies operated, representing 1.3 percent of the world total. Federal law limits common stock and mortgage investments of life insurance firms.

Historically, the Latin American insurance market has been small. While roughly 8 percent of the world's population resides in this region, Latin American life insurance premiums in 1996 represented only 0.58 percent of total life premiums. Several factors suggest that the industry may experience significant growth in the future:

- Latin American pension systems are being liberalized to allow for more private-sector involvement.
- Economic conditions have stablized in contrast to hyperinflation of the 1980s, improving the climate for all financial services, including insurance.
- Latin America has a relatively young population, suggesting potentially strong demand for insurance products.

Europe represented 26.4 percent of total life insurance premiums in 1996. Previously, laws governing the industry in Europe varied significantly. Diversity of rules and regulations makes it somewhat difficult for firms to operate across national borders. However, member countries adopted several directives aimed at harmonizing (coordinating) company requirements and insurance coverage throughout the European Union. The European insurance market likely will become more competitive in light of the implementation in 1994 of the single EU license.

- Insurance companies registered in their home country are permitted to transact insurance business anywhere in the European Union.
- The amount of insurance regulation has been reduced – prices and terms of insurance may now be negotiated between the insurer and the insured.

In 1996, Asia represented 47.5 percent of world life insurance premiums, with Japan alone accounting for 41.3 percent. A high savings rate contributes to this concentration of insurance activity. Also, the relatively slow development of public pensions encouraged growth in Japan's private insurance sector. Elsewhere in Asia, the trend toward privatization of public pension systems suggests growth potential for private-sector insurance companies.

Assets and Liabilities

3.1 LIFE INSURANCE COMPANIES

Changes in the mix of life insurance business have, of course, affected the industry's balance sheet. In the asset section (Exhibit 30.5):

- Equity investments are an increasingly larger part of the general accounts, growing from 5.5 percent of financial assets to 26 percent.
- Corporate and foreign bonds have consistently commanded between 35 and 42 percent. Most of these are high quality corporate bonds. Only a small share is composed of junk bonds.
- Mortgage loans have become less important. However, within the mortgage category, the share of assets devoted to home mortgages declined most during the period shown (from 19.7 percent of financial assets in 1964 to 0.3 percent in 1998), while commercial mortgages increased in importance and then declined (from 10.4 percent in 1964 to 16.3 percent in 1989 to 6.4 percent in 1998).

In the liability section (Exhibit 30.6), the shift in industry emphasis is even clearer. In 1964, life insurance and pension reserves represented 70 percent and 19 percent of liabilities, respectively. By 1998, their relative positions were reversed, with life insurance and pension reserves constituting 26 percent and 53 percent of liabilities, respectively.

	1964	1969	1974	1979	1984	1989	1994	1998
Financial assets ($billion)	$144.9	$191.3	$255.0	$419.3	$692.9	$1,138.6	$1,882.7	$2,693.3
Checkable deposits and currency	1.0%	0.8%	0.8%	0.6%	0.7%	0.3%	0.3%	0.1%
Money market fund shares	–	–	–	0.2	1.0	0.7	0.8	2.5
Cash & cash equivalents	1.0	0.8	0.8	0.8	1.7	1.0	1.1	2.6
Equity investments:								
Mutual fund shares	0.1	0.3	0.2	0.2	0.4	1.2	0.4	2.4
Other corporate equities	5.4	6.9	8.3	9.3	8.7	9.0	14.6	23.6
Total equities	5.5	7.2	8.5	9.5	9.1	10.2	15.0	26.0
Debt instruments:								
Federal Govt:								
Treasury issues	3.9	2.2	1.3	1.2	6.0	5.4	5.7	3.4
Agency issues	0.1	0.2	0.4	2.3	5.3	6.6	12.4	8.9
Total Govt	4.0	2.4	1.7	3.5	11.3	12.0	18.1	12.3
Tax-exempt	2.6	1.7	1.5	1.5	1.3	1.0	0.7	1.4
Corporate & foreign bonds	40.2	38.0	37.8	40.6	35.0	39.1	41.4	39.2
Mortgages:								
Home	19.7	14.4	7.4	3.8	2.0	1.4	0.4	0.3
Multifamily	5.0	7.4	7.7	4.6	2.7	2.1	1.3	0.9
Commercial	10.4	12.8	16.2	16.9	16.1	16.3	9.2	6.4
Farm	2.9	3.0	2.5	2.9	1.8	0.9	0.5	0.4
Total mortgages	38.0	37.6	33.8	28.2	22.6	20.7	11.4	8.0
Commercial paper and banker's acceptances	0.1	0.7	1.6	1.7	3.2	3.6	2.8	2.6
Policy loans	4.9	7.2	9.0	8.3	7.9	4.7	4.5	3.9
Total debt instruments	89.8	87.6	85.4	83.8	81.3	81.1	78.9	67.4
Miscellaneous	3.7	4.4	5.3	5.9	7.9	7.7	5.0	4.0
Totals:	100.0%	100.0%	100.0%	100.0%	100.0%	100.0%	100.0%	100.0%

◆ **Exhibit 30.5: Financial assets of US life insurance companies, 1964–98**

◆ *Source:* Board of Governors of the Federal Reserve System, *Flow of Funds Accounts, Financial Assets and Liabilities*, various issues.

	1964	1969	1974	1979	1984	1989	1994	1998
Financial liabilities ($billions)	$134.0	$177.5	$243.9	$396.9	$665.3	$1,069.5	$1,773.5	$2,513.5
Life insurance reserves	70.0%	66.5%	61.7%	49.8%	35.5%	28.3%	27.7%	26.0%
Pension fund reserves	18.9	21.2	24.8	36.2	49.8	61.0	50.6	52.7
Taxes payable	0.4	0.4	0.3	0.4	0.1	0.1	0.1	0.7
Miscellaneous	10.4	11.9	13.2	13.6	14.6	10.6	21.6	20.6
Totals:	100.0%	100.0%	100.0%	100.0%	100.0%	100.0%	100.0%	100.0%

◆ **Exhibit 30.6: Liabilities of US life insurance companies, 1964–98**

◈ *Source:* Board of Governors of the Federal Reserve System, *Flow of Funds Accounts, Financial Assets and Liabilities*, various issues.

	1964	1969	1974	1979	1984	1989	1994	1998
Financial assets ($billion)	$34.9	$45.5	$67.9	$155.1	$241.0	$460.1	$676.3	$888.6
Checkable deposits and currency	4.0%	2.9%	2.4%	1.9%	1.3%	1.3%	0.7%	0.4%
Security repos	–	–	–	–	7.4	6.1	4.3	4.1
Cash and short-term investments	4.0	2.9	2.4	1.9	8.7	7.4	5.0	4.5
Corporate equities[1]	32.7	29.2	18.8	16.0	18.5	17.2	16.6	23.0
Debt instruments:								
Federal Govt:								
Treasury issues	16.0	7.5	4.3	6.9	9.7	11.1	19.7	10.5
Agency issues	1.4	2.9	2.4	1.9	8.7	7.4	6.8	8.1
Total Govt	17.4	11.0	8.3	10.8	15.5	17.7	26.5	18.6
Tax-exempt	31.5	34.1	45.2	46.9	35.1	34.0	22.7	22.3
Corporate & foreign bonds	6.9	13.8	14.7	15.2	10.7	14.0	16.3	18.3
Commercial mortgages	0.3	0.4	0.3	0.4	1.1	1.0	0.6	0.2
Total debt instruments	56.1	59.3	68.5	73.3	62.4	66.7	66.1	59.4
Trade credit	7.2	8.6	10.3	8.8	10.4	8.7	7.8	7.1
Miscellaneous	–	–	–	–	–	–	4.5	6.0
Totals:	100.0%	100.0%	100.0%	100.0%	100.0%	100.0%	100.0%	100.0%

◆ **Exhibit 30.7: Financial assets of US property and casualty insurance companies, 1964–98**

◈ *Note:* 1 Does not include mutual fund shares

◆ *Sources:* Board of Governors of the Federal Reserve System, *Flow of Funds Accounts, Financial Assets and Liabilities*, various issues.

3.2 PROPERTY AND CASUALTY COMPANIES

Property and casualty companies have reduced their proportional holdings of equities in favor of corporate and foreign bonds, in search of higher returns from 1964 to 1979. Then equity holdings increased somewhat during the 1980s and 1990s – during a period of strong stock market growth. As shown in Exhibit 30.7, the share of financial assets devoted to Treasury securities declined and then increased somewhat. Repurchase agreements and government agency securities have generally become more important over time. These changes reflect efforts to continually improve investment income results, efforts also observed in the case of other financial institutions.

 Summary

US insurance companies have traditionally performed the function of risk-sharing (property and casualty firms) and savings (life companies). The industry underwent few changes until the 1970s and 1980s when inflation pushed the cost of claims beyond the level of premium receipts in the nonlife industry and prompted disintermediation in the life industry. The result has been restructuring of premium schedules and the introduction of new product lines and services.

 End-of-chapter Questions

1. For a particular insurance policy, explain why the sum of premiums paid is less than the face value of the protection that is provided. Include a discussion of both life and nonlife coverage.
2. Describe three common attributes of property and casualty insurance.
3. What are the basic principles of insurance?
4. Identify the primary components of insurance company income and expense.
5. Why are life insurance policies commonly considered savings vehicles? Why are nonlife policies not so classified?
6. What factors have contributed to dominance of the Japanese market in the life insurance industry?
7. What factors could lead to higher growth in the life insurance industry in Latin America?
8. Why are life insurance company profits not taxed?
9. How has the Single European Market changed the way insurance business in Europe is conducted?
10. Many of the insurance policies that have been sold to the public in recent years have been purchased in order to provide retirement income for millions of people. If insurance companies fail, what role do you think the federal government should play in this restructuring?

SELECTED REFERENCES

American Council of Life Insurance. *1996 Life Insurance Fact Book*, Washington, DC, 1996.

American Council of Life Insurance. *1997 Life Insurance Fact Book*, Washington, DC, 1997.

Board of Governors of the Federal Reserve System. *Flow of Funds Accounts; Financial Assets and Liabilities*, various issues.

MacAvoy, Paul, ed. *Federal–State Regulation of the Pricing and Marketing of Insurance*, American Enterprise Institute for Public Policy Research, Washington, DC, 1977.

Neave, Edwin H. *Canada's Financial System*, John Wiley and Sons Canada, Toronto, 1981.

Sametz, Arnold, W. *The Emerging Financial Industry: Implications for Insurance Products, Portfolios, and Planning*, Lexington Books, Lexington, Mass. 1984.

Wasow, Bernard and Raymond D. Hill, eds. *The Insurance Industry in Economic Developments*, New York University Press, New York, 1986.

US Dept of Commerce, Bureau of the Census. *Statistical Abstract of the United States, 1989*, Washington, DC, 1989.

US Dept of Commerce, Bureau of the Census. *Statistical Abstract of the United States, 1996*, Washington, DC, 1996.

Finance Companies

chapter 31

Introduction

Finance companies have evolved from modest, one location operations to multibillion-dollar enterprises. Some of the largest now offer bank-like services to industry, while others remain focused on the consumer market. The services available from finance companies include consumer installment loans, real estate loans, business inventory and mortgage financing, and money market accounts. Freedom from federal regulation enables finance companies to have this wide scope of operation and to avoid the expense of regulatory compliance. As a result, finance companies now compete vigorously with commercial banks.

 The Early Years

For 100 years, finance companies have offered services to fill the gap between (1) the needs of industrial and consumer clients and (2) the services provided by commercial banks. At the inception of the finance company industry, three types of firms emerged:

- Commercial finance companies
- Sales finance companies
- Consumer finance companies

1.1 COMMERCIAL FINANCE COMPANIES

Early in the twentieth century commercial banks did not offer loans to industrial firms that used their accounts receivable as collateral because the Federal Reserve only discounted, or bought, promissory notes that were related to productive purposes. A firm's receivables frequently arose from retail sales – that is, consumer purchases – not purchases by industrial concerns.

Commercial finance companies filled this void by making loans to industrial firms on the basis of accounts receivable. In exchange for the loan, the borrowing firm signed over its right to the receivables to the finance company and, upon collecting the receivables, turned over all proceeds to the finance company. Since the borrowing firm's original customer was not aware of this arrangement, the technique became known as *nonnotification accounts receivable financing*.

Nonnotification accounts receivable financing:
Method of obtaining a loan by assigning the future collection of accounts receivable to a financial institution without disclosing this arrangement to the customers that gave rise to the receivables.

Commercial banks did not begin to participate in this form of financing until the Great Depression in the 1930s and then only in those cases that the borrower's ability to repay was questionable. Thus, commercial banks associated accounts receivable financing with financial distress and did not adopt it as a standard method of banking. At the same time, commercial finance companies expanded their use of collateralized lending to accommodate their industrial customers. Soon finance companies were offering loans collateralized by equipment and inventory and gaining the reputation of finding innovative ways to finance small businesses.

1.2 SALES FINANCE COMPANIES

When mass production of automobiles began in the early twentieth century, banks did not offer automobile loans again because the auto purchases were considered consumer purchases, not productive investment. Commercial finance companies started sales finance departments or subsidiaries that offered installment loans. Soon firms exclusively involved in sales finance sprang up and were so successful that they began to finance also the retail purchases of radios, refrigerators, washing machines, dryers, furniture, vacuum cleaners, and other consumer durables.

Automobile manufacturers expected their dealers to accept an even flow of car shipments to keep auto factories running smoothly year-round. The pattern of consumer purchases, however, was subject to seasonal peaks and valleys, giving rise to the need for inventory financing during slow-selling seasons. Sales finance companies arranged "floor plans," wholesale financing that involved placing a lien on each automobile in the showroom or warehouse, with the arrangement documented in a trust receipt.

Floor planning:
> Loan(s) made to finance a dealer's inventory, usually durable goods with broad consumer appeal. The dealer issues a trust receipt to the lender. The lender is repaid when the inventory is sold.

Trust receipt (floor planning):
> A security agreement between a lender and a durable goods dealer that permits the dealer to have possession of the inventory while it is being offered for sale. Payments to the lender are paid from a trust account as the durable goods are sold.

Effectively, the sales finance company owned the autos until they were sold to the dealers' customers, at which time the finance company received wholesale cost plus accrued interest. It was not long before floor plans and consumer installment financing were being handled by the same sales finance company. This process was then replicated in the sales of other consumer durables such as washing machines, dryers, and television sets.

Some sales finance companies operated as *captive finance companies*. The first captive finance company, formed in 1919, was General Motors Acceptance Corporation (GMAC). Similar institutions were formed by Ford, Chrysler, and General Electric a few years later. Over time, many others followed.

> **Captive finance company:**
>   A finance company that is wholly owned by a manufacturing firm and handles the retail and wholesale financing of only that manufacturer.

1.3 CONSUMER FINANCE COMPANIES

Other consumer finance companies developed in the early 1900s that were not involved exclusively in sales finance. These companies made loans available to wage earners on the basis of their gainful employment for purposes including medical expense and emergency needs. Frequently, household furnishings were used as collateral. Customers of these firms were generally considered to be high credit risks and unable to obtain financing from commercial banks.

② The Industry Today

As is true in the financial services industry in general, previous distinctions between commercial, sales, and consumer finance companies have blurred and each now offers a wider range of services. In the late 1960s there was another important addition to the list of services – second mortgage loans, introduced in California by Beneficial Finance, one of the earliest consumer finance companies. Since then, second mortgage lending has become a fast-growing segment of the market.

Exhibit 31.1 shows the breakdown of all finance company loans in 1996. The largest category of loans is business loans – 57.4 percent of the total. Personal or consumer loans represent 29.4 percent and real estate loans the remainder.

To illustrate the expanding scope of finance company operations in these areas, five major firms are discussed in this chapter. The firms (and their 1995 total assets) are:

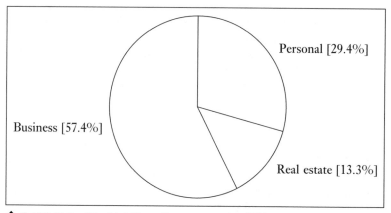

◆ **Exhibit 31.1: Mix of total loans finance companies, 1996**

◆ *Source*:   Author's calculations and graphic based on data from:
                    Federal Reserve Statistical Release; Finance Companies;
                    September 1996.

- General Motors Acceptance Corporation (GMAC – $95 billion)
- Ford Credit Company (Ford – $113 billion)
- General Electric Capital Corporation (GECC – $161 billion)
- Household International (Household – $29 billion)
- Beneficial Corporation (Beneficial – $16 billion)

GMAC and Ford are captive sales finance companies, wholly owned by their automobile manufacturing parent companies. GECC is also a captive finance company owned by its manufacturing parent, but has diversified far beyond its original purpose. Household and Beneficial are consumer finance companies that have also become more widely diversified.

2.1 CONSUMER SERVICES

2.1.1 FINANCING RETAIL PURCHASES

Automobile financing was the cornerstone of the consumer finance industry and remains its most important category, representing in 1996 over 51 percent of all consumer loans (motor vehicles plus securitized motor vehicle) excluding mortgages as indicated in Exhibit 31.2. Securitized automobile loans represented 16 percent of total consumer loans, underscoring the impact that securitization has had on the finance company industry. (See chapter 4 for a description of securitization.) Personal cash loans, mobile home loans, and loans to purchase other consumer goods (appliances, apparel, and general merchandise) constitute the remainder of finance company consumer loans outstanding in 1996 (other consumer and securitized other consumer). Again, securitized other consumer loans represented a significant share (10 percent of total consumer loans).

Finance companies remain strong in most of their traditional markets and are making significant inroads into other consumer finance areas, such as:

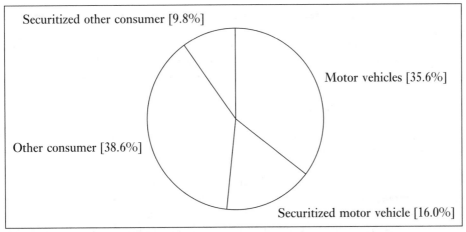

◆ **Exhibit 31.2:** Mix of consumer loans (other than mortgages) finance companies, 1996

◆ *Source*: Author's calculations and graphic based on data from: *Federal Reserve Statistical Release; Finance Companies; September 1996.*

- Credit cards
- Bank activities
- Investment products

GMAC and Ford purchase *closed-end retail installment contracts* from affiliated vehicle dealers as the core of their operations. Recently, captive finance companies have added leasing plans to their consumer offerings through dealers. Since 1986, the marine division of GMAC has extended installment and lease financing to boat dealers affiliated with Sea Ray and Boston Whaler.

> **Closed-end retail installment contract:**
> A contract that obligates a consumer that is purchasing goods to pay the lender specified installments for a specified period of time.

GECC purchases closed-end consumer installment contracts from a wide variety of retail establishments, including those that sell General Electric products. Leasing plans are offered through dealers of automobiles, manufactured housing, recreational vehicles, and boats. Household and Beneficial also purchase closed-end retail installment contracts from a large number of retailers.

2.1.2 CREDIT CARDS

GECC issues credit cards directly to consumers through a *credit card bank* called Monogram Bank. Until 1995, Household issued credit cards directly to consumers through its credit card bank, Household Bank, NA, operating throughout the United States. In 1995, Household sold all but its Illinois network to capitalize on its strong presence in that state. In 1986, Beneficial sold its purely credit card operation, as well as insurance and mail-order divisions, in order to focus more on its traditional consumer business.

> **Credit card bank:**
> A bank designated to conduct primarily credit card business and is thus not subjected to the same regulatory constraints as commercial banks.

2.1.3 BANK ACTIVITIES

Even the captive auto finance companies are involved in bank activities. For example, in 1995, GMAC, the Polish-American Enterprise Fund (PAEF) and Polish Private Equity Funds (investment companies) purchased the controlling interest of Polbank SA. This bank continued its traditional banking business and offered automobile financing to Opel dealers (General Motors affiliates in Europe) and their customers in the Polish market. Also, Ford is affiliated with California-based First Nationwide in the Ford Financial Services Group.

Also, finance companies have become involved in the banking industry through acquisitions of thrift institutions. Beneficial Savings Bank is based in Florida. Household Bank, FSB (federal savings bank), operates a branch network, direct mail marketing, telemarketing, and direct marketing to universities. Household Bank services include checking accounts, savings and money market accounts, youth savings accounts, certificates of deposit, individual retirement accounts (IRAs), personal loans, student loans, credit cards, debit cards, and business banking services.

Beneficial National Bank is based is based in Wilmington, Delaware and is Beneficial's commercial banking subsidiary. Services include commercial and consumer banking services to small- and medium-sized businesses and consumers in Delaware and surrounding markets. Also, Beneficial National Bank provides corporate cash management and treasury services to Beneficial and its operating subsidiaries. As these cases illustrate, the extent of finance company diversification is substantial.

2.1.4 INVESTMENT PRODUCTS

Another area into which finance companies have expanded is investment products. For example, in 1993, GECC purchased an annuity business. Also finance companies now offer money market accounts – technically only permitted for regulated depository institutions and money market mutual funds. For example, Ford offers money market accounts that are administered by Northern Trust of Chicago.

The range of consumer services available through finance companies is extensive:

- Competitive automobile loans
- Other convenient retail installment contracts
- Cash loans
- Leasing
- Credit cards
- Other bank services
- Money market accounts

The lack of federal regulation as compared to banks gives these companies a competitive edge.

2.2 Mortgages

Residential and commercial mortgages are now a major component of finance company operations. Some firms make direct loans, while others solicit the mortgages, package them, and resell them as securitized assets. (See chapter 4 for a description of mortgages and securitization.)

GMAC Mortgage Corporation originates first mortgages on both single-family residences and commercial real estate throughout the United States, but does not hold the mortgages in its portfolio. The loans are securitized and sold to investors. In some states, GMAC Mortgage Corporation also issues home equity loans or second mortgages. In 1990, GMAC purchased Residential Funding Corporation (GMAC RFC) to act entirely in the wholesale secondary mortgage market. GMAC RFC purchases single family mortgages from the original lenders, securitizes and sells them to investors. Once sold, GMAC continues to service the underlying mortgages. Because of these transactions, GMAC's mortgage activity is essentially "off balance sheet," that is, the loans are not reflected as receivables by the company. In 1995, GMAC RFC was the largest nongovernmental sponsor of mortgage-backed securities. Also in 1995, GMAC formed GMAC Commercial Mortgage Corporation – currently the largest servicer of commercial and multifamily loans in the United States.

GECC has extensive holdings in real estate. The company provides financing for the acquisition, development, refinancing, and renovation of primarily commercial property. Most of the loans are in the form of intermediate-term senior or subordinated floating rate loans secured by existing income-producing commercial property such as office buildings, rental apartments, shopping centers, hotels, industrial buildings, and warehouses. Over 90 percent of the loans are senior mortgages, receiving first priority in any liquidation. GECC also makes loans for the construction of commercial projects and for the acquisition and development of large parcels of land for single-family homes. Most of these loans also have senior status.

In 1995, Household stopped writing first mortgages as these loans represented a low-margin (low profit) segment of the business. Home equity loans, that is, second mortgages, continue to be available through Household's consumer division.

Beneficial remains committed to real estate using direct-response television advertising as its primary marketing strategy. Beneficial Mortgage Corporation solicits, packages, and then sells first mortgages to investors, but the second mortgages stay on their books.

In general, home equity loans have become a lucrative business for finance companies because the bad debt expense and administrative costs on these loans are much lower than those on unsecured loans. The borrowers essentially must qualify for the loans on the basis of their income, or ability to repay, so that the real estate collateral essentially becomes an additional assurance of repayment.

2.3 BUSINESS SERVICES

Finance companies provide comprehensive services for industrial firms. As shown in Exhibit 31.3, the major categories are retail, wholesale, and leasing services with the largest category being leasing – 50 percent of all finance company business receivables in 1996 (including a small percentage securitized). Retail financing services were 8 percent of the total (1 percent securitized) and wholesale 26 percent (6 percent securitized). *Retail financing* facilitates transactions between a retail seller of goods and the ultimate consumer. *Wholesale financing* accommodates transactions between parties other than the consuming public, for example, between a manufacturer and a distributor.

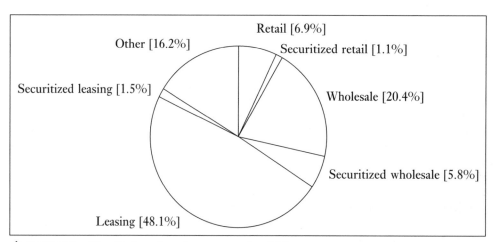

◆ **Exhibit 31.3:   Mix of business loans finance companies, 1996**

◆ *Source*:   Author's calculations and graphic based on data from: *Federal Reserve Statistical Release; Finance Companies; September 1996.*

The provision of securitized financing for industrial firms was the industry's strongest contribution as it developed years ago and this is still its competitive advantage. The principle now applies to many classifications of collateral – inventory, transportation equipment, and industrial goods.

GMAC provides wholesale financing to GM dealers for inventory floor plans and to firms that lease, rather than sell, GM vehicles. Several boat dealers are also entitled to these services. GMAC's wholesale leasing activities extend to industrial equipment, with either GMAC owning and leasing the equipment directly to its industrial customer or providing the financial backing for a leveraged lease, that is, one in which the customer leases the equipment from another party with money borrowed from GMAC. GM dealers may also receive from GMAC working capital cash loans and loans to purchase or remodel their dealership locations.

Ford offers much the same type of wholesale inventory, working capital, real estate, and capital improvement loans to dealers as GMAC. Furthermore, in its diversified financing division, the company invests in corporate preferred stock and other equity. Under a special program, Ford dealers can purchase used cars at auctions throughout the country and merely sign for them instead of having to pay for them on the spot. Lastly, an electronic funds transfer system between the Ford and the dealers makes payment delivery to the dealers as expedient as possible. Commercial receivables comprise 31 percent of Ford's loan portfolio.

GECC provides wholesale inventory financing for firms that manufacture, distribute, and retail GE products. In addition, GECC provides the important retail service of *private label credit card programs*. GECC's private label credit cards constitute one of the largest such operations in the United States and include the accounts of Macy's. Household also is a major provider of private label credit cards. Companies for which Household manages credit card programs include General Motors, Ameritech, Pacific Bell, US West, Charles Schwab, Carlson Wagonlit Travel, Mitsubishi Consumer Electronics, and Culligan.

Private label credit card program:
A program in which a finance company manages the credit card operation of a retailer, including promotion, credit evaluations, billing, and accounting, all in the retailer's name.

For its commercial clients, GECC also finances fleets of automobiles, trucks, and buses. The company provides wholesale loans for manufacturing equipment, corporate aircraft, construction equipment, business communications equipment, and high-tech equipment, including computers and scientific equipment.

Finance companies, in general, have been aggressive in the provision of commercial services. Their interest rates and fees are competitive and they are comfortable with using asset-based lending. The commercial services available from finance companies include:

- Inventory floor plans for company products
- Wholesale purchase and lease financing for other equipment
- Transportation fleet financing
- Real estate loans
- Working capital loans
- Private label credit cards

	1964	1969	1974	1979	1984	1989	1994	1998
Financial assets ($billion)	$39.7	$61.6	$98.5	$189.1	$301.6	$502.4	$734.4	$795.5
Demand deposits and currency	4.5%	3.9%	3.8%	2.4%	1.5%	2.0%	1.7%	2.7%
Consumer loans	56.4	51.9	45.2	38.1	37.8	36.5	18.4	19.4
Mortgages:								
Home	8.6	7.9	8.9	12.3	13.1	12.2	10.7	7.8
Multifamily	1.0	1.1	2.5	1.0	0.6	0.3	–	0.4
Commercial	0.3	0.3	1.9	1.5	1.3	0.9	–	3.1
Total mortgages	9.9	9.3	13.3	14.8	15.0	13.4	10.7	11.3
Business loans	29.2	34.9	37.7	44.7	45.7	48.1	46.0	42.1
Miscellaneous	–	–	–	–	–	–	23.2	24.5
Totals:	100.0%	100.0%	100.0%	100.0%	100.0%	100.0%	100.0%	100.0%

◆ **Exhibit 31.4: Financial assets of finance companies, 1964–98**

◆ *Note:* The percentage breakdown of assets in this exhibit, based on Federal Reserve Flow of Funds data, differs from that in Exhibit 31.1, which is based on the Federal Reserve Statistical Release for finance companies. The Statistical Release analyzes only the receivables of finance companies and includes those which have been securitized (that is, are no longer reflected on the balance sheet of the originators). On the other hand, this exhibit includes demand deposits, currency, and miscellaneous financial assets. Also, this exhibit is consistent with other exhibits throughout the text that show trends over time.

◆ *Source:* Author's calculations based on data from: Board of Governors of the Federal Reserve System, *Flow of Funds Accounts; Financial Assets and Liabilities*, various issues.

Assets and Liabilities

Finance companies have grown rapidly in the last two decades. The asset mix has changed over time to reflect the industry's diversification and much of its growth has been financed in the commercial paper market.

3.1 ASSETS

Exhibit 31.4 includes both the dollar amount of total financial assets and the major categories. In 1964, consumer loans were 56 percent of the portfolio, but by 1998, they represented only 19 percent. Both mortgages and business loans grew substantially, going from a combined 39 percent of assets in 1964 to 53 percent in 1998. Home mortgage loans are the most significant component of mortgages. The industry's expansive range of business services has driven the increase in business loans. As a result of these changes, the finance company industry may accurately be described as mature and diversified.

3.2 LIABILITIES

Exhibit 31.5 illustrates how the industry has been financed. In 1964, finance companies depended on bond issues and commercial bank loans for 64 percent of funding. In the next 34 years, the use of bond financing continued to be an important source of funds, remaining a fairly stable percentage of total liabilities over time. The use of bank financing, however, declined dramatically from 28 percent in 1964 to less than 3 percent in 1998.

Finance companies have become largely independent of the banking system as a source of funds. The first commercial paper was issued by GMAC. Commercial paper began in the 1960s essentially as a viable alternative to bank loans for finance companies, institutions that had earned the reputation of devising innovative and imaginative ways to fund other companies. In 1964, finance companies issued 87 percent of all commercial paper outstanding. The use of the new method of direct short-term financing by other firms also grew. By 1996, the finance-company share of commercial paper had declined to 20 percent, with asset-backed securities issuers and nonfinancial corporate businesses having taken advantage of this funding source. Even in devising a short-term alternative for its own use, the finance company industry brought innovation to industry and finance.

Summary

The early finance companies provided services that commercial banks did not, pioneering the field of asset-based lending for industrial firms and consumers. Major manufacturers of vehicles and other products developed well-functioning captive finance companies.

Today consumers may obtain small loans for a wide variety of purposes and larger second mortgage loans. Through finance companies consumers also may purchase high-ticket items and arrange financing with retail installment contracts. Some finance companies issue credit cards and own savings banks. Industrial firms have an even greater selection of services, including inventory floor plans, working capital loans, lease financing, highly leveraged transaction loans, and private label credit cards.

	1964	1969	1974	1979	1984	1989	1994	1998
Liabilities ($billion)	$34.2	$57.1	$96.6	$193.9	$291.5	$574.0	$658.6	$815.2
Commercial paper	21.3%	40.3%	28.3%	31.3%	34.6%	49.9%	28.0%	27.7%
Bonds	35.4	26.4	29.0	27.0	26.5	27.0	35.7	42.8
Bank loans	28.4	16.8	19.5	11.2	5.2	-3.7*	3.2	2.7
Taxes payable	0.6	0.4	0.3	0.2	–	0.1	0.2	0.8
Miscellaneous	14.3	16.1	17.7	17.9	17.8	5.4	25.2	18.6
Funds from parent company	–	–	5.2	12.4	15.9	21.3	7.7	7.4
Totals:	100.0%	100.0%	100.0%	100.0%	100.0%	100.0%	100.0%	100.0%

◆ **Exhibit 31.5: Liabilities of finance companies, 1964–98**

*In 1989, finance companies were net creditors of commercial banks providing loans to banks of 3.7 percent of finance company total liabilities

◆ *Source:* Author's calculations based on data from: Board of Governors of the Federal Reserve System, *Flow of Funds Accounts; Financial Assets and Liabilities*, various issues.

End-of-chapter Questions

1. What was the first type of financial service that finance companies offered industrial firms?

2. What is the difference between a sales finance company and a consumer finance company?

3. Given what you know about consumer loans (excluding mortgages) in finance companies, why do you think that commercial banks did not pursue this segment of the loan market in the early 1900s when finance companies developed?

4. What single factor contributed most to the popularity of second mortgages? (Hint: Review tax law changes in the 1980s.)

5. How did nonnotification accounts receivable financing help establish finance companies in industrial finance?

6. How does a closed-end retail installment contract differ from a credit card account?

7. Why is the interest rate for an unsecured consumer loan at a finance company higher than at a commercial bank?

8. Why do you think automobile loans represent such a large share of total consumer loans outstanding (excluding mortgage loans) in the finance company industry?

9. Given that finance company unsecured personal loans carry a higher interest rate than second mortgages, why have finance companies so actively pursued the second mortgage market?

10. General Motors Acceptance Corporation actively originates single family and commercial mortgages. Why then do you think that the company packages and sells them instead of holding them in their own portfolio? (Hint: Consider the firm's balance sheet composition.)

11. Why might a retailer prefer to participate in a private label credit card program available through a finance company rather than develop its own program?

12. What advantage accrued to finance companies when they started to issue commercial paper to finance their operations?

13. Obtain the annual reports of a major bank and a major finance company. Compare and contrast their credit operations and funding bases.

14. In your opinion, should finance companies be allowed to own commercial banks? Why or why not?

SELECTED REFERENCES

Beneficial Corporation Annual Report 1995, Wilmington, Del.

Captive Finance Companies: The Why and How of Credit Subsidiaries, American Management Association, Finance Division, 1966.

Chapman, John M. and Frederick W. Jones. *Finance Companies: How and Where They Obtain Their Funds*, Graduate School of Business, Columbia University, New York, 1959.

Federal Reserve Statistical Release; Finance Companies, Board of Governors of the Federal Reserve System, monthly series.

Ford Credit Annual Report 1995, Dearborn, Michigan.

General Electric Capital Corporation Annual Report 1995, Stamford, Conn.

General Motors Acceptance Corporation Annual Report 1995, Detroit, Mich.

Household International Annual Report 1995, Prospect Heights, Ill.

McAleer, Ysabel Burns. *Finance Companies in 1989; American Financial Services Association Research Report and Second Mortgage Lending Report*, American Financial Services Association, Washington, DC, 1990.

Appendix A

Present Value of $1

$$PVIF = \frac{1}{(1+k)^n}$$

Periods	1%	2%	3%	4%	5%	6%	7%	8%	9%
1	0.9901	0.9804	0.9709	0.9615	0.9524	0.9434	0.9346	0.9259	0.9174
2	0.9803	0.9612	0.9426	0.9246	0.9070	0.8900	0.8734	0.8573	0.8417
3	0.9706	0.9423	0.9151	0.8890	0.8638	0.8396	0.8163	0.7938	0.7722
4	0.9610	0.9238	0.8885	0.8548	0.8227	0.7921	0.7629	0.7350	0.7084
5	0.9515	0.9057	0.8626	0.8219	0.7835	0.7473	0.7130	0.6806	0.6499
6	0.9420	0.8880	0.8375	0.7903	0.7462	0.7050	0.6663	0.6302	0.5963
7	0.9327	0.8706	0.8131	0.7599	0.7107	0.6651	0.6227	0.5835	0.5470
8	0.9235	0.8535	0.7894	0.7307	0.6768	0.6274	0.5820	0.5403	0.5019
9	0.9143	0.8368	0.7664	0.7026	0.6446	0.5919	0.5439	0.5002	0.4604
10	0.9053	0.8203	0.7441	0.6756	0.6139	0.5584	0.5083	0.4632	0.4224
11	0.8963	0.8043	0.7224	0.6496	0.5847	0.5268	0.4751	0.4289	0.3875
12	0.8874	0.7885	0.7014	0.6246	0.5568	0.4970	0.4440	0.3971	0.3555
13	0.8787	0.7730	0.6810	0.6006	0.5303	0.4688	0.4150	0.3677	0.3262
14	0.8700	0.7579	0.6611	0.5775	0.5051	0.4423	0.3878	0.3405	0.2992
15	0.8613	0.7430	0.6419	0.5553	0.4810	0.4173	0.3624	0.3152	0.2745
16	0.8528	0.7284	0.6232	0.5339	0.4581	0.3936	0.3387	0.2919	0.2519
17	0.8444	0.7142	0.6050	0.5134	0.4363	0.3714	0.3166	0.2703	0.2311
18	0.8360	0.7002	0.5874	0.4936	0.4155	0.3503	0.2959	0.2502	0.2120
19	0.8277	0.6864	0.5703	0.4746	0.3957	0.3305	0.2765	0.2317	0.1945
20	0.8195	0.6730	0.5537	0.4564	0.3769	0.3118	0.2584	0.2145	0.1784
25	0.7798	0.6095	0.4776	0.3751	0.2953	0.2330	0.1842	0.1460	0.1160
30	0.7419	0.5521	0.4120	0.3083	0.2314	0.1741	0.1314	0.0994	0.0754
35	0.7059	0.5000	0.3554	0.2534	0.1813	0.1301	0.0937	0.0676	0.0490
40	0.6717	0.4529	0.3066	0.2083	0.1420	0.0972	0.0668	0.0460	0.0318
45	0.6391	0.4102	0.2644	0.1712	0.1113	0.0727	0.0476	0.0313	0.0207
50	1.0000	0.3715	0.2281	0.1407	0.0872	0.0543	0.0339	0.0213	0.0134

10%	11%	12%	13%	14%	15%	16%	17%	18%	19%	20%
0.9091	0.9009	0.8929	0.8850	0.8772	0.8696	0.8621	0.8547	0.8475	0.8403	0.8333
0.8264	0.8116	0.7972	0.7831	0.7695	0.7561	0.7432	0.7305	0.7182	0.7062	0.6944
0.7513	0.7312	0.7118	0.6931	0.6750	0.6575	0.6407	0.6244	0.6086	0.5934	0.5787
0.6830	0.6587	0.6355	0.6133	0.5921	0.5718	0.5523	0.5337	0.5158	0.4987	0.4823
0.6209	0.5935	0.5674	0.5428	0.5194	0.4972	0.4761	0.4561	0.4371	0.4190	0.4019
0.5645	0.5346	0.5066	0.4803	0.4556	0.4323	0.4104	0.3898	0.3704	0.3521	0.3349
0.5132	0.4817	0.4523	0.4251	0.3996	0.3759	0.3538	0.3332	0.3139	0.2959	0.2791
0.4665	0.4339	0.4039	0.3762	0.3506	0.3269	0.3050	0.2848	0.2660	0.2487	0.2326
0.4241	0.3909	0.3606	0.3329	0.3075	0.2843	0.2630	0.2434	0.2255	0.2090	0.1938
0.3855	0.3522	0.3220	0.2946	0.2697	0.2472	0.2267	0.2080	0.1911	0.1756	0.1615
0.3505	0.3173	0.2875	0.2607	0.2366	0.2149	0.1954	0.1778	0.1619	0.1476	0.1346
0.3186	0.2858	0.2567	0.2307	0.2076	0.1869	0.1685	0.1520	0.1372	0.1240	0.1122
0.2897	0.2575	0.2292	0.2042	0.1821	0.1625	0.1452	0.1299	0.1163	0.1042	0.0935
0.2633	0.2320	0.2046	0.1807	0.1597	0.1413	0.1252	0.1110	0.0985	0.0876	0.0779
0.2394	0.2090	0.1827	0.1599	0.1401	0.1229	0.1079	0.0949	0.0835	0.0736	0.0649
0.2176	0.1883	0.1631	0.1415	0.1229	0.1069	0.0930	0.0811	0.0708	0.0618	0.0541
0.1978	0.1696	0.1456	0.1252	0.1078	0.0929	0.0802	0.0693	0.0600	0.0520	0.0451
0.1799	0.1528	0.1300	0.1108	0.0946	0.0808	0.0691	0.0592	0.0508	0.0437	0.0376
0.1635	0.1377	0.1161	0.0981	0.0829	0.0703	0.0596	0.0506	0.0431	0.0367	0.0313
0.1486	0.1240	0.1037	0.0868	0.0728	0.0611	0.0514	0.0433	0.0365	0.0308	0.0261
0.0923	0.0736	0.0588	0.0471	0.0378	0.0304	0.0245	0.0197	0.0160	0.0129	0.0105
0.0573	0.0437	0.0334	0.0256	0.0196	0.0151	0.0116	0.0090	0.0070	0.0054	0.0042
0.0356	0.0259	0.0189	0.0139	0.0102	0.0075	0.0055	0.0041	0.0030	0.0023	0.0017
0.0221	0.0154	0.0107	0.0075	0.0053	0.0037	0.0026	0.0019	0.0013	0.0010	0.0007
0.0137	0.0091	0.0061	0.0041	0.0027	0.0019	0.0013	0.0009	0.0006	0.0004	0.0003
0.0085	0.0054	0.0035	0.0022	0.0014	0.0009	0.0006	0.0004	0.0003	0.0002	0.0001

Present Value of an Annuity of $1

$$PVIFA = \left(\frac{1}{k}\right)\left(1 - \frac{1}{(1+k)^n}\right)$$

Periods	1%	2%	3%	4%	5%	6%	7%	8%	9%
1	0.9901	0.9804	0.9709	0.9615	0.9524	0.9434	0.9346	0.9259	0.9174
2	1.9704	1.9416	1.9135	1.8861	1.8594	1.8334	1.8080	1.7833	1.7591
3	2.9410	2.8839	2.8286	2.7751	2.7232	2.6730	2.6243	2.5771	2.5313
4	3.9020	3.8077	3.7171	3.6299	3.5460	3.4651	3.3872	3.3121	3.2397
5	4.8534	4.7135	4.5797	4.4518	4.3295	4.2124	4.1002	3.9927	3.8897
6	5.7955	5.6014	5.4172	5.2421	5.0757	4.9173	4.7665	4.6229	4.4859
7	6.7282	6.4720	6.2303	6.0021	5.7864	5.5824	5.3893	5.2064	5.0330
8	7.6517	7.3255	7.0197	6.7327	6.4632	6.2098	5.9713	5.7466	5.5348
9	8.5660	8.1622	7.7861	7.4353	7.1078	6.8017	6.5152	6.2469	5.9952
10	9.4713	8.9826	8.5302	8.1109	7.7217	7.3601	7.0236	6.7101	6.4177
11	10.3676	9.7868	9.2526	8.7605	8.3064	7.8869	7.4987	7.1390	6.8052
12	11.2551	10.5753	9.9540	9.3851	8.8633	8.3838	7.9427	7.5361	7.1607
13	12.1337	11.3484	10.6350	9.9856	9.3936	8.8527	8.3577	7.9038	7.4869
14	13.0037	12.1062	11.2961	10.5631	9.8986	9.2950	8.7455	8.2442	7.7862
15	13.8651	12.8493	11.9379	11.1184	10.3797	9.7122	9.1079	8.5595	8.0607
16	14.7179	13.5777	12.5611	11.6523	10.8378	10.1059	9.4466	8.8514	8.3126
17	15.5623	14.2919	13.1661	12.1657	11.2741	10.4773	9.7632	9.1216	8.5436
18	16.3983	14.9920	13.7535	12.6593	11.6896	10.8276	10.0591	9.3719	8.7556
19	17.2260	15.6785	14.3238	13.1339	12.0853	11.1581	10.3356	9.6036	8.9501
20	18.0456	16.3514	14.8775	13.5903	12.4622	11.4699	10.5940	9.8181	9.1285
25	22.0232	19.5235	17.4131	15.6221	14.0939	12.7834	11.6536	10.6748	9.8226
30	25.8077	22.3965	19.6004	17.2920	15.3725	13.7648	12.4090	11.2578	10.2737
35	29.4086	24.9986	21.4872	18.6646	16.3742	14.4982	12.9477	11.6546	10.5668
40	32.8347	27.3555	23.1148	19.7928	17.1591	15.0463	13.3317	11.9246	10.7574
45	36.0945	29.4902	24.5187	20.7200	17.7741	15.4558	13.6055	12.1084	10.8812
50	39.1961	31.4236	25.7298	21.4822	18.2559	15.7619	13.8007	12.2335	10.9617

10%	11%	12%	13%	14%	15%	16%	17%	18%	19%	20%
0.9091	0.9009	0.8929	0.8850	0.8772	0.8696	0.8621	0.8547	0.8475	0.8403	0.8333
1.7355	1.7125	1.6901	1.6681	1.6467	1.6257	1.6052	1.5852	1.5656	1.5465	1.5278
2.4869	2.4437	2.4018	2.3612	2.3216	2.2832	2.2459	2.2096	2.1743	2.1399	2.1065
3.1699	3.1024	3.0373	2.9745	2.9137	2.8550	2.7982	2.7432	2.6901	2.6386	2.5887
3.7908	3.6959	3.6048	3.5172	3.4331	3.3522	3.2743	3.1993	3.1272	3.0576	2.9906
4.3553	4.2305	4.1114	3.9975	3.8887	3.7845	3.6847	3.5892	3.4976	3.4098	3.3255
4.8684	4.7122	4.5638	4.4226	4.2883	4.1604	4.0386	3.9224	3.8115	3.7057	3.6046
5.3349	5.1461	4.9676	4.7988	4.6389	4.4873	4.3436	4.2072	4.0776	3.9544	3.8372
5.7590	5.5370	5.3282	5.1317	4.9464	4.7716	4.6065	4.4506	4.3030	4.1633	4.0310
6.1446	5.8892	5.6502	5.4262	5.2161	5.0188	4.8332	4.6586	4.4941	4.3389	4.1925
6.4951	6.2065	5.9377	5.6869	5.4527	5.2337	5.0286	4.8364	4.6560	4.4865	4.3271
6.8137	6.4924	6.1944	5.9176	5.6603	5.4206	5.1971	4.9884	4.7932	4.6105	4.4392
7.1034	6.7499	6.4235	6.1218	5.8424	5.5831	5.3423	5.1183	4.9095	4.7147	4.5327
7.3667	6.9819	6.6282	6.3025	6.0021	5.7245	5.4675	5.2293	5.0081	4.8023	4.6106
7.6061	7.1909	6.8109	6.4624	6.1422	5.8474	5.5755	5.3242	5.0916	4.8759	4.6755
7.8237	7.3792	6.9740	6.6039	6.2651	5.9542	5.6685	5.4053	5.1624	4.9377	4.7296
8.0216	7.5488	7.1196	6.7291	6.3729	6.0472	5.7487	5.4746	5.2223	4.9897	4.7746
8.2014	7.7016	7.2497	6.8399	6.4674	6.1280	5.8178	5.5339	5.2732	5.0333	4.8122
8.3649	7.8393	7.3658	6.9380	6.5504	6.1982	5.8775	5.5845	5.3162	5.0700	4.8435
8.5136	7.9633	7.4694	7.0248	6.6231	6.2593	5.9288	5.6278	5.3527	5.1009	4.8696
9.0770	8.4217	7.8431	7.3300	6.8729	6.4641	6.0971	5.7662	5.4669	5.1951	4.9476
9.4269	8.6938	8.0552	7.4957	7.0027	6.5660	6.1772	5.8294	5.5168	5.2347	4.9789
9.6442	8.8552	8.1755	7.5856	7.0700	6.6166	6.2153	5.8582	5.5386	5.2512	4.9915
9.7791	8.9511	8.2438	7.6344	7.1050	6.6418	6.2335	5.8713	5.5482	5.2582	4.9966
9.8628	9.0079	8.2825	7.6609	7.1232	6.6543	6.2421	5.8773	5.5523	5.2611	4.9986
9.9148	9.0417	8.3045	7.6752	7.1327	6.6605	6.2463	5.8801	5.5541	5.2623	4.9995

Future Value of $1

$FVIF = (1+k)^n$

Periods	1%	2%	3%	4%	5%	6%	7%	8%	9%	10%
1	1.0100	1.0200	1.0300	1.0400	1.0500	1.0600	1.0700	1.0800	1.0900	1.1000
2	1.0201	1.0404	1.0609	1.0816	1.1025	1.1236	1.1449	1.1664	1.1881	1.2100
3	1.0303	1.0612	1.0927	1.1249	1.1576	1.1910	1.2250	1.2597	1.2950	1.3310
4	1.0406	1.0824	1.1255	1.1699	1.2155	1.2625	1.3108	1.3605	1.4116	1.4641
5	1.0510	1.1041	1.1593	1.2167	1.2763	1.3382	1.4026	1.4693	1.5386	1.6105
6	1.0615	1.1262	1.1941	1.2653	1.3401	1.4185	1.5007	1.5869	1.6771	1.7716
7	1.0721	1.1487	1.2299	1.3159	1.4071	1.5036	1.6058	1.7138	1.8280	1.9487
8	1.0829	1.1717	1.2668	1.3686	1.4775	1.5938	1.7182	1.8509	1.9926	2.1436
9	1.0937	1.1951	1.3048	1.4233	1.5513	1.6895	1.8385	1.9990	2.1719	2.3579
10	1.1046	1.2190	1.3439	1.4802	1.6289	1.7908	1.9672	2.1589	2.3674	2.5937
11	1.1157	1.2434	1.3842	1.5395	1.7103	1.8983	2.1049	2.3316	2.5804	2.8531
12	1.1268	1.2682	1.4258	1.6010	1.7959	2.0122	2.2522	2.5182	2.8127	3.1384
13	1.1381	1.2936	1.4685	1.6651	1.8856	2.1329	2.4098	2.7196	3.0658	3.4523
14	1.1495	1.3195	1.5126	1.7317	1.9799	2.2609	2.5785	2.9372	3.3417	3.7975
15	1.1610	1.3459	1.5580	1.8009	2.0789	2.3966	2.7590	3.1722	3.6425	4.1772
16	1.1726	1.3728	1.6047	1.8730	2.1829	2.5404	2.9522	3.4259	3.9703	4.5950
17	1.1843	1.4002	1.6528	1.9479	2.2920	2.6928	3.1588	3.7000	4.3276	5.0545
18	1.1961	1.4282	1.7024	2.0258	2.4066	2.8543	3.3799	3.9960	4.7171	5.5599
19	1.2081	1.4568	1.7535	2.1068	2.5270	3.0256	3.6165	4.3157	5.1417	6.1159
20	1.2202	1.4859	1.8061	2.1911	2.6533	3.2071	3.8697	4.6610	5.6044	6.7275
25	1.2824	1.6406	2.0938	2.6658	3.3864	4.2919	5.4274	6.8485	8.6231	10.8347
30	1.3478	1.8114	2.4273	3.2434	4.3219	5.7435	7.6123	10.0627	13.2677	17.4494
35	1.4166	1.9999	2.8139	3.9461	5.5160	7.6861	10.6766	14.7853	20.4140	28.1024
40	1.4889	2.2080	3.2620	4.8010	7.0400	10.2857	14.9745	21.7245	31.4094	45.2593
45	1.5648	2.4379	3.7816	5.8412	8.9850	13.7646	21.0025	31.9204	48.3273	72.8905
50	1.6446	2.6916	4.3839	7.1067	11.4674	18.4202	29.4570	46.9016	74.3575	117.3909

11%	12%	13%	14%	15%	16%	17%	18%	19%	20%
1.1100	1.1200	1.1300	1.1400	1.1500	1.1600	1.1700	1.1800	1.1900	1.2000
1.2321	1.2544	1.2769	1.2996	1.3225	1.3456	1.3689	1.3924	1.4161	1.4400
1.3676	1.4049	1.4429	1.4815	1.5209	1.5609	1.6016	1.6430	1.6852	1.7280
1.5181	1.5735	1.6305	1.6890	1.7490	1.8106	1.8739	1.9388	2.0053	2.0736
1.6851	1.7623	1.8424	1.9254	2.0114	2.1003	2.1924	2.2878	2.3864	2.4883
1.8704	1.9738	2.0820	2.1950	2.3131	2.4364	2.5652	2.6996	2.8398	2.9860
2.0762	2.2107	2.3526	2.5023	2.6600	2.8262	3.0012	3.1855	3.3793	3.5832
2.3045	2.4760	2.6584	2.8526	3.0590	3.2784	3.5115	3.7589	4.0214	4.2998
2.5580	2.7731	3.0040	3.2519	3.5179	3.8030	4.1084	4.4355	4.7854	5.1598
2.8394	3.1058	3.3946	3.7072	4.0456	4.4114	4.8068	5.2338	5.6947	6.1917
3.1518	3.4785	3.8359	4.2262	4.6524	5.1173	5.6240	6.1759	6.7767	7.4301
3.4985	3.8960	4.3345	4.8179	5.3503	5.9360	6.5801	7.2876	8.0642	8.9161
3.8833	4.3635	4.8980	5.4924	6.1528	6.8858	7.6987	8.5994	9.5964	10.6993
4.3104	4.8871	5.5348	6.2613	7.0757	7.9875	9.0075	10.1472	11.4198	12.8392
4.7846	5.4736	6.2543	7.1379	8.1371	9.2655	10.5387	11.9737	13.5895	15.4070
5.3109	6.1304	7.0673	8.1372	9.3576	10.7480	12.3303	14.1290	16.1715	18.4884
5.8951	6.8660	7.9861	9.2765	10.7613	12.4677	14.4265	16.6722	19.2441	22.1861
6.5436	7.6900	9.0243	10.5752	12.3755	14.4625	16.8790	19.6733	22.9005	26.6233
7.2633	8.6128	10.1974	12.0557	14.2318	16.7765	19.7484	23.2144	27.2516	31.9480
8.0623	9.6463	11.5231	13.7435	16.3665	19.4608	23.1056	27.3930	32.4294	38.3376
13.5855	17.0001	21.2305	26.4619	32.9190	40.8742	50.6578	62.6686	77.3881	95.3962
22.8923	29.9599	39.1159	50.9502	66.2118	85.8499	111.0647	143.3706	184.6753	237.3763
38.5749	52.7996	72.0685	98.1002	133.1755	180.3141	243.5035	327.9973	440.7006	590.6682
65.0009	93.0510	132.7816	188.8835	267.8635	378.7212	533.8687	750.3783	1.05e+03	1.47e+03
109.5302	163.9876	244.6414	363.6791	538.7693	795.4438	1.17e+03	1.72e+03	2.51e+03	3.66e+03
184.5648	289.0022	450.7359	700.2330	1.08e+03	1.67e+03	2.57e+03	3.93e+03	5.99e+03	9.10e+03

Future Value of an Annuity of $1

$$FVIFA = \left(\frac{1}{k}\right)\left((1 + k)^n - 1\right)$$

Periods	1%	2%	3%	4%	5%	6%	7%	8%	9%	10%
1	1.0000	1.0000	1.0000	1.0000	1.0000	1.0000	1.0000	1.0000	1.0000	1.0000
2	2.0100	2.0200	2.0300	2.0400	2.0500	2.0600	2.0700	2.0800	2.0900	2.1000
3	3.0301	3.0604	3.0909	3.1216	3.1525	3.1836	3.2149	3.2464	3.2781	3.3100
4	4.0604	4.1216	4.1836	4.2465	4.3101	4.3746	4.4399	4.5061	4.5731	4.6410
5	5.1010	5.2040	5.3091	5.4163	5.5256	5.6371	5.7507	5.8666	5.9847	6.1051
6	6.1520	6.3081	6.4684	6.6330	6.8019	6.9753	7.1533	7.3359	7.5233	7.7156
7	7.2135	7.4343	7.6625	7.8983	8.1420	8.3938	8.6540	8.9228	9.2004	9.4872
8	8.2857	8.5830	8.8923	9.2142	9.5491	9.8975	10.2598	10.6366	11.0285	11.4359
9	9.3685	9.7546	10.1591	10.5828	11.0266	11.4913	11.9780	12.4876	13.0210	13.5795
10	10.4622	10.9497	11.4639	12.0061	12.5779	13.1808	13.8164	14.4866	15.1929	15.9374
11	11.5668	12.1687	12.8078	13.4864	14.2068	14.9716	15.7836	16.6455	17.5603	18.5312
12	12.6825	13.4121	14.1920	15.0258	15.9171	16.8699	17.8885	18.9771	20.1407	21.3843
13	13.8093	14.6803	15.6178	16.6268	17.7130	18.8821	20.1406	21.4953	22.9534	24.5227
14	14.9474	15.9739	17.0863	18.2919	19.5986	21.0151	22.5505	24.2149	26.0192	27.9750
15	16.0969	17.2934	18.5989	20.0236	21.5786	23.2760	25.1290	27.1521	29.3609	31.7725
16	17.2579	18.6393	20.1569	21.8245	23.6575	25.6725	27.8881	30.3243	33.0034	35.9497
17	18.4304	20.0121	21.7616	23.6975	25.8404	28.2129	30.8402	33.7502	36.9737	40.5447
18	19.6147	21.4123	23.4144	25.6454	28.1324	30.9057	33.9990	37.4502	41.3013	45.5992
19	20.8109	22.8406	25.1169	27.6712	30.5390	33.7600	37.3790	41.4463	46.0185	51.1591
20	22.0190	24.2974	26.8704	29.7781	33.0660	36.7856	40.9955	45.7620	51.1601	57.2750
25	28.2432	32.0303	36.4593	41.6459	47.7271	54.8645	63.2490	73.1059	84.7009	98.3471
30	34.7849	40.5681	47.5754	56.0849	66.4388	79.0582	94.4608	113.2832	136.3075	164.4940
35	41.6603	49.9945	60.4621	73.6522	90.3203	111.4348	138.2369	172.3168	215.7108	271.0244
40	48.8864	60.4020	75.4013	95.0255	120.7998	154.7620	199.6351	259.0565	337.8824	442.5926
45	56.4811	71.8927	92.7199	121.0294	159.7002	212.7435	285.7493	386.5056	525.8587	718.9048
50	64.4632	84.5794	112.7969	152.6671	209.3480	290.3359	406.5289	573.7702	815.0836	1.16e+03

11%	12%	13%	14%	15%	16%	17%	18%	19%	20%
1.0000	1.0000	1.0000	1.0000	1.0000	1.0000	1.0000	1.0000	1.0000	1.0000
2.1100	2.1200	2.1300	2.1400	2.1500	2.1600	2.1700	2.1800	2.1900	2.2000
3.3421	3.3744	3.4069	3.4396	3.4725	3.5056	3.5389	3.5724	3.6061	3.6400
4.7097	4.7793	4.8498	4.9211	4.9934	5.0665	5.1405	5.2154	5.2913	5.3680
6.2278	6.3528	6.4803	6.6101	6.7424	6.8771	7.0144	7.1542	7.2966	7.4416
7.9129	8.1152	8.3227	8.5355	8.7537	8.9775	9.2068	9.4420	9.6830	9.9299
9.7833	10.0890	10.4047	10.7305	11.0668	11.4139	11.7720	12.1415	12.5227	12.9159
11.8594	12.2997	12.7573	13.2328	13.7268	14.2401	14.7733	15.3270	15.9020	16.4991
14.1640	14.7757	15.4157	16.0853	16.7858	17.5185	18.2847	19.0859	19.9234	20.7989
16.7220	17.5487	18.4197	19.3373	20.3037	21.3215	22.3931	23.5213	24.7089	25.9587
19.5614	20.6546	21.8143	23.0445	24.3493	25.7329	27.1999	28.7551	30.4035	32.1504
22.7132	24.1331	25.6502	27.2707	29.0017	30.8502	32.8239	34.9311	37.1802	39.5805
26.2116	28.0291	29.9847	32.0887	34.3519	36.7862	39.4040	42.2187	45.2445	48.4966
30.0949	32.3926	34.8827	37.5811	40.5047	43.6720	47.1027	50.8180	54.8409	59.1959
34.4054	37.2797	40.4175	43.8424	47.5804	51.6595	56.1101	60.9653	66.2607	72.0351
39.1899	42.7533	46.6717	50.9804	55.7175	60.9250	66.6488	72.9390	79.8502	87.4421
44.5008	48.8837	53.7391	59.1176	65.0751	71.6730	78.9792	87.0680	96.0218	105.9306
50.3959	55.7497	61.7251	68.3941	75.8364	84.1407	93.4056	103.7403	115.2659	128.1167
56.9395	63.4397	70.7494	78.9692	88.2118	98.6032	110.2846	123.4135	138.1664	154.7400
64.2028	72.0524	80.9468	91.0249	102.4436	115.3797	130.0329	146.6280	165.4180	186.6880
114.4133	133.3339	155.6196	181.8708	212.7930	249.2140	292.1049	342.6035	402.0425	471.9811
199.0209	241.3327	293.1992	356.7868	434.7451	530.3117	647.4391	790.9480	966.7122	1.18e+03
341.5896	431.6635	546.6808	693.5727	881.1702	1.12e+03	1.43e+03	1.82e+03	2.31e+03	2.95e+03
581.8261	767.0914	1.01e+03	1.34e+03	1.78e+03	2.36e+03	3.13e+03	4.16e+03	5.53e+03	7.34e+03
986.6386	1.36e+03	1.87e+03	2.59e+03	3.59e+03	4.97e+03	6.88e+03	9.53e+03	1.32e+04	1.83e+04
1.67e+03	2.40e+03	3.46e+03	4.99e+03	7.22e+03	1.04e+04	1.51e+04	2.18e+04	3.15e+04	4.55e+04

Index